The Limits of Social Cohesion

THE LIMITS OF SOCIAL COHESION

Conflict and Mediation in Pluralist Societies

A Report of the Bertelsmann Foundation to the Club of Rome

EDITED BY

Peter L. Berger

WestviewPress

A Division of HarperCollinsPublishers

Copyright © 1998 by Bertelsmann Foundation Publishers
Original title: *Die Grenzen der Gemeinschaft: Konflikt und Vermittlung in pluralistischen Gesellschaften* herausgegeben von Peter L. Berger

Published in 1998 in the United States of America by Westview Press, 5500 Central Avenue, Boulder, Colorado 80301-2877, and in the United Kingdom by Westview Press, 12 Hid's Copse Road, Cumnor Hill, Oxford OX2 9JJ

Library of Congress Cataloging-in-Publication Data
The limits of social cohesion : conflict and mediation in pluralist
    societies : a report of the Bertelsmann Foundation to the Club
    of Rome/ edited by Peter L. Berger.
        p. cm.
    Includes bibliographical references and index.
    ISBN 0-8133-3401-2 (cloth)
    1. Social conflict.   2. Social norms.   3. Conflict management.
4. Mediation.   I. Berger, Peter L.
HM136.L525   1998
303.6—dc21   97-25243
                                                                                               CIP

The paper used in this publication meets the requirements of the American National Standard for Permanence of Paper for Printed Library Materials Z39.48-1984.

10   9   8   7   6   5   4   3   2   1

Contents

Preface

by Werner Weidenfeld

Member of the Board of
the Bertelsmann Foundation

This report is the result of years of close cooperation between the Club of Rome and the Bertelsmann Science Foundation. The President of the Club of Rome, Ricardo Díez-Hochleitner, and other distinguished members of the Club of Rome like Bertrand Schneider, Klaus von Dohnanyi, Eberhard von Koerber, and Ruud Lubbers are working in close connection with our foundation. In the context of this dialogue we developed the idea that the Club of Rome should work on the basic issue of social cohesion in our societies as the crucial challenge on a future-oriented agenda.

Future historians looking back on our epoch will define our time as one of the periods with the most profound changes ever experienced in our history. As contemporaries of such times of change, we remain focused essentially on the surface of the spectacular current events, frequently failing to notice the shifts behind the scenes and in the deep dimensions of attitudes, values, and mentalities, and failing to come to terms with the tectonic changes of power and culture constellations.

Yet it is precisely these shifts that really deserve our attention. We are currently experiencing history in rapid motion:

- The Cold War has ended, and therefore the mental dividing lines of world politics, which provided patterns of explanation for international organizations and legitimation as well as for the internal cohesion of many societies, have disappeared.
- An ideology with a claim to universal dominance has vanished, and hence manifold distinctive enemy images and projections have lost their justification.
- Fixed political bloc formations and thus the segmentation of power have ended, and a variety of conflicts originating from numerous causes have emerged. Ethnic and nationalistic conflicts

have resurfaced, and solutions must be sought, bringing with
them new risks and dangers.

In those periods of dramatic changes with breathtaking opportunities for
freedom, security, and wealth but also with explosive risks for the peaceful coexistence of peoples, fundamental questions of social and political
life are again raised:

- How do we perceive our identity, both in individual and
  collective terms?
- How do pluralistic societies develop cultural and normative
  orientations?
- How can normative conflicts be solved in an acceptable,
  constructive way?
- What holds a society together?

All of these questions must be considered in the light of an extensive international interdependence in the economic, political, and cultural
spheres.

In the new world political era, the cultural resources that lead to social
cohesion and the limits of that cohesion in our societies are of the utmost
importance. It will be the primary task for societies to promote social cohesion as the basic source of economic development and ecological sensi-
bility. The cultural foundations of society deserve our full attention as a
basis of sustainable development.

In the past the debate about the limits to growth created a certain understanding, namely, that economic activities consume the resources on
which the existence of mankind is dependent. The discussions caused remarkable changes in our thinking and led to the conviction that we
should not consume the very basis that our economic and human survival depends on. This is the contribution of the Club of Rome to recent
history, having created an awareness and having fostered discussion irrespective of the scientific exactness of the developed scenarios.

A comparative effort now lies ahead for our societies to make clear that
there are not only limits to growth but also limits to the social cohesion
on which our survival as human beings in peaceful societal circumstances depends. This report is intended to deliver the message to the
Club of Rome and the general public that we all have to be very sensitive
and very careful in dealing with the cultural resources of our societies,
with norms, values, and social attitudes.

Sensitivity and care should be directed in particular toward generating
a tolerant dialogue on norms and values within and between societies.
Our interest should focus on mediating structures that allow societies to

cope with conflict. Mediation is required to allow varied normative positions to coexist and different value systems to be maintained without inimical consequences to equally legitimate and respect-deserving positions of others. This very subject deserves our full attention and requires major efforts in the near future to develop paths that can be distinguished and widened to become roads to peace and mutual understanding.

This report was developed over the last few years by an international team of fourteen outstanding researchers representing many cultures of the world under the chairmanship of Professor Peter L. Berger from Boston University. Dirk Rumberg and Volker Then from the Bertelsmann Foundation assisted in coordinating the project team and making this joint effort possible. With its extensive project on normative conflicts, the Bertelsmann Science Foundation laid down the basis for this report. The research team analyzed eleven countries, raising the central question of how societies can solve normative conflicts and therefore maintain social cohesion. The report assesses the question of social cohesion from a comparative perspective, taking into account questions of international and intercultural comparison. The countries included are Chile, France, Germany, Hungary, India, Indonesia, Japan, South Africa, Taiwan, Turkey, and the United States.

The work started from the guiding question: How do societies cope with normative conflicts under the conditions of pluralism? It is evident that in pluralistic societies there are different communication structures and different ways of conflict resolution. It is precisely these structures of information processing and value-oriented communication that we focused on in our analysis. These are the so-called "intermediary institutions," or "mediating structures," as Peter Berger has termed them.

In a systematic approach we therefore try to answer four key questions in this report:

- What are the central value conflicts of the countries concerned and what are the orientations and cultural patterns that clash in this situation?
- Which "intermediary institutions" become active in mediating in these conflicts?
- Under what conditions can these mediating structures perform their tasks more effectively, and what are possible obstacles in their way?
- Which consequences have to be drawn from these analytic results to establish future methods of conflict resolution in societies and between societies or cultures?

All our findings point in the direction that communication and the potential for dialogue have to be improved. Therefore I wish the message of this report to be that greatly increased efforts at creating and strengthening mediating structures in the communication between differing value and normative systems in the world is of foremost importance. May this be the message of the Club of Rome for the twenty-first century: Take care of the cultural basis of human coexistence!

Preface

by Ricardo Díez-Hochleitner

President of the Club of Rome

There is a growing sense of uncertainty and anxiety the world over on the eve of the third millennium. Despite the many important achievements of our times, the roots of the unease lie largely in the profound change inherent in the transition toward a new global society, over and above the nation-state. Moreover, what some enlightened citizens see as a great opportunity, others regard as a very serious threat.

In any case, almost in every country—irrespective of the level of development or cultural background—there are limits to social cohesion.

The Club of Rome, with its one hundred members from over fifty countries—together with its honorary, associated, and institutional members and national associates—is concerned with the world *problématique* and regards itself as a catalyst of change and a center of innovation and initiatives for solutions contained in the studies and debates it conducts in a context of complete intellectual independence.

In line with the above, the Club of Rome commissioned the present study on normative conflicts and mediation to the Bertelsmann Foundation—to be carried out as part of its long-term program on cultural orientation—under the general cooperative agreement previously reached with the chairman of its board, Reinhard Mohn, and following an outline worked out by Professor Werner Weidenfeld in consultation with our club. The Bertelsmann Foundation in turn entrusted Professor Peter L. Berger with the intellectual leadership of the study. The systemic and all-embracing methodology deployed has involved research work conducted by eminent specialists from different countries and regions of the world.

The ensuing report to the Club of Rome provides opportunities for in-depth debate and discussion, promoted by our club. We know that some of the ideas presented here to public and to professional opinion are likely to be controversial. However, this report should be considered as a first step toward a better understanding of the limits to social cohesion and the increasing role of intermediate institutions or, lacking that, of individual leaders in the mediation of normative conflicts. The preliminary conclusions reached by Professor Berger in the final chapter of the volume provide much sound substance for further reflection and constitute a practical guide for action.

The very nature of this report is in itself a contribution to an increasingly necessary worldwide cultural dialogue. In this regard, more specific references to normative conflicts resulting from exacerbated nationalism and concurrent cultural identities would have been welcome. In addition, further studies on mechanisms for *preventing* conflicts also seem to be needed. Moreover, an analysis of the role of public institutions as well as of intermediate institutions in the event of international conflicts should be undertaken later on, and may prove to be extremely useful.

We are firmly convinced that the report's holistic approach and its many innovative ideas merit the highest level of public attention, especially from public and private leaders, academics, educators, mass media professionals, and others who are concerned with solidarity and cooperation as avenues for developing peaceful societies, democratic stability, and social justice.

The suggestions contained in the report have been the subject of intense discussion among the members of the Club of Rome, both by its Executive Committee and during its annual conference held in Ponce, Puerto Rico, in December 1996. The complexity and uncertainty of world affairs preclude, nowadays, quick and easy solutions. For these reasons the Club of Rome welcomes this report as an important contribution to the necessary public debate on one of the most fundamental issues of the times, although this does not necessarily imply that all its members fully agree with its contents.

The members of the Executive Committee of the Club of Rome:

Ricardo Díez-Hochleitner, Ruth Bamela Engo-Tjega, Belisario Betancur, Umberto Colombo, Orio Giarini, Bohdan Hawrylyshyn, Alexander King, Eberhard von Koerber, Ruud Lubbers, Manfred Max-Neef, Samuel Nana-Sinkam, and Bertrand Schneider.

Introduction

by Volker Then

In a world of increasing public concern with conflict, this report is intended to examine normative conflicts and divisions in modern societies. At the same time, it aims at identifying solutions to these conflicts or strategies of mediation between the contending parties. The underlying research design is based on an international and intercultural comparative perspective, and the study embraces eleven countries representing many of the major cultures and regions of the world.

As modern pluralist developments eroded the unity of value systems, there is a range of potential reactions that societies and their responsible political leaders may resort to with regard to social cohesion. It would be futile to consider a "rollback strategy" to be a sustainable option in any regard. The solution to the problem cannot be found in the restoration of seemingly lost values of the past. Unanimity on normative positions cannot be forged in the melting pot of pluralist societies without doing harm to the very core of their pluralist character. Nor would a "laissez-faire" approach toward all normative positions be an appropriate notion on which to base social cohesion. Rather this study seeks the solution in a third strategy—a strategy of containment, a strategy of accepting the diversity of different normative positions in society that at the same time is concerned with those mechanisms that help them to coexist. This report is therefore an assessment of the functioning of "mediating institutions," mechanisms of mediation that prevent normative clashes from becoming violent and that allow society to negotiate a settlement between the parties in conflict.

Today pluralism is not only a phenomenon *within* societies but also *between* them. In a world of globalized communications the interaction between nations inevitably involves normative conflicts of one kind or another, no matter whether the normative differences are genuinely believed in or only used to justify conflicting vested interests. Thus the issues discussed in this book concern not only domestic politics but international relations as well. This aspect of the matter has attained particular relevance as a result of the controversy swirling around the recent publication of Samuel Huntington's *The Clash of Civilizations and the Remaking of World Order*. Huntington's thesis (or, as he cautiously labels it, hypothesis) is that in the wake of the Cold War international conflicts will increasingly occur around the fault lines between civilizations. He ends his book with a call for a dialogue between civilizations so as to minimize the threat of violent clashes between them. In other words, the search for normative mediations is not only of great importance for the social cohesion of individual societies, but also of possibly even greater importance in the building of a peaceful international order.

Virtually all human societies have conflicts, such as those caused by divergent class interests, political aspirations, or ethnic animosities. The focus of this report is on one particular sort of conflict (though of course this is frequently linked with the aforementioned social cleavages)—namely, conflicts that entail differences concerning the normative character of the society in question. Examples of such conflicts in the contemporary world include differences: over the definition of national identity and purpose, such as in the debate over "Japaneseness" in that country; over the relation between religion and the modern state, such as in Islamic countries, or in India over the status of religious law, or in France over *"laïcité"*; over the capacity of the society to adapt to other cultures, such as in the disputes over multiculturalism in the United States and Europe; over both the practical and the moral scope of the welfare state, which occur virtually everywhere, though with distinctive features in Latin America and the former communist countries in Central and Eastern Europe; over the applicability of Western notions of human rights in non-Western societies (particularly in Asia); over the public and legal status of issues of personal morality, such as those of the "culture wars" in the United States; over the rival claims of individual rights and equity between groups, such as in debates over "affirmative action," in India and South Africa today; over the role of "civil society" as against the institutions of the state—in contemporary reassessment almost everywhere. This is by no means an exhaustive list, but it may serve to concretize what is meant here by "normative conflicts."

A human society is held together by a variety of forces—common interests, sheer habit, the absence of alternatives, reasonable levels of affluence, common historical experience, shared notions of adversaries—and these are all fortified through institutions (positive law being the most obvious case). But one does not have to be an orthodox Durkheimian sociologist to agree that a society will sooner or later be in serious trouble if it is not also held together by common normative orientations (*conscience collective* or *Geistige Orientierung*). These are not always promulgated through formal institutions (such as the state, or a church, or this or that ideological movement). There are taken-for-granted normative traditions dispersed throughout a population, maintained by what Thomas Luckmann has called "moral communication in everyday life." But in a strict sociological use of the term, these too are institutionalized (even if the relevant institutions are not "phone book institutions"—they do not have an address, a staff, written constitutions, or budgets; they are not listed or registered anywhere). Such institutions may include regular meetings of neighbors (the German *Stammtisch*), networks of like-minded people communicating by telephone or Internet, spontaneous gatherings of people around local issues of concern (such as the plethora of ad hoc action or support groups in the United States).

But then there are more formal institutions maintaining, promulgating, and disseminating norms. These range from those at the local level (the local church, political party, labor union) through those at the intermediate levels (say, the Massachusetts chapter of the American Civil Liberties Union) to those at the national level (the state itself, the media of mass communication, national nongovernmental organizations). All of these may serve to mediate normative conflicts—that is, they may serve as mediating institutions. But conversely, at all these levels there are institutions that maintain and aggravate normative conflicts—rival meetings of neighbors, networks of people whose like-mindedness is based precisely on a common position of opposition to other groups, national organizations pitted against other national organizations. Normative conflicts, from the merely verbal to the physically violent, are fought at all these levels. Naturally it is easier to organize both for conflict and for mediation under a democratic regime that guarantees rights of free speech and association, but comparable processes also occur under dictatorial regimes, and often they are more violent precisely because of the repression imposed on them.

The term "mediating institutions" as used here is not synonymous with the term "mediating structures," which Peter Berger used in earlier work. The latter term referred to any institution that linked individuals in their private sphere to the "megastructures" of a modern society. But some "mediating structures," in that sense, aggravate conflict, whereas others mitigate it. Conversely, "megastructures" may serve as "mediating institutions" in situations of normative conflict. Thus a forum for discussion and compromise may occur on television or under the sponsorship of a national religious organization—or, indeed, of the state.

In each of the examples of normative conflict cited above, there are institutions that mobilize people on each side. It is important to understand what these stand for, and to understand their social base and the vested interests with which they may be linked. But the main interest of the report is in the mediating institutions, both those that exist now and those that might come into being. The practical goal would then be to determine possibilities of how to support the former and help to stimulate the latter.

It is important to recognize that the same institution may sometimes succeed and sometimes fail in mediation. To take another American example: The civil rights struggle of the 1960s was effectively mediated by the democratic process, culminating in legislation based on commonly accepted norms that in the end brought over the majority of white Southerners. The "New South" is not just the result of a practical compromise, but of a wide normative consensus. The democratic process has not succeeded thus far in mediating the current "culture wars" (as notably on the abortion issue). On the contrary, the democratic process itself has become a prime arena of conflict.

In Western societies many of the mediating institutions may be subsumed under the currently fashionable term "civil society." These are groupings based on voluntary association, standing outside and often pitted against the state. It has been recognized for a long time (at least since the Enlightenment) that these groupings play an important role in social cohesion, and this insight has been revitalized recently in the struggle against communist totalitarianism in Europe. But it cannot be assumed that all non-Western societies share this propensity toward voluntary association. Therefore, a particular interest of the report is to explore two questions of great relevance in Asia and Africa: What are the prospects for civil-society institutions in non-Western societies? And what mediating institutions based on traditional customs and norms (that is, not based on Western-type voluntary association) are to be found in those societies? These could be institutions based on extended kinship, caste, ethnicity, and (probably most important) religion.

From this research design resulted guiding principal questions to be addressed by each contributor that were the basis for the comparability of the findings and provided good grounds for summing up results based on generalizable evidence. Therefore, it was the task of each contributor, first, to determine the major normative conflicts and the clashing normative orientations and cultural patterns of the society; second, to analyze the institutions, structures, movements, and groupings that mobilize people on the opposing sides of the cleavage; and third, to explore mediating institutions and strategies as well as the conditions for their effectiveness.

According to this framework, eleven countries were studied: Chile, France, Germany, Hungary, India, Indonesia, Japan, South Africa, Taiwan, Turkey, and the United States. Under the chairmanship of Peter Berger and in cooperation with Dirk Rumberg and Volker Then of the Bertelsmann Foundation, the team of authors met several times to coordinate its efforts, to establish a common frame of reference, and to discuss draft versions of the contributions. Consulting members of the project team were: Thomas Luckmann, Theo Hanf, and Anton Zijderveld, who kindly played the role of critics. The results that reach beyond individual national interest are summed up in concluding observations by Peter Berger, establishing general directions for dealing with normative differences and cultural pluralism. It is the hope of the participants that this report will contribute to the capacity of modern pluralist societies to deal with normative conflicts and social cohesion.

1

The American Culture War

James Davison Hunter

As the Enlightenment architects designed the *novus ordo seclorum,* they deliberately restricted the role of religious ideals and religious institutions in the ordering of public life. They advanced this agenda not simply because religion violated their intellectual and aesthetic sensibilities but because they were determined to secularize public affairs in order to avoid the conflict that competing religious faiths often engendered—conflict that was frequently unwieldy, entrenched, and more often than not, bloody. The Enlightenment architects regarded secularization of the public sphere through the privatization of religion as an innovative solution to the conundrum of pluralism and the conflict that pluralism inevitably fostered. Despite the intellectual establishment's smug confidence over the past two centuries that history was steadily progressing on this enlightened path, the "new order of the ages" has yet to witness the end to normative conflict. Indeed, conflict remains a defining feature of public life even in the most "enlightened" societies of the Western world. One explanation for this is that much of today's conflict remains fundamentally religious in nature—if not in explicitly institutional form, then certainly in character. Nowhere in the West is this more true than in the United States, where normative conflict manifests itself as a moral and even quasi-religious struggle to define the meaning of America. Thus, the ancient and abiding problem of societal conflict rooted in opposing "faiths" and contradictory ideals of national identity has not passed into memory as was once hoped. Rather, the United States (at least) has seen this conflict transformed. For better or for worse, the quandary of how democracy will arbitrate such conflict remains as pressing today as ever.

America at War with Itself

On the surface, normative conflict in the United States takes shape as a series of public policy battles between those who are ostensibly either conservative or liberal on a wide range of domestic issues—abortion and reproductive technologies, sexuality, the family, the teaching of values in the public schools, multiculturalism, funding for the arts, the relationship between church and state, the role of religion in politics, and so on. It is essential to note, however, that there are layers of subterranean friction and hostility that animate these disputes over governmental policy. For example, the controversy over abortion is more than a conflict over the politics of reproduction. Rather, it is a debate over the meaning of motherhood and the nature and extent of individual liberty. So too, the dispute over the National Endowment for the Arts and its funding of controversial art is more than a disagreement over the politics of governmental patronage. It is a serious debate over what constitutes "art" and what normative ideals art will represent. Likewise, the quarrels over textbooks in public schools are more than conflicts over the politics of educational curricula. Instead they are disagreements over the national ideals bequeathed to America's next generation. Similarly, the antagonisms over domestic partnerships and other gay rights concerns are more than squabbles over the legal rights of homosexuals. They represent a serious debate over the fundamental definition of "the family." And the brawls over crèche scenes on public property or prayer at school-sponsored sporting events are more than examples of the politics of church and state. Rather, they portray the evolving public debate over the role of religious institutions and religious authority in an increasingly secular society.[1] And so it goes. The family, the arts, faith, education, the media, law, and government—each realm is beset by a myriad of political controversies that themselves signal yet deeper crises over the very meaning and purpose of the core institutions of American society.

And percolating just under the surface of these conflicts over the meaning and purpose of American institutions are competing moral ideals of how citizens ought to order and maintain public life. These ideals are not mere political ideologies, reducible to party platforms. Rather, they are the moral visions that fuel vehement disagreements over policy and politics. Definitions of these ideals will be varied and nuanced. That is, citizens tend to articulate their moral ideals in a variety of ways. But when activists use the symbols of public discourse to translate these ideals, the ideals invariably come to represent sharply antagonistic tendencies. One moral vision is predicated upon the assurance that the achievements and traditions of the past should serve as the foundation of communal life and guide us in negotiating today's and tomorrow's challenges. Though often tinged with nostalgia, this vision is misunderstood by those who label it as reactionary. In fact, this vision is neither regressive nor static, but rather is both syncretic and dynamic. Nevertheless, the order of life sustained by this vision does seek deliberate continuity with the guiding principles inherited from the past. The goal of this vision is the reinvigoration and realization in our society of what traditionalists consider to be the noblest ideals and achievements of civilization. Against this traditionalism is a moral vision that is ambivalent about the legacy of the past—it regards the past in part as a curiosity, in part an irrelevance, in part a useful point of reference, and in part a source of oppression. The order of life embraced by this vision idealizes experimentation and, thus, adaptation and innovation according to the changing circumstances of our time. Its aim is the further emancipation of the human spirit.

But again, there is more. Underneath it all—beneath the public policy disputes, the institutional crises, the conflicting moral visions—are different and competing understandings of what is real and the means by which we can know what is real; different and competing understandings of what is good and true and the means by which we can know what is good and true. These conflicting cultural impulses, and the moral visions that give them form, are, at their core, animated by conflicting metaphysical assumptions—realist and antirealist.

Historical Transformations

In the United States today, rudimentary metaphysical disputes over what is real and what is good and true—with all of their social and political consequences—stem from the nation's founding and the cultural impulses that dominated that historical period some two hundred years ago. These cultural impulses consisted of Enlightenment rationalism (rooted in the urban elite of Boston, Philadelphia, and the southern states) and the biblical pietism of Reformed Protestantism (which defined the theological core of most Protestant sects). In the years leading up to the American Revolution, the Enlightenment and Calvinist revolutionaries made strategic alliances with each other in opposition to British rule. But these political associations were always strained and provisional.

Particularly after the Revolution, Enlightenment and Calvinist revolutionaries no longer regarded their strategic alliance as necessary. Jedidiah Morse's Fast Day sermon delivered on May 9, 1798, set the mood for the decades to follow: "[L]et us beware," he proclaimed, ". . . of blending the end with the means. Because atheism and licentiousness are employed as instruments, by divine providence, to subvert and overthrow popery and despotism, it does not follow that atheism and licentiousness are in themselves good things, and worthy of approbation."[2] In this post-Revo-

lutionary social and political environment, the tension between the "infi-
del philosophers" and the preachers of "superstition and bigotry" was
unrelenting and the rhetoric often fierce. This tension manifested itself
most infamously in the hostility between Timothy Dwight (the grandson
of Jonathan Edwards and at the time president of Yale University) and
Thomas Jefferson. Dwight accused Jefferson of being an atheist and predicted that if Jefferson were elected to the presidency he would bring
about the destruction of Christianity in America.[3]

By the early decades of the nineteenth century public manifestations of
the conflict between the advocates of secular rationalism and the advocates of biblical faith had been buried—the powerful institutions of reformed Protestantism did not so much defeat as assimilate the ideas and
institutions of the Enlightenment. A critical reason for this assimilation
was that early nineteenth-century America remained agrarian, localistic,
and communal. Well over nine out of ten Americans lived in rural and
agrarian communities, communities with populations typically no larger
than 500 to 1,000. The residents of these communities were overwhelmingly Protestant, if not formally, then in background and disposition. Enlightenment ideas, which were at that point congenial only to a small urban elite, simply could not penetrate this environment or the public
imagination cultivated by this environment. Nor could these Enlightenment ideas penetrate beyond the indigenous hostility of Protestantism's
local clerical establishments; local clerical elites were much more influential on the population and on public culture than were the national elites
with whom we typically associate the founding period and the early
decades of the Republic.

Throughout most of the nineteenth century and early twentieth century, the influx of Catholics from Ireland, Germany, Italy, and Eastern Europe (1830–1860), and the influx of Jews primarily from Germany
(1880–1920), posed the greatest challenge to Protestant domination in
America.[4] Needless to say, the transformation in the religious and ethnic
content of the American population during this period spurred an intense
economic and political rivalry, most often expressed through religious animus. Anti-Catholicism and anti-Semitism remained defining features of
American politics and culture beyond the mid–twentieth century.

But times have changed. In the post–World War II period, and especially around the mid-1960s, one sees a dramatic transformation of
American public culture—an unmistakable trend of tolerance among
Protestants, Catholics, and Jews (as well as Mormons and others) became
evident. One series of national surveys conducted between 1966 and
1984, for example, shows that during this period strong prejudicial feeling both for and against different religious faiths declined. Neutrality
among Catholics, Protestants, and Jews generally increased, and antipa-

thy toward various religious groups subsided.[5] Most scholarly research conducted on interreligious and cultural conflict in the post–World War II period focused on anti-Semitism. And once again, the empirical data demonstrate a dramatic decrease during this period in the proportion of the population holding negative perceptions of Jews.[6] Even among white Evangelical Protestants, who represent the sector of the population historically most hostile to Jews, anti-Semitic feeling was quite low. According to one survey conducted in 1986 for the Anti-Defamation League of B'nai B'rith, there is no longer any "strong direct evidence" suggesting that "most Evangelical Christians consciously use their deeply held Christian faith and convictions as justification for anti-Semitic views."[7]

This expansion of interreligious tolerance is not an isolated phenomenon but has taken place in concert with the slow but steady expansion of social and political tolerance (toward communists and atheists), racial tolerance (toward Blacks and Hispanics), and even sexual tolerance (toward homosexuals and those cohabiting outside of marriage).[8]

No scholar would argue that interreligious and inter-ideological tension of the kind that prevailed in the nineteenth and early twentieth centuries has disappeared altogether—nor, in all likelihood, will this tension ever disappear entirely. Even so, the evidence overwhelmingly demonstrates that the social ethos of the late twentieth century has changed dramatically from that which prevailed during the preceding century and a half. The older manifestations of normative conflict have steadily waned.

The New Cultural Divide

While the older, traditional prejudices between religious factions no longer resonate throughout the populace, previous intolerances—albeit somewhat transformed—have reemerged. This reemergence has resulted in a historically unprecedented realignment of American public culture. The politically consequential divisions in the United States are no longer theological and ecclesiastical but are "cosmological." They no longer revolve around specific doctrinal issues or styles of religious practice and organization; they revolve around Americans' fundamental understandings of value, purpose, truth, freedom, and collective identity. A cultural fault line that was initially evident in the Enlightenment era but was subsequently obscured during the nineteenth century by interreligious rivalry has reemerged, wider and deeper, dividing cultural conservatives and cultural progressives. This realignment is most clearly visible in the developments within particular ecclesiastical and philosophical traditions. Hence politically relevant divisions no longer divide Protestant from Catholic, Protestant from Jew, or Catholic from Jew, but rather divide, on the basis of their metaphysical differences, "orthodox" and "progressive" within each religious tradition. Conservative Catholics, Evangelical Protestants, Orthodox Jews, and even secular Platonists have more in common with one another than with those in their own faith traditions who are progressives. Likewise, liberal Protestants, progressive Catholics, Reformed and secular Jews, and secular postmodernists have more in common with one another than with those in their own traditions who are theologically orthodox (or, in the case of secularists, who are metaphysical realists).

What animates each of the opposing sides and is at the heart of this normative conflict is differences over moral authority. Among citizens and within institutions one can find nearly infinite variation in definitions of moral authority. As these definitions filter into the grammar of public discourse, however, two different and competing impulses emerge. One impulse is characterized by a sense that ultimate reality is rooted in the transcendent. Whether apprehended through Nature or Scripture or Tradition itself, the "orthodox" view of reality allows its adherents to discern and articulate relatively fixed, even eternal, standards by which one's personal existence and the community's corporate existence can be organized and regulated. Such objective and transcendent authority defines, at least in the abstract, a consistent, immutable measure of value, purpose, goodness, and identity. It tells us what is good, what is true, how we should live, and who we are. It is an authority that is universal in its reach and sufficient for all time. It is these *formal* metaphysical properties that provide the common ground for Evangelical Protestants (in their commitment to the authority of Scripture), orthodox Catholics (in their commitment to the traditions of the Church and the teachings of the magisterium), Orthodox Jews (in their commitment to Torah and to the integrity of the community that lives and interprets the Torah), and secular Platonists (in their commitment to a high view of Nature and natural law).

Animating the other side of the cultural divide is a sense of ultimate reality that rejects the possibility of fixed standards outside of human experience, privileging instead what we can apprehend through our senses in our personal experience. Truth, if not verified through scientific observation, is therefore personal; it emerges out of experience and is necessarily contingent. According to this view, what is "real" or what is "good" is not so much constant and enduring as conditional and more or less relative.

These two competing moral visions—the orthodox and the progressive—represent the twin metaphysical traditions of the secular Enlightenment, positivism and subjectivism. Today's postmodernism is now rejecting the former and eagerly embracing the latter.

Though these sketches of the orthodox and progressive sides in today's culture war are broad and tentative, they nevertheless provide insight into the political debate over abortion, gay rights, education policy, and a host of other issues. In particular, the coexistence of discrete sources of moral authority helps to explain the nature of the present conflict over issues concerning the human body.

To cultural progressives, the individual's right to formulate his or her own views on the meaning of life is indisputable. This stems in large part from the progressivist notion (whether conscious or unconscious) of individual autonomy, which draws on the Enlightenment's project of liberating the self. According to progressives, reality is fluid, a product of one's creative engagement with the world. Based in part on this intellectual foundation, the progressivist conception of moral authority generates a loose assortment of precepts. These precepts may include the idea that personhood begins more or less at birth (or when science determines), that gender difference is essentially biological, and that the common understanding of "female" and "male" is merely the product of accretion and social construction. It follows from these premises that human sexuality represents a biological need that can be met in any number of ways, the best of which takes place in the context of a caring and healthy relationship. Additionally, marriage and family structures are culturally determined and open to variation.

For the orthodox, the individual is secondary to the religious tradition. The universality of orthodox moral authority prevents the individual from claiming an independent moral space. Rather, moral law applies equally to the skeptic and the faithful. This means that one's views on the nature of human life—particularly its origin in conception and its subsequent sacredness—carry more than the weight of any one individual's conviction. There is little room for negotiation and compromise. As the existence of a Transcendent Reality is not held to be an individual projection, neither is the application of this Reality limited to the individual. Rather, traditionalists decide moral questions based on universally applied moral laws. Just as disbelief in the law of gravity does not exempt one from gravity's effects, neither does disbelief in the orthodox version of moral authority free one from responsibility before the universal law.

Passion and Sacredness

In tracing this debate over moral authority back in this way, it is clear that what is at the center of today's normative conflict is more than "values" and "opinions." Such language misconstrues the nature of the cultural forces at play and the moral commitments of those individuals and groups involved. The language of "values" reduces moral commitment to preferences and "lifestyle" choices. Today's conflict burrows deeper into the culture and deeper into people's pretheoretical consciousness.

What we are dealing with here are two fundamentally different conceptions of the "sacred" and the moral authority by which people apprehend the sacred. To speak of the sacred is to speak of our most basic assumptions and intuitions—assumptions and intuitions that inform our moral imagination about what is good and true and right. At this level, it is not easy to negotiate in the American culture war. Nothing else can account for the extraordinary energy and emotional intensity of the conflict except that what is at stake in the culture war are people's most cherished ideals and commitments.

In this light, it should be clear that normative conflict is not merely a manifestation of the antagonism between religious faith and secular reason. Such a formulation presupposes that religion is sectarian and particularistic, whereas the secular is common to all, and therefore morally and politically neutral. Rather, what I am talking about illustrates what Michael Polanyi referred to as the "fiduciary nature" of knowledge.[9] The idea that the secular is any less particularistic—and therefore less "sectarian"—than theistic religion is philosophically naive and sociologically untenable. What we have in the contemporary American culture war are competing understandings of the sacred, competing faiths—in reality, competing parochialisms. And this fierce competition is all about which moral vision will prevail.

Institutional Factors

Though normative conflict in the United States is rooted in competing cultural systems and worldviews, these cultural systems and worldviews are not free-floating in the social world. They take concrete institutional form in the class structure, party system, and the voluntary sector of American society, as well as in the institutions of American public discourse.

Class and Social Location

Traditional class-based theories explain very little of what is going on in the United States today. The culture war is not between haves and have-nots; not between the urban proletariat and the upper middle class of owners and managers. Rather, the culture war plays itself out within the white middle classes. The principal players on both sides of the cultural conflict are the cultural elites—those who derive their livelihood from the knowledge sector of the economy. How could it be otherwise? As this is a struggle to define the normative realities of public life, the primary actors are those elites in reality-defining institutions—the media, universities, think tanks, voluntary organizations, special-interest groups, and so on.

There is a key social difference among these primary actors, however, which falls along status lines. While virtually all cultural elites have college or university degrees, and often professional degrees, cultural conservatives (as in the leadership of the pro-life movement, the legal defense establishment, the public policy pressure groups, and the literary establishment) tend to draw their degrees from denominationally affiliated colleges (those within the religious orbit of orthodoxy) and second-tier state universities. In contrast, the leadership of progressive causes tends to draw its credentials from the elite private schools of the Ivy League and the prestigious public universities. As to social location, it is important to point out that the respective centers of orthodox and progressive activism differ as well. A survey of more than 400 public affairs organizations found that the overwhelming majority (83 percent) of those that were committed to progressivist causes were located in Washington and New York as well as Boston, Chicago, and Los Angeles, whereas only about half (56 percent) of those committed to conservative causes were located in these cities. The remainder of the conservative organizations were located in towns and small cities (such as Colorado Springs, Colorado; Lynchburg, Virginia; Wheaton, Illinois); one-fifth of these organizations were located in the South.[10]

Clearly these geographic differences reflect the social location of each side's respective constituencies. The constituencies that support culturally conservative issues are disproportionately from the lower-middle-class occupations from the suburban and small-town areas of the South and the Midwest. These conservative constituencies are also found in the traditionally ethnic neighborhoods in urban areas. (In all areas, these conservative supporters are older than the general population and disproportionately female.) By contrast, the grassroots membership of progressive causes is disproportionately represented by the highly educated, professionally oriented, mobile upper middle classes from the metropolitan areas on both coasts. (The majority are also younger than the general population and disproportionately male.) The key distinguishing factor between the opposing constituencies, however, is higher education.

Politics

Perhaps the most visible manifestation of the American culture war is in the party system. Cultural conservatives have a dominant voice in the Republican Party and cultural progressives hold sway over the Democratic Party. This has not always been the case, however. Historically, Southerners—Southern Evangelicals, in particular—could be counted upon to vote with the Democratic Party. So too, northern and Midwestern Catholics were typically Democratic Party loyalists. As Archbishop John

Whealon explains, "I [was] a somewhat typical example of [the] link between U.S. Catholics and Democrats. In my childhood home, God and Jesus Christ were first, the Catholic Church second, and the Democratic Party was third."[11] Yet in the presidential elections, both Southerners in general and white Southern Evangelicals in particular fled the Democratic Party in droves in the 1980s to support Republican candidates: 61 percent went for Ronald Reagan in 1980; 79 percent went for Reagan in 1984; and 72 percent went for George Bush in 1988. Likewise, Catholic voters could no longer be relied upon as a Democratic voting bloc—the more traditional Catholics voted for conservative Republicans, and the more progressive Catholics voted for liberal Democrats.[12] The same tendencies are at play within the Jewish community.

Political scientists have viewed this shift in political constituencies with astonishment, as though the shifts in party affiliation and voting behavior by Evangelicals, Catholics, and Jews means something important; they have assumed that the electorate has changed in a meaningful way. In fact the substantive change is not in these voters (who at least on cultural issues were always conservative and remain so) but in the parties that presume to represent them. As Archbishop Whealon puts it, "The nation needed Franklin Roosevelt and the Democrats to bring legal power to the trade unions, security for the elderly, subsidies to the farmers, and special help to the poor. But by its repeated stance in favor of abortion, the Democratic Party has abandoned the Catholic Church and fragmented a Catholic bloc."[13]

The Voluntary Sector

The principal way in which Americans have institutionalized normative conflict is in the voluntary sector and, most prominently, in the special agenda organizations. It is here that people formulate and publicize opposing moral visions, giving them power in social life and endurance over time. Thus, the special agenda organizations have become the chief carriers of the culture war.

Historically, special agenda organizations have come and gone with the passing of issues.[14] Even so, their presence and prominence in public affairs have grown dramatically since the mid-1960s. One observer who closely monitors all such organizations describes this growth as "unparalleled in American history."[15] It is probably impossible to obtain an accurate total number of special agenda organizations today, but the best estimates place the figure around 3,000, most of which were founded after 1970.[16] Since the beginning of that decade, for example, activists have founded 89 women's groups, 86 peace groups, 58 civil liberties groups, about 50 politically oriented consumer groups, 45 or so gay and lesbian rights organizations, roughly the same number of conservative social groups, 36 or more environmentalist groups, and nearly a dozen antipornography groups. The number of special agenda organizations that are religious in character has more than doubled in the last half century—from approximately 400 in 1945 to more than a thousand today. All of these special agenda organizations are national in scope, and all, along with their related political action committees (PACs),[17] continue to exert influence today.[18]

To get a sense of the resources involved, consider as an example the special agenda organizations involved in the abortion controversy. On the abortion rights side, there is the National Organization for Women (NOW), with a staff of 28 and an annual budget of $6.2 million. NOW also claims 250,000 members, 9 regional offices, 50 state groups, and 800 local chapters. Planned Parenthood has a staff of 227, a budget of $300 million, and 20,000 volunteers. (The large budget is derived primarily from government contracts and the income from Planned Parenthood clinics.) The National Abortion Rights Action League (NARAL) has a staff of 34 (most of whom are professionals), 250,000 members, and a budget of $4 million. Besides its national organization, it also has 41 state groups. The Religious Coalition for Abortion Rights has a staff of 9, a total of 27 state groups, and an annual budget of over $1.3 million. Not least is the American Civil Liberties Union (ACLU) Reproductive Rights Project, which has a budget of $2 million.[19] These groups comprise the central institutions committed to sustaining liberal abortion policy.

On the pro-life side are such organizations as Concerned Women for America (CWA), the conservative counterpart to NOW. Like NOW, CWA is not exclusively concerned with abortion. It has a staff of 29, a membership of over 500,000, a total of 1,800 local chapters in all 50 states, and a budget of over $7 million. Then there is the National Right to Life Committee (NRLC). Clearly the largest of the pro-life organizations, it has a staff of 39, a membership of 11 million, 50 state groups, and 2,500 local chapters. The American Life League has a staff of 31, a membership of 270,000, a total of 16 branches, and a budget of nearly $10 million. Likewise, the American Life Lobby has a staff of about 30, nearly 300,000 members, a group in every state, and a budget of $2.5 million.

On its own, the expansion of these special agenda structures in the post–World War II period would seem a rather insignificant development. But coupled with the weakening of denominational ties, this expansion has fostered the deepening of century-old intrafaith divisions. In fact, most special agenda organizations coalesce fairly tightly around the poles—conservative or progressive—of the new cultural axis.

At the same time, special agenda organizations increasingly provide the institutional framework for the broader realignment of public culture. Within the parameters of their political mission, activists in these organizations communicate with one another and even draw direct support from one another. For example, in a survey of forty-seven public affairs organizations, leaders from every organization claimed to be in communication with individuals or groups outside of their own religious or philosophical tradition. Most of these leaders had even engaged at one point or another in active cooperation. The public affairs office of the Orthodox Jewish organization Agudath Israel, for example, regularly allies itself with Catholics on issues concerning private education, and with conservative Protestants on moral issues. Grassroots contributions supported the overwhelming majority of the forty-seven public affairs organizations surveyed. In fact, all but one or two public affairs organizations claimed to receive contributions from Protestants, Catholics, Eastern Orthodox, and Jews. The Religious Coalition for Abortion Rights, for example, had 31 member organizations by 1988, including such diverse groups as the American Jewish Congress, Catholics for a Free Choice, the American Humanist Association, the YWCA, the United Methodist Church, and the Women's League for Conservative Judaism.

Despite this diverse grassroots support, special agenda organizations tend to become autonomous from the people they represent and hence develop something of a life of their own.[20] This is particularly evident in the ideological character of their work and the zealotry of the professionals who promote their agenda.[21] As studies have repeatedly shown, the attitudes and agenda of movement elites are nearly always more extreme than the attitudes and agenda of the constituencies they purportedly represent.[22] The "win at all cost" orientation of movement elites is reinforced by their reliance on litigation.[23] By its very nature, litigation polarizes people as adversaries in the zero-sum logic of winner take all.

The consequences of all this activist litigation are substantial. Political analysts have repeatedly observed that special agenda organizations and their PACs have eclipsed the power of the traditional party system, rendering the parties as tools of the competing interests and of the agendas of the culture war. Then-President George Bush acknowledged as much in a speech in 1989 when he said that special agenda organizations "and their $160 million war chests overshadow the great parties of Thomas Jefferson and Abraham Lincoln."[24]

Another consequence of the prominence of special agenda organizations in public life is that these organizations have come to dominate the content and conduct of public debate.

Public Discourse

Special agenda organizations provide the dominant voices in the evolving public debate over everything from educational vouchers to abortion rights to funding for the arts. Not only are special agenda organizations active in initiating litigation and other policy battles, but also they shape the public commentary about these contests. According to a study of the media coverage of the 1989 *Webster* decision, for example, special agenda activists accounted for 42 percent of all sources quoted.[25] Of 869 citations, the National Organization for Women had the most, with 75 citations; the National Abortion Rights Action League followed with 72; the National Right to Life Committee was next, with 65 citations; Operation Rescue had 28; and the ACLU, especially its Reproductive Rights Project, followed with 20 citations. It is not just that special agenda organizations offer the loudest and most prominent voices in the "debate," they also (and just as important) establish the *framework* for the debate. They do this through a strategy of aggressive litigation and the careful use of new communications technologies such as direct mail, sound bites, talk shows, political advertisements, the Internet, and so on. These new communications technologies are especially important because they are resistant to public accountability. This lack of accountability explains why public rhetoric is so often shrill and extreme, concerned less with making credible and compelling arguments than with discrediting the opposition.

This brings us to the unique complexity of the normative conflict taking place in the United States. The form in which the dynamics of faith and culture are played out most sharply is not in the accumulated subjective attitudes of independent citizens but rather in the competing moral visions in public culture that have evolved and crystallized over the past several decades—the institutions and elites that produce them and the structures of rhetoric by which they are framed and articulated. It is through the social organization and articulation of these moral visions within the culture-forming institutions of public discourse that they become a reality sui generis—ultimately a reality larger than and independent (in the sense of disembodied) from those who give it expression. The intentions behind speech acts and any qualification or nuance that public speakers might offer become irrelevant. In this Durkheimian sense, the speakers—both individuals and organizations—become separated from their own speech.

It is in this Durkheimian sense that the idea of the "culture war"—with its implied stridency, polarization, and mobilization of resources—assumes its greatest conceptual force. Culture is certainly complicated. On the one hand, there are strong impulses—philosophical and sociological—toward moral and political consistency, such that individuals who hold strong opinions on one issue will hold comparable opinions on other issues. Yet the evidence suggests that people's polarized reactions to public policy differ from one issue to the next. People can hold liberal views on some matters and conservative views on others. This is also true for organizations. For example, the *New York Times* may take progressive editorial positions on some issues and moderate and conservative positions on others. The central point is this: However individuals or organizations align themselves on particular issues, they become subservient to—and if unwilling to submit, must struggle against—the dominating and virtually irresistible categories and logic of the culture war. Activists tend to force attitudes and opinions into the grid of rhetorical extremes.

This has consequences for the majority of Americans who occupy the vast middle ground between opposing cultural poles. In most cases, the middle is eclipsed by the stridency of the extremes. It is for precisely this reason that public discourse in the United States is more polarized than are Americans themselves.

Normative Conflict and America's Legitimation Crisis

This polarized discourse and the ensuing normative conflict constitute a peculiar predicament for the state: the problem of sustaining its own legitimacy. In short, normative conflicts in the United States, in particular those fundamental controversies over what is good and true and just, posit a crisis of legitimacy for those who govern. In practical terms this means that people on opposing sides of the cultural divide operate with fundamentally different criteria of legitimacy: What one side regards as good law, the other side regards as bad law, and vice versa. The state, then, is caught in a zero-sum bind. Its legitimacy is contingent on embracing what some fundamentally reject as illegitimate. On every issue, no matter what position the government takes, some powerful faction will call the government's authority into question.

In a more traditional setting, when facing a crisis the state could invoke the common values and ideals rooted in traditional religion or folk culture or even nationalist identity as the means to maintain social integration and to buttress the state's own flagging authority. But these older cultural resources no longer resonate deeply in the collective consciousness of the United States. Pluralism has rendered them weak. Instead the modern state increasingly has had to rely on procedural norms concerned with the legality and constitutionality of its actions as its source of justification. The problem is that the procedures themselves, not to mention the institutions established to put these procedures into effect, are also vulnerable to public scrutiny, doubt, criticism, and cynicism.

It is clear now just how unique and historically contingent the earlier normative consensus in the United States was. In the context of the present normative conflict, that consensus has all but completely unraveled—deconstructed by postmodernist philosophy, and rendered practically implausible by pluralism itself.[26] To the extent that a "moral center" does exist, it has been effectively silenced by the acerbic and seemingly autonomous rhetoric of the extremes. As moral philosophers are fond of saying, the disagreements go all the way down. They even extend to those civic institutions that should, in fact, mitigate conflict.

Civil Society

Ancient philosophers as well as the framers of the American Constitution all anticipated that the democratic ideal would be founded on the participation of an informed citizenry in government. "Whenever people are well-informed," Jefferson wrote, "they can be trusted with their own government; [so] that whenever things get so far wrong as to attract their notice, they may be relied on to set them to rights."[27] For this reason Jefferson, like Washington, Madison, and Adams, among others, advocated education for the common people. "Let our countrymen know, that the people alone can protect us against these evils [of tyranny], and that the tax which will be paid for this purpose, is not more than the thousandth part of what will be paid to kings, priests and nobles, who will rise up among us if we leave the people in ignorance."[28] But by what means can the common people—comprising individuals and groups holding fundamentally different conceptions of the moral order—participate in one, unified government?

Clearly public education of one sort or another is essential to the creation of an informed and civic-minded populace. But public education is just one of a wide range of institutions that comprise "civil society," institutions that stand between the individual and the state, *mediating* between private interests and government functions—the press, professional organizations, philanthropic institutions, and institutions of faith (churches, synagogues, denominations, and the like). Unlike the special agenda organizations that by charter stand for one set of interests or another, these institutions, in principle, exist for all citizens. They are not exclusive but rather exist as a central component of common life, providing either a forum for public debate, a stimulus to public debate, or the information that makes substantive public debate possible. In theory, they bridge the gap between antagonists, thereby transforming cultural conflict into civil conversation.

Philanthropy and Foundations: A Case Study

Consider one such mediating institution—public philanthropy and, in particular, the public role of private foundations. Philanthropy is an interesting case study for three reasons: It is quintessentially American; as an institution it characterizes the vitality and power of civil society as it is uniquely positioned within society to play a role in ameliorating normative conflict; and it exemplifies many of the difficulties attending today's institutions of civil society.

American Exceptionalism

Philanthropy, both individual and institutional, is part of the fabric of American volunteerism. What in France was accomplished through the state and in Britain through the aristocracy, was in America, as Tocqueville observed, accomplished through its own citizens in voluntary associations.[29] Rooted in a Puritan legacy that affirmed the interrelationship between individual prosperity, virtue, charity, and community well-being, philanthropy was an ingrained habit of otherwise individualistic Americans—Americans who would routinely pool private resources and form voluntary associations to promote collective interests and the common good, whether this meant aiding those who had fallen on hard times, building a library, or founding a school.

Today this Puritan legacy remains intact. Indeed, a majority of Americans remain committed sponsors of the nonprofit or so-called "third sector." These Americans believe that helping others is a fundamental moral obligation.[30] In 1994, for example, reported philanthropic contributions in the United States totaled $129.9 billion, or approximately 2 percent of the gross national product. This excludes the value of volunteer labor, which is worth more than all the cash and in-kind gifts that nonprofit organizations receive combined. In 1994, individuals, via living and willed gifts combined, gave almost 88 percent of all contributions to nonprofits.[31] According to estimates provided by the American Association for Fund-Raising Council Trust for Philanthropy, total giving from living individuals in 1994 amounted to $105.1 billion.[32] Since 1995 giving has grown every year in current dollars, although in one-quarter of the years it has lost ground to inflation.[33] In 1993 approximately 73 percent of American households reported giving an average of 1.84 percent of their household income to charitable causes.[34] It is not just the wealthy who represent the bulk of personal giving. Indeed, just about half of all charity dollars come from families with incomes of under $25,000. In addition, people with incomes of $5,000 to $10,000 contribute two and one-half times more of their income than do people with incomes of $50,000 to $100,000 (3.9 percent compared to 1.6 percent). Even in families with incomes of $5,000 or less, the average given in 1981 was $238, about 5 percent of their total income.[35]

Cross-national comparisons highlight the exceptionalism of American philanthropy. The Johns Hopkins Comparative Nonprofit Sector Project found in its national surveys of giving and volunteering in the United States, France, and Germany in the early 1990s that 7 out of 10 Americans had donated money in the previous 12 months, compared to 4 out of 10 German and French citizens. Not only was the overall proportion of givers in the population significantly higher in the United States, but also the average contribution made by Americans was 7 or 8 times larger than the average French or German contribution. The average sum of money donated during the previous year amounted to $851 in the United States, $120 in Germany, and $96 in France. And whereas one-half of all individual donations in the United States were $300 or higher, the median German and French donations were about $40—13 to 15 percent of the U.S. figure. The Johns Hopkins researchers found that Americans donated on average about 1.2 percent of their annual income, Germans donated 0.3 percent, and the French donated 0.15 percent.[36] Researchers have compared national giving as a percentage of personal income. In 1985 Canadians gave on average just 0.76 percent of their total annual income, and the average British citizen gave 0.52 percent. In sum, "as a proportion of personal income, Americans give about four times more than the British and about two and a half times more than the Canadians."[37] In the Western industrialized world outside of the United States, the apparatus of the state tends to affect virtually every aspect of life and consequently leaves little room for public activity that is genuinely autonomous from the state or the market.[38] In most Western nations the state virtually monopolizes institutions for public care and welfare—including the church.[39] In Japan voluntary nonprofits are, for all intents and purposes, also nonexistent. Here too the lack of an independent philanthropic sector stems from the fact that the state has joined hands with powerful market forces "in such a way that it is extremely difficult to discern the existence of a public sphere standing between the two."[40]

Of course, the philanthropic spirit in the United States is not in the least bit dampened by the government's unique support for the nonprofit sector in its tax codes. Two cornerstones underlie U.S. tax policy toward charitable activity: the deductions for contributions allowed in major federal taxes (the personal income tax, the corporate tax, and the estate tax); and the tax-exempt status generally accorded nonprofit institutions.[41] As a case in point, most millionaires who are philanthropically inclined admit that they give up to the maximum for which they can receive a deduction, but not much more. In one study of the giving patterns of 135 wealthy donors, fewer than ten claimed that taxes had no important impact on their giving decisions.[42]

Foundations and Public Life

Clearly a favorable tax environment also has encouraged the proliferation of philanthropic foundations in the United States.[43] By the mid-1980s the *Foundation Directory* listed more than 25,000 foundations, each with assets of over $1 million and/or donations of at least $100,000 annually.[44] The years 1980–1989 represent a peak in foundation establishment. More than 3,000 foundations with assets of at least $1 million and/or grants of at least $100,000 were formed during the 1980s. Of the 37,000 foundations in existence today, 13,000 were formed since 1980.[45] Approximately 80 percent of foundations today are funded from a single donor and are known as independent foundations.[46] In the past twenty-five years the assets of American foundations (including corporate foundations) have more than tripled and now stand at approximately $189.2 billion. In 1994 foundations gave away more than $10 billion in grants.[47] As Waldemar Nielsen observed in 1985, "No other nation in the world has such an array of aggregations of private wealth devoted to public purposes; no other nation has been so encouraging to donors to create such philanthropic institutions; no other has given them, once created, such freedom of action; and in no other have foundations played such a significant role in a nation's life."[48]

The most interesting change in the foundation world in the post–World War II period is the increasing involvement of foundations in public affairs advocacy of one sort or another.[49] Until this time, the charitable activities of foundations were relatively uncontroversial. Foundations supported medical and scientific research, they funded scholarship and the arts, they focused on education and conservation. Even as foundations began to turn to the amelioration of social problems, their strategy was to maximize the use of university-based knowledge to solve problems. Thus the famous liberal foundations (e.g., Carnegie, Ford, and Rockefeller) gave enormous sums for research in both the natural and social sciences to further societal problem solving, whereas the more conservative foundations continued to support "concrete" projects like building libraries.[50] Even when foundations did focus on building projects and scientific research, it was assumed that the larger, more forward-looking foundations were ultimately supposed to influence public policy. During the 1960s, for example, especially during the Kennedy administration, foundation specialists worked closely with their counterparts in the federal government. According to the accepted wisdom of the time, philanthropy was to create "pilot programs for government to take over."[51]

Since the early 1970s, however, there has been a shift in project funding away from both university-based research and "bricks and mortar" projects (the building of hospitals, libraries, and community centers) toward the direct support of advocacy groups and public policy. Today a significant segment of the foundation elite envision themselves on the cutting edge of practical social innovation; they aim to fund projects that seek massive changes in American society.[52] There is a widespread assumption today that in order for a philanthropic foundation to be in the vanguard, that is, to be living up to its full potential, it must recognize its obligation to bring about constructive social change.[53] Today the majority of foundations have come to equate "public purpose" with influencing the policies of the federal government.

But what is the cumulative effect of this effort, particularly in relation to normative conflict in the United States? Do the foundations provide a bridge between the opposing sides in the culture war? As a matter of fact, foundation insiders view themselves and the foundations they lead as bridge builders. They are quick to contend that only a small proportion of foundations fund politicized grants. These insiders also contend that foundations represent a diversity that is typical of the nation as a whole. As Robert Payton, former president of the Exxon Education Foundation, put it, "If the marketplace is indifferent, the government is incompetent. What we've done in our society, therefore, has been to develop the philanthropic alternative. Within it there is so much diversity that it is unthinkable that anybody is dominating anything."[54]

Payton's point has some merit. According to J. Craig Jenkins, an authority on the foundation patronage of social movement organizations, foundations that fund social movements are "innovative and relatively unconventional actors within their own world." Jenkins asserts that at its peak in 1977, foundation giving to social movements accounted for barely 0.69 percent of total foundation giving and averaged only 0.24 percent of total giving. In 1977 only 131 of a possible 22,000 active grant-giving foundations funded a social movement project.[55] Nevertheless, foundations, which accounted for a mere 7.6 percent of total giving in 1994,[56] have the assets and inclination to target their grants strategically; this gives foundations inordinate influence in the third sector and in public policy. With their flexibility, their commitment to innovation, and their freedom to engage both the state and the market, foundations exercise tremendous influence. In short, the largest foundations have a disproportionate potential to shape and alter the course of public affairs. They have "critical mass," and consequently "their funds have leverage."[57]

Partisanship in the Foundation World

Certainly one can give foundation elites the benefit of the doubt; they are undeniably sincere in their efforts to seek the public good. But when American public culture is so divided over the nature and content of the public good, it is not surprising that controversies over the definition of "the public good" will spill over into the world of philanthropy and, in particular, the world of the foundations. Foundations themselves are divided along the fault line of the contemporary culture war. Both conser-

TABLE 1.1   Twenty Most Partisan Foundations (Based on the Number of Progressive or Conservative Grants)

Ten Most Liberal		Ten Most Conservative	
Foundation	*Number of Grants*	*Foundation*	*Number of Grants*
Ford Foundation	262	John M. Olin Foundation	75
John D. and Catherine MacArthur Foundation	96	Smith Richardson Foundation	74
J. Roderick MacArthur Foundation	82	Amoco Foundation	41
Public Welfare Foundation	63	Bradley Foundation	37
New World Foundation	55	Sarah Scaife Foundation	33
ARCO Foundation	54	J. M. Foundation	17
Carnegie Corporation of New York	49	Alcoa Foundation	15
Rockefeller Family Fund	47	Rockwell International Corp. Trust	14
Rockefeller Foundation	44	Samuel Roberts Noble Foundation	14
George Gund Foundation	43	Ford Motor Company Fund	12

Source: Althea Nagai, Robert Lerner, and Stanley Rothman, *The Culture of Philanthropy: Foundations and Public Policy* (Washington, D.C.: Capital Research Center, 1991), 21–23.

vative and progressive foundations provide the resources for the advancement of competing cultural and policy agendas. Yet the foundation world is not evenly divided. Consider the funding patterns of the largest, most partisan foundations, as listed in Tables 1.1 and 1.2.

One can make a few quick observations about these funding patterns. First, a comparison of those foundations that give the most to progressivist causes with those that give the most to conservative causes illustrates the statistical preponderance of progressivist grant giving. No foundation awards as many grants to conservative groups as Ford and the two MacArthur foundations each make to progressivist causes. In sum, the ten most progressivist foundations make an average of 795 liberal grants in the course of a year, whereas the ten most conservative foundations make an average of only 332 conservative grants in that same period—a ratio of approximately 2.5 to 1. Despite this preponderance of progressivist grants, conservative projects receive considerably more per grant. On average, the typical foundation gives $49,340 per liberal grant and $112,756 per conservative grant. (This may reflect the fact that there are more liberal recipients competing for available funds.[58]) Most conservative grant proposals that receive funding are for research,

TABLE 1.2   Twenty Most Partisan Foundations (Based on Mean Dollar Amount per Progressive or Conservative Grant)

Ten Most Liberal		Ten Most Conservative	
Foundation	*Mean Amount/ Grant*	*Foundation*	*Mean Amount/ Grant*
MacArthur Foundation	$437,159/96	A. Burnett and C. Tandy Foundation	$2,000,000/1
R. W. Johnson Foundation	$381,932/15	Conrad N. Hilton Foundation	$1,594,878/1
R. K. Mellon Foundation	$366,667/3	McCune Foundation	$750,000/1
Andrew Mellon Foundation	$362,857/14	J. Howard Pew Freedom Trust	$280,000/4
Joan B. Kroc Foundation	$303,333/3	John Hartford Foundation	$260,476/2
Jessie B. DuPont Fund	$255,000/1	Sarah Scaife Foundation	$136,667/33
W. K. Kellogg Foundation	$211,867/20	Bradley Foundation	$109,519/37
Pew Memorial Trust	$191,750/4	Smith Richardson Foundation	$76,156/74
Wm. and Flora Hewlett Foundation	$183,700/20	M. J. Murdock Foundation	$70,640/5
H. J. Kaiser Family Foundation	$176,016/6	John M. Olin Foundation	$55,600/75

Source: Althea Nagai, Robert Lerner, and Stanley Rothman, *The Culture of Philanthropy: Foundations and Public Policy* (Washington D.C.: Capital Research Center, 1991), 21–23.

whereas liberal proposals tend to be for action-oriented projects. That is, among conservative grants given, 55 percent were for research projects, 42 percent were oriented toward "doing something," and 3 percent were for conferences or workshops. By contrast, 25 percent of liberal grants were awarded for research purposes, 71 percent for "action" projects, and 4 percent for conferences.[59]

Other studies confirm that foundation giving is not at all balanced. In a study of 844 foundations, which gave over $1 million in grants to various nonprofit enterprises in at least several cities, Althea Nagai, Robert Lerner, and Stanley Rothman found that foundation leaders' "theoretical commitment to philanthropic pluralism does not extend to the ideological sphere."[60] The majority of foundation leaders and foundations promote an "adversary viewpoint" and push for social change, most often in the liberal direction.[61] To be sure, though only a small proportion of foundations fund politicized grants, when the typical foundation does involve itself in public policy matters, "it most often supports a liberal [progressivist] project (such as reproductive rights) and sometimes prominent liberal recipients such as the American Civil Liberties Union."[62] Because, "unlike the media, [foundation elites] see little reason to maintain any ideological balance in their grant-making, when ideological factors do come into play, most [foundation elites] continue to favor progressivist recipients by an overwhelming margin."[63] Thus when foundations award grants with an ideological slant, they make nearly four times as many liberal as conservative grants. Of the 4,738 public policy grants in Nagai et al.'s study, 57 percent were politicized: 44 percent were liberal and 13 percent were conservative. When Nagai et al. categorized these grants in terms of total dollars awarded, of the $386,470,000 distributed in public policy grants, $212,839,800 (roughly 55 percent) went to politicized groups, with progressivist groups receiving about four times as much as conservative recipients.[64]

The Emergence of Adversary Philanthropy

The preponderance of progressives in the foundation world invites some explanation. After all, the big donors who originally set up these foundations tended to be entrepreneurs and "self-made men."[65] Teresa Odendahl, in her study of big donors, discovered that "[w]hatever their political perspectives, [generous philanthropists] had strong anti–welfare state ideologies."[66] In general these donors mistrust the federal bureaucracy and worry about excessive governmental intervention in the form of the welfare state. As John D. MacArthur put it, "the only thing that will save this country is a paper shortage." And yet, over the course of two generations or so, foundations have tended to turn in a direction that their founders would likely have found dubious—namely, exhibiting a propensity to become more liberal and adversarial over time. While individual donors themselves prefer to support traditional civic projects such as university buildings and hospitals, the arts, well-known charities, and churches, foundations are susceptible to the allure of funding "dramatic change." Consider the evolution of two philanthropic institutions: Carnegie and Pew.

The Carnegie Corporation was founded by Andrew Carnegie in 1911. Starting out in this country as an impoverished Scottish immigrant, Carnegie—with a mixture of brilliant business acumen, hard work, and unflagging energy—was a millionaire by his mid-thirties. According to biographer Martin Wooster, Carnegie was "an articulate champion of free enterprise and opponent of government."[67]

Throughout his life he made huge philanthropic donations, but even with such generous giving, his personal fortune continued to increase. In 1911 he created a trust, the broad purpose of which was "the advancement and diffusion of knowledge and understanding among the people of the United States and the British Dominions and colonies."[68] In particular, Carnegie made a list of seven priorities: funding universities; establishing libraries; establishing hospitals, medical colleges, and laboratories; providing land for development of public parks; constructing meeting places and concert halls; constructing swimming facilities (which today would most likely translate into recreational facilities of all kinds); and constructing church buildings.[69] According to Carnegie, all of these benefactions would assist the industrious poor while dodging the claims of "irreclaimably destitute, shiftless, and worthless" idlers who refused to work.[70] Historically, the Carnegie Corporation generally followed Carnegie's priorities. The Corporation, along with other large American foundations (Rockefeller and Ford in particular), sponsored the discovery of insulin and the development of the polio vaccine. It supported the research that discerned the double-helical structure of DNA. It made grants that led to the control of hookworm and yellow fever. It financed the Green Revolution and supported research into birth control. Carnegie alone endowed 2,811 libraries in the United States and Britain.[71]

In his bequest, Carnegie granted the Corporation "full authority to change policy or causes hitherto aided, from time to time, when this, in their opinion, has become necessary or desirable. They shall best conform to my wishes by using their own judgment."[72] Not surprisingly, over the years priorities did shift. During the 1970s the Carnegie Corporation focused its attention on the problems of the disadvantaged, targeting its programs toward a "comprehensive strategy of social change." It especially supported those programs most concerned with social justice, equality, and human resource development. By the mid-1980s the Carnegie Corporation was at the forefront of progressivist foundations; one sympathetic observer described it as "the quintessential liberal, activist, entrepreneurial foundation: more a combat force than a conventional charity."[73] Today Carnegie's grant recipients include such progressive activist groups as the ACLU Foundation, the Children's Defense Fund, the National Council of La Raza, the International Peace Academy, the Council of Economic Priorities, and the Arms Control Association.

The Pew Memorial Trust and the J. Howard Pew Freedom Trust, established originally by the Pews of Philadelphia with the wealth accrued in Sun Oil and Sun Shipping, offers another illustration. The Pews were fundamentalist Christians. Originally the Pew family established the Pew Memorial Trust "to meet human needs through financial support of charitable organizations or institutions in the area[s] of education, social services, religion, health care and medical research."[74] The Pew family provided more specific directives for the J. Howard Pew Freedom Trust, however. These directives reflected the Pews' strong fundamentalist beliefs and support for free enterprise. During the 1970s the Pew trusts were mostly involved in "bricks and mortar" projects. They also supported numerous religious organizations, including the Billy Graham Evangelistic Association, the National Association of Evangelicals, and the Moody Bible Institute. The Freedom Trust also supported the Hoover Institute and the American Enterprise Institute.

Following the deaths of the senior members of the Pew family, dramatic changes took place at the Pew Foundation. Grants from the Pew Memorial Trust to conservative policy-oriented institutions became fewer and by the 1980s had virtually disappeared. Likewise, in the 1980s the Pew Memorial Trust stopped funding hospital construction and renovation, and discontinued support for research into specific diseases. Pew also overhauled its funding for higher education. It dropped all grants to private Christian schools and focused on big research universities. Today Pew no longer funds conventional, religiously based health services ministries. Instead, in recent years, Pew's grants have gone to Planned Parenthood and the Center for Community Change in Washington, D.C.—"liberal and activist agencies that would never have been found on a Pew grant list even a few years earlier."[75] In contrast to Pew Memorial Trust, the narrow directives of the donor have constrained the liberalization of the J. Howard Pew Freedom Trust. Thus today the Freedom Trust administers many of the Pew Memorial Trust's former grants to religious activity.

This tale of foundation liberalization repeats itself time and time again. In the case of the Ford Foundation (a foundation with a $6.7 billion endowment and yearly grants of upwards of $285 million in 1994), the shift in grants policy was so dramatic that Ford's heir, Henry Ford II, resigned in 1977 after thirty-four years of service on the foundation's board of directors. In his letter of resignation, Ford argued that the foundation had shown no interest in the health of the American economy that made its benefactions possible: "I'm not playing the role of the hard-headed tycoon who thinks all philanthropoids are socialists and all university professors are communist," wrote Ford. "I'm just suggesting to the trustees and the staff that the system that makes the Foundation possible very probably is worth preserving. . . ."[76]

In 1990 the Ford Foundation launched its "Campus Diversity Project" with an initial investment of $1.6 million. At the University of Iowa, readings for a mandatory freshman rhetoric class have included "Against Ageism" and "Good-bye Sexist Pig—Say Hello to the New Old Boy." A new multicultural reader paid for by the Ford Foundation inspired these readings. Similarly, the City University of New York recently launched a three-year fellowship program with $250,000 from the Rockefeller Foundation. Suggested topics for study included projects in transgender phenomena such as transsexualism and other cross-gender figures. The Rockefeller Foundation has also bankrolled the Center for Advanced Feminist Studies at the University of Minnesota.[77]

One explanation for this liberal activism on the part of foundations is the relatively recent emergence of a new stratum of foundation elites. Fewer than one in ten of all active foundations existed before World War II. The majority of foundations, then, are relatively new and the elites of these foundations, according to David Samuel and other commentators, tend to share the same social characteristics and social location of progressive elites generally.[78] Once their original donors have died, foundations are often free from external constraints. Thus, foundation elites are free to pursue their own progressive agendas. Says one observer, "The preponderance of foundation grants to advocacy groups . . . suggests that foundations are less devoted to the reasoned pursuit of the public good than to the multiculturalist dogmas propounded by their staff."[79]

Interestingly, foundations and the elites who run them are a study in contrasts. Despite foundations' unprecedented private wealth and generous grant-making potential, foundation elites tend to view their own power quite modestly. Nevertheless, they prefer to use their "modest" means as societal innovators. Yet another paradox of foundations is that although they are dependent on the goodwill of the people and the peoples' formulation of and support for beneficial tax codes, the foundation elites have felt no need to justify their foundations' work to the public, preferring to stay out of the public eye. In fact, only a handful of foundations even publish public reports. As the authors of a study entitled *Foundations, Private Giving, and Public Policy* state, foundations "have tended to overestimate their immunity from public criticism and from accountability to the public."[80]

Conservative Backlash

Since the late 1970s a growing number of conservative foundations have challenged the domination of the foundation world by progressives and challenged as well the notion that constructive social change is "always something [the] government does for people."[81] Since the mid-1980s conservative foundations have become increasingly sophisticated in their attack on the dominant liberal ethos of foundation giving. They have funded conservative think tanks, supported conservative publications, and nurtured conservative scholarship. This rise of conservative work in philanthropic circles has not gone unnoticed and has not escaped criticism.

One critic, Leon Howell, notes that today's most prominent neoconservative thinkers have been especially successful in communicating their views and rallying their followers because conservative-leaning foundations support them financially. Howell cites four conservative foundations (Bradley, Olin, Smith Richardson, and Scaife—sometimes called the "Four Sisters" because they act in concert) as the prime supporters of a conservative vanguard. In 1993 these four foundations made grants totaling some $57 million. This is by no means a large figure in foundation circles, but it has had an influential impact on normative conflict because it is funneled directly to the front lines of the intellectual battlegrounds.

Some of the recipients of this funding included the Heritage Foundation, the American Enterprise Institute, Weyrich's Free Congress Foundation, the Manhattan Institute, the Institute on Religion and Democracy, and the Institute on Religion and Public Life. In ominous tones, Howell implies a sort of covert conspiracy in which numerous conservative organizations rely on the same funding sources, leading to a situation where "some of the prominent actors in the culture wars may be more closely related than observers would otherwise assume."[82]

Despite the attention some conservative foundations have received of late, it is important to reiterate that conservative foundations are vastly outnumbered by their liberal counterparts. "[A] critical mass of social-change foundations attempts to push the national agenda in a liberal direction, despite the prominence of a few conservative foundations," Nagai et al. note.[83] After studying their data, they emphasize that relatively few foundations fund projects explicitly aimed at building support for democratic capitalism. Such foundations "correctly regard themselves as a small minority in the foundation world."[84] Irving Kristol came to the same conclusion in 1978 when he wrote: "The majority of the large foundations in this country, like most of the major universities, exude a climate of opinion wherein an anti-business bent becomes a perfectly natural inclination."[85] A decade later, William Simon, president of the John M. Olin Foundation, harshly criticized the liberal bent of corporate philanthropy (and foundations): "[L]eaders of the American free enterprise system—or people acting in their name and with their corporate profits—are financing the destruction of their own system and ultimately of our free society."[86]

Reality Check

The liberalization of foundations is interesting in light of the larger context of American philanthropy. Overwhelmingly, ordinary American citizens are giving to religion. In 1994, 45.3 percent of all funds contributed went to churches and other religious organizations. In fact, over the past two decades, Americans have devoted nearly half of all philanthropic dollars to the promotion of religion and religious institutions.[87] Giving to religious organizations increased by approximately 4.5 percent in the last year—amounting to $58.87 billion in 1994.[88] Notably, while over half of all individual giving goes to churches, almost no foundation giving goes to religious endeavors.[89]

It is not just that religion receives massive outlays of individual charitable dollars, but religious faith is also an important motivating factor when it comes to the proportion of dollars that citizens give and the number of hours that they volunteer. Moreover, the most generous of givers tend to be those who are active in a religious body.[90]

Conclusions

As disheartening an end as this inquiry seems to lead to, it is important to step back and consider the story within a larger frame of reference. In global terms, of course, public life in the United States is still serene, markedly so. Normative conflict is not open warfare or anything close to it. Critics have a point, then, when they say that the term "culture war" is a serious overstatement when applied to the American case. The "things aren't so bad" perspective gains credibility when the vitality of American civic institutions is considered. It is not just private philanthropy that is so vigorous in the United States, but American institutions of public education, the press, professional life, and religion too are as healthy and dynamic as can be found anywhere in the world. In this light, there really is little about which to be concerned. American democratic institutions are not in serious jeopardy.

Fair enough. But normative conflict still exists and its character is different from anything we have ever before witnessed. The question is what, if anything, does it portend? The answer, I believe, can be found in a reexamination of the Enlightenment solution to normative conflict and its fate.

The Enlightenment solution to the problem of normative conflict worked pretty well so long as the main normative cleavages in the social order remained bounded by a diffused biblical culture. This is to say that the potential conflict between various Protestant, Catholic, and Jewish faiths could be kept under reasonable control to the extent that there remained at least minimal compatibility between the particular, and therefore *private* aspects of religious faith and the normative parameters of the *public* culture. On these terms, disagreements could flourish in private, yet on matters relating to the ordering of public life—the nature of justice, freedom, and tolerance, the proper structuring of family life, the purposes of education, the focus of public welfare, and the aims of artistic expression—there would be general agreement. This public agreement was certainly imperfect and often strained, but as a working agreement it evolved and over time came to function reasonably well. Religious warfare did, after all, stop. And while anti-Semitism and anti-Catholicism have not disappeared, they have certainly lessened in intensity.

It was because of this agreement on the ordering of the public domain that the public realm could be viewed, for all intents and purposes, as neutral territory. It was often mistakenly understood to be a secular territory, but in fact it was nothing of the sort. Ideals of justice and freedom remained informed by biblical and classical categories; the definition of the family, the direction of education, the impetus behind public welfare, and the like were all framed by the still powerful residue of a biblical culture. As such, it was shared in common by people of all faith traditions.

But as American public culture has secularized, as in the secularization of family policy, public education, arts policy, not to mention First Amendment jurisprudence, the rough compatibility between the particularities of traditional religious faith and the normative codes of the public culture began to disintegrate.

Concurrent with this development in the public culture was a transformation of the mosaic of American pluralism in ways that supported this development. The most significant way in which the mosaic changed was in the expansion of the minority of Americans who claimed to have no religious faith—"secularists," as they are called in survey research. The percentage of secularists in the United States grew from 2 percent of the general population in 1962 to 5 percent in 1972, 8 percent in 1982, and 11 percent in 1989. These individuals are disproportionately well-educated and in white-collar professions. Kindred spirits, in many ways, was the significant faction of people in the traditional faiths who also embraced this increasingly secularized public order. Chief among them were mainline religious leaders.

Given the nature of public culture today, the Enlightenment solution to the problem of normative conflict has now become part of the problem. Public culture is no longer regarded as neutral but rather as contested.

Here it is worth offering a quick aside. Even if the contested realm of public life is mostly symbolic rather than martial, we know that these are intimately related to each other. Rarely if ever is there a conflict of force that is not preceded by a conflict of normative ideals. In the course of violent conflict, the symbolic conflict provides the competing justifications for the harm done to opponents. For this reason, one can never minimize the status or consequences of normative conflict, even absent violence. Where violence is present, as it is in the conflict over race and the conflict over abortion and homosexuality, it is easy to imagine, and perhaps safe to predict, an escalation. This is particularly so in a cultural context where rhetorical extremism is so prevalent.

There is yet another problem. In the midst of the evolving normative conflict, the Enlightenment ideals of public trust and civic tolerance central to liberal democracy and the peaceable resolution of conflict have also lost credibility. The very idea of a social order in which individual interests and the larger social good would be reconciled, if not synthesized, has all but completely unraveled—deconstructed by postmodernist philosophy and social science, and rendered practically implausible by pluralism itself. To the extent that a "moral center" does exist in American public culture, it has been effectively eclipsed by the acerbic rhetoric of the social and political extremes.

In the absence of common values and ideals as the means to maintain social integration and to buttress its own flagging authority, the modern state has increasingly had to rely on procedural norms concerned with the legality and constitutionality of decisions as its source of justification. The problem is that the legitimacy of the procedures themselves, not to mention the institutions established to put them into effect, are also vulnerable to public scrutiny, doubt, criticism, and cynicism.

Despite the relative tranquillity of American social life, the question implied in the normative conflict of the late twentieth century and the failure of the Enlightenment solution to address it is: On what terms can democratic institutions and ideals be sustained?

Sociologically, it would seem essential for civil society to operate within some normative framework in which ideals of civility, sociality, and fairness are taken for granted. And yet there are those who suggest that the very search for common normative grounds is merely a cloak for a new tyranny of the majority. There are others who say that the pragmatism of procedural rationality is enough to sustain the democratic project, but this, critics point out, is probably a naive hope.

The cultural capital that has long sustained democratic institutions and practices is evaporating, that much is certain. How long it will be capable of lubricating the mechanisms of democratic life is simply unknown. It is also unknown what cultural agreements, if any, might revive democratic ideals. If there is a democratic way forward it is not likely come from the state but rather from democratic institutions themselves. Most important of these are the institutions of civil society—the strategic and cooperative effort of civic institutions like private philanthropy, the schools, civic organizations, churches, and the like. The challenge they face in the United States of somehow transcending the pressures of partisanship in the ongoing normative conflict is formidable, to be sure, but by no means impossible.

Notes

1. This general argument is elaborated in my book, *Culture Wars: The Struggle to Define America* (New York: Basic Books, 1991).

2. Henry May, *The Enlightenment in America* (Oxford: Oxford University Press, 1977), xiv.

3. The hostility between progressives and traditionalists was also institutionalized. Enlightenment progressives and political radicals, both before and after the Revolution, organized local Democratic Clubs that proliferated during this era. Deists often led these clubs, which were frequently and publicly antagonistic toward superstition and the clerisy. Though they proliferated, they did so mostly in cities, and their numbers remained relatively small. By contrast, the opposition to the ideas of the Enlightenment was organized within Federalism, a political movement that was institutionally broader and stronger. Conservatives of all stripes feared the forces of radical democracy, particularly in the wake of the Ja-

cobin uprising in France and the Reign of Terror that followed. Reformed Protestants provided just one voice of opposition, made powerful by virtue of Protestantism's ability (through the churches) to mobilize populist resentment.

4. By 1880 there were over 6 million Catholics in the United States—about 12 percent of the population. By the 1920s Catholics comprised roughly 17 percent of the American population. Between 1880 and the mid-1920s, the number of Jews increased from roughly 300,000 to 4 million—from only about one-half of one percent of the American population to a full 3 percent, all in the course of four decades.

5. Interestingly, while neutrality increased and antipathy declined, close identification among various denominations (as measured by "feelings of warmth") did not increase. These findings are a part of the University of Michigan surveys on American Presidential Politics. The "feeling thermometer" these Michigan researchers employed was a 100-point scale on which respondents located themselves according to the coldness or warmth they felt for different groups. Coldness was measured as a score between 1 and 40, neutrality between 41 and 69, and warmth between 70 and 100. For the general population, coldness toward Catholics decreased from 13 percent of the population to 9.9 percent in 1984. (Comparable figures were not available for Protestants and Jews, but for Blacks, the figure dropped from 15 percent to 11 percent.) Those neutral toward Catholics grew from 39 percent in 1966 to 46 percent in 1984. Those neutral toward Protestants grew from 27 percent in 1966 to 47 percent in 1976. And those neutral toward Jews grew from 47 percent in 1966 to 56 percent in 1976. Again Protestants and Jews were omitted from the 1984 survey. Another general indication of a growing interreligious tolerance among the American population is found in the questions surrounding the suitability of presidential candidates who personally identify with one or another religious tradition. In 1958 one of every four Americans claimed to be opposed to a nominee who was Catholic, but by 1987 the proportion had decreased to only 8 percent. Likewise, in 1958, 28 percent said that they would not vote for a candidate who was Jewish. Nearly thirty years later this figure had dropped to only 10 percent. The earlier figures were taken from a 1958 Gallup Poll, and the more current figures come from the *Williamsburg Charter Survey on Religion and Public Life*, conducted in December 1987.

6. Thus, for example, non-Jews are now far less likely to believe that Jews "have a lot of irritating faults," such as being "unscrupulous," or being "more willing than others to use shady practices to get what they want," or that they "always like to be at the head of things," or that they are "objectionable neighbors." Non-Jews are also far less likely to believe that Jews "have too much power," that they "don't care what happens to anyone but their own kind," and that they "are more loyal to Israel than to America." One can find a review of this literature in Hunter, *Culture Wars*.

7. See V. Tarrance, C. Hill, F. Newport, and M. Ryan, "Nationwide Attitudes Survey—September, 1986: A Confidential Report Presented to the Anti-Defamation League of B'nai B'rith." See also Bruce Bursma, "Anti-Semitism Fading for Some," *Chicago Tribune*, 9 January 1987, and Marjorie Hyer, "Poll Finds No Rise in Anti-Semitism: Most Evangelicals Reject Jewish Stereotypes," *Washington Post*, 10 January 1987.

8. See John Lawrence Sullivan, James Piereson, and George E. Marcus, *Political Tolerance and American Democracy* (Chicago: University of Chicago Press, 1982), for a summary of the data.

9. Michael Polanyi, *Personal Knowledge* (Chicago: University of Chicago Press, 1958).

10. See Hunter, *Culture Wars.*

11. Archbishop John F. Whealon, "The Democratic and Republican Platforms," *Crisis* (October 1988): 36–37.

12. The key measure here for Catholics is "belief orthodoxy," not measures of piety such as church attendance. These voting patterns do not show up at all on the basis of church attendance.

13. Archbishop Whealon, "Democratic and Republican Platforms," 36–37. See also Peter Occhiogrosso, "Born Again Politics: Why a Catholic Housewife Is Organizing the Midwest for Pat Robertson," *Crisis* (February 1988): 19–24.

14. One can think back to the nineteenth century, when activists founded such organizations as the Women's Christian Temperance Union (1874), the Society of Christian Socialists (1889), the National American Woman Suffrage Association (1890), the Anti-Saloon League (1895), the National League for the Protection of the Family (1896), and the Jewish Labor Bund (1897). By the end of World War II, the number of such organizations grew to about 500, each with offices in Washington, D.C.

15. John M. Holcomb, "Introduction," in *Public Interest Profiles, 1988–1989* (Washington, D.C.: Congressional Quarterly, 1989), 1.

16. See David Knoke, "Associations and Interest Groups," *American Review of Sociology* 12 (1986): 1–21. Knoke says that "[o]f the nearly 7,000 organizations that maintain a continuing presence in Washington, either by keeping an office or hiring counsels to represent them, nearly half are corporations." See also K. L. Schlozman and J. T. Tierney, *Organized Interests and American Democracy* (New York: Harper and Row, 1985). The figures that follow in this paragraph are derived from *The Encyclopedia of Associations* (Detroit: Gale Research Co., 1995).

17. With the reform of political campaign laws in the early 1970s (to curb the political influence of wealthy individuals, corporations, and powerful labor unions), PACs began to flourish. In 1974 there were just over 600 PACs registered with the Federal Election Commission. By 1991 there were over 4,600, and PACs were providing an ever increasing share of candidates' election money. (This figure comes from the Federal Election Commission, in a telephone conversation with Eric Morrison of the Public Records Department, 17 September 1991.) See also Larry Makinson, "Open Secrets," in *The Almanac of Federal PACs* (Washington, D.C.: Congressional Quarterly, 1990), 3. In 1974 about 17 percent of all campaign revenue for House candidates came from PACs. In 1988 it was 37 percent. The greatest share of PAC money is still organized by corporations and labor unions, but a substantial amount is also affiliated with the special agenda organizations for no other purpose than to purchase influence in governmental affairs.

18. The names of the most powerful of these are well known: the National Organization for Women operates with an annual budget of $6.2 million; the American Civil Liberties Union works with a budget of $14.4 million; People for the American Way carries out its agenda with a budget of $5.3 million; Common

Cause operates with a yearly budget of over $11 million; and the National Rifle Association throws its weight around with an annual budget of over $50 million.

19. This $2 million comes out of the ACLU's total budget of $14.4 million. The Reproductive Rights Project has a staff of 16 attorneys and 10 support personnel.

20. The composition of today's special agenda organizations completely reverses the composition of earlier activist organizations. These days the overriding tendency is to build such organizations from the top down rather than from the bottom up. In other words, the organizations that are so prominent on the political scene today were typically founded *as* national organizations; as they grew, they grew downward into regional, statewide, and sometimes local chapters. The truth, of course, is that membership means very little. Individuals who constitute the membership of these organizations are at best "checkbook members" who make a tax-deductible gift to the organization but are never involved in the organization's operation. Such donors set no goals for the group and have no role in directing its day-to-day or long-term affairs, and the group itself is in no way accountable to them for its actions. The same is true for PACs. In principle, PACs are mechanisms for providing citizen-based financial support for political candidates. In this way campaign funding is supposedly democratized. In fact, however, only a small number of people contribute to PACs and even fewer direct its resources. "Individual PAC donors," as Mark Green puts it, "participate in the least participatory way. PACs take small contributions from donors but the donors have little say over how the money is disbursed" (Mark Green, "When Money Talks, Is It Democracy?" *The Nation* [5 September 1984]: 200–204).

21. The most powerful people on the staff at special agenda organizations, those who make policy decisions for the organization, are not volunteers or local advocates but professionals—lawyers, Ph.D.s, accountants, public relations experts, and the like. This is significant because special-interest organizers and managers are very much "elites" by virtue of their educational credentials, their salary, and the power they wield.

22. It is only logical that when movement elites lobby political leaders on an issue, or represent their case to the public as a whole, they do so in ways that serve to sharpen and polarize what were already distinct and opposing moral positions.

23. The ACLU and the National Association for the Advancement of Colored People (NAACP) Legal Defense Fund pioneered public-interest legal involvement and became models for others that followed. Though the apex of public-interest law firm foundings was reached in the 1970s and early 1980s, the number of public interest law firms still hovers around 150 or so. Each of these law firms is involved in litigating the various issues of the culture war. Sometimes these firms are attached to special agenda organizations, but more often than not the special agenda organizations have a legal staff of their own. All tallied, the legal initiatives of the special agenda activists greatly influence both the nature of the legal debate and the substance of the outcome. See Gregory A. Caldeira and John R. Wright, "Organized Interests and Agenda Setting in the U.S. Supreme Court," *American Political Science Review* 82, no. 4 (December 1988): 1109–1127.

24. Quoted in Mark Green, "Take the Money and Reform," *The New Republic* (14 May 1990): 28.

25. "Roe v. Webster: Media Coverage of the Abortion Debate," *Media Monitor* 3, no. 8 (Washington, D.C.: Center for Media and Public Affairs, October 1989). The study included 118 stories on the ABC, CBS, and NBC evening news (7 hours, 19 minutes of air time) and 179 news stories and 36 opinion pieces in the *New York Times* and the *Washington Post*.

26. The best recent summary of this predicament is found in Adam Seligman's *The Idea of Civil Society* (New York: Free Press, 1992).

27. Quoted in Thomas Jefferson, *Democracy*, ed. Saul K. Padover (New York: D. Appleton-Century, 1939), 135.

28. Quoted in Jefferson, *Democracy*, 134.

29. Michael Novak, "An Essay on 'Public' and 'Private,'" in *Philanthropy: Four Views*, ed. Robert Payton, Michael Novak, Brian O'Connell, and Peter Dobkin Hall (New Brunswick, N.J.: Transaction Books, Social Philosophy and Policy Center, 1988), 12.

30. A 1991 survey sponsored by the Independent Sector found that three-quarters of survey respondents thought that it was in their power to do things to improve the welfare of others. Also, two-thirds rejected the notion that individuals could do little to alleviate suffering in the world. When similar questions were asked in Great Britain in the 1988 Charity Household Survey, only 46 percent of respondents considered it the responsibility of people to give what they could to charity. Eighty percent thought that it was the responsibility of the government to take care of people who could not care for themselves. See Virginia A. Hodgkinson, "Civic Participation in America: Volunteering and Contributing," *The Public Perspective* 5, no. 3 (March/April 1994): 14–15. For additional information on Great Britain, see also James A. Beckford, "Great Britain: Voluntarism and Sectional Interests," in *Between States and Markets: The Voluntary Sector in Comparative Perspective*, ed. Robert Wuthnow (Princeton: Princeton University Press, 1991), 59.

31. American Association for Fund-Raising Council (AAFRC) Trust for Philanthropy, *Giving USA: 1995*, 12 and 24–25.

32. Ibid., 47.

33. Ibid., 25.

34. Ibid., 47–48.

35. Brian O'Connell, "Private Philanthropy and the Preservation of a Free and Democratic Society," in *Philanthropy: Four Views*, ed. Payton et al., 29.

36. Helmut K. Anheier, Lester M. Salamon, and Edith Archamboult, "Participating Citizens: U.S.-Europe Comparisons in Volunteer Action," *The Public Perspective* 5, no. 3 (March/April 1994): 16–18, 34. Other studies confirm these patterns. The 1989 study by the Laboratoire D'Economie Sociale and the Fondation de France found that 43 percent of French respondents reported contributing an average of $213. In the United States the same year, 75 percent of Americans reported average household contributions of $978. Overall, about twice as many Americans contributed and three times as many volunteered. (Hodgkinson, "Civic Participation," 15.)

37. Hodgkinson, "Civic Participation," 15. The following anecdote relayed by journalist Bill Bryson in November of 1995 illustrates Britain's unfamiliarity with philanthropic giving: In 1986 an American professor arrived at Oxford University to set up a fund-raising campaign, a complete novelty in Britain, where the gov-

ernment has traditionally provided the vast majority of university funding. (In other words, the alumni of Oxford have, until now, been blissfully spared those frequent dinnertime "Capital Campaign" calls that are so familiar to American college graduates.) As the American academic, Henry Drucker, later recalled, "Oxford had no experience with this sort of thing. It didn't even have a list of its alumni." Subsequently, an American firm was hired as a consultant, and the campaign was soon underway. By its conclusion, Oxford had procured £341 million, an astronomical amount, more than a third of it stemming from North America. (Bill Bryson, "Oxford," *National Geographic,* November 1995, 132.)

38. For elaboration on this point, see Beckford, "Great Britain: Voluntarism and Sectional Interests," 59.

39. The Swedish Secretariat for Futures Studies (SFS), the Swedish equivalent to a top U.S. presidential commission, recently issued a report entitled "Care and Welfare at the Crossroad," in which it recommends that the Swedish government not only levy taxes but also levy compulsory time. Every Swede aged 19 to 65 would be compelled to donate 4 to 6 hours a week to volunteer activities: "The state will now re-create the private sector by state coercion." See Novak, "An Essay on 'Public' and 'Private,'" 13, and John Boli, "Sweden: Is There a Viable Third Sector?" in *Between States and Markets,* ed. Wuthnow, 94–124.

40. Helen Hardacre, "Japan: the Public Sphere in a Non-Western Setting," in *Between States and Markets,* ed. Wuthnow, 219.

41. Charles Clotfelter, "Federal Tax Policy and Charitable Giving," in *Philanthropic Giving: Studies in Varieties and Goals,* ed. Richard Magat (New York: Oxford Press, 1989), 111.

42. Teresa Odendahl, "Independent Foundations and Wealthy Donors," in *Philanthropic Giving,* ed. Magat, 167. See also AAFRC Trust for Philanthropy, *Giving USA: 1995,* 50.

43. Though the first American foundations appeared before the enactment of an income tax, the greatest number of foundation creations coincided with the highest income inheritance tax rates (Odendahl, "Independent Foundations," 167).

44. Althea Nagai, Robert Lerner, and Stanley Rothman, *Giving for Social Change: Foundations, Public Policy, and the American Agenda* (Westport, Conn.: Praeger, 1994), 24.

45. AAFRC Trust for Philanthropy, *Giving USA: 1995,* 63. According to the AAFRC Trust for Philanthropy, one possible catalyst for the impressive surge in foundation foundings in the last decade was the tax treatment of gifts of appreciated securities. "In 1984, living donors gained permission to deduct as charitable contributions the full market value of gifts of publicly traded stock to private foundations. Previously, only the cost basis—the price originally paid for the stock—could be deducted. This provision was passed as part of the Tax Reform Act of 1984 and was scheduled to expire at the end of 1994" (p. 63).

46. In 1980 there were some 700,000 millionaires alive and prospering, several hundred centimillionaires, and a dozen or two billionaires. (Waldemar A. Nielsen, *The Golden Donors* [New York: Truman Talley Books/E. P. Dutton, 1985], 3.) In 1993, gifts to foundations increased 26 percent, and the number of gifts of $5 million or more increased by 25 percent. (AAFRC Trust for Philanthropy, *Giving USA: 1995,* 63.)

47. David Samuels, "Philanthropical Correctness: The Failure of American Foundations," *The New Republic*, 18 and 25 September 1995, 28.

48. Nielsen, *The Golden Donors*, 3–4. Nielsen goes on to say that as a group, foundations are "like no others, operating in their own unique degree of abstraction from external pressures and controls, according to their own largely self-imposed rules. They are private, and yet their activities cut across a broad spectrum of public concerns and public issues. They are the only important power centers in American life not controlled by market forces, electoral constituencies, bodies of members, or even formally established canons of conduct, all of which give them their extraordinary flexibility and potential influence. Yet they remain little known and even less understood, shrouded in mystery, inspiring in some the highest hopes and expectations and in others dark fears and resentments."

49. Tremendous affluence has encouraged the expansion of all benevolence beyond the constraints of one-to-one charity. The increasing professionalization of philanthropic giving means that paid professionals serve as intermediaries between philanthropists and recipients. Professionalization encouraged the idea that the goal of philanthropy is to engage in society-wide change and not simply to solve individual problems. Jane Mavity and Paul Ylvisaker cited these factors as contributing to the increasing tendency of foundations to engage in public affairs in their testimony before the 1970s Government Commission on Private Philanthropy and Public Needs (better known as the Filer Commission). See Althea Nagai, Robert Lerner, and Stanley Rothman, *The Culture of Philanthropy: Foundations and Public Policy*, Studies in Philanthropy No. 8 (Washington D.C.: Capital Research Center, 1991), 6.

50. Nagai et al., *Giving for Social Change*, 103.

51. Ibid., 99.

52. Ibid., 5, 99.

53. Waldemar Nielsen, author of *The Golden Donors*, is an outspoken proponent of this idea.

54. Quoted in Kenneth Thompson, ed., *Philanthropy, Private Means, Public Ends* (New York: University Press of America, 1987), 14. As another apologist put it: "The foundations are, quite literally, far too motley to constitute a concerted striking force on behalf of anyone's political cause." See John Simon, "Foundations and Public Controversy: An Affirmative View," in *The Future of Foundations*, ed. Fritz Heimann (Englewood Cliffs, N.J.: Spectrum, 1973), 86.

55. Jenkins, J. Craig, *Social Movement Philanthropy and American Democracy*, in *Philanthropic Giving*, ed. Magart, 294.

56. Foundations contributed an estimated $9.91 billion to nonprofit organizations in 1994, a 4 percent increase over giving in 1993. (AAFRC Trust for Philanthropy, *Giving USA: 1995*, 63.)

57. Nielsen, *Golden Donors*, 7.

58. Ibid., 22.

59. Ibid., 24.

60. Nagai et al., *Giving for Social Change*, xiii–xiv.

61. Ibid., 166.

62. Ibid., 123.

63. Nagai, et al., *Culture of Philanthropy*, 67.

64. Of their sample of foundations, 65 percent were liberal, 18 percent were conservative, and the remaining 17 percent were neutral. In addition, "[a]t the ex-

tremes, 91 foundations supported only liberal causes while a mere 15 supported only conservative groups." Nagai et al., *Culture of Philanthropy,* 19–21.

65. Nielsen, *Golden Donors,* 13.

66. Odendahl, "Independent Foundations," 171.

67. Martin Morse Wooster, quoted in Nagai et al., *Giving for Social Change,* 105.

68. Nielsen, *Golden Donors,* 136.

69. Robert Payton, "Philanthropic Values," in *Philanthropic Giving,* 38–39. See also Kathleen McCarthy, "The Gospel of Wealth: American Giving in Theory and Practice," *in Philanthropic Giving,* ed. Richard Magat (New York: Oxford University Press, 1989), 50–51.

70. Carnegie, quoted in McCarthy, "The Gospel of Wealth," 50.

71. Thomas Parrish, "The Foundation: 'A Special American Institution,' " in *The Future of Foundations,* ed. Heimann, 11.

72. Carnegie, quoted in Nagai et al., *Giving for Social Change,* 105.

73. Nielsen, *Golden Donors,* 133–134.

74. Pew Memorial Charter, quoted in Nielsen, *Golden Donors,* 173.

75. Nielsen, *Golden Donors,* 179.

76. Henry Ford II, quoted in Nielsen, *Golden Donors,* 71–72.

77. Evan Gahr, "Paymasters of the PC Brigades," *The Wall Street Journal,* 27 January 1995.

78. Other recent studies have discovered that the foundation elites are now one of the most ideologically polarized of all elite groups. (Nagai et al., *Giving for Social Change,* 69.)

79. David Samuels, "Philanthropical Correctness: The Failure of American Foundations," *The New Republic,* 18 and 25 September 1995, 32.

80. *Foundations, Private Giving, and Public Policy: Report and Recommendations of the Committee of Foundations and Private Philanthropy* (Chicago: University of Chicago Press, 1970), 71.

81. Nagai et al., *Giving for Social Change,* 65.

82. Leon Howell, "Funding the War of Ideas," *Christian Century* 11, no. 22 (19–26 July 1995): 702. Howell goes on to quote Michael Lind, who suggests in the winter 1995 edition of *Dissent* that this neoconservative dependency on funding from the four sisters has inevitably "promoted groupthink."

83. Nagai et al., *Giving for Social Change,* 1.

84. Nagai et al., *Culture of Philanthropy,* 3.

85. Irving Kristol, quoted in Nagai et al., *Giving for Social Change,* 65.

86. William Simon, quoted in Nagai et al., *Giving for Social Change,* 65.

87. AAFRC Trust for Philanthropy, *Giving USA: 1988,* 4.

88. AAFRC Trust for Philanthropy, *Giving USA: 1995,* 85.

89. Nielsen, *Golden Donors,* 34. According to the AAFRC Trust for Philanthropy, in *Giving USA: 1995,* only 2 percent of all foundation grants go to religion.

90. In a 1993 survey entitled *Giving and Volunteering,* sponsored by Independent Sector, the percentage of respondents reporting household contributions to charity was 57 percent for those who did not attend religious services at all and 85 percent among those who attended religious services weekly. Similarly, the proportion of volunteers was 34 percent among nonattenders and 64 percent among those who attended religious services weekly. In addition, when the same

survey asked respondents to rank their confidence level in a variety of charitable institutions, religious institutions came out at the top of the list, with 50 percent of respondents expressing "a great deal" or "quite a lot" of confidence in them. Less than 20 percent of respondents reported confidence in major corporations, the federal government, political organizations, lobby groups, or Congress. *Giving and Volunteering in the United States: Findings from a National Survey, 1994 Edition* (Washington, D.C.: The Independent Sector).

2

The Past in the Present: Redefining *Laïcité* in Multicultural France

Danièle Hervieu-Léger

Modern societies are usually described as societies of change. It is not this movement as such, however, that sets them apart from traditional societies, which are often wrongly thought of as being static. The particularities of one kind or the other depend on the manner in which each evaluates change. Traditional societies are above all concerned with maintaining their rules, regulations, and organization. Modern societies, in contrast, value change: They claim innovation as the key to their development. They are even governed by the "imperative of change" (Gauchet, 1985). Not only are they capable of modifying their norms and functioning in response to new situations, but also they are constantly creating new orientations that induce social change as much as they are a reflection of it.

Any consideration of the crisis and the conflicts facing modern societies must be made in the light of this very capacity for "self-regulation" in these societies (Touraine, 1973). The notion of "crisis" suggests that available methods of control and regulation are insufficient to counter the instability that change continuously infuses into the social system. All change, no matter how sectorial, involves working toward redressing the upset balance. It calls into question established situations once again; it compels a reorganization of power relations, a reconsideration of what is customary, a reorganization of methods of thinking and ways of doing things, and so on. In complex societies subjected to increasingly rapid processes of change, a "crisis" does not simply imply a temporary dysfunctioning of a system preparing, in a state of significant turbulence, a new phase of stabilization. Rather, insofar as the constitutive elements of the social system are in perpetual movement, developing at different rhythms according to potentially contradictory tendencies, "crisis" has become the structural condition of modern societies. This dynamic of imbalance continuously modifies the system of tensions between order and movement that constitutes the very fiber of social existence. It involves the constant adjustment of relations between the various social agents through conflicts that modify the map of social, political, and cultural problems that society must confront and the field of debate through which it defines itself. The normative conflicts characteristic of a given society emerge at the precise point where the ideological process of definition and redefinition of collective orientations (which are at once induced by change and generators of change) meets the concrete processes involved in the readjustment of relations between social agents. Accordingly, they constitute cultural conflicts that must be seized not as dysfunctions or miscarriages of the social system but as the very dynamic through which society creates itself.

In a given society, in order to pinpoint the truly significant normative conflicts, an effort must be made to identify those that call into question the definition that the society gives of itself—in other words, conflicts that strongly influence the construction of collective identity, the management of memory, and the definition of the foundations on which social cohesion is, or should be, based. In the case of France, it seems that one of the most decisive changes that have occurred since the beginning of the 1980s has been the transformation of a society in which cultural homogeneity seemed assured within the normative space defined by the great republican referents, to a multicultural society in which the most radically foreign element to the "Republican Pact" (in which the State and the public school are the two pillars) is now emerging: that is the claim for communitarian difference. The question of Islam, which has become the second religion in France after Catholicism—ahead of Protestantism and Judaism—constitutes the highly sensitive point of crystallization of a problem that is much more vast: the question of the relation between particularity and universality in the very definition of French identity.

It would go beyond the scope of the present contribution to embrace all aspects of this cultural change—aspects that take shape in multiple normative conflicts. Only one of its dimensions shall thus be treated: that concerning the reevaluation of both the ideological and practical meanings of *laïcité*. The primary reason for this choice is that the untranslatable concept of *laïcité* (roughly, "secularism" or "secularity") has been, for more than a century, a highly specific constituent of the French identity. It retains today—even though its stakes have changed considerably—a remarkable capacity to crystallize public debate. Via the apparently abstract question of the redefinition of *laïcité* comes to light the whole range of problems related to the construction and preservation of

social ties, in a society whose historical ideal of integration (political, administrative, linguistic, ideological, and cultural) is now confronted with
a new configuration of social and cultural relations characterized by pluralization and fragmentation. In fact, contrary to the first impression that
one might have from looking over the past two centuries of French history, the redefinition of *laïcité* today constitutes neither a new point of
conflict between the Catholic Church and the State nor a new episode of
the historical "War of the Two Frances": hierarchical, conservative, and
Catholic on the one hand, and modern, progressive, and republican on
the other (Poulat, 1987). It concerns rather the relation of national common values (shaped at the crossroads of a Catholic civilization and a revolutionary-republican tradition) to community values held by minority
groups that claim their "right to be different" in the very name of democracy. The school is emerging as the favored ground on which to stake
such claims: The question of Muslim girls' right to wear the Islamic veil
at school is currently emblematic of this debate. In relation to these phenomena of self-assertion of communities, the State, the Catholic Church,
and Protestant and Jewish institutions representing minorities "assimilated" into a republican culture that they have helped to create are striving to re-create, from the standpoint of their own traditions, a body of
common values. Among themselves, they are entering into unprecedented levels of cooperation, through which has come into play an extremely interesting redefinition of relations between the Republic and
the different "spiritual families" that constitute the French identity. In
these redistributions, the question of the memory of the different traditions that make up French identity is particularly important: These traditions are once more elaborated and re-created with regard to present
problems. The present analysis shall attempt to demonstrate that this
question is at the center of the mediating processes through which the
normative conflicts giving rise to the redefinition of *laïcité* are capable—
under certain conditions—of contributing to the formation of a common
identity in today's multicultural France.

Laïcité in the Course of History:
From Confrontation to Compromise

"France is an indivisible and *laïque* Republic."[1] The first sentence of the
Constitution of 27 October 1946, retained by the Constitution of 1958,
solemnly confirms that the *laïcité* of the State is a fundamental component of the republican tradition. Outside of France this phrase is often
seen as being mysterious, and some are even shocked when they perceive it as being associated with the idea of a battle against religion,
clashing with the idea of tolerance in a pluralistic society. To avoid mis-

conceptions, it is necessary to recall the historical genesis of French-style *laïcité*, whose most distant origins probably lie in the age-old struggle led by French kings to escape the yoke of the Roman Catholic Church. *Laïcité* does not primarily oppose religion in itself, but rather any clerical tutelage that religious institution imposes on the powers of State. There exists, from this standpoint, a significant connection between the secularist tradition and the Gallican tradition that dominated the history of the French Church until the middle of the nineteenth century.

On the eve of the Revolution of 1789, Catholicism was present throughout French society: It legitimated the political institutions; it governed the time and space of collective life; it controlled the registry office, the teaching, medical, and social institutions. In a matter of months (between May and September 1789) the Ancien Régime collapsed, and the succeeding constitutional monarchy is characterized by the immediate *laïcisation* of the political system. The legitimacy of the monarchy lost its religious foundation: It was henceforth based on a contract struck between the king and the nation (Langlois, 1988). The citizen now defined himself through his belonging to the nation (as a community), and his confessional leaning could not be seized upon to prevent him from participating in political life. The proclamation of the principle of religious freedom in Article 10 of the Declaration of the Rights of Man and of the Citizen (1789) represents a decisive step in this political transformation. Religious minorities were gradually granted all the rights associated with citizenship. The rights of Protestants to vote and to be elected to public office as well as their admission to all employment were rapidly established. Jewish emancipation was effected in September 1791, involving the abnegation of former community privileges. The constitution adopted on 3 September 1791 guaranteed as a "natural and civil right" the freedom of each citizen to "practice the religion to which he is devoted." But the very question of religious freedom raises the issue of the status of Catholicism in the society—an issue that led to the break between the new regime and the Church. Several times the Assembly turned down the demand that Catholicism be recognized as the State religion. The entire modern construction of *laïcité*, which culminated with the Separation Law in 1905, is contained, in embryonic form, in this first setting down of the relation between the Church and the State. It corresponds to "a political conception implying the separation of civil society and religious society, the State exerting no religious power, and the churches no political power" (Capitant, 1936).

Why has this process of the dissociation of religion and politics (which characterizes all modern countries) taken on in France, for more than a century, such an intensely conflictive aspect? The main reason is that the historical symbiosis between the Catholic institution and the absolute monarchy lent to the process of political modernization (nevertheless acquired with the support of part of the clergy) the dimension of a veritable religious conflict, which divided the Church itself. The radicalization of the opposing positions came to enjoin, for each, the exclusion of its adversary; the Republic could only triumph in bringing down the Church—but this constituted the victory of one-half of France over the other (Winock, 1989). By breaching his contract with the nation (his attempt to escape abroad, cut short at Varennes in June 1791), the king disrupted the first balance established by the Constitutional Assembly or National Assembly and spurred on the establishment of the Republic. In response to attempts to restore the Ancien Régime, *laïcisation* measures directly attacked the social power of the Church. The registry office, which was held by the clergy, was placed in the hands of municipalities; marriage as a civil contract was clearly separated from its religious celebration; the dioceses and parishes were divided into administrative districts; the choice of bishops and parish priests was made by election.

Nevertheless, the revolutionaries of 1791 did not call into question the importance of religion in society. Their objective was to "regenerate" the ecclesiastical institution (M. Ozouf, 1989), to "force it into marriage with civil society, so it can always be the source of social morals" (Baubérot, 1990b: 20). The instrument of this policy was the Civil Constitution of the Clergy, promulgated in 1789, which required members of the clergy to take an oath to the new regime. Its application, dividing the clergy between constitutional "juror" (sworn) priests rallied around the new regime and refractory "nonjuror" priests immediately suspected of being political opponents, contributed to the irremediable radicalization of the conflict. In 1791 "jurors" constituted 52 to 55 percent of priests. French Catholicism was thus split into two opposing factions: one supporting the new regime, the other maintaining an increasingly resolute opposition to the order established by the Revolution. The hardening of this opposition, the increasing repression brought to bear on the nonjuror priests, and the authoritarian radicalization and religious meandering of the regime born in 1789 (the establishment of the revolutionary cult occurred in 1793, coinciding with the beginning of the Terror) drew France into a religious conflict of astounding violence. They created the causative conditions of the "War of the Two Frances" (Poulat, 1987), which marked the entire course of French history up until World War I—and which left traces that still have not faded from collective memory.

After the ravages of the preceding period, the Concordat signed by Bonaparte in 1801 constituted a pacifying element. Catholicism, though proclaimed "the religion of the majority of the French," did not regain its status as the state religion. The State, assuming the position of arbitrator, took charge of the protection of the authorized denominations that were supposed to assure public morality and materially supported their ministers. For the Catholic Church this system achieved, from a purely administrative standpoint, the Gallican ambition for autonomy from Rome. But it did not solve the problem of the imbalance between minority religions (Protestantism, Judaism) and Catholicism, which claimed—as the religion of the majority of the French—to be recognized as incarnating the religion of the nation. Within the Church, a liberal current stemming from the constitutional Church and inspired by the Gallican and Jansenist traditions asserted that conciliation was possible between Catholicism and democracy. It was sharply fought by an intransigent Catholicism that rejected outright the "pretensions of reason" and the principles of 1789 and wanted to rebuild the historical influence of the Roman Church on society. This opposition, which was the axis of French history until the twentieth century, ended with the victory of democracy.

The political tribulations of the nineteenth century (an alternation of revolutionary clashes and conservative hardenings) and the magnitude of social movements tied to France's accelerated industrialization and urbanization entailed a simplification and new radicalization of opposing positions. The Catholic Church appeared definitely tied to the "side of order" even as, in the mid–nineteenth century, what Gabriel Le Bras (1955–1956) described as "the great toing and froing of the classes on the steps of the Church" was taking place: The liberal, Voltairian middle class was seen to be leaning on the Catholic institution to defend proprietorship, while at the same time a part of the popular masses, migrating from the countryside to the factories in the cities, was leaving the Church. This period was marked by the intransigent stiffening of a Roman Church that was wholly mobilized—the proclamations of the Syllabus of Errors of 1864 in hand—by the struggle against liberal modernity and the individual liberties it promoted. But this period was also one of intensive spiritual renewal for a French Catholicism strongly identified with the nation's rural origins, and which was fervently reconstructing the past memory of France as a shield against the turbulence of the modern world (Langlois, 1980: 231–406).

Over and beyond the sensitive issue of the legal regulation of the relationship between Church and State was the confrontation of two worldviews, of two value and normative systems in the process of crystallization. According to the dogmatic vision of the intransigent Catholicism, truth was substantial, positive, given once and for all, and all-encompassing. From this standpoint, the political autonomy set down in the principles of 1789, along with the critical posture of modern science, was intolerable. Being faithful implied absolute submission to the legitimate authority (the magisterium) that guaranteed the endurance of truth. The strengthening of the institution's hierarchical character was, from this point of view, inseparable from the war it was waging—throughout the nineteenth century until the Second Vatican Council (1962–1965)—against liberalism (and against the perverse offspring of liberalism, which was, in its eyes, socialism) (Poulat, 1987).

On the political scene, this major ideological conflict crystallized in the confrontation between the Catholic institution, a besieged fortress aspiring to retrieve its lost powers, and the republicans, who intended to see realized the process of religious emancipation of the State and society. Within this process the struggle against the power of religious orders took on a major and practical significance. Although the diocesan clergy gradually accepted the rallying to the Republic as admonished by Pope Leo XIII, the orders remained pivotal to the antirepublican and antidemocratic movements. Bringing down the "black party" by way of religious orders became a republican obsession: The objective of counteracting their particularly strong influence in the area of education was an important part of the anticlerical radicalization of school policy under the Third Republic. In prohibiting members of orders from teaching, the republicans, sons of the *Encyclopédie* and the French Enlightenment, considered finishing with what the Protestant Fernand Buisson, instigator and theoretician of the *laïque* school, called "the freedom to monopolize consciences" reserved for Catholic religious orders. In expelling the orders by force, the government of radical Emile Combes transformed the conflict between clerical France and *laïque* France into a veritable pitched battle. The ancient seminarist, whom Pope Pius X called the "satanic Monsieur Combes," embodied an extremist conception of the anticlerical struggle: an extremism exacerbated by the fact that the successor to Leo XIII identified himself with an equally rigid version of intransigent Catholicism. The conflict over the status of religious orders led to a pointed power struggle between Rome and France, which degraded into a break of diplomatic relations between the French State and the Holy See. The false steps made by the papacy and the escalating anticlericalism of the radicals and socialists made inevitable the Separation Law, promulgated on 11 December 1905.

Voted in "an atmosphere of religious war" (Rémond, 1974: 199), the Separation Law, which conclusively separated Church and State, was not, however, a law of war against religion. In bringing the conflict to a head, it can be considered as a mediating device, permitting the appeasement and control of conflicting passions that had, by the end of the nineteenth century, entered the critical phase. Above all, the Separation Law represented the passing over from a primary threshold of *laïcisation* (that of the Concordat system) to a second threshold of *laïcisation* (Baubérot, 1990a). Over the preceding period, the social utility of religion had been publicly recognized. Religious institutions were treated as public institutions and placed under State control. Under the new conditions established for religion in 1905, religion was considered a private affair, and religious freedom was just one of many public freedoms. The State guaranteed each citizen the freedom to declare religious affiliation, and severe penalties were reserved for those who tried to stand in the way of the normal functioning of cultural life. Religion was now a strictly personal and optional affair; consequently, the Republic did "not recognize, payroll and subsidize any religious group" (Article 2 of the law of 1905). The privatization of religion in France resulted as much from government policy as from the culmination of a cultural process witnessed, moreover, in all modern societies.

The implementing of this policy, which initially the hierarchy of the Catholic Church opposed with all its might, precipitated violent confrontations, notably on the occasion of the inventories of ecclesiastical assets before they were consigned to cultural associations (by law, private). Nevertheless, and in spite of the pope's condemnation, the law found support among Catholic currents who recognized its potential as an instrument of legal mediation in the inexpugnable conflict of the two Frances—which was effectively the case. Two elements came into play here:

Firstly, the law itself was a text of compromise between several competing conceptions of *laïcité:* Combes had dreamed of dismantling all the churches, forbidding them any national organization. But the Separation Law, drawn up by the Protestant Méjean and marked by the influence of the socialists Jaurès and Briand, led to the prevalence of a liberal inspiration that respected the internal organization of the churches. The system of 1905 united, with the intention of peace, the various traditions of the *laïque* camp: the Enlightenment spirit of Voltaire, Diderot, and Condorcet; the scientific positivism of Auguste Comte; and the different currents of freemasonry. It also integrated the expectations of the Protestant (Encrevé and Richard, 1979) and Jewish (Birnbaum, 1992) minorities, deeply suspicious of the intentions of the dominant religion. The religious minorities contributed decisively to the mediation of the conflict in assuring, in the face of Catholic totalitarian pretensions, the cultural integration of *laïque* ideals by religion and of religious ideals by the Republic. In valuing the individual and his liberty, the French Protestants, numerous among the great figures of *laïque* thought, played a major role in the elaboration of republican conceptions of morality, educative responsibility, and civility. But the law of 1905 was also suited to a liberal Catholicism trying to reconcile religion and the principles of 1789: Despite its marginal impact on Roman Catholic orientations since the middle of the nineteenth century, this liberal Catholicism remained very vivid in French intellectual and religious life.

Secondly, in the course of the nineteenth century, the vast majority of Catholics progressively rallied to the republican regime. At the beginning of the twentieth century, the form of the regime—monarchical or republican—ceased to be at the center of the public debate. Religious passions, as much as anticlerical passions, were subsiding. World War I, in demonstrating the possibility of a "sacred union" of *laïques* and Catholics against an outside enemy, brought the process to a close. The "War of the two Frances" ended, in a sense, in the trenches.

After a *laïcité* of confrontation, the post–World War II climate gave rise to a new period: that of a *laïcité* of compromise. The Church more or less accepted the principles of freedom and pluralism—those of modern democratic societies. At the same time, *laïcité* lost much of its anticlerical passion and was able to become "a solution of neutrality, permitting the cohabitation of children belonging to different and respectable families" (Winock, 1989). This does not mean—far from it—that the two different political, moral, and spiritual worlds became homogenized. On the contrary, they retained, and have for the French today, a strong potential for symbolic identification. The interpretation of the "Republican Pact" remained an object of debate. But the original system established by the law of 1905, along with the idea that the State shall remain above and beyond all ideological and religious components of civil society, was henceforth the object of a very broad consensus.

Persistence and Topicality of the School Question, or "The Present Encumbered by the Past"

With the situation settled overall, how may it be explained that at regular intervals, and always with regard to the schools, there is a resurgence of conflicts reactualizing—with an intensity surprising to foreign observers—ideological conflicts that are supposed to be over? In 1984, for example, in reaction to the Socialist government's proposal to create a "great, broad, unified and *laïque* public service of education," after numerous provincial demonstrations, 800,000 people took to the streets in Versailles on the 4th of March to defend the "freedom of education." Ten years later, in January 1994, a similar but opposite scenario drew hundreds of thousands of demonstrators to the streets in protest against the conservative government's bill to authorize local authorities to finance as they please—above the 10 percent allowed by the Falloux Law of 1850—the investment expenditure of private schools. In each of these cases, the political dimension of the movement is obvious: In 1984, the defense of the private school mobilized all right-wing components, from the center to the extreme right; in 1994, the defense of the public school[2] rallied the left against a right-wing movement. Is it possible not to see, in these twin episodes, a new outbreak of the "War of the Two Frances"? The present appears "encumbered by history" (Rémond, 1984b). In order to understand why the school question remains the point of crystallization of an always vivid normative conflict in France, it is useful to grasp how these events fit indisputably into the continuity of a particular course of history, and also where and why they diverge from it.

Already central, before the Revolution, to the undertakings of the Catholic Counter Reformation to thwart the influence of Protestantism, the question of education is at the heart of Revolution (M. Ozouf, 1989). But it was the founding of the Imperial University, endowed by Napoleon with the monopoly of higher education, that marks the flash point of the school conflict. The Church could not accept that the State take charge, exclusively, of the development of minds and spirits, and it put forward the demand for freedom of education. The resulting conflict, which lasted three-quarters of a century, presents the peculiarity that the Catholic Church, the resolute adversary of modern liberties in all domains, was fighting for freedom of education while, at the same time, the liberal inheritors of the age of Enlightenment were defending the monopoly of education in order to thwart the antidemocratic influence of the Roman Church. Despite evolutions on either side of the conflict, something of these perspectives remains in the background of the present conflicts (Rémond, 1984a).

Under the July Monarchy the question of educating the people, at the primary school level, became a veritable "affair of State" (Nique, 1990). The Guizot Law of 1833 established, in each region, a college of education in order to train primary school teachers, and required every city with a population of more than 500 to have a primary school for boys. The figure of the *"laïque* cleric," the *instituteur* (primary school teacher), asserting himself in a position opposing that of the parish priest, came out of this period: Their opposition crystallizes the contradiction between two types of education and values and two types of social authority. In each village the relationship between the parish priest and the *instituteur* closely reflected the turbulence of sociopolitical relations in post-Revolutionary France. The republicans' first concern was to emancipate young minds from the obscurantist and antiscientific influence of the Church. Conversely, when the conditions seemed ripe for a monarchical restoration (i.e., after the defeat suffered at the hands of the Prussians in 1871 and the crushing of the Paris Commune), the Catholic side mobilized with a view to restoring the Church's grasp over all institutions (justice, army, social assistance, medical, etc.), and especially over schools. In return, the electoral defeat of Mac-Mahon and the institutional stabilization of the Republic after 1877 involved an opposing movement to emancipate the State from any religious tutelage and the separation of the Church and the school. If the school question remains so charged with emotion in France today, it is because it has crystallized, in the course of history, all the conflicts that have accompanied the establishment of political modernity.

Indeed, for the republicans, if generalized education is the inseparable corollary of universal suffrage, the separation of primary school teacher and priest is both the condition and the guarantee of political autonomy, given that the Church that does not separate the assertion of its spiritual authority from the reconquest of the social positions it occupied before the Revolution. It is thus significant that the first of the great school laws (1881–1886), which carries the name of Jules Ferry, minister of public education from 1879 to 1883, concerned the creation of a women's college of education in each region. The law was intended to curtail the antidemocratic influence maintained by the Church through women. The law of 28 March 1882 made primary education mandatory, free, and *laïque*, the latter disposition signifying that religious questions had no place in education. The law gave rise to lively debate among the republicans themselves. Certain among them could easily have imagined that at school children could be spoken to of God in a nondenominational way. The most radical dreamed of a monopolistic model of education, conceived to end clerical schooling once and for all. As it was, the general legislative pattern initiated by Ferry did not imply a State monopoly on the schools: It establishes a public education service in which, to this day, the principle of philosophic neutrality remains the foundation. One day a week (other than Sunday) is reserved for religious instruction, which must be given outside the school and according to parents' wishes. The primary school teacher has neither to extol a particular religion, nor voice antireligious views; he is required, in respect of pupils' consciences, to preach a moral code capable of transcending the different existing metaphysic and religious systems, a code that complies with the stringency of the scientific method and that can serve as the basis of a new consensus among the French. This moral dimension of the Third Republic's school work (which Emile Durkheim made the main stream of his republican commitment as much as sociology) is fundamental. The school is charged with developing the individual and the citizen as much as with passing on knowledge. All elements contributing to the undertaking of political and cultural—as well as ethical and symbolic—unification of the nation are contained in this program: The "schoolmasters"—these "black hussars of the Republic," according to writer Charles Péguy (1873–1914)—took it in their charge as a veritable religious ministry (J. Ozouf, 1973). Nevertheless, the republicans did not suppress private education: Not only in the Christian regions, a tightly knit network of primary and secondary schools as well as technical colleges was maintained where teaching faithfulness to the Church was rarely separated—at least until the eve of World War I—from a hostility more or less obviously directed toward the Republic and its policy (Rémond, 1984b).

In the years before World War II, the positions were evolving. In 1929 the encyclical of Pope Pius XI, *Divini illus magistry,* acknowledged that the State has an educational responsibility (while continually reaffirming the right of Catholics to have their own schools and the duty of the faithful to enroll their children in them). Catholics, without accepting the principle of a public education administered by the State, abandoned the idea of suppressing it or controlling it. More particularly, they discovered that *laïque* neutrality was not to be confused with antireligious *laïcité*: A growing number of Catholics chose public schools for their children, without sensing a conflict of interest with their faith, and often in the very name of their faith. Priests stopped thundering on the pulpit against the "school of the devil." Nevertheless, the presence in numerous cities and villages in France of two competing schools—one of the Republic, the other of the Church—kept indefinitely in evidence an ideological conflict, which endured by progressively changing its stakes during the Fourth Republic (Gauthier, 1994).

At the end of World War II, the commission presided over by the Protestant André Philip and instructed—after the dark years of Vichy— to reconstruct the school system in the spirit of the Resistance, had to try once again to regulate the opposition between two extremist, but efficiently organized, minority camps: one preaching the nationalization of denominational schools, the other wanting to establish the autonomy of private denominational schools, subsidized by the State. The conflict was ideological and political; it continued to involve the mutual facing down of two contradictory value systems, but the tenor of the confrontation had changed. In the past, for the republican statesmen rising to power in 1789, the duality of educational practices constituted, in a country cut in two by the Church's attitude toward political democracy, a "mortal, dividing germ in the social body" (Rémond, 1984a). This hard-fought unity, won against the many particularisms, privileges, and social inequalities characteristic of the Ancien Régime, could not be conceived by these republicans, the sons of the Revolution, as serving other than to uniformize and homogenize differences (E. Weber, 1983). The school of the Republic was, in their minds, the favored instrument of this unification.

However, as soon as national unification was institutionally and legally accomplished, the question of unity acquired an altogether different bearing, related to the capacity of the community to generate common values and political consensus among the French people. The struggles over school issues that erupted after World War II crystallized—in the ultra-ideologized form that has always invested public debate in France—a debate much more vast, bearing on the conception of pluralism in a modern democracy. "The school war is no longer a conflict between the Republican State and the Church: the struggle no longer revolves around one side's seeking to impose the idea of a teaching Republic, while the other side fights for freedom in education." Via the prickly question of the public financing of private schools, a "direct struggle for the equal sharing of children" had come into play (Coq, 1995: 49).

Since the Republic was reconfirmed, the compromise established by the Fourth Republic created a new balance in favor of private education. In recognizing, in the terms of a contract, the role of private education (which in France is largely religious and Catholic) and its commitment for public interest, the Debré Law of 1959 assured a balance between the different components of the education system. Private schools that enter into a contract with the State accept the State's rules on the content of programs, the recruitment of teachers, and the enrollment of pupils (in particular, they have to accept pupils of all religious denominations); in return, the State contributes financially to their operation. The "noncontracted" private school cannot claim the same recognition on behalf of the public authority. The effectiveness of this legislative arrangement was clearly demonstrated during the 1984 and 1994 conflicts: In both cases the government's retreat in response to pressure from symmetrically opposite social movements assumed the very form of a return to the rules of the game as defined by the Debré Law.

This law is still challenged, marginally, by small cells of resolute *laïques* intransigently adhering to the sacrosanct slogan "To public schools, public funds; to private schools, private funds." It is equally criticized on the Catholic side, both by conservative movements—which fear that the State will interpret too freely its contractual powers and arrogate the right to scrutinize the teaching programs of denominational schools— and by progressive movements, which consider the existence of the denominational school network (where Catholic children grow up with only other Catholic children) to be a barrier to the pastoral mission of the Church that should be present throughout society. The law has nonetheless become, according to one staunch supporter of *laïcité*, "an established point of reference for French-style *laïcité*" (Coq, 1995).

The mediating quality of the contractual system, which was introduced during a phase of (relative) waning of the symbolic importance of the school question, from the viewpoint of the relation between the religious and the political in France, has proved effective. It has benefited from—while also accelerating—sociocultural developments since the end of the 1960s. Private denominational schools have become secularized; the vast majority of their teachers are laypersons, and the reasons cited by families for enrolling their children at private schools are not, in a Catholic country as little devout as France, primarily religious. Only an estimated 20 percent of parents enroll their children in Catholic schools for religious motives. With regard to the teachers in the public sector, they partake of a *laïque* culture notably free of passion.

This development is in keeping with a much broader redefinition of "public" and "private": Over the past fifty years, the role of the State and how it perceives its mission have been profoundly transformed. It is now widely recognized that the welfare state assumes a responsibility toward economic, social, and cultural activities lying beyond its powers of direct initiative. In the domain of education, the idea of a certain sharing of tasks between the public school and the private school, corresponding to different services and educative styles, is tending to command attention from either side, while parents are adopting the habit of turning alternately from one system to the other according to their children's needs. It is not uncommon to see the head of a public school orienting (discreetly) a student in difficulty toward a private school, and vice versa. The competition between the public and private school systems still exists, but it is more concerned with the "educational benefits" offered by one or the other than with the teachers' philosophical leanings. The episcopate has taken a moderate line, and contrary to what might be expected, the left's (thus the *laïques'*) rise to power in 1981 served to reinforce that moderation: far from being openly defiant, the bishops clearly let it be known that concern for their flock includes concern for the whole of society's youth (and not only for young people educated in Catholic schools) and that they oppose the instrumentalization of the question of educational freedom by the right-wing parties.

If the situation has on the whole been settled, what explanation may be offered for the great recurrent battles over the school question, which consistently see part of France taking to the streets? In order to interpret correctly the social and cultural significance of the conflicts of 1984 and 1994, their apparent similarities must be held at a distance so that their differences may be observed more closely.

1. The 1984 conflict was sparked off by the Socialist government's initiative to give new impetus to the idea—which had been part of candidate François Mitterrand's "110 proposals for France" during the electoral campaign—of a "large, unified public education service." In 1984 the Socialist government, confronted with the reality of handling political affairs in a difficult international economic context, had to face up, on all fronts, to the disintegration of the socialist utopia. The policy of nationalizations of the new septennate (presidential election period, administration of President Mitterrand) had met with a check; from 1983, the government undertook a policy of severe economic and financial measures far from resembling the dreams it had entertained to stem the tide of capitalism. This swift and brutal conversion to a market economy and liberalism, which accompanied the modernization of the French left in the early 1980s, gave rise to a decline of the great symbolic ideals that made up the memory of the "people of the left."

In this climate of political disenchantment, the question of education took on, for many of those who had brought the left to power, an aspect of considerable emotional and symbolic bearing: It had become, in a way, the refuge of a lost utopia. Presided over in tones of strict moderation by the minister of education, Alain Savary, negotiations were begun in 1982 on the government's proposal. It immediately aroused latent passions. The *laïque* camp, represented by the National Committee of *Laïque*[3] Action (CANL) and the public schools' teachers' unions on one side, and the private education camp led by the National Union of the Parents' Association for Free Education (UNAPEL) and by Canon Paul Guiberteau, secretary-general of the National Center of Catholic Education (CNEC) on the other, immediately got down to a show of force. Proclamations and demonstrations followed from both sides. One rallied against the menace the omnipotence of the modern State represents for basic civil liberties and for the freedom of the communities that make up the "wealth of the nation" (Guiberteau, 1984) to express their values. The other deplored the political deviation of the debate and the "exorbitant demands" of the episcopate. Indeed, the latter refused, among various counterproposals, to make civil servants of private school teachers. It claimed, rather, a specific status for these teachers along with an administrative structure for the management of private schools "equivalent," according to *laïques* (who clearly reject this idea), "to a veritable public service of Catholic education" (Bouchacheirass, 1984).

In retrospect, the 1982–1984 conflict highlights, strikingly, from the government's moderate proposal and the first reactions of the bishops, the escalation of the symbolic importance of what was at stake. The bill itself, in the form it was in when first laid on the bench of the National Assembly, in no way threatened the existence of private education. Contrary to declarations made during the electoral campaign, it did not abolish the contractual system established by the Debré Law, and it even recognized the possibility of spiritual considerations peculiar to denominational schools. The main preoccupation of the bishops, at the beginning of the negotiations, concerned the weight of the anticipated administrative machinery. In allowing for amendments on a second reading, the minister of education was clearly aiming at conciliation. The hard line came from the prime minister, Pierre Mauroy, who chose to forgo the admittedly tenuous stability, and, using Article 49.3 of the Constitution,[4] entered into an ideological conflict toward which the Socialist Party, led by its most uncompromising *laïque* elements, cleared the way.

The consequence was the immediate dramatization of the conflict. In an interview accorded to the daily newspaper *Le Monde* under the headline (intensely emotionally charged) *"J'accuse,"*[5] Cardinal Lustiger, archbishop of Paris, spoke bitterly of his humiliation and charged the government with "not keeping its word." The large demonstration of 24 June marked the climax of the mobilization. The private education bill was withdrawn from the parliamentary agenda of 12 July. On 14 July, the national commemoration day, President Mitterrand announced the withdrawal of the Savary bill. The minister of education, who had so actively sought a compromise (Savary, 1985), had to resign, as did Prime Minister Mauroy. The new minister of education of the Fabius government, Jean-Pierre Chevènement, announced on 29 August "simple and practical measures" to quell the conflict over private education. These arrangements aimed at solving the problem of the public administration's financing of private schools. They involved, according to the minister, "a republican law" signaling a "return to the Debré Law." Can it consequently be claimed, however, that the 1984 conflict led to nothing, a kind of swan song for the "War of the Two Frances"? In fact, 1984 bears witness to the *mediating conflictivization* of a debate that permitted, in playing itself out in entirely symbolic terms, to diffuse almost completely what had historically been at stake in the school conflict: for both sides, the disappearance of the "school of the others." In seizing upon (without Alain Savary's spirit of conciliation) the theme of a "public education service," and in renewing by this tack the link with the strongest symbols of its own tradition, the Socialist Party strove to avert the collapse of the socialist dream. At the same time, however, it had to take into account that 70 percent of French people (thus a significant part of its electorate) had just declared themselves in favor of freedom of education. As several observers—including the sociologist Michel Crozier—remarked at the time, the school battle of 1984 particularly reveals the very strong need of the French for freedom, "a need that has nothing to do with religion or political affiliation" but which demonstrates a wish to see the State limit its intervention in daily life, leaving to parents alone the responsibility for the educational directions of their children (Crozier, 1984). As for the bishops, they have come a long way from the rigid stances taken by their predecessors. One of Canon Guiberteau's messages, repeated continually by loudspeakers during the course of the demonstration of 24 June, is revealing in this regard: "We're not demonstrating against *laïque* schools, but against a disastrous law. The government wants the demonstration to be, at all costs, a demonstration that pits the right against the left, which is totally ridiculous." Respect for the *laïque* school, refusal of any political interpretation of the conflict—this was the overall attitude of the bishops. Consequently, those most involved in the debate (Monsignor Vilnet, Monsignor Lustiger, and Monsignor Honoré) chose not to take part in the demonstrations, satisfied with being present on the morning of the 24th for the start of the march. At no time was there any question of the State's abolishing private education, nor of the Church's challenging the legitimacy of the Republic's educational role. The symbolic representation of the conflict between the "*laïques*" and the "religious" has become, through this affair, and having taken into account the bearing of the past, the paradoxical means of a significant de-ideologization of the political debate over what constitutes the ideal of freedom in a modern society.

2. At first glance, the 1994 conflict seems to be a repetition of the preceding scenario, allowing the process of mediating conflictivization to come into play in the opposite way, via the mass demonstration of defenders of *laïque* values against the perceived abuses of a right-wing government. But the analysis cannot stop there, for the elements of another normative conflict appear, beyond taking up classic ideological themes. A better understanding of these new developments may be gained through a brief examination of the chronology of events.

On 13 June 1992, an agreement was signed between the minister of education, Jack Lang, and the new secretary-general of Catholic Education, Father Max Cloupet, in order to assure definitively the parity between the public and private sectors. After the turbulence of 1984, a period of peace seemed finally to have arrived. Nevertheless, a question was left in abeyance: that of teacher training. A complementary agreement dated 11 January 1993, which aimed at solving this question, stated that private school teachers would thenceforth undergo the same education and be subject to the same examinations as their public school colleagues. This agreement gave rise to stiff opposition from both intransigent *laïques* and "staunch Catholics." So as not to aggravate the conflict, the minister withdrew the agreement.

At the same time, the right's platform for the legislative elections of 1993 predicted that "local governments could in all fairness finance investments for private schools, in the way they do for public schools." Immediately after the victory of the new majority, private schools pressured the Edouard Balladur government to keep the promises it had made during the electoral campaign and rescind the Falloux Law, which fixed the possible public contribution to investments in private establishments at 10 percent. The revision process began in the Assembly in June 1993. At the end of a long debate, the Assembly adopted the law modifying the Falloux Law. For the law to be promulgated definitively, it had to be passed with the same wording in the Senate.

In the meantime, a report made at the demand of the minister of education, François Bayrou, by a commission presided over by Dean Vedel, a distinguished professor of law and former member of the Constitutional Council, was published. It was an alarming exposé of the real estate situation of private schools, from the point of view of pupils' security. Cries of indignation were heard from the public schools, whose real estate situation is at least as poor, if not worse. The work of the Vedel Commission appeared, in this context, as an opportunistic undertaking designed to justify, in the name of pupils' security, the government's particular concern for private education. The expeditious passing through the Senate, in a night's sitting, in December 1993, of the revision of the Falloux Law instigated a vigorous mobilization of the *laïque* camp (and a strike of public school teachers). In order to defuse the movement, Prime Minister Balladur announced a commission to evaluate security in public and private schools, followed, at the beginning of January 1994, by the installment of a five-year plan for public education, matched with 500 million francs[6] intended for security-oriented renovations in public schools.

Despite this, the movement in favor of public education grew stronger and more vigorous. Three days after the Constitutional Council had passed a vote of censure on Article 2 of the law amending the Falloux Law (the article authorizing public contributions of more than 10 percent for investments in private schools), a massive demonstration of almost a million people passed through the streets of Paris, from the Place de la République to the Place de la Nation. Along the route, which had been that of all the great workers' demonstrations of the past, slogans took up, in an often most imaginative way, the old themes of the conflict between the two schools: "*Laïques* in the street, frogs in the holy-water basins!", "Private is selection; public is integration", "The only free school is no school!", not to mention, "Come back Jules!"[7] But the most revealing slogan was one borrowed from the poet Paul Verlaine: "There is weeping in our hearts like the rain in our classes."[8]

Even as it reaffirmed the values of *laïcité*, the January 1994 demonstration bears witness to the misgivings the French have when confronted with the deterioration of their public school system. Over and beyond the problems posed by the lack of material means allocated by the government to the schools, the recognition of the fundamental mission of public education to integrate all young people into the heart of the French community had been called into question. The competition with private education for a slice of State aid gives rise to more fundamental questions regarding the ultimate goal of the public education service. This questioning is strongly intensified by the criticism, becoming widespread in the 1990s, opposing the ideal of a "public service" shared by both public school teachers and Catholic school officials. The "privatization" stakes have changed: They now have less to do with the denominational character of education than with the aim of the educative mission. Stating the faults of the existing system, certain parties—such as the Association of School Makers, founded in 1992 by Guy Bourgeois—preach the complete autonomy of schools, which would be able to choose freely their teachers and their pupils as well as to enter into a contract with the State and local authorities. The project goes further than the simple freedom granted to private initiatives to develop, autonomously, original educative experiences (a freedom that already exists for private "noncontracted" schools not benefiting from State financial aid): It is a matter of offering to all establishment heads (public or private) the possibility of becoming, at their own choosing, "school entrepreneurs," thus to be responsible for defining the various programs of their respective establishments and to submit these curricula to the discretion of the administration with a view to obtaining subsidies. This clearly engenders—as Guy Coq has remarked—a proposal to "privatize public schools," which calls into question the idea—constitutive of the republican ideal—according to which educational responsibility involves the entire nation (as a community) and demands a national policy implemented by the people's representatives.

After the Jospin Law of 1989 (voted by a socialist majority), local educational initiatives were given much latitude, at departmental and regional levels, to help students who were in difficulties. This opening—which corresponds to a general policy of decentralization, paradoxically put into play since 1981 by a left with a reputation for being Jacobin and centralizing—incites the opposition of the most resolute *laïque* movements that fear losing the "unified" character of the public education service, even as it rallies all those who perceive it as a modernization of the education system. The tendency outlined by the subsequent "school entrepreneurs" proposal, which seduces the ultraliberal movements of the right now back in power, is of an altogether different nature: It aims at making education a purely private affair, in which the "educative entrepreneurs" offer the "school customers" (Ballion, 1982) services evaluated according to criteria over which the nation (as a community) is not consulted. Calling into question the "economic distress of public schools" and thus the weakness of the State's commitment, the mobilization of 1994 is more or less explicitly in reaction to the aim of privatizing the education system, an aim that fundamentally opposes not only the classic republican conception of education but also the general principles of the national political culture. The government well understands the message: Not only is the Bourg-Broc Law, which reforms the Falloux Law, promulgated by the president of the Republic without Article 2, thus putting an end to the 10 percent rule, but also the minister of education undertakes, in the form of a "conference for education" held throughout France, a vast consultation of the various unions and administrations involved in the education system.

Even though the symbolic conflictivization of 1984 constitutes the final moment in the process of de-ideologization of the school war, progressively pacified by the contractual system established in 1959, the *laïque* show of force of 1994—led formally against "the securing of public funds by denominational education"—opens a much more decisive normative conflict: that concerning the possible preservation of the ideal of a "public education service," in a society where the objective of the integration of the nation (as a community)—which is the political foundation of the republican identity—is called into question.

French *Laïcité* as Challenged by Minorities

Since the Revolution, the construction of French identity has depended on the idea that citizenship should transcend community ties and define, beyond all particularisms, a national "we" with which each person can identify. Over and beyond the "War of the Two Frances," the country's religious homogeneity—given the vast presence of Roman Catholicism— once constituted, well before the revolutionaries, a foundation for the monarchy's aim of political unity. The historical confrontation between Catholic France and *laïque* France stemmed from the incompatibility of two absolute conceptions of the collective identity: one firmly entrenched in a religious vision of the world, the other based on a political vision of society. The triumph of the second over the first spelled not the end of re-ligious France but the establishment of a specific identity: that of a "*laïque* country of Catholic culture*" (Willaime, 1996). Today, this synthesis of identity is suffering a change that sends tremors through all its dimen-sions—religious, cultural, social, and political.

In the religious domain, the principal concern is the current phenome-non of religious diversification, occurring even as the socioreligious links forged over centuries by Catholicism continue to give way. Initiated after World War I, the destructuring of the "parish civilization," which framed the spatial, temporal, and symbolic dimensions of Catholic France, dra-matically accelerated after World War II (Lambert, 1985). The subsidence of regular religious practice (around 10 percent in 1995), the collapse of sacerdotal vocations (45,000 priests in France in 1945; 27,000 in 1994; ap-proximately 2,000 in 2010 if current trends continue), and the more recent fall in the number of Catholic baptisms and marriages, bear witness to the waning of the world of observances structured by Catholicism (Maître et al., 1991). While French Catholicism is not without vitality, these days this is measured in terms of the proliferation of small groups of volunteers who are viewed (and see themselves thus) as a part of a mi-nority in a society dominated by religious indifference. More signifi-cantly, since the mid-1980s there has been a marked fall in the nominal identification with Catholicism: In 1985, 82 percent of French people who were asked the question, "Do you have a religion?" called themselves "Catholics." In 1994, this proportion had dropped to 67 percent.[9] This drop includes the increasing number of those who describe themselves as having "no religion," but it equally corresponds to the redrafting of the distribution of the religious minorities present at the heart of the na-tional community.

The traditional religious minorities (Judaism and Protestantism) have always played an extremely important role on the national stage, and the contribution of the Protestant community to setting in place the Republic's ideals was mentioned earlier. French Protestants (mostly Calvinists) currently represent 1.7 million people, or 3 percent of the French population, yet their social influence seems out of proportion to the demographic significance of Protestant churches. This fact is partly linked to the social composition of the Protestant group: Except in eastern regions, where a veritable working-class Protestantism exists, blue-collar and lower-level white-collar workers are clearly underrepresented in the Protestant population, when compared to executives, teachers, and members of the intellectual professions. In French public opinion, this image of a "social elite" Protestantism, oriented toward progress and inclined to the left, is particularly strong, and it is reinforced by the outstanding role played by Protestants in the fields of high finance, business, and high public service as well as in political life.[10] Behind this image lies a history of a minority whose identity awareness still bears the marks of a tradition of resistance and struggle: resistance to the persecutions inflicted—from the repeal of the Edict of Nantes in 1685 to the Edict of Tolerance of 1787—in the name of the State religion, and constant struggle, in the name of the individual and his conscience, against the crushing monopoly of Catholicism, all of which explains the vigorous Protestant support for laïque modernity, particularly in national education,[11] and in public health and hygiene. But will the social success of French Protestantism, directly linked to the positive rapport it maintains with the political modernity incarnated by the Republic, spell, paradoxically, the decline of the Protestant community? Certain studies published at the end of the 1980s underline a tendency toward the loss of identity of a community actively engaged in ecumenical dialogue and relatively dispersed (Baubérot, 1988). Recent studies, however, indicate on the contrary the force of attraction exerted by "Protestant values"—the preeminence of the individual conscience, the zeal for democracy, the sense of social responsibility and fellowship, the insistence on everyone's right of access to culture and knowledge—on the Catholic population. In 1995, 27 percent of people who declare themselves "close to Protestantism" belonged to the Catholic Church. Herein lies a particularly interesting indicator of the developments that affect the formation of religious identities in French society.

The French Jewish population, on French soil since Gallo-Roman times and highly assimilated and deeply devoted to the ideals of the French Revolution, was enhanced at the end of the nineteenth century by the first wave of Ashkenazi immigrants. While interrupted by World War II (95,000 Jews living in France were victims of the genocide), the integration of Central European Jews occurred rapidly, in the space of two or three generations. Furthermore, the process of decolonization in the Maghreb and the development of the Israeli-Arab conflict in the Middle East provoked, in the 1950s and 1960s a new influx of migrants, which had a redynamizing effect on community-oriented Jewish life. These Sephardic Jews are more deeply rooted in diverse traditional cultures, but also more familiar with the French language, and many were already of French nationality. Once again, the dialectic of assimilation and of the reassertion of identity, for an estimated Jewish population of 600,000 people, is entered into. In the case of Judaism, as in the case of Protestantism mentioned earlier, the question of community identity and that of the reevaluation of the relation to modernity seem closely correlated.

Today, however, it is the presence of a numerically significant Muslim community, increasingly revealing of its particular identity, that has once again brought to light, and in completely new terms, the question of the relation between these diverse community realities and a French identity built up over the centuries with minority assimilation as its keynote. Estimated at 4 million people, the Muslim population currently constitutes France's second largest religion. It includes foreign nationals from Muslim countries (mostly from the Maghreb: between 1.8 and 2 million people), French Muslims (the "harkis," who opted to settle in France during the independence of North African countries, and their descendants, totaling 500,000 people), young Franco-Maghrebi or "*beurs*"[12] from the second generation (of French nationality), a small group of French converted to Islam, and naturalized Muslims.

The Muslim presence in France is not, as such, a new phenomenon. Nevertheless, it seems as if the French are currently "discovering" its magnitude. This sudden awareness appears to be linked to the psychological shock created in public opinion by the Iranian Revolution and by the general rise of Islamic movements in all Islamic countries, particularly in Algeria, a country that has always generated extremely strong feelings in France. Recent events—from the Salman Rushdie affair to the recent bombings in Paris—have, in the eyes of the public, given content to the image of an Islam that is closed off to the world, refractory in response to modernity, and fanatical—possessed by a spirit of conquest liable to put in danger both the "French identity" and the security of the population. The extreme right has exploited this widespread anxiety with regard to Islam in order to incite hatred toward "the immigrant"—a ploy that has served as its electoral stock-in-trade.

The passionate character of public debate over the greater assertion of the Muslim presence in France serves to cloud the appreciation—in itself difficult because of the composite character of Islam in France—of the reality of this presence. The French Muslims, repatriated from North

Africa, who form the oldest, most established component of the Muslim population, differ markedly from the immigrant Muslims, who have been progressively "sedentarized" in France. This "precarious sedentarization" (Kepel, 1987) has been one of the unintentional effects of the July 1974 law suspending the migratory influx of workers. A great number of workers who moved regularly between their countries of origin (where they had left their families) and France opted, as a result, to move permanently to French soil, benefiting from the provisions (which had not been suspended) entitling families to regroup. Previously these workers, who lived between the factory and their lodgings, had limited contact with French society at large. The arrival of women and children upset this state of "invisibility": The "immigrants" are now present in urban districts, in working-class high-rise estates, and in schools. They progressively assert their own specific culture, one dimension of which is Islam. The social conflicts of the 1980s (particularly the car industry strikes of 1982–1983) in which large numbers of immigrant workers were involved, contributed to enhancing this cultural and religious assertion from an implied, private register to one that is evident and public. Ever since, the number of places of worship (11 in 1970, 274 in 1980, 1,000 to 1,500 in 1990, twice that today) as well as the number of Islamic associations, hallal butchers, libraries, and so on concurrently undergo expansion. Further, the cultural assertion of Islam takes on a broader aspect with the coming of age of a generation of young people born of the Maghrebi immigration who suffer acutely at school and in seeking employment from the difficulties of an integration that becomes, with the fading of the dream of "going back home," imperative. These young *beurs* insist on the right to an overt and collective expression of Islam, which constitutes a fundamental dimension of their cultural identity in French society. The question of whether young Muslim women should wear the *hijeb* (the veil) in public schools has brought to light a striking example of the normative conflicts capable of inducing such a public expression of Islam in a *laïque* society. From many angles—the neutrality of schools, the private nature of religious expression, the status of women, paternal authority, but also the acceptability and regulation of certain religious practices, such as the sacrifice of a sheep during the major festival of *al-'Id al-Kabir*[13] (Brisebarre, 1989)—this public expression of Islam sets the most assured aspects of French modernity off balance.

The problems posed by the reality of the Muslim presence are complicated by a great uncertainty in relation to Islamic representative institutions in France: A great number of Muslims take exception to the privilege bestowed on the Paris Mosque (linked to Algerian Islam) of representing Islam in France. Ethnic and political conflicts, as much as those of a theological nature, come to complicate an organizational process already made difficult by the rejection—by certain Islamic fundamentalist movements—of all forms of compromise with the State, its laws, and the profane society it embodies. If modernity has defied the religious culture of immigrants in search of ways to integrate, it seems evident that today, in return, Islam defies the assimilating culture of the French Republic (Leveau and Kepel, 1988).

The normative conflict thus engendered between an integrationist conception of the national identity and a differentialist conception of community identities produces two kinds of effects, the juxtaposition of which sends tremors through the classic conceptions of *laïcité*.

1. First, the conflict highlights (and contributes to accelerating) the process of disenchantment that affects, in this last decade of the twentieth century, the political ideals on which the Republic was founded, and more precisely, the truly religious form in which the founding conflict between the Catholic Church and the State contributed to the institutionalization of these ideals. The historian Pierre Nora has emphasized, along with many others, that the Republic established itself in France in the form of a "veritable civil religion that has endowed itself with a Pantheon, a martyrology, a hagiography, a plural, multiform, and ubiquitous liturgy; it has invented its myths, its rites, its altars, constructed its temples and multiplied its props—statues, frescos, street signs, school manuals—being a permanent educative spectacle" (Nora, 1984: 651). This alternative religious structure has striven to replace the educative spectacle offered over the centuries by Catholicism: that of steeples, processions, and the calvaries and spandrels of cathedrals. This very situation leads English sociologist David Martin to remark judiciously that "The secular religions produced by France are sometimes a form of Catholicism without Christianity" (Martin, 1979: 24). Fundamentally, this religion of the Republic is based on a universalistic ideal capable of subsuming all the particularisms in a veritable "citizens' communion," the secular version—may it be said—of the "Saints Communion" of Catholicism. Excluded from the economic, cultural, and political benefits promised to them by this utopia, the young *beurs* have created for themselves a specific identity by appropriating a Muslim culture that their parents have mostly not passed on to them. But this claiming and assuming of Islam is in itself a way of revealing a draining of the Republic's secular eschatology: Over and above their desire to affiliate themselves with the *umma* (the community of believers in Islam), these new faithful drive French society to measure the loss of plausibility of the foundation myths that feed the dominant political discourse, that of the left as of the right. The increasing number of calls currently heard for a "new *laïque* pact" can be interpreted as many attempts to face up to the symbolic deficiency on the political side that has resulted in this disenchantment.

2. There are other ways, though, to confront this symbolic void. The subsidence of the vision of an integrated community of citizens (Schnapper, 1994) and the concurrent pluralization of the religious domain are, moreover, encouraging a tendency toward the assertion of the ethical, cultural, and symbolic particularities of the different communities, aside from the particular case of the Muslims. The political scientist Pierre Birnbaum has undertaken in-depth studies of the force of the ties that unite Franco-Judaism to the Republic (Birnbaum, 1992), despite the shock of the Dreyfus affair and despite the divisions caused by the rise of anti-Semitism at the end of the nineteenth century (Birnbaum, 1988). In a brilliant and provocative work recently published (Birnbaum, 1995), he puts forward the hypothesis that these ties are currently becoming undone, not only because a movement for identity renewal has tended to gain momentum since the 1980s (particularly among the younger generations, who have known neither the persecutions nor the Shoah and who are hardly at all involved in the network of organizations of institutional Judaism) but also because public opinion and the political community—which by a vast majority reject the anti-Semitic provocations of the extreme-right—demonstrate a tendency to want to "recommunitarize" the Jewish population. The huge demonstrations of protest that took place throughout France in May 1990, following the profanation of Jewish tombs in the Carpentras cemetery, seem to Birnbaum to have signaled the return, in the minds of both Jews and non-Jews, of an "imaginary community" to which the solemn intervention of political leaders lent a certain substance. While the conflict surrounding the Dreyfus affair had its origins in the universalism of the Enlightenment, Birnbaum notes that "a philo-Semitic mobilization is now being realized in the name of a community paradigm" (p. 258). Nevertheless, he is careful to point out that not long before Carpentras, the French president, François Mitterrand, had presided, on the occasion of the bicentennial celebrations of the Revolution, over the solemn placing of the ashes of the priest Grégoire—the democrat who in 1791 was the great advocate of Jewish emancipation and of their "regeneration" as citizens—and of René Cassin, a great Jewish statesman anxious to impose upon the world, through the United Nations Declaration of Human Rights, the universal virtues of 1789. According to Birnbaum, "One could scarcely dream of a better symbol of the strength of republican ideals: a Jewish statesman solemnly placed in the Pantheon at the same time as the priest Grégoire, figurehead of the emancipating Enlightenment!" Nevertheless, this belated public consecration occurs, paradoxically, when the Republic is preparing to turn its back on certain 1789 assimilating ideals: "as if rendering homage to an epoch almost past, it was enacted at the moment when the processes of communitarization are severely diminishing the ties of citizenship in the name of

respect for identities" (p. 259). It might well be that for those who are not French, what is at stake in the conflict highlighted by Birnbaum between the republican conception of citizenship and the absolute assertion of the "right to difference" should seem extraordinarily mysterious. Nevertheless, it is at the center of all normative conflicts involving the definition of the national identity.

These conflicts do not find expression only by way of debates whose ideological implications are formalized and dramatized by intellectuals. The shift that has for the past twenty years taken place at the heart of the Jewish population in France, from the ideal of citizen assimilation to that of the self-assertion of communities (Cohen, 1993), equally shows itself in the form of concrete demands. The wish to give Jewish life more social visibility no longer exclusively concerns the minority groups of ultrareligious Jews (the Hassidim of Lubavitch have less than 10,000 faithful in France), but it currently mobilizes various much broader movements of French Judaism, whose demands can be passed on to the public authorities by the Chief Rabbi. The negotiations undertaken over the past few years over permitting Jewish pupils to be exempt from school obligations on Saturdays so that they might observe the Sabbath illustrates this new tendency. A circular letter in 1989 made it possible for the school calendar to be planned around the major religious festivals, taking into account all denominations, including Muslims and Armenians. When confronted by the repeated demands of Jewish students for leaves of absence on Saturdays, however, a statutory order on 18 February 1991 on pupils' rights and obligations strictly recalled the principle of obligatory school attendance. The Central Consistory and two Jewish associations responded by lodging an appeal to the Council of State. The controversy was particularly divisive within the Jewish population itself, with the *laïque* movements (represented especially by the Association for a Humanist and *Laïque* Judaism, and the *Laïque* Jewish Center) forcefully opposing community orientation as defined by the Chief Rabbi.

Ultimately it was the public affairs tribunal that mediated in the conflict, on the one hand recalling principles, and on the other discouraging any rigidity in their application. In 1993 a Jewish (senior) secondary school student in Nice was expelled for repeated absences from his Saturday lessons. The Nice Public Affairs Tribunal ruled in favor of the school, which led to an appeal before the Council of State in 1995. The Council rejected the appeal insofar as it was attempting to win a general leave of absence for Jewish pupils on the Sabbath. But it stopped short of confirming school attendance as being absolutely obligatory: Pupils who request leave could be authorized not to attend, as long as those absences are "not in contradiction with the tasks inherent in their studies" and "that they do not disrupt public order within the establishment."[14] The

adopted solution thus consisted of authorizing the heads of school establishments to evaluate and act upon specific situations. This "decentralization" of the decisionmaking process (foreign to French political and
administrative traditions) appears to be the principal fruit—beyond the
case of Jewish celebrations—of the mediating interventions by the public
affairs tribunal in conflicts regarding community claims in the social
sphere and especially in school. The solution outlined a new and practical (rather than ideological) method of regulating *laïcité*.

Could this type of juridico-administrative mediation work in all cases?
The answer to this question remains uncertain. Over and beyond the practical developments demanded by "communal" movements within the
Jewish population (regarding the school calendar, but also regarding Jewish cemetery plots, the dates of elections, etc.), the fundamental stakes are
those of the "right to community differences," which are placed all the
more radically by the processes of (re)Islamization of France's Muslim
population. It is further significant, from this point of view, that the Chief
Rabbi's most solemn public demands concerning the right of Jewish pupils
not to go to school on Saturdays[15] should coincide precisely with two particularly heated moments during the "veil affair," which in effect concentrated all aspects—administrative, political, but especially symbolic and
ideological—of the current debate over the redefinition of *laïcité*.

Mediating in a Deadlock: The "Veil Affair"

In describing the extent to which public opinion is divided over the "veil
affair," certain commentators have found therein a "new Dreyfus affair."
Nevertheless, the event at the origin of the extraordinary unleashing of
passions that has accompanied this polemic over several long months
may seem of negligible importance to someone observing events from
the outside. In June 1989 the board of a (junior) secondary school in Creil,
in the Val d'Oise department, met to work on the "school project," a document stating the school's objectives for the coming years. In this school,
situated in the outer suburbs north of Paris, there were no less than
twenty-five different nationalities. A large group of Jewish children had
for the previous several years fallen into the habit of missing school on
Saturdays and on days of Jewish celebrations. In coping with this situation, the teachers decided to include in the project a clause on *laïcité*, stating that (1) absence from class due to religious reasons will no longer be
permitted, effective from the beginning of the next school year, and
(2) that discretion is required regarding the wearing of distinctive religious insignia. The teachers immediately brought up the case of three
Muslim girls wearing the *hijeb*: what shall these girls be told if Jewish
children are asked to respect the *laïque* nature of the institution?

When classes resumed, a note from the board called upon teachers of the Creil school to refuse classroom access to girls wearing the Islamic veil. Two girls refused to accede to this request. One of their fathers came to the school accompanied by an imam and accused the headmaster (himself from Martinique) of racism. A few days later the headmaster informed three girls wearing the *hijeb* that they were provisionally suspended from classes, on the grounds that wearing the veil represents "a blow struck both at *laïcité* and at the neutrality of the public school." A compromise was finally reached during a meeting of the school board in the presence of the parents of the three pupils and the presidents of Tunisian, Moroccan, and Algerian *laïque* associations: The girls would keep their veils on within the school bounds, but they would take them off during classes, letting them fall to their shoulders. Furthermore, they would undertake to attend all classes, including natural science and sports.

In the interim, however, at first the local and then the national press gave the affair broad coverage. On the cover of *Nouvel Observateur* magazine is a veiled girl and the title "Fanaticism: The Religious Menace." Two weeks later *Express* magazine, in turn, carried the headline "Danger for the *Laïque* School—Fundamentalists: Their Strategy." Against the red background of the cover, a veiled schoolgirl is turning her back on the photographer. This process of media dramatization of the "veil affair" occurred in parallel with the ideological amplification of the controversy on a national scale. The Socialist (and Protestant) minister for national education, Lionel Jospin, adopted a balanced position, which remained his approach. "It has to do," he said, "with demonstrating respect for the *laïcité* of schools by not flaunting signs of one's religious affiliation." He nevertheless added that "Schools are made to welcome children, not to exclude them," a position reaffirmed in his speech before the National Assembly on 25 October 1989. *Laïcité*, he said, no longer needed to be "a *laïcité* of conflict. On the contrary, it must be a kind, generous, good-willed *laïcité*, made for the very reason of avoiding conflict, including religious conflict. . . . It would be a serious fault," he added, "to adopt an inflexible attitude, to unite—by the reflex of solidarity—the whole of the community around a few isolated elements. It is not by refusal, in practicing exclusion, that the evolution of Islam in the Western world is to be favored. Who is to say that in ten years' time, these Muslim girls who are today making headlines shall still be wearing veils, that they shall not be emancipated?"

This moderate position was clearly supported by François Mitterrand and the prime minister (also Protestant), Michel Rocard. But it clashed with the radicalization of positions, which thenceforth confronted each other publicly. Schools witnessed a rapid increase in conflicts; provocation on the one side and exclusion on the other were mutually reinforced.

At Creil, the symbolic place of conflict, the pupils breached the compromise by wearing their veils during classes. This reversal occurred in the wake of a meeting their fathers had with a representative of the National Federation of French Muslims, which defended the idea that wearing the veil is "an affair of modesty," and "that there can be no compromise with religion." The girls were immediately suspended from classes (but allowed onto the school grounds and to the library). A committee supporting the girls of Creil was set up, and an action was brought against the school for "racial discrimination." But a march organized by two Muslim fundamentalist organizations in Paris for 22 October 1989 (and attended by only 600 people) was repudiated by the Paris Mosque and the National Federation of French Muslims.

This split among the Muslim associations regarding the strategy to adopt in reaction to measures that had, according to them, a "discriminatory" and "intolerant" character highlights a more general fact: that of the split introduced by the "veil affair" into all families of thought—political, religious, and ideological—as much as among intellectuals, who put their quills to work dramatizing the conflict. On the side of the laïque organizations, they were far from unifying their positions. While the most resolute elements among them called for a general ban on wearing the veil, more progressive movements argued, to the contrary, for an "open laïcité." Michel Morineau, national secretary of the Education Association (guiding light of the laïque movements) asked "if these girls really have demonstrated the wish to influence their classmates, if they have openly said their prayers in class and express their hostility toward Catholics, Protestants, Israelites, or atheists, if they have refused to attend certain courses? If not, they should keep their veils! A rule is neither sacred nor eternal, and laïcité does not imply maintaining, at all costs, the established order" (Le Monde, 26 October 1989). The Fédération des Conseils de Parents d'Elèves (FCPE), the parents' association, clearly oriented toward the left and firmly attached to the established laïcité of public schools, also had doubts: "What to preach? Certainly not exclusion, which categorically rejects the people concerned, certainly not strict rules of the road to be applied nationally. We must tread the narrow path between rejection, the easy solution, and abdication, the pernicious" (Statement of 24 October 1989). The teachers' unions assumed the opposite position, strictly opposed to any conciliation in the belief that a dam is the answer to the rising tide of religious fundamentalism, and in the name of sexual equality, which is spurned by the forced wearing of the veil. In the name of women's rights too, the feminist associations became mobilized against what they saw as the overly conciliatory position of the government and the minister of national education. The French Grand Orient (freemasons) supported this stance. However, the antiracist organizations and the associations for the defense of the rights of immigrants were divided. SOS-Racism (tending to the left) rejected the terms of the debate: "The real question," insisted its president, Harlem Désir, "is not to be for or against the veil in public schools, but to know which schools these children will go to and how best to bring about their integration" (Statement of 15 October 1989), and the president of France-Plus (of liberal orientation) called upon Lionel Jospin "urgently to assure the respect of *laïcité* in the face of veils, kippas, and all other religious insignia which risk disturbing the peace at school" (15 October 1989).

The positions of non-Muslim religious institutions demonstrated a diversity of opinions. The Jewish organizations supported demands for the free expression of religious beliefs in schools, inasmuch as "there is no risk of destabilizing the society." According to the Protestants, "there is no reason to forbid wearing the veil in school unless it is used as some form of proselytism," but, they add, "there must be an absolute respect for *laïcité*" (Statement of the Protestant Federation of France, 24 October 1989). The Catholic Church shared this view and sought, moreover, through the words of Monsignor Lustiger, cardinal-archbishop of Paris, to dedramatize the affair: "Perhaps the only significant aspect of wearing the veil is that it signifies opposition, something like a Rasta haircut. Let's not go to war with adolescent *beurs*. Cease fire! Let's not confuse the problem of Islam with that of adolescence. Let's stop this debate until the Muslim authorities explain to us the precise meaning of the veil, so that we can understand whether or not it contradicts the French definition of *Laïcité*" (Interview with *Agence France-Presse*, 19 October 1989).

In the process of the ideologico-political radicalization of the debate—which occasionally led to the quite unnatural convergence, and meeting, of certain intransigent, antireligious *laïque* movements and the rejection of Islam (as practiced by immigrants) by certain movements of the conservative, nationalist right—intellectuals with opposite visions concerning the "mission of the left" equally had their say. On 2 November 1989 the *Nouvel Observateur* published, under the title "Teachers, Don't Give In!" a letter signed by five prominent intellectuals (E. Badinter, R. Debray, A. Finkielkraut, E. de Fontenay, and C. Kintzler) opposed to wearing the veil. This text expressed, in the most dramatic, incandescent way, the position of the defenders of republican purity, in face of the assertion of community identities and the increase in particularisms. The tone was set by the first line of the letter addressed to the minister: "The future will decide," announced the signatories, "if the bicentenary year will have seen the Munich of republican schools." Several days later, a letter signed by other, no less known personalities (J. Kaufmann, H. Désir, R. Dumont, G. Perrault, and A. Touraine) retorted that the "obligation" they preach "to forbid" will lead to a cul-de-sac in regard to integration. Exclusion, they asserted, is the cradle of fundamentalism, and of Jean-Marie Le Pen's National Front.[16] "Will those who today conjure up the Munich of republican schools give rise to the Vichy of the integration of immigrants?" (*Politis*, no. 79, 9–15 November 1989).

These quotations are indicative of the passionate tone that invested the controversy. It gave rise to an enormous amount of documents, articles, and manifestos. It was responsible for an avalanche of letters (each arguing strongly for one side or the other) from ordinary citizens to the editors of all French newspapers and magazines. Positions seeking appeasement nevertheless found expression. They aimed to dedramatize the stakes of the conflict, to evaluate the regulating role of Islam in France (e.g., Roux, 1990), or, further, to transpose the problem to the pedagogical and educative domains by asking, for example, how to help the Muslim girls (who are often forced by their fathers or brothers to wear a veil against their wishes) to secure, within the framework of the school, a true personal autonomy.

These efforts toward rationalization carried little weight in face of the outbursts of anathemas. In this context of ideological war, the minister of national education attempted a mediation "from above." He asked for the advice of the Council of State (the supreme administrative tribunal). The judgment, handed down on 27 November 1989, was balanced: "Pupils' wearing religious insignia is not incompatible with *laïcité*," the text pointed out, as long as the signs do not assume "a character of ostentation or protest." This advice left to the schools "the careful task of assessing, case by case and under the judges' control, the limits of this tolerance." The minister thereupon published a memorandum that recalled the principles set forth by the Council of State: It gave priority to talks in the case of pupils' wearing religious insignia (provided these external signs are not aimed at promoting a religious belief), but it advocated rigidity if the principles of neutrality and class attendance are at risk. This attempt to introduce a case-by-case ruling of "veil affairs" failed to create the dynamism of discussion to which the minister had appealed. Its "ambiguity" gave rise to criticism from teachers' unions unwilling to see their teachers burdened with having to take on the main responsibility of the decision. Lively reactions were seen among the most resolute anticommunitarian advocates of *laïcité* as well as from feminist movements. Furthermore, the right wing, in order to thwart the growing appeal of Le Pen's National Front (Le Pen continually cried out against the menace of an "Islamic invasion") among the most conservative sector of its electorate, also seized upon the "veil affairs" to denounce the government as being "too soft" overall and to call into question the policy of integration adopted with regard to immigrants.

In the absence of a coherent negotiating strategy, 1991 and 1992 were characterized by both the increase in and standardization of "veil affairs," according to a repetitive scenario: The cases of suspension from classes (a few dozen since 1989) were brought by their families before the public affairs tribunals, which generally confirmed the decision of exclusion. Appeals against this judgment were heard by the Council of State, which quashed any rules that might have allowed the case to act as a precedent for the generalization of exclusion. This arbitration by the tribunals allowed the independent, case-by-case treatment of the girls' situations. They either agreed in the end not to wear their veils, opted for schooling by correspondence, or were accepted with their veils (while agreeing to abstain from all forms of proselytism) by private Catholic schools. At Creil, it must be noted, it was only the direct intervention by the King of Morocco—the Commander of Believers—asking Moroccan girls expressly to take off their veils and to accept the ground rules of French *laïcité*, that allowed their integration in the secondary school.

The dramatization of the "veil affair" and the failure of attempts at mediation that tended to promote a negotiated solution to the conflict took place against the background of a more fundamental social and cultural conflict: the question of the space to be allowed, in a democratic society destabilized by unemployment, to immigrant communities and thus to Islam as their point of reference. The interference by these two problems appeared more evident in the second heated phase of the "veil affair." It began with the new school year in 1993 at the (junior) secondary school of Nantua in the Jura region, with the suspension of four Turkish girls who refused to remove their veils during sports classes. Over and beyond the strictly school-related problem, the crisis revealed the rejection of a populous Turkish community, whose withdrawal among themselves was compounded by the language barrier (thus differing from the Maghrebi communities, who speak French), and whose religious manifestations crystallized an adherence to their own traditions. But the "Nantua affair" also brought to light the directly political dimension of the conflict, which found vigorous expression in positions directly associating the total prohibition of the veil in schools with the limitation of immigration and the expulsion of illegal immigrants. A short time afterward, in the National Assembly, the (centrist) education minister of the right-wing government now back in power, François Bayrou, was called upon by the most conservative elements of his majority to finish with the "institutional vandalism" allowed by the Jospin Law of 1989. This law, they claimed, encouraged the pursuit of a Muslim-led "insidious jihad" in the midst of schools. To defuse the situation (and to reassure school heads who feared the judicial reversal of their decisions), Bayrou published, on 27 October 1993, a memorandum, the main part of which recalled the terms of the Jospin memorandum and the decision of the Council of State of November 1989. The fundamental principles are noted: "the school is a place where children are to be found; its role is to promote integration, not division. Respect for the principle of *laïcité* is imperative." But the text more sternly stressed the responsibility expected of school heads, who were asked to react rapidly and firmly in the face of any pressure, provocation, or proselytism seen as threatening public order. After the deepening of various local conflicts, a second memorandum dated 20 September 1994 went further in defining the wearing of religious insignia as wearing "symbols that are in themselves elements of proselytism," and in asking school heads to "propose to the board, in relation to school rules, that religious symbols worn ostentatiously shall be prohibited, whereas the presence of more discreet signs, reflecting a personal conviction, shall not be called into question." Clearly, the notion of "ostentatious symbols" is expressly aimed at the Islamic veil, while the cross and the kippa are considered as "discreet signs." Issued under the pressure of a political majority bent on defending a conception of French identity as being endangered by immigration, the second Bayrou memorandum had the effect of systematizing the procedures of exclusion by making them commonplace. Like his socialist predecessor, the minister wanted to "convince without constraint," but the results of his intervention seem just as mixed: Since 1989, if 1,500 girls have chosen to abandon their veils, 150 others have been suspended from their schools. This significant number of exclusions not only demonstrates the failure of a "certain idea of school"; the failure to initiate a procedure permitting differential solutions according to the comportment of individual Muslim girls[17] in regard to the veil demonstrates that the national psychodrama born at Creil in 1989 has not given rise to a conflict capable of producing new norms, which would have led to a renewal and enrichment of questioning in regard to *laïcité*.[18]

From Appeased *Laïcité* to *Laïcité* as Mediator: The Case of the 1988 Conflict in New Caledonia

The "veil affair" reveals, in the always highly symbolic domain of the school, the particular kind of contradictory political instrumentalizations of which *laïque* values can again become the object, as soon as the problem of the cultural integration of Islam into modernity has been attached to the debate over immigration and the integration of immigrants into French society. Is this to say that the "Republican Pact" is spent, and that the normative conflicts still in play in its regard are no more than the exacerbated manifestation of a collective "work of mourning" around the defunct ideals of the Republic? The picture is in fact more contrasted. It is to be observed that the threats hanging over the historico-symbolic heritage of *laïcité* are at the same time favorable to a work of assessment and replenishment of this symbolic capital that serves to mobilize, together, the different families of thought and assures the involvement of the State. Yesterday's adversaries, confronted by the risk of the disintegration of social ties, can pool the symbolic resources constituted in the historical conflict that opposed them, in order to contribute together to the safeguarding and recharging of the collective memory. The *laïque* Republic thus watches with the utmost care over the maintenance and valorization of the common heritage constituted by the churches and religious buildings of France. There is an increasingly clear tendency of *laïcité* to incorporate explicitly the national religious memory into the development and celebration of the cultural continuity of the nation. From this point of view, the vast (and peaceful) debate recently opened over pupils' lack of religious education, the necessity of introducing into public schools the teaching of the various "religious cultures" and the need to develop the place allocated for religious considerations in the study of history, languages, philosophy, literature, music, or geography are very significant (Hervieu-Léger, 1990; Messner, 1995).

This cooperation between the different families of thought not only concerns the preservation of the common memory; it also has a place in the important ethical debates over the future of society and humanity, concerning, for example, the management of progress in biological and genetic research, or the struggle against AIDS. The "spiritual families" are represented in the Ethical Advisory Committee for the Life and Health Sciences, created in 1983, and in the National AIDS Council, created in 1989. Aside from these official expressions of an "ecumenism of the rights of man" (Willaime, 1996) to deal with the great ethical questions posed by the contemporary world, a multiplicity of initiatives have attempted clearly to make this ethical convergence of the great religious and *laïque* "belief traditions" known in a situation of increasing instances of racism and anti-Semitism. This convergence is also increasing in the domains of social action and solidarity. The public authorities recognize the major role of religious institutions in this area and make a point of calling upon them in the struggle against social exclusion. Though commonplace in many countries, this mutual legitimation of the social action of the State and that of the churches constitutes a new element on the French scene.

Could this "ecumenism of the rights of man" develop to the point of constituting a major mediating vector in conflicts that are at once the expression and the result of the crisis of republican normativity? A remarkable example in this domain has come to light in the manner in which a solution was found, in 1988, to a violent conflict between the Melanesian and European communities in New Caledonia. It would go beyond the scope of this contribution to provide a detailed account of the origins of the conflict between the Melanesian population, present on the land before 1853, and the nonnative population, which has been established for a little more than a century and comprises the descendants of nineteenth-century colonizers. The European population holds the reins of economic and social power. It is concentrated in the region of Nouméa, whereas the smaller Melanesian population (30 percent of the total population) is a rural population, dispersed over a vast territory carved into parcels, and profoundly traumatized (at least until the land reforms of 1978) by the dispossession of their land and the administrative divisions imposed in the nineteenth century. During the years of economic boom (1969–1972), the marked ethnic and socioeconomic divisions that had arisen in the relations between the urban area and the countryside found a "solution" in the fact that the rural dwellers were drawn to and integrated in the economy of services linked to a growing urban sector. The following economic crisis brutally revealed the inequalities that had endured beneath the façade of economic expansion. The Kanak demands for independence are the logical culmination of a conflictive process between a multicentered power (that of the traditional chieftaincies) proud of its traditions, and a State power that is doubtful about its own values (Doumergue, 1994).

To see nothing more in this conflict than a mere struggle for colonial emancipation would nevertheless be a simplification. The nonnative population—which is demanding economic development for the country—is itself a composite, made up of various elements from former colonizers as well as from Asia (Vietnamese, Indonesians, etc.) and Oceania (Polynesians, Loyalty Islanders, etc.) forming rigidly structured communities. In an attempt to deal with this situation, in 1983 the socialist government gathered together in France representatives of the principal communities. Together they recognized, by a common declaration, their identity and their respective rights.[19] A commission headed by Edgard Pisani, a former minister in the de Gaulle government, went to New Caledonia with the intention of establishing a plan of regionalization permitting the Kanaks, wherever they are in the majority, to institute policies aimed at developments (notably in the agriculture and education) corresponding to their specific needs. The beginning of the return to civil peace was abruptly interrupted by the decision of the Chirac government (while the right was back in power from 1986 to 1988) to accelerate the process in the institutional domain. The idea was that in order to solve the problems posed by these far-off shores, they should be granted the broadest possible administrative autonomy. Such a policy was tantamount to assigning an inequitable distribution of territorial power to the profit of one community over the other, under cover of a legal majority. The announcement of a referendum on the new bylaw promulgated on 22 January 1988, whose provisions were unacceptable to the Kanak community, lit the fuse. On 22 February, a commando of the Kanak Socialist National Liberation Front (FLNKS) took nine gendarmes hostage. Their liberation by force led to numerous arrests. On 22 April, during an attack on a gendarmerie at Fayaoué, four gendarmes were killed and twenty-two taken hostage along with a magistrate. Under pressure from the right wing of his majority and from the National Front, Jacques Chirac refused the intervention of a mediator requested by the leaders of the FLNKS, Jean-Marie Tjibaou and Léopold Jorédié; but President Mitterrand, in favor of mediation, opposed the disbanding of the FLNKS. New Caledonia fell into civil war. In the presidential elections of April 1988, Mitterrand was reelected in a landslide. On 5 May, however, before the new socialist government was nominated, the Chirac government still in office gave the order for parachutists, gendarmes, and marines to launch an assault on the grotto of Ouvéa, where the hostage-takers had taken refuge. Two gendarmes and nineteen members of the independence movement were killed in this operation.

This chronology of events is indispensable to understanding the far-reaching effects of the initiative taken by the new prime minister, Michel Rocard, as soon as he was appointed. After having assigned the portfolio of the Overseas Departments and Territories to a centrist with a reputation for having an open mind, Olivier Stirn,[20] he appointed a commission of six people charged with the task of "appreciating the situation in New Caledonia and reestablishing talks." This commission, which was to spend a month on the scene, had no precise guidelines; it had to establish its own contacts and offer the conciliatory gestures indispensable to the reestablishment of talks between the communities.

The choice of the members of the commission is particularly interesting. Its coordinator, charged with drafting the final report destined to inform the government, was the prefect Christian Blanc, who had been Edgard Pisani's right-hand man during the first commission and who knew the New Caledonia file very well. At his side were two other higher civil servants: the vice-prefect Pierre Steinmetz, a close collaborator of Raymond Barre, whose presence showed clearly that the resolution of the New Caledonian situation would have to transcend habitual political differences; and Jean-Claude Périer, a state councillor and former director of the Gendarmerie, whose wise actions had been much appreciated in May 1968 and whose participation was a guarantee for the army and the police forces. These three representatives of the Republic were supported by three members of the "spiritual families" strongly present on New Caledonian soil. The first was Monsignor Paul Guiberteau, rector at the Catholic Institute of Paris, former director of Catholic Education, and a prominent figure in the 1984 conflict over private schools. Though the only member of the commission without New Caledonian experience, he was nonetheless a remarkable figure in French Catholicism. Apart from Catholicism's being by a large majority the religion of European New Caledonians, his presence in the commission allowed Rocard to intimate that the school quarrel belonged to the past. The second was the pastor Jacques Stewart, president of the Protestant Federation of France, whose presence was even more important, as great numbers of Melanesians belong to the (notably Presbyterian) evangelical churches. The third was Roger Leray, a former Grand Master of the Grand Lodge of France who had already been approached by Mitterrand in the pre-conflict phase about being the mediator. The freemasonry has a strong presence on the island, and the two leaders of the independence movement (Jean-Marie Tjibaou), and the loyalists (Jacques Lafleur) are both freemasons. The arrival of the commission was greeted with skepticism, even with coldness, both on the side of the FLNKS and on that of the Rally for New Caledonia in the Republic (RPCR), the New Caledonian branch of Chirac's political party, with which the great majority of European New Caledonians identifies.

The work of the commission comprised two distinct phases. The first, from 20 to 28 May 1988, aimed at reaching two principal objectives: on the one hand, to reconstitute talks between the different communities of New Caledonia and the State while restoring the discredited legitimacy of the Republic on the island, and on the other, to establish a social and political diagnosis of the situation. The most remarkable aspect was the place allowed, in this phase, for symbolic gestures rather than discussions. After preliminary meetings with representatives of the communities, churches, political parties, trade unions, and social and professional organizations, the "missionaries" began their fieldwork at Ouvéa, an area populated by Melanesians. They met the traditional chiefs, undertook the customary exchange of words, and visited the common grave in which the nineteen hostage-takers killed during the assault on the grotto were buried and where the Kanak flag flies. "We have come to salute the dead," they stated, "not a flag. And if this emblem stands as a claim of identity and dignity, why should we be shocked? Surely it is better to fight with a flag than with a gun?" (*Libération*, 26 May 1988). Though it engendered indignation among the loyalists, this approach led to an opening on the side of the independence movement. It signaled the beginning of a symbolic course during which the use of silence had as much importance as verbal exchanges. At the grotto itself, the prefect Blanc made only the following statement: "Very hard things happened here. I do not want to make a speech. We come to share the silence with you." There was a similar silence at the Fayaoué gendarmerie where four gendarmes had been massacred in April. Paying respects to the dead was the first condition of the talks.

On 26 May the commission met with Jean-Marie Tjibaou in his village, Hienghène. This meeting with the man who remained, despite pressure from the most extreme partisans of independence, the symbol of the Kanak struggle, announced the mediation's entry into the second phase: that of negotiation. After visits to the traditional chiefs and the missionaries' lunch with the tribe, Tjibaou cleared the way for talks. "There can be an end to the troubles," he stated, "if there are glimmers of hope. We must meet to set out our problems, and then each side shall talk of its concerns, its demands, its claim on the future. In this way, we can treat the problems one by one, see what can be discussed, the possible solutions, and set them out over time. Each of us will make concessions. At first, each shall begin by putting the bar as high as possible, which is to be expected. And then, during the talks, we shall see if the interests of one and the other are negotiable. It is imperative that, around a table, a way is found to gratify Kanak demands" (*Le Figaro,* 27 May 1988). The commission collected the propositions of the Front for Independence. At the same time, it met with the youth, the "bushmen" (loyalist peasants), and the representatives of the New Caledonian, Wallis Islander, Futuna Islander, Polynesian, and Vietnamese communities, and so on. On the ground, the situation was extremely tense, but the joint interviews of the commission with all the social groups created the minimum conditions of confidence needed to enter into a phase of discussions. These talks lasted from 26 May to 6 June. Périer spent a day with the State security police; Pastor Stewart met, at the Tjibaou's request, with the committees supporting the Kanak struggle; Canon Guiberteau took part in the first pilgrimage that included all of the communities mixed together, organized by all of the churches; and Blanc and Steinmetz met secretly with the two leaders of the independence movement, Tjibaou and Yeiwéné Yeivéné, then (again away from the presence of the media) with Lafleur, leader of the European New Caledonians.

On 1 June Lafleur stated on the radio that he was ready for talks to begin. For the first time, he recognized the ethnic dimension of the New Caledonian question, admitting that if sacrifices were to be demanded of those who claimed independence "in the name of the first occupant," then "we must also give and freely consent to sacrifices." On 4 June, at the conclusion of these multiple consultations with the interested parties, the commission began drafting the report that the prefect Blanc subsequently handed to Michel Rocard. It proposed a new status for the territory: a partitioning into federal districts or autonomous regions respecting the distribution of community populations, and a referendum in ten years' time through which the two federal districts would decide whether to remain a French overseas territory or to become independent.

After returning to France on 7 June, the commission was received by the prime minister. He concluded that the commission's work had brought hope and opened "perspectives for direct talks between the communities, with arbitration, and under State authority." On 15 June Tjibaou and Lafleur met for three hours in Rocard's office. Meetings between the two New Caledonian delegations continued from 23 June: The State had given the protagonists fifteen days to resolve all litigious points (the questions of the boundaries between regions, the date of the referendum on self-determination, etc.), based on a nine-point document proposed by Rocard. Christian Blanc shuttled between the two camps in order to untangle points of contention and to decide with his collaborators on the final text. The Matignon Agreement was signed on 26 June, two days ahead of schedule. Over the following days, the agreement was largely acclaimed by political figures on all sides as well as by the newspapers as an unprecedented success, due first and foremost to the "Rocard method."

The Matignon Agreement did not solve all of New Caledonia's problems. As early as 5 June 1988, Monsignor Guiberteau and the pastor Stewart emphasized, during a common press conference, that it was exceedingly urgent that not only the political, but also the economic and social balance of the communities be restored in New Caledonia. Christian Blanc's commission, however, had done more than reestablish the conditions of public order and set down guidelines for a civil peace that remains fragile. It had restored, particularly, not only for New Caledonians, but for all French citizens, the credibility of republican ideals, over and above the ideological conflict between political movements favoring the immediate realization of decolonization (in contempt of the country's social reality) and partisans of the intransigent preservation of a united territory (even at the price of violence). The principal strength of the commission was, under the circumstances, its modesty. At the time he had appointed the committee, Michel Rocard had stated, "We shall not turn anything upside down; we want to listen to everyone." Olivier Stirn had stated, "It would be imprudent, at least certainly premature, today, to have a ready-made view, a plan outlined. . . . It is neither an administrative commission nor a technical commission; it is composed of men who represent the values of our country, and who have been charged, in the name of these values, in the name of civil society, to try to thaw a situation that is blocked" (*Le Monde*, 1 June 1988).

It is not necessary to draw attention to the unprecedented nature of this approach in the over-ideologized context of the French political scene. Nevertheless, its interest does not lie merely in its pragmatic approach to the reality: It resides particularly in the type of ethical mobilization that it sets in the center of political action. The commission was not charged with proposing a program for New Caledonia: It was there to listen to and to take seriously what the various social agents had to say. It invited them to come up with values that could serve to reestablish talks between them, in allowing them to bear witness to the "republican convergence" of traditions incarnated by each of the commission's members—the tradition of the public service, the tradition of the army, the traditions of the Christian churches, the traditions of rational free thought, and so on. These traditions outlined very precisely (with the exception of the Jewish component not represented by the commission because it is nonexistent in New Caledonia) the constellation of a deconflictivized *laïcité*, that has become the chief principle of common and pluralistic values. "Our role, all things considered," as Canon Guiberteau summarized in returning from the commission, "will have been that of catalysts." In light of the social turbulence currently sweeping France, one comes to regret that the example of the New Caledonian commission should have been, in the end, so minor an object of meditation by politicians.

Conclusion: Prescribe the Norm, Organize the Debate, Create the Ties—From One Kind of Mediation to Another

In order to understand the presentation and analysis of the normative conflicts characteristic of the present recompositions of French-style *laïcité*, it has been necessary to engage in a lengthy historical perspective. This is not only because France is a country with a long history: All normative conflicts, while they involve different or contradictory visions of the world, are conflicts constituted in the long term, structuring the collective memory of the nation. At stake in the mediation of these conflicts is the transformation from open defiance to a process leading to the creation of new norms. This dynamic conversion of the conflict intervenes insofar as these contradictory visions of the world find a regulating principle for their relating within the rules of the game authorized by the different parties in the conflict. This signifies in particular that the pretension borne by each of these visions of the world to represent the truth must henceforth find expression in the competition they legitimately maintain in order to emphasize their validity within the framework set down by these rules of the game. This competition—which is the very dynamic of a pluralistic society—allows whatever might be common among the aspirations expressed through these visions of the world to come to light. Moreover, at the same time it makes possible the permanent restarting of the contestation of new norms in which this "common part" inevitably tends to become fixed. By way of this movement, competition structures the strata of the collective memory, strata in which are registered the successive steps of this normative self-creation of the society. Such as it has been sketched out here, the theoretical scheme of the historical course of normative conflicts through which the present form of French-style *laïcité* has been constructed could certainly benefit from further validation and refinement. Nevertheless, it permits the identification, in an ideal-typical manner, of four "scenarios of mediation"[21] through which it is possible to evaluate the various remarkable situations offered by history, whether long ago or more recently:

1. The first scenario concerns *imperative mediation,* according to which an end is brought to a given conflict by the formal fixing of common obligations and rules to which the protagonists are obliged to submit. It might not be acknowledged that this first scenario has the quality of a scenario of mediation, since an exterior intervention imposes upon the different parties of the conflict a modus vivendi that they have not themselves chosen, but which is enforced as a system of rules. Insofar as the content of these rules of the game as established by an exterior arbitrator (the legislator, the administration, the judge, etc.) puts an end to the direct and open defiance between different visions of the world (held by struggling social groups) that aim to eliminate one another, we can nonetheless, in this case, speak of mediation. The enacting terms of the Separation Law of 1905 in France could thus be analyzed as a case of imperative mediation: In placing a formal separation between the irreconcilable, the law also constituted a point of departure whence the relations between the two visions of the world—Catholic and Republican—were able to find a form enabling the two sides to live peacefully together.

2. The second scenario is that of *prescriptive mediation,* which consists, for the mediator, of defining a body of references (a collection of shared significations) that is capable, in transcending the normative conflict under way, of marking out a possible space for communications between the conflicting visions of the world. Prescriptive mediation tends in this way to organize a negotiating space permitting the rapprochement of points of view between the social actors holding these visions of the world. A kind of application of prescriptive mediation was put to work on the occasion of the "veil affair"—for example, while attempts were being made to set forth categorically which particular fundamental principles ought to govern the existence of public schools (admitting all children, philosophical neutrality in the classroom, equality of the sexes regarding access to knowledge, etc.). It was hoped that the strict clarification of these principles would allow the different points of view to reach a common ground. This was unfortunately not the case.

3. The failure of prescriptive mediation led to the emergence of another type of mediation, which can be called *pragmatic mediation:* In default of arriving at a compromise on the principles capable of transcending the normative conflict, the aim of this type of intervention is to arrive at a common qualification of practices acceptable to all (in defining, for example, what constitutes the "discreet" as opposed to the "ostentatious"

wearing of religious insignia). This limited practice of mediation, which can be employed on a case-by-case basis by diverse authorities—individuals or institutions (parents' associations, religious associations, etc.)—acting in an intermediary capacity between the conflicting parties, seeks not to go beyond the normative conflict but to define the tolerable modes of behavior that would make the nonviolent cohabitation of the protagonists possible.

4. The fourth scenario is that of *expressive mediation,* which became a possibility in the case of the conflict in New Caledonia. It consists of allowing each of the various social agents the greatest possible opportunity to express his vision of the world. It is concerned with either restoring, renewing, or establishing—out of the diversity and contradictions to which these expressions give rise—ties between the social agents involved in the conflict. The work of reconciling the different points of view is accomplished, in this scenario, by the (re)constitution of a social fabric that allows the establishment of relations based on confidence and cooperation. In this process the mediator does not intervene from the outside; rather, he involves himself personally, as he himself is one of the social agents.

Imperative mediation imposes from the outside, from above, rules of cohabitation between the different points of view (and between the groups concerned). *Prescriptive mediation* gives rise, in a more dynamic way, to the involvement of the protagonists in the elaboration of a possible manner of living together, but it does it through establishing, from the outside, the framework and the elementary principles of their coexistence. *Pragmatic mediation* tends to help the interested parties to define ways of doing things that are tolerable for one and the other, without requiring them to agree on common norms other than those that are strictly practical. Each of these three types of mediation constitutes a possible modality (there are certainly others) of an application of mediation *ad extra,* which leads to the intervention of an external arbitration authority. *Expressive mediation* can, on the contrary, be defined as a mediation *ad intra,* in which the mediator acts as the catalyst of a joint process of elaboration of a new norm capable of transcending initial conflicts.[22] If the course of French-style *laïcité* were related to this preliminary typology, it might be suggested that the *laïcité* imposed by the imperative mediation of policy at the beginning of the twentieth century has progressively become the prescriptive/pragmatic framework of the mediation of conflicts linked to the assertion of community identities in today's multicultural France. *Laïcité* is, as has been shown above, the *lieu de mémoire*—the commemorative symbol—of the collective identity and the symbolic medium through which the French conception of citizenship forged by history is expressed. The question directly posed by the challenge of communities in France today is the following: Is *laïcité* able to regenerate and renew its ideals through nourishing the practice of expressive mediation in new conflicts confronting a society troubled by the advance of internationalization?

Notes

1. Translator's note: The French adjective *laïque*, meaning "having the quality of *laïcité*," or elsewhere in the chapter, "partisans of *laïcité*," has been left in italics, as has the word *laïcité*. (*Laïc*, which means "lay person," has been translated as such.)

2. Translator's note: "Public school" throughout the chapter refers to a school provided at taxpayers' expense and managed by public authority, as part of a system of free, *laïque*, public education.

3. Translator's italics.

4. Article 49.3 of the Constitution allows a bill to be considered as passed if, consequent to the government's having fully committed itself to the text, a vote of censure moved by the opposition is rejected by the majority. This procedure allows the government to pass a bill "outright," without subjecting it to the discussion and the amendments of the Assembly.

5. "*J'accuse*" was the title of Zola's famous article, which appeared on page one of *L'Aurore* during the Dreyfus affair. (Translator's note: The article was a violent denunciation of the French general staff during the Dreyfus affair.)

6. Translator's note: Circa US$100 million.

7. Presumably Jules Ferry.

8. Translator's note: These lines are adapted from the first lines of Verlaine's poem "Il pleure dans mon coeur": "*Il pleure dans mon coeur / Comme il pleut sur la ville*": "There is weeping in my heart like the rain on the city."

9. CSA opinion poll, *L'actualité religieuse dans le monde*.

10. From Maurice Couve de Murville, one of Charles de Gaulle's ministers, to Michel Rocard, including Gaston Defferre, Pierre Joxe, or Lionel Jospin, the French political community counts numerous Protestants, whose prominence further increased during the fourteen-year socialist presidency of François Mitterrand. Highlighting this affinity between the left and French Protestantism is not to ignore the pluralism that all the same exists within this denomination. Meanwhile, it maintains the "progressionist" image generally associated with Protestantism in France.

11. In 1882 the Protestants voluntarily handed over their 1,500 schools to the Republic in order to integrate them into the public education system.

12. Translator's note: "*Beur*" is French slang, from the reversal of sounds in the word *arabe* (Arab).

13. Translator's note: "*al-'Id al-Kabir*" is also known as Kurban Bayram.

14. *Le Monde*, 2–3 April 1995; 16–17 April 1995.

15. Interview in *Le Monde* of 11 November 1989, bearing on the redefinition of *laïcité*: "What is a *laïcité* that wants to be secular at any price?"; Meeting at the official residence of the President of the Republic, François Mitterrand, 16 November 1993.

16. Translator's note: The *Front National* is the principal far-right-wing political party in France.

17. A shrewd and thorough investigation by two sociologists regarding Muslim girls effectively showed that among them a range of attitudes toward wearing the veil was to be found—rejection, forced wearing, nonchalant wearing, voluntary wearing as a sign of personal engagement, militant wearing, and so on (Gaspard and Khosrowkhavar, 1995).

18. A judgment handed down by the Lille Islamic tribunal concerning several cases of expulsion occurring after the publication of the second ministerial memorandum nevertheless contradicts this evidence in confirming three cases of expulsion by reason of disrupting the public order (disorder created in classes by girls and their brothers; refusal to participate in swimming classes), while at the same time canceling the expulsion of a girl who had always worn a veil "without her behavior's being regarded as interfering with the freedom of others" (Judgment of 13 April 1995). Wearing a veil is not in itself "ostentatious": It is the manner in which it is exhibited in schools that is called into question. This balanced decision will probably come into its own in opening up the possibility of differential solutions (*Le Monde*, 15 April 1995).

19. The Declaration of Nainville-les-Roches, 12 July 1983.

20. Olivier Stirn had also been assigned the Overseas Departments and Territories portfolio during Valéry Giscard d'Estaing's presidency, where he paved the way for Djibouti's accession to independence.

21. In designating scenarios in the present discussion, terms have been borrowed freely from the philosophy of mediation developed by Mark Hunyadi, in *La vertu du conflit: Pour une morale de la médiation* (Paris: Cerf, 1995).

22. These distinctions closely overlap with, yet without actually covering, the mutual opposition set down by Jean-François Six between *institutional* mediation (which is an application of arbitration) and *citizen* mediation, an open mediation in which the mediator acts as a "frontier runner" between the agents engaged in the conflict. See J. F. Six, *Dynamique de la médiation* (Paris: Desclée de Brouwer, 1995).

References

Ballion, R. 1982. *Les consommateurs d'école*. Paris, Stock.

Baubérot, J. 1988. *Le protestantisme doit-il mourir?* Paris, Seuil.

_____. 1990a. *Vers un nouveau pacte laïque?* Paris, Seuil.

_____. 1990b. *La laïcité, quel héritage? De 1789 à nos jours*. Genève, Labor et Fides.

Birnbaum, P. 1988. *Un mythe politique: La "république juive."* Paris, Gallimard.

_____. 1992. *Les fous de la République: Histoire politique des juifs d'Etat, de Gambetta à Vichy*. Paris, Fayard.

_____. 1995. *Destins juifs: De la Révolution française à Carpentras*. Paris, Calmann-Lévy.

Bouchacheirass, M. 1984. "Ne pas capituler." *Le Monde*, 3 March.

Brisebarre, A. M. 1989. "La célébration de l'Ayd-el-Kabir en France: Les enjeux du sacrifice." *Archives de Sciences Sociales des Religions* 68(1), July-December.

Capitant, H. (ed.) 1936. *Vocabulaire juridique*. Paris, PUF.

Cohen, M. 1993. "Les juifs de France: Affirmations identitaires et évolution du modèle d'intégration." *Le Débat* 75, May-August.

Crozier, M. 1984. "La rue n'appartenait plus à la gauche." *La Croix,* 23–24 June.

Coq, G. 1995. *Laïcité et République: Le lien nécessaire.* Paris, Félin.

Doumergue, J. P. 1994. "L'enracinement des mouvements politiques en Nouvelle-Calédonie." *Acta Geographica* 98, 20–42.

Encrevé, A., and Richard, M. (eds.) 1979. *Les protestants dans les débuts de la IIIe République (1871–1885).* Paris, Société de l'Histoire du Protestantisme Français.

Gauchet, M. 1985. *Le désenchantement du monde: Une histoire politique de la religion.* Paris, Gallimard.

Gauthier, G. 1994. *Un village, deux écoles.* Paris, Panoramiques.

Gaspard, F., and Khosrowkhavar, F. 1995. *Le voile et la République.* Paris, La Découverte.

Guiberteau, P. 1984. "La richesse d'une nation." *Le Monde,* 3 March.

Hervieu-Léger, D. (ed.) 1990. *La religion au lycée: Conférences au lycée Buffon.* Paris, Cerf.

Hunyadi, M. 1995. *La vertu du conflit: Pour une morale de la médiation.* Paris, Cerf.

Kepel, G. 1987. *Les banlieues de l'islam: Naissance d'une religion en France.* Paris, Seuil.

Lambert, Y. 1985. *Rien change en Bretagne: La religion à Limerzel de 1900 à nos jours.* Paris.

Langlois, C. 1980. "Permanence, renouveaux, et affrontements (1830–1880)." In F. Lebrun, ed., *Histoire des catholiques en France* (Paris, Privat/Hachette), 321–406.

———. 1988. "L'héritage de la Révolution française: Les trois cercles de laïcisation." *Projet,* September-October.

Le Bras, G. 1955–1956. *Etudes de sociologie religieuse,* vols. 1–2. Paris, PUF.

Leveau, R., and Kepel, G. (eds.) 1988. *Les musulmans dans la société française.* Paris, Presses de la Fondation Nationale des Sciences Politiques.

Maître, J., Michelat, G., et al. 1991. *Les Français sont-ils encore catholiques?* Paris, Cerf.

Martin, D. 1979. *A General Theory of Secularization.* London, Harper.

Messner, F. (ed.) 1995. *La culture religieuse à l'école.* Paris, Cerf.

Nique, C. 1990. *Comment l'école devint affaire d'Etat (1815–1840).* Paris, Nathan.

Nora, P. (ed.) 1984–1987. *Lieux de mémoire.* Vol. 1, *La République;* Vols. 2–4, *La Nation.* Paris, Gallimard.

Ozouf, J. 1973. *Nous les maîtres d'école: Autobiographies d'instituteurs de la Belle Epoque.* Paris, Seuil.

Ozouf, M. 1989. *L'homme régénéré: Essais sur la Révolution française.* Paris, Gallimard.

Poulat, E. 1977. *Eglise contre bourgeoisie.* Paris, Castermann.

———. 1987. *Liberté, laïcité: La guerre des deux France et le principe de la modernité.* Paris, Cujas/Cerf.

Rémond, R. 1974. *Introduction à l'histoire de notre temps.* Vol. 2, *Le XIXe siècle, 1815–1914.* Paris, Seuil.

———. 1984a. "La laïcité n'est plus ce qu'elle était." *Etudes,* April, 439–448.

———. 1984b. "Le présent encombré par l'histoire." *Le Monde,* 3 March.

Roux, M. 1990. "Vers un islam français." *Hommes et Migrations,* no. 1129–1130, February-March.

Savary, A. 1985. *En toute liberté.* Paris, Hachette.

Schnapper, D. 1994. *La communauté des citoyens: Sur l'idée moderne de nation.* Paris, Gallimard.

Six, J. F. 1995. *Dynamique de la médiation.* Paris, Desclée de Brouwer.

Touraine, A. 1973. *Production de la société.* Paris, Seuil.

Willaime, J. P. 1992. "La laïcité française au miroir du foulard." *Le Supplément,* no. 181, July.

_____. 1996. "Laïcité et religion en France." In G. Davie and D. Hervieu-Léger, *Les identités religieuses des européens.* Paris, La Découverte.

Weber, E. 1983. *La fin des terreurs: La modernisation de la France rurale, 1870–1914.* Paris. (Originally published in English under the title *Peasants into Frenchmen,* Stanford University Press, 1976).

Winock, M. 1989. "Les combats de la laïcité." *L'Histoire,* no. 128, December.

3

Normative Conflicts in Germany: Basic Consensus, Changing Values, and Social Movements

Franz-Xaver Kaufmann

If the extent of normative conflicts in Germany since World War II is measured by the virulence of traditional areas of conflict—religion, ethnic origin, class—the level of conflict proves to be surprisingly low. Overt normative conflicts have emerged primarily in connection with the formation of new social movements that have left a characteristic mark on the "old" Federal Republic and its politics. However, more recent developments, in the period since the unification of the two postwar Germanies, raise the question of whether normative conflicts of the older type are not reemerging.

In the context of the project on normative conflicts embodied in this volume, the analysis of the German case study has particular problems to contend with. In comparison to its European neighbors, Germany is a "belated nation" (H. Plessner) whose regional and political unity is also marked by clear ruptures. The unification of Germany as a nation-state did not occur until the years from 1866 to 1871 under Prussian leadership. Once created, the German Empire (Deutsches Reich) gained and lost considerable territories in this century in connection with the two world wars and, in the aftermath of World War II and the course of the Cold War, was divided into East and West. Two independent states, the Federal Republic of Germany and the German Democratic Republic, emerged out of the four Allied zones of occupation. This led to the fundamental normative conflict between capitalism and socialism being, as it were, externalized, as was the traditional Protestant predominance. This study, as far as it is concerned with the period 1945 to 1990, is limited to the Federal Republic.

Although little appears to have changed in West Germany[1] as a result of reunification, there have been changes in the political coordinates. A major feature of West German cohesion was rejecting East German socialism and perceiving it as a threat. This essential element of cohesion is now gone. In addition, the domestic political situation was altered by the East German states' joining those of the West on an equal basis. This new constellation did not, however, lead to any clear reorientation or to new and clear fronts. This is true for both domestic and foreign policy and in particular for the German intelligentsia, which has still hardly dared to attempt a comprehensive diagnosis of the situation. There is not so much being heard from the "new social movements" nowadays. Apparently disastrous, constantly rising unemployment was the first central problem to enter into the public consciousness after unification. Thus the following analysis and its conclusions are perforce based on a past whose validity for the foreseeable future is less than certain.

This study deals with normative conflicts and their mediation at state level. Normative conflicts are defined as those conflicts in which there is a question not only of conflicting interests but also of conflicting "principles" that permit no compromise and the pursuit of which may outlive any possible defeats in the process of political decisionmaking or judicial scrutiny. At the root of normative conflicts lie different values and, arising from this, different evaluations of the situation, which prevent the parties in conflict from recognizing one another's point of view. Normative conflicts are therefore *insoluble in principle:* Direct confrontation may lead at best to their being avoided, defused, mitigated by a third party, or suppressed, but never to their being solved. At worst they may escalate to involve violence, since each side has a "clear conscience" by virtue of its adherence to different values.

The level of analysis required here concerns societies constituted as nation-states. Thus only those normative conflicts are of concern that have weighed on the political events of a country with a certain continuity. Particularly in democratic societies, politics is the most important arena for normative conflict. An outbreak of normative conflicts in politics assumes the existence of collective agents of differing orientations who seek to mobilize the support of a wider group of sympathizers through their activities. The strategies employed can differ greatly, and it is not rare for these differences in strategy themselves to be a substantial medium of escalation.

In the following I am concerned not only with the description of normative conflicts and the explanation of their existence but also with ways of dealing with them, of reducing the chances of their escalating, of mediating between hostile parties, and so on. In this connection we must also look at contexts in which we would expect normative conflicts but where they are missing. In the case of Germany the low level of conflict in classical areas of normative conflicts demands an explanation in itself.

Classic Normative Conflicts: Overcome or Suppressed?

Religion

The territory of present-day Germany can be seen as the central region of the Reformation. The difference in creed between Lutherans, Calvinists, and Catholics has greatly influenced German history on various levels. After Prussia had forced the Lutherans and the Reformed Church to unite (1811), antagonisms within the Protestant movement receded. The conflict between the Catholics and the Prussian government, however, intensified after the imprisonment of the archbishop of Cologne (1837) and culminated in the Kulturkampf between church and state from 1871 to 1878. Within the German Empire the Catholics subsequently made up a well-organized minority with an influential political party, the Zentrum (Center). The Protestants were organized in conservative and liberal parties while the majority of the working class kept apart from these denominational differences and joined the Socialist or Social Democratic parties. Hence the spectrum of political parties in the German Empire was based on ideological differences that were rooted in different social backgrounds.[2]

The traumatic experience of National Socialism contributed greatly to these ideological differences' being overcome. Members of the "Bekennende Kirche" (professing church), who had also been the first to formulate the points of doctrine uniting Protestantism in the "Barmer Confession" (1934), drew closer to the Catholics, the majority of whom were also skeptical of the Third Reich. This permitted the early foundation of a Christian political party irrespective of denominational differences in 1945. In West Germany the separation of Central Germany also led to approximate religious parity. As a result of the supremacy of the predominantly Catholic Christian Democratic Party (CDU) and the long period of office of its chancellor, Konrad Adenauer, the Catholics completely lost their sense of being a minority group. The Social Democratic Party (SPD) also surrendered its detachment from the churches as it reoriented itself from being a party of a class to a party of the people (Volkspartei). In addition, flight and migration caused a general spatial reshuffle of the denominations that encouraged their ecumenical rapprochement. We can therefore say that the conflict of denominations has been more or less overcome in Germany.

However, it is still an open question as to how far the widespread secularization of East Germany and the increase of skepticism toward the church on the part of the younger generation in West Germany will affect legal aspects connecting the state and the established church, largely determined since 1919 by the idea of a "balanced separation between church and state" (E. W. Böckenförde). Attempts by the smaller parties (the Free Democratic Party, the Greens) to alter this relationship in favor of reducing the influence of the church have met with little political response.

One of the more far-reaching ideological issues that involved the Catholic Church in particular on the one hand and groups unconnected with the church on the other was the question of the legality of abortion (§ 218 StGB/Penal Code). This was one of the few points for which an interim agreement was expressly conceded for East Germany, permitting its former liberal ruling to be retained during a transition period. This conflict has been brought before the Federal Constitutional Court several times. The point of issue was the priority of conflicting values—the inviolability of human life or women's right to self-determination. The supporters of a liberal ruling for abortion were not in fact questioning the supremacy of human life but rather defined the situation differently, that is, the concept of *human life* was understood in a narrower sense that excluded the first weeks of pregnancy. This conflict was resolved after a complicated to and fro between the legislators and the Federal Court and finally concluded with a compromise requiring compulsory counseling for women in conflict over their pregnancies. This was unsatisfactory for both sides but restored the public peace.

It remains to be seen to what extent the Islamic minority in Germany will develop a potential for conflict. The traditionally low degree of centralization in the Muslim religious community and the insignificance of fundamentalist groups would suggest that it will not. The two Christian churches together with their associated social services also keep up an open relationship with the Muslims. In my opinion, we can assume therefore that for the time being the conflict of religious ideologies has been largely overcome by the fact that the churches succeeded in emphasizing their common factors rather than the potentially divisive factors and so have moved closer together.

Ethnic Conflict

Apart from the grave exception of the Nazis' murderous racial madness, ethnic conflicts have played only a subordinate role in German history. The deliberate persecution and elimination of "non-Aryans" was moreover aimed at sections of the population that were reasonably well integrated, such as the German Jews. In spite of a massive influx of immigrants in the postwar period, particularly Turks, there has been no significant mobilization of ethnic minorities until now.

In the face of the still vivid memories of racist crimes during the Third Reich, the Germans seem little disposed to define social conflict in the sense of ethnic conflict. In real terms, however, Germany practices a particularly strict policy of discrimination between natives and foreigners in comparison with the rest of the world. This goes back to the ius sanguinis (right of blood) which was first introduced in Prussia in 1842 and which is the basis of the Act of Citizenship of Reich and State of 1913, still in force today. Its principle is still upheld by the present political majority. In contrast to most other countries, while descendants of Germans who have been living out of the country for generations can assert a claim to citizenship, it cannot be acquired even after years of residence and cultural integration in Germany. Naturalization is at the discretion of the authorities and remains an "act of administrative mercy."[3] As a rule naturalization is granted on condition that any previous citizenships are relinquished, so dual nationality is not permitted. Movements to permit foreigners to participate in the political decisionmaking process also still seem to be up against apparently insurmountable opposition. Presumably this attitude is even more widespread among East Germans than in the West.

There exists here, then, a latent potential for conflict whose normative charge has, however, been so far successfully defused. On the whole this may originate with the fact that in practice foreigners resident for a longer period are subject to conditions of residence similar to those of native Germans, and while foreigners are doubtless discriminated against on an interactive level, discrimination is universally publicly rejected. Prevailing opinion seems to tolerate characteristics of national culture so long as they are restricted to the private sphere, yet to reject outright the political principle of "multiculturalism"—a compromise that has also been respected so far by the majority of foreigners.

Class Conflict

Whereas theoretical reflections on the conflict between capital and labor have gained considerable weight in German sociology as the historically crucial class conflict, real class conflict during industrialization was in effect relatively mild compared to England and particularly France. Although there was political opposition to the labor movement's being organized into socialist trade unions and parties (Anti-Socialist Act, 1878), their organization proceeded more or less uninterruptedly. Revolutionary minorities were not able to gain control. State social policy developed roughly parallel to industrialization and orientated itself primarily toward the "labor question" (Arbeiterfrage). During World War I workers' representatives were already given first rights of codetermination, and an agreement between representatives from industry and from the socialist trade unions (Stinnes-Legien agreement, 1918) laid the foundations for the Weimar State constitution, which included important economic and social rights. The termination of the eight-hour day by heavy industry and its subsequent state legalization (1923) led to renewed alienation of the parties to the wage agreements and to bitter disputes in the later Weimar period, which contributed to the rise of the Nazis.

After the existing organizations and their structures had been dissolved under Nazi rule and replaced by the "German Labor Front," the fresh start in 1945 brought with it a fundamental reorientation. The former ideologically oriented political trade unions were replaced by the principle of the ideologically neutral industrial union linked to certain branches of industry. Since the workers also tended to group together quite naturally according to the interests of their particular branch of industry, a system of negotiation between the partners to the wage agreements, extremely effective by international comparison, was successfully created and subsequently made legally binding. Thus industrial relations in Germany are said to be *corporatistic*, that is, there are essentially large regionally structured organizations for each branch of industry that negotiate a collective wage agreement defining the minimum terms of employment.

While both partners were more or less able to retain the right to industrial disputes (strikes, lockouts), these are only used comparatively sparingly and deliberately. As will be shown in the next section, soon after its foundation the social and economic order in Germany was carried by a broad consensus that included both parties to the collective wage agreements. Various different developments in the postwar period, particularly increasing internationalization and tertiarization in trade and industry, have contributed to the breakup of homogeneous class layers and at the same time to a diversification of interests on the side of both the employers and the employed. Not least, the rise of new social movements (discussed later) resulted in their both frequently pursuing similar interests, even such as in environmental matters or the question of subsidies as well as some sociopolitical measures.

To sum up, then, in the Federal Republic the economic and social conditions that led to the development of distinct class conflict have mainly disappeared. This does not mean that economic and social inequality have vanished or even been noticeably reduced, but their dimensions have changed and different types of social deprivation only appear to accumulate in what have been up to now smaller fringe groups. However, the recent trend of rising unemployment may well cause the number of groups that are disadvantaged in more than one way to increase, and so new forms of structured poverty may be expected. Since we are dealing here with groups that tend to be excluded from participation in the manufacturing process, the development of a social class in the traditional sense is not to be expected. German sociologists now no longer consider social inequality in the light of social class but of differing ways of life and lifestyles.[4]

The study of social inequality in the light of "class," as was first undertaken by the French socialists, reveals in itself a certain implicitly normative definition of the situation. It assumes a common interest among all those addressed as one class (workers) and provides them with another class as clear opponents (capitalists). Karl Marx and Friedrich Engels were the first to approach this problem of class consciousness by differentiating between *Klasse an sich* (class in itself) and *Klasse für sich* (class for itself). With their notion that "all history is the history of class struggle" they elevated the self-evident fact of there being opposing class groups to the level of historical philosophy. If class antagonism has become implausible today, this naturally does not mean that social inequalities could no longer be normatively charged. There have been repeated attempts at this from various sides in the Federal Republic, but they have never resulted in a broad mobilization in favor of people defined as disadvantaged in this way. This is precisely what we mean by saying that normative conflicts are lacking in the dimension of class. The elimination of this area of conflict is largely a consequence of developments that will be discussed in the following section.

Basic Consensus: Basic Law and Social Market Economy

Memories of the atrocities committed during Hitler's Third Reich in the name of the "nation" have more or less robbed this concept of any legitimizing power in Germany. In addition, the amalgamation of the three occupied zones to form a single state signified more of an adaptation to the political circumstances of the Cold War than a fundamental political decision. The reservations associated with being *provisional* haunted politics in Bonn from the start. The only thing that lent this state a certain identity and authority was the negotiation and passing of the Basic Law in 1949. It not only comprises the organizational rights of the state and the classical rights of liberty but also expresses moral convictions: the inviolable dignity of the individual, social justice, the importance of private property, family, and religion. The legal and moral form of the social community is expressed in the four principles of article 20 of the Basic Law: constitutionality, democracy, the welfare state, and federalism. Together with human dignity, these four principles are considered unalterable (Basic Law articles 79, 3) and, should they be threatened by any state authority, resistance would be legitimate (Basic Law, articles 20, 4). These clauses of the constitution testify to the memory of the perversion of justice and the constitution under Nazi rule.

The Basic Law, which became the definitive constitution after the unification of West and East Germany in 1990, comprises not only a legal but also a moral consensus, at least in West Germany. The state as a moral concept may be foreign to Anglo-Saxon thinking, but it has a long tradition in Germany, dating back to G. W. F. Hegel's *Rechtsphilosophie (Legal Philosophy)* of 1821. The Basic Law can therefore be credited with civil religious properties. Even progressive intellectuals such as Jürgen Habermas see an appropriate form of collective identity in "constitutional patriotism."

Correlating to this "faith in the state" is the high regard paid to *legality* in Germany. In accordance with the principle of constitutionality, any state action will be judged by its conformity to the constitution. Political conflicts are increasingly referred to the Federal Constitutional Court for a legal solution. Constitutionality and the idea of the welfare state are seen equally as the expression of moral virtues, such as social justice.

The extent to which these ideas that foster a collective identification are also being adopted by the citizens of East Germany remains to be seen. While for the Bonn republic the passing of the Basic Law meant that a basis for a new collective identity had been created within it, which gradually flourished under legislation and social and economic developments, for the East Germans the old socialist system of power was replaced by an apparently complex and scarcely comprehensible German legal order, which, apart from a few exceptions like the abortion ruling, was to be unconditionally accepted. Even though the majority of the population wanted and welcomed unification, both in the East and the West the problems resulting from it had been underestimated. A collective sense of dissatisfaction arose out of hopes that had been unrealistic but nonetheless disappointed, and the struggle over how to share the costs of unification continues, not least in the current attempt to reduce the rate of increase in government expenditure *(Staatsquote)* it caused (which will be addressed later in the chapter).

In 1949 the Basic Law left the question of the future economic and social order of the new political state open. The political inclinations of the time went from a liberal market economy to democratic socialism. Hence the question of the future economic order posed a normative conflict that could not or would not be resolved by the constitutional assembly (the Parliamentary Council). The positions of the two larger parties were overshadowed by the relatively unsuccessful practical attempts made by the Weimar Republic to codify economic and social rights, and they hoped to win a majority in the parliament yet to be elected. Hence they agreed on an open policy toward the economic and social order in the constitution while setting down extensive sociopolitical jurisdiction for the federal legislators in article 74.

In the elections to the first federal German parliament, the Bundestag, in September 1949, Konrad Adenauer was elected chancellor with a very slim majority—allegedly only that of his own vote. Adenauer appointed Ludwig Erhard to his cabinet as minister for economic affairs. As director of Bizonal economic affairs in Frankfurt (Main), Erhard had already pursued liberal economic policies.

However, Erhard's liberal ideas differed characteristically from those of Anglo-Saxon liberals. A free-market economy was now no longer expected as a consequence of state abstinence in economic matters and unrestricted economic liberty but as a product of a political choice of economic order and its legal enforcement. It was considered the task of the state to guarantee the conditions required for free competition; the protection of private property, a noncompetitive monetary and financial order, the regulation of competition, and the prevention of monopolistic mergers. This idea of the "conscious creation of a social and economic order which is free in principle but at the same time bears social responsibilities and its guarantee by a strong state"[5] developed within the framework of the so-called "ordo-liberal" Freiburg School of National Economy during World War II, with which Erhard was associated.

The term "social market economy," which was coined by Alfred Müller-Armack, undersecretary in Erhard's ministry for economic affairs, advanced to become the keyword for the program of the new economic order. Since then a seemingly never-ending dispute has raged as to the nature of the *social* element of this market economy. Influenced by the experience of political interventionism in the period between the wars and of a controlled economy during the war years, Erhard himself emphasized the importance of a controlling state framework for the development of free economic activity, optimized by competition. This was the essential ingredient for "prosperity for everyone." Economic growth and full employment were to guarantee the stability of a liberal social order—this was his "social" ideal. Erhard accepted the need for a supplementary welfare policy for blue-collar workers and lower paid white-collar workers; the self-employed and higher paid employed, however, were to be responsible for their own social security. In his opinion a national insurance scheme would be the expression of an "attitude of dependence on the state."[6] However, his chief interest was in an economic policy that encouraged productivity and growth. Coupled with widespread wealth, a successful economic policy should keep the need for sociopolitical measures to a minimum.

It was this "ordo-liberal" idea that was the principal determining factor for economic policy throughout the Adenauer period, although it was at times faced with opposition from large-scale industry, which wanted to prevent the passing of antitrust laws. In the 1950s the so-called economic miracle, that is, massive economic growth of an annual average of 8 percent, also won over the majority of trade unionists and Social Democrats who had initially been skeptical and had in many cases advocated a state-controlled economy.

The question of worker participation in management became a key factor for gaining the support of the trade unions for the new economic order. During the Weimar period, the call for "economic democracy" had already influenced the position of the free trade unions, but the relevant provisions in the Weimar Constitution had been only partially realized because of opposition in management circles. Thus the constitution of 1949 laid down no requirements, and with a Social Democratic minority in the first German parliament the chance of pushing through a system of intercompany forums for worker participation in management in the sense of "democratic socialism" seemed very slim. Hence the trade unions fought all the more to preserve the system of "equal representation" that had initially been offered on a voluntary basis by the large enterprises of the *Montan* industries—the iron, coal, and steel industries. After a threat of sweeping strikes this finally led to the legislation of the so-called "Montan system of worker participation." In 1952 the Works Constitution Act *(Betriebsverfassungsgesetz),* which regulated worker participation in all large companies outside the iron, coal, and steel industries, was less far-reaching and strengthened the negotiation level within the individual companies by providing for the works councils to be independent of the trade unions. The compromise situation that this established has subsequently proved to be considerably stable. Industrial tribunals including representatives of both management and workers had been created in the Weimar period and were then reinstated. They have proved to be the most important regulatory factor in industrial relations, which are now virtually independent of state influence.

In its "Godesberger Program" of 1959 the Social Democratic Party finally abandoned its demands for a change of economic order. Since then the principles of a market economy supported by sociopolitical measures form part of the basic consensus within the large national political parties and industrial organizations.

Market Economy *and* or *anti* the Welfare State?

Sociopolitical developments have moved a long way from Erhard's minimum. Apart from a brief crisis in 1966 and 1967, the German economy expanded continuously from 1949 to 1973, thus providing sufficient leeway for the expansion of the existing national insurance network and the development of new welfare benefits. Both the fact that the expansion of the welfare system was virtually unaffected by a change of government and the results of the relevant polls[7] show that state-aided social security is highly valued by the Germans and is not considered an alternative to making private provisions but as a basis for it.

The signal for further extensions to the welfare state was given by the pension reform of 1957, which guaranteed a rise of pensions for those no longer in employment proportionate to the general increase in wages. Following Erhard's model, however, employees with higher incomes and the self-employed were initially excluded from the pension scheme altogether, until in 1972 they were offered unduly favorable conditions to join the scheme belatedly as its scope was generally widened. Apart from state employees, who are provided for under a separate system and hence do not need to contribute to the national insurance system, practically the whole of the population is protected by the national health insurance scheme. As far as illness and old age are concerned, it can be said of the present-day Federal Republic that there is more or less complete coverage by national insurance for everyone, even if its organization has yet to be standardized.[8] Together these two insurance risks make up 70 percent of total welfare expenditures and have proved particularly expansive as far as cost is concerned.

In addition to the improvement of welfare, the public purse has been stretched by spending in the areas of education, health, and other public services. The social-liberal coalition that was in power from 1969 to 1982 under the chancellors Willy Brandt and Helmut Schmidt was particularly committed to the concept of an active social policy for "a better quality of life," its manifesto slogan. Hence measures were taken to redevelop decaying urban areas, to improve the transport system, to develop the universities and hospitals, and to provide more educational opportunities for the "educationally remote" section of the population (the working class, the rural population, girls). Since most of these measures came under the jurisdiction of the individual *Länder* (the federal states), the federal government intervened essentially by setting up coordinating groups *(Bund-Länder Kommissionen)*, by providing the legal framework, and by giving generous subsidies to projects developed by the states and local authorities. Government social policy also discovered new target groups. As early as 1953 when child benefits were introduced, the Federal Ministry for the Family was set up; it was consolidated in 1957 as the Ministry for Family and Youth; in 1986 it was extended to include "Women"; and in 1991 "Senior Citizens" were added as well.

The postwar "economic miracle" made it possible to provide work not only for the existing population of West Germany but also for several million refugees and people driven out of the separated eastern territories. Before long there were not enough of the indigenous population to continue economic expansion, and in the 1960s an influx of foreign workers began. This trend toward overemployment was brought to an abrupt halt by the international oil crisis (1973). In spite of further reductions in working hours the unemployment rate rose from 1 percent in 1973 to over 4 percent in 1975, and again to over 9 percent between 1980 and 1983. This level was exceeded in West Germany after 1994 following a drop to less than 7 percent in 1991. Consequently the costs of unemployment benefits and social benefits paid by local government have increased enormously, while at the same time the proportion of the population paying social security contributions and income tax is decreasing.

The growth of unemployment was still more dramatic in East Germany. In the German Democratic Republic there was officially no unemployment—both economic and social policies were oriented toward maximum possible employment for the adult population. The majority of women were in full-time employment, made possible by a well-developed system of collective child care. The low productivity of East German industry, the collapse of socialism in the traditional East German markets, and the swift integration into West German industry have all contributed to the current high rate of unemployment (17 percent in March 1996), in spite of various publicly financed employment schemes.

A further point was that the treaty of unification provided for the West German national insurance system to be applicable to East Germany. Its provisions were to remain below the level of those in the West, but only by degrees. For the East, decisive factors were the favorable change to parity of the currencies and the wage level negotiated by the trade unions, which was far higher than the comparable average level of productivity. Pensions are linked to these wage levels and, since the Democratic Republic had a much higher rate of employment, are based on a period of insurance that is on average much longer than in the West. So the insurance authorities are forced to pay out far more for pensions in East Germany than corresponds to the level of contributions. The same is true for unemployment benefits. In East Germany the costs of health insurance have developed more slowly as a result of the necessary restructuring of the health care system, but there too, they exceed the revenue from insurance contributions. Consequently, both the employers and the insured in West Germany have to share the costs of several dozens of billions of deutsche marks annually for national insurance in East Germany. This has led to a considerable rise in the level of contributions. In 1996 statutory national insurance contributions accounted for 41 percent of gross earnings (within certain assessment limits). Reliable estimates indicate that if it were not for these payments stipulated by the unification, which are "extraneous to the insurance," contributions would only have to comprise between 33 and 35 percent of gross earnings. After it had become clear that the economic problems of the East would not to be solved by a "new economic miracle" merely in the conversion to a market economy but only by a massive process of public redistribution, there was a renewed increase in public expenditure, which had been reduced in the 1980s, and in particular in the national debt.

The present socioeconomic situation in Germany is burdened by a series of factors that inevitably cause an intensification of the conflict over distribution. These include the increasing "maturity" (in Schumpeter's sense) of important branches of German industry, the comparatively limited expansion of the German domestic market, the high level of wages and of average welfare benefits, the advanced demographic aging process, and finally, the discipline imposed on financial and economic policies by the Maastricht treaties in view of European monetary union. Added to these factors, which affect most European states to a greater or lesser extent, are the particular burdens of German unification. The current complaints from employers about the high level of ancillary wage costs thus have two different causes—one is the increase in competition from countries with considerably lower wage levels, and the other is the increase in ancillary wage costs caused by unification.

Thus it is hardly surprising that conflict over the distribution of the national income has recently come into the open. Employers and that part of the media which supports industry are now making public demands for a "reduction of the welfare state," the government is calling for it to be "restructured," and the trade unions are calling for its "preservation." So the lines are clearly drawn on the normative values front. Previously the basic consensus in Germany had taken a complementary relationship between economic and social development for granted, so that although there may have been occasional disagreement on priorities, economic and social policy were seen as two areas of state activity that, in principle, supported and promoted each other. Now, however, conflict is being built up between them, particularly on the part of the market economists, and a reduction of social policy expenditures is seen as the key to the success of economic policy.

Nevertheless, the normative conflict suggested by this difference, seen as the "market economy" versus the "welfare state," has remained very basic until now. There are few new points to be found in the store of normative arguments of either side, but old ones are expounded with all the more urgency. Remarkably enough, the dispute has so far been restricted to advocates of the employers or the trade unions. No interest has been roused either within the large national political parties or among the public at large.[9] If we look more closely at current problems it is clear that they are not likely to be solved by a strategy concerning either the market economy or the welfare state as alternatives. The phenomenon that is generally accepted as being the problem is the upward trend of unemployment, which proves a loosening of the link between economic growth and full employment. However, the discussion of the reasons for this and hence of a successful "therapy" is extremely controversial and seems itself to be determined by the assumption that the option for a solution lies either with the market economy or the welfare state.

Orthodox market economists blame rising unemployment in Germany primarily on high wage levels (including high ancillary wage costs) and/or the downward inflexibility of wages. Even though the system of collective bargaining in Germany is based almost exclusively on agreements negotiated freely between the two partners, it is true that attempts to reduce levels of wages or welfare payments have hardly ever been successful. As the current argument over the reduction of sick pay shows, any challenge to "social progress" must expect to be faced with strong opposition from the trade unions. However, it is an open question as to whether a general reduction in wage levels would in fact lead to a corresponding expansion of the volume of work, considering the economy as a whole.

A second view is that the reason for rising unemployment lies in the fact that conditions for Keynesian full employment no longer exist. The national debt, which had been accumulating over a long period and was given a new and lasting boost by the need to finance the costs of unification and the growing burden of interest on it, makes increasing demands on public expenditure. However, not only the size of the national debt but also, especially, the increasing Europeanization of economic policy and globalization of financial and commodity markets have an adverse effect on the ability of the individual states to operate economic policies and make the prospect of Keynesian employment policies seem unlikely. The lowering of wage costs recommended by market economists appears dangerous from a Keynesian point of view, since this would reduce the already insufficient demand for consumer goods.

A third view sees the cause of rising unemployment in the continued improvement in labor productivity. Ever-widening areas of industry are affected by technical and organizational improvements, and industrial goods and relevant services in particular can be produced with a constant reduction of the working time required. Increasing foreign competition in particular forces a corresponding rationalization in Germany. While it is to be supposed that there are considerable unfulfilled needs in the area of personal services, they are becoming increasingly expensive in comparison to other types of production, precisely because they cannot be easily rationalized and are therefore beyond the means of large sections of the population. It is no coincidence that the increase of jobs during the past two decades has been largely in posts in education, health, or social services, that is, personal services that are publicly funded or organized or financed by the national insurance scheme. However, this publicly financed expansion is limited by the slow growth of the market sector. From this point of view the most rational strategy would seem to be further massive reductions in working hours or a redistribution of labor in order to prevent the spread of public redistribution of income.

A fourth view points out that a large proportion of the unemployed are problem cases—people who are difficult to place.[10] It is difficult to imagine that employers will be found to give new employment prospects to these particular people. In spite of the current unemployment, employers are frequently to be heard complaining that there is insufficient *suitable* manpower. It can be shown that the more intensively capital is invested, the more unprofitable is the employment of workers who are less than optimally productive. Thus it can be expected that these people will be increasingly excluded from the typical entrepreneurial forms of labor. For them to be employed, even for moderate wages, special arrangements with low fixed costs and transaction costs would be required.

It thus becomes evident that the crux of these particular debates is not orientation toward differing values but *differing definitions of the situation*. An unbiased observer might suppose that each of these views presents an accurate picture of *one specific aspect* of the current employment problem. Even though the reduction of unit labor costs is undoubtedly of considerable importance for the competitiveness of German industry in foreign trade, the reinstatement of full employment based on the free market economy seems an unrealistic prospect. Industry's labor requirements concentrate on the most productive section of the working population, and the only sector of German industry in which costs compare favorably is in high-performance production. Therefore, the redistribution of available work to those already unemployed is only of limited practical use. Both demographic developments and the structure of the labor market suggest that in the long term a shrinking section of the earning population will have to finance a growing section of nonearning people.

Traditionally this would essentially be the task of the welfare state in Germany. However, since, for the reasons just discussed, we can expect at best long-term growth of the economy as a whole but no improvement in real income for individuals, the conflict over distribution is bound to get worse. To what extent normative conflicts will develop out of this will depend to a great extent on how political parties and associations handle the problems and on the subsequent reaction of the population. Since all those involved are well aware of the value of the wage bargaining partnership and the basic consensus connected with it, it is justifiable, in my opinion, to expect that even if verbal attacks become stronger and there are more labor conflicts, a big fuss over legislation, and even some cases brought before the highest courts, in the end the necessary restructuring will proceed relatively peacefully.

New Social Movements as Catalysts for Normative Conflicts?

Whereas the classic areas of normative conflict have hitherto found remarkably little expression in the history of the Federal Republic, we must not fail to emphasize the development of new areas of conflict. Conflicts with a longer-term political development can generally be categorized under the headings of "armament and peace" and "environment." Several other conflicts besides have enjoyed short-lived popularity: sexual liberation, the process of democratization in universities and colleges, participation in political planning, the question of women's rights, housing shortages, politically disciplinary measures *(Berufsverbote)*, the "exploitation of the Third World," and resistance to certain technologies (nuclear power, genetic engineering). Before we look more closely at the two main areas of conflict, we need at least to outline the common factors and underlying structures of these "new social movements."

Although a common feature of all social movements is opposition to existing social structures, protest groups in the Federal Republic differ from those connected with the labor movement because of their social base. Typical activists are young adults and youths, particularly students and secondary school pupils and "people employed in the social service sector, social workers, teachers, priests, doctors, artists musicians and actors, journalists, academic sociologists, etc."[11] The potential for protest appears to be more closely connected to attitude than to a particular problem. This basic attitude is often described as being "critical of modernity" or as "postmaterialistic."[12]

The mentality underlying this attitude seems to be specific not only to social class but also to a certain generation. The "extraparliamentary opposition" that came into being during the "Grand Coalition" (1966–1969) and the subsequent student protest movement, which spread throughout the country after the student Benno Ohnesorg was shot by the police on June 2, 1967, can be seen as pioneering movements that influenced a whole generation. It was a protest against more than the Emergency Powers Act *(Notstandsgesetze)*, passed to ensure the functioning of government even in states of political emergency, and it was more than a mere continuation of the protest against rearmament. Even the semi-provocative, semi-ironic demystification of German universities ("under the gowns, a thousand years of dust") was only one aspect of the much more fundamental criticism of the "CDU state," of the restoration tendencies of the postwar period and of the concepts of political and moral order that appeared far too restrictive in the light of the enormous increase in affluence and the wider opportunities it afforded.

This German movement was also a part of the new international phenomenon of youth protest groups, which began in 1963 with criticism of the Vietnam War but soon escalated to become a movement toward liberation from the prescribed patterns of the bourgeois moral order. Many universities and their academic environment became the test beds for new ways of life that were equally threatening to the middle-class family, the capitalist economy, the political establishment, and bourgeois forms of the Christian Church.

What distinguishes the development in Germany from that in most other countries is that the potential for protest has continued and become increasingly politically organized over the past thirty years. Although the student movement broke up around 1970 into various "left-wing" factions, other groups outside the universities then began to use their ideas of participatory democracy and their provocative techniques to draw attention to their own concerns. At the end of the 1960s a wave of local protest groups *(Bürgerinitiativen)*, which were highly decentralized, began to concern themselves with all kinds of local grievances and saw themselves as a constituent part of what appeared to be a changing political system following the instigation of a coalition of the Social Democrats and the Liberal Democrats in 1969. However, as the limits of the new government's political flexibility became clear, and particularly as nuclear power stations began to be built in many places, these local protest groups began to develop into a supraregional protest movement. It was directed primarily against the use of nuclear power for nonmilitary purposes, but it soon comprised a broader thrust.

The Ecological Movement

In 1972 the Club of Rome published the report "Limits to Growth," which caused a stir internationally and suddenly made the public aware of the ecological problems that the experts had been gradually beginning to acknowledge since the 1960s. The question of the use of nuclear power was then put in a broader ecological context, and no later than 1972 a federal association for environmental protest groups *(Bundesverband Bürgerinitiativen Umweltschutz*, BBU) was founded to organize and coordinate the ecological movement and to give the various local issues a nationwide platform. By occupying the sites of nuclear power stations (Wyhl in 1975, Brokdorf in 1976/77), protesters drew public attention to the issue, and protest was mobilized throughout the country. Since 1977 the environment has become a central political issue that the established parties also began to take up. At the same time, opposition to it built up, starting with the nuclear industry itself and scientists in its service but soon spreading to the trade unions, who largely supported the atomic industry and its promise of widespread jobs and who opposed ecological arguments against economic growth. Within the established parties, especially in the Free Democratic Party (FDP) and the SPD, the active environmentalists were forced increasingly onto the defensive. It was in Bremen, in 1978, that they first drew the necessary conclusions by leaving their party and attempting to found a new one.

The reasons for the ecological movement's rapid restructuring into a political party rather than a protest movement have to do with radical encounters with the increasing deployment of state power against opponents of nuclear energy. The collapse of the student movement had not only led to the development of terrorist groups like the Red Army Faction (RAF), who were responsible for the spectacular murder of three prominent figures in 1977, but also to the emergence of groups, particularly connected with the "autonomous" squatter scene, that were prepared to use violence. The participation of these potentially violent groups in the protests led to an increase in the number of violent clashes with the police and to the authorities' taking an increasingly firm line against organized mass protests. What had begun as an unconventional expression of protest was now threatened more and more frequently with violent escalation.

The greater majority of those engaged on the ecological front rejected violence as a means of pursuing ecological aims. In addition, the violent confrontations harmed the popularity of the movement. This explains why it split into a majority who accepted the methods of conventional politics and made increasing use of them and a minority more inclined to political hooliganism than to furthering ecological aims.

This led to the ecological movement's becoming more conventional. Besides the continuation of existing groups and organizations, it adopted the form of a political party, which saw itself initially as a convinced opposition party and refused to take any kind of political responsibility. Hence it remained a party of fundamental political opposition that then adopted nearly every "alternative" political issue—from the liberalization of sexual relations to the peace movement, from genetic engineering to the national census. At the same time, rules were agreed that differed from the established running of politics (e.g., the rotation of posts) and that were to ensure that the representatives of the Green movement kept in close touch with the grass roots of the party. However, everyday political life soon convinced some of them that nothing could be achieved by fundamental opposition. This resulted in the formation of two factions within the Green Party, the "fundamentalists" (Fundis) and the "realists" (Realos).

The Greens were founded as a national party at the end of 1979, and as early as 1983, on their second attempt, they succeeded in gaining seats in the German Bundestag, to which they have belonged ever since. In many federal states and in the Bundestag they have now progressed to become the third largest party. As a result of the increasing influence of the realist faction, the Greens now form part of the government of the largest federal state, North Rhine Westphalia, and of several smaller states. In most respects the Greens have become a normal party. They mobilize large sections of the "self-fulfillment milieu"[13] in particular, whose members feel poorly represented by the mainstream parties.

About the same time as the Greens became more conventional, the aims that the ecological movement was fighting for established themselves as part of a basic political consensus. Nowadays there is no opposition to ecological demands in principle but only objections to particular projects when they do not appear opportune. Support for ecological aims has a much broader basis than the Green Party itself and comprises not only environmental groups but also, among others, large parts of the Christian churches and groups in other political parties. It was Helmut Kohl's conservative-liberal coalition that set up a Ministry of Environment in 1986 and headed it with one of the coalition's most able ministers. Environmental protection has advanced from being merely a programmatic term to being professionalized (e.g., environment officers) as well as incorporated into everyday reality (e.g., the sorting of garbage). German industry owes its leading international position in the field of environmental technologies to the effectiveness of its ecological movement. Environmental issues still have considerable normative power and the potential to mobilize on a moral issue, as the recent reaction of the German population to the Greenpeace campaign against the sinking of the oil platform Brent Spar demonstrates. The reaction to the infection of British and Swiss cattle with bovine spongiform encephalitis (BSE) was also not restricted to the political arena but spread to everyday behavior, as can be seen by the decrease in beef consumption. Regardless of how justified the ecological objections are in each individual case, the ability to respond and react to ecological topics is particularly pronounced in Germany.

The Peace Movement

The ecological movement can be seen as a success story in two senses: for the movement itself and for the adaptability of the political system. In comparison, the peace movement was nowhere near as successful.

The origins of the peace movement can be traced to the protests against the rearmament of Germany and the introduction of general military service (1951–1955), which were, as we know, unsuccessful. This struggle originated in circles of the Protestant church that sympathized with the Bekennende Kirche in the Third Reich, but its legitimacy was impaired by simultaneous communist agitation. A similarly structured, new wave of opposition came into being in connection with the question of nuclear weapons. It was able to mobilize much larger sections of society, but a referendum was prohibited by the Federal Constitutional Court (1958). The "Fight Atomic Death" campaign subsequently dissolved. However, the remnants of it reassembled after 1960 as the Easter marches movement, which was able to mobilize 300,000 people in 1968 at the height of the dispute over the Emergency Powers Act (*Notstandsgesetze*). The Easter marches were discontinued while the SPD/FDP coalition was in power and were not resumed until the North Atlantic Treaty Organization (NATO) resolution to rearm using medium-range missiles directed toward the Soviet Union. The peace demonstrations between 1981 and 1986 brought more people into the streets than the movement against the Emergency Powers Act but were still unable to prevent the missiles from being stationed as planned. The change in the Soviet Union's attitude and its final collapse brought the cause for further rearmament to an end and with it the peace movement's ability to mobilize support.

After reunification Germany was increasingly required and expected to accept international responsibility, which could involve the deployment of federal troops outside NATO areas. This consideration has led to nothing like the same level of public protest. The view that the violence in the Balkans might have to be counteracted by similar means if necessary has spread even into some circles of the Green Party.

In contrast to the aims of the ecological movement, the official aims of the peace movement were reasonable right from the start and capable of finding a consensus throughout society. Nobody in Germany dared to advocate publicly the use of force in the national interest—memories of World War II, which had been started by Germany, were still too vivid both at home and abroad. However, the means of securing peace were deeply controversial. Normative conflict here, then, concerned the means, not the ends. While the peace movement hoped to be able to initiate an international pacifist movement by the possible demilitarization of Germany, those in government circles who were on the side of further armament built on the old Roman principle of *"si vis pacem, para bellum."* The peace movement was also unable to shake off the suspicion of being partly infiltrated by communists and exploited and supported by the socialist bloc as "useful idiots."

The fact that the demonstrations were more disciplined and more peaceful than those of the environmental movement was a condition for the credibility of the movement and prevented an escalation of the confrontations with the authorities. Although we can surmise that there was also conflict over the aims and not only over the means between representatives of government policy and considerable sections of the peace movement who were working against the containment of Soviet power in Europe, this was never brought out into the open. There is also no denying that the majority of those in the peace movement, whose center was in the progressive wing of the Protestant church, were primarily committed to solving conflicts by peaceful means. Their influence may be partially responsible for a marked increase in tolerance and the widespread rejection of military force, expressed, for example, by the chains of light, kilometers long, against the outbreak of the Gulf War. The comparatively liberal ruling for those who object to doing military service can probably also be attributed to the effect of the peace movement. And in the final analysis the Germans are still living in peace today. Although the peace movement had minimal political success as far as methods of securing peace are concerned, the influence it had on current mentality should not be underrated. Even if the exclusively defensive character of German anticommunism was dictated by prudence in foreign affairs, the widespread rejection of military solutions to conflicts in Germany will be a result of the constant public discussion of the peace issue.

The Dispute over Atomic Energy

Cause for a lasting normative dispute in the Federal Republic has been given in particular by the phenomenon of the nuclear industry and the problems resulting from it. Here issues from the peace movement and the environmental movement, whose circles of sympathizers overlap to a large degree in any case, combine in the collective consciousness. It is in all likelihood precisely this double horizon of associations that, important as it is both economically and politically, explains why there is such a deep rift between, on the one hand, the nuclear industry and those sections of the political system associated with it, and on the other, wide sections of the population. In the course of this dispute, which has been going on for more than four decades, nuclear energy has become a politically unviable form of technology, in spite of the technological lead that German companies have in some areas of the nuclear industry. The fact that "the narrow interests of the pro–nuclear power coalition and the bloc in power were opposed by the equally narrow-minded anti–nuclear power coalition with its short-term, negative demands and its romantic, unpolitical visions"[14] revealed the extent to which it was an issue involving fundamental principles. But the antagonism is in itself based on much more deep-rooted factors, namely, on a considerable social division between those actively involved and those affected. This is symptomatic of most risks based on large-scale technologies.

A large number of nuclear projects have been dropped (e.g., "fast breeders," Kalkar; the reprocessing plant in Wackersdorf), and approval for new ones has been delayed by diverse misgivings and legal restrictions, so plans for new atomic power stations in Germany have more or less been abandoned. Nevertheless, the normative conflict has by no means been ironed out. The unrelenting positions on both sides point to nothing other than a religious war, with the supporters of peaceful uses of nuclear energy seeing it as the "cleanest" and most environmentally friendly source of energy, whereas its opponents cannot ignore the possible consequences of relatively improbable breakdowns and nuclear energy's presumed wide-sweeping political and social effects. In Germany at present there is no sign of a discussion that could serve as a common platform to argue out practicable, partial solutions to this conflict.

What Can the German Example Teach Us
About Handling Normative Conflicts?

Normative conflicts here are understood to mean practical disputes and the sets of opinion legitimizing them that appear to exclude any direct compromise between opponents by virtue of the fundamental character of the issue at stake and the involvement of individual, personal values. Basically, social alliances can be founded on three principles: on power on the one hand and fear on the other; on complementary interests; or on shared values. Usually at least two of these are of simultaneous importance. Stable common values go hand in hand with solidary social relations, whereby mutual reinforcement usually takes place. The collective character of a social context, that is, the high level of identification its participants have, depends as a rule on shared norms and values; these will also, however, be reinforced and strengthened in the collective character of the social context. Thus solidary alliances tend to be closed outwardly and to exclude the "unknown." This is particularly true when the common element has gradually become habit—that is, *tradition*.

Normative conflicts do not have an independent source but derive from something else: They appear when differing value-based convictions take effect between social groups who have to deal with an issue of common concern. The simplest method of avoiding normative conflict is therefore to separate the potential partners to the conflict, to minimize common elements that are likely to cause conflict. This, however, assumes spatial and political conditions that are increasingly disappearing in modernizing societies. Modernization processes are linked with increasing interdependence: Higher population density, the expansion of markets, and the development of transport and communication systems make up the most effective elements of increasing interlinking and possible interaction.

Increasing interdependence makes it possible for social units to grow. The development of European nation-states can be seen as an increase of internal interdependence and an external line of demarcation. To create states effectively it was assumed that a common history and culture (tradition) should already exist or be invented—say, in the shape of a "national character." Nationalist movements such as those in Italy and Germany in the nineteenth century proved to be important promoters of a new common consciousness. Social movements regularly play an important role when *new* social values are being created. By propagating new values they replace tradition as the basis for solidarity, which can then be experienced within the movement itself. The democratic movement deserves mention in this context since it emphasizes the equality of everyone involved and hence counteracts inner social barriers. The fact that the nationalist and democratic movements in Germany were not able to cooperate, so that the Weimar Republic was not a form of government that united the Germans, was an important contributory factor to the rise of the Third Reich.

Political unification of territories that were formerly separate is a regular cause of normative conflict, as it was in the case of German unification. Physical proximity generally leads to social proximity unless it is prevented by social boundaries (e.g., class boundaries) that have been consciously erected and are protected by certain values. Ethnic and religious ties have proved to be particularly resistant in the course of unification and often cause normative conflict. A historically successful way of weakening their significance in all modern democracies has been the formation of political parties. They enable particular social communities to be preserved and integrated within the nation-state threatening them, by permitting them to form political organizations and participate in the political decisionmaking process. This assumes that the principle of majority is respected, which, in the case of fundamental, identity-threatening conflicts, often serves to escalate rather than defuse the conflict. The recognition of the rights of minorities (especially in education) has frequently proved to be a useful corrective for majority democracy.

As we have seen, the common ground on which the Federal Republic is founded and which excludes fundamental religious and ethnic conflicts was prepared by the experience of the catastrophe of the Third Reich. Common values emerged as a reaction to this experience and are deeply embedded in the collective memory. In contrast to the French Revolution, which could likewise be seen as a catastrophe leading to the creation of a new state, the interpretation of the Nazi disaster is not controversial in principle but made the constitutional consensus possible on which the Basic Law was based. Thus, in a historically badly structured situation, the Basic Law created the foundation for a state identity, within which the national element was rendered insignificant.

Nowadays there seem to be two reservations about the effect this foundation has on creating identity. On the one hand, the relative importance of the social order established by the Basic Law must be assessed as markedly different in East Germany from in the West. Whether there will be a common interpretation of the unification process seems doubtful. It seems more likely that in future it will meet with controversial interpretations. On the other hand, the fact that the theme of nationalism has been transferred in the collective consciousness from Germany to Europe should not hide the considerable tendency toward political exclusion as regards citizenship and the treatment of immigrants from other countries. The Federal Republic has never consciously faced the fact that in spite of the protestations of the Federal Constitutional Court to the contrary, it is de facto an immigration country. For this reason it has not yet developed clear policies toward long-term residents from other countries. This could lead to normative conflict, particularly in connection with a rapid spread of Islam.

Class conflict, that is, the common social factors and differences formed by different relationships to the process of production in a society and the normative articulation of them, usually only emerges during the process of industrialization or democratization. Naturally social inequality was not unknown to advanced civilizations of the past, and indeed, it played a much greater role then. Inequality was then considered legitimate and was essentially related to rank or rights and not to a person's economic situation. Class conflict first emerged on the horizon of the normative conception of political liberty and equality, that is, the values of the democratic movement. The annoying thing about class differences is precisely the fact that they make social inequality visible. This is something for which a culture molded by the Christian conception of equality and the Enlightenment idea of liberty may find a pragmatic reason but not a satisfactory normative one.

For this reason it is far easier to find pragmatic solutions for the causes and characteristics of social inequality than to find a basic solution. If we turn to basic principles, then the problems of social inequality are related to the economic order. Market economies based on private capitalism basically tie income opportunity to the value of production factors based on supply and demand. Therefore they exclude anyone from earning an income who cannot offer any productive services. Socialist economic orders based on collective ownership, in contrast, are perfectly capable of organizing the distribution of income as required. Past experience shows, however, that they are not able to ensure the necessary incentives for efficient, consumer-oriented production at the same time. The basic normative conflict over the economic order was also rife during the foundation phase of the Federal Republic. The majority decision in favor of what was in principle a free-market economy, but with sociopolitical corrections to soften the effect of the inequality it tends to reinforce, proved less coherent than the formula "social market economy" suggested. However, the immediate success of this decision, the so-called economic miracle, put a stop to any basic criticism of it. Capitalism did not meet with fundamental criticism again until it was revived by the Marxist-inspired section of the student movement—though it was unable to inspire any lasting response. The pragmatic way of regulating autonomy in wage negotiations, of gradually extending the system of social security and the social services while at the same time insisting on economic productivity, has proved extremely successful until now. Constant economic growth has continued to open up new scope for the distribution of wealth without having too detrimental an effect on industry's profits.

Now, however, this satisfactory constellation seems to be crumbling. Growing competition on the world market, more favorable opportunities for investment abroad, easier openings for the exodus of capital, the increasing national debt, and last but not least, the increasing Europeanization of economic policy—all these factors are having a dampening effect on the growth of the German economy and on the scope the state has for economic and sociopolitical maneuver. While the proportion of retired and unemployed people who can claim social security is increasing, public income from taxes and insurance contributions is decreasing. It is no longer a question of distributing additional resources but of drawing on and interfering with acquired assets. It is already evident that this is leading to more intensive conflict over distribution.

In order to judge to what extent a rekindling of normative conflicts may be expected, it is advisable to examine more closely the conditions under which class conflict loses its normative relevance. The normative dramatization of the conflict between capital and labor regularly originated with the workers, since the interests of industry beyond the guarantee of private property and economic liberty evidently require no additional normative justification as basic components of the liberal creed. The typical reaction of capital to a worsening of its chances of utilization is *exodus*—that is, the *avoidance* of conflict rather than *opposition* or conflict. The typical reaction of the workers, on the other hand, was to protest, to put up a moralizing struggle by appealing to the common values of a bourgeois society molded by Christianity and the Enlightenment.[15] The normative dramatization of the demands of the labor movement relaxed to the same extent as its basic demands for the recognition of the right of coalition and for the participation in the making of decisions concerning conditions of pay and employment were fulfilled. There are essentially two forms of mediation that have proved effective in defusing normative conflict: *enabling the formation of organizations* and *proceduralizing the conflict.*

There are no significant legal restrictions on the right to form organizations in the Federal Republic. Though organizations that are considered to be "hostile to the constitution" can be prohibited by the state, this ruling has seldom been implemented and is subject to judicial review. The decisive factor for the relatively low level of normative conflict in the Federal Republic is the proceduralization of conflicts. In the context of capital and labor it is manifested mainly in the creation of statutory systems of negotiation and the restoration of a system of industrial tribunals with representatives of both sides to the wage agreements. These systems of negotiation exist on an intercompany level in the form of negotiations for a collective wage agreement and on an intracompany level in the form of various arrangements for worker participation. Industrial law in

Germany has essentially developed into law on collective wage agreements as well as case law (the decisions of the Federal Industrial Court serve as precedents). The legislator is active only in protecting health and guaranteeing minimum working conditions.

For the legally controlled system of wage bargaining to be effective, it is necessary for the partners to the negotiations to be organized and committed. Only when industrial organizations and trade unions can depend on their members to follow their advice can they act as reliable partners in the process of negotiating their interests and can keep up the other side's interest in maintaining the negotiation system. Until now this condition was generally fulfilled, but there are signs, both on the side of industry and on that of the unions, whose level of organization is sinking, of first symptoms of the erosion of individual willingness to comply. Whether the intensification of the conflict over distribution will lead to a consolidation or a fragmentation of the wage agreement partners can hardly be predicted—either is possible.

The topics causing conflict and the willingness to behave with solidarity in the new social movements are less affected by direct material interests. Many of the activists are also directly involved, such as people living near a nuclear power station or homeless squatters. But they are a minority who would not be able to produce a comparable reaction for their cause alone. The fact that reaction is widespread in society arises from the *normative dramatization* of these issues, which are interpreted as symptoms of a fundamental connection, such as the endangerment of nature, a threat to future generations, or the exploitative nature of capitalism.

In sociological literature the articulation of these kinds of interests is interpreted as *postmodern* and is thought to derive from a fundamental change in values. This results from the interaction between changes in society on the whole on the one hand, such as increasing affluence, continuing peace, technological progress, developing education, and the greater influence of the mass media, and individual experience on the other hand. It is the younger generations in particular, and among them the better educated, who display these new, postmaterialist or posttraditionalist patterns of thinking. For the new social movements, they are also potential recruits and primary responders.

In this unavoidably brief outline we have seen that the political success of the topics articulated in the "milieu" of these movements has been very varied. The environment and women's rights have both been topics that have brought about a change of attitude reaching far beyond the ecological or women's movements. These became everyday topics, that is, they lost their normative urgency in a similar way as class conflict. The self-organization of the social movement was consolidated in the form of organized groups and a political party, and the themes of conflict were proceduralized by legal means, for example, by testing for damage to the environment or introducing the post of a representative for women's affairs with corresponding influence and rights. Lastly, these topics were taken up by other parties apart from the Greens and thus integrated into the prevailing structure of consensus.

In contrast, other topics such as the lack of cheap housing or the question of the use of nuclear power turned out to be more unwieldy. Here the demands of the social movement came up against the entrenched economic interests of private individuals, who fought back using political and legal means. Political or legal decisions did not generally lead to the resolution of the conflict if they protected existing property rights and commitments and thus did not correspond to the demands of the movement. As a result the active core of the movement became increasingly radical, and there were violent clashes. The use of violence had a different effect in each case. The "autonomous" squatter scene was isolated, whereas the antinuclear movement did not noticeably lose support for its cause as a result.

New studies in the sociology of risk show that advanced technologies divide the population into two groups. One is made up of those people who make decisions about these technologies and hope to profit from them; they *participate*. The other group are those who will possibly have to face incalculable consequences; they are *affected*.[16] It is much more difficult to find a balance of interests between these two groups than between, say, capital and labor, since proceduralization of the conflict does not work. The decisionmakers insist on keeping calculated risks within the limits of sums that can be covered by insurance, whereas those affected suspect possible risks for which insurances would not be prepared to pay. Although experts have put forward several proposals for models in which people affected could also become participants, they have hardly been discussed politically. An attempt at proceduralization by using a system of testing or legal proceedings did not go far enough for the antinuclear movement. Since the reactor catastrophe in Chernobyl the dangers of nuclear power have become firmly entrenched in the public consciousness. There is thus no end in sight to this conflict, which has been rearing its head constantly for forty years.

The proceduralization of conflicts renders them less dramatic by fragmenting them and allowing them to be worked on piece by piece within the framework of systems of negotiation in which the parties to the conflict participate. In the case of Germany this has proved extremely effective in the context of democratic and administrative processes. Proceduralization fails, however, when "everything is at stake." In German society it has become standard opinion that nuclear power threatens the life of future generations. No credit is given to promises of increasingly strict security standards, since their international implementation remains unlikely. Neither an ethical nor a political or procedural solution has yet been found to the conflict between those affected by decisions made about advanced technologies but excluded from them and those participating in those decisions. It would appear to be a characteristic type of normative conflict in advanced industrial societies.

Notes

1. The area belonging to the Federal Republic until 1990 is called "West Germany" here, and that of the former Democratic Republic "East Germany," according to customary but imprecise usage.

2. M. R. Lepsius, "Parteiensystem und Sozialstruktur: Zum Problem der Demokratisierung der deutschen Gesellschaft," in W. Abel, ed., *Wirtschaft, Geschichte und Wirtschaftsgeschichte* (Stuttgart, 1966).

3. Mathias Bös, "Ethnisierung des Rechts? Staatsbürgerschaft in Deutschland, Frankreich, Großbritannien und den USA," *Kölner Zeitschrift für Soziologie und Sozialpsychologie* 45, 4 (1993):628.

4. H.-P. Müller, *Sozialstruktur und Lebensstile* (Frankfurt am Main, 1992).

5. H. Lampert, *Die Wirtschafts- und Sozialordnung der Bundesrepublik Deutschland,* 12th ed. (Munich, 1995), p. 85.

6. L. Erhard, "Grundbedingungen einer freiheitlichen Sozialordnung," in H. F. Wünsche, ed., *Grundtexte zur sozialen Marktwirtschaft,* vol. 2 (Stuttgart and New York, 1956), pp. 13–16.

7. E. Roller, *Einstellungen der Bürger zum Wohlfahrtsstaat der Bundesrepublik Deutschland* (Opladen, 1992).

8. F.-X. Kaufmann, "Die Soziale Sicherheit in der Bundesrepublik Deutschland," in W. Weidenfeld and H. Zimmermann, eds., *Deutschland-Handbuch: Eine doppelte Bilanz 1949 to 1989* (Munich, 1989), pp. 308–325.

9. Fortunate circumstances have made it possible to study the different sociopolitical interpretations of the current situation in an authentic concentration. At the end of 1994 the German (Catholic) Bishops' Conference and the Council of the Protestant Church in Germany published the basis for discussion of a joint declaration of the churches, "On the economic and social situation in Germany," asking people to participate in a "process of consultation" on it. It met with a remarkably wide response and at an estimated 4,000 public events this draft was used as the basis for discussion and interpretation. Apart from numerous publications on the topic, by April 1996 the official church addressees had received approximately 2,400 submissions and comments, amounting to a total of 25,000 pages. These include comments from all the political parties and most larger organizations, but also from private individuals, church groups, and others. The comments are being catalogued according to keywords and made accessible to computer evaluation. As far as it was accessible in February 1996 the material was examined with reference to the present study. The results can only be briefly incorporated as far as the limited available space permits.

10. Of the 1.7 million unemployed registered in September 1990, 1.2 million (70 percent) counted as problem cases on account of insufficient education, health problems, and/or a period of unemployment longer than a year. This proportion was also valid for the 1990s. B. Hof, *Für mehr Verantwortung—Langzeitarbeitslosigkeit und soziale Marktwirtschaft* (Cologne, 1991).

11. K.-W. Brand, D. Büsser, D. Rucht, *Aufbruch in eine andere Gesellschaft: Neue soziale Bewegungen in der Bundesrepublik* (Frankfurt, 1983), p. 35.

12. Thus we can assume a close correlation with the so-called "changing values," that is, with the change in attitude that leads from the traditional value of duty to that of self-fulfillment. This aspect cannot be followed up here; see O. W. Gabriel, *Politische Kultur, Postmaterialismus und Materialismus in der Bundesrepublik Deutschland* (Opladen, 1986); M. Greiffenhagen and S. Greiffenhagen, *Ein schwieriges Vaterland: Zur politischen Kultur im vereinigten Deutschland* (Munich and Leipzig, 1993), pp. 156ff., 221ff.; and K.-U. Hellmann, *Systemtheorie und neue soziale Bewegungen* (Opladen, 1996), pp. 188ff.

13. G. Schulze, *Die Erlebnisgesellschaft: Kultursoziologie der Gegenwart* (Frankfurt and New York, 1992), pp. 312ff.

14. H. Kitschelt, *Kernenergiepolitik-Arena eines gesellschaftlichen Konflikts* (Frankfurt and New York, 1980), pp. 318ff.

15. E. Heimann, *Soziale Theorie des Kapitalismus-Theorie der Sozialpolitik* (Frankfurt am Main, 1990 [orig. 1929]).

16. N. Luhmann, *Soziologie des Risikos* (Berlin, 1991), pp. 93ff.

4

Uncertain Ghosts: Populists and Urbans in Postcommunist Hungary

János Mátyás Kovács

Q: Why do the Populists dislike the Urbans?
A: Because they both enjoy sitting in the same cafés, but the Urbans sing folk songs so loudly that the Populists cannot hear themselves talk business.

—**A Budapest joke from 1993**

Populists and Westernizers in Eastern Europe

There was a moment in the history of Eastern Europe at the end of the 1980s when the optimistic observers believed that the century-long cleavage between the so-called "Populists" (traditionalists, nativists, nationalists) and "Westernizers" (modernizers, cosmopolitans, liberals) would fade away from the intellectual and political life of the region. Today we know that the rapprochement of the national(ist) and liberal strains of anticommunism was due to the common enemy rather than to normative cohesion. The compromise between the dissenters/dissidents proved to be provisional: It evaporated in the course of the first free elections. Political discourse has been refilled with well-known symbols of conflict, including even extreme forms of demonization such as the identification of national revival with Nazism and, conversely, liberal politics with Jewish conspiracy. Accordingly, the optimistic prognosis of a sweeping victory of "liberalism with a national face" in Eastern Europe had to be revised. Today, instead of a kind of *Verfassungspatriotismus*, nationalism, authoritarianism, and neosocialism are ascendant in many of the new democracies. In most governments of the region, fragmented liberal policies are implemented by illiberal or expressly antiliberal parties.

Was the temporary compromise broken by the nationalists, who reconciled themselves with the old *nomenklatura* (e.g., "red-brown" coalitions) in most of the countries? Not infrequently, ethnic cleansing was the result of this reconciliation. Was the rapprochement ended by the liberals, whose pro-capitalist programs were regarded by many as a betrayal of national traditions and a violation of social justice? Is the new rivalry a natural consequence of the emerging multiparty system, in which an original division of the political space is taking place? Was the compromise canceled by the fact that in certain postcommunist states the old cleavage took the form of national conflict whereby "West-oriented" Czechs, Lithuanians, or Slovenes were confronting the "East-oriented" Slovaks, Russians, or Serbs? Questions without answers. . . .

In most postcommunist societies the major normative conflicts are still ritually attached to (and derived from) comprehensive visions of nativist-traditionalist or West-oriented development. Since 1989 noncapitalist "Third Road" programs have been competing with Grand Designs of catching up with the West. Their followers accuse each other respectively of indulging in a servile imitation of false (unnatural, alien, unorganic, etc.) patterns of progress and taking romantic pride in backwardness (ignorance, obscurity, parochialism, etc.).

The passionate debates trickle down from the scientific and political level of the rival world outlooks and permeate all possible conflicts between cultures, religions, ethnic groups, genders, and so on, on the level of moral attitudes, behavioral patterns, everyday fashions, and literary styles. For example, a typical nationalist theorist/politician in Eastern Europe would fight any extension of gay and lesbian rights supported by the liberals in the following way: He would begin with the abstract concepts of nation and family as society's fundamental components; then he would stress the moral duty of the individual to save the nation by stopping the decline of birth rates in the country (at this point he would also refer to Christian ethical rules of childbearing); historical examples would follow in solemn sentences about the manly virtues of national heroes, the idyllic large families in the countryside, and the heroism of mothers; next he would list a couple of quasi-pragmatic arguments concerning AIDS, the defense capability of the country, and the welfare budget; thereafter instructions would be given on "normal" sexual behavior (possibly caricaturing those with "perverse" habits by using vulgar terms of slang) and on the role of the government in correctly educating the citizens and strictly punishing sexual crimes; then the materialism, godlessness, and relativism of the West would be accused (probably with anti-Semitic overtones); and finally our nationalist, if he is not short of demagogy, would warn the nation that excessive permissiveness may turn into new totalitarianism, and sooner or later gayness will become obligatory.

How would a typical Westernizing liberal support the emancipation of homosexuals? First of all, he would stress that contrary to the accusations, he is not speaking out of self-interest. He would simply like to protect universal human rights that belong to man by birth. Then he would refer to recent liberal legislation in advanced Western countries and to current scientific evidence (e.g., the genetic roots of homosexuality) to prove that the extension of gay and lesbian rights does not lead to rising criminality, falling birth rates, and the spread of sexually transmitted diseases. Just the opposite is true, he would argue: It is the illegal conditions under which the homosexuals are forced to live that increase morbidity and criminality. Most likely, our imaginary liberal would not confine himself to "cold" argumentation but he would draw passionate parallels between political, racial, ethnic, and sexual discrimination, using the example of the Holocaust and Stalin's terror. Finally (if he is not short of demagogy) he would ridicule some of the national heroes by pointing to the fallibility of their character (womanizing, rude sexual habits, etc.) and ask irreverently: So what if the nation slowly dies out? That already happened to higher cultures in the world.

In the Prison of a Dichotomy

Is it appropriate to use the old designations and call the current confrontation a struggle between "Populists" and "Westernizers"? Nothing is more comfortable than falling back on a routine language with flexible vocabulary. In witnessing the renaissance of a somewhat familiar political discourse in the postcommunist countries, the observers appear to be satisfied with the old clichés about the *Slavophils* and the *zapadniks* formed in nineteenth-century Russia and later applied to similar normative cleavages in East-Central Europe between the two wars.[1] Obviously, these clichés lost some of their relevance during the Communist period. (For instance, it proved to be very difficult to situate the Communists with their pseudo-internationalist nationalism and outmoded modernization ideology within the Populist–Westernizer scheme.) Now there is a temptation to reactivate this old dichotomy with the help of the so-called "refrigerator thesis," according to which communism only froze the old normative conflicts in Eastern Europe, which reappeared in full strength after the refrigerator door had been opened in 1989.

The thesis is usually supported by horror-examples of wild nationalism ranging from the Russian *Pamiat'* movement to the Serb *cetniks*. The protracted and ambiguous revival of Eastern European liberalism apparently does not fit in well with the metaphor of the refrigerator.[2] I am afraid that postcommunist affairs hardly lend themselves to an analysis based on simple dual schemes. Nationalist/populist rhetoric may hide resolutely liberal economic measures (Hungary 1990–1994, Slovakia 1993–1996) and proudly liberal governments may pursue populist-style policies of mass privatization (Czech Republic). People who call themselves liberal in economic matters may vote for restrictive abortion laws or lobby against the separation of the church from the state (Poland). Allegedly West-oriented Czech or Slovene politicians still use quasi-nationalist arguments when justifying the secession, not to mention the liberals in the Baltic states. Croatian Catholicism is regarded by many as a Western feature as opposed to Serbian Orthodoxy, while Catholicism in Slovakia is treated as "less Western" than Czech Protestantism.

Typically the political parties in the region are divided into a number of rival factions (not simply into two platforms), and the similar groups do not join forces across party lines or national borders to create two distinct political blocs. The same applies to their academic and artistic entourage. To take an extreme example, cooperation between a Serb and a Croat liberal against their nationalist opponents is almost as unlikely as an alliance between the nationalists themselves. In many countries no significant liberal force exists in the political and intellectual arena. Here, if there is a cleavage at all, it occurs between the representatives of moderate and radical nationalism/populism. It is also very difficult to find a place for the rapidly rising neosocialists or the unexpectedly weak environmentalists in a Populist–Westernizer dichotomy.

The semantic obstacles are also immense. Mutual stigmatization by the rival camps has resulted in strange synonyms (populist, nationalist, and conservative on the one hand; Westernizer, cosmopolitan, democrat, and liberal on the other), which are often used against each other as four-letter words. As a consequence, hybrid solutions such as Christian democracy, Christian socialism, and social democracy are ab ovo excluded from the classification. Recurrent attempts of analysts using the left-right distinction in the same context (they ask, for example, whether the new Eastern European nationalists are rightists or rather leftists) is a further complication. Umbrella concepts such as populism (which originally referred to Russian *narodnichestvo* and not to a certain technique of political mobilization and manipulation) and Westernism (which is based on an image of the future that changes along with Western capitalism) are contrasted as if their meanings were unambiguous. Sometimes it is simply futile to look for any coherent meaning at all (e.g., Zhirinovsky's "liberal-democratic" party in Russia), because the so-called New Populists in Eastern Europe try to follow both their "premodern" predecessors and their "postmodern" colleagues in the West.[3]

In the literature of the Populist–Westernizer debate a whole catalogue of antagonisms was created to support a dichotomic model of East and West: tradition versus modernity, collectivism vs. individualism, informal relations vs. formalized institutions, direct vs. indirect democracy, egalitarianism vs. meritocracy, fundamentalism vs. pragmatism, dogmatism vs. relativism, romanticism vs. realism, nation vs. citizen, religion vs. secularization, past vs. future, localism vs. universalism, village vs. city, agrarian vs. industrial development, nature vs. technical civilization, closed vs. open society, and so on. One could list such pairs of concepts almost indefinitely. Probably these concepts were helpful in comprehending the normative cleavages in Eastern Europe during the nineteenth and the first half of the twentieth century. Since then, however, both the Eastern and Western pillars of the Populist–Westernizer paradigm have undergone substantial changes. Today any dichotomic structure may turn out to be a straitjacket. Something may have happened in that communist refrigerator. Perhaps it was unplugged from time to time, or its door was opened repeatedly, because some of the old conflicts had rotted by 1989. Nonetheless, some others, while hibernated, have been able to adjust to the changing environment. To avoid this nonsense in biophysics, I prefer to use a less scientific metaphor, the metaphor of the ghosts who were periodically allowed by the Communist rulers to rise from their graves, to scare each other and see the world develop. To put it simply, the Populists were reactivated when the Communist elite needed patriotic legitimation, and the Westernizers were sought when the *nomenklatura* wanted to initiate limited market reforms and open up a little to the West. Small wonder that our ghosts have become uncertain during the decades of their disappearance and reappearance.

Rivalry in Indecision

East and West—what do they mean? Central Europe's separation from Eastern Europe, the Russian crisis, the survival of communism in China, and so on are exciting puzzles, which show a great variety of "Eastern" developments. Even if one disregards the question of what "East" means after the collapse of the Eastern Bloc, who would dare specify the notion of *the* West, which—depending on how you see it—has reached its postmodern stage or is just celebrating the triumph of liberalism? For the sake of a thought experiment let us accept the latter. If liberal ideas have conquered the world, which current of liberalism could Eastern Europe join? In American conservative thought, for instance, both Eastern European nationalists and liberals may easily find firm points of reference, depending on whether they choose the communitarian or the free-market message of the various theories. Or let us take the example of egalitarian (communitarian, multicultural) liberalism: Would it be a Populist or a Westernizer project if it were accepted by wide circles of intellectuals in Eastern Europe? "Beyond the age of Enlightenment," is there still a quintessence of Western civilization that may serve as a universal goal for postcommunist transformers? Whether or not we accept postmodern skepticism or liberal euphoria, the transformers are faced by both.

As regards real capitalism, West may in fact mean East (Asia) or South (Europe) for the Westernizers of our time when they search for success stories to study. In other words, less and more liberal options are equally offered in the marketplace of ideas. A Westernizer today sees a much more colorful mixture of capitalisms than his *zapadnik* predecessor at the end of the nineteenth century, even if he is presented with the idea of the united Europe as an almost mandatory destination of the Westernizing project. The Westernizer is also disturbed by the fact that he recognizes a great number of "Eastern" elements in the daily workings of Western capitalism (French separatism in Quebec, religious strife in Northern Ireland, organized corruption in Italy or Japan, romantic anticapitalism in the European Green movements, state-led modernization in Southeast Asia, resurgent right-wing populism in Western Europe, national rivalry within the European Union, etc.). With a slight exaggeration, the only thing he knows for sure is that (re)joining the West may be the sole guarantee for his country to remain in the North. At the same time, even the most dedicated Westernizers feel a bit betrayed by Western politicians, who in 1989 promised more assistance and less "entrance examination" to Eastern Europe.

The Populist, while enjoying the inconsistency of the Westernization project, probably encounters even greater difficulties when defining the national traditions he would like to preserve. Where is the peasantry ("the cornerstone of the nation") he wishes to emancipate? Where is the rural idyll he swore to protect? What does national culture mean in the age of the Internet and cable TV? How can one preach isolation and egalitarianism and advocate Grand Social Experiments after so many decades of communist autarchy, leveling, and permanent experimentation? State paternalism, collectivism, social protection, and so on have also partly been discredited by the ancien régime. Anticapitalism needs existing capitalism first. Anti-Semitism has changed its utility in political programs since the Holocaust. Ethnicity and religion (i.e., two weak points in standard liberal theory) remain the trumps in the hands of the Eastern European Populist until emerging capitalism delivers the arguments against itself. Or he may rely on nostalgic communism. After a while these three sources (ethnic nationalism, renascent anticapitalism, and whitewashed communism) can merge, and the Populist may add the principle of social responsibility, firm moral standards, and law and order to the trumps just mentioned. With a partial devaluation of nationalism by the Yugoslav and post-Soviet wars, it is the critique of "Wild-East" capitalism that is currently occupying the center of populist discourse in Eastern Europe. Will this new compound save populism or destroy it? Will the flirt with nostalgic communism prove a fatal embrace? These dilemmas should encourage the Eastern European analysts to update, attenuate, and open up the old dichotomies.

To reform our conceptual schemes is all the more urgent because the Populists and Westernizers have already begun to reform their agendas. Let me refer to my original field, the current history of economic thought, and take an example from there. During the early to mid-1990s, the liberal economists of Eastern Europe had to accept the paradox that the market cannot be exclusively created by the market, the state may be an agent of deregulation, and liberalization needs social support. Accordingly, their Westernization ideals have rapidly moved from a less interventionist, occasionally neoliberal model of capitalism to the more interventionist concept of *Soziale Marktwirtschaft*.[4] At the same time, the populist-minded economists had to come to terms with severe constraints of national isolation, state dirigism, small entrepreneurship, agrarian and social protectionism, and anticonsumerism in a global economy or in the process of European integration. Until now, neither neoliberal nor Latin-American-type populist revolutions have taken place in the former Eastern Bloc.[5] While the latter may break out in the Eastern part of the region at any time, a gradual and limited rapprochement of the two camps' programs seems more likely. Certain forms of conservatism, communitarian liberalism, environmentalism, etc. may prove to be appropriate fields in which they can meet. Another option would be that the difficulties in formulating coherent Populist and Westernizer agendas lead the antagonists to ignore the Grand Ideologies and experiment with a postmodern "anything goes" mixture of concepts. Today two major political groups are making attempts to neglect or ridicule the old normative cleavage: the Neo-Socialists and the New Populists. These ghosts are far from being uncertain. . . .

Why Hungary?

Although in present-day Eastern Europe it is rather difficult to squeeze the tradition versus modernity, nationalism versus liberalism, etc. debates into the Populist–Westernizer model, there is a country in the region, Hungary, in which these types of normative cleavages can be observed (1) in a transparent dichotomic breakdown and (2) in a surprising historical continuity.[6]

The country exhibits: powerful but only half-successful attempts at embourgeoisement from the early nineteenth century onward, which have created an oversized group of intellectuals without eliminating the peasant question (i.e., the armies were ready to fight and the ammunition was abundant); a brief period of hard-line communism followed by three decades of a relatively permissive reform-communist regime (i.e., the belligerents were allowed—occasionally urged—to shoot at each other); ethnic homogeneity, large Hungarian minorities in the neighboring countries, and a large Jewish community in Budapest (i.e., the front line between "Hungarian nationalists" and the "Jewish liberals" was relatively stable); no dominant church and a high degree of secularization (i.e., no religion could reconcile the fighters or cross-cut the conflict). As a result, one sees two large camps of intellectuals and politicians concentrated in the capital who still call themselves (and each other) "Populists" or "National-Populists" and "Urbans" or "Westernizers." Today they use terms that were coined back in the nineteenth and early twentieth centuries and do not cease to consider their confrontation a regular cultural war that goes beyond conventional political struggle.

In this chapter I will try to explain why the Populist–Urban (PU) conflict[7] in Hungary shows such a high degree of continuity. What happened in the "communist refrigerator"? How could the PU cleavage almost outcompete even the communism-capitalism clash inherent in the 1989 revolution? I will also examine why reconciliation has proved unsuccessful so far, and how truce can be converted into peace. Finally, I will meditate on mediation between the belligerents. What can be its final goal: mutual tolerance or cultural synthesis? Which patterns of mediation have failed and which promise success? Can the Populist–Urban conflict be buried for good?

In Hungary the PU cleavage is considered an eternal fact of social life. The Populists write tragic ballads, the Urbans ironic studies about why their conflict can*not* be resolved. While I am also skeptical about the Big Solutions, I would like to examine the small ones.

Populists and Urbans in Hungary (1930s–1990s)

The Prewar Debate and the "Original Sin"

"Garden Hungary," "elevation of the peasantry into the nation," "qualitative socialism," "Third Road," "*ex oriente lux,*" breaking the monopoly of the feudal aristocracy, the Catholic Church and Jewish/German capitalism, "guilty Budapest," "deep" versus "diluted" Hungarians, and so on—these were standard phrases in populist terminology during the period between the late 1920s, when the first manifestos[8] were published by populist ideologues, and the 1943 Szárszó meeting, their last public gathering before the end of the war.[9]

With a few exceptions, they were all writers, some of them widely educated talents, no more than two dozen intellectuals altogether who had no formal organizations, only one or two literary journals. The Populists managed to launch short-lived political actions (such as the "New Spiritual Front" in 1935 and the "March Front" in 1937) and lasting cultural initiatives (studies in rural sociology, "People's Colleges") rather than new political movements or parties. Being devoted to a kind of plebeian radicalism against the aristocracy and the so-called Christian middle class (including the gentry), they equally flirted with the communists and the protofascists. In other words, as followers of the tradition of agrarian socialism (many of them were born in the countryside), they could equally criticize feudal and capitalist exploitation and represent *"Blut und Boden"* vitalism, frequently mixing anti-German, anti-Soviet, and anti-Semitic arguments.

The Third Road, the synthetic concept of populist theory in Hungary, meant avoiding Western (above all, German and Jewish) capitalism without choosing Russian communism. According to this idea, there was a sort of national-oriented agrarian socialism in the middle, which seemed to be the best (and a morally superior) way to overcome feudalism and solve the "peasant question," the crucial problem of Hungarian society. Land reform and cultural emancipation of the peasants were the fundamental claims in the populist program. The idealization of national self-reliance, the identification of the nation with the People and the People with the peasantry, a Protestant-style anti-Catholic rhetoric and social responsibility for the poor (the "three million beggars" of Hungary) were also important ingredients of this single-issue movement of *Volkstümlich* intellectuals. In contrast to the prevailing ideology of the time, the Populists' nationalism initially was not irredentist. Instead of taking a revanchist approach to the Trianon peace treaty that deprived Hungary of two-thirds of its territory, many Populists cherished the nineteenth-century idea of a Danubian confederation of the "clean, young peoples" with their autarkic economic systems. Also, they were not dogmatically anti-modernist; they only represented a peculiar, "organic" strategy of modernization from below, which originates in the countryside and relies not on "parasitic aliens" but on indigenous small entrepreneurs, their cooperatives and banks. The industrial workers as well as the urban middle class escaped the Populists' attention.

In this program the merciless critique of Hungarian feudalism and the claims of romantic anticapitalism (anti-Westernism) were interconnected. This was what fundamentally challenged the liberal thinkers, while, of course, they also felt provoked by the racist and nationalist arguments of the Populists. The Urbans[10] did not represent the protofascist Miklós Horthy regime prevailing in Hungary between the two wars. Nevertheless, they—that is, a small group of writers and journalists (who were even less organized than their opponents)—became targets of vigorous populist criticism in the middle of the 1930s. The intellectual/ideological explosives of the controversy had already been accumulated at the end of the 1920s, and only a spark was lacking to set the normative conflict into flames. It was provided by an article written in 1934 by the "pope" of populism, László Németh, on the necessity of limiting the influence of Jews on Hungarian literature. The counterattack was inevitable: A leading representative of the Urbans accused Németh of being a spiritual terrorist. He responded by using the analogy of Shylock from *The Merchant of Venice*, thereby cementing the debate in a Jewish versus non-Jewish dimension. Since this duel, there has been no durable peace along the PU front line in Hungary.

The Urbans felt offended by a brief flirtation in 1935 between the populist writers and the radical nationalist prime minister, Gyula Gömbös, which openly broke the solidarity within the group of critical intellectuals. This episode was regarded by the liberals as the "original sin." Even if there had been a rational dispute between the two groups before, the support (or tacit acceptance) by many Populists of the Nuremberg-style anti-Jewish legislation in Hungary during the second half of the 1930s certainly excluded reconciliation. This entire drama happened in Budapest, sometimes at the neighboring tables of the same café. And it ended with the physical liquidation of a great number of Urbans and with the unholy alliance of the Populists with the right-wing regime or its communist opposition during the war.

The Urbans were on the defensive throughout the PU controversy of the 1930s. They did their best to save as much from the capitalist modernization project as possible during the low tide of liberalism after World War I and the Great Depression. With only a few elitist liberals in their ranks, the Urbans were essentially social democrats of the time who expected growing welfare for the working classes (including the peasantry and the urban middle strata) from capitalist progress without strong state interference and social protectionism. They could not offer, however, quick solutions for the problems of rural unemployment, mass poverty, emigration, and so on. In an understandable lack of clear economic visions about the immediate future of capitalism, they gave elementary lectures to the Populists on the advantages of industrialization, foreign trade, and banking, or instead, focused on the defense of human and civic liberties endangered by the upsurge of national socialism. The Urbans were anxious about the possible links between populist and fascist theories. Therefore, they stressed the differences between mythical and rational reasoning, the ethnic and political concepts of nation, decadence, and civilization, rural idyll and economic progress, etc. And, loyal to the label of "urbanness," they protected the idea of the city, in particular that of the cosmopolitan metropolis, against the "virgin provinces."

The majority of Urbans came from Jewish middle-class families. Despite the political diversity of their group (there were anarchists, radical and conservative liberals, social democrats, even communists among them), its normative cohesion with regard to some basic issues of liberalism was strong. They named their cultic journal "West" and desperately preached the "European values" of civilization in an era of a grave crisis of European identity. Small wonder that they were not able to touch the souls of even the most moderate Populists. Yet, in retrospect, one can perhaps define a middle ground, where the warriors might have met to bury their hatchets. In principle, a New Deal–type social-democratic economic program with an emphasis on agriculture could have served as a compromise. The common enemy could have been found in the so-called "neo-baroque" regime of Admiral Horthy, German fascism, and Soviet communism. Instead of this, if there occurred any rapprochement between the two sides (e.g., the March Front), it followed the logic of populist arguments. Due to mutual stigmatization ("snobs" and "peasants," "aliens" and "anti-Semites," etc.), group solidarities became extremely strong. No influential mediators appeared in the controversy, and there was virtually no migration (no converts, no traitors) between the two camps. Personal quarrels, nasty revenges, malicious gossip, prejudices and denunciations were all components of a hostile relationship bordering on tribalism. The rivalry of vested interests in the intellectual marketplace and the intrigues of the government (although the confrontation was not channeled into party politics) may be additional reasons for the lack of reconciliation.

Quarrel Under Communist Control

Serving the Lord.   The postwar years in Hungary, with their emotional blend of reconstruction euphoria, repentance, and a fresh start in democratic politics, could have become an era of PU peace if the Communists had not joined the confrontation. Actually, quite a few young Marxists were already active participants in the polemic during the 1930s as members of the populist movement. With the gradual *Gleichschaltung* of the peasant parties by the Communists in the second half of the 1940s, a great number of former Populists converted to the new faith. Opportunism aside, they were enchanted by the fact that the Communists borrowed their land reform project and many of their egalitarian, social-protectionist ideas. Furthermore, they loved the antireactionary rhetoric and grassroots activism of the new rulers, and, for some years, believed in their generous promises concerning free agricultural cooperatives, rural banks, and so on.

The Communists, whose top leaders were without exception Jews belonging to the Muscovite faction of the party, had an enormous deficit in patriotic image. In order to counterbalance the "alien" character of the Marxist-Leninist program, they invented a new, people-and-nation-based interpretation of Hungarian history. According to this approach, the Communist regime was an inevitable result of a long series of fights for national independence and social justice; that is, communism was an ultimate embodiment of plebeian truth. The peasants, stylized as agrarian proletarians, were co-opted in the working class, so populism could be harmonized with the Marxian theory of class struggle. The two thought worlds also overlapped in terms of the idealization of the "People." The beginning of the Cold War, the ferocious anti-West campaign in the Soviet Union, and the nationalist zeal of the *Zhdanovschina* provided a firm background to this spiritual coalition.

Strangely enough, the alliance of the Populists and the Communists survived (1) the forced establishment of the *kolkhoz* system and the impoverishment of the villages in the late 1940s and early 1950s; (2) the crushing of the 1956 revolution and the following "socialist consolidation" crowned by a new wave of violent collectivization in agriculture; and (3) the quasi-liberal economic reforms of János Kádár during the 1960s and 1970s, which brought about income differentiation, Westernization of lifestyles and consumption patterns, etc.—all anathemas in populist ideology. This paradox needs a more profound explanation than a simple reference to opportunistic behavior. Most Populists were not only corrupted by spectacular though second-rate jobs in the government. They were also attracted first—between 1953 and 1956—by the program of the pro-peasant faction of the Communist Party, led by the prime minister of the 1956 revolution, Imre Nagy, and later by Kádár's pragmatic agrarian policy based on semiprivate cooperatives, which by and large solved the peasant question in Hungary. By the 1980s quite a few Populist radicals of the younger generation believed that the Hungarian nation paid an unfairly high cultural price for economic welfare in the provinces. However, instead of turning their back to the Communists for good, they found a "godfather" again in the Communist leadership in the person of Imre Pozsgay. Pozsgay, a self-made party intellectual from the countryside, was at that time competing with György Aczél, Kádár's chief ideologue since 1956, and who was also an urban Jew.

What kind of roles were assigned by the Communists to the few remaining representatives of the Urban camp after the war? In contrast to the Populists, they were not commissioned to serve as "moral entrepreneurs." While suffering from a lack of patriotic legitimacy, the Communists thought they had no modernization deficit. Hence they treated the liberals with contempt as "bourgeois reactionaries" and the social democrats, who were rivals in Marxist theory, with suspicion and feelings of inferiority. None of the Urban groups were of any use for the new regime. With the exception of a few leftist social democrats, who helped the Communists unite the two parties, the Urbans of the 1930s rejected collaboration by leaving the country or choosing passive resistance. Those who remained were marginalized from the very beginning, not infrequently in an aura of anti-Semitic allusions—an exercise by the Communist leaders in overcompensation. At the same time, the Communists commissioned young intellectuals (many of them were Jews) from their own ranks to perform the daily tasks of "agitation and propaganda." Many of these writers, journalists, philosophers and social scientists became members of the old generation of Hungarian liberals by 1989. However, on their way to liberalism they had to go through several phases of the Communist Purgatory. Needless to say, they were regarded by the Populists as natural heirs of the prewar Urbans. Their own "original sin" of having served the Communists between 1945 and 1953 has not been forgiven, even now.

As time passed in the early 1950s, the Stalinist regime in Hungary proved unable to domesticate its own intelligentsia. Unwillingly, it created a great many PU-neutral intellectuals, a large group of dissenters who came, for example, from among those country boys and girls who were students in the legendary People's Colleges closed down by the Communists in the late 1940s as well as from among those young communist intellectuals who felt ashamed to have written long articles in the party newspaper to justify the eradication of these institutions. They became the core of the revolutionary generation in 1956. Their PU immunity stemmed from many sources: the joint frustration of being cheated by the Communist oligarchy; the widely accepted idea of making communism democratic and patriotic; the continued exclusion of the older generation of the Populists and Urbans from the public discussions even after Stalin's death in 1953 (with the exception of the revolutionary weeks in 1956); the participation of a large group of social scientists, economists, lawyers, and engineers in the debates; and the short-lived experiment with democratic politics in 1956, which did not allow for the renascent parties to sharpen the PU conflict. In other words, 1956 provided the following lessons in conflict resolution: If there is a common enemy (hardliner Communists) and a joint ideology (democratic/patriotic socialism), if the protagonists do not carry the moral burden of former fights and the language of the debate is increasingly rational (i.e., the discourse of the new professional participants cannot be arranged in bipolar schemes as easily as the prophetic visions of writers), and if there is no electoral competition, then the Populists and the Urbans can forget their normative cleavages for a while.

The PU peace of 1953–1956 was prolonged by Soviet occupation and Communist oppression during the late 1950s and early 1960s. Prison is an appropriate place for normative cohesion, at least for political victims. Once again, reconciliation along the PU front line was disturbed by the Communists. After 1956, the Kádár regime expected assistance not only from Populist patriots but also from social engineers, above all economists, who could deliver the reform programs of market socialism,[11] to reduce popular discontent. This dual strategy presupposed a controlled involvement of both camps of intellectuals in the upper-middle levels of policymaking. Kádár and Aczél applied the classical warfare of *divide et impera* in the form of what they called the strategy of "two-front struggle" and the "3T principle" (constructed from the first letters of the Hungarian words for prohibition, toleration, and support). The Communists situated themselves at the center of the political space and distanced their position from the imaginary—nationalist and liberal—extremes, the "two fronts," left and right, as they simplistically depicted them. The prohibitive regulations of censorship were gradually softened, the scope of toleration was broadened as self-censorship became habitual, and support was given in small doses to the Populists and the Urbans alternately.

The Urbans, now a large group of ex-communist intellectuals (many of the 1956 vintage) as well as a growing number of nonparty experts, moved closer to social-liberalism. The Prague Spring in 1968, the Solidarity movement in 1980/81 (neither of which concerned the Populists), and the ups and downs of the Hungarian economic reforms between 1964 and 1989 were crucial stages of the learning process leading from neo-Marxism and market socialism to liberalism. This was the first time throughout the PU controversy when the identification of liberalism and Jewishness became a mathematical nonsense. True, quite a few members of the Lukács School (Kindergarten and Creche)[12] as well as many of the so-called reform economists, that is, the two major groups of opinion leaders among the future liberals, were born in urban Jewish families. Nonetheless, they represented a diminishing share of liberal-minded professionals that rapidly grew in number (a sign of Kádárist modernization, by the way).

The redirection of the PU debate to the "Jewish versus non-Jewish" track presupposed the amortization of the Kádárist social contract of "small freedoms." The radical wing of the liberals (the so-called *samizdat* group or Democratic Opposition) rejected self-censorship at the end of the 1970s, whereas the Populists, who were still led by writers, looked for new protectors in the ruling elite to compensate for the deterioration of their relative position. This deterioration was a consequence of the devaluation of populist ideas in the eyes of the Communists, who gradually established their own—profane—principle of national legitimation based on the pride of managing "the happiest barrack in the communist camp." This management required a limited liberalization of the economy and

Westernization of the society, that is, professional (Urban) recipes rather than fine words on national virtues or anxieties about the Hungarians abroad. The secularization of communism was a menace to national romanticism: In terms of normative cohesion, a cynical communist might be closer to an Urban than to a Populist, or at least this is how the latter tended to interpret the triangle. Materialism, moral relativism, cosmopolitanism, and so on were products of a communist-liberal conspiracy, they argued, and it was not too difficult to find the obligatory Jewish intriguers in the persons of Aczél and Lukács to complete the theory.

Imre Pozsgay, who in the second half of the 1980s replaced Aczél in the job of the chief ideologue, took over part of this criticism, translated the Populists' discourse into communist language, and applied their basic themes (which ranged from social anomie, through cultural colonization to the tragedy of Hungarian minorities) in the power struggle within the party. At that time, there was once again a growing demand for the national-romanticist views of the Populists among some ruling Communists, who were frustrated by the stagnation and decay of Kádár's "economic miracle" under the aging leader. Hence the Populists regained part of their role of a spiritual *Hoflieferant*, though for their services they got too little, too late.

Playing the Game. In the first section I talked about the ghosts of Populists and Westernizers who were allowed by the Communists to rise from their graves—a risky enterprise anyway. How could their earthly activities be controlled? In the period between 1945 and 1948 the reemergence of the PU divide was inhibited by the fresh memory of the war. Quite a few Populists felt sorry for having indirectly assisted the Holocaust and regretted the myopic attitude of having quarreled with the Urbans even on the eve of the Nazi occupation of Hungary. They were not dishonest in regarding the death or the emigration of their antagonists as a victory in the normative conflict. The PU cleavage was not deepened by the new democratic polity either, because it opened a large window of opportunity to overcome the feudal legacies of the Horthy era in a joint effort.

From 1948/49 on, with the exception of the 1956 revolution, it was the Communists who controlled the development of the PU confrontation by constantly modifying the relative position of the two camps. They used stick-and-carrot techniques to balance the relationship between the nationalists and the liberals and behind-the-scenes machinations to prevent them from joining forces. By fine-tuning the rules of censorship after 1956,[13] the Communists could define the ideological frontiers as well as the main actors, themes, and languages of the PU controversy until the formation of the *samizdat* movement in the late 1970s. During the 1960s and 1970s, at least two dozen major public debates took place in Hungary. Their participants regularly used the "Populist" and "Urban" designations when interpreting the conflict in private. (In the 1980s these adjectives reappeared in public discussions as well.) What for the outside world often seemed to be a fight between Communist reformers and hard-liners, national-minded and Muscovite Communists, or conservative Marxist-Leninists and neo-Marxists frequently hid a typical PU debate as well.

The PU controversy under Communist control displayed a large variety of subjects, whereas the structure of the debates was relatively stable. As a rule, someone (either a Populist or an Urban) challenged, upon his own initiative or suggestions "from above," what was thought to be the official party line. While the Communist leaders were bargaining among themselves about the ultimate word of the party in the discussion, they mobilized their nationalist or liberal clients in and outside the party to respond to the initial challenge. The debates almost automatically turned into multilateral fights with a great many intermediary positions until the party intervened, now publicly, and playing as unbiased referee, closed the discussion by specifying the "truth" between two extremes. It was precisely this artificial definition of the extreme positions that prolonged the PU conflict through a polarization of the political discourse. No matter whether the discussions focused on "consumer socialism" or the subsidization of cultural goods in the 1960s, birth control or alcoholism in the 1970s, or the shadow economy or welfare reform in the 1980s, just to name a few,[14] they usually ended with a simultaneous disapproval of the "leftist" and "rightist" protagonists.

This was a trap because any opting out of the game would have meant risking the turn of Communist policies toward the rival group of intellectuals. And conversely, remaining in the game promised a gradual modification of the party directives in favor of one's own program. Both camps tried to exclude certain combinations. The Urbans feared the alliance of the Populists and the Communist hard-liners, and the Populists wanted to avoid the coalition of the Urbans with the reform Communists—a special version of the Prisoners' Dilemma. To many of the players who developed a sort of *Hassliebe* with each other, the art of politicking became an obsession. This game was played until some of the PU participants realized that there were chances for an agreement outside the Communist framework and its price was not prohibitively high.[15] At the end of the 1970s, the two camps ceased to communicate with each other exclusively via the weakening Communist Party. Indirect rivalry was complemented with direct—occasionally, public—cooperation for some years. The memory of the 1956 revolution, the oeuvre of the democratic theorist István Bibó (one of the few non-Populist yet non-Urban intellectuals in Hungary),[16] common anxieties about national independence, the Hungarian minorities, economic decline, pollution, and so on served as bridges between the old antagonists. "Why should we not conclude a peace treaty?" some leading Populists and Urbans began to ask themselves.

In fact, there were many reasons in favor of reconciliation. The old generation of Populist-collaborators was dying out. Many of the younger Populists still came from literary circles; nonetheless, their thought patterns were less abstract and archaic than those of their predecessors.[17] On the other side, the liberal dissidents distanced themselves from the top ideological clientele of the Communist leadership, the "Aczél boys" who were discredited in the eyes of the Populists during the "two-front battles" of the party. In principle, the noncommunist groups could have started peace negotiations with a joint agenda, because some typically populist themes (national self-determination, poverty under communism, rural stratification, critique of communist history-writing, etc.) were cultivated or even introduced in public discussions by the liberals themselves. They were no laissez-faire fundamentalists, and the Populists did not dream about "Garden Hungary" any more. The two camps were able to agree on the persons of the mediators (members of the 1956 generation), who managed to organize two major common events unprecedented in the history of anticommunist resistance after the revolution: the *samizdat* publication of the Bibó memorial volume in 1979 and the Monor meeting of intellectuals in 1985. One might have believed that the PU peace of 1956 could be repeated.

However, the Communist control proved to be effective again, the last time before 1989. The Populists, who wanted to save their integrity as a loose spiritual movement of dissenters, considered the Monor meeting as too courageous a first step in anticommunist institution building. In order to avoid the image of hard-core dissidents, they accepted the informal offer made by the Pozsgay group in the Communist leadership concerning a better protection of Hungarian national interests in and outside the country and the provision of certain cultural privileges (e.g., a new journal) for the "patriotic forces." This flirtation brought the motives of treason and sin back into the discussion and prevented the noncommunist groups from blurring the PU boundaries before the 1989 revolution. Instead, the communism-capitalism cleavage became blurred, a tragedy of most Eastern European transitions.

An Old Cleavage in a New Democracy (1989–1996)

From the Roundtable to the Pact

Western observers loved to call the year 1989 *annus mirabilis*. Dissidents in Eastern Europe were also under the spell of the unexpected implosion of communism and the rapid disintegration of the *nomenklatura*. In Hungary there was only one thing that enchanted the oppositionists more:

their own unity. The small Hungarian miracle of 1989 was "cheap" in terms of physical destruction and the Grand Deal that has informally compensated the Communist ruling elite for peaceful resignation.[18] It also proved to be inexpensive because during the so-called "constitutional" revolution, cooperation between the various groups of the anticommunist opposition (and between them and the reformist wing of the Communists) minimized the political costs of the first stages of the transition. No tanks, no strikes, no constitutional vacuum. . . .

Despite the fact that following the 1985 Monor meeting of dissidents the Populist and Urban intellectuals were busy organizing their own— National-Conservative and Liberal—political movements and building up their own parties,[19] the two camps displayed harmony on many crucial issues of the new constitution in the course of the roundtable talks during 1989. True, this harmony was disturbed by mutual suspicion in a conventional PU-style radicalism-versus-moderation debate. The Liberals tended to believe that the National-Conservatives had struck a secret deal with the nationalist wing of the Communist Party, whereas the National-Conservatives were scared by the militant moves of the Liberals. They feared that the acceleration of the revolutionary process might help unite the dislocated groups of the *nomenklatura* and provoke retaliation from Moscow.

There were serious conflicts between the former oppositionists concerning the concessions to be made to the Communists in order to buy their benevolence. (The dismantling of the secret police and the party militia, and the mode of presidential elections, were among the burning questions.) However, the common fear of missing the historical chance for holding free parliamentary elections helped them close their ranks and continue the roundtable talks. Behind the façade of recurrent rhetorical assaults on each other, a unique opportunity for PU peace seemed to crystallize. The constitution-making and the preparations for the elections produced professional players in the center of the political space. It was not only with the Communists that most of the hard-liners were marginalized in the course of the negotiations. The National-Conservatives also strengthened their West-oriented, Christian-Democratic ("national-liberal") faction to the detriment of the radical populist group in the leadership, and the Liberals, too, succeeded in placing a number of young experts (of non-Jewish origin) in the foreground of political bargaining. Optimistic observers believed at that time that a *modus vivendi* existed in the PU confrontation along the lines of liberal patriotism between social (communitarian) liberalism and "decent" nationalism. By 1989 the Liberals qualified themselves as pioneers of national independence vis-à-vis the Soviet Union and as leading activists in the environmental movement and poverty relief while coquetting with collectivist forms of ownership. At the same time, part of the National-Conservatives was ready to accept a number of liberal claims ranging from the protection of human rights to privatization. One did not have to be extremely naive to think that the two groups would skip the memory of PU strife and reach back to the common tradition of coupling "progress" with "fatherland": that is, either to the 1956 revolution, or—if it were considered too socialist oriented—to the 1848 and the 1918 revolutions, which tried to combine capitalist development with national independence in Hungary.[20]

Cooperation between the emerging political parties was first endangered by the referendum on the mode of presidential elections, which was initiated by the Liberals at the end of 1989 to prevent the National-Conservatives from tacitly supporting the Communist candidate. The Liberals won the referendum by cleverly defining its questions, which trick was considered by many of their opponents a *casus belli*. Then the fragile peace was severely hurt by the parliamentary elections during the spring of 1990, which brought a rivalry between Populists and Urbans within a modern democratic framework. After the ex-Communists had lost the competition in the first round, the National-Conservatives and Liberals wounded each other deeply in an outburst of repressed indignation and hatred. The populist radicals were eagerly searching for communist Jews in the families of the "nationless" Liberal candidates, while some of the Liberals questioned the good faith, the expertise, and the "Europeanness" of their National-Conservative rivals. As far as the respective political programs were concerned, the National-Conservatives took pride in national liberation, Hungarian traditions, Christian values, and the like and promised a smooth transition in the economy, and the Liberals emphasized the constitutional elements of the revolution (parliamentary democracy, rule of law, human rights, private ownership, and so on) and predicted a bumpy road of the economic transformation. In occupying the National-Conservative and the Liberal halves of the political field, the two camps blamed each other for expropriating and distorting the patriotic and the democratic messages, respectively, and excluding the rival parties from a valuable part of the political discourse.

The damage was partly repaired by the last piece of anticommunist realpolitik right after the elections that ended with a victory of the three National-Conservative parties. A few prominent representatives of the two leading parties in the government and the opposition signed a *sub rosa* pact of power sharing, which reinforced the National-Conservative government vis-à-vis the Parliament but placed the executive branch under Liberal supervision by the president of the Republic, a president who was practically appointed by the opposition. This was the first (and so far the last) major agreement between Populist and Urban forces that followed pragmatic routines of political cooperation.

The Erosion of the Pact and the Birth of the Charta

Although the Liberals attained a landslide victory in the local elections held during the autumn of 1990, providing an opportunity for power sharing between the central and local governments, that is, between the National-Conservatives and the Liberals, a series of highly emotional quarrels erupted instead. The populist radicals, who had not been consulted before the pact was signed, accused the moderates in their own camp of compromising the democratic elections by behind-the-scenes deals with the archenemy. They tried to discipline their colleagues by launching heavy ideological offensives against the Liberals, who were depicted in a familiar style: (1) as urban Jews who, instead of allowing themselves to be assimilated, make successful efforts to assimilate the ethnic Hungarians; and (2) as demagogues who cannot represent the nation with as much moral devotion as the real patriots.[21]

The Liberals in turn were embarrassed by the rapid establishment of new clientelist networks under National-Conservative leadership, the spread of state intervention in business, and the extension of government control in the media, in education, and in the private lives of the citizens under the banner of authoritarian, nationalist slogans from the 1930s. As a typical overreaction, the Liberals did not exclude the possibility of dismissing the government through civil disobedience in the course of a nationwide cab drivers' strike in October 1990—a strike that might have had a violent end if the Liberal president of the Republic had not ruled out the use of force by the government (a typical overreaction on the opposite side).

As a consequence, by the winter of 1990/91, that is, one year after the conclusion of the Roundtable Agreement and half a year after the parliamentary elections, PU relations were again animated by scandals.[22] The influence of the mediating personalities weakened, and negotiated compromises were replaced by rhetorical intransigence. To a certain degree, the mutual accusations became self-fulfilling prophecies. Those blamed as protofascists among the National-Conservatives approached the political right; and those blamed as "Liberal-Bolsheviks" joined forces with the moderate faction of the Neo-Socialists in the Democratic Charta, a loose organization created by leftist liberal intellectuals to prevent the authoritarian degeneration of the revolution. This is where the PU dialogue finally came to a standstill. The moderate National-Conservatives broke with the radical Populists in their ranks too late (in 1993), while the Liberals allowed the Neo-Socialists to come out of political quarantine too early (in 1991). And the two camps did not stop quarreling with each other even when the army of the Neo-Socialists stood already *ante portas*.

The Neo-Socialist Breakthrough

The birth of the Charta marks not only the end of rational political strategies to bridge the PU gap through internal agreements. It also indicates the beginning of a new kind of rationality, namely, a pragmatic strategy to circumvent and neglect the entire controversy. This strategy was formulated by the Young Liberals, then adopted by the Neo-Socialists. Ironically, the old pupil proved to be smarter than his young teacher. The Neo-Socialists managed to abstain from the PU debate and enfranchise their own Urban and Populist sympathizers under the flexible heading of social democracy (something considered European *and* patriotic, liberal *and* solidaristic, modern *and* traditional). At the same time, the Young Liberals alienated a great number of intellectuals (and a much greater number of voters) by emphatically rejecting the whole debate, yet simultaneously flirting with both camps. Eventually, they could not help drifting into the PU conflict.

The Young Liberals embarked upon democratic politics in 1989 with a clear program of PU neutrality. They declared the cleavage to be anachronistic, tragicomic, and inconceivable in terms of pragmatic policymaking.[23] In this spirit, they often distanced themselves from their liberal allies in opposition whenever the latter engaged in an ideological quarrel with the National-Conservatives on national symbols (holidays, coat of arms, anthem, etc.), the interpretation of history (fascism and communism in Hungary, retroactive justice, etc.), and human rights. The Young Liberals regarded the communist versus noncommunist divide as more important than the PU conflict within the noncommunist half of the political spectrum. Doubting the social democratic conversion of the former Communists, they came closer to the National-Conservative parties at the right-of-center. By now the language the Young Liberals use fits in well with the PU framework in many respects (they identify the Liberals with the Neo-Socialists and blame them for free-market orthodoxy, for disregarding family, church, and national issues, for sacrificing the domestic small entrepreneurs and monopolizing the public media, etc.). Nevertheless, this kind of populism (currently they call themselves "civic democrats") is less traditionalist and more liberal than the populism still represented by the radicals in the National-Conservative camp.

Until now, the Neo-Socialists have been able to resist the temptation to get involved in the PU conflict. As with the Young Liberals, this was a deliberate action in order for them to qualify as modern pragmatists, the only label that might cover the seamy side of the Communist Party's past. This label required deep silence on the PU controversy and on any ideology-based division, be it a left-right, a Populist-Urban, or a capitalist-communist typology. Otherwise, these classification schemes would have harmed the image of the Neo-Socialists, striving for relegitimation, who embodied all contradictions reflected by these schemes. Their election program went like this: reformation with a human face, social market economy, capitalism with national specifics—this is what we—that is, the liberal and patriotic factions of the Hungarian Communists—wanted to achieve from the 1960s on. We will be proud to perform the hard task of "building up capitalism" with social and national responsibility, the Neo-Socialist ideologues said, cross-cutting the traditional PU divide well before their victory in 1994. We are the only guarantee that the pointless ideological debates between self-interested groups of Budapest intellectuals will be terminated and replaced by real progress in transformation. We will act, not talk, and find the middle ground between liberal and national-conservative fundamentalism. . . .

Disillusionment and Fatigue

Half of this prediction was correct. The PU controversy lost much of its fervor in 1995 and 1996, although this was partly because of the lack of the promised "real progress" in transformative politics. A substantial part of the PU conflict has been absorbed by the Neo-Socialist–Liberal coalition. The liberal program has become an amorphous practical project because it has repeatedly been subdued by the Neo-Socialists within the government. True, in principle the very fact of the government coalition can rekindle the embers of the confrontation at any time, but so far the references to the "worldwide Jewish conspiracy of the Communists and the Liberals" have come basically from outside the Parliament.

Thanks to the weakening of the radicals among the National-Conservatives following their election defeat and the growing influence of the Young Liberals in the opposition, illiberal voices in the Parliament are most often heard in the ranks of the Smallholders, a party of—let us call it—post-PU (or postmodern) populism. Although this party had much to do with the Hungarian peasantry before World War II, in its program agrarian populism has always been mixed with the vision of medium-sized capitalist enterprise in the countryside and entrepreneurship in urban areas. After 1989 the Smallholders borrowed part of the radical discourse of the National-Conservatives; now they would like to represent the underclass against any establishment. There is no intellectual coherence in their political moves, and there are no visionary intellectuals in the leadership of the party. The political engineers of the Smallholders are not blurring or denying (like the Neo-Socialists and the Young Liberals) the PU cleavages but alternately or simultaneously representing the conflicting, even the diametrically opposing, visions. Accordingly, while insisting on a generalized antiestablishment rhetoric and using all technical instruments of populism (exaggerated promises, mass mobilization, charismatic leader, etc.), they ridicule the basics of the PU controversy.[24]

In 1998 there will be parliamentary elections in Hungary again. By extrapolating the 1990–1994 cycle of PU quarrels, one could predict the resurgence of heated debates in the political arena very soon. By now, however, a substantial part of the classical PU arguments has become irrelevant, and the marginal electoral profits that can be earned by sharpening the PU conflict seem to be comparatively small. The compromise between the Liberals and the Neo-Socialists devalued some of the typical accusations (lack of social responsibility, obsession with the free market, etc.) leveled at the Liberals by the National-Conservatives. Moreover, the Liberals and the National-Conservatives learned from the success of Neo-Socialists (the *lachende Dritte*) that a deep involvement in the PU controversy can backfire. Finally, the danger of postmodern (unpredictable because unprincipled) populism may bring together the moderates in the respective PU camps against the common enemy.

In other words, the political space in Hungary is becoming composed of three segments: a social-liberal, a moderate conservative, and a radical nationalist-populist segment. Purely for mathematical reasons, a three-person game offers more opportunity for cooperation and cross-cutting conflicts than a two-person game with relatively homogeneous blocs of Liberals and National-Conservatives. The professionalization of postcommunist politics, that is, the replacement of visionary intellectuals by clerks in the new parties, also contributes to reconciliation. Intellectuals in both PU camps feel betrayed by the growing cynicism of the "political animals" within their own parties and frustrated by the recurrent compromises in the political game and the corruption across party lines. The disenchantment that followed an already none-too-enchanting revolution has gradually deprived the PU confrontation of its romantic overtones.[25] The participants in the controversy also recognize that the narrow space for maneuvering in the postcommunist transformation and the complicated procedures of democratic decisionmaking often reduce the large ideological distances between the Populist and Urban positions to minuscule intervals. The parliamentary discussions of the laws on abortion, reprivatization, or teaching religion at schools (just to select three heated debates from the early 1990s) evidenced this convergence in legislation. Business as usual in postcommunist political life results in a growing fatigue for the participants in the PU confrontation. Would rapprochement be based on disillusionment and fatigue?

Resolving or Civilizing the Conflict?

Changing the Plot and Keeping the Scenes

Modern democratic politics has instrumentalized—revitalized, exploited, and partly moderated—a traditional normative conflict in Hungary. Politics was, however, not only a villain but also a victim in the PU play. In 1989 the confrontation between the Populists and the Urbans was already precoded in the mentality of the new political class. Even if the first noncommunist leaders had arrived in Hungary from the moon, they would not have been able to recruit their entourage from among intellectuals who did not think and speak in PU terms at all, whose life stories were not permeated with the memory of the debate, and whose social networks and cultural institutions were not shaped by personal PU commitments. In any event, recruitment had an opposite direction. The potential advisers became politicians almost overnight. It was exactly these members of the Hungarian intelligentsia (primarily social scientists and writers) who occupied the commanding heights of the transformation and entered the first free "Parliament of historians, poets, and lawyers."

They brought along their friends and colleagues (and not infrequently, their clients and family members), with all their political preferences, language routines, and images of the enemy, the past, and the future. The typical "revolutionary" in Hungary was no Young Liberal allegedly immune to the PU discourse but a gentleman from the 1956 or the 1968 generation, that is, males with university background who were between forty and sixty and who had not been dissidents—on the contrary, normal citizens of "goulash communism," former Communist Party members or adherents to—at least partly—collectivist ideologies (Marxism, social-liberalism, nationalism, authoritarian conservativism, etc.). Hence, the normative toolboxes of the new political actors were almost full; one could reach into them with a reflex motion at the first occasion of conflict. In 1989 the militant strategies of the PU confrontation were fresh not because they had been kept in the "communist refrigerator" for forty years but because they had not been frozen in 1948/49.

Unfortunately, in 1989 the very possibility of the transition from communism reinforced the beliefs of the two camps in the conventional dichotomies. At first sight, the whole *problématique* of the transformation seemed to revalidate the old alternatives of modernization: joining Western capitalism in a European framework or taking one of the Third Roads within national boundaries? imitation or experimentation? progress or fatherland? Both approaches involved a return to history to find "clean sources" before they had become poisoned by the Communists. Under the shock of the unexpected fall of the Soviet system and the pressure of rapid identity creation, the new political elite did not have much time to disentangle the complicated web of similarities and differences between the 1930s, the postwar years, 1956, and the 1990s. As a consequence, very few intellectuals bothered themselves with second thoughts about the obsolescence of some old PU conflicts and the rapprochement between the original positions under (and because of) communism.

This also explains the remarkable continuity of the PU controversy in Hungary. It was not only a political but also a rhetorical drama that contributed to the prolongation of the old debate. "Back to the 1930s: Changing the Plot and Keeping the Scenes"—this is how I would entitle the play.[26] While the Urbans were looking for their ancestors primarily in the 1956 revolution and the short-lived democracy of 1945–1948, the Populists found their golden age between the two wars. Probably the 1930s would not have irritated the Liberals so much, if that decade had only symbolized the plebeian tradition of antiliberalism. However, the Christian Democratic allies of the Populists within the ruling party found their heroes in the same period, emphasizing the Christian, national, and middle-class oriented character of the Horthy regime. This combination of plebeian and elitist symbols (a historical nonsense by the way) could have simply made the Liberals laugh. They exploded instead as they heard the familiar passwords: Trianon, Christian middle class, Jewish capitalism, heroism of the Hungarian soldiers in World War II, etc. The Urbans, who were always accused by the Populists of being ahistorical, let themselves be directed by their memory.

The scene of the PU play of the 1930s was rapidly reconstructed, so it took some years for the actors to realize that the plot has grossly changed in the meantime. The economic programs of the political parties converged[27] and the main lines of the liberal-democratic constitution written by the participants of the roundtable talks in 1989 were not questioned by the National-Conservatives. The controversy of the 1930s was essentially a pre-totalitarianism controversy. In the 1990s, that is, in a post-totalitarian phase and in a Western (or global) environment, it became rather difficult to represent utopian, dirigist, autocratic, etc. programs, at least on the level of practical policymaking. In other words, the Urbans, whoever they were, have won the cultural war in Hungary: The convergence took place on their half of the scene rather than somewhere in the middle. Nevertheless, the defeat has incited the radical Populists to start desperate rear-guard battles on the level of political rhetoric with the aim of reconquering the scene until the lease of the theater (i.e., the Parliament) expires.

With the benefit of hindsight, one can state that these were typical ersatz-fights, although they were instrumental in destroying some bridges over the PU gap. It did not make a great difference when the members of the Parliament were discussing for weeks whether the royal crown should feature in the national coat of arms, whether a politician may call his colleague unpatriotic, or whether it had been correct to attack the Soviet Union in 1941. At the same time, the rhetorical quarrels created a cultural atmosphere in which vital questions of daily transformative politics such as privatization, economic stabilization, welfare reform, local self-government, and the like could not be answered in pragmatic terms, and similarly vital issues of human and civic rights such as abortion, the legal position of the church, media control, and so on, could not be discussed in a relatively detached manner. The passions prevented a reasonable compromise between the converging programs. It became clear that the two camps can dislike each other even in the lack of dictators to flirt with.

Meditation on Mediation

The rhetorical prolongation of the debate notwithstanding, the passionate outbursts were less frequent in 1995 and 1996. If we review the various techniques of PU conflict resolution over the past six decades, we do not find a single negotiated peace settlement. Rather, provisional truces were fabricated without firm peacekeeping arrangements. Even the most recent cease-fire (more exactly, "low-intensity warfare") is only partly intentional: It stems to a large extent from common frustration. Denying, ignoring, or ridiculing the confrontation, that is, the latest innovations in PU peacemaking, seem to be helpful in immediate crisis prevention. Although even the imminent danger of a Neo-Socialist breakthrough did not lead to a reduction in the grand gap between the Populists and the Urbans, the bridging of smaller gaps has begun under the pressure of parliamentary realpolitik. The Liberals and the Neo-Socialists on the one hand and the Young Liberals and the National-Conservatives on the other have got closer to each other. Because of these rearrangements there is a growing conviction in Hungary that the PU conflict has no cultural-ideological but "only" civilized, pragmatic solutions. The conflict can be moderated, swept under the carpet, or in the best case, left behind and forgotten, but not resolved. Like a subterranean river, it can break out onto the surface at any time.

The participants in the PU debate have understood that competitive democracy is no panacea: It may cyclically sharpen the conflicts, as well as prevent them from developing into a cultural war. Prevention would mean self-defense, that is, a consensus based on the vested interests of the potential belligerents in the political class to freeze, delay, and thus probably outlive the confrontations. Can this spontaneous process be accelerated by mediation? If one meant by mediation a kind of Freudian therapy whereby prejudices and suppressed aggressive feelings are articulated and memories are mobilized and interpreted to liberate the "patient," I would be rather skeptical about the result of the treatment. The naming of the various stigmas and allegations can revive the hostilities, particularly if no impartial mediator is available. Human speech may be dangerous: In a cultural war that from time to time has been associated with real wars, you can kill with words. Also, it may happen that one of the conflicting partners ab ovo rejects rational dispute as part and parcel of the opponent's cultural heritage. In any event, mediation requires from the antagonists a certain extent of sobriety, an ability to engage in a dialogue and to accept an arbitrator. What if the patients do not want to see the doctor? "Hate speech," stigmatization, and scapegoating are not the most favorable preconditions for mediation. Self-appointed mediators such as the revolutionaries of 1956, the financier George Soros, or the writer Péter Esterházy (a liberal-minded aristocrat), who all acted in good faith, have not been able to attain lasting results thus far.

Would it be better to leave the collective subconscious as it is, to avoid clear language ("don't ask who shot first," "call the massacre a sad event"), and to accept a kind of moratorium on the therapy? Postwar Germany, France, Austria, and others provide—better or worse—examples for postponing the payment of historical bills and replacing memory with oblivion/amnesia.[28] Also, I wonder if one can advise a "forget rather than talk" moratorium after so many decades of another moratorium under communism that converted almost the same topics of the PU controversy into taboos? Should we create institutions instead that—in contrast to the psychiatrist—perform mediation in an impersonal manner? Western observers tend to trust the emerging civil society in Eastern Europe. Its institutions may localize, fragment, and intersect the big normative conflicts, they say. Will the Populists and the Urbans reconcile with each other if they join the same club of stamp collectors? It may be, especially if one has in mind other, quasi-political organizations of the civil society such as professional associations, single-issue movements, or the church. Unfortunately, the current experience in Hungary shows the duplication of civic initiatives and their integration by the parties: Probably we already have a Populist and an Urban club of stamp collectors. Should one then long for a common enemy (an imperialist Russia, chauvinists in the neighborhood, unreconstructed Communists, and postmodern populists at home or—*horribile dictu*—an ultracentralist European Union) again? Or should we prefer the Yugoslav solution of pushing the confrontation to its extremes in order to compromise it forever? Hopefully, there are less painful ways of PU peacemaking.

Since 1989 democracy has taught the participants in the PU debate to negotiate with each other and honor second-best solutions in the political process. They learned that the language of professional policymaking is rarely bipolar. Multiparty politics with all its lobbying mechanisms helped break the PU dichotomy by cross-cutting the confrontation. Conflicting norms were translated into conflicting interests; business groups entered the scene; new buffer zones emerged; and it turned out that there *are* common solutions. Neither of the two groups could find its "one and only" electorate. Hungarian society did not allow itself to be segmented into two halves such as the winners and losers of the postcommunist transformation, Western or Eastern Hungary, towns and villages, etc. Representative democracy forced the antagonists to pluralize their agendas, and pluralization meant overlapping programs. Parliamentarism urged many Populists to accept bargaining as such, to obey constitutional procedures and to exchange romantic language for professional discourse. Similarly, it convinced the Urbans that the Populists are inferior partners in a rational discussion only until they learn to accept the rules of the game. Then a veritable rivalry begins between the two sides, neither of which can be sure about his superiority in professional, ideological, or moral terms. So much for the sunny side of democracy.

However cynical it may sound, I would put much faith also in the deficiencies of parliamentary politics and the fin de siècle uncertainty in the field of political ideologies. Ironically, the symptoms of decay, which Western analysts like to enumerate when burying their old democracies (popular distrust of institutions, large-scale corruption, overcomplicated procedures, unfair coalitions, the relativization of political philosophies, etc.), in the new democracies of Eastern Europe may well promote reconciliation through common frustration along the PU front line. True, like in the West, the weakening of liberalism and the success of postmodern populism may be the price of this frustration. Nevertheless, the imperfections of the democratic system work against liberal complacency and reduce the humiliation of the Populist losers: It is not a winner-take-all situation. As a consequence, the demand for prophecies may diminish on both sides. In the optimal case, a common search for non-utopian solutions may follow, in which the former antagonists subscribe to a common minimum of democratic/liberal rules, and in a joint effort, discipline the radicals and exclude the extremists from parliamentary communication.

In a sense, this end-of-century-style democracy made the "uncertain ghosts" of both camps even more uncertain and reduced their direct political activity. The exodus of the party intellectuals from politics has already begun. On the one hand, they were pushed out by professionals, and on the other, they could no longer tolerate that the rank and file betrayed the "sacred" principles of their parties. This largely reduced the heat of the PU strife. A further reduction is expected from the ongoing marketization of the cultural spheres, marketization that should wash away the difference between the state-sponsored intellectuals and the "pariahs"—Populists or Urbans, depending on which camp is in the government.

In 1994 it was the Hungarian citizens who voted for a desacralization in party politics. They made the political class understand that they are not really interested in symbols and memories. By elevating the Neo-Socialists to the government, the electorate happened to be the most powerful mediator in the history of the *Kulturkampf*. All things considered, it was the voters who started to "civilize" the conflict, that is, like in advanced Western democracies, to keep the hostilities under control (or outside the Parliament). The former enemies feel a bit uneasy in the new atmosphere of partial tolerance. In some years, however, the repeated political compromises between them may result in some cultural synthesis of national-conservativism and social liberalism.[29] Until then, I would not speak of conflict resolution.

With all my respect for the merits as well as the shortcomings of democracy, let me doubt that without a Hungarian *Wirtschaftswunder*, the road leading from truce to peace can be substantially shortened and the ghosts sent back to their graves. The German, Japanese, and other economic miracles after the war were contingent upon normative mediation from outside (not to mention generous economic assistance by the West). In a sense, the losers were sentenced to democratization and liberalization. In contrast to these "happy" losers, those who were defeated in the Cold War forty-four years later receive comparatively less economic aid and even less normative assistance. In Hungary, if one disregards the initiatives of some foreign (primarily German and American) foundations to bring the quarreling parties closer to each other, the International Monetary Fund and the World Bank were the only external mediators, as a Budapest joke says. Why them, precisely? Because with their unavoidable austerity packages they achieved what no one could achieve in the history of the PU conflict: Half of the liberals converted to populism.

In the absence of Western occupation and a new Marshall Plan, the Populists and the Urbans in Hungary have to work hard to build some kind of normative cohesion from inside. If they succeed, it will be such a formidable accomplishment that even the driest liberals will be imbued with national pride. But how will the nationalists tolerate that?

Notes

I wish to express my gratitude to Éva Kovács for her comments on the manuscript for this chapter.

1. In these clichés the elitist and mystical Slavophils are identified with the later *narodniks*, the real forefathers of Eastern European populists, who were radical agrarian socialists (anarchists) rather than devoted nationalists. For a conceptual clarification, see Daniel Chirot, "Ideology, Reality, and Competing Models of Development in Eastern Europe Between the Two World Wars," *East European Politics and Societies* 3 (1989); Ernest Gellner, *Nationalismus in Osteuropa* (Vienna, 1992); Ernest Gellner, *Encounters with Nationalism* (Oxford, 1994); Liah Greenfeld, *Nationalism: Five Roads to Modernity* (Cambridge, Mass., 1992); Ghita Ionescu and Ernest Gellner, eds., *Populism, Its Meanings and National Characteristics* (London, 1969); George Schöpflin, "Conservatism in Central and Eastern Europe," in J. M. Kovács, ed., *Transition to Capitalism? The Communist Legacy in Eastern Europe* (New

Brunswick, N.J., 1994); F. Venturi, *Les intellectuels, le Peuple at la Révolution: Histoire du populisme russe* (Paris, 1972); Andrzej Walicki, *Legal Philosophies of Russian Liberalism* (Oxford, 1967); Andrzej Walicki, *The Controversy over Capitalism* (Oxford, 1969); Andrzej Walicki, *The Slavophile Controversy* (Oxford, 1975).

2. See Jerzy Szacki, *Liberalism After Communism* (Budapest, 1995); J. M. Kovács, ed., "Rediscovery of Liberalism in Eastern Europe," *East European Politics and Societies*, special issue, Winter 1991.

3. In my view, postmodern populists in Eastern Europe such as Vladimir Meciar, Voislav Sheshel', József Torgyán, Stanislaw Tyminski, and Vladimir Zhirinovsky rely on a traditional antiestablishment discourse, that is, a basically premodern critique of competitive democracy while relativizing the romantic anticapitalist message of their predecessors. For the similarity of their programs with those of Umberto Bossi, Pat Buchanan, Jörg Haider, Jean-Marie Le Pen, or Ross Perot, see J. M. Kovács: "Haider in Ungarn: Notizen zum postmodernen Populismus," *Transit* 11 (1996).

4. See J. M. Kovács, "Which Institutionalism? Searching for Paradigms of Transformation in Eastern European Economic Thought," in Hans-Jürgen Wagener, ed., *The Political Economy of Transformation* (Heidelberg, 1993).

5. See Béla Greskovits, "Demagogic Populism in Eastern Europe?" *Telos*, Winter 1995.

6. Probably a comparative study of the Czech Republic, Hungary, Poland, and some of the ex-Yugoslav republics would deliver the most balanced history of the Populist–Westernizer conflict in Eastern Europe. Bulgaria, Romania, Slovakia, and the ex-Soviet countries show a shorter period of embourgeoisement and/or a longer phase of hard-line communism. Unfortunately, with Russia one loses a well-cultivated, broad research field and the most spectacular confrontation in the nineteenth century. In the case of Yugoslavia the recurrent ethnic fights camouflage (or suspend) the conflicts between the Populists and the Westernizers. In modern Czech history the agrarian question was always less important than in other countries of the region; nonetheless, the Slavophil connection in the nineteenth century reinforced the populist option. Also, the revival of hard-line communism after the Prague Spring prolonged the break in the Populist–Westernizer controversy. As regards Poland, the hegemony of Catholicism may hide deep cleavages between the nationalists and the liberals. The belonging to Western Christianity and the incessant claim for independence from Russia made Polish populism less "Eastern."

7. Below I will formally accept these self-designations but challenge their contents step by step.

8. The roots of the PU debate in Hungary go back to the nineteenth century, although then the principles of "fatherland" and "progress," to use the terminology of the time, still seemed to be complementary for a large part of the political and cultural elite. The collapse of the Austro-Hungarian monarchy, the Trianon peace treaty, the massive assimilation of Jews, the rapidly growing number of the intelligentsia, the communist dictatorship in 1919, the postwar stagnation, the Great Depression, and the delaying of agrarian reforms in the 1920s were all essential reasons for the separation of the two principles in the first decades of the twentieth century.

9. For a literature on the first round of the PU controversy, see Gyula Borbándi, *Der ungarische Populismus* (Munich, 1976); Ferenc Donáth, *A Márciusi Fronttól Monorig* [From the March Front to Monor] (Budapest, 1992); Ferenc Fejtö, *Budapesttöl Párizsig* [From Budapest to Párizs] (Budapest, 1990); Ferenc Fejtö, "A zsidóság és a népi-urbánus vita" [The Jewry and the Populist-Urban Debate] *Századvég* 2 (1990); Gyula Juhász, *Uralkodó eszmék Magyarországon (1939–1944)* [Dominant Ideas in Hungary] (Budapest, 1983); Miklós Lackó, *Korszellem és tudomány* [Zeitgeist and Science] (Budapest, 1988); András Lengyel, *Utak és csapdák* [Roads and Traps] (Budapest, 1994); Péter Sz. Nagy, ed., *A népi-urbánus vita dokumentumai (1932–1947)* [Anthology of the Populist-Urban Debate] (Budapest, 1990); Dénes Némedi, ed., *A népi szociográfia* [The Populist Sociography] (Budapest, 1985); György Poszler, "Görbe tükör és forgatókönyv: Népiek és urbánusok a marxista kritikában (1937–1943)" [Populists and Urbans in Marxist Critique], *Társadalmi Szemle* 2 (1993); Konrád Salamon, *Utak a Márciusi Front felé* [Roads to the March Front] (Budapest, 1982); Miklós Szabó, *Politikai kultúra Magyarországon* [Political Culture in Hungary] (Budapest, 1989).

10. While the word "Populist" (*népi, népies*) had appeared already in the nineteenth century, the designation "Urban" (*urbánus*) was first used, characteristically in its Latin version, in the late 1920s. The liberals applied it as a synonym of educated, modern, sophisticated, "European" world outlook to contrast it with the backwardness of the countryside, whereas the Populists associated the term with adjectives such as alien, artificial, criminal, and the like (See András Lengyel, op. cit.). The only participant in the debate who acquired world fame is the Paris historian François Fejtö from the Urban group.

11. See György Konrád and Iván Szelényi, *The Intellectuals on the Road to Class Power* (New York, 1979); J. M. Kovács, "Compassionate Doubts About Reform Economics (Science, Ideology, Politics)," in J. M. Kovács and M. Tardos, eds., *Reform and Transformation: Eastern European Economics on the Threshold of Change* (London, 1992); J. M. Kovács, "Planning the Transformation? Notes About the Legacy of the Reform Economists," in J. M. Kovács, ed., *Transition to Capitalism?* op. cit.

12. See Marc Rakovski (György Bence and János Kis), *Towards an East-European Marxism* (London, 1978).

13. See Miklós Haraszti, *The Velvet Prison: Artists Under State Socialism* (New York, 1987).

14. See Ervin Csizmadia, *A magyar demokratikus ellenzék (1968–1988)* [The Democratic Opposition in Hungary] (Budapest, 1995); Mária Heller, Dénes Némedi, and Agnes Rényi, "Népesedési viták" [Debates on Population Growth], *Századvég* 2 (1990); "A magyar nyilvánosság szerkezetváltozásai a Kádár-rendszerben" [Structural Changes in Hungarian Public Life Under the Kádár Regime], in Péter Somlai, ed., *Ertékrendek és társadalmi-kulturális változások* (Budapest, 1992).

15. The lures of the Communist trap were partly neutralized by the philanthropic activities of the Hungarian-born Jewish American businessman, George Soros, who launched his aid program in Hungary in the middle of the 1980s with the sincere aim of filling the gap between Populists and Urbans. Besides Aczél and Lukács, he became the third demon in the new anti-Semitic mythology of the 1990s.

16. See István Bibó, *Zur Judenfrage: Am Beispiel Ungarns nach 1944* (Frankfurt, 1990); István Bibó, *Die Misere der osteuropäischen Kleinstaaterei* (Frankfurt, 1992); Ferenc Donáth, op. cit.

17. Eva Standeisky, "A népi irók és a hatalom" [The Populist Writers and the Communist Power], *Holmi* 10 (1994); Mária Heller, Dénes Némedi, and Agnes Rényi, "A népies beszédmód alakváltozásai az elmúlt harminc évben" [Changes in the Populist Discourse over the Last Thirty Years], in *Közelítések* (Budapest, 1991).

18. Elemér Hankiss, *Eastern European Alternatives: Are There Any?* (Oxford, 1990); László Bruszt and David Stark, "Remaking the Political Field in Hungary: From the Politics of Confrontation to the Politics of Competition," in Ivo Banac, ed., *Eastern Europe in Revolution* (Ithaca, 1991); András Bozóki, "Hungary's Road to Systemic Change: The Opposition Roundtable," *East European Politics and Societies*, Spring 1993.

19. The *dramatis personae* are as follows: The *National-Conservatives* comprised the Hungarian Democratic Forum; the Christian Democratic People's Party (Christian-Democrats); and the Independent Smallholders' Party (Smallholders). The *Liberals* comprised the Alliance of Free Democrats (Liberals) and the Alliance of Young Democrats (Young Liberals). The *Neo-Socialists* on the scene were in the Hungarian Socialist Party (successor of the reformist majority of the former Communist Party). From 1990 to 1994 the leading force of the National-Conservative government coalition was the Hungarian Democratic Forum. Since 1994 its popularity has decreased (in 1996 the party split in two), while that of the Smallholders has grown. The Christian-Democrats' position has not changed. The Free Democrats were the leading party of the opposition from 1990 to 1994. In 1994, after the landslide victory of the Socialist Party (formerly the smallest in the opposition) the Free Democrats joined them in the government. Since then both of them have lost much of their popularity. The Young Democrats, who had been close allies of the Free Democrats, started to cooperate with the National-Conservatives in the opposition after the 1994 elections. Their popularity is growing.

20. For the post-1989 round of the PU controversy, see Gyula Borbándi, "A népiségkritika nyomorúsága" [The Misery of Criticizing the Populists], *Valóság* 4 (1993); András Bozóki, "Vázlat három populizmusról" [An Outline of Three Populisms], *Politikatudományi Szemle* 3 (1994); Mária Heller and Agnes Rényi, "Discourse Strategies in the New Hungarian Public Sphere: From the Populist–Urban Controversy to the Hungarian-Jewish Confrontation," in Krisztina Mänicke-Gyöngyösi, ed., *Öffentliche Konfliktdiskurse um Restitution von Gerechtigkeit, politische Verantwortung und nationale Identität* (Frankfurt, 1996); Eva Kovács, "Volkstümliche und Urbanisten," *Österreichische Zeitschrift für Geschichte* 6 (1994); Péter Kende, "A lovagi ütközet vége?" [Will the Knightly Struggle End?], *Mozgó Világ* 11 (1994); Miklós Lackó, "Népiesség tegnap és ma" [Populism Yesterday and Today], *2000* 10 (1992); Sándor Radnóti, "A populizmusról" [On Populism], *Kritika* 6 (1992); G. M. Tamás, "Farewell to the Left," *East European Politics and Societies*, Winter 1991; G. M. Tamás, "Ahogyan az ember forgószélben viselkedik" [As One Behaves in a Tornado], *Valóság* 10 (1992). See also the special issue of the journal *Századvég* 2 (1990): *Népiek és urbánusok—egy mitosz vége?* [Populists and Urbans—End of a Myth?], especially the response to its questionnaire by András Gergely,

András Gerö, Géza Hegedüs, Péter Kende, László Lengyel, György Litván, György Szabad, Iván Szelényi, Akos Szilágyi, G. M. Tamás, and Mihály Vajda.

21. See Sándor Csoóri, *Nappali hold* [Moon by Day] (Budapest, 1991); Sándor Radnóti, "Etnosz és démosz" [Ethnos and Demos], *Holmi* 6 (1992).

22. See István Csurka, *Uj magyar önépítés* [New Hungarian Self-Construction] (Budapest, 1991); István Csurka, "Néhány gondolat a rendszerváltozásról" [Thoughts about the Change of the System], *Magyar Fórum*, August 20, 1992.

23. See "Népiek és urbánusok," *Századvég*, op. cit.; János Gyurgyák, "Valahol megint utat vesztettünk" [Somewhere we have lost our way again], *2000* 9 (1994).

24. See J. M. Kovács: "Haider in Ungarn," op. cit.

25. The 1989 revolution in Hungary was not glorious, if one does not admire its pragmatic sequence. The first prime minister in the new democracy was no dissident under the Communists, he directed a museum; the second worked as a typical manager of a socialist firm; the third (present) was a member of the Communist terror groups after 1956. One of the chairmen of the two radical populist parties admitted that he served as a secret police agent in the 1960s; the other is still denying that he did.

26. See the articles cited earlier by Kende, Lackó (1992), Radnóti, and Tamás.

27. See Béla Greskovits, "Populista átmenet-programok Magyarországon" [Populist Programs of the Transition in Hungary], *2000* 7 (1996).

28. See Tony Judt, "The Past Is Another Country," *Daedalus*, Fall 1992.

29. It is difficult to predict whether this rapprochement can take place on the level of party politics. Today, the Liberals are embraced by the Neo-Socialists, and the Young Liberals seem to oscillate between moderate and radical National-Conservatives. In any case, it would not harm the peace process if it were preceded by an "apolitical dialogue." See János Kis, "Túl a nemzetállamon" [Beyond the Nation State], *Beszélö* 3/4 (1996).

5

Revolution from the Top and Horizontal Mediation: The Case of Chile's Transition to Democracy

Arturo Fontaine Talavera

From the Cleavage of Marxism to the Cleavage of the Military Government

In the early 1930s the following thesis spread in Chilean society as in many other places: Bourgeois society, which was liberal, democratic, and capitalist, was dying and would inevitably disappear.[1] One alternative, the most attractive, widespread, and promising, was Marx's historical materialism. Another was fascism, which never achieved in Chile the status of a popular movement of any significance. The other was the *terza via* (third way) favored by the social doctrine of the Catholic Church. The issue of poverty became the most pressing and what to do about it was the defining problem. The cleavage thus became socioeconomic.

Marxism was disseminated from state-run universities, and it quickly attracted leading cultural figures who would soon play important roles. Pablo Neruda and Violeta Parra were communists. Poetry and musical folklore became "committed" and "revolutionary." Many scientists and humanists felt that their thoughts were congruently or congenially interpreted. The foundation of the Communist Party in 1917, led by Luis Emilio Recabarren, gave the intellectual élite a chance to set up an alliance with labor union leaders. The latter, grouped in Federación Obrera de Chile (Chilean Labor Federation, FOCH) joined the International Red Union, with headquarters in Moscow, that same year. From its inception, the Chilean Communist Party had a twofold source of support: the intellectuals, often the sons and daughters of European immigrants, and the unions. The size of the Communist project in Chile was not measured only by the number of votes. Proof of its influence was observed in the effect it had on other parties.

For instance, the breakup of the Conservative Party and the emergence of the Christian Democratic Party were to a considerable extent the result of the need felt by youthful leaders to raise a new project against Communism. Eduardo Frei Montalva would come to office in 1964 with the slogan "Revolution in freedom," as opposed to the "Socialist revolution" represented by Salvador Allende. In the 1960s, during the Frei administration, the Christian Democrats would divide once and then again in the early days of the Allende administration, because certain groups would declare themselves Socialist. The Radical Party, which embraced the social democratic ideal, was split on the issue of Marxism. One fraction opposed Allende because it considered his Marxism to be contrary to democracy in the long run. Another, Socialist, portion joined the alliance as a minority partner of the two Marxist parties, which now became known as Unidad Popular. In sum, the key strategic decisions of the parties from the 1940s on cannot be understood except as responses and reactions to what was often called "the Marxist threat."

Marxism penetrated even to the interior of Masonic lodges. Catholicism too was shaken by Marxism. With the dissemination of liberation theology and "base communities," many priests and believers even professed themselves Marxist or at least accepted Marx's social and economic analysis.

By the time of the presidential election of 1964, Chilean society was profoundly polarized for or against the Marxist option represented by Salvador Allende. The Cold War atmosphere contributed to this situation. For example, the Central Intelligence Agency (CIA) channeled substantial funds into Chile. In fact, the CIA that year spent more money per voter in Chile than Barry Goldwater and Lyndon Johnson did in their respective campaigns that same year.[2] Chile was a battlefield between Communism and the Free World, and Chileans, of course, conceived the country's political struggle in those terms.

Once Allende was elected in 1970, polarization of Chilean society advanced rapidly. In a few months, at all elections, even for student bodies at elementary and secondary schools, partisans and opponents of Marxist parties faced off. In 1973, when the Supreme Court and the majority of the Chilean Congress declared Salvador Allende's administration to be unconstitutional, they opened the door for the military to take over the government. That is why the major leaders of the Christian Democrats, Eduardo Frei Montalva and Patricio Aylwin, publicly supported the military coup of 1973.

The prolonged duration of the military régime brought about profound transformations and generated a further cleavage. The régime intended to "extirpate the cancer of Marxism," which meant, first of all, controlling public policy and repressing all paramilitary, partisan, union, and cultural Marxist organizations together with their mass media. To this end the military government unleashed a violent repression that caused deep wounds, which in turn would hinder a swift return to democracy.

The dismantling of the Marxist parties' organizations and traditional means of communication was effective. It is true that the Communist Party managed to survive clandestinely. In 1988 its armed branch, known as *Frente Manuel Rodríguez*, attempted to assassinate General Pinochet and very nearly succeeded. Nevertheless, there is no doubt that in 1973 the military managed in a very short time to defeat through fear the popular-based Marxist forces, that is, to break down their will to fight. Resistance lasted only a few hours.

For many the attraction of Marxism lay, to a considerable extent, in the fact that the future was viewed as belonging to them. The coming confrontation had been announced for many months. What else did Fidel Castro speak about during the two months he spent in Chile? Among the people, who watched on television the soldiers in Allende's home, counting his many suits of clothes and showing his store of Chivas Regal, who saw detachments of soldiers with painted faces and armed to the teeth coming and going along the streets, who heard about searches and arrests, the general impression was of a speedy and complete defeat of the left.

The Marxist movement as the incarnation of promised victory for the poor classes collapsed in the minds of the people. The project suddenly became illusory. It should be borne in mind, too, that despite Marxist assumptions in Chile the class division never ran parallel to the political division. For example, the right wing has always had about one-third of the popular vote. This means that at all levels of society every supporter of Allende knew that on the same street lived an enemy of Allende, now a supporter of the military, with all that this might come to imply.

The régime, for its part, was bent on transforming the overregulated economy into a free-market economy. The purpose was to produce rapid economic growth. The assumption, according to a well-known political theory recently reformulated by Francis Fukuyama,[3] was that economic development would result in development of a stable democracy. The military government also decided to reformulate the future institutional framework of the country by drafting a new political constitution and new legislation in key political areas.[4]

The government junta took up "exercise of all functions of individuals and bodies composing the Legislature and the Executive, consequently Constitutional authority." The judiciary would retain its autonomy, although its functions were curtailed under various decree-laws. For example, the country was declared in a "state of siege" (D.L. No. 3, September 11, 1973), which was renewed from time to time until the election of 1988. The state of siege was construed as "wartime conditions," for the purposes of penalties provided under the Code of Military Justice (D.L. No. 5). The juridical effect pursued was to transfer to military justice in wartime the hearing of cases arising out of the application of provisions in effect in the state of siege. Despite the fact that certain jurists objected to this step as unconstitutional, the Supreme Court ruled on September 13, 1973, and August 21, 1974, that military courts in wartime were not subject to supervision by the Supreme Court. The operation of a parallel judiciary was thus legitimated. It has been proved that between 1973 and 1990 there were 2,115 fatal victims, including deaths by Councils of War, during demonstrations, while attempting to escape, under torture, and of persons arrested and missing.[5] This issue, particularly the trials involving arrested and missing persons, continues to divide Chilean society even today. Indeed, *A Nation of Enemies* is the title given to a book on the military régime by a pair of social scientists well acquainted with Chilean history.[6]

The Catholic Church rapidly turned into an institution critical of the government, of its violations of human rights, its capitalist economic project, its social insensitivity, and its nondemocratic nature. The Church's Vicaría de la Solidaridad registered and documented violations of human rights, and its lawyers helped the victims' relatives. The Christian Democrats, who had supported the military régime in the early days, gradually withdrew to a distance and eventually, in alliance with the bulk of left-wing forces, formed the opposition bloc that defeated the supporters of the military régime in the elections of 1988 and 1989.

The cleavage, however, continues.[7]

To imagine a military government confronting a civilian population barred from power and simply subjected is to understand little or nothing of the Chilean case. A more accurate depiction would show the civil society divided into two blocs and the military governing with the support of one of them (Pinochet got 43 percent of the vote in 1988). Neither was the relation between civilians and military within the governing bloc one of subordinates and superiors. There was rather a sharing of functions and tasks. This sharing generated friction inside the régime over the greater or lesser military participation of one group versus another.

In economic affairs the military administration was guided by a team of economists mostly from Universidad Católica who had studied at the University of Chicago or adhered to its tenets. The diagnosis and basic program of reforms began long before the military régime. The basic approach, indeed, arose in the 1960s, during the administration of Eduardo Frei Montalva, and in the Jorge Alessandri presidential campaign of 1970. Both under the Christian Democratic government and during the right-wing campaign, the new economic free-market-oriented ideas were strongly resisted. Gradually, however, they came to be shared by thousands of economics and business graduates from Universidad Católica or the business school connected with Fundación Adolfo Ibáñez. In addition, these ideas had been widely disseminated since the 1960s by *El Mercurio*, a highly influential daily paper.[8] In the advance and consolidation of the economic project, the network of economists that spread through the administration, universities, institutes, corporations, and banks, plus *El Mercurio*, composed a most powerful alliance. In political affairs, after considerable internal tension, the government eventually took up a democratic constitutional outlook of a strongly presidential cut, long before the military régime. In that respect, too, the alliance between certain ministers and civilian collaborators of the régime, together with *El Mercurio*, was crucial.

In this chapter I seek to show that the transformation of Chilean society took place primarily along two axes: one vertical, from the top down, conducted by the administration (economic and institutional matters), and one horizontal (cultural). It is worth noting, however, that the reforms introduced from the top also rest on a prior cultural movement, namely, the influence of the Chicago school and the Chilean presidential political theory. The most influential ministers and collaborators of the régime were well-known present or former university professors.[9]

The Social Effect of "Revolution from the Top": Economic Reform and Political-Institutional Reform

In 1985 the thesis that Chile was on the way to becoming "another Nicaragua" was widely held, and analysts of various leanings shared the diagnosis.[10] "Pinochet: The Next Somoza" was the title of an article published in the Heritage Foundation's journal *Policy Review*.[11] An article in *Foreign Policy* was entitled "Is Chile Next?"[12] U.S. diplomacy during the Ronald Reagan administration favored this view to the extent of declining to vote in favor of substantial World Bank loans in 1985 and 1986. (The loans were granted nonetheless.) The Reagan administration adopted a vote of censure on Chile for abuses in the field of human rights. Elliott Abrams, assistant secretary of state for Inter-American Affairs, stated that "he was skeptical that Pinochet wants any kind of transitions."[13] Nonetheless, in March 1990 Chile made the transition to democracy. Overnight, the Chilean nightmare ceased and Chile became a success story. What allowed a peaceful agreed transfer of power to take place from the military to a civilian government led by a coalition of opponents of the authoritarian régime? How did the mediation process come about?

The transition was agreed because the projects of both government supporters and opposition were to some extent frustrated. In early 1982, the former believed that General Pinochet could remain in office until 1996, legitimated by a referendum to be held in 1988. Subsequent transit to democracy was conceived as something gradual, remote, peaceful, and unilateral. Substantial economic development would uphold the popularity of both the régime and its political successors. For the other side, the régime had to be overthrown, as had happened with the Shah of Iran or Somoza in Nicaragua. There would be no transition to democracy nor reconciliation while General Pinochet remained in power. His economic structure must be dismantled for the new democratic Chile to be reborn.

The question is, What made the negotiation successful? How was the basic consensus arrived at to give it life? To begin with, a large number of elements were involved. It cannot be denied, for instance, that U.S. diplomatic pressure was instrumental in letting the régime see the high cost of evading a democratic outcome. It is quite likely that the legality of elections and the opportunity given to the opposition to conduct its political campaign were linked to pressure from foreign governments, including the United States, as well as to a vast number of international and foreign agencies.[14] The hierarchy of the Roman Catholic Church did something similar. Of course, many political, economic, and cultural elements were involved. Which of these were the most significant? How did they mesh together?

Economic development is a possible hypothesis. Was it not true that those who foretold the coming of a crisis in Chile and who saw how the nation became more and more polarized from day to day lost sight of the beneficent influence of economic well-being? From an economic standpoint, Chile is today an exemplar in Latin America. The bulk of the reforms that radically transformed the economy were completed under the military administration.[15] Was that not the key to the transition? In 1970 Chilean society was profoundly divided and polarized. In 1990 the reigning atmosphere was one of consensus. Is the economic well-being achieved after nearly two decades of capitalism the reason for the difference?

Of course, the project entertained by the more lucid collaborators of the military régime was always to transform politics starting from economics. The notion of eradicating communism by eradicating extreme poverty was particularly attractive.[16] It would be oversimplifying, however, to think that economic development was made solely responsible for remodeling politics. The régime also undertook vast political and constitutional work. This position, disseminated far and wide by the media during the entire military régime, drove deep into military and business circles. The cultural and ideological differences, the disparity of political concepts, which had sundered the nation for the past fifty years, would vanish thanks to economic growth and the new political institutions.

The difficulty with the hypothesis that attempts to explain transition to democracy as a by-product of economic growth is that the per capita income in real terms in 1970 was very similar to that of 1987. Adjusted by the terms of trade, gross domestic product (GDP) per capita was equal to US$3,882 in 1970; $4,087 in 1972; $3,821 in 1987; and $4,098 in 1988.[17] After eighteen years per capita income was $216 higher, or, if annualized, 0.3%. In 1972, in the midst of political polarization, per capita gross national product (GNP) was fairly comparable (only $11, or 0.04% less) to what it would be twenty years later, at a time of orchestrating widespread consensus and a spirit of reconciliation. Another indicator, per capita consumption of calories and protein, was lower in 1981, 1982, and 1988 than in 1972.[18] A number of reasons, for the most part of external origin, led Chile to a serious recession in 1975, which was followed by several years of growth averaging more than 7% per annum and by a second recession in 1982. On these occasions, GDP dropped by 13% and 14%, respectively. As a result, not only was GDP the same after twenty years, but also the population had undergone the effects of two substantial reductions in GDP with their natural sequels of unemployment and lost purchasing power of wages. Unemployment remained much higher than historic averages for most of the period; it rose to over 30% in 1982, fell to 27.7% in 1983 and continued downward in subsequent years, and was still at 16.7% in 1986. (These figures include the minimum employment program and the employment program for heads of households, both public emergency employment programs with minimal compensation.) Private per capita consumption in 1987 was 9.7% lower than in 1970, and 2.6% lower in 1988, the year of the referendum, than in 1970. Private per capita consumption fell by 21.8% between 1972 and 1987.[19]

The 1982 recession was particularly serious, as it occurred after several years of high growth, giving rise to a general belief that the economy had "taken off" for good. The grievous - 14.09% of 1982 had the régime tottering and opened a space where the true transition began. In early 1984 per capita consumption was 18.3% lower than in 1981. After 1984, while Hernán Büchi was minister of finance, there was high economic growth and speedy expansion of employment. For many people, however, the first fruits of economic reforms were not felt until the first few years of democratic government, that is, from 1990 on. The incipient democracy inherited, then, a sound economy, with appropriate institutions for capitalist development and a technocratic business class with the expertise and training to face the challenges of competition. Naturally, this helped to decompress the political system and to dilute pressures in the first few years of democracy.

Poll data fail to support the widely disseminated theory that the people were pleased with the economy and displeased with General Pinochet's dictatorship and its behavior in the area of human rights. Centro de Estudios Públicos-Adimark (CEP-Adimark) surveys show that in 1988, at the time of the referendum that General Pinochet lost, 56.9% of respondents "disagreed with the current economic policy." Indeed, when asked for the reasons for voting "No" (i.e., against Pinochet's continuing in office), the reasons most frequently given were of an economic nature: "economic situation," "poverty," "no jobs," "I don't like the economic policy." Against expectations, reasons linked to human rights were relatively less important. At the same time, the main reasons given for voting "Yes," that is, for Pinochet, were "order," "peace and quiet," "doesn't want changes." Reasons referring to order, peace, and quiet were mentioned more times than the "economic situation" or "economic policy."[20]

It was not therefore GDP growth as such that paved the way for democracy. Does this suggest that economic matters played no major role in political affairs? Not at all—only that the issue is somewhat more complex and less mechanical than it might seem at first sight. First, in spite of unemployment and two recessions, extreme poverty could be reduced. For example, in 1970, 79.3 infants under one year of age died per thousand live births; by 1980 the figure had dropped to 31.8 deaths per thousand live births.[21] This was the combined effect of growth, opening to foreign trade, and social policies with government and foreign support (e.g., from the World Bank). These actions included food for school-aged children and nutrition for mothers during pregnancy and the child's first year. The schoolchildren's food program was channeled through private firms that efficiently supplied thousands of children at their schools. Mass supply of plots complete with deed of ownership, electric light, water, and a minimum facility containing kitchen and bathroom, allowed low-income owners gradually to complete their own definitive dwellings, which opened up for them a possible, concrete, horizon.

A figure capable of suggesting the magnitude of the structural change that overtook the Chilean economy is perhaps the relative proportion of exports and imports as percentage of GDP. Exports accounted for 11.5% of GDP in 1970, 24.1% in 1988, and 36.5% in 1994. Exports and imports together accounted for 35.5% of total GDP in 1970, 52.0% in 1988, and 77.6% in 1994.[22] As may be observed, it is a profound change, whose nature is not fully reflected in GDP growth figures. Tariff reduction and the end of protectionism meant that a large number of items that symbolize status came within the reach of vast groups of people. For example, in 1970, of every ten thousand inhabitants, 72 owned a refrigerator against 958 in 1988; 52 against 871 owned a washing machine; 415 against 735 had a telephone; 189 against 790 owned an automobile.[23] Color television arrived in Chile in 1979. In greater Santiago, 42.8% of homes had color television in 1982; 59.8% of the urban population in 1992. In 1992, 89.1% of the total population had color or black-and-white television.[24]

Perhaps the most important step, sociologically speaking, was the provision allowing import of second-hand clothing. Barefoot children and rural workers wearing the traditional peasant sandal known as *ojota* rapidly disappeared. From the United States came second-hand shoes, sneakers, plastic footwear, at minimal prices. The poorest neighborhoods were flooded with T-shirts bearing such legends as "University of Oregon" or "Free Sex." The poncho was replaced by the anorak made in Korea, purchased and worn in the United States, and resold in Chile. Macroeconomic figures are too large to supply details on the significance of such transformations. After this, was it possible, for example, to promote a return to the protectionist economy that resulted in domestic but expensive clothing, Chilean-made but extremely expensive television sets, now clearly of lower quality than the Japanese product? Even with a population critical of the economic policy because it caused widespread unemployment and low wages, could they be expected to give up these consumption patterns and expectations? It must be remembered that the rapid spread of television simultaneously triggered an equally rapid dissemination of such consumption patterns, so that the population felt that by wearing an anorak instead of a poncho they were part of a contemporary way of life prevailing in more prosperous and educated societies. In other words, for a dweller in La Pintana, the poorest urban area in Chile, the anorak became a symbol of progress.

Many side effects took place also. For instance, television advertising for Isapres (health insurance) contributed to disseminating the habit of medical checkups and appropriate food during pregnancy.

Something similar happened in the rural areas. The military government distributed among rural workers the lands expropriated during the Allende administration and held until then in the so-called "social area," or, for all practical purposes, under government control. Competition kept most land holdings from being economically efficient, and they passed from the hands of former workers to those of agricultural businessmen filled with a new spirit. Many of these belonged to the traditional landed families and reassembled their property, adding plots to the core of land retained as "reserve" after expropriation; others were physicians, agronomists, accountants, tradesmen, notaries, technicians, or owners of farm machinery who bought up several plots and organized a farm from scratch. The approach, however, was "modern," "technified," "economic." Splitting up the land increased the value of machinery; in general terms, successful farming was more capital-intensive. The memory of takeovers of farms in the 1960s and early 1970s inclined the new farmers to hire a minimum of labor.

The new horizon was export. In 1973 copper accounted for 80.1% of total exports; in 1983 it was only 48.9%. Export of fresh fruit (grapes, apples, nectarines, kiwis, etc.) to countries in the Northern Hemisphere, taking advantage of the off-season period, had a profound effect on lifestyles.

Farming activities became industrialized.[25] Some of the workers no longer lived on the land but came to work on bicycles, like industrial workers. Women joined the work force. At harvest time, women became responsible for the delicate job of selecting and packing fruit at the packing plants. As a result, in families of two or more daughters, the women began to contribute as much or more yearly income as the husband. In addition, women, transported to work in buses and on trailers across fields and villages, began to travel to their packing jobs, where they came across the world of male work. Added to the onrush of television, it is not surprising that in rural areas the anorak should have replaced the traditional poncho of the Andes. The left thus lost sight of its cultural symbols.

Furthermore, the rapid increase of formerly traditional nonmining exports generated a sense of the ability to integrate with the rest of the world and of pride, both powerful sentiments in a small country located at the end of the world. This feeling is particularly strong among the business sectors recently engaging in the new areas of export and import, as well as services. They became the allies of the new free-market policies and of the military government that implemented them. Wide expansion arose in the financial area of banking and insurance. The newest development, however, took place in health and social security. A number of private firms, subject to various regulations, were allowed to manage the funds mandatorily discounted every month from salaries for this purpose. The pension funds (AFPs) and health insurance institutions (Isapres) were to become important elements in the new composition of Chilean business.

In the field of labor, the initially repressive methods were replaced by a full labor reform, providing, for example, for election of union leaders by secret ballot, leader irremovability while in office, and the right to strike. The employer, however, was allowed to hire temporary workers, under the same terms and conditions that prevailed before the strike. Collective bargaining by trade was not allowed. Such legislation, which was ardently opposed at first by union leadership, was now beginning to work. From an economic standpoint the law became more flexible, so that the value of labor was fixed by the market. From a political standpoint, it dismantled the large federations and confederations of unions, which as members of the nationwide Central Unica de Trabajadores (CUT) had provided the mainstay for the Communist Party. At the same time, it provided a channel for union participation, limited but far more effective than the prohibitions and delegates of the early Pinochet years. In the final years of the régime, labor legislation expedited a speedy rise in employment.

In 1983, in spite of having little if any formal representation, CUT, with international funding, nevertheless became the hub of the nighttime demonstrations of that year. It failed to organize strikes or paralyze production, but succeeded in leading political protest. Next to it, political leaders became visible, having returned from forced or voluntary exile or having simply bided their time in Chile.

The new business class, to the extent that it became consolidated, acquired a long-term view. Its support to the military government was primarily support for its economic policy. Without prejudice to seeking to prolong General Pinochet's administration as much as possible, they were concerned about the institutions of the future. They knew that perpetuation of a "military state," as some wanted, was not feasible, given the Chilean democratic tradition and the atmosphere prevailing in modern societies.[26] What worried them most was rather the transition and how to ensure that tomorrow's decisions, under democracy, would be "rational." That is why they supported the collaborators of the régime engaged in economic policy and those politically active in designing mechanisms and institutions intended to preserve current achievements on issues of private property and economic policy, and to put a brake on populism. There was to be no turning back, at any cost. This entailed making a correct diagnosis of what caused the expansion of Marxism and the Allende administration as well as which political institutions would be right for the future. This was the point where the economic met the political and intellectual interests of the social sciences—economists, sociologists, political analysts, philosophers, and others.

Meanwhile, the opponents of the régime had little by little set up private institutes devoted to the social sciences and critical of the economic model: CIEPLAN, FLACSO, CIDE, CPU, CED, SUR, ICHEH, CISOC, CERC, CENECA, Vector, etc.[27] They received funding from abroad and hence enjoyed great autonomy vis-à-vis local pressures. They were think tanks and meeting places. They published copiously, and through courses, lectures, and seminars without university or official recognition they were in fact training a considerable portion of the ablest university students. Their research and analyses fed the press. It was difficult for journalists to ignore them, especially when—as in the case of CIEPLAN economists—they provided data that belied the economic authorities of the administration on such technical issues as the calculation of inflation and the effect thereof on real government contributions in the social area. Some of those intellectuals began to appear in magazines and papers as regular columnists, though their writings were cautious and carefully edited. The authors were backed by academic degrees obtained from renowned foreign universities and by their publications. Nevertheless, though firmly anchored in modernity, it was clear that they failed to share the business view of the military régime. They criticized the economic model, politics, and ethics. Their view of the future was also different. In this context, with a view to validating the market economy in intellectual circles beyond purely specialized economics, and thinking above all of the conceptual discussions that would shape the future democracy, in 1980 a group of businessmen founded the Centro de Estudios Públicos (Center for Policy Studies), which was to contribute to legitimating in the democratic intellectual world contrary to the régime a new set of ideas arising in the society: the so-called neoliberalism, which in fact is only classic liberalism reborn. It was instrumental in translating and discussing in Chile a whole group of thinkers that were virtually unknown in the country at the time (Hayek, Berlin, and Rawls, for example). Other such institutes were formed as well; one of the major ones was the Instituto de la Sociedad Libre (Free Society Institute), which published the journal *Realidad* and would become the core from which one of the two current right-wing parties was to spring: Unión Democrática Independiente (UDI).

In sum, the economic system undoubtedly weighed on the transformation of the political atmosphere that eventually led to agreed transition. More important than economic growth per se, however, were the economic institutions and, of course, the interests built around them. Here it should be pointed out that the world of the free market, with its opportunities, patterns of consumption, and ways of life, does not make it difficult to vote Socialist; but it does put up rather severe obstacles to a Radical Socialist program.[28] The new free-market society opened options and possibilities, pointed to new ways and new styles. Having lost faith in the prospect of collective political action, confidence was reinforced in individual improvement and the private world. The new economic system emphasized just that. New promises had arisen.

In 1986 a CEP opinion poll was conducted to find out how people explained personal economic success or failure. The options offered included "economic status of parents," "government economic measures," "financial assistance from government," "educational status," "personal initiative," "responsible work," and so on, from which respondents were asked to select two (so the results add up to more than 100%): 54.5% selected "responsible work" and 45.7% selected "personal initiative" as the main reason for success.[29] The options offered for the reasons for poverty included "government economic policies," "lack of financial assistance from government," "abuses and injustice of the system," "scarce job opportunities," "lack of education," "vices and alcoholism," and finally "laziness and lack of initiative." The latter, "laziness and lack of initiative," was the most frequently mentioned reason (more than 50% of responses), followed by "lack of education" and "vices and alcoholism." The result is the same among responses in the low-income sector.[30] This suggests that a perception was socialized to the effect that economic progress and social mobility were associated with individual effort rather

than with the expectation of structural change: "The population generally associates the problem of poverty with conditions linked to individual behavior rather than with external circumstances."[31] Such data suggest that Marxism and the radical left wing in general had little social
support.

In conjunction with economic reform, the military régime set about
preparing the institutional stage for future democracy. The significance
of this side of the work done by the military régime is perhaps not always acknowledged. The underlying diagnosis was that the crisis of
democracy that led to the events of 1973 was partly the result of its own
ineffectiveness. In a nutshell, this ineffectiveness was blamed on the
power of Congress to obstruct the policies of the elected government.
The importance of the vertical reform "from above" has yet to be properly recognized, for it became effective as recently as 1990 and is still, to a
considerable extent, under debate. The fact is, however, as was stated
earlier, that the régime adopted a strongly presidential constitution and a
complete set of supplementary political laws.

Thus, for example, it was provided that members of Congress were not
entitled to raise draft laws involving public expenditure. This was the exclusive prerogative of the president. Special quorum requirements were
set higher than before to hinder easy amendment of particularly significant legislation, such as labor and electoral laws. Election districts were
redesigned. A new electoral system was devised providing for the election of two members of Congress per district in order to penalize party
scattering. The effect of this was to force parties into broad electoral alliances that now divide the nation into two major blocs. The Senate was
increased by a number of senators not elected directly by the citizens but
designated by various institutions. The high command of the armed
forces, once designated, no longer consisted of confidential officials under the president, but remained in office for one term, unless found to be
unfit. Finally, it was determined that General Pinochet would remain at
the head of the army until 1998. Many other legal provisions were
amended under the reform agreed in June 1989; the items just listed are
some of those that were retained.

In brief, the régime's jurists performed a vast task of political engineering designed to remodel political activity, build juridical dams to contain
populism, and often to protect the régime's achievements and institutions
and to empower its supporters—criticized by opponents of such institutions as "lock-in laws." Government-sponsored attempts at reform succeed one another and are rejected by the present opposition. Still, Chile
has been governed from this institutional base, which has to a considerable extent conditioned the action of political leaders and parties. However, given that this institutional base began to operate properly under the

new democracy and that the economy has had an important but limited social effect, other complementary factors must be investigated to explain the profound change in Chilean politics. That change was visible already in 1986, with the execution of the *Acuerdo Nacional*, or National Accord.

A Case of Horizontal Mediation: Agreed Transition and Private Academic Institutes

From 1980, about fifteen transitions to democracy took place in Latin America. In all cases, military, political, business, and press leaders played an important part, as did U.S. diplomacy and economic factors. The unique trait of the Chilean case is that the transition involved not only resuming an interrupted democratic tradition of long standing but also a profound change in political style and supply of social projects. The most plausible explanation of this is the part performed by intellectuals in the social sciences grouped in private academic think tanks. There is a growing body of literature on the subject.

According to Jeffrey Puryear, "Most analyses emphasize initiatives taken from within authoritarian régimes to institute transitions to democratic rule, and the role of élites more generally in leading the shift from authoritarian to democratic values. But the élites mentioned are, for the most part, military, political, or economic. Intellectual élites virtually never appear. Yet our review of Chile's experience suggests that intellectuals have positive roles to play in democratic transitions."[32] More specifically, he says, "Chile's transition was shaped not by a cross-section of the country's intelligentsia but by a sophisticated group of foreign-trained social scientists."[33] In fact, a study by José Joaquín Brunner published in 1985 concluded that "there are in Chile today about thirty-five private academic centers, staffed by about 470 professionals. It is estimated that approximately 300 work as full-time researchers, not considering research assistants."[34] And María Teresa Lladser documented in 1986 the work and characteristics of some forty nongovernmental study centers.[35]

A review of the publications of these think tanks reveals that they focused on a vast array of public issues. Behind such a varied range of topics, however, the affairs of special interest tended to define the political order and the socioeconomic order of the future. Initially, this work was conducted in the privacy of each institute, without communicating with those who thought differently. Later, as some common ground was found, not always an easy task, discussion seminars were initiated.[36]

Marxist intellectuals in general returned from exile with a much more critical view of what might be expected from the Socialist revolution. Repression in Chile had given new value to such formal institutions in traditional law as the habeas corpus. Contemporary publications allow a reconstruction to be made of the itinerary of gradually increasing reliance on the values and institutions of bourgeois democracy. Books were exchanged, and international reading and experiences were discussed. At the centers "the renewal of the left began. There was a serious reflection on our failures, a rethinking of our entire role."[37] Marxism was fast losing its appeal. It was not to recover from this critique.

One recurring set of topics of papers and seminars was the nature of totalitarian society, the critique of Leninism that pervaded the minds of Chilean Marxist parties, and the notion of the rule of law. In this context, one debate, for example, focused on whether a free press is possible under a régime that rejects private property or bans commercial advertising. The argument hinged on transition to democracy and the costs involved in terms of making doctrinaire and testimonial positions flexible. Other questions of interest were the role of church and state in configuring the national identity, if there was such a thing, and the possibility that a liberal society might take root given the ethos of Chilean society. Particular importance was attached to the issue of a minimum of socioeconomic agreement to sustain a democracy, widespread ownership, inequality of income and power, and ways to consolidate democracy. A profound analysis was conducted on the causes of the crisis of democracy. Contrary to expectations, the conclusion was that the delegitimation of democracy was not the outcome of economic or social conditions but basically of a cultural phenomenon. For example, Tomás Moulián, a sociologist returned from Marxism, argued that "the Chilean left, in its recent history, has thought of democracy in a double dimension: as a given and as an obstacle."[38] For some twenty intellectuals of diverse leanings, such as Góngora, Moulián, Valenzuela, Garretón, Foxley, and others, the radicalization and polarization of Chilean politics is basically the work of intellectual and political élites.[39] Self-criticism emphasized a cultural approach to explaining the undermining of the democratic tradition. For example, Mario Góngora, a distinguished conservative historian, criticized the "overall planning" reflected in the Christian Democratic projects of the 1960s, the Unidad Popular, and the military régime.[40] If that was the case, then the intellectuals would be basically responsible for reconstructing the language of public life so that it would allow for encountering democracy afresh. Thus not only visions of future society were engendered at the private think tanks but also a recomposition of the past.

At the same time, the free-market-oriented economic reforms of the military régime were working a profound transformation in Chilean society. The very structural reforms that the régime was introducing offered an intellectual challenge. There was, in fact, a new and daring agenda induced by the authorities and enjoying a theoretical and technical backing that could not be ignored.

All these issues were the object not only of serious academic research but also of countless seminars and panel discussions, in which many of the régime's technocrats and ideologues also took part. At these meetings a gradual change and the emergence of a new consensus became increasingly clear.

An historic circumstance empowered the work of these think tanks. The golden age for study centers stretched from 1982 to 1986. In 1982, as mentioned earlier, a severe exchange crisis made the régime's economic model totter. The government put banks under intervention together with economic groups symbolizing the new capitalism. In 1983 mass protests, led by trade union leaders and politicians, became general. The stability of the military régime itself was called into question. General Pinochet appointed a right-wing politician as minister and he began to talk to the opposition leaders. These leaders, overestimating their power, asked the general to step down. The conversations failed, and the régime hardened. However, the existence of an opposition had been recognized and legitimated. What was later to be known as "the opening" had begun.[41]

The severe recession of 1982 had serious political effects in that the régime's project, its raison d'être, hinged at that time on accelerated economic growth. The vulnerable nature of the "economic model" brought politics and ideological discussion into play. Why did the traditional revolutionary left not gather more strength? Street riots began, together with terrorism, nighttime protests after placing bombs on high-voltage towers and plunging whole sections or the whole city in darkness. Popular mobilization had revived, after ten years. What the analysts feared when they saw Chile as a "new Nicaragua" and Pinochet as a "new Somoza" was the emergence of a radical left. Why did the position of leaders such as Volodia Teitelboim, at the head of the Communist movement, fail to take hold? The true transition, different from the unilateral one planned by the régime in the Constitution of 1980, was to be a process shared by government and opposition. "Give-and-take" situations so common in political life became frequent. Why then did a revolutionary left not lead the protest as of old? What made the new leaders moderate and of a Social Democrat bent? One explanation is that in the institute network Marxism and radical strategies were losing validity. These institutions gradually filtered and processed the Chilean historic experience, together with the international intellectual and political atmosphere. For instance, in 1984 a Communist-inspired institute[42] was founded that began to teach courses, publish a quarterly review, and the like, but it failed to acquire legitimacy.

The intellectuals feverishly devoted their efforts to writing articles and books, to discussing them at seminars, and to teaching courses. Traditional politicians were somewhat bewildered, university students looked for new horizons, businessmen worried about what would happen after

Pinochet, and journalists needed to renew their instruments of analysis. It was a time of major debates as well as of uncertainty, fear, and hope.

Did this work by intellectuals have any political effect? In fact it did. The press was the first to be influenced by the work of private think tanks. Their research offered a base for reports, and many intellectuals sat on editorial committees or were themselves columnists. Public opinion polls, in particular, which were published openly since 1986 by CERC, CED-FLACSO, and CEP, served as a bridge between élites and population. After fifteen years of dictatorship they proved immensely interesting and useful. Many conceptions and prejudices fell in the face of the information collected in the course of such social research. The society was less polarized than the élites, which reinforces the thesis that in the past the élites had radicalized political strife.

The press and the political leadership found, often to their astonishment, that moderation reigned among the majority. For instance, the left virtually gave up writing and drawing on walls, which was part of their traditional style and had become a kind of popular art, given the general disapproval it caused. It was also significant that the majority wished to reform the Constitution of 1980 rather than attempt a new one. The polls gave no sign that the "Allende myth"[43] and the Communist Party had revived, as many had foretold.

Consensuses arrived at in the intellectual field were conveyed to the political arena and took the form, for instance, of the National Accord of 1976, which brought together a vast array of right-wing and left-wing leaders, from Andrés Allamand, current chairman of Renovación Nacional, one of the two right-wing parties, to the socialist Ricardo Lagos, later minister of education under President Aylwin, minister of public works under President Frei, and leader of the left. The National Accord became one of the milestones of the transition; it failed to produce the intended effect because the military government did not share the diagnosis. The accord implied, in effect, the advance resignation of General Pinochet before he attempted to remain in office beyond 1989, following a referendum. At the time, the more lucid supporters of the régime believed that General Pinochet might feasibly carry and win the referendum without negotiations or compromises. From then on, however, political leaders took up the new notions, the language and style validated by the intellectuals.

The conceptual origins of the National Accord may be traced, for example, in *Orden Económico y Democracia* (Economic Order and Democracy), edited by Edgardo Boeninger, who later drafted the text of the accord and was a key minister in the Aylwin administration. His examination may illustrate the type of influence obtained on the basis of institute activities. The book contains a set of papers and comments presented at a Centro de

Estudios del Desarrollo (CED) seminar in 1984, encompassing a variety of tendencies and views, from liberal to socialist. Boeninger's central point, however, is that "to consolidate democracy, respect for democratic procedures is neither sufficient nor possible in the absence of some degree of agreement on fundamentals, particularly as regards the economic order, which is perhaps the area of most extensive political and social conflict in Chile . . ." He opposed the idea of "a unilateral imposition of necessary austerity and sacrifice, which assumes a new form of dictatorial rule," that of a "political and social concertation." ("Concertación" was to become the name of the alliance of political forces that defeated Pinochet in 1988 and Büchi in 1989.) The volume stated that "Chile urgently demands a basic political agreement based on economic order."[44]

The idea of minimum consensus is not new; the régime upheld it from the beginning, and it had adherents among the opposition.[45] What was new was the procedure and its virtual materialization. Rather than wait for consensus to arise, basically as a by-product of economic growth, future juridical institutions, and economic and political reeducation to socialize the principles of the régime's supporters in a significant sector of the population, it was expected to emerge from political negotiation recognizing the variety in Chilean society as it stood. Not only was the objective suggested but also a study over one hundred pages long attempted to set the bases of what such an accord might contain and exclude. All of this was based on an exercise in personal critical judgment applied to the other papers contained in the same book, which had been discussed face-to-face at previous seminars. The author, quoting studies and proposals current at the time, opposed the Chilean radical left, which shared "an approach contrary to the existence of large private corporations and private education" and held "that a development strategy requires centralized control of the surplus."[46] The attitude in question contended that Chile enjoys relative advantages only in a few areas linked to natural resources, namely, mining, industrial fisheries, lumber and pulp, and fresh fruit—all highly capital-intensive activities. There were two alternatives: Either such surpluses are to be controlled by a small number of separate, private economic groups or by the State. If the former, it must be admitted that power would concentrate in the hands of a minimal minority. Only under State control would true democracy be possible. Otherwise, power inequalities would make a mockery of democracy. At a time when the large economic groups had fallen, such a position was not unattractive. The idea, however, with its traditional burden, as presented in a number of seminars, failed to take hold among the élite. This is one concrete example of how a certain form of proposal from the traditional left can lose legitimacy.

Nevertheless, Boeninger stated that "the economic policy of the military régime has been harshly criticized, particularly the so-called 'Chicago model,' which ended in a resounding failure." This gives an idea of the sense then prevailing of the régime's vulnerability. Objections were also raised against liberal postures that, while admitting the pressing nature of the struggle against poverty and a government commitment to it, oppose any attempt at income redistribution beyond minimum sustainability, intended to correct the inequalities and seek some ideal of maximum permissible inequalities for the society as a whole.

The study combined economic, political, and philosophic elements. Apart from Chilean authors, studies, and reports, the citations and discussion included Arrow, Dahl, Duverger, Friedman, Heilbroner, Rawls, and others. All, however, focused on the country's problems and the specific aim proposed: the pursuit of a "convergence in the economic and social field, however minimal, among the political projects of the various ideological movements and political parties striving for power." The perception is to be avoided that taking turns in government is "an intolerable threat to minority sectors." This is not intended to mean giving up "Utopias or long-term ideal views."

In sum, the author suggested a "mixed economy" recognizing "appreciable degrees of economic freedom as one of the manifestations that democratic freedoms are in effect and a condition for the development of creativity," which implies "recognizing the predominant role of the market and conventional private property"; granting priority to "economic growth" to prevent "the distribution problem" from becoming "a zero sum game leading unavoidably to social confrontation"; and, finally, to engage in a gradual process led by the government for "overcoming extreme poverty and progressively reducing inequalities." Until a short time ago, to suggest that proposals such as these might be part of a nationwide consensus would have been, simply, nonsense. The Chilean Christian Democratic Party would have found such language difficult to accept. The very élite of the institute network had moved perceptibly toward liberalism. A summary of such ideas became the National Accord, which was formally proposed and sponsored by Francisco Cardinal Fresno, archbishop of Santiago. The U.S. government provided explicit support.

The "National Accord" was resisted by a substantial portion of the right wing, including both political leaders (Jaime Guzmán, for one) and major media (*El Mercurio*, the magazine *Economía y Sociedad*), as well as most businessmen. The opposing argument was that the economy had to be allowed time to recover. Any sign of agreement or negotiation would be a sign of weakness and fuel the struggle against Pinochet until he was overthrown. Underlying this, however, was something more significant: mistrust for the opposition leadership that signed the accord. This became abundantly clear on the issue of property and the economy.[47]

The failure of the accord revealed that confidence and trust were essential to restoring democracy. The loss of mutual trust within Chile's leadership is of course one of the reasons for the prolonged duration of the military régime. The network of contacts that had been formed through the institutes was to play a major role in restoring such confidence. In the process, the traditional liberal institutions continued to gain ground among their former opposition. How? More and more seminars, more and more publications, more and more debates. "It is the horizontal penetration of liberalism. If the régime was the equivalent of 'enlightened despotism' in our time, the institutes were its 'literary salons.'"[48]

In institutional circles, the recovery of trust owed much to two major political decisions made by the authorities. One, by the Constitutional Court, was a ruling to the effect that the referendum of 1988 was to be governed by the regulations in force for normal elections, implying that the process was to be overseen by the Electoral Court. This was a novel decision, for the issue was unclear. The régime, which had created the Constitutional Court, abided by the ruling and so tied its own hands. The other arose in the Ministry of Interior, with the enactment of a law to govern the process that made fraud extremely difficult. Taken together, the decisions ensured that elections would be truly free.

Although the accord with the military régime failed, it was possible to overcome relatively quickly the fear of the void that prevailed when thinking of how the established régime was to be replaced. The "No" vote won, and that very evening, September 4, 1988, in a historic appearance on television, lawyer Sergio Fernández, minister of interior, acknowledged the defeat. This was the democratic beginning of the régime and the new institutions created thereby. The quiet that reigned that night, and the tranquil withdrawal of the military, would have been difficult indeed had there not been a modicum of confidence in what might be expected from the leadership of the opposition. A crucial contribution to this came from the faith in the National Accord, in addition, of course, to the trust placed by the military in the institutional framework designed by the régime and watched over by General Pinochet himself as captain general of the army.

One of the focal points of the mediation performed by the think tanks was the reform of the Constitution of 1980, which went through a referendum in early 1989 and allowed for an agreed transition. Intellectuals linked to think tanks took part at meetings where such reforms were discussed and negotiated. The main collaborators of the régime, including those who opposed the National Accord, pressured for concessions and to have the constitution validated by a referendum. Thus vertical mediation took place, that is, mediation involving the political authorities.

Apart from the issues already discussed, what elements allowed the centers to fill a mediating role? In times of dictatorship think tanks became meeting-points for the élite. Even years after the coup the supporters and the opponents of the military régime had avoided meeting. In a very real sense, they had nothing to say to one another. The think tanks with their little rituals—the papers, the comments, the panel discussions—gave people something to say. As often happens in such cases, the most serious issues were not mentioned; the talk was dotted with painful areas that were omitted. The object, the required goal, was to keep up some form of conversation, however imperfect and incomplete. This necessary restraint, designed to capture the other's sympathy, as Adam Smith said so many years ago, brought about a certain peace of the soul. The most meaningful mediation was not the mediation conducted outward, from one ideological sector to another, but that conducted inward: the reprocessing of ideas, histories, and experiences, that the small think tank makes possible. Politicians, businessmen, clergy, union leaders, foreign intellectuals—all found in these centers a relaxed environment for reflection.

Another factor was the ideological nature of Chilean political tradition. Chile has offset the spirit of caudillismo prevalent in other Latin American societies with a high appreciation for political and socioeconomic doctrines, for the currents and doctrines of thinking. The price of this has been that Chile has performed as a sort of guinea pig for one doctrine or another. Chilean society is remarkably permeable to political ideals. It rapidly clusters around poles of action and social mobilization.

Another factor was the previous existence of groups of highly qualified social scientists with a university tradition. These university centers (Centro de Estudios de la Realidad Contemporánea [CEREN] and Corporación de Investigaciones Económicas para Latinoamérica [CIEPLAN] of Universidad Católica, and the oldest of all, the Centro de Estudios Internacionales, of Universidad de Chile, for example) became the predecessors of those that proliferated during the military régime.[49] There were also cases of study centers with private funding, such as CESEC, founded in the late 1960s. The institutes, in turn, worked a great deal with university academics. They should be seen as poles of influence and coordination integrated into a much more extensive cultural system, where universities are the fundamental institutions. In other words, without a high-quality, thriving university system, the work of the study centers would not have been possible.

Another factor was international funding from European and U.S. foundations, which foresaw the effect that the intellectual élite might have on Chile's transition to democracy. Financing from private enterprise, except in the case of CEP and one or two others, was not significant, which gave them autonomy. Initially many were backed by the Roman Catholic Church. Another factor was international experience, particularly that of socialism in Spain, under Felipe González. Subsequently, of course, the debate was closed by the collapse of the Berlin Wall.

A very significant condition was the press. Although the authoritarian régime possessed the legal tools to control the media, it handled them in such a way as to leave some room for opposing publications. In addition, such dailies as *El Mercurio, La Segunda, Las Ultimas Noticias,* and *La Tercera* kept up a degree of autonomy and capacity for criticism. *El Mercurio* was constantly providing abundant information and editorializing on current public issues. Public opinion in favor of the régime concentrated around it, but the paper's influence reached far beyond. Others, like *La Segunda,* went to the length of pushing for political opening. The administration, however, retained a measure of control over television by appointing the rectors of the universities; the latter, under the legislation prevailing at the time, were the only institutions allowed to own and operate television stations.

The situation broke down when, one month before the referendum, the régime set up a mandatory nightly television spot of fifteen minutes for free advertising by each of the "Yes" and "No" vote campaigns. This decision was designed to ensure that electoral competition would be fair and that the opposition would have access to the media. Polls later showed that most of the "No" voters arrived at their decision by watching this television advertising campaign. The concept of the messages and their appropriation by opposition leaders were, as we know, the work of certain study centers.[50] The "No" vote campaign revealed that a major political transformation had taken place within the opposition leadership.

In time, as noted earlier, free-market ideas took their place in the intellectual community. Chilean thinking has returned to the tradition of freedoms that characterized it in the nineteenth and early twentieth centuries. When various major intellectuals came to the Aylwin administration as ministers of finance, directors of the budget, ministers of communications, and so on, they were characterized in part by their support of the market economy within their political coalition. While helping to mediate, the institutes became incubators of leaders.[51] From the return to democracy, the economy has grown by 5.4 percent per capita per annum and private investment has been greater than under the administration of General Pinochet.

But is it not true that intellectuals should be against capitalism and the market economy? The Chilean case shows that this may not always be the case. Just as socialism and central planning was fashionable among intellectuals, at a certain point this began to change. Just as psychoanalysis was extremely popular in such circles and now it is in good taste to satirize it, today (for how long?) statism is improper. In the 1960s democracy and its formal rights, capitalism and the *bourgeoisie* were ridiculed in Latin American intellectual circles. Now it is just the opposite.

The agreed and peaceful transition was of course the outcome of a multitude of factors. I think I have covered the most significant, including the political effect produced by the coup and the dismantling of Marxist organizations, the social effect of transformation of the economic system, the institutional channels set up by the régime, the critical posture of the Roman Catholic Church, international pressures, and the institutes that played a mediating role. The theories and leaders favoring radicalized positions were not legitimated by the institutes' intellectual network.

However, might not these institutions have acted as radicalizing agents and helped to polarize conflicts? Indeed, they could have, and in fact some of them attempted to do so. What this experience suggests is that a core of intellectuals may well exert a mediating influence in the case of a radical conflict. This does not mean that such an eventuality may be counted on. In the Chilean experience, institutes became places from which to reweave, in freedom, the collective conscience of a society jolted by traumatic shocks.

Notes

I acknowledge and appreciate the comments and cooperation of Harald Beyer.

1. François Furet, *Le passé d'une illusion* (Paris: Robert Laffont/Calmann-Lévy, 1995).

2. Arturo Valenzuela, *The Breakdown of Chilean Democracy* (Baltimore: Johns Hopkins University Press, 1978), p. 35 and note 21, p. 118.

3. Francis Fukuyama, *The End of History and the Last Man* (New York: Free Press, 1992). See also Larry Diamond and Mark F. Plattner, eds., *Capitalism, Socialism, and Democracy Revisited* (Baltimore: Johns Hopkins University Press, 1993). Originally the link between economic development and democracy was formulated in the classic book *Political Man: The Social Bases of Politics*, published by Seymour Martin Lipset in 1959.

4. About the foundational character of the régime, see Sergio De Castro et al., *El Ladrillo*, which circulated in a mimeographed version before the coup and was republished by Centro de Estudios Públicos in 1993; see also the journal *Economía y Sociedad* (particularly the regime's first stage) and the magazine *Realidad*. For a critical analysis, see Manuel Antonio Garretón, *El proceso político chileno* (Santiago: FLACSO, 1983) and comments by David Gallagher in *Estudios Públicos*, no. 13, 1984.

5. "Informe de la Comisión Nacional de Verdad y Reconciliación." See extracted version in *Estudios Públicos*, no. 41 (Summer 1991).

6. Pamela Constable and Arturo Valenzuela, *A Nation of Enemies: Chile Under Pinochet* (New York: Norton, 1991).

7. Arturo Fontaine Talavera, "Significado del eje derecha-izquierda," *Estudios Públicos*, no. 58, 1995.

8. See Juan Gabriel Valdés, *La escuela de Chicago, operación Chile* (Buenos Aires: Editorial Zeta, 1998); and Guillermo Sunkel, *El Mercurio: 10 años de educación político-ideológica 1969–1979* (Santiago: Estudios ILET, 1983). See also Arturo

Fontaine Talavera, "Acerca del pecado original de la revolución capitalista chilena," in Barry B. Levine, *El Desafío Neoliberal* (Bogotá: Grupo Editorial Norma, 1993).

9. For instance, the men who set the course for economic policy, such as ministers Jorge Cauas, Sergio De Castro, Pablo Baraona, Sergio de la Cuadra. In the political and institutional area, Sergio Fernández (twice minister of the interior) and Jaime Guzmán (political adviser) were professors of law.

10. Mark Falcoff, Susan Kaufman Purcell, and Arturo Valenzuela, *Chile: Prospects for Democracy* (New York: Council on Foreign Relations, 1988).

11. Mark Falcoff, "Pinochet: The Next Somoza," *Policy Review* 34 (Fall 1985).

12. Pamela Constable and Arturo Valenzuela, "Is Chile Next?" *Foreign Policy* 63 (Summer 1986).

13. Constable and Valenzuela, *A Nation of Enemies*, p. 291.

14. The National Endowment for Democracy (NED) was important because: (1) it funded CEP and CED-FLACSO independent polls, which were the first bridges between citizenry and leadership after nearly two decades of dictatorship; (2) it helped with funding and advice to mobilize citizens to register and vote; and (3) it monitored the election itself, both as to laws and regulations and the actual counting of votes. A survey of selected polling points allowed an accurate estimate of the outcome to be broadcast by radio before the official result was out. It is clear, moreover, that negotiating loans with the World Bank and the International Monetary Fund forced the régime's technocrats and businessmen to pay heed to political variables that they had previously been able to disregard.

15. For an economic analysis of these reforms, see Sebastian Edwards y Alejandra Cox, *Monetarism and Liberalization* (Chicago: University of Chicago Press, 1991), and Juan Andrés Fontaine, "Transición económica y política en Chile," *Estudios Públicos*, 1993.

16. See, for instance, José Piñera, "Hacia un nuevo modelo político," *Economía y Sociedad*, no. 2 (April 1976), and Jaime Guzmán, "El camino político," *Realidad*, no. 7, 1979. Piñera was one of the principal ministers of the economic area under General Pinochet, responsible for important labor and social security reforms. Guzmán was Pinochet's main political adviser and had considerable influence on the Constitution of 1980 and the schedule for transition established at that time.

17. A. Summer and R. Heston, *World Press Tables*, NBER, Version 5.6.

18. Bela Balassa, "Experimentos de política económica en Chile," *Estudios Públicos*, no. 14 (Fall 1984), p. 80. For 1988, Banco Mundial, *Informe de Desarrollo Humano 1992* (Washington, D.C., 1993). Figures are in 1985 dollars.

19. Figures estimated on the basis of data contained in Banco Central, *Informe económico y social 1960–1988*.

20. Roberto Méndez, Oscar Godoy, Enrique Barros, and Arturo Fontaine Talavera, "Por qué ganó el NO?" *Estudios Públicos*, no. 33 (Summer 1989).

21. Tarsicio Castañeda, "Contexto socioeconómico y causas del descenso de la mortalidad infantil en Chile," *Estudios Públicos*, no. 16 (Spring 1984).

22. Bela Balassa, "Experimentos de política económica en Chile," *Estudios Públicos*, no. 14 (Fall 1984), p. 80.

23. Bela Balassa, op. cit. For 1988, telephone figures are from Banco Mundial, *Informe de desarrollo humano 1992* (Washington, D.C., 1992). Automobile figures

are based on Instituto Nacional de Estadísticas, *Compendio estadístico 1991* (Santiago, 1993). Washing machine and refrigerator figures are inferred from *Censo de Población 1992*. Assume income elasticities of 1.5 and population elasticities of 1.

24. Gallup, *Indice Gallup de opinión y mercado*, Santiago, October 1982, p. 9; and *Censo Nacional de población y vivienda* (Santiago: Instituto Nacional de Estadísticas, 1994).

25. Traditional crops also became modernized. In 1970 production of wheat and maize per hectare was 13.9 metric quintals and 31.1 metric quintals, respectively; in 1988, it was 24 metric quintals of wheat and 75.3 metric quintals of maize. See Héctor Véliz, "La agricultura chilena y los indicadores sectoriales internacionales," *Estudios Públicos,* no. 30, 1989.

26. See Sergio Fernández, *Mi lucha por la democracia* (Santiago: Editorial Los Andes, 1984).

27. Corporación de Investigaciones Económicas para Latinoamérica (CIEPLAN); Facultad Latinamericana de Ciencias Sociales (FLACSO); Centro de Investigación y Desarrollo de la Educación (CIDE); Corporación de Promoción Universitaria (CPU); Centro de Estudios del Desarrollo (CED); Centro de Estudios Sociales y Educación (SUR); Instituto Chileno de Estudios Humanísticos (ICHEH); Centro de Investigaciones Socioculturales (CISOC); Centro de Estudios de la Realidad Contemporánea (CERC); Centro de Indagación y Expresión Cultural y Artística (CENECA).

28. See Arturo Fontaine Talavera, "Riqueza y estabilidad," *Economía y Sociedad,* no. 24 (April 1984).

29. "Estudio social y de Opinión Pública en la Población de Santiago," Santiago, Centro de Estudios Públicos, *Documento de Trabajo* No. 83, 1987.

30. Centro de Estudios Públicos, *Documento de Trabajo* No. 102, 1988, and No. 151, 1991.

31. Ignacio Irarrázaval, "Una mirada diferente al estrato socioeconómico bajo," *Estudios Públicos,* no. 43 (Winter 1993).

32. Jeffrey Puryear, *Thinking Politics* (Baltimore: Johns Hopkins University Press, 1994), p. 161.

33. Ibid., p. 164.

34. José Joaquín Brunner, "La participación de los centros académicos privados," *Estudios Públicos,* no. 19 (Winter 1985), p. 166.

35. María Teresa Lladser, *Centros Privados de Investigación en Ciencias Sociales en Chile* (Santiago: Academia de Humanismo Cristiano/FLACSO 1986).

36. Publications that covered these seminars most extensively included books published by CED and *Estudios Públicos*.

37. José Joaquín Brunner, quoted in Constable and Valenzuela, *A Nation of Enemies*, p. 252. At present Brunner is minister secretary-general of government.

38. Tomás Moulián, "Estabilidad Democrática en Chile: Una Mirada Histórica," in CIEPLAN, *Democracia en Chile: Doce Conferencias* (Santiago: CIEPLAN, 1986).

39. Jeffrey Puryear, op. cit., pp. 25–32.

40. Mario Góngora, *Ensayo Histórico sobre la Noción de Estado en Chile en los Siglos XIX y XX* (Santiago: Editorial Universitaria, 1986; first edition, Ediciones La Ciudad, 1981).

41. See Carlos Hunneus, "La política de la apertura y sus implicancias para la inauguración de la democracia en Chile," *Revista de Ciencia Política,* vol. 7, no. 1, Instituto de Ciencias Políticas, Universidad Católica de Chile, 1985.

42. The Instituto de Ciencias Alejandro Lipschutz (ICAL). See María Teresa Lladser, op. cit.

43. A CEP poll conducted in 1988 found, for instance, that 14 percent of respondents wished that "the political, economic, and social ideas of the next president" would be closer to those of President Allende. Centro de Estudios Públicos, *Documento de Trabajo* No. 102, 1988.

44. Edgardo Boeninger et al., *Orden Económico y Democracia* (Santiago: Centro de Estudios del Desarrollo [CED], 1985), pp. 23 and 85.

45. See, for instance, Alejandro Foxley, "Algunas condiciones para una democracia estable: El caso de Chile," Santiago, Colección *Estudios Cieplán,* November 1982; and "Después del monetarismo," in *Reconstrucción Económica para la democracia* (Santiago: Cieplán, Editorial Aconcagua, 1983). See also Alejandro Foxley et al., *El futuro democrático de Chile: 4 visiones* (Santiago: Centro de Estudios del Desarrollo, 1984).

46. This view was presented by, among others, Eduardo García, "Papel del estado como promotor y regulador del proceso de desarrollo económico," *Chile económico* (Santiago: Vector, 1984). See also Taller de industrias de la agrupación de economistas socialistas, "Una estrategia de industrialización" (Santiago: Vector, 1984).

47. For a discussion of the accord with the main supporters and detractors, see Tamara Avetikian, "El Acuerdo Nacional y la democracia," *Estudios Públicos,* no. 21, 1986.

48. See Arturo Fontaine Talavera, "Acerca del pecado original de la transformación capitalista chilena" (op. cit.). This text contains a more detailed examination of studies, papers, and persons who led the study center network.

49. CEREN, for instance, was closed down by the Universidad Católica after the coup. Several of its researchers later returned to Chile and joined FLACSO.

50. This has been amply documented. See Eugenio Tironi, *La campaña del no vista por sus creadores* (Santiago: Ediciones Melquíades 1989), and Guillermo Sunkel, "El uso político de las encuestas de opinión pública," *Documento de Trabajo* No. 18, Serie Educación y Cultura (Santiago: FLACSO, 1992).

51. Especially noteworthy were, for example, Alejandro Foxley, minister of finance, former director of CIEPLAN; Edgardo Boeninger, minister secretary-general of government, former director of CED, and his closest collaborator, Angel Flisfish, political analyst with FLACSO; Eugenio Tironi, undersecretary for communications, former director of SUR; René Cortázar, minister of labor, CIEPLAN economist; and José Pablo Arellano, director of the budget, CIEPLAN economist.

6

South Africa: Normative Conflicts, Social Cohesion, and Mediating Institutions

Ann Bernstein

South Africa in the 1990s is a society undergoing a fundamental transformation. This transformation is taking place in every aspect of South African life and it is radical in its implications. In some areas of the society the transition toward a nonracial and democratic society has been rapid and relatively untraumatic (thus far) for those involved. In other areas change is only now starting to bubble to the surface, and the full implications of the transition at work are not yet clear. This chapter is therefore written about a society undergoing a profound revolution, albeit a negotiated one. As will be apparent, this makes it difficult to isolate and select a defining normative conflict for South Africa that seems central to its past, present, and future, and so I have structured the essay perhaps rather differently from what might have been anticipated.

The chapter begins with a discussion of the historic and central South African conflict of apartheid and the way in which this has affected every aspect of South African life for the past four and a half decades. This fundamental, all-pervasive, normative conflict about the nature and future of South Africa in turn gave rise to a series of important strategic, political, and ultimately normative divides among apartheid's opponents (both inside the country and outside) about how to oppose the system. I describe and define these different normative conflicts, which contained within them numerous assumptions about the nature of change in a developing society and the relationship between ends and means in the

The assistance of Judi Hudson, research coordinator at the Centre for Development and Enterprise, is acknowledged in writing this chapter.

struggle to transform South Africa and create a better system of government for the country. And all of these different approaches to how to oppose and change apartheid South Africa involve issues that are already appearing and will certainly reappear in postapartheid South Africa.

The chapter then moves on to look at the remarkable political transition that has taken place in South Africa since 1991. In assessing and attempting to understand this unique transition many commentators have concentrated only on the dramatic and highly visible political developments since President Frederik W. de Klerk announced the unbanning of the African National Congress (ANC), the South African Communist Party (SACP), and others as well as the release of Nelson Mandela from prison. I argue that there have been two related but rather different and very important components to the—thus far—astoundingly successful transformation. After looking at aspects of what has been called, respectively, "the silent revolution" of de facto desegregation and growing black empowerment, and "the small miracle" of political negotiation and the relatively peaceful introduction of democracy into South Africa for the first time in its history, I go on to examine the role of business as a mediating institution; that section looks at business's role under apartheid and during the transition toward a new democratic order.

I then go on to explore the new normative conflicts and major issues that face South Africa now. In examining some of the potential divisions and conflicts that confront the "new South Africa," I focus on one particular challenge, that of the reestablishment of rule by law inside the country. The important mediating role of the legal system and the punishments that flow from its abrogation are looked at in this context. The concluding section of the chapter looks at mediating institutions more generally.

The South African Conflict

Until 1994 there was one central normative conflict that dominated and overshadowed all else in and about South Africa. Apartheid consisted of a package of values and actions comprising a very strong normative position imposed by a small group on everyone else in society. This set of norms turned around the most fundamental issues of national life—who is a South African citizen, what rights do they have, and what is their relationship with the state and each other? Ever since 1652, when Jan van Riebeek arrived from Holland and established a settlement at the Cape of Good Hope, most white people in South Africa have believed in their superiority to black South Africans and their right to rule the larger and larger amounts of territory they were able to subjugate under their military control.

By the middle of the twentieth century the prevailing white ethos of superiority, segregation, and discrimination toward black South Africans was slowly being undermined and eroded by the inexorable forces of urban industrialization and worldwide trends and attitudes following World War II. Instead of an acceleration of this process, which might have been anticipated in the light of trends throughout the continent, the succession to power of the Afrikaner-dominated National Party led to a reversal of this gradual loosening of racial segregation. From 1948 the policy that came to be known as apartheid took segregation to its logical conclusion. Apartheid amounted to a more systematic, more monolithic set of policies and programs and was far more ruthlessly enforced than earlier approaches to segregation. By the late 1950s and into the 1960s this new and more formal ideology of race discrimination had developed into a highly complex system of political, social, and economic rules and regulations coupled with racist norms and ideas that dominated the entire country.

At the core of apartheid thinking was the search for a system and in effect a rationalization of the core South African dilemma, as members of the National Party (NP) would define it. Here at the bottom tip of Africa was a country consisting of many different racial and tribal groups. The international experience showed, so the Nationalists thought, not only that such diverse groups could not live together happily and successfully but also that violence was inevitable if they tried to do so. Hence the evolution of what came to be the complex system of apartheid with its grandiose plan to mark off parts of the country (consisting mainly of the poorest and least modern areas) and designate them as homelands for the different tribal groups of black South Africa. In 1970 apartheid planners went so far as to state that in time there would be no black South African citizens. This amazing proposition was argued on the basis that in time all black people would be citizens of their designated homeland, even if they had never been there, did not speak the language of the area, and had no desire to live there.

In many respects apartheid can be understood as an extremely complex policy to prevent the natural and inevitable political and social consequences of economic growth. In the belief that blacks were citizens not of the whole of South Africa but only of their particular rural reserve (all nine of which occupied only some 13% of the country's land area) apartheid apologists could justify the exclusion of black people from any permanent presence in the burgeoning urban areas and from the commercial white farming areas. Black South Africans then could come to the cities and the farms to work for white people, but their real future and homes and thus the places where they would exercise their political rights were in the rural reserves or Bantustans. Considerable state resources were put into the implementation and enforcement of this policy. Millions of people were forcibly removed from their homes and land. Hundreds of thousands of bureaucrats, police, inspectors, soldiers, and ultimately weapons were used to keep the apartheid policies on track and dissent quelled. Apartheid created small, grossly overcrowded rural reserves with few economic prospects and even less in the way of infrastructure, education, or social facilities. The growing poverty, deprivation, and desperation in these areas then acted as a "push" factor in driving people to migrate to the centers of opportunity and growth in the country—the very cities and towns that the apartheid policy was designed to "preserve" as white. And there, because they were denied all rights of citizenship and had to live in appalling conditions, the very violence and unrest the ideologues had hoped to prevent grew as a consequence of the discrimination and deprivation of the policy.

Historically many of the opponents of apartheid thinking and ideas from within both white and black South Africa saw the growing, modern, and inevitably urban economy as the key mediating institution through which the many different people of South Africa could build a common country and find a common identity. This theme of the market economy as a vital magnet to pull people together and provide a binding common purpose and culture for all the different people who live in South Africa (and southern Africa) will be developed more fully in a later section of this chapter. For now it suffices to state the argument and turn to the normative conflicts that arose in response to the imposition of apartheid by a small (albeit militarily and politically powerful) minority on the vast majority of the inhabitants of the country.

As can be imagined, the apartheid policy—its norms and effects—had an enormous counterreaction, which in turn gave rise to other equally heated and pervasive normative schisms. From the early days of its imposition on the country, different forms of opposition were hotly debated even in white circles, and much more vigorously in black politics. The multifaceted debate on how to respond to apartheid, how to live with it, and how to oppose it led to many diverse and heated points of view. I will now turn to examining the essentially different forms of opposition, as they raise important normative issues in themselves and highlight themes that underlie many aspects of South African politics today.

The response to apartheid evoked five different types of reaction. The first type can be classified as the route followed by the ANC, that of "violent opposition." In the early years of apartheid, when the ANC was legal, it organized internally to oppose apartheid laws and to resist their enforcement. A small organization with never more than a million members, they were unable to stop the imposition of apartheid laws through peaceful internal resistance. The state responded to their actions with repression and jailing for leaders. Within some twelve years of NP rule the ANC was banned, and the organization went into exile and formed a guerrilla movement.

It has been said that the ANC had the least effective armed wing on the continent and had decided to tackle the strongest state on the continent at its most powerful point, its military might. The ANC in exile was a far more successful operator in the world of international diplomacy and was able in time to position itself brilliantly as the single legitimate voice for all black South Africans and the rightful heir to the apartheid regime. They also played an important role in influencing how the Western world understood and dealt with the South African issue, particularly in the final stages of the 1980s. The essence of this approach to opposition was the belief that the rigid authoritarian state that had been built up by the NP could only be fought through a strategy that combined violent opposition (of different kinds), total international isolation of "the racist regime," and economic boycotts to weaken the "white economy." This strategy assumed a static regime inside the country and believed in the desirability of what could be called "total revolution" as an effective mechanism of changing South Africa.

The second type of response to apartheid was the development of mass internal organizations starting in the 1970s and into the 1980s. In many respects these were what might be termed "revolutionary incrementalists" rather than advocates of violent one-off change from outside the country. With the growth of the South African economy and the increasing numbers of black people in industry and the urban areas, first trade unions and then urban community organizations started to develop and become powerful actors in the domestic politics of the country. Emphasizing internal democracy and mandating for representative leadership, these organizations became powerful actors in the domestic politics of the country and shaped the nature of opposition from within its borders. In many ways these were the most effective and powerful opponents of the apartheid regime. Their links with the exiled ANC movement were complex. Emotionally most internal resisters saw themselves as one with the ANC, but in many respects their strategy of change and assumptions about the ruling regime were different. Moreover, their location within the country led to a far more pragmatic "something is better than nothing" approach. Although many individuals might have assisted the ANC in aspects of its clandestine armed struggle, most were far more intimately involved in the complex business of internal resistance to apartheid laws and practices on the factory floor or in the cities and towns. The Congress of South African Trade Unions (Cosatu) and the collection of civic and community organizations that formed the United Democratic Front (UDF) were totally immersed in the detailed and incremental business of fashioning an industrial relations system that could work in the South African context or in arguing the implications of "one city one economy" in the many cities and towns throughout the country.

The third response to apartheid involved a very different kind of internal actor. These were people opposed to apartheid but who had decided through force of circumstance or opportunity, because of their particular identity or position, to oppose the system from within it. An example of this type of actor is Chief Mangosuthu Buthelezi and his Inkatha movement (which became a political party in the 1990s, the Inkatha Freedom Party). In the 1970s and 1980s Chief Buthelezi's refusal to accept independence for the KwaZulu homeland prevented the apartheid regime from denying some 6 million Zulu South Africans their South African citizenship. In so doing they played an important role in forcing many within the ruling NP to rethink the premises of the grand apartheid strategy of "no black South African citizens." Another type of incrementalist change agent from within the system was the white opposition party, the Progressive Party. In the role pioneered by their sole representative for some thirteen years (Mrs. Helen Suzman) this small liberal party fought every piece of apartheid legislation from their parliamentary base and used this platform (and its protection and privileges) to obtain factual information about the effect of apartheid policies on the society as a whole and the millions caught up in its terrible consequences, to educate white (and black) South Africans about the effects of apartheid legislation, and to help keep alive democratic and nonracial ideals in the public arena.

The fourth response to apartheid can be described as those who put their heads down and tried to get on with their lives. For some (mainly whites) this entailed leading a relatively normal existence; others (mainly black South Africans) endured tremendous suffering as a result of apartheid policies (forced removals in urban and rural areas; denial of opportunity in schooling, university, workplace, and so on).

The fifth type of response to apartheid involved a large number of people who can be said to have joined the system—collaborated in one way or another. It is often forgotten that there are a significant number of black South Africans who benefited from the system of apartheid and made careers and relative fortunes for themselves. This was done through participating in the system of token political representation established through apartheid laws, and in finding economic opportunities in the interstices of segregation and its erosion.

The adoption of such varying responses to apartheid involved significant normative differences between many of these actors. Conceptually these differences ranged over issues as wide and as fundamental as the relationship between apartheid and capitalism in South Africa; violent revolution versus nonviolent incremental change; the ultimate goals of such change and how best to get there but also in terms of how change happens in modern industrializing societies—a single route to the "new utopia" or multifaceted approaches to changing a vast and complex social system; attitudes toward violence and the consequences of such violence against the regime and within communities; the nature of the South African state and how best to find its weakest points, oppose its policies, and make inroads in building a nonracial society. These different worldviews not only encompassed how to oppose apartheid but also how to manage the transition to a new political order and, importantly, what kind of new society should replace the apartheid order (a Western-type human rights constitutional regime or an Eastern bloc–style socialist state)? It could be said that at the root of the differences between apartheid and its different opponents was a desire for power, but coupled with this were very different conceptions of the norms and values that should underlie South African society.

It is important to point out that in the 1980s conflict between proponents of different forms of opposition to the apartheid regime was not only at the conceptual level. ANC operatives were involved in brutal battles with supporters of Chief Buthelezi, and the struggle between them continues to this day in the bloody conflicts that plague the province of KwaZulu/Natal. Since September 1987 there has not been a peaceful month in the region; between January 1991 and December 1994 over 5,000 people were killed (Hudson 1995, 10). The region is awash with lethal weapons, many of them assault rifles supplied under a cloak of secrecy by the South African Defence Force to the Mozambique National Resistance (MNR or RENAMO) that began to flow back from across the border. Other weapons came from secret arms caches stored by Umkhonto we Sizwe when the ANC suspended its guerrilla war against white minority rule.

South Africa's Negotiated Revolution

South Africa's political transition in the 1990s is a remarkable story. The political action starts in Nelson Mandela's jail cell and his attempts to start the negotiations for a peaceful transition in South Africa from the mid-1980s. It is supplemented by conversations in British and Swiss hotel rooms between members of the banned ANC and leaders of its "terrorist" army, initially with Afrikaner academics and then with members of the country's intelligence service. This amazing "behind-the-scenes" process became public in 1990 when President Frederik W. de Klerk started a high-stakes political poker game with the announcement in the "white" parliament that he would be releasing Nelson Mandela and unbanning the ANC and allied organizations simultaneously. After decades of the liberation movement and its leaders being portrayed as the "terrorist" and "communist" dominated enemy, the significance of such developments cannot be underestimated. Nine days later Nelson Rolihlahla Mandela walked free from the Victor Verster Prison after serving twenty-seven years, six months, and one week of a life sentence for sabotage and conspiracy to overthrow the white minority government. Mandela's historic release signaled the beginning of a process of negotiations that would culminate in a new constitution for South Africa four years later and Mandela's inauguration as president on 10 May 1994.

Revelers celebrating his release thronged the streets in the city centers around the country. It was reported that most were "well-behaved" but also that a "handful of blacks (in Johannesburg) taunted whites, yelling "Freedom is coming. Whites get out!" (*The Star,* 12 February 1990). Not everyone was happy. Shocked that the Nationalist government could be contemplating negotiating with "terrorists," a crowd of about 2,000 Afrikaner Weerstandbeweging (AWB) members and a group of neo-Nazi supporters marched through the Pretoria city center in protest against the state president's reform initiatives. Shouts of "Hang Mandela!" rang out over placards saying "Reform stinks"; one man dangled a black doll from a piece of string shouting, "This is Mandela!" The AWB leader, Eugene Terreblanche, and the Boerestaat Party leader tried to hand over thirty pieces of silver and a white coffin to leading members of the NP. When the latter refused it, the bag was thrown on top of a coffin (*Sunday Times,* 11 February 1990; *Business Day,* 16 February 1990).

The transition period was a time of great danger and uncertainty for the society, with Mandela and de Klerk buffeted by extremists on their left and right, respectively, and by crises occasioned most often by outbreaks of violence in one or another segment of a large and diverse population. Many actors and institutions played a role in helping to keep negotiations on track and mediate the crises. These "mediating actors" included foreign governments watching and nurturing the process in various ways; the church within South Africa, which also played its part with all the relevant parties; the South African business sector, which helped the process along in different ways; individuals such as Professor Okumu from Kenya, who played a critical role in Inkatha's decision to participate in the elections. Before looking in detail at the mediating role of business, it is necessary to give a brief description of the process of negotiations.

The first phase of the process can be termed "the talks about talks" phase. Until the beginning of negotiations proper at the Convention for a Democratic South Africa (CODESA), talks consisted mainly in establishing the circumstances within which negotiations could begin. In May

1990 Mandela headed the first round of official negotiations with the government at the presidential residence, Groote Schuur, which resulted in an agreement on a peaceful negotiation process. The Groote Schuur Minute, as it came to be known, was to facilitate the release of political prisoners, the return of exiles, and the amendment of security legislation. All this was necessary to enable the ANC to operate within the country. The next important phase in negotiations was the signing of the Pretoria Minute in August when the ANC renounced its armed struggle. Most of 1991 was taken up with efforts to prepare the country for the constitutional negotiations. In May of that year the ANC suspended negotiations with the government, accusing it of complicity in political violence. By September, however, the foundations for the multiparty negotiations had been laid with the signing of the National Peace Accord (NPA) brokered by important members of the church and business communities. Little more than a month later, negotiations for a new South African constitution got under way. CODESA had been born.

A total of eighteen organizations were present at these negotiations. The white right wing as well as some groups to the left of the ANC were notable in their absence. Significant agreements were reached before CODESA's breakdown in June 1992: the shape of an interim government was decided; it would consist of a national assembly and a senate, which would operate according to special majorities and wide constitutional principles. However, fundamental divisions between the chief protagonists—the ANC and the South African government—proved too deep and intractable to allow extensive progress at this first bargaining forum. The ANC sought a rapid transition to majority rule whereas the government remained wedded to a slower transition that would make binding decisions, thus giving minority parties effective say in deciding constitutional principles. More time was needed by both sides. Negotiators needed to ensure that their parties were supportive of the dynamics developing in the talks, and many needed to see and be reminded of "the alternative that was too ghastly to contemplate" if talks were to break down. CODESA, however, set the ground for the successful negotiations of 1993.

By the time a new round of multiparty talks started in 1993, the ANC and the government had recognized that negotiations were the only game in town—and that both parties had now staked their own futures on the success of such negotiations. In the stormy seas of South Africa in the midst of transition from the old order to the new, de Klerk and Mandela needed each other to get to the other side safely. The irony of the nature of South Africa's transition is in part its great strength. The key protagonists in the South African drama—Afrikaner and African nationalists—now had to work with each other and together carve out a viable compromise that would provide the only weapon either of them had with which to deal with the more radical forces opposed to a workable deal. Within nine months a new constitution had been negotiated, and the country could move toward its first democratic election in 1994.

In the run-up to the first nonracial elections, twenty-nine political parties registered. The Inkatha Freedom Party (IFP) was conspicuously absent and remained so until a week before the elections, when its leader, Chief Buthelezi, agreed to participate. After three days of voting, between 26 and 29 April, the ANC emerged victorious, winning 62.6% of the national vote and all but two of the provinces—a landslide victory. The NP got 20.4% and to the surprise of many, the IFP polled 10.5% of the national vote and won the KwaZulu legislature with 50.3% of the vote—the ANC polling 32.2% of this province's vote. In the wake of the election the Government of National Unity (GNU) was established, comprising most major political parties, with NP leader de Klerk elected as one of two deputy presidents. (See box on chronology of South Africa's transition.)

A revealing illustration of South Africa's fragile new unity as a nation can be found in two sporting events, which, in view of the high priority many South Africans (black and white) give to sport, are significant. The first took place in late 1994. The World Cup Rugby Games were held in South Africa for the first time and represented the first major sporting event to be hosted in the country now that it was back in the community of nations. Rugby has traditionally been a "white" sport and identified with Afrikaner dominance, bullying, and power. For the first time ever, black and white South Africans identified with the national team, even though the vast majority of team members are white. Media reports focused on interviewing black cabinet ministers in the new GNU and ordinary black citizens concerning their reaction to both watching their first rugby match and cheering for a South African national team for the first time. Most reported wonder, novelty, and excitement at this unusual experience. The second sporting event was the African Nations Cup, the most important soccer event on the continent, also held in South Africa for the first time, and the first time in thirty years that South Africa was allowed to participate in it. Soccer is traditionally seen as a black sport in the country. Coming after the rugby tournament and the remarkable sense of common nationhood that event and South Africa's victory in it produced, it became very important for the newly united nation that soccer not be seen as the poorer second cousin of "white man's" rugby. Considerable effort was made by politicians, white sports writers, and public commentators generally exhorting whites to show the same national spirit for the soccer team as blacks did for the rugby team. Businesses' advertising too was very careful to show that they were as committed to this mainly "black sport" as they were to rugby. It was clear that black politicians who had gone considerable distance to identifying with the spirit of

CHRONOLOGY 6.1   Brief Chronology of South Africa's Transition

---

1990

February	De Klerk lifts the ban on the ANC, PAC, SACP and other organizations and releases Nelson Mandela from prison.
April	Exiled ANC leaders return to South Africa to begin talks with the SAG.
May	ANC and SAG sign Groote Schuur Minute facilitating the release of political prisoners and the return of exiles.
June	State of emergency lifted everywhere except Natal.
August	Pretoria Minute signed between ANC and SAG, ending the ANC's armed struggle.

1991

April	ANC accuses SAG of complicity in violence and threatens to withdraw from negotiations.
May	ANC withdraws from talks with SAG and announces mass action campaign.
September	National Peace Accord signed by all major players apart from the right wing.
December	Constitutional negotiations begin with the formation of CODESA.

1992

March	Whites-only referendum gives de Klerk support for reform process.
May	CODESA ends in deadlock after working group on constitution-making fails to produce results.
June	ANC suspends negotiation with SAG and begins "rolling mass action" campaign.
September	ANC and SAG sign Record of Understanding: certain political prisoners released, CODESA 2 deadlock resolves, some hostels fenced, and carrying of traditional weapons banned.
October	Concerned South Africans Group (Cosag) formed, which included IFP, right-wing leaders, and leaders of Ciskei, Bophuthatswana, and KwaZulu.

1993

April	Negotiations resume with Multi-Party Negotiation Process.
June	IFP and CP quit talks over "sufficient consensus" mode of decision-making.
November	Constitutional negotiations come to an end with agreement on interim constitution.

1994

March	Twenty-nine political parties register for April elections. Afrikaner Volksfront leader, Constand Viljoen, registers Freedom Front at last moment, splitting the right wing. International mediation issue on the role of Zulu King Goodwill Zwelithini bedevils negotiations.
April	Buthelezi registers IFP at eleventh hour.
	South Africa's first general election is held.
	ANC emerges victorious in elections for the National Assembly and wins all the provinces except KwaZulu/Natal and the Western Cape.
May	GNU formed to lead South Africa over the next five years.

Source: Adapted from the *Mail and Guardian*, 15 April 1994.

reconciliation and nationhood embodied in the very idea of black people supporting a South African rugby team were concerned that their white compatriots should now play the game and support soccer. This seems to have been the case with, for example, the mainly white rugby team appearing at the soccer game with a big sign indicating their support for the South African national soccer team. This window into South Africa as it is now is revealing because it tells us so much about the divided society that apartheid had created and also some of the fragility of the mood of reconciliation and "togetherness" of the "rainbow nation."

South Africa's "Silent Revolution"

Many commentators on the South African transition have focused primarily on the dramatic and highly visible political developments since 1990, which started with de Klerk's now famous 2 February 1990 speech. This remarkable period of negotiation, conflict, breakdowns, and the ultimately successful and relatively peaceful transition is only one part of the South African revolution. In this section I will place this "small miracle" of the political transition in the context of what John Kane-Berman has called in a book of the same name the "silent revolution" of desegregation, economic growth, and integration that has taken place in South Africa since the 1970s, despite apartheid policies and often in defiance of them.

While formal opponents of the apartheid regime talked long and loud about its evils and what was needed to bring it down, fundamental processes were at work within South Africa itself. The effect of these changes was to undermine and remove much of the rationale and relevance of apartheid laws and thinking from the emerging new society. Starting in the 1970s and increasingly throughout the 1980s, developments were taking place outside of the formal arrangements of power (still strictly segregated) of profound importance and significance.

Apartheid ideologues had always understood the paradox that faced a segregated South Africa. Since the discovery of diamonds and gold in the late nineteenth century the fortunes of the country rested on the development of a thriving and increasingly diversified single national economy. This project required black labor, and in time it was to require skilled black workers and then managers. How to do this while simultaneously enforcing political, social, educational, and other aspects of economic segregation would, of course, be a problem. This dilemma was expressed best by a right-wing (i.e., to the right of the NP) slogan in the 1960s: "The choice is simple—poor and white or rich and mixed." The story of South Africa over the past century demonstrates the almost inexorable and very powerful role of the market economy in drawing people into a single, urban-based industrializing and modernizing economy. In a sense it is the market that has been South Africa's most powerful and significant mediating institution, and it has done this in spite of the apartheid laws that often worked to prevent this role and make it harder for growth to happen.

The industrial color bar whereby blacks were able to perform only certain jobs in industry was formally entrenched in law in the 1920s but had to be gradually relaxed (albeit extremely grudgingly) in the first two decades of apartheid as more and more black people moved into skilled jobs, in line with the economy's growing needs. The manufacturing sector, given a boost by the wartime conditions of the 1940s, had by the mid-1960s overtaken mining and agriculture as the dominant sector of the economy. This emergence of manufacturing as the leading sector of the South African economy required a shift from a mainly unskilled migratory workforce to an economy that needed trained, technically competent, and more literate workers. According to the state-appointed 1977 Wiehahn Commission, "There were simply not enough skilled workers available to fill all the vacancies . . . with the result that increasing numbers of unskilled and semi-skilled workers, particularly blacks, had to be trained and utilized to perform higher-level skilled jobs" (Wiehahn Commission Report 1982, p. 1, quoted in Price 1991, 31). In 1965 middle-level manpower was only 20% black; twenty years later, in 1985, the proportion had doubled to 40%; over the same period the black contribution to high-level manpower jumped from 25% to 32%. In 1968 the country's largest bank reported that 1% of its clerical staff was black, and by 1983 the proportion was 23%; a large industrial company reported in 1988 that the proportion of black skilled employees in their company had risen from 0.4% to 16.5% over the preceding ten years; in 1990 there were 5,000 black people in the mining industry doing jobs previously reserved for whites (see Kane-Berman 1990, 9). The economy's increasing reliance on skilled black manpower increased black workers' bargaining power and also put pressure on segregated education, since a more effective education system for blacks was required to meet skilled labor demands.

Linked to the use of black people in skilled jobs is the increase in the numbers of black students at white universities by the 1970s. The number of African students attending the "white" universities increased more than twofold between 1974, when only 309 African students had been granted government permission to attend, and 1980, when the number attending was 788 (Price 1991, 109). In 1983 the government conceded that the permit system had broken down, and by 1986 Africans enrolled at the English-speaking "white" universities numbered 3,428, and by 1990 about 22% of all students at these universities were black (including "coloureds" and Asians). With respect to schooling, the story is even more dramatic.

By the early 1970s the governing elite had begun to acknowledge that the shortage of skilled labor had become a threat to continued economic

TABLE 6.1   Racial Shares of Personal Income (in percent)

	1985	1990	1995
Whites	58.7	54.0	51.7
Coloureds	8.2	8.8	9.2
Asians	4.3	4.7	5.0
Blacks	28.8	32.5	34.1

Source: A. Bernstein, ed., "Post-Apartheid Population and Income Trends," Centre for Development and Enterprise, CDE Research No. 1, Johannesburg, 1995, p. 16.

growth and that something had to change. In the early 1970s government was spending some eighteen times as much money on a white pupil as on an African student. Over the next eighteen to twenty years state spending on African education was to increase by nearly 6,000% from R70 million to R4,097 million. As a result of this greater allocation of resources to Africans the racial expenditure ratio dropped to about 4.6 to 1 by 1987/88.

Racial shares of personal income started to change in the 1970s. According to Kane-Berman, the 1970s saw a redistribution of income from (relatively) rich white people to poor black people. This trend has continued into the 1980s and early 1990s. Between 1980 and 1986 real African personal disposable income rose, albeit very slightly (0.8%), but that of whites declined by nearly 16%. Recent research published by the Centre for Development and Enterprise finds that between 1985 and 1995 average per capita income rose for all groups except whites, who suffered a small decline, as shown in Table 6.1.

Apartheid policy was originally premised on the notion of "the cities as the white man's creation," with Africans participating in the urban economy on a migratory basis as and when white needs determined. This destructive and rather fanciful notion had started to erode from the earliest urban settlements in South Africa. Nonetheless, the acquisition of power by the NP at midcentury led to a rigid intensification of the system of influx control designed to enforce black outmigration and to control the general flow of people into and out of the cities. By the late 1970s there were already numerous indicators of the functional failure of this system. No fewer than 17.12 million people were arrested under the pass laws between 1916 and 1981—which averages out to 721 arrests every day, nonstop, for sixty-five years (Kane-Berman, "The [White] Lie of the NP's Election Campaign," *Mail and Guardian*, 4 March 1994). Despite this enormous government expenditure on armies of bureaucrats and police to apprehend, prosecute, imprison, and deport pass law offenders, the black population in South Africa's urban areas continued to grow. This growth was fueled in part by people "voting with their feet" and ignoring the prohibitions on migration and urban settlement and in part by the natural increase of the existing urban population.

The 1985 census showed that there were already more black people living in "white urban areas" of South Africa (some 7 million) than there were white people in the country (some 5 million). The projected increases in these figures were enough to make the dream of "black homeland independence" little more than a bad joke. As the business-funded Urban Foundation stated in 1990, South Africa is in a period of "fundamental transition towards large, predominantly black metropolitan areas" (*Private Sector Council*, no. 1, p. 24).

The Group Areas Act whereby residential and commercial areas in the cities and towns were strictly segregated by race had begun disintegrating steadily some time before its repeal in 1991. It is estimated that at least 150,000 black people were living unlawfully in white group areas at the end of the 1980s. Indeed, according to a newspaper report of the time: "So extensively had the Act broken down that one estate agent said of a conservative threat to take her to court for selling a house in a white area to Indians that the conservative would have to hire the Ellis Park Rugby Stadium for all the prosecutions he would have to conduct" (*The Weekly Mail*, 10 February 1989).

There are many other important examples of the way in which the inexorable forces of the market and urbanization were undermining the legal structures of apartheid. Mention should be made of the growth of the black trade union movement centered in mining and manufacturing, which was to grow to 1 million members, with considerable influence in the country; the growing power of black consumers, who were increasingly starting to dominate critical market sectors; and the minibus taxi industry (operating outside the law and in competition with a subsidized bus service), which grew its share of African commuter transport to some 44% in the space of a decade during the 1980s and which by the 1990s provided four motor manufacturing companies with a turnover of some R2 billion a year, representing a capital investment of about R3 billion and creating some 300,000 jobs (Cooper et al. 1992, 175). And finally, although it was not until 1983 that shebeen owners (illegal bars in black urban townships) could even apply for liquor licenses, it was estimated in 1993 that some 45% of the volume of beer manufactured in the country was distributed and sold through shebeens (Sidiropoulos 1993, 29).

In parallel with these trends "on the ground," as it were, white and black attitudes about the future and about each other were changing as well. In two important studies undertaken in the 1970s it was found that three-quarters of the blacks interviewed desired economic improvement, and two-thirds gave this as their top priority. At the same time, about 80% of the white electorate accepted in principle the idea of higher wages and a better standard of living for blacks, with some two-thirds accepting the principle of equal pay for equal work irrespective of race. While the majority of whites were not yet prepared to grant full job equality to black people, openness on this issue grew over the period of study. In 1974 only 13% of Afrikaners and 44% of English speakers were prepared to work under a black person; by 1977 this had risen to 24% and 55% respectively. By 1974 one-third of whites were prepared to accept the closing of the wage gap between blacks and whites even at the cost of additional inflation (see Hanf et al. 1981).

Although at this time the ANC and most other black political groupings argued for a socialist or even communist system, the study noted that a large majority of blacks accepted a free-market economy. "What blacks want is a better and more appropriate position in the existing economic system. Were this not the case—if for instance the majority of blacks preferred some form of state economy or a socialist economic system—the economic conflict could also become fundamental and thus far more difficult to settle by negotiation" (Hanf et al. 1981, 369). According to the study, blacks showed an "extraordinary high tolerance . . . towards the economic role of whites and Indians in a hypothetical future society." Black people are well aware of the whites' usefulness for the functioning of the South African economy. "They do not want to expropriate white and Indian businesses; they rather want their own businesses and a share of the fruits of a booming economy" (p. 369). It was clear from these findings that openness on the part of the whites was close to the expectations of blacks on the issue of economic conflict. "To abolish administrative and legal discrimination, introduce equal opportunities and dismantle inequality are goals of peaceful change which cause no fundamental conflict between blacks and whites" (p. 371).

According to the same study social segregation was an issue of prime concern to white people. Almost 60% of whites were not amenable to any peaceful change in the field of social relations, and about 30% were prepared to accept at best marginal changes; only 10% were ready to accept the abolition of enforced social segregation. These attitudes did not change much between 1974 and 1977. Luckily for South Africa one of the important findings of the study was that discrimination by whites had not given rise to racism in reverse. The authors found that urban black people in fact showed "remarkable tolerance towards white and Indian minorities in a future society." While black people found institutional segregation to be insulting, only about 10% regarded the abolition of social discrimination as a matter of prime concern.

In this regard it is also interesting to note the results of studies conducted to assess the views of young black people. It was originally thought that one of the greatest threats to both the transition and the new regime would come from young black South Africans. There was a widely held notion that the young urban black teenagers and those slightly older who had been at the forefront of so much of the internal resistance and disturbances throughout the 1980s and into the 1990s would pose the greatest threat to the stability of the new order. Considerable research has now shown that this fear, like that of virulent black racism in reverse, was misplaced and exaggerated.

It is generally acknowledged that "without doubt it was the youth— university students, schoolchildren, and unemployed people—who provided the cutting edge of the political radicalism in the 1980s" (Lodge and Nasson 1991, 38). Once regarded by many as the brave foot soldiers of the liberation struggle, the "politically fired-up" youth who made their own rules and would not listen to any form of authority seemed to pose enormous problems for stabilizing the society. Writing for the *Washington Post,* the South African correspondent said, "A demographic time-bomb—black youths who came of age on the liberation slogans of the 1980s—has tick-ticked into a lost generation of crime-prone young adults. They are without education, skills, job prospects or hope—but they do have plenty of guns" (*Washington Post,* 4 September 1992). Dr. Gomolemo Mokae from Azapo (a small, intellectual left-wing political party) said in 1992, "We are reaping a whirlwind of the 1985–86 era when youths were given licenses to kill in the name of liberation. They were made to understand that what they were doing by becoming a law unto themselves was the right thing" (*City Press,* 30 August 1992).

In the early 1990s there was considerable talk about "the lost generation"—young people in the townships who were undereducated, highly politicized and radicalized, and through the ANC campaign of ungovernability and government repression, no longer respected or listened to any figures of authority at all. For many they were seen as the "wild card" in South Africa's transition to inclusive rule (Schlemmer 1991, 16). However, when serious investigation was undertaken into what young people in the townships felt and wanted, commentators were surprised at the results. Three different studies were conducted. One compared the views of young black people (16–24 years old) with those of older people. The second interviewed a sample of some 2,200 people of all races aged between 16 and 30 and covered all the different parts of the country. The third interviewed white and black youths in metropolitan centers. The findings of all three studies contradict the notion of "the lost generation" that would threaten the transition and the fragile new democracy.

The studies found too that young South Africans are serious about religion. According to the sample survey, 56% of young women attend church once a week or more. Young men attend church slightly less frequently; even so, 37% went once a week or more. Only 9% of young people never attend church at all, and more than half (53%) of the younger age category (16–20 years) attend church once a week or more. Many young South Africans feel that education is the way to a secure future. One of the polls showed that as many as 80% of those interviewed felt that there should be more discipline both at school and at home. Of those young people who did not continue studying as far as they had planned, only 2% cited "politics" as the reason for not completing their education. This finding was much higher among "coloured" young people, at 10%, than among African youth, at 1%. Only 12% of the young people are members of political organizations, and here the percentage was higher among men than women. This figure was slightly higher at 15% among young Africans. Surprisingly, many of the people surveyed were involved in church choirs (38%) and in sports organizations (32%) (see Everatt and Orkin 1993).

In comparing young people to older South Africans it was found that the younger group does not support the South African Communist Party (SACP) to a greater extent than older people, nor do they appear to be drawing away from the ANC in favor of the more radical Azapo or Pan African Congress (PAC). The youth on average are more likely than the oldest group of township residents to feel close to the ANC and the de Klerk administration. (See Table 6.2.) Young people are only marginally more likely to support boycotts and stayaways, demonstrations and marches than their elders. They are no more likely to support violence and the armed struggle and just as likely as older people to support negotiations with the government. As one of the country's senior social scientists concluded: "Clearly the stereotype of a 'lost generation' is based on the posture and actions of a highly mobilised activist minority and on the behaviour of an anti-social minority" (Schlemmer 1991, 23).

In the general study conducted by Hanf et al. published in 1981, the authors argued from their findings that white people "are far more open to concessions in the economic sphere than they are to initiating peaceful change in the sphere of social relations." It is instructive to look at the possible reasons for this. In the economic sphere white people were coming into contact with blacks all the time and on an increasingly equal basis. They depended on each other in many different ways and knew that the economy would not grow without both black and white participation. Increasingly white public figures in business, media, and in time politics would be arguing the economic case for progress and providing leadership on these issues. All of these factors had an impact on white attitudes. In the social sphere, however, it was still possible to lead highly segregated lives and to assume that this was quite normal and a viable way for social matters to be organized. It was only as everyday events started to contradict and challenge old white attitudes, and when their political leaders took a stand, that attitudes would change. The examples of the re-

TABLE 6.2   Identification with Organizations

	16–24 yrs	*25–34 yrs*	*35–49 yrs*	*50+ yrs*
Feel "very close" to or "close" to:				
Church	75%	70%	65%	69%
Employer	34%	47%	51%	39%
Street committee	38%	44%	47%	28%
Civic association	43%	49%	48%	33%
SACP	36%	45%	38%	23%
PAC	17%	24%	24%	13%
De Klerk government	66%	64%	62%	53%
ANC	67%	71%	62%	57%
Sample *N*	281	244	217	163

Source: L. Schlemmer, "Black Township Residents Amidst Protest, Violence, and Negotiation," Centre for Policy Studies, Research Report No. 15, Johannesburg, 1991, p. 17.

peal of apartheid in elevators in the 1970s, of influx control in 1986, and of the Group Areas Act in 1990 all demonstrate the remarkable phenomenon of changes in public policy and political justification leading to a change in white attitudes. These were all good omens for the state president to take a decisive political lead in 1990 and feel confident that the majority of his supporters would back his decisions and leadership role.

It is in this context of what has been called "the silent revolution" of change on the ground and in white people's attitudes that the dramatic political developments of the 1990s need to be understood. The main struts of the apartheid system were systematically being undermined by the realities of a growing single economy, an integrating workplace and consumer market, and the actions of ordinary people doing what they could to survive in difficult circumstances and taking opportunities where they were. In the process the building blocks for a new and very different kind of society were created.

Business in South Africa:
An Unusual Mediating Institution

The South African economy has been a critically important factor in exposing the irrationality of apartheid policies. Building on this point, the focus in this section is on an institution that played an unusual and remarkable role in the fight against apartheid and in the transition to a new political and social order, namely, the business sector. Three different aspects will be highlighted: business and its growing opposition to apartheid laws; business and the political negotiations; and business and the peace process.

Any discussion about business as an "institution" must start by clarifying what is meant by the term business itself. In the South African context (and in many other countries) "business" is used very loosely to refer to whatever the user would like it to mean. The term itself can be used to refer to two different entities. The first is the firm itself: the category of individuals and organizations that are engaged in the production of goods and services for profit. The idea of the firm spans a spectrum from the multinational corporation to the one-person enterprise. The second entity is the business organization: the voluntary association of a number of firms into chambers of commerce and industry that could represent sectors or geographic regions or businesses within the country as a whole. In addition, the term is often and somewhat misleadingly used to describe the activities or views of a vaguely defined collectivity of "tycoons"—the owners and executives of the largest business groups. In addition to these analytic distinctions there are three other factors that can often affect the precise meaning of the term business. The first is ethnicity; for example, in South Africa the vast majority of corporations and business organizations are controlled and managed by white people. The second factor concerns size. In South Africa the economy is dominated by some six very large corporations that own many subsidiary businesses. The third factor concerns ownership and whether or not the business is owned and controlled by permanent residents of a particular country or foreigners. In South Africa this is not an issue, as the majority of large corporations are at least domestic, albeit white controlled.

The role of business in South Africa during the apartheid era is a complex and mixed one. In general it can be said that, like businesses elsewhere, they accommodated themselves to the prevailing politics of apartheid for most of the period, and it was only in the 1980s, when the immediate interests of many corporations were affected, that business leaders started systematically to speak out against the government and act in ways that were directly counter to apartheid policies. Throughout the earlier period business organizations would indicate their opposition to government policies as these affected the workplace and economic issues and then get back to business. Relations between the government and the business sector were always strained, and it is significant that Harry Oppenheimer, the country's leading businessman and head of its largest corporation, never actually met the man who was state president (P. W. Botha) throughout the turbulent 1980s.

Business, Apartheid, and the Urban Foundation

In 1976 South African business came together to form the Urban Foundation. In the words of H. F. Oppenheimer, head of South Africa's largest corporation, Anglo American Corporation of South Africa, speaking at the Founding Conference of the Urban Foundation in November 1976: "We in South Africa are going through a very critical time and of all the difficulties we face one of the most serious factors, perhaps the most serious factor, is the quality of life in our urban communities. Business people have a very important role to play and it is in order to organise business people that this conference has been arranged."

This organization was to perform a remarkable and unique role over the next fifteen years. There are separate business organizations in South Africa for English and Afrikaans business, and one of the unusual aspects of the Urban Foundation was that it was the first time that English and Afrikaans businessmen had come together in the same organization. Thus indirectly the organization was to play a "mediating role" between these two historically estranged and sometimes antagonistic groups.

Originally set up "to improve the quality of life in urban black communities," the Foundation's role grew far beyond this initial idea. By the end of the 1980s the organization was the country's leading development agent, demonstrating through practical projects innovative ways of tackling the massive development challenges that would face a government committed to housing, educating, and servicing all the country's citizens. The organization was also leading the business sector in its opposition to the country's key apartheid laws. Thus it was the Foundation that educated and informed business leaders about the negative ramifications of influx control on the economy and all South Africans; mobilized the international and domestic research evidence and arguments to counter government and conservative thinking on the necessity of retaining controls over black movement to the cities; mobilized business resources and influence to persuade the government that influx control must go; publicly lobbied and galvanized others to join in this campaign; and then, having obtained government support in principle for the abolition of this key pillar of the apartheid system, ensured that the actual legislation came to parliament as quickly as possible and that it carried through the intentions of abolition in all respects. With this victory under its belt, the Foundation then embarked on a five-year campaign to educate and mobilize business and then other interests around the removal of the other key pillars of apartheid, namely, the Land Acts (dealing with rural segregation—ownership of land), the Group Areas Act, and the enforcement of segregated local government.

Through its work the Foundation became an institution in apartheid South Africa where black and white South Africans could come together to discuss issues of national concern in an open and constructive environment. It was a place where projects could be initiated and then jointly managed by black South Africans and Foundation staff. Through the support of key business leaders and their organizations the Foundation could play a leadership role with respect to ideas, development programs, and policies. Through its support for a set of values that, taken to their logical conclusion, were clearly in opposition to those of apartheid, the Foundation was a bridgehead in the world of the white establishment for a new South Africa not based on race. Perhaps as important as its other roles was that the Foundation provided a place where many professionals and activists could come together and think creatively about the development needs of a new South Africa and how a government could effectively start to deal with those burgeoning needs. Through the use of statistics and sound local and international research the Foundation was able to take highly emotional issues in the South African context (segregated education, for instance) and place them into a more technical and neutral environment, thus making them more susceptible to rational discussion and action. In the middle to late 1980s the Foundation played a unique mediating role between the values and concerns of business, the interests of urban communities, and those within government starting to want to move away from the rigidities of apartheid.

*Business, Negotiations, and the Consultative Business Movement**

In the late 1980s South Africa was undergoing successive states of emergency as the only way the government had of curbing the heightened militancy and unrest throughout many parts of the country and particularly the urban areas. It was in this environment that some parts of the business sector got together to form an organization called the Consultative Business Movement (CBM). Initially it played a facilitating role, organizing meetings throughout the country to enable business people and leadership in the internal and increasingly the external black political movements to get together. These informal meetings played a role in helping to prepare the white elite for the period of political negotiations. By this time business was finally acutely aware of the impact of apartheid policies on the environment for doing business: In short, it was a disaster for the country's business sectors. The economy had been straitjacketed by short-sighted and counterproductive policies that failed to train skilled workers adequately, that inhibited commercial development in black areas, that put numerous obstacles in the way of commercial, residential, and other kinds of development. Importantly, the international sanctions and boycotts were starting to bite, and certain sectors

---

*This section has benefited from an interview by the author with Colin Coleman, assistant director of the then Consultative Business Movement, interviewed in Johannesburg on 12 December 1995.

of the economy were suffering badly; international investment, always essential for South Africa's growth, had come to a halt, and there was net disinvestment taking place. Internal stability seemed to be an illusion of the past, and current policies seemed to provide no way out of the downward spiral in economics and politics.

The CBM was established in 1989 to "build better understanding between business and the different political and economic actors" in the country. Through workshops and discussions it was to play a bridging role between different parts of the political and economic worlds at a time of heightened conflict and estrangement. At the end of 1991 a range of political parties requested the CBM to render process and secretarial services to the negotiations at CODESA. At a time when the state was weak and ineffective and had lost the confidence of most sectors of the society both in terms of its efficiency and its ability to be neutral, a business-funded organization was seen as the most neutral "civil service" that could be obtained for the negotiations. The CBM, funded by corporate South Africa, was to perform the secretariat function for the negotiations all the way through to their conclusion. In this role they were sometimes in a position to brief business leaders on sticky patches in the process and together with them find ways out of these difficulties.

Once a political settlement was reached and preparations had to commence for the country's first nationwide elections to be held, business played an important role in this respect as well. Here, because of legitimacy problems, a new institution—the Independent Electoral Commission (IEC)—was created to design and manage an election for 20 million mainly first-time voters. The capacity problems of this agency were a feature of the election. What is notable is the extensive role played by corporations in enfranchising millions of voters in their workplaces; running voter education programs for virtually all formally employed persons; running important parts of the election machine, including voter stations on election day; and intervening at critical moments when both the election itself and vote counting threatened to collapse.

Business and the National Peace Accord

In 1990, with political negotiations on the horizon, the high levels of tension and intercommunity violence threatened to derail progress and continued economic activity. It was in this context that business organizations locally and business leaders nationally were drawn into discussions about the political violence to help keep the political transition process on track. The increasing violence not only threatened the ANC's ability and willingness to participate in the negotiation process at this time but also showed the need for people other than politicians to intervene.

TABLE 6.3   Political Violence Fatalities in South Africa

	1985	1986	1987	1988	1989	1990	1991	1992	1993	1994
January	4	105	40	211	126	210	187	139	135	239
February	35	112	22	107	95	283	129	238	148	259
March	76	179	40	62	89	458	351	348	143	537
April	46	145	40	48	99	283	270	300	212	436
May	66	221	33	58	89	208	318	230	339	207
June	45	212	36	76	38	150	150	324	309	119
July	96	122	39	94	96	247	164	278	547	136
August	163	76	35	112	104	698	184	331	430	106
September	69	40	73	108	135	417	282	298	376	109
October	86	16	93	90	116	162	218	229	361	103
November	101	37	89	85	129	316	283	246	351	80
December	92	33	121	98	287	267	170	141	285	103
Total	879	1,278	661	1,149	1,403	3,699	2,706	3,102	3,706	2,434

Source: Race Relations News, 1994, p. 10, and C. Cooper et al., "Race Relations Survey," South African Institute of Race Relations, Johannesburg, 1995, p. 438.

South Africa's "small miracle" of a negotiated settlement has to be balanced with the reality of a country molded by violent conflict as well. There is considerable controversy about the causes and perpetrators of violence in South Africa during its years of transition. Nonetheless, it is possible to provide an impression of the extent of "political" violence for the period between 1985 and December 1994. As Table 6.3 shows, fatalities increased substantially in the 1990s.

Violence was also expensive. For example, the cost to the economy of political violence in the Transvaal province during the first half of 1991 was estimated at R3 billion. This included 1,800 deaths, the destruction of 2,000 shops and factories, lost production in national and regional strikes protesting the killings and spending on security forces. In Natal investors were apparently scared off by the toll of deaths, boycotts and strikes linked to the violence (*Financial Mail,* 14 June 1991). Some businesses were directly affected by the conflict, and this often prompted individual businessmen into action. The managing director of a large company in South Africa's industrial manufacturing belt near Johannesburg got involved in the peace process when his workers were killed in political and ethnic clashes that swept through their hostels.

Early in June 1991 business leaders announced that they would join church leaders in the effort to end violence and intimidation. A joint committee was formed with the aim of bringing together political leaders to "deal with the violence and intimidation problems in South Africa." The committee would act "merely as a low-profile catalyst to bring leadership together." As a result of this initiative the National Peace Accord was signed by all the leaders of the key political parties. The accord included codes of conduct for the political parties, police, and army; set the ground rules for free political activity; and laid down the brief for a commission of inquiry (to be chaired by a Supreme Court judge) to investigate cases of public violence and relevant laws and regulations along with ombudsmen for complaints about police behavior. The accord also included provisions for the establishment of peace committees at national, regional, and local levels that would monitor and facilitate public political activity (marches, rallies and so on), intervene in crises and resolve disputes in cases of violence and potential violence, and also become involved in socioeconomic reconstruction and development. The overriding aim of the peace committees was to establish communication between the leaders of parties in conflict and "put out fires." By late 1993 eleven regional and 120 local peace committees had been established around the country.

Business's role was explicitly recognized in the accord, which provides that the chair or deputy chair of the National Peace Committee must come from business. From inception to closure, the chair of the committee was a senior executive from the country's leading industrial corporation. Sections of business played an important role not only in giving shape and energy to the process but also in making staff and resources available. These included conference rooms, training facilities, food and drink, legal assistance, advertising and printing, and vehicles for peace monitors. The involvement of business brought more than only material resources to the peace process. Business leaders made time to chair regional peace committees and to get involved in helping to resolve conflicts. Because of their standing in the white community, business people's interventions in conflict situations were often treated with more respect than those of black activists, white police, and local authorities. Seen as a mediator not beholden to any political group, the business community could also get warring parties together. This was particularly significant in crisis times, given the extent of polarization and mistrust in South African society. Business people also brought their skills into the process and the ability to get things done. "Many local peace committees were chaired by businessmen, who knew how to run conflictual meetings and how to get plans implemented . . . skills often rare in the townships" (Charney 1994).

Since 1991 sections of business contributed resources, leadership, and authority to the creation and operation of national, regional, and local peace structures. Business played a brokerage role helping to create and lead forums for dialogue among parties and also a stabilizing role ensuring the continuation of the process despite limited government funding or violent disruptions. Through the interventions of business not only were some of the edges around hostile relations between warring parties softened, but also the National Peace Accord helped to create the right climate for negotiations to continue.

Transition to What? New Normative Conflicts in South Africa

South Africa's negotiated transition to a democratic and nonracial society, culminating in the successful elections of 1994, removed the long and dark shadow of apartheid norms, policies, and attitudes that had dominated South Africa for so long. In its place is emerging a far more complex society than that conveyed by the "black/white" morality play of the past. In the remarkable and extremely fast-moving changes that are taking place throughout every facet and building block that comprise this society, new perceptions of what South Africans have in common and what might pull them apart are starting to emerge. It is worth pointing out that apartheid's blinkers have left behind a society that is only now starting to look more honestly at itself. More time is required to understand fully the different groups, classes, issues, and interests that have been hidden and submerged for so long behind the all-encompassing and blanket terms of "black" and "white."

As a new and emerging democracy (democratic local government elections were only held in November 1995, and two large parts of the country did not hold these elections until May and June 1996), South Africa today has a fluid political situation. South Africans, led by a remarkable state president (a mediating institution all on his own), are still in the very basic and important process of discovering their common country and the interests and norms that they do share, decades of apartheid notwithstanding. The new interim constitution and bill of rights provide not a definition but a framework within which this process of discovery will unfold.

There are many areas in which enormous conflict was anticipated but in which events are actually proceeding peacefully and relatively smoothly. Whites are taking instructions from blacks in the police, the army, the traffic department, and all branches of the civil service; school integration proceeds apace; public facilities are now open to all citizens; the local government transition is well under way; the integration of the South African Defence Force and the previous guerrilla armies has proceeded; and so on. It is against this background of a South Africa where both leaders and ordinary citizens are at last finding so much in common as equal citizens of the same country that I will turn now to look at emerging normative divides within the "new South Africa." It is a sign of the increasing normality of the country that many of the issues that confront South Africans now sound like those of other countries and are not all derived solely from questions of race. Of course the legacy of apartheid in its many different forms looms large for the new society.

A first major theme around which many differences will undoubtedly arise concerns the nature of the new South African democracy. The structures of this new democracy will need to be created from the old segregated institutions or by building new institutions altogether. From the legislature to all the branches of the executive to the judiciary, complex questions about the nature of government and the interrelationship of its executive, legislative, and judicial arms will need to be debated and resolved. An issue currently absorbing considerable heat and energy concerns the powers of the central and the provincial tiers of government and increasingly the metropolitan level—how federal will a democratic South Africa become? Simultaneously a formerly participatory culture of democratic participation that characterized the internal resistance movement must adapt to the rigors of representative parliamentary democracy and in time to the culture of tolerance implicit in the notion of a multiparty democracy and party system. Thirdly, the "democratic centralism" of the underground and exile resistance movements must find its place in a "new, transparent and open democratic culture." A relatively tolerant and peaceful but nonetheless nationalist movement turned government must come to terms with a very complex country and the inevitability of political difference and opposition.

A further emerging issue concerns social policy and the balance between direct referenda of the population and letting elected representatives make decisions. In the case of capital punishment, for example, the ANC as a party is opposed to it, and this is now the accepted government position. The opposition NP has called for a referendum on the issue in which citizens would vote directly, indicating their preference on the matter. There is little doubt that if such a referendum were held capital punishment would be reinstated in the country. A recent national survey found that most South Africans support the death penalty in principle: 62% wanted capital punishment to remain legal. So the ANC is faced with the question of how much democracy it wants between elections and who exactly its party activists represent.

A second major theme around which many differences will emerge concerns what might be called the tension between democracy and delivery. The development challenge that faces the Government of National Unity (GNU) is enormous (although it must be said that this has been exaggerated by the media). The government inherits a backlog of neglect and deliberate failure in the provision of services and infrastructure. Some examples of this serve to provide some indication of the scale of the challenge. Close to 40% of South African households live below the minimum poverty line; some 12 million South Africans (30% of the population) do not have access to clean water; 70% of the population do not have electricity, and one-quarter of the society relies on wood for energy. More than 7 million people live in informal housing circumstances—shacks, backyard structures, garages, and the like. The major crisis area lies in unemployment, with some 40% of the laboring population unemployed. The government has also inherited a civil service that is demoralized and without the skills necessary to build a productive nation.

Simultaneously the government is committed to introduce some form of reasonably rapid affirmative action to ensure a civil service whose composition is more closely aligned with the country's demographic profile. The big normative test will come when, at the micro level, government gets tired of the trade-off between endless consultation with "the community" and actually getting projects on the ground, and at the macro level, government finds it harder to deliver on a massive scale than it originally thought and pressures rise for less-than-democratic measures to quell popular discontent. It must be said that the country is a long way from this at present. Nonetheless, there is already rising tension about these issues, particularly with respect to issues of "law and order."

A third major area of difference will concern the relationship between the new South African state, the individual, and independent organizations. First, will South Africa become a country where people are provided with equal opportunities with individuals competing on their merits? Or will the state succumb to demands for groups to be entitled to special dispensations and privileges? This is the key issue in the debate on affirmative action and how it will be applied in government, educational institutions, and the private sector. Will race be allowed to reemerge in the country as the critical selector of jobs and opportunities? Is it possible to build a nonracial state based on a nonracial constitution and have special privileges for some people purely because of their race? Second, will the state allow independent organizations that criticize its policies to continue to operate? How far will government tolerate dissent? Is it true that one of the root causes of the violence in KwaZulu/Natal is that the ANC is not comfortable with the idea of a powerful alternative black political party? Will future criticism of government policy be seen as a resurgence of white racism or "apartheid puppets" or the emergence of new enemies of the democratic nonracial project? Third, will the state allow South Africa to develop an uninhibited market system, and to what extent will it allow the black business and professional middle class to dictate the agenda for change in this area?

Perhaps the most important normative conflict currently facing the country and posing a growing challenge to the new and fragile democracy is the general question of order. In many realms of South African life the country is sliding toward a form of anarchy. There are different components to this phenomenon, each with its own set of reasons and histories, but there can be little doubt that the new government is finding it difficult to restore law and order. A state in transition such as South Africa's from the momentous announcement of February 1990 until the inauguration of a new president in May 1994 will also lose some measure of authority. Couple this with the following additional factors and one is amazed that the society came through the transition and is as stable as postapartheid South Africa now is:

- a high level of violence, general unrest, and turbulence together with elements of the state security forces operating to undermine the transition;
- "no-go areas" where state officials were under constant siege and in which it was a toss-up as to whether the police or their township opponents had more or better weapons;
- former members of the ANC and other black liberation movements' armed wings now back in the country and in many cases still armed;
- a ready supply of cheap weapons from Mozambique; and
- disaffected white members or former members of the security forces with access to large quantities of arms.

However, the new government has to deal with a more disturbing legacy than the situation they inherited after the transition. There are five other factors working to undermine some of the most basic rules that hold a society together. The first factor is the state of the South African criminal justice system. It sounds counterintuitive to state that South Africa—"the apartheid police state"—is underpoliced. South Africa has one policeman for every 358 people, one of the lowest ratios in the developed world. In the country's large and growing cities, "the thin blue line" is too narrow, demoralized, and underresourced to perform adequately. Violent behavior has often been allowed to go unchecked through lack of resources to deal with it. This in turn has given criminals enormous confidence in their ability to escape arrest or defeat prosecution. In 1994 "the police solved fewer than half of all serious crimes. . . . In the case of vehicle theft, which has risen faster than any other crime, police managed to solve only 16%" (*Financial Mail*, 2 December 1994).

Crime is a serious problem in South Africa. This is indicated by research that shows a murder rate in South Africa of 45 per 100,000 people in 1994 (the international average for 122 countries studied was 5.5) and an assault rate of 840 per 100,000 (compared with an international average of 142). For seventy-two countries for which a full range of crime figures are available, murder and assault make up an average of 3% of reported crime. In South Africa the figure is 16% (*Saturday Star,* 11 November 1995). In South Africa there is:

- one vehicle hijacking every 54 minutes, 27 hijackings a day;
- one murder every 30 minutes, 48 murders a day; and
- one rape every 18 minutes, 80 rapes a day (*Saturday Star,* 11 November 1995).

In the ten years from 1983 to 1992 the murder rate increased by 135%, robbery by 109%, burglary by 71%, car theft by 64%, rape by 62%, and serious assault by 13% (*Fast Facts,* no. 3, 1993, 3).

The increasing "Wild West" atmosphere and the infrequency of police patrols has led whites to turn to private security firms to guard their homes and increasingly their streets and neighborhoods. This would seem to signal that they have "given up on the police as a protective force." Black people living in townships resorted to a variety of means, such as setting up self-defense units, organizing street patrols to protect communities, and holding impromptu "people's courts" that punished alleged wrongdoers. The other side of this "double whammy" is the efficacy of the criminal justice system. Jails are overcrowded, and people seem to come out of them better schooled for a life of crime than before they went in; criminals have been released as part of the amnesties for political activists; and convicts are now being released because there is no room for them in the jails.

The second factor in the breakdown of adherence to society's laws concerns the rent, services, and bond boycotts in the townships. Originally these boycotts were introduced as a part of the ANC "ungovernability" strategy in the mid-1980s—a popular move especially as many people were not receiving adequate services anyway and payment was becoming more onerous in a situation of rising unemployment. With the arrears now totaling billions of rands, the new government is finding it extremely difficult to persuade citizens to start paying once again. In October 1994 the government announced a nationwide campaign, "Operation Masakhane" (self-reliance), which would try to persuade people to start paying. At the end of 1995 it was being acknowledged openly that the campaign had failed. In the words of the business weekly, the *Financial Mail,* "Even the ANC and the populist organisations accept that there is no longer any need for boycotts. The trouble is that their strategy worked too well: the townships were indeed made ungovernable and in many cases they still are. It will not be easy to restore respect for authority (if ever respect existed)" (*Financial Mail,* 2 December 1994).

The second part of the boycott problem concerns the failure to repay housing mortgage loans in the townships. It has been estimated that one-third of the 30,000 mortgage loans to African families since 1986 are in arrears. This situation has led the president of the Association of Mortgage Lenders to say that the risks of mortgage lending to low-income people has increased to such a level that it was not "prudent" to lend to them. If a bank tries to repossess the house and sell it to a new homeowner, local activists either prevent the new family from moving in at all or make their lives impossible and dangerous once they are in.

The third factor contributing to lawlessness is the general level of corruption in and around the state and its former homeland dependencies. Over forty years of effective "single-party rule" led to considerable nepotism and abuse of position in the apartheid government. The tin-pot administrations in most of the homelands created a black "comprador" class and a system built on corruption. In the dying days of apartheid numerous schemes were put into effect (only some of which have been uncovered) to enable bureaucrats to garner as many state resources as they possibly could. Homeland leaders have been found to have properties and large bank accounts in Western Europe. State officials have been found to have unheard-of sinecures.

The fourth factor is an insidious legacy of apartheid. Many black people spent their lives evading unjust and intrusive apartheid laws. Alienated from the government and the totally undemocratic process whereby laws were made, many people felt no obligation to pay taxes, traffic fines, or numerous other bills. This might now be the "new South Africa" with Mandela as president, but old habits die hard.

The fifth component in this litany is a consequence of the country's growing rate of urbanization and thus rapid expansion of its cities. Large cities need tough laws and city governments with the muscle to enforce them. Traffic departments need to have regulations, and these must be applied consistently. South African cities are in the midst of a difficult transition from being small, orderly, and white to being large, interracial, intercultural, and with a lot more infringement of the rules. Some rules will need to go, and the sooner the better, but unless there is strict enforcement of traffic, sanitation, and other health and safety regulations, the city will cease to be effective as an arena for economic activity or as a viable place in which to work or live.

All these factors—a struggling criminal justice system, rent and bond boycotts, corruption in and around officials and institutions of the former apartheid state, the apartheid legacy of alienation from the laws of the land and evasion of selected laws, and the need for city managers to adapt to larger populations and more complex circumstances—combine to present a real threat to the economic and political prospects of the new democracy. In a synergistic way they all underline the importance of a mediating institution that most Western societies take completely for granted. Unless a society agrees on the process whereby laws are made and the means whereby these laws are enforced and offenders punished, it becomes very difficult to keep social systems functioning.

Mediating Institutions

This recounting of the South African conflict and transition to democracy has revealed the presence of a number of mediating institutions. The list is an interesting mix of rather diverse phenomena:

An integrated modern economy worked (unintentionally) to undermine the rationale and basis for apartheid and the grand project of separate in-dependent homeland states. In an indirect way participation in firms, corporations, and enterprises of an industrializing economy worked to build relationships and conceptions between and about South Africans that had less and less to do with race. The functional relationships of the workplace (however imperfectly impaired by discrimination) are built on rather different notions about people than either those of traditional tribal society or white racism. In the new South Africa the economic mo-tor might start to function in a different way if affirmative action (race and gender) is reintroduced into the workplace.

The role of leaders (both black and white) at critical times in the country's history has also played an important mediating role. When white figures of authority finally spoke out against segregation legislation and rede-fined white interests as dependent on the abolition of discrimination, public opinion followed their lead remarkably quickly. Nelson Mandela has through his actions and statements played a phenomenal personal role in mediating between black and white South Africa and starting to build a common sense of citizenship and nationhood. That these leaders could be so powerful and effective is related partly to the fact that they were responding to and reflecting the realities of everyday life for most South Africans: day-to-day dependence on one another (in white peo-ple's homes through their dependence on black domestic labor; in public institutions such as buses, the telephone system, the post office, etc.); and mutual participation in a common economy and the social world of work and the workplace. They were also tapping into the attitudes that black and white people shared, such as the Christian values that are important for the vast majority of South Africans.

The business sector inside the country played an unusual role for commer-cial enterprises over the past twenty years. Through business-funded and -supported institutions they played a leading role (albeit belatedly) in the battle against apartheid legislation, especially where it hindered economic growth and relations with the country's trading partners. They also played an important role in helping to create the climate in the white establishment for political negotiations and then facilitated these negotiations by funding and supporting the secretariat (effectively a transitional civil service) for them. In playing this role the business community was driven by its concerns with economic issues and the effect of apartheid restrictions and the consequent opposition, unrest, and international opprobrium on their material interests. But many leading business people were concerned about the country's future and willing to put time and effort into these "extracurricular" activities because they saw their future in South Africa and as ordinary citizens wanted to help bring about change.

Business has always acted in terms of its interests (and its perception of those interests), and it will continue to do so. Now that South Africa is a democracy with a legitimate government, the role of the business sector as a "social actor" will change. Increasingly it will be an interest among others within a plural and diverse democracy. It will need to move beyond the role of facilitator, of a seemingly neutral intermediary of the transition period, and into the challenging role of participant in the public debate and tussle of interests of a more open marketplace of ideas. The behind-the-scenes role of business intervention that characterizes authoritarian regimes will need to be supplemented by the public role in which the business community will have to argue the case for the policies it wants in terms of the national interest and persuade many different politicians. In so doing business will need allies who share the values of capitalism and competitive allocation of resources (Bernstein, Godsell, and Berger 1996).

At a very fundamental level one of society's most important mediating institutions is *the constitution and the legal system for regulating competition, dispute, and conflict between citizens.* Countries start to slide into anarchy if there is no law and order; economic growth becomes more and more difficult, and retaining the benefits of such growth for individuals, companies, and governments becomes more and more arbitrary. In South Africa's long haul back to a "civil society" the effective maintenance of law and order will be of paramount importance. The potential for establishing equality before the law for the first time in the country's history needs to be bolstered by the building of an effective police and overall criminal justice system. The values of adherence to properly formulated and legitimately adopted laws and regulations will need to be inculcated and then enforced if this most basic of mediating processes in a modern society is to work properly. This will entail tough measures on the part of government, which will need to use its hard-won democratic legitimacy to change the "Wild West" culture prevailing in many parts of the country.

The final mediating institution, though it has not received sufficient attention in this chapter, is a political institution. South Africa was extremely fortunate that when the opportunity for a negotiated resolution to its historic conflicts arose there was an opposition movement strong enough to act as an effective partner to the government. The *ANC-led alliance* is an extremely broad front spanning views that stretch from devout Christians, Muslims, and atheists to communists, socialists, rampant capitalists, and militant trade unionists. The movement incorporates whites with a strong sense of guilt about the past, covert black racists, and committed African nationalists. The glue that has held this broad coalition together was its opposition to apartheid. In some respects this was very lucky for the country. Instead of a divided and fractious set of opposition groupings, the ANC provided a powerful leadership and organizational vehicle to help lead South Africa away from apartheid and into the democratic era.

The ANC in government faces many different challenges, and its broad front and diverse composition is under threat. Effective economic growth for a middle-income developing country will entail some tough choices, and the ANC will need to confront the trade union movement (after all only a small minority of the population, albeit well organized). There are other elements in the ANC alliance that will find it harder and harder to live with a middle-of-the-road social-democratic government. Thus, the kind of mediating role the ANC was able to play at a critically important time in the country's history will change.

References

Bernstein, A. (ed.). 1995. "Post-Apartheid Population and Income Trends." CDE Research No. 1, Centre for Development and Enterprise, Johannesburg.

Bernstein, A., Godsell, B., and Berger, P. 1996. "Business and Democracy: Cohabitation or Contradiction?" Development and Democracy No. 10, Centre for Development and Enterprise, Johannesburg.

Charney, C. 1994. "Political Violence, Local Elites and Democratic Transition: Business and the Peace Process in South Africa." Unpublished paper commissioned by the Development Strategy and Policy Unit, Urban Foundation.

Cooper, C., et al. 1992. "Race Relations Survey." South African Institute of Race Relations, Johannesburg.

_____. 1995. "Race Relations Survey." South African Institute of Race Relations, Johannesburg.

Everatt, D., and Orkin, M. (eds.) 1993. *"Growing Up Tough": A National Survey of South African Youth.* Johannesburg: Community Agency for Social Enquiry.

Hanf, T., et al. 1981. *South Africa: The Prospects of Peaceful Change: An Empirical Enquiry into the Possibility of Democratic Conflict Regulation.* London: Rex Collings.

Hudson, J. 1995. "The Hidden War: Violence in KwaZulu/Natal." Lecture at King's College, University of London, 14 March 1995.

Kane-Berman, J. 1990. *South Africa's Silent Revolution.* Johannesburg: Southern Books.

Lodge, T., and Nasson, B. 1991. *All Here and Now: Black Politics in the 1980s.* Cape Town: Ford Foundation–David Philip.

Price, R. 1991. *Apartheid State in Crisis: Political Transformation in South Africa, 1975–1990.* New York: Oxford University Press.

Schlemmer, L. 1991. "Black Township Residents Amidst Protest, Violence, and Negotiation." Research Report No. 15, Centre for Policy Studies, Johannesburg.

Sidiropoulos, E. 1993. "Black Economic Empowerment." Spotlight No. 2/93, September, South African Institute of Race Relations, Johannesburg.

7

Some Notes on Normative Conflicts in Turkey

Serif Mardin

Two preliminary issues set the stage for our investigation of normative conflicts. First, there is no unique venue, no methodological canon for the study of normative conflict, whatever society is under scrutiny. Second, in the case of Turkey, one has to take into account problems related to the transition of an "ancien regime," an Empire, to the building of a "modern" society and a nation-state.

A description of this Turkish transition process may be the most appropriate way of substantiating my first point, namely, the variety of conceptual approaches that may be used in the study of normative issues. But we first need to recall some of the fundamental features of the Ottoman ancien regime, in which we find the source of today's major normative conflicts.

Foundations of the Ottoman System

The Ottoman sociopolitical formula was a sophisticated elaboration of a system known as patrimonialism/sultanism.[1] The power of the center was not, as is often believed, derived from the sultan's power as head of the Muslim community (i.e., his status as caliph) but from an intricate military and administrative machine staffed by the protobureaucratic "slave" officials of the sultan, a system that only had some overlap with Islamic institutions.[2] Ottoman society, which claimed to be the latest torchbearer of Islam, therefore showed an unacknowledged internal fault line, an area of constant friction between the sultan's administrators and the Muslim clerical establishment (ulema). The history of modern Turkey since the nineteenth century may be seen as an unfolding, a projection into the future of aspects of this dichotomous structure at a time when

new ideas and institutions began to be copied from the West at an accelerated rate. It is in the intricacies of this unfolding that we may isolate the
many possible configurations suitable for the study of our problem.

We have, first, the general process of centralization and secularization
promoted initially by the sultan's officials and then by the founders of the
Turkish Republic (1923) as well as the various normative problems that—
paradoxically—derived from the relatively successful elaboration of this
project. Second, we may look at the characteristics of the geographical setting of this reform policy, an area that, before World War I, included the
Balkans, but after 1918 was bounded by Turkey in Asia Minor (Anatolia).
Here we still encounter a gradient of "development" going from West to
East with "modernity"/economic development appearing as a characteristic of the West and "traditionalism"/underdevelopment a character of
the Eastern region. These two terms involve the polarity modernity/con-
servative-Islamic (or localistic) *values* and generate a subset of normative
conflict. The more general way of looking at this subset would be to consider it under the rubric of rural-urban differences. And yet this seems a
simplistic dichotomy, since the point here is that localism is structured by
a long history of *local power* and of power groups' having challenged the
idea of a centralized state.

A more abstract version of this dichotomy, of which we have already
seen two variants, would be what has been named the Ottoman center-
periphery cleavage, center and periphery carrying antagonistic sets of values. Here the contrast between center and periphery has much more
clearly the connotation of power relations. This particular polarity has endured long enough to function as one of the main axes of modern Turkish
politics. One of its current versions emerged during the municipal elections of March 1994. At that time the Islamic Welfare Party represented the
political and cultural periphery, the "province," and also Islam, whereas
the Social Democratic Action Party represented the center—the concentration of power in the state and secularism as a state policy. The same alignment appeared in the general election of 24 December 1995.

Another dyad that shows family resemblances with the center-periphery pair is universalism-particularism. It has risen in importance in
Turkey as the result of recent (beginning in 1950) massive migration from
rural to urban areas. This demographic shift has promoted a form of particularism that runs counter to the values of the founding fathers of the
Turkish Republic. The new demographic picture has activated the partic-
ularist term of this polarity in ways that have created new areas of social
identity building and therefore issues for normative dissension.

A more concrete focus for similar normative clashes would be the residual scope of kinship groups, tribal affiliation, and religious sect membership in their promoting affiliation and solidarity with these collectivities.

The Turkish Republic attempted to replace these focal points of allegiance with the notion of a Turkish citizenship, but the process is still ongoing.

Some overlap with this type of kinship-related structure appears in the transition from the patriarchal to the nuclear family. Tribes and sects are ruled by elders and come with values of respect for established authority that, when modernity emerges, pit sons against fathers, contemporary graduates of the secular lycées and universities against seniority, young political activists against persons in positions of authority, and so on.[3] A striking example of this divide is in the book written in the 1960s by a twenty-six-year-old lower-rank religious functionary of Kurdish origin. This work was the first of the bottom-up, "populist" analyses and critiques of the system of hegemony of notables and tribal leaders prevailing in (Kurdish-speaking) Eastern Turkey *(Doguda Agalik-Seyhlik)*.

Finally, in the economic sphere, Turkey gradually moved from an Ottoman society of consumer protection, price fixing, and monopolies and an Islamic society of interest camouflage to one of an increasingly free economic market. The "etatist" economic features of the early Turkish Republic were partly a carryover from the empire. The structural conflicts that arose during the transformation of the economy are well known to students of contemporary Turkey, namely, the diminished role of military and civilian officialdom in a market economy and their revolutionary sequels. But this structural clash between entrepreneurs and bureaucrats has a value component—the false (i.e., self-serving) consciousness of officialdom as carrier of the values of populist, redistributional, modern Jacobin Kemalism.[4] Typical in this sphere are some recent decisions of higher courts. Judges of the Supreme Court as well as those of the Council of State (an administrative court) both consider themselves to be the guardians of Kemalism and have fought what they consider to be violations of the Kemalist social contract, such as the privatization of state industries.

I shall concentrate on a hereby *reconstituted* set of the normative conflicts that I have outlined in the preceding:

1. The state, the center, and the bureaucracy and its associated values versus the periphery, the province, and "personalistic" networks.
2. Secularism versus religion.
3. Traditional kinship group affiliation, patriarchalism, and the family and women.

The description of the normative conflicts that I survey covers, primarily, different viewpoints held by constituencies or *groups*, but as will be apparent in a number of instances, two variants of this approach arise.

First, conflicts may be internal to the social setting, in other words to a dichotomous *system*. Imagine an apartment with two "social" rooms, one a European "salon," the other a traditional Ottoman guest room. One family alternately uses one and the other according to the type of social event during the same day. Imagine the amount of cultural confusion. Second, the conflict may be internal to a subject or actor who is torn between conflicting values. A tentative description of these phenomena is presented at the end of this chapter.

A tangential point about theories of society is that Turkish society and social change in Turkey cannot be understood from a purely structural vantage point, nor can the normative conflicts we have to uncover be located in that never-never land of "values" as an autonomous area of study.

Cultural Differences

A latent theme that underlies this chapter is that cultural differences are really different. These differences inhere in the interstices of language as well as in lifestyles, forms of the private sphere approximating what has been termed "civil society" in the West, and in the reverberation of these in the material conditions of life. This does not mean that cultures are totally untranslatable but that the equipment of Western social science does the job poorly. The following are some considerations concerning this weakness.

A summary Western social science–oriented evaluation of the main points of my description of value conflicts would be that Turkish society has moved away from being knit together (or capped) by respect for status and has stumbled into a somewhat perplexing landscape where such ties are no longer central. But this would neglect a number of important elements. One would be the multiplex role of religion in "traditional" pre-republican Turkish society. It is tempting to see this role as that of an "intermediate" institution in the Tocquevillian sense. In fact, a more accurate description of this role would be to see it as a net of mediating mechanisms operating within the frame of Islam. Second, as has been pointed out many times—and most recently by Anthony Giddens—questions related to the changing focus of trust during modernization have not decreased but increased the clientele for this diffuse type of intermediation.[5]

Cultural elements enable people to make distinctions in their everyday life. Major changes occur during modernity in the way in which culture intervenes, but the foundation of the cultural pattern remains active because of the range of functions it controls. The specific patterning of the constituent pieces of the culture, the stamp or formula of a culture—a dynamic principle of constant reformulation—has been described by French students of society as an *imaginaire,* among others by Cornelius Castoriadis.[6] While Castoriadis's definition of the *imaginaire* is not always clear, the following of his statements shows in what measure it was used here:

> If the theoretician distinguishes between a religious aspect and a legal aspect in the activities of a given traditional or archaic society, which, in itself does not distinguish between them, this is not due to the progress of knowledge or to the purification and the refinement of reason but to the fact that the society in which the theoretician lives, has for a long period of time instituted its own legal categories as relatively distinct.[7]

The terms in which persons organize "views of themselves, of others, as well as the world in which they live"[8] brings in a second dimension of the dynamic of the *imaginaire,*[9] and that is the drive to retrieve and tell a story in which one has a central role. "We achieve our personal identities and self-concept through the use of the narrative configuration, and make our existence into a whole by understanding it is an expression of a single unfolding and developing story. We are in the middle of our stories and cannot be sure how they will end. We constantly have to revise the plot as new events are added to our lives."[10]

Richard Kearney expresses the same thought by pointing out that "subjects, individual or communal, come to imagine and know themselves in the stories they tell about themselves."[11] The preceding quotations are simply meant to refer to the wider contributions of Paul Ricoeur and Jerome Bruner, on which I constantly rely.

In a number of cases I shall be describing "personalistic" relations. This is a means of bringing to center stage in my description the belief or view that some Ottomans had of society as being made up of persons, somewhat in the sense of Max Scheler's concept of *Gesamtpersonen.*[12] In Ottoman society this view, which builds an alternative to what social science terms collective identity, works in tandem with the extremely restricted availability of a concept of corporate personality. It is the circulation of this view of persons-in-society that enables the building of the sense of *belonging,* a category that in modern society is replaced by the mechanistic membership-citizenship link to the collective.

Another explanatory scheme that I shall keep in mind is one offered by Victor Turner, who states in a passage summarizing his views:

"Field experience and general reading in the arts and humanities convinced me that 'social' is not identical with 'social-structural.' There are other modalities of social relationships. . . . Communitas is a relationship between concrete, historical, idiosyncratic individuals. These individuals are not segmentalized into roles and statuses but confront one another in the manner of Martin Buber's 'I and Thou.' Along with this direct, immediate and total confrontation of human identities, there tends to go a model of society as a homogeneous and unstructured communitas."[13]

The most important single fact concerning value conflicts in Turkey is that Turkey now lives in a shuffling of two cultures: the West, with its own dream or *telos,* and the Ottoman Islamic culture, with its own latent directional thrusts, which has not been allowed to develop since the nineteenth century and which is now a thing of bits and pieces. The current jumble of Turkish values (Western-Islamic-consumerist-econo-puritanical) makes part of a population, already displaced geographically by the great influx to the cities of the past fifty years, yearn for a return to an imagined seamless Islamic society. The point I want to make here is that "imagined," in this context, also refers to a nostalgia for the return to some "real," quasi-structural items of Ottoman society that provided the process of intermediation between state and society but that have disappeared during modernization.

The State Versus Interpersonal Networks

In the perspective of the past two centuries, no issue of sociopolitical organization has been more central and conflictual in Turkey than the centralization of the state that has run parallel to the wholesale importation of Western European institutions and the "from the top down" secularization of society. This process is usually dated from a series of defeats in the Ottoman Empire between 1699 and 1720. To become more statelike meant to shift resources from the traditional imbrication of religion and the state—already a structure that gave more weight to the Ottoman state than the rest of the Islamic culture area allowed—increasingly toward the state itself. The destabilizing force of this shift can only be understood in relation to what may be termed the original triangular organization of the Ottoman state: The central power took up matters of military organization, administration, and tax collection; the clerics, the doctors of Islamic law (ulema), filled the position of judges, professors, part-administrators, prayer leaders, theologians; and a third social vector, the Sufi orders, ministered to the day-to-day cares of artisans and citizens of various nonofficial statuses.

The organic connection of the ulema to the Ottoman center, through the state's control of the prebends of those highest in the hierarchic scale, meant that the theoretical resources of the clerics were used to build what was in reality an "administrative Islam." An overlapping branch of the religious establishment, the Sufi brotherhoods, by contrast, targeted a popular rather than an official clientele. These orders constituted the third leg of the Ottoman political formula and were able to fill functions of social services, education, and the placating of heterodox trends by incorporating them. The Sufi orders, functioning as networks of its members, saw social relations in a somewhat different light than the Ottoman state. They conceived society as made of an interlinking of persons—a view that was widely diffused. After the Republic banned Sufi orders in 1925 pious Turkish Muslims refigured this view of society and now took it to be *the* single principle that regulated Ottoman society, a principle that they would have liked to be incorporated in modern Turkish society. This ideological reformulation process is still important today.

In the Ottoman Empire the palace and the Sufi orders were both centers for the inculcation of a type of Ottoman/Islamic civility that went by the name of *adab*.[14] *Adab* was not simply a veneer of bureaucratic and Sufi life but must be understood as *constitutive* of Ottoman society, as part of a social equilibrium based on the foundational use of personal relations and as a social-structuring element enabling one to question, if not often to oppose, official acts.

To the triangular Ottoman structure corresponded three types of values: First, the ideology of service to the state commingled with the ideal of the gentleman courtier in the chanceries of state; second, orthodox-official Islam; and third, a Sufi latitudinarianism that often took in folk motifs as well as irony as worldview. All three of these have residues in modern Turkey. The value conflicts associated with them consist in their continued rivalry with the values of modernity. But once again one has to stress that in the rebuilding of society what is involved is not only the loss of old values but often the combination and permutation of old and new values as well. "Loss" can be described further as referring to the loss of tacit understandings regarding the Ottoman social contract that, though they remained unstated, were nevertheless part of the fabric of society as a whole.[15]

Altogether, then, Ottoman Islam, in its ability to counterpoise religious law, ritual, and effective institutions such as the Sufi orders to the mechanism of the state, may be seen as a source of the "civil society" operating outside the Ottoman state. The introduction of printing (1727–1729), a state enterprise for the benefit of bureaucrats aimed at increasing the power of officials, was typical of the way new institutions were to undermine the Ottoman system. It impaired the foundations of Ottoman social relations, based as they were on interpersonal relations and the use of a religious discourse of legitimation. Here orality as much as scripturality had a basic role to play. Modernity created a field of "imagined" relations, that is, "a public" that was distant, impersonal, and emptied of sacred time and that was linked to the new idea of a collectivity of which the people were supposed to be a part, but without the intermediation of the former Ottoman "civil society." Modernity was therefore, in the long run (i.e., in the eighteenth to the twentieth centuries), more than an importation of different institutions. It was an undermining of the specific equilibrium mechanisms of Ottoman society.

Language in the sense of "discourse" (not the use of the term by Foucault but in its original meaning in French of a "spiel") had been part of this mechanism. The Republic's "language reform" of the 1930s was therefore another force shattering the mechanism for cohesion in Ottoman society. This reform consisted of the systematic elimination of words with Arabic or Persian roots from the written language and their replacement by neologisms purportedly drawn out of the "pure" Central Asian Turkic dialects. One of the consequences of this "purification" was that the Ottoman, pre-Republican sociopolitical vocabulary and rhetoric was eliminated, thus forcing people who were arguing about foundations of society to learn a new way of formulation and debating issues related to an ideal "good society" or then relegating them to the political mutes, which often happened.

Alaturca-Alafranga

While normative conflicts raised by the religious/secular dyad may be discussed in this chapter in terms understandable to an educated and cosmopolitan audience, the local conceptualization of these matters and the conflict to which they give rise are expressed in Turkish. The words used to discuss matters related to the polarity have come out of the cultural history of Turkey. The thrust of these Turkish expressions must be recaptured, since they transpose the discussion on a slightly different plane than when they are expressed in translation as I have done in this chapter. In Turkey the doublet in which disputes of the religious/secular type are debated refer to "Musluman"/"Yabanci" (Muslim/Foreign), or in a wider context, "alaturca"/"alafranga." Here the dissonance has a cultural valence involving not only religion but lifestyle, tastes in music, and ritual cleanliness. "Alaturca"/"alafranga" is one of the most ubiquitous normative fault lines in modern Turkey, albeit diffuse, yet full of connoted, not clearly expressed, meaning.

Sencer Ayata, a Turkish sociologist, has studied the instability created within a family by the mixture of alaturca and alafranga in their everyday life. He noted that the "salon," a new type of room in Turkish domestic arrangements, was kept for more "Western" occasions: with a glass cupboard, bottles of banana liqueur, and tea with cakes. Serving nonalcoholic beverages and traditional sweets and sitting in one's pajama was the character of the sparsely furnished (i.e., Ottoman), much more relaxedly used, "rec room."[16] The sense of disorientation created by this seesaw is the main point of Ayata's study. The sense of disorientation, by the way, does derives not only from the to and from, that is, the physical alternation between rooms, but also from the Turkish "alafranga"/"alaturca" vocabulary that is used in each compartment.

The Nineteenth Century

Defeats on the battlefield and the recasting of the military (eighteenth to nineteenth century) meant an acceleration of the process by which resources were directed toward the construction of the reformed Ottoman state, which was inspired by European enlightened despotism and its theoretical version, namely, cameralism. A parallel component of the same historical trend was the progressive asymptotic weakening of the role of religion in the Ottoman state during the nineteenth century. It was asymptotic in the sense that it took more than a century for the dereliction of Islamic institutions, of which eventually only a shell remained, to appear.

The acceleration of this process of modern state construction appears in its clearest form in a long-ranging project of reform in the Ottoman Empire known as the Tanzimat (1839–1876). The Tanzimat was engineered by advisers in the chanceries of the sultan, who, for all practical purposes, had taken the reins of government into their hands by 1840. They comprised a rather formidable array of officials who also instituted consultative arrangements that grew throughout the nineteenth century. Paradoxically, their project of reform eventually created a new opposition to the extent that it depended on the nurturing of a new class of Western-inspired guardians of communications who, as journalists, crafted a new field for themselves. Here they could express the first modern critique of centralization and their support of parliamentary government and democracy.

Poles of Normative Dissensus

Elite Versus Mass. Ottoman officialdom and its literati were self-consciously elitist. Islam required them to consider men as made in God's image, but few of them drew this item out of their cultural knapsack. This attitude was taken over by the founding fathers of the Republic, but with a different venue: Georges Sorel, Gustave Le Bon, the general interest in pre-fascist thought, and the ideas of late-nineteenth-century Europe are known to have overdetermined an already existing foundation of elitism.[17] The first comprehensive detailed modern work on total war, Colmar von der Goltz's (later to be known as Goltz Pasha) *Das Volk in Waffen* (1885), set the ideology of modern warmaking for the Young Turks.[18] The founding fathers of the Turkish Republic and their heirs time and again underlined that the people were sovereign but that their first task as leaders was to find a means of mobilizing Turks en masse—and therefore that they had a role to play as a vanguard of the people. Long after the single party that ruled over Turkey until 1950 had its teeth filed, Kemalism, its ideology, and the idea that the educated had the right to rule "for, but also against" the people, survived. This attitude still forces apart Kemalist Jacobins and the citizens who have a stake in Turkish democracy in the present system.

One of the Kemalist elites' tinkerings with the system was—as I have already noted—their search for a "pure" Turkish language. In Turkey political radicalism—Marxism and socialism as well as Kemalism—has for many years automatically meant support for linguistic reform. This is still a lively issue, as a recent debate in the daily *Cumhuriyet* has demonstrated. The latest military intervention in 1980 brought with it a purge of all state institutions in which linguistic purists, that is, radicals, which is to say purported leftists, socialists, and Marxists, had filled directing roles. In the 1990s radical secularist Kemalists are still carrying on a battle for the use of "pure" Turkish, whereas a less puritanical attitude toward language is promoted by groups with more centrist or conservative views. Although the issue is rarely discussed in these terms in Turkish society, it is a reality of the Turkish scene.

Universalism-Particularism.   Turkish republican reform underlined its commitment to universalism in its political compact (as appeared in the Constitution of 1924). The populations of Anatolia, the territory left to Turks after the demise of the empire, were not to be labeled any more as Lazes or Kurds—as had been the case before 1918—but as Turkish citizens. All Turkish citizens were considered by the founding fathers to be integral components of the unfolding of a general, unlabeled "civilization" (i.e., the civilization of the West) and of Comtian "humanity."

Particularism as an abstraction had no meaning for Ottoman Turks whose own terms (Laz, etc.) were ethnic labels. The accommodational Ottoman system kept these subunits relatively undisturbed; autonomous community organization took care of local matters. In modern Turkey a structural development, rural to urban migration, changed the social conditions after 1946, promoting particularistic identities and bringing the concept of particularism into the political debate. This development was used by the "universalists" to express their apprehension of a direction of social change they feared.

The way in which social change had recast the new social equilibrium that the Republic was trying to establish was that Islamists began to deny that universalist abstractions such as civilization and humanity had any meaning. They challenged the universalism of the early Republic by referring to "our" civilization, that is, the civilization of Islam as the civilization of the Turks.

Another development, less ideological and more structural, has reinforced—albeit tangentially—the Islamic critique of Republican universalism. Since 1950 Turkey has experienced an extraordinarily large migration from the countryside to major urban centers. Metropolitan Istanbul, with a population of 950,000 in the early 1950s, is estimated to be a city of 12 million today. It is estimated that 3,000 persons a day enter the city for permanent settlement. This has created boroughs with inhabitants who have clustered around earlier migrants from their own subprovince, town, or even village of origin. A type of localism has developed within these boroughs that is the most practical and efficacious frame of social identity for the migrants in view of the resources that these informal networks command. As a consequence, no political party can go to the polls without having one person on its electoral list from the specific provincial locality that has stamped its mark on the borough. The Polish vote in Chicago is a reminder that similar situations exist outside Turkey, but the situation is somewhat more complex.

For one thing, some political issues make the picture less clear. There is little doubt that a number of these transplanted provincials gave some thought to the inclusion of Turkey in the European Customs Union when they voted for parties that supported it. The normative conflict, however, appears in political choices of a somewhat different nature. Cem Boyner, a wealthy industrialist, is the founder of a new political party, the New Democratic Party (December 1994) and a political liberal with populist sympathies. He was nevertheless treated of no account throughout these settlements. The opinion held about him was that he was an honorable man but not sufficiently "upcountry." Indeed, some sign of sympathy for the "local/provincial" has become a preferred trait of leaders of all types.

The modern Turkish secular intelligentsia has maintained its universalism and shown it in the energy it devotes to following the development of "global" trends. It also pays attention to what it considers the requirements of global civilization, but it is increasingly distanced from the population of the wide belt of shantytowns around Istanbul.

Military Versus Civilian.   A subset of the elitist-mass cluster may be the dividing line between military and civilian rule. The Turkish army has always seen itself as the guardian of basic foundational principles of the Republic, namely, that the latter was *une et indivisible*, populist, etatist, secular, and revolutionary. Above all, the military has been intent on protecting the state and *raison d'état*.[19]

In 1950 a new political party, the Demokrat Party (DP), had begun to challenge the one-party regime that had lasted until 1946. The DP was expected to turn the whole system around in the first exercise in free, multiparty elections. The main slogan of the DP, "Enough," attacked one-party authoritarianism. The army was apprehensive that the coalition of landowners, businessmen, and "provincials" with strong Muslim values would subvert the Republican order, and indeed a strong if unvoiced propellant of the DP was the antimilitaristic stance of some of its supporters, who associated Kemalism cum militarism with etatism and its limitation on opportunities for development. Ismet Inonu, the president and a former general, stopped the army from nullifying the elections in 1950. In 1961, following a military coup against the DP that involved the same principles, he once again stopped the perpetuation of military rule. In 1971 the military intervened again, because of the fear of left-"anarchism" on university campuses. By this time the civilian reactions were strong enough to force free elections in 1973.[20]

In 1980 the Turkish army once again staged a coup at a time when the nationalist right and a variety of Marxist groups were engaged in daily battles. The extraordinarily utopian project of the military to establish a system of three "domesticated" parties—left, center, and right—ended in fiasco. Recently (December 20, 1995) the news was that at a meeting of the Turkish National Security Council a military member voiced the possibility of military intervention were the (Islamic) Welfare Party to take the lead in the general election of December 24, 1995. These rumors, however, met with disapproval in the Turkish press. For a large sector of the population in Turkey "civil society" is understood as *civilian* society with its democratic institutions. Military rule is opposed by all who see an opportunity for political participation for themselves as actors in the present system. But the Kemalists' fear of Islam sometimes overwhelms their democratic inclinations. In the interlude between the election of December 1995 and the negotiations for a center-right coalition the Istanbul press continuously deplored an outcome government in which the Welfare Party (which obtained a plurality of votes) would be represented. This attitude continued after the Welfare Party formed a government with the True Path Party in the summer of 1996. As the Washington, D.C., *Turkish Probe* (March 21, 1997) stated, the Istanbul press had more than one aim in encouraging a military coup.

Secularism Versus Religion.   I shall not recapitulate the details of the secularization of Turkish society since 1923. The abolition of the sultanate and of the caliphate, the state's declared monopoly of education and the elimination of the Ministry of Religious Affairs, the adoption of the Swiss Civil Code, the Latinization of the alphabet, the striking of the sentence in the Constitution of the Republic to the effect that the religion of Turks was Islam, the abolition of the Sufi orders, all have been described elsewhere.[21]

What these steps provided was a focus for a new Turkish social and national identity and a venue into a future democracy. Many modern critics consider the democratic goal to have been rhetoric pure and simple.[22] The main reform project of the Republic, secularization, did not penetrate effectively into rural Turkey. The consequence was a structural conflict between the secularization of a Kemalist elite and the Islamic everyday life of the provinces and the villages, where community action and the construction of the self was still a function of Islam. For the new middle class this area was a void where Islamic values were in reality taken for granted but not consciously acknowledged. Among the secularist-activist founding fathers, this value set provided a subconscious moral frame that was simply residual, that is, what was left of Ottoman culture, and therefore had flimsy foundations. A society based on the market would quickly undermine these unanchored values and create perplexity or cynicism among later generations, as has been the case since the 1960s among young Turkish Marxists.

Buried in the depths of Turks' endorsement of the republican regime and its cult of popular sovereignty lie some concealed issues brought to center stage by the recent Islamic revival and publicized by some Islamic radicals. One such issue is the foundation of the Republic's legitimacy. By Islamic standards it is God and his sovereignty that legitimate any political system. Obviously, it is the "people," and not God, who provide the ultimate legitimization of the Turkish Republic. However, Islamic theory of this level of analysis has not had much resonance in Turkish public opinion. This silence connotes the real popularity and acceptance of Turkish democracy in its present form by Turks of all walks of life.

In the 1950s multiparty politics brought to the fore new forces that attempted to mobilize rural Turkey and used (or had to use) the existing Islamic networks and values to promote political party success. But there are three more dimensions of this revitalization that should be kept in mind and that are less directly political. First, a mobilized, modernizing society promoted individual vertical and geographic mobility, which brought to the forefront of society and to parliament people from the cultural (i.e., Islamic) periphery. Second, many of the people educated in the Republic's secular universities began to question the values of Kemalism as superficial. And third, many people who had been projected out of their everyday setting by modernity began a more conscious search for value moorings that Kemalism did not provide. In the long run, all elements of Turkish society have had to accept Turkey's Islamic inheritance as central to life in Turkey, but the controversy continues as to the extent to which these values should inform Turkish society. This is of central interest for the project embodied in the present volume. One of the major areas where value conflicts have developed has been the well-publicized "head-scarf" issue. In the 1980s a number of women students in universities began to appear wearing head-scarves and ankle-length dresses.[23] The connotation was that they were observant Muslims and took the Qur'anic injunction "not to display their adornments."[24] What was called the "turban" issue was immediately interpreted by Kemalists as a "provocation" aiming to bring symbols of religiosity into secular schools. Further research has shown that some of these students were using that very Islamic symbol to differentiate themselves from the patriarchal authority of a *secular* father.[25] It is these "wheels within wheels" that make the study of Turkish society so challenging.

Secularism Versus Religion in Education. Kemalists today decry the fact that "Imam-Hatip" schools (secondary level "seminaries") have now taken up a hefty portion of the national education budget. In fact, this is a means for the rural poor to promote an education that the state had denied them for years. This denial is not written in any document but is a result of the privileges of the sons of the secular elite, who are privileged as candidates for the modern sector by the very circumstances of their birth, that is, as persons whose fathers have books or encyclopedias in their home. The conflict between secular and religious schools is clearly structural, but it emerges and is fought out as value differences. Many of my own university students in Turkey were completely ignorant of such elements of modern Islamic religiosity as sect membership and local religious organization and looked at these features as promoted by backward people who would soon abandon their ancient ways.[26] Value conflicts are generated at this very threshold of Kemalist views of the world and the reality of Turkish Islam.

An interesting consequence of value differences appears in the life expectations and strategies of "secular" and "religious" Turks. Graduates of Muslim seminaries expect to emerge into a society based on personal networks and *discourse* (a nostalgia for the old mechanism of Ottoman civil society?), whereas Turkish society already operates with *institutions*.[27] The contrast between these naive expectations of seminarians and the real institutional focus of Turkish society makes them prisoners of a modern *state dynamic* that they are at a loss to understand. Religiously trained persons, when they have risen in politics, have therefore often limited their influence to clientelism and are inept at institution building of a new type. By contrast, they have been much more successful in building economic associations with communal/petty bourgeois/religious foundations that have gone on to prosper and step into qualitatively different, much larger spheres of economic enterprise and associations, such as the Islamic businessmen's association, MUSIAD.

The strongest force for the continuation of conflicts discussed in this section has been the obduracy of some secularists in recognizing that religion is a sociologically relevant datum and is thus also relevant for education. The history of education in France does not seem to have alerted them to the tenacity of the issue.

Secularism, Religion, and Art. Plastic arts in the Turkish Republic and art in general have been based on a repudiation of Ottoman art. Two examples will suffice. Plastic art with calligraphy as the canonical form was replaced partially during the nineteenth century and then completely after the foundation of the Republic by Western, "advanced" pictorial representations. Surprisingly, the self-conscious copies of Western painting in the early years of the nineteenth century were quickly overtaken by technically competent painters. But this was the achievement of an elite. Modern Turkish painting does not often appear on the walls of provincial houses, but samples of Islamic calligraphy do.

The mayor of Ankara, elected in 1994 on the ticket of the Welfare Party (i.e., the Islamist Party) has vowed to bring down the many public sculptures in the "proletkult" genre with half-naked men lifting torches to the sky to illuminate the way of half-naked women, both ubiquitous symbols of republican dynamism. While the nude has since the late nineteenth century been a motif in Turkish Western painting, it is still deeply shocking for devout Muslims. Yet the genre does continue to inspire the modernist art sector. Possibly a congruence of streams with respect to values in art may take place as abstract expressionism becomes a more fashionable source of inspiration for Turkish painters.

Music has had a similar history. Atatürk attempted to "shape the musical tastes of the masses from above,"[28] giving full official support to Western music. The failure of this movement is indicated by the heated discussion that for more than fifteen years has been promoted by bureaucrats and intellectuals concerning a new, "degenerate" musical form, *Arabesk* (imitation Arab). The Turkish state attempted to exercise censorship to control and limit access of this musical art form. State national radio and television broadcasts ignored it. Local recording and film industries, however, have contributed in a major way to the unrivaled popularity it has experienced in the past decades through the creative efforts of its expanding network of Arabesk "star performers."[29] With their usual susceptibility to financial success, Turkish modernist music experts have both crafted a new, profitable rock-Arabesk and began to integrate Arabesk into legitimate folk culture.

Women: Patriarchy, the Kemalist Ideal, and the Feminist Movement in Turkey

Like Russian matrioshka dolls, three issues that raise normative problems in Turkey overlap and may be studied under one general heading: tribal, or localistic affiliations; issues involving patriarchal relations; and the status of women in society. All of these bring with them conflicts in which inherited notions of social roles clash with newer views delineating these roles.

One of the structures inherited by modern Turkey from the Ottoman Empire has been what scholars have termed its mosaiclike social structure. This description covers a variety of formations: tribes, heterodox variants of main religious communities, geographical enclaves forgotten by history. Existing Turkish tribal formations, whether nomadic or sedentary, function with "maps" of patrilineal descent that are often "imagined" rather than "real" but that nevertheless shape social relations, depending as they do on the concept of a forebearer and his male issue. This frame for action is patriarchal both in the sense of an image of a founder whose male descendants inherit his charisma and in the everyday aspect of the power he exercises over the tribe as a whole. The fact that women usually do not inherit movable or immovable property in the tribal sector (the result of illegal "arrangements") adds an extra twist to patriarchal rule.[30]

The system brings with it a legitimation of hierarchical-authoritarian-paternalistic roles that was, from the very beginning of the republican system, seen as inconsistent with Kemalist Man. This Kemalist Man was expected to have divested himself of affiliations that impeded his functioning as a citizen of the Republic. In practice, the Turkish Republic involved itself in some major contradictions, which I shall describe presently. This does not stop today's custodians of Kemalist values, that is, groups of schoolteachers, intellectuals, and bureaucrats, from combating what they see as "feudal remnants." Central to this contestation has been the figure of the "Aga"—the traditional tribal leader, the local provincial notable, or the "fathers" (Babas), the title given to leaders of the heterodox Alevi community. The somewhat unidimensional portrait of the Agas' oppressive presence in rural Turkey has been continuously used as a focus for the condemnation of patriarchal-patrimonial rule.

In many ways this tribal patriarchal structure is replicated in the role of the male and the father in the family. Although there are a number of subtleties in this relation, prominent contemporary students of the Turkish family have made it the centerpiece of their analyses.[31]

Everyday relations in Turkey constantly confirm the lingering of patriarchalism. For a taxi driver with whom I had a conversation a few years ago, the most telling sign of the decline of Turkish society was obvious: "My son does not listen to me anymore." This, of course, was a feature of Turkish families undergoing change that had been discovered many years earlier by M. Kiray.[32]

The contradictory stand taken by the fathers of the Turkish Republic concerning patriarchalism in the family did not keep them from undertaking reforms that clearly targeted patriarchalism, the strongest of which appeared in the secularization of the Family Code of 1926. As to the contradictions in which the founders of the Republic involved themselves, these only surface in a detailed history of the Kemalist stand toward women and their role in society.

An area where normative differences are still central in Turkey today is the role of women in society. Women were a preferred icon of Kemalist ideology. A number of women's rights were first targeted by the Young Turks' Family Code of 1917. The Turkish Civil Code (October 4, 1926, free translation of the Swiss Civil Code) brought in the following items: monogamy, mutual agreement in divorce, equality in testimony, equality as a basis of the marriage contract, equality in rights of parents over children, free choice of marriage partner, the legitimization of marriage by civil contract, the setting of marriageable ages. The same law, however, retained the concept of the male as the family head, the use of the man's family name for the woman, the woman's responsibility for work in the household, and the woman's obligation to receive her husband's consent for work outside the household. In the Municipal Electoral Law of 1930, women over eighteen years of age were given the right to vote, to be chosen ward director *(muhtar)* or mayor. In 1934 men and women over twenty-two were given the right to vote for national elections to parliament and those over thirty to be elected to parliament.

Some of the ways in which these values are still the center of conflict in Turkey are visible in the fact that although the Turkish Constitutional Court has ruled against the permission-to-work clause, the Turkish Grand National Assembly has not taken it off its books. Some of the foundations of this conflict are clearly inheritances from the Ottoman Empire.

In Ottoman society the role allocated to women marked the boundary between private and public space. Private space was that delineated by the women's space in the household. Public space was the space occupied by men: the street, the work locale, and even the shop, the latter a liminal, rather dangerous area kept under observation by the police. In an article written long ago I attempted to show how the republican construction of public parks was part of the effort to break this dichotomy. Today's mayor in Tehran has somewhat more cautiously tried to promote a similar policy.[33] In contemporary Turkey an aspect of normative conflict is still the clash between the contending values of woman as "street-broom" (an old Turkish expression referring to women who were always in the street) and "woman at home." This is a conflict that becomes one between real actors, the emancipated-Westernized woman being criticized and sometimes shamed both by men *and* women with conservative views. Its perpetuation is linked to a pair of notions that form the cornerstone of Turkish patriarchal society, namely, the concepts of *şeref* (honor) and *namus* (purity). But in this case too there are some interesting reversals that have to be brought into the picture. A recent article on Turkish women described as follows the career of a woman who was the editor of an Islamic women's periodical:

She was a graduate of Atatürk Kiz Lisesi (a prominent secular high school for girls in Istanbul) and the Business School of Istanbul University. In her own words she came from a "modern family"; however, what did modern mean? In the university, together with some other friends, she began questioning the meaning of modernity, and discussed what "God's path" was. This same group decided they would not be seduced into imitation of the West. They denounced blue jeans and low-cut dresses and covered themselves up. Their families reacted to their daughters' clothing but the daughters persisted. After covering herself up, our assistant editor did not want to work outside, despite her high level of education because she felt she would be harassed as a covered person; this job was perfectly suited to her.[34]

There are a considerable number of women who have identified with Kemalist reform, who have endorsed the role of women highlighted by these reforms, and who occupy professional or political positions. The case of the Turkish prime minister is well known. In general, women's success in this area has been outstanding, even though sustaining these roles demands real commitment and determination. But Turkish feminists have pointed out that such roles are self-limiting.

The unveiled "new woman" of the Republic embodied a whole code and language to delimit new boundaries; two-piece suits, simple short hairstyles, and a lack of make-up were not simply the predilection of the working woman who had no time for frivolity but could also act as a powerful symbolic armor. Even Arat's relatively recent study of women politicians conveys the continuing pressure on women in public roles to act as "honorary men" and de-emphasize their gender identity.[35]

This is a plausible argument to which one should nevertheless add that Turkish feminism has had a century-old history, beginning with themes that appear in late-nineteenth-century Ottoman literature, a feminism that then goes on to surface as feminist activism after the Young Turk revolution of 1908. The first contemporary organized feminist movement of any strength appeared after the 1980 military coup as part of a protest against it.

After the reintroduction of parliamentary rule in 1983, feminism became truly active.

In 1983 feminist groups collaborated in the weekly *Somut* with a page in which they shared with the public their new discoveries about women's issues. . . . In 1986 Istanbul and Ankara feminist groups together organized a petition campaign in order to ask the government to comply with the UN convention about the Abolitions of all Discrimination Against Women (1979). . . . About 7,000 women signed this petition.[36]

In 1990 two important institutions for the protection of women were founded in Istanbul, the Purple Roof Shelter for battered wives and the Women's Library and Information Center.

The right to form associations under current Turkish law, as well as the sympathetic view of major media, will continue to provide support for women's causes. Even the Islamic Welfare Party has had to involve its female members in electoral canvassing. The fact that no women appeared on Welfare Party's list has caused criticism among the very women who worked for it. Moreover, the involvement of these women has not escaped the notice of the popular press; in a recent cartoon featured in the daily *Sabah* a woman in traditional Muslim dress was pictured carrying her husband to the polling both. Things are now moving more rapidly than ever, but some of the problems we are studying in this volume's project are latent and invisible in Turkey, and it is therefore difficult to see the entire picture from the information I have provided to this point.

Epilogue

The main conclusion to be drawn from the preceding is that in Turkey one major normative problem, namely, that of religion versus secularism, heads all others. In fact, many of the conflicts I have enumerated—center versus periphery, elite versus mass, and so on—overlap with that of Islam versus republican secularism. The historical events of the past century and a half provide the details of the way this major duality has been unfolding. They show that a prime element in the historical process leading to the present fluid social equilibrium in these matters has been the eclipse of diffuse Ottoman "intermediating" processes. These consisted of the Sufi orders and the ability of private individuals to refer to the Sufi orders' or other local institutions' assistance where the state or its representatives were absent or oppressive. Their right to invoke religious law when pressed by the administrative state, the use of a view of society as made up of persons, and the sense of belonging to it also promoted the discourse that enabled these strategies to be pursued.

The Republic did attempt to establish its own intermediate *institutions*—People's Houses, clubs, cultural associations, and of course the Republican People's Party, the single party of the Republic until 1946. But these institutions operated according to principles that were completely foreign to the rural Turks' everyday life. Possibly even more important was that these Republican institutions had no familiar mythological resonance, no vocabulary of solicitude for the person, and no practical elements for the construction of the self or the person-in-society in the rural setting.

With the inauguration of the multiparty government, the tempering of secularist campaigns, and the appearance on party electoral lists of individuals who were known to respect Islamic lifestyles, a change came about. These persons were now propelled into politics and representation in parliament. "Traditional" Turks whose cultural premises had been invalidated believed that this new choice would bring back the old inter-mediating processes. This was a mistake. Old personalistic networks—once intertwined with and synchronized with religious discourse—now appeared in the form of institutionalized, mechanical clientalism. Islam acquired a new ideological-political dimension. But there were also other developments among the secularists that precipitated this rush to redeem Islamic institutions. The founding fathers of the Republic had a sophisti-cated, cosmopolitan, imperial background. In the 1940s their more com-plex view of the world was replaced by a simplistic, pedantic, and schoolmarmish version of Kemalism, which, in many quarters, endures to this day. Obviously modifications on both sides of the equation had changed the nature of the polarity. In both cases, today's Islamic actors are unaware that they are using a refiguring of the past in which in many cases the elements of an earlier discourse now appear as an unintegrated jumble. For the majority of the population this disarray will continue for a long time. So much for a pessimistic version of the issue.

The following may be said for the optimistic view, however. Protago-nists on both sides of the issue have considerably increased their stock of knowledge. The idea that antagonistic views can be publicly debated has been a contribution of the infiltration of "American" culture and its diffu-sion in erstwhile missionary schools as well as its appearance in today's Turkish television. Turkish television has a number of debating programs with an enormous clientele; programs sometimes last until 5:00 A.M. There is a sizable community of Islamic intellectuals who write articles informed by a reading of Western philosophy and sociology and who publish books with a sophisticated understanding of the role of Islam in Turkish society. Islamic knowledge itself has grown exponentially through the publication of Islamic classics and the translation of Islamic literature published outside Turkey. Whether this will promote the build-ing of a more unified culture is still to be seen. I believe one can still be in-spired by the views of William Kornhauser, who, deploring the decline of intermediary institutions in Europe in his *Politics of Mass Society* (1960), added, "These conditions of modern life carry with them both the height-ened possibility of social alienation *and* enhanced opportunities for the creation of new forms of association."[37] To some extent this may be wit-nessed during the tenure (beginning in March 1994) of religious forces in the Istanbul municipality.

The Islamic Welfare Party, which has controlled the municipality of Is-tanbul since 1994, has encouraged a number of activities that the more secular political movements have met with grudging admiration. For the metropolitan mayoralty this has consisted of attending to municipal ser-vices with unusual seriousness, having trash collected with unprece-dented regularity (making trains run on time?), but also engaging in wider campaigns of beautification such as the planting of 50,000 trees. The submayoral unit of the district of Kâğithane, in particular, has promoted a local version of direct democracy constructed on the convening of "town meetings" in which citizens are asked to criticize the municipality for its failings and bring their suggestions regularly. Kâğithane has also organized seminars on city life and cultural programs such as "Soviet Film Week." Two characteristics of these activities have been reported: the attendance of seminars by a large proportion of young, scarf-wearing women, and the sophistication of the politicocultural fare that is offered.

We have here once more what are clearly unanticipated consequences of "fundamentalist" behavior and a sign indicating the creation of a new "discursive sphere" within the Islamic fold. An aspect of the solution that we have been seeking in this project would be to take this activity at face value, that is, as showing some of the elements of resolving value conflicts.

The preceding has primarily been a description of normative conflicts that emerge in the social behavior of groups. However, much more important than conflict between groups are the built-in contradictions of the system of modernity in Turkey. Just as important are the conflicts that may be located in the "internal states" of modern Turks. Both demand more serious study than has been accorded them. The following simply underlines the issue.

Istanbul: An Example of Dissonance Within an Urban System

Istanbul is a cosmopolitan city. What is meant by this is its openness to the world. On the other hand, Istanbul is spatially divided between Islamic "Istanbul" and "Western," secular, Beyoğlu, the nineteenth-century Pera. The Golden Horn physically sets apart the two worlds. Conservative Istanbul is framed by five imposing mosques: Aya Sofya, Sultan Ahmet, Fatih, Bayezid, and Suleymaniye. Intimations for the daily life of its population radiate from these centers. Smaller domes of bazaars and pious foundations replicate the form of the mosque. Public fountains for drinking or ablution—long dried up—point to the generosity of its Muslim founders; women circulate with head-scarves, and restaurants do not serve alcohol. Beyoğlu, with its extensions of Levent, Şişli, and Bebek, is another thing. Formerly the abode of the Frank and Levantine, it makes its mark with its boutiques, beer parlors, and restaurants in which there is a continuous flow of ninety-proof *raki*. In Beyoğlu, in 1994, the person who paid the highest personal (national and municipal) income tax was a certain Madame, who served more than Turkish coffee in her various "houses." Yeniköy, by now an extension of Beyoğlu, can boast of a three-tiered night club, the first level of which closes at 1:00 A.M., the second,

which offers a psychedelic dance floor, at 3:00 A.M., and the third, fre-
quented by the "white" golden youth, at 6:00 A.M.

Featured in the Turkish dailies with the highest circulation, which have
a Beyoğlu view of the world but which ironically are printed on the Istanbul side of the city, are European, American, and—increasingly—
Turkish fashion models in a state of undress that would raise eyebrows
even in the United States.

There has been much circulation between Istanbul and Beyoğlu, in the
past as in the present. Only at night, when the population of both parts of
the city have gone back to their homes, can one distinguish the inhabitants of either part. Istanbul has always resented the life of Beyoğlu, and
it has also provided the highest number of votes for parties that represent
Islam. In March 1994, as the consequence of the encroachment of many
new settlements on the Beyoğlu area, the elections for the Istanbul metropolitan mayoralty were won by the Islamic Welfare Party. Numerous
schemes are planned nowadays for making Beyoğlu a more Islamic
place. The one that has caused the most heated discussion is the Islamist
project to build a large mosque in Taksim. Taksim Square is the traditional center of Beyoğlu and at present is dominated by a large nineteenth-century Greek Orthodox church, the Atatürk Cultural Center, and
a number of upper-class hotels. This project, which may now be revived
since the Islamic Welfare Party became the leader in the December 1995
elections, represents a potentially explosive development.

This field of inner systemic contradictions is, obviously, an extremely
important area that overlaps with the specific focus of our normative
conflicts project. The example I have provided is simply an illustration of
the many issues that await investigation.

The Quandaries of a Young Islamic Leader

In 1993 a book appeared in Istanbul entitled *The Powerless Breviary (Mizraksiz Ilmihal).* The author, writing under the pseudonym Mehmet Efe, was a
twenty-three-year-old ex–Islamist intellectual and youth leader who had
given up his leadership role and was working in publishing. The title of
the book was a play on the title of one of the most popular Turkish bre-
viaries: *The Breviary with a Lance.*[38] Efe's book is an autobiographical novel
that centers on the author's short-lived platonic relationship with a young
woman of his age whom he met while he was an Islamist leader. It is also
the frame for the description of the doubts that eventually led him to abandon Islamic student politics. The book is written in student slang and had
an especially evocative quality, deriving from its language.

The narrator begins his university career in the Faculty of Communications, Istanbul University. He is the first in his peasant family to reach
this level of education. His acceptance to the university coincides with

the government policy that took shape in the early 1980s: the exclusion from the university of women students who insist on wearing a scarf to adhere to Islamic precepts. The policy causes a violent protest in which Efe participates and which he recollects at the beginning of his book:

> Either you jettison what you believe in or you are expelled from school, said the state. Sticking to one's belief means becoming a second-rate citizen. . . . Retracting your belief means you can stay in school. . . . We linked together and saw that we were supported by people who had never taken the time to support any group before. This interdiction had given us the means of practicing everything we had read, everything we had accumulated [i.e., the concept of liberty as it had been taught to the author in republican schools]. Then, protests, action, forums, discussions, speeches, meetings, petitions, arrests, court appearances, newspaper and magazine articles, etc.[39]

With time, some of the contradictions he notices in the group with which he is affiliated begin to disturb him:

> I had a friend by the name of Hayrettin who lived in the same house. He used to say, "It is sinful to speak to girls." . . . One day I saw him on one of the benches at school with a girl wearing a head-scarf; I overheard him promoting a somewhat different line: "I think of a woman as a mother, a fighter for the cause, a symbol of purity, virginity and beauty." Later they got engaged, but within a month they separated. When I asked why, he answered: "These girls have been spoiled to the core. It's the school that has done it to them. I'm going to get a girl from my village."[40]

In the novel, Efe claims to have found the following passage in his girlfriend's dairy, which in fact expresses his own view:

> We look at the writings of eminent writers in novels and magazines or refer to the punditry of Freud or Eric Fromm to find truths that have already been vouchsafed to us by Islam. . . . I cannot forget how our friend, the psychology student, on the panel on "The Muslim's Construction of His Identity," was referring to Fromm's view on early education and yet completely oblivious to the Qur'anic passages and traditions that taught us the very same truths.[41]

Efe's final assessment is one in which he begins to question his own activist role:

> We say these times are evil, that our Muslim brethren are unaware of their religious obligations. We are in a country where the Archfiend is in power, so what can we do? The system itself is rotten.
> It's the system that is rotting us through, it is the Prince of Darkness who Disintegrates us and yet it is the ignorant who have led us to the pass. These are the Circumstances. So what can we do?
> Proclaim the creed!

All right, let us destroy the system, destroy the established order, proclaim the truth to ignorant Muslims so that consciousness among them increases.

So how shall we do it?

Let's get together, organize, establish Muslim pious foundations, do "Islamic work," publish journals, organize night watches, meetings, revolutionary demonstrations.

But then what happens?

Everything we have learned has turned to ammunition. We read books in order to have the means of conscientizing people, we conscientize people to bring them into an organization, our organization exists for us to take leave of our inner self.[42]

Efe's narrative is only one variety of the inner conflicts that riddle youth in Turkey. The very ability of a Muslim youth leader to write a book like *The Powerless Breviary,* however, would have been unthinkable a few decades ago. The book is altogether a fair treatment of ideological issues. It has had record sales in Turkey and would seem to be the product of a society in which the public discussion of key issues has become generalized. This is in fact a type of "intermediation" that hopefully will diffuse some of the violence of the conflicts that are internal to modern Turks.

Finally: A Word About Non-Value Conflicts

The existing value conflicts in Turkey seem to have shifted to a new, dangerous structural divide, namely, the growth of extreme left radicalism among the youth in the shantytown suburbs of Istanbul, as was shown in the riots of May 1, 1996. These huge agglomerations, the buildings of which are no longer tin huts but flimsy and ugly apartment buildings built in concrete, have a young population that has clustered into subreligious (Alevi) groups that are increasingly politicized. Youth in these sections are bombarded by television programs that describe a life they cannot afford and show the corruption of those who can get to the top. A recent study indicated that the main value in this setting was force: the force that enabled some inhabitants to get electricity (by "bleeding" existing lines), water (through similar strategies), and land. Force has thus become the fulcrum of life in these areas. A possible solution here would seem to be for national and international organizations to take the "shantytown" as a serious unit for immediate attention. The Habitat II meeting, which met in June 1996 in Istanbul, may have contributed something to the solution of the problem, but we have not as yet seen anything of relevance for these problems.

Notes

1. For patrimonialism, see Stephen Kalberg, *Max Weber's Comparative-Historical Sociology* (Chicago: University of Chicago Press, 1994), pp. 96–98.

2. This is a view on Ottoman institutions that we owe to Professor Halil Inalcik. See his *The Ottoman Empire: The Classical Age, 1300–1600,* translated by Norman Itzkowitz and Colin Imber (London: Weidenfeld and Nicholson, 1973), pp. 70–104, 163–173, 186 ff.

3. See Lale Yalcin-Heckmann, *Tribe and Kinship Among the Kurds* (Frankfurt: Peter Lang, 1991).

4. Kemalism is the general rubric that comprises the ideology of reform promoted by the founding fathers of the Turkish Republic. See Bernard Lewis, *The Emergence of Modern Turkey,* 2d ed. (London: Oxford University Press, 1968), pp. 239–293.

5. Anthony Giddens, *Modernity and Self-Identity* (Stanford: Stanford University Press, 1991), p. 207.

6. See Cornelius Castoriadis, *The Imaginary Institution of Society,* translated by Kathleen Blaney (Cambridge: Polity Press, 1987); Jacques Le Goff, *L'imaginaire médiéval* (Paris: Gallimard, 1985), "Preface," pp. i–xxi.

7. Castoriadis, *The Imaginary Institution of Society,* pp. 237–238.

8. Jerome Bruner, *Acts of Meaning* (Cambridge, Mass.: Harvard University Press, 1990), p. 137.

9. Ibid., pp. 112–113.

10. Donald Polkinhorne, *Narrative Knowing and the Human Sciences* (Albany, State University of New York Press, 1988), p. 150, quoted in Bruner, *Acts of Meaning,* pp. 115–116.

11. Richard Kearney, "Narrative Imagination Between Ethics and Poetics," *Philosophy and Social Criticism* 21 (1995):182.

12. I realize that in Scheler the problem to be solved with regard to the person is one of ontology. But there exists an argument of Scheler to the effect that the ultimate salvation of the person is totally independent of his relation with the state, which is closer to what I mean. See Max Scheler, *Formalism in Ethics and Non-formal Ethics of Values,* translated by Manfred S. Fring and Roger L. Funk (Evanston, Ill.: Northwestern University Press, 1973), pp. 512–519. This argument is also one of the main arguments of Islamic thinkers of note. It is a moral that also appears in Ottoman folk tales. Although this would appear as a weak element for the comparability of cultures, in fact the structuralist bias of Western social thought immediately brings about a bifurcation. The *person,* not the collective, is the primary element of Ottoman folklore where it takes up a story concerning the state.

13. Victor Turner, *The Ritual Process: Structure and Anti-Structure* (Chicago: Aldine, 1969).

14. "Edeb," *Osmanli Tarih Deyimleri ve Terimleri Sozlugu* (Istanbul: Milli Egitim Basimevi, 1971), p. 501, which in a short paragraph underlines the sense of a value setting the "right path for any official or private actor."

15. For this contract, see my "Freedom in an Ottoman Perspective," in *State, Democracy, and the Military: Turkey in the 1980s,* edited by Metin Heper and Ahmet Evin (Berlin and New York: Walter de Gruyter, 1988), pp. 23–35.

16. Sencer Ayata, "Statu Yarismasi ve Salon Kullanimi," *Toplum ve Bilim*, no. 42 (1988):5–25.

17. See my *Jon Turklerin Siyasi Fikirleri* (Ankara, 1964), passim.

18. M. Sukru Hanioglu, *The Young Turks in Opposition* (New York: Oxford University Press, 1995), p. 211.

19. See William Hale, *Turkish Politics and the Military* (London: Routledge, 1994).

20. Ibid., pp. 216 ff.

21. See, for example, Erik Jan Zurcher, *Turkey: A Modern History* (London and New York: I. B. Tauris, 1993).

22. Mete Tuncay, *Turkiye Cumhuriyetinde Tek-Parti Yonetiminin Kurulmasi (1923–1931)* (Ankara: Yurt Yayinlari, 1981).

23. Ayse Saktanber, "Becoming the 'Other' as a Muslim in Turkey: Turkish Women vs. Islamist Women," in *New Perspectives in Turkey*, no. 11 (Fall 1994):99.

24. Qur'an, 24:30–31.

25. Nilufer Gole, *Modern Mahrem* (Istanbul: Metis, 1992).

26. The new expression in use among Turks is "black Turk," i.e., provincial, Muslim, rural versus "white Turk," i.e., educated, urban, Western-oriented.

27. For the sense in which I use this term—that is, "The principle [through which] activities are carried on by individuals not qua individuals, but in their capacity as holder of offices"—see Gianfranco Poggi, *The State: Its Nature, Development, and Prospects* (Stanford: Stanford University Press, 1990), p. 75.

28. Irene Markhoff, "Popular Culture, State Ideology, and National Identity in Turkey: The Arabesk Polemic," in *Cultural Transitions in the Middle East*, edited by Serif Mardin (Leiden: E. J. Brill, 1994), p. 227.

29. Ibid., p. 225.

30. Lale Yalcin-Heckmann, "Gender Roles and Female Strategies Among the Nomadic and Semi-nomadic Kurdish Tribes of Turkey," in *Women in Modern Turkish Society*, ed. by Sirin Tekeli (London: Zed Books, 1995), p. 220.

31. Deniz Kandiyoti, "Patterns of Patriarchy: Notes for an Analysis of Male Domination in Turkish Society," in Tekeli, *Women in Modern Turkish Society*, pp. 306–318.

32. M. Kiray, "Changing Roles of Mothers: Changing Intra-family Relations in a Turkish Town," in *Mediterranean Family Structure*, edited by J. Peristiany (Cambridge: Cambridge University Press, 1976).

33. See Fariba Adelkah, "Quand les impôts fleurissent à Teheran: Taxes municipales et formation de l'espace public," *Cahiers de CERI*, no. 12, 1995.

34. Yesim Arat, "Feminism and Islam: Considerations on the Journal *Kadin ve Aile*," in Tekeli, *Women in Modern Turkish Society*, pp. 73–74.

35. Kandiyoti, "Patterns of Patriarchy," p. 315.

36. Sirin Tekeli, "Introduction," in *Women in Modern Turkish Society*, p. 14.

37. William Kornhauser, *The Politics of Mass Society* (London: Routledge and Kegan Paul, 1960), p. 237.

38. Mehmet Efe, *Mizraksiz Ilmihal* (Istanbul: Yerli Yayinlari, 1993).

39. Ibid., p. 15.

40. Ibid., p. 19.

41. Ibid., p. 67.

42. Ibid., p. 159.

8

Islamic Tolerance: The Struggle for a Pluralist Ethics in Contemporary Indonesia

Robert W. Hefner

Viewed from afar, few countries in the modern world seem as unlikely a candidate for the development of a civil and tolerant political culture as does the Southeast Asian nation of Indonesia. Here is a nation, after all, composed of more than three hundred ethnic groups living on some six thousand inhabited islands historically separated by marked divisions of religion, language, and culture. Though some 88 percent of all Indonesians officially profess Islam, the Muslim community is itself cross-cut by deep divisions of theological orientation and political ideology. During the 1950s and early 1960s, Muslim discontent in several portions of the archipelago fueled secessionist rebellions aimed at, among other things, the establishment of an Islamic Republic independent from the Javanese-dominated and, at the time, left-leaning central government. Even as these rebellions raged, however, half of the Muslims on the island of Java, where some 60 percent of Indonesians live, threw their support to secular parties, usually either the Indonesian Nationalist Party (PNI) or the Communist Party (PKI). By the early 1960s this predominantly Muslim country had the unusual distinction of having the largest communist party in the noncommunist world.

Hostility between advocates of an Islamic state and their communist and nationalist rivals only fueled secessionist discontent in Indonesia's outer islands. These and other events in turn contributed to the tensions that engendered the awful bloodletting of 1965–1966, one of the twentieth century's worst incidents of civil violence. In the months following a failed leftist coup, the armed forces and Muslim organizations joined forces to round up and execute the communist leadership and hundreds of thousands of their supporters. Most of the condemned leftists, of course, were also nominal Muslims. Over the next few years, some 2 million nominally Islamic Javanese reacted against the violence of their Muslim brethren by converting to Christianity or Hinduism.[1]

Normative divides within the Muslim community are further complicated by those between Muslims and non-Muslims. Under the terms of the national ideological charter known as the Pancasila ("five principles"), all Indonesians are obliged to profess one from among the five religions recognized by the Indonesian government: Islam, Protestant Christianity, Catholicism, Hinduism, or Buddhism. At some 6 percent of the population, Protestant Christians are the largest minority, followed by Catholics (about 3 percent), Hindus (2 percent), and Buddhists (1 percent). Though their absolute numbers are small, Protestants and Catholics are disproportionately represented in the ranks of the middle and professional classes as well as, not insignificantly, the military. Originating in the preferential access to education enjoyed by Christians in colonial times, this imbalance has also been a recurring source of social tension.

The religious landscape is further complicated by divisions of ethnicity and class. Though a handful have converted to Islam, most Chinese Indonesians profess a minority religion, typically either Christianity or Buddhism.[2] More significantly, although they comprise just 3 percent of the national population, Chinese Indonesians own an estimated 75 percent of mid- and large-scale private enterprise; they are thought to control an even larger proportion of the shares traded on the recently established Jakarta stock exchange. Chinese economic dominance originated in precolonial and colonial times, when government officials preferred to give economic concessions to the economically savvy—and politically docile—Chinese rather than native entrepreneurs. Despite a series of government-run affirmative action programs, Chinese economic dominance in the (post-1945) independence era has, if anything, only increased, widening the normative divide between Chinese and Muslims. Since the mid-1960s, in particular, Muslim-owned enterprise has experienced a precipitous decline while Chinese firms have flourished, in part as a result of sweetheart deals between Chinese businesses and Indonesian politicians.[3]

Given this history of religious tensions, economic segmentation, ethnic rivalries, and occasional mass violence, it may appear surprising that Indonesia is today the center of one of the world's largest and most influential movements for a democratic and pluralist Islam. A key feature of this movement has been the effort to provide normative sanctions for democracy and religious tolerance. Another element in this Muslim program has been the rejection of the idea that Islam requires the establishment of an Islamic state. In place of a formally Islamic state, these Muslim activists advocate the substantive realization of the values they regard as most central to Islam—equality, freedom, and social justice—through the strengthening of civil society and constitutional democracy.

To the degree that it is taking hold, the emergence of this type of politically reformist Islam is a remarkable event in its own right. It is all the more significant, however, in light of the fact that Indonesia is the fourth most populous country in the world, and the largest majority-Muslim society. In recent years Indonesia has attracted the attention of observers in other Muslim countries, not least because, with an average annual gross domestic product growth of 6 percent over the past quarter century, the country has achieved a combination of social stability and growth sorely lacking in most of the Muslim world. For all these reasons, the Muslim experience here is of interest far beyond Indonesia's shores.

In what follows, I want to examine the social and historical background to this movement for a democratic pluralist Islam, and then to examine some of the challenges the movement now faces. One irony of the movement's recent success is that as the Islamization of Indonesian society has deepened, it has given rise to social forces opposed to these efforts to develop Islamic sanctions for democracy and civil tolerance. This kind of tension is not peculiar to Indonesia but endemic to many parts of the modern Muslim world. As we shall see, however, the tension has as much or even more to do with structural tensions within the Indonesian political system itself as it does anything peculiar to Islam.

At a time when some Western observers speak of a potential "clash of civilizations" between Islam and the West,[4] the Indonesian example provides a local illustration of a general fact: that throughout the Muslim world, there are intellectuals and activists struggling to devise an Islamic framework for democratic pluralism and tolerance. The example also underscores the important fact that, just as in the earlier Christian West, the outcome of this effort will be determined not merely by the good intent and theological sophistication of religious actors—though these qualities *are* deeply important—but by the larger balance of social and political forces with which these actors must contend.

Islam and National Integration

Disagreements as to the role Islam should play in the legal and constitutional apparatus of the country have long been one of the sharpest normative divides in modern Indonesia. The first mass-based organization for native political rights, the Sarikat Islam, was established in 1912 and quickly achieved a mass following in central portions of the archipelago, especially on the island of Java.[5] Though originally established to defend the interests of Muslim merchants, Sarikat Islam quickly developed an internal divide between members committed to the organization's original Islamic principles and those inclined toward Marxism and secular nationalism. Influenced by socialist and communist advances in postwar Europe, the organization's leftist membership succeeded in giving a socialist emphasis to the proceedings of the third national congress in October 1918. In 1921 the rivalry between the Muslim and Marxist factions came to a climax with the expulsion of communists from the organization. Over the next five years leftists and Muslims vied for control of Sarikat Islam's many local chapters. In conjunction with growing state repression, the rivalry shattered the organization and left the native movement for independence in disarray. The conflict laid the foundation for a normative tension between Muslims and secular-nationalists that has continued to this day.

In the last years of Dutch colonialism, leadership of the nationalist struggle passed from Sarikat Islam into the hands of the Indonesian Nationalist Party (PNI). Established in 1927 under the chairmanship of a young engineer, Soekarno, the PNI was committed to the idea that multiethnic nationalism *(kebangsaan)*, not religion or ethnoregionalism, must be the basis of an independent Indonesia. Though familiarized with Islamic doctrine in his youth, Soekarno received his higher education in the multiethnic and multireligious environment of colonial schools. He was, in other words, an almost prototypical example of the "creole functionary" whom Benedict Anderson, in his study of the origins and genesis of nationalism, has identified as the carrier of postcolonial nationalism.[6] Educated at a time when the colonial state required growing numbers of native functionaries, Soekarno learned Dutch and was deeply affected by the modernist ideas of European liberalism. Yet, for him and many other native intellectuals, this education only served to highlight the gap between liberal ideals and colonial realities. Ultimately, as with many of his fellows, Soekarno's educational pilgrimage inspired a strong commitment to the idea of an Indonesian nationalism transcending ethnicity, region, and religion.

Soekarno's conviction was reinforced by his belief that the "historical Islam" of the modern world had diverged from Islam's original ideals; in so doing, he felt, this Islam had only exacerbated the Muslim world's backwardness. Influenced by the ideas of nationalist reformers in Turkey and the Middle East, Soekarno argued that the union of state and religion common in classical Islamic governance was a prime cause of the Muslim world's stagnation and allowed Islam to be used for oppressive ends.[7] By contrast, Soekarno argued, separation of Islam from state would actually free Islam from state tutelage. Significantly, in presenting this argument, Soekarno took pains to point out that although he rejected the formal union of Islam and state, he felt that religious disestablishment would and *should* contribute to the substantive realization of Islamic values in society.

In the eyes of many Muslim political thinkers, however, nationalism seemed a shallow basis on which to build a new political order. While a small segment of the native population had been afforded the privilege of Western education, many more had made a very different educational pilgrimage, through a network of mosques and religious schools that stretched across western and central portions of the Indonesian archipelago. The speed with which Middle Eastern reformist ideas spread through this network in the last half of the nineteenth century provided striking testimony to its effectiveness as a vehicle of social integration and anticolonial aspiration.[8] Though Hindu Bali, the remote interiors of some larger islands, and the desperately poor islands of eastern Indonesia remained outside this Muslim circuit, its influence otherwise reached deep into all of the archipelago's central territories. Not surprisingly, in the early colonial era many of the most prolonged struggles against the Europeans were conducted under the banner of Islam.

In light of this historical precedent, many Muslim intellectuals were convinced that Islam, not nationalism, was the proper ground on which to build the independence struggle. For these thinkers, Soekarno-style nationalism was merely a modern version of the tribal and ethnic divisions (*'asabiyah*) that had divided the Arabs in pre-Islamic times and against which Muhammad himself had inveighed.[9] Would not adoption of this foreign ideology separate Indonesians from their Muslim brothers at a time of growing pan-Islamic consciousness?[10] Was not Islam, therefore, a more meaningful ground for national integration than the Western-derived notion of nationalism? Besides, many Muslim leaders argued, Islam is not merely a matter of personal piety and inner belief, like modern Christianity. It is a civilization and social order, which is to say a complete and self-sufficient "system" in itself. This idea of Islam as a complete social order (*al-nizam al-islami*) has been a recurrent theme in Islamist politics throughout the Muslim world, and it remains a contentious issue dividing the Indonesian Islamic community today.[11]

However, Soekarno was not the only Muslim leader to find the modernist and progressive ideals of nationalism more appealing than those of pan-Islam. Many among the early supporters of nonconfessional nationalism were, in fact, devout Muslims.[12] Some were attracted to nationalist ideals on purely practical grounds, recognizing that the fledgling nation might disintegrate were it declared an Islamic state. Though they comprised only about 10 percent of the Indonesian population, non-Muslims were not concentrated in easily controllable cities or dispersed among the general population, as with Christian minorities in countries like Egypt and Syria. Instead they lived primarily in remote regions, especially in eastern Indonesia, where state administration was weak, and where a strong secessionist movement might well challenge the young republic.

The political appeal of nonconfessional nationalism was also reinforced by the fact that a substantial number of Indonesian leaders from Muslim backgrounds were themselves uneasy about the idea of Islamic government. This was especially true on the heavily populated island of Java. The ethnic Javanese, who comprised 75 percent of that island's population (and about 45 percent of Indonesia's population as a whole) were renowned for the divide between those who were orthodox in their profession of Islam, sometimes known as *santri*, and those who were more lax in their devotional duties or who mixed the profession of their faith with a variety of Javanese ritual and aesthetic traditions.[13] From the first days of the nationalist movement, *santri* Javanese had thrown their support to Islamic political parties, while the latter group, known as Javanists or *abangan*, tended to identify with nationalist and communist causes. At several points in the independence struggle Muslim politicians overestimated their strength by failing to recognize the seriousness of this normative divide among Javanese Muslims.

Against this historical backdrop, it is perhaps not surprising that every effort to create an explicitly Islamic state in the early independence era failed. There were, for example, fierce ideological debates over the legal and constitutional grounds of the new state in the weeks leading up to the Indonesian declaration of independence in August 1945. A few months earlier, in the last days of their occupation, the Japanese had allowed the native community to form a Preparatory Committee for Indonesian Independence. The assembly was able to reach agreement on the outlines of the new state on all points except the future role of Islam. Soekarno attempted to break the deadlock by proposing five principles as the philosophical basis of the country, principles that later came to be known as the Pancasila. Among the principles was *ketuhanan*, or belief in God, a clear concession to supporters of an Islamic state. Later, in the face of continuing pressures from this group, a small committee expanded this principle to read, "Belief in God *with the obligation to carry out Islamic law [shariah] for its adherents*." Known as the Jakarta Charter, this principle of state support for Islamic law would be a bone of contention between Islamists and nonconfessionalists for years to come.[14]

In the end, one day after the August 17, 1945, declaration of independence, Soekarno yielded to the appeals of Christians, Hindus, and nonconfessionalists by ignoring the recommendation of the preparatory committee and dropping the Jakarta Charter from the preamble to the Indonesian constitution. As a concession to Muslim leaders, he added a clause to the first principle of the Pancasila so that it became not merely "belief in God" but "belief in a singular God" (*ketuhanan yang Maha Esa*).

This revised formulation brought the Pancasila closer to Muslim ideas on the unity of God *(tauhid)*. In addition, it had the very serious effect of proscribing animism and polytheism as legitimate religious options for citizens in an independent Indonesia. In the years since independence, most animists have felt compelled to convert to Christianity or Islam. Buddhists and Hindus have been obliged to reformulate their beliefs in a manner that, at least publicly, brings them into line with monotheistic notions of divinity, no small matter in the case of Hinduism.[15]

In any case, during the first years of postrevolutionary independence, this compromise formulation seemed to mediate the normative divide between Muslims and secular nationalists well enough. Between 1950 and 1957, a period today regarded as the heyday of parliamentary democracy, three of the seven cabinets that governed were led by the modernist Muslim party, Masyumi. Though the leaders of this party were among the most forceful proponents of an Islamic state, they made no move when in power to upset the compromise worked out in the first days of independence. Moreover, they showed themselves to be among the most conscientious supporters of constitutional law and parliamentary procedure.[16]

In the aftermath of the first national elections in 1955, however, the country began a rapid descent into presidential authoritarianism and a fierce, three-sided rivalry between the Communist Party (PKI), Muslim parties, and the military. To the surprise of most observers, the 1955 elections resulted not in an outright Muslim victory but in an unstable standoff between Muslim parties and their nationalist and communist rivals. The elections that year also brought a Constituent Assembly into existence, whose task it was to draft a definitive constitution for the young republic. (The two previous constitutions had been regarded as temporary or "working" constitutions.) As in parliament, the balance of power in the Constituent Assembly was more or less evenly divided between nonconfessionalist nationalists and supporters of an Islamic state. While the Assembly managed to reach agreement on many important matters, it deadlocked on the question of the degree to which Islam should be accommodated within the legal and political structures of the state.[17] The normative divide between Muslim and secular nationalists seemed as great as ever.

Frustrated by this impasse—and convinced that he himself was the sole guarantor of the Indonesian revolution's continuing progress—President Soekarno took advantage of this crisis to announce a return to the Constitution of 1945 and the creation of a "Guided Democracy." This new political system transferred power away from parliament and into the hands of the president. Though the nationalist and communist leadership eventually went along with the president's initiative, the modernist Masyumi, the largest of the Muslim parties, vehemently opposed it. Annoyed by the ferocity of the Masyumi opposition, the president simply ignored constitutional procedure, dissolved the Constituent Assembly, and declared a return to the executive-heavy Constitution of 1945. A year later, as the country was shaken by regional rebellions, Soekarno struck back at his most virulent critics, Masyumi and the social-democratic Indonesian Socialist Party (PSI). Citing the failure of their leaders to condemn the rebellions, the president banned both parties. Shortly thereafter, to the dismay of Muslim and social democrats alike, he imprisoned most of their leadership. Muslim (and social democratic) fidelity to constitutional democracy had yielded a bitter fruit indeed.

While the president's Muslim opponents were thus marginalized, the PKI during these same years transformed itself into the country's most powerful party. The party benefited from the growing support of President Soekarno. Though he was the founding father of the Indonesian Nationalist Party, during his final years in office Soekarno was locked in a power struggle with the armed forces, who were unhappy with his economic policies and his tilt toward Beijing. Frustrated by continuing military opposition, Soekarno looked to the communists to provide him with a mass base with which to outflank his military rivals.

The PKI was able to expand also because, more than its rivals, it found itself able to take advantage of the precipitous decline of the national economy by mobilizing the rural poor, especially in Java. In late 1963 the party launched a campaign to implement the sharecropping and land-reform laws of 1959–1960. As its campaign advanced, it encountered fierce resistance from landlords and, especially in East Java, devout Muslims, many of whom were more consistently targeted for PKI actions than were their nationalist or communist counterparts. In several instances, the campaign escalated into fierce battles between communists and Muslims, creating tensions that would shortly feed into the violence of 1965–1966.[18] The normative cleavage between Muslims and secular nationalists had taken a new and dangerous form.

In the end, political tensions escalated to the point that leftist junior officers in Jakarta launched a coup the night of September 30, 1965, ostensibly to preempt what they claimed was a planned coup by conservative generals. The coup leaders bungled the effort, but, by killing five senior generals and forging ties with at least some of the PKI leadership, they also handed their enemies the pretext for a massive counterattack against the communist left. From October 1965 through March 1966 President Soekarno tried desperately to save the crippled party. However, a complex (and regionally variable) alliance of military, Muslim, and even Hindu and Christian organizations struck back with deadly effect, destroying the vast party apparatus and tens of thousands of party members. In March 1966 President Soekarno relinquished power to the military leader of the anticommunist forces, General Soeharto. The "New Order" era had begun.

From Center to Margin

It would take us beyond the confines of this chapter to provide a detailed account of the normative conflict between Islam and secular nationalism under the New Order. However, before describing the rise of what I refer to here as a "civic pluralist" Islam, let me briefly outline the unusual course of events that followed the destruction of the PKI and the ascent of the New Order government.

During the first four years of the New Order regime, Muslim-state relations went from cordial to strained. As reward for their assistance in forcing President Soekarno from power and crushing the PKI, Muslim leaders at first expected to be welcomed into government or, at the very least, allowed to play an active role in the next national elections. Muslim activists—and apparently a few military leaders as well—were convinced that with the communists destroyed and the Nationalist Party discredited, Muslim parties might well be able to take an electoral road to power.

It was not long, however, before the military-dominated government indicated that it had no intention of holding early national elections or allowing Muslim organizations much organizational latitude when they finally did. Among other things, regime spokesmen reiterated their opposition to any effort to revive the Jakarta Charter, the 1945 document that had affirmed the state's obligation to implement Islamic law among Muslims. This was the first indication of a notable cooling toward Muslim organizations on the part of the government. A bit later, regime spokesmen denied requests for the rehabilitation of what had earlier been the largest of the Islamic parties, the Masyumi, which had bitterly opposed President Soekarno before it was banned in 1960. At first the government appeared to sweeten this bitter pill by agreeing to allow the formation of a new Islamic party. But it soon revealed the limited nature of that concession by refusing to allow ex-Masyumi officials to play a leadership role in the new party.

All this was part of a broader effort on the part of Indonesia's military leadership to prevent a recurrence of the mass-based political struggles of the 1950s. The military was concerned about the nation's normative fissures too, and had concluded that the best way to deal with them was to demobilize political society. At the center of this strategy lay a plan to reorganize the whole of Indonesian society into government-controlled corporatist groups, known generically as "functional groups" (*golkar* or *golongan karya).* Though the system would allow for national elections, electoral campaigns would be restricted to the days immediately before the elections, and political parties (with the notable exception of the government party) would be otherwise barred from the countryside. Rather than the revolutionary mobilization of the Soekarno era, the populace was to be transformed into a "floating mass" primarily concerned with the practical task of economic development.

From the early 1970s to the mid-1980s this strategy of political containment advanced through several stages. Before the 1971 elections the government announced a policy of "single loyalty" *(monoloyalitas)* forbidding members of the armed forces and many civil servants to hold membership in any political party other than the government party, Golkar. In the course of the 1971 campaign, there were numerous reports of intimidation of voters in an effort to expand support for Golkar. Golkar went on to win the election with 63 percent of the vote. Two years later the government announced even firmer measures against the political parties, consolidating the nine surviving parties into two umbrella groups. One was nominally Islamic, and the other an unwieldy amalgam of Christians, Hindus, democratic socialists, and nationalists. Needless to say, this forced consolidation destroyed the autonomy of those parties that had survived the 1965–1966 violence. It also provided the government with a new opportunity to intervene in party affairs. Government officials now asserted the right to screen lists of candidates for election, influence the selection of party leaders, and approve the final wording of party platforms.[19]

The decisive blow against the last bastions of Muslim party power, however, occurred with the government's announcement in 1983 that from 1985 on, all political organizations would have to accept the Pancasila as the sole basis *(asas tunggal)* of their ideology. Though Christians also resented the new regulation, Muslim organizations were its primary target, since, in effect, it required them to forswear any commitment to the idea of establishing an Islamic state. Though it sowed deep discord in their ranks, in the end all Islamic organizations except one went along with the government regulation. The traditionalist Muslim organization Nahdlatul Ulama—once one of Indonesia's most powerful political parties and now a faction within the consolidated Islamic party—accepted the policy but also withdrew from formal politics.[20] By the mid-1980s the regime's ability to set the terms of national politics seemed complete and its political opposition in disarray. As we shall see, however, it was less clear that the normative divide between secular and Muslim nationalists had finally been resolved.

There had always been Muslim activists who were unhappy with their community's preoccupation with power politics. During the turbulent

1960s, when the very survival of Muslim organizations seemed in question, their voices had been drowned out by those of politicians. However, the regime's restrictions on party politics led some Muslim leaders to reassess the merits of a strategy so thoroughly centered on state politics. By the late 1960s, as many Muslim leaders saw their hopes for a heightened political role fade, these once-marginal ideas again began to be aired in some Muslim circles. A number of young Islamic leaders criticized the senior leadership's preoccupation with party politics. They called for a commitment to Islamic renewal not through political parties and the state but through programs of social and educational reform. Eventually these calls gave rise to a powerful new initiative for Muslim pluralism and civil revival known as the "renewal" *(pembaruan)* movement. This Islamic movement would seek to come to grips once and for all with Indonesia's normative divides.

Toward a Civil-Pluralist Islam?

The idea that Muslims' preoccupation with party politics was misplaced and what was needed was a commitment to a pluralist and revitalized Islam originated among activists in several centers of Islamic learning. Some of the most influential figures, however, were associated with the powerful Association of Islamic Students or HMI *(Himpunan Mahasiswa Islam)*, an organization established in 1947 as an umbrella group for Muslim students, primarily of a modernist theological persuasion. From a comparative Islamic perspective, the HMI is interesting because it is a striking example of a much-discussed species of Islamic organization that became widespread in the Muslim world in the 1950s and a major force in Islamic politics in the 1970s. This is to say that, in an Indonesian setting, the HMI is the organizational embodiment *par excellence* of a group commonly described in Islamic studies as the "new Muslim intellectuals."

Whether in Indonesia or the Middle East, the new Muslim intellectuals emerged with the expansion of mass higher education, a development that began in earnest in most Muslim countries only in the 1950s. With the socialization of large numbers of youths in the abstract and relatively open (relative, that is, to traditional institutions of Islamic learning) environment of the university, mass higher education exposed Muslim youth to a new way of accessing and organizing knowledge. In many Muslim countries, including Indonesia, it also pushed pious Muslim youth into contact with nationalist, socialist, and Marxist activists. In so doing, the educational process encouraged the youth to compare their religious beliefs with those of their ideological rivals. As a result of this exercise, they came to view Islam as an objective system that could be compared and opposed to other ideologies.[21] Though this objectification and ideologization of Islam was intended to defend its traditional authority, in fact it represents a decidedly modern way of understanding and utilizing religion.

The emergence of this class of educated activists fragmented patterns of authority within the Muslim community. Dale F. Eickelman's description of the nature of these changes in Oman has direct parallels in Indonesia:

> Oman provides a recent example of a general shift to a religious activism that marginalized the authority of traditional leaders. . . . With this transformation, religious authority shifts from elite specialists recognized as masters of religious texts and often inaccessible rhetorical forms to religious and political activists who seek open religious discussion and action and whose authority is based upon persuasion and the interpretation of accessible texts.[22]

The HMI was a vehicle of just such a dispersion of religious authority. With its ascent, traditional and modernist leaders saw their public authority challenged by university-trained intellectuals with an activist understanding of religion.

Given the fact that in some countries new Muslim intellectuals have a reputation for Islamic fundamentalism,[23] the HMI might at first sight seem an unlikely source for democratic pluralist ideas. This paradox is all the more striking in light of the political history of the organization in the last years of the Soekarno era. At that time, this small organization was pushed into an increasingly militant posture when it became the target of a bitter campaign by the more powerful PKI. The PKI was convinced, quite rightly it turned out, that some of its most skilled Muslim foes lay in the HMI's ranks and its associated alumni organization. Thus, in the aftermath of President Soekarno's 1960 banning of Masyumi, the PKI launched a vigorous campaign to portray the HMI as equally "counterrevolutionary" and to have it declared illegal as well. President Soekarno resisted these pressures, apparently because there were still several HMI supporters among his advisers. HMI thus survived and remained one of the most effective Muslim critics of the PKI throughout the early 1960s.

Not surprisingly given this history, the HMI was also one of the first organizations to respond to the attempted coup of September 30, 1965. On the first day of the coup the HMI leadership moved quickly to make contact with anticommunist military leaders. When the coup collapsed, HMI leaders worked to devise a strategy for a broader assault against communist power. Through demonstrations and, in several instances, outright attacks on PKI facilities, the organization worked with anticommunist military officers to limit President Soekarno's authority and, more specifically, to frustrate his efforts to save the PKI. When President Soekarno attempted in early 1966 to regroup his supporters and restore his faltering power, the HMI, in conjunction with other student organizations assembled as the Indonesian Student Action Group (KAMI), spearheaded a campaign to block the president's efforts. In March 1966 this combination of military pressures and student demonstrations effectively forced a transfer of power from Soekarno to General Soeharto and the military. Shortly thereafter, the already-decimated PKI was abolished and leftist officials in government fired or imprisoned.[24] Though its precise role varied from province to province, segments of the HMI were also active in the "cleansing" campaign conducted from late 1965 to late 1966 against the rural PKI organization.[25]

Given the HMI's role in the anti-Soekarno and anticommunist campaigns, one would not expect it to become a center of civil pluralist ideals. But this is exactly what happened. The reasons for this development remain one of the great mysteries of early New Order politics. Part of its explanation is that even at the height of its struggle against the PKI, the HMI harbored a diverse array of political actors. In the 1950s, for example, certain HMI activists had been among the first and only Muslim leaders to declare that the Pancasila, with its vision of a nonconfessional republic, was consistent with Islam. Though many HMI figures had personal ties to Masyumi, HMI as an organization always made a point of guarding its independence from any single party. A few in the HMI leadership had even been vocal supporters of President Soekarno.

From early on, then, some in the HMI developed a principled commitment to ideological diversity and political independence. These attitudes proved to have a critical influence on the reaction of the HMI leadership to the unexpected course of events during the first years of the New Order.[26] In the months following the Soekarno regime's collapse, many among the "generation of 1966," as they were known, were intoxicated with their achievement and what they felt was a new freedom to voice opinions illegal just a few months earlier. Many were also convinced that a new and genuinely democratic era had dawned. Adnan Buyung Nasution—a well-known activist at this time who today has become the distinguished and outspoken director of Indonesia's foremost legal rights center—described the heady triumphalism of the era in this way:

> When I look back on that period, it was like a dream. I was naive and didn't understand the politics of the time. In my own thoughts, I saw myself at the time as rising to resist the authoritarian Sukarno regime. I felt he had stripped the country of its constitutional guarantees and was using appeals to what he said were Indonesian ideals to limit the rule of law and democracy. But I didn't understand the power politics taking place.[27]

Though not a member of the HMI, Nasution was a founder of the postgraduate action group known as KASI (Kesatuan Aksi Sarjana Indonesia). He cooperated closely with HMI activists in the campaign to ban the

communist party and bring down Soekarno.[28] His surprise at the undemocratic evolution of the New Order led him to reexamine his earlier actions and eventually to become one of Indonesia's most courageous
spokespersons for constitutional government and the rule of law.

Though the practical focus of their effort might differ, many HMI leaders experienced a political awakening not unlike that of Nasution. Just
two years after the establishment of the New Order, many in this Muslim
organization began privately to express doubts about the political order
they had helped to usher in. They were concerned not merely about new
government restrictions on political activity, however, but also about
what they felt was the tendency of the Muslim leadership to react to the
situation with the same tired strategy of confrontation and mobilization.
Some young Muslim leaders began to wonder whether the time were not
ripe for a new approach to Indonesian politics and renewal.

We know from the posthumously published diaries of Ahmad Wahib,
for example, that at this time there were HMI members in the organization's powerful Yogyakarta chapter that were rethinking the relationship
of Islam to party politics. Killed in a motorcycle accident in 1973, Wahib
was a young and highly original intellectual active in HMI circles in that
Javanese city. Through an Islamic study group known as the "Limited
Discussion Group," he and his friends were preoccupied with the question how to revitalize Islamic culture and politics.[29] Along with such re-
newalist thinkers as Djohan Effendi and Dawam Rahardjo, and under the
tolerant sponsorship of Mukti Ali, a professor at an Islamic university
who would later become minister of religion, Wahib and his associates
expressed frustration at what they regarded as the stagnation of Islamic
modernism. Having originated as a bold and dynamic response to
modernity, Wahib felt, modernism had degenerated into an orthodoxy
that hindered freedom of thought. He blamed the subordination of Islam
to party politics for much of this stagnation. By so singularly emphasizing party politics over cultural renewal, Wahib argued, the Muslim leadership had ideologized Islam and undermined Muslims' ability to create
a free and modern Islam.

Not coincidentally, as early as mid-1967, arguments like these led
Wahib and his Yogyakarta colleagues to argue that the HMI should repudiate the idea of an Islamic state and embrace the Pancasila as a sign of
their commitment to a pluralist and tolerant Islam. Their public expression of this opinion during 1968 and 1969 excited strong condemnation
by the Jakarta branch of the HMI, which accused the Jogja chapter of secular and "socialist" thought.[30]

In fact, however, no less a figure than the national chairman of the
HMI, Nurcholish Madjid, was privately moving toward a similar conclusion at this same time. Chairman of the HMI for two terms from 1966 to

1971, Madjid was widely regarded as a rising young star in the modernist Muslim community. As president of the Union of Southeast Asian Islamic students (1967–1969) and assistant secretary-general of the International Islamic Federation of Student Organizations (1968–1971), he had also achieved international recognition. Secretly, however, Madjid was troubled by the Muslim community's deadlock with the government. Though he recognized that some of the blame for the impasse lay in government officials' attitudes, he also felt that the Muslim community's obsession with party politics and, more generally, the establishment of an Islamic state, created an all-or-nothing attitude that made it impossible for Muslims to respond to the challenges of the age. Muslim politicians had confused the worldly and merely instrumental with what was essential to Islam.[31]

In January 1970 Madjid's reservations were made public with the leaking to the press of one of his position papers. The article decried the continuing Muslim obsession with party politics and called for a bold new program of intellectual and social renewal. A key feature of this renewal, Madjid argued, must be a "secularization" *(sekularisasi)* of Islamic thought, which is to say a principled and consistent effort to distinguish what was lasting and sacred in Islamic tradition from what was merely worldly and temporal. This effort at desacralization, Madjid asserted, is required by the most cherished of Islamic principles itself, *tauhid*, the affirmation of God's absolute oneness. *Tauhid*, Madjid argued, obliges Muslims to distinguish mere politics from divine commands. Only the latter are absolute; by contrast, human understanding of God's commandments is relative and incomplete. More specifically, the idea of an Islamic state, and even the need for an Islamic party, must be desacralized and replaced with an enduring commitment to intellectual openness and political pluralism.[32] With the publication of this work, the renewal movement moved from private dialogue to public debate.

Madjid's article immediately excited a storm of protest. His comments, coming as they did on the heels of government restrictions on political organizations, were seen by many older Muslim leaders as an opportunistic attempt to court government favor. Madjid was promptly and bitterly denounced by such Muslim luminaries as Hamka, Muhammad Natsir (the former head of Masyumi), and H. M. Rasjidi.[33] Curiously, however, some of the most biting criticism concerned not Madjid's reflections on the government or political parties but his call for the secularization of Muslim thought *(sekularisasi)*. Though Madjid took great care to distinguish his commitment to *secularization* from the antireligious ideology of *secularism*, he was tarred by his opponents as a secularist and Westernizer.

Though in private interviews today he acknowledges that his use of the term secularization was not "efficient" since the term lent itself to misconstrual,[34] Madjid has not ceased to insist that Muslims distinguish what is essential and sacred in their religion from what is merely worldly and temporal.[35] Among the latter values, he still asserts, is the idea that a formally Islamic government is either required by or good for Islam. Madjid's critics counter that such an argument amounts to a "Christian" understanding of Islam. They insist that Madjid's view replaces the actions and sayings of the Prophet (the *sunnah*) with an ethically "interiorized" understanding of religion. Islam, they insisted, is a "system" and total way of life, of which state politics is a vital ingredient.

Madjid has responded to these arguments not by denying that Islam influences the apprehension of all aspects of life but by insisting that Islam's completeness lies not in some once-and-for-all political formula but in the infusion of enduring values into the culture and politics of society. In my conversations with him, Madjid compares his position to the much-discussed role of civil religion in the United States.[36] "I believe that the true role of Islam should be quite similar to that of civil religion in America. It is not a structure of government that is required, but a general ethos of justice and universal dignity running through society." Closer to the Islamic tradition, he and many like-minded Indonesians see a precedent for just such an approach in the experience of the Prophet Muhammad in Medina. There Muslims, Jews, and polytheists worked together in a pluralist environment in which there was no formally established Islamic state.[37]

In this and other examples, the style of Madjid's argument, with its unselfconscious drawing of parallels between Western and Islamic history, illustrates the openness generally characteristic of Indonesia's democratic pluralist Muslims, including many in such mainstream organizations as Nahdlatul Ulama and the Muhammadiyah.[38] Like Dawam Rahardjo, Ahmad Wahib, and Djohan Effendi, or Abdurrahman Wahid in Nahdlatul Ulama, or Abdul Munir Mulkhan and Ahmad Syafii Maarif in the Muhammadiyah, Madjid eagerly mines Western as well as Islamic sources in an effort to discover intellectual resources applicable to the challenges of the modern era. Such deliberate and critical eclecticism distinguishes these writers from the traditionally trained jurists of Islamic jurisprudence, the ulema, many of whom insist that theologically persuasive arguments can only be derived directly from recognized sources in Islamic tradition.[39] On this point, at least, the approach of these Indonesian writers resembles new Muslim intellectuals in many other Muslim countries. All of them draw on an array of intellectual sources, typically including Western philosophy and social commentary as well as texts from the Islamic tradition.

On two important points, however, these Indonesian thinkers differ profoundly from at least some of their counterparts in the Middle East. First, their invocation of Western scholarship is devoid of the apologetics and polemics common in much Middle Eastern scholarship. Rather than citing Western works so as to draw a sharper line between Islam and the West, the tendency of these thinkers is to emphasize the universality of human experience and, more specifically, the shared nature of the problems faced by humanity in the modern era. The Indonesian title of Madjid's most recent work is indicative of this style: *Islam, Humanity's Religion (Islam, Agama Kemanusiaan).*

The second feature that distinguishes these writers from many of their Middle Eastern counterparts is their interest not merely in the slogans but in the practical workings of democracy and civil pluralism. Each author, of course, has a different intellectual background, and their writing styles reflect this diversity. Ahmad Wahib was a romantic and freewheeling existentialist. Nurcholish Madjid tends to present his arguments with extensive comparisons of Western and Islamic ethical philosophy. Dawam Rahardjo is well versed in Western economic and political theory and juxtaposes it with remarkable skill to the Islamic tradition. Writers from the modernist Muhammadiyah organization, such as Ahmad Syafii Maarif and Abdul Munir Mulkhan, bring a deep engagement with Western political theory to their scholarship. A leader of the 30 million–strong Nahdlatul Ulama, Abdurrahman Wahid speaks to a mass following and thus feels obliged to express his political views in an earthy and often jocular shorthand. But he has been an ardent promoter of small business and democratic capitalism and, through his joint ventures with Chinese Indonesians, has worked tirelessly to reduce tensions between Chinese and Muslim Indonesians. He was also a founding member of the Democratic Forum, a discussion group dedicated to democratization and multireligious pluralism.

The point to note here is that the commentaries of all these authors show none of the characteristics that Olivier Roy, in *The Failure of Political Islam*, associates with the new Islamist intellectuals in the Middle East.[40] The claim that all human knowledge is present in the Qur'an (and thus modern science is nothing new); the emphasis on an immediate and ideologized Qur'anic truth; and the rejection of the human sciences in favor of a mechanical application of Islamic formulae—all these themes are notable by their absence in these authors' work. One finds instead a thoughtful emphasis on the complexity of the modern challenge, the universality of the human experience, and a need for openness to other cultural and religious as well as political perspectives.

The Dilemma of Success

I have described elsewhere the nature of the Islamic revival that swept Indonesian society, especially its urban middle classes, in the 1980s and early

1990s.[41] Here I would like to make just two points concerning the revival and its impact on the effort to develop a pluralistic and democratic Islam.

The first point concerns the nature of the sociopolitical alliance associated with the Islamic revival. Though the Indonesian press has sometimes spoken as if proponents of civil Islam dominate the revival, the development has in fact been the work of a complex and unstable alliance of groups. For example, in addition to proponents of civil Islam, the revival was also supported by at least some government officials, especially high-ranking officials in the Department of Religion. Numerous nongovernmental Muslim organizations such as the Muhammadiyah and the Nahdlatul Ulama also played an important role. Among these last groups there was a branch of the old modernist Muslim leadership descended from Masyumi. Most of these figures were committed to a more conventional, even conservative understanding of Islam and politics. Since each of these groupings is vying for influence in the Muslim community today, a few words need to be said about their relative interests and capacities.

Western scholars have often portrayed the New Order regime as an ideological monolith. A characteristic of this monolith, according to these observers, is the ruling elite's commitment to mystically Javanese (and, from an Islamic perspective, deeply heterodox) spirituality rather than Islam. Though there is little question that some among the ruling elite have been interested in various forms of Javanese mysticism,[42] this characterization overlooks the important fact that from early on in the New Order, some government officials were deeply committed to Islam and thus unhappy with the tension between the government and Muslims. Quietly and patiently, these officials worked to improve government-Muslim relations. Some of the most influential of these figures were in the Department of Religion. The second largest of all ministries in the government (in terms of staff) and responsible for an enormous array of educational and social programs, the Department of Religion has played a major role in the Islamic revival.[43]

Even as the public relationship between the government and Muslim political organizations degenerated in the 1970s, officials in the Department of Religion worked behind the scenes to advance the Muslim cause. For them, as for the civil pluralists, what was important was not party politics but the long-term effort to improve the social circumstances of Muslims and to deepen popular commitment to a pluralist understanding of Islamic values. Two of the most prominent officials in this effort were the ministers of religion during these years: Mukti Ali, who had acted as the sponsor of the "Limited Group" in Yogyakarta before becoming minister of religion in 1973, and Munawir Sjadzali, minister of religion during the critical transition years of 1983–1993.[44]

Slowly, the efforts of these and other officials working "in the system" began to bear fruit. Their success was evident in the Department of Religion's Decision No. 70 in 1978 limiting the activities of Christian missionaries;[45] in the enormous expansion of government aid to State Islamic Institute Colleges (IAIN) during the 1970s and 1980s; in a near 75 percent increase in the number of mosques in Central and East Java; and in an ambitious program of government-financed religious proselytization *(dakwah)*.[46] In the late 1980s and early 1990s this stream of state concessions to the Muslim community grew into a flood. A new education law in 1988 strengthened the requirement for religious education in all grades and schools; in 1989 a law on Islamic courts extended their authority in matters of marriage, divorce, and inheritance; in 1991 the government began a compilation of Islamic law so as to coordinate legal procedures across provinces; in that same year, the government sponsored its first Islamic cultural festival *(Festival Istiqlal)*, repudiated regulations barring female high school students from wearing religious head coverings *(jilbab, hijab)*, and established the country's first Islamic bank. In late 1990 the government also allowed the formation of an Association of Indonesian Muslim Intellectuals known as ICMI. Over the next five years this association turned itself into one of the most significant interest groups in the government, providing a critical line of access to the highest echelons of power.[47] As the 1990s progressed, even stern Islamist critics of the government could be heard declaring that the New Order had dramatically changed its policy on Islam.[48]

Indeed, the very breadth of the Islamic revival, and the government's courtship of the Muslim leadership, has presented the advocates of a civil and democratic Islam with a dilemma. Again, the Islamic revival was pioneered by an array of organizations with different interests. All shared a concern with strengthening Islamic values and institutions in society. But the parties differed dramatically on their understanding of just what those values and institutions might entail in the long run. Thus some proponents of Islamic revitalization saw it as a way to do away once and for all with the "fetishism" of the Islamic state (as one activist put the matter to me), and to encourage a decisive turn toward civil, pluralist, and democratic values. But others saw the strengthening of Islamic culture as a temporizing strategy, intended to strengthen Muslim associations as a prelude to a more direct Muslim penetration of government. Members of this latter group, state-oriented Islamists, had learned that it was no longer efficient to attack the Pancasila or to call openly for the establishment of an Islamic state. A few, in fact, had learned to live with the Pancasila, believing that although it was not a particularly compelling ideology, it was not a serious obstacle to a more Islamic form of government. However, if some of them could live with the Pancasila, none of these assertive Islamists were comfortable with the civil-pluralist Islam promoted by people like Nurcholish Madjid, Dawam Rahardjo, Abdurrahman Wahid, or Djohan Effendi: In conservative Islamist eyes, these thinkers had betrayed the promise of Islam and its demand for the creation of an all-encompassing Islamic "system."

Let me cite an incident that illustrates potential conflicts between these two groups and their different visions of Islam. On March 31, 1995, the official newspaper of the ICMI, known as *Republika,* ran a two-page article commemorating the work of Ahmad Wahib. Recall that Wahib was the author of a posthumously published diary that became a bestseller in the 1980s, renowned for his existentialist-like questioning of faith (even as, in the end, he resoundingly affirmed that faith) and his forceful criticism of the Muslim community's mainstream leadership. Though the thoughts presented in his diaries are not as well developed as those of his longer-lived associates, Wahib has become a popular symbol of civil Islam. Written by two bright junior staffers at *Republika,* the article on Wahib presented an overview of his life and ideas, and, in gentle terms, celebrated his legacy.

Three days after the article's appearance about seventy demonstrators appeared outside the *Republika* building, angrily crying "God is Great" and calling for the resignation or even imprisonment of the journalists responsible for the story. The demonstrators accused Wahib of being a Zionist and an agent of the U.S. Central Intelligence Agency. While a student in Yogyakarta, they said, Wahib had lived in a Catholic boarding house, and his religious views had, essentially, been Christianized. The demonstrators presented a list of thirty-one passages from Wahib's diaries where they claimed Wahib had slandered Islam, the Prophet, and the Qur'an. The list included a number of Wahib's most painfully probing reflections, including such expressions as "Islam is static," "Religion is dead," "The Qur'an has many verses which are not used any longer," and "I am looking for a different kind of God than one who is in contradiction with humankind."

As the demonstration progressed, the calls from the crowd became fiercer, leading some *Republika* staff to take shelter in the back rooms of their building. Eventually the protesters surged into the building's front lobby demanding to see the editors. Clad in a red head scarf, the leader of the assault screamed at representatives from the newspaper, "I have many red *surban* [head scarves]!" A red head scarf is conventionally seen as an item of apparel worn by Muslim warriors when they prepare for martyrdom. Terrified that they were about to be assaulted and their building burned, newspaper officials did their best to calm the crowd, saying they would investigate the story and take disciplinary action where required.

This was only the beginning, however, of a larger drama. In the days following the demonstration, the minister of information, Harmoko, intervened on the side of the demonstrators. He called in *Republika*'s editors and demanded that the reporters responsible for the Wahib story be fired. Not coincidentally, he also used the occasion to raise questions about the commitment of the *Republika* staff to "national stability," noting that the newspaper had been responsible for articles that had "confused the Muslim religious community [*ummat*]." Parni Hadi, the editor in chief of *Republika,* was deeply upset by this exchange. A soft-spoken, decent man, Parni had a long history of amicable collaboration with Harmoko. In earlier years he had worked for the government-linked Indonesian press agency, Antara, over which Harmoko, as minister of information, exercised considerable control. Parni's appointment to the editorship position at *Republika* had been arranged by government officials concerned that the new Muslim newspaper, supported in part by government funds, might prove obstreperous under a more independent editor. (Dawam Rahardjo—a close friend of Nurcholish Madjid and a colleague of Ahmad Wahib—had earlier been viewed as the most likely candidate for the editorship.) As editor, Parni had exercised his authority gently and taken pains to allow a diversity of opinion among staff writers. Lacking an independent base of support in the military or bureaucracy and dependent as he was on Harmoko's good favor, however, he was keenly aware of the limits of his authority, and he encouraged his team to take care in writing stories challenging government policy.

In the end, high-ranking officials from ICMI intervened on the side of the newspaper and defended its right to publish the story on Ahmad Wahib. Dawam Rahardjo and Nurcholish Madjid—civil pluralists who, though associated with ICMI, were careful to maintain their independence from direct government controls—played a pivotal role in mobilizing support for the newspaper. The reporters responsible for the Wahib story were not fired, but as a minor concession to the protesters they were quietly shifted to less prominent positions in the newspaper's research department.

A message had nonetheless been conveyed: The government wanted *Republika* to take greater care in its presentation of stories and to avoid disseminating stories that challenged the government or "sowed confusion in the *ummat*." A similar message was conveyed several weeks later, when *Republika* ran another story in which a reporter discussed the importance of "deregulation" in the political as well as economic sphere. In a meeting of the presidential cabinet, several ministers are said to have loudly criticized the ICMI chairman, Dr. B. J. Habibie, a respected government minister, over the content of the articles. Embarrassed by the incident, someone from Habibie's staff is reported to have telephoned the newspaper to say that if any such articles were run in the future he would make sure that all staff members up to the position of editor in chief were fired.

This was but one of several incidents between 1992 and 1995 that illustrated the divisions between civil pluralist and less tolerant Muslims, and the vulnerability of certain Islamic institutions to political pressures. The protesters at the *Republika* office were conservative Islamists opposed to civil Islam. The protesters had been recruited from three groups: nearby Qur'anic boarding schools renowned for their hard-line views; a faction from the Dewan Dakwah Islamiyah, a proselytizing group established by former members of the Masyumi after that party's abolition in 1960; and several members of the HMI leadership who in recent years have turned against the civil-pluralist ideals of Nurcholish Madjid and other HMI alumni. All three of these groups included in their ranks a number of people who had studied either in Egypt or Saudi Arabia, many with Saudi financing, where some had been attracted to the conservative ideas of the Islamic Brotherhoods.

What unites all these people is that they are dedicated to the idea that Islam is itself an all-encompassing sociopolitical system and not in need of the mediating compromise promoted by people like Ahmad Wahib, Nurcholish Madjid, or Abdurrahman Wahib. For these critics of civil Islam, the borders of the Muslim community must be fortified, not blurred. What is required for such a strengthening is, above all, a more formal linkage between Islam and government.

Let me illustrate this same tension with one last incident. On December 21, 1992, Nurcholish Madjid and several of his associates held a gathering at the Jakarta Cultural Center known as Taman Ismail Marzuki. The event was organized in response to a series of incidents earlier in the year. These included rising criticism of Protestant proselytization by provincial Muslim leaders and several nasty incidents in which Protestant churches were set ablaze after large demonstrations. Coming as they did on the heels of the government's rapprochement with the Muslim leadership, the incidents sent a shock wave through Christian and other minority communities and raised fears that as the government moved to strengthen ties with Muslims, it might lessen its commitment to religious tolerance.

At the December meeting Madjid presented a paper in which he made several daring arguments to underline what he feels are the Islamic grounds for interreligious tolerance. Perhaps the most striking of these was his assertion that the term *Islam* should not be understood as referring to a bounded religious community but as an attitude toward God not limited to Muslims but found among all people of good faith. Madjid based his argument on his reading of a Qur'anic verse (3:19) that asserts that the true attitude of submission recognized by God is that of absolute surrender to God's Truth.[49] Islam literally means "surrender," and Madjid asserted that the spiritual quality of this act is not guaranteed merely by one's professed religious affiliation. Nor is this vital act of surrendering unique to people who call themselves Muslim. There were additional details to Nurcholish's argument, all intended to demonstrate the consistency of his argument with Islamic tradition. But his basic point was to challenge the arrogance of those who think that by the simple act of formal adherence to Islam, one is necessarily faithful to God's commands.

Whatever its complexity, the implications of this argument were not lost on Madjid's critics. They responded to his appeal with a vituperative press campaign the likes of which had not been seen since the leaking of his "renewal" speech in January 1970. His critics attacked Madjid as a blasphemer, a Christianizer, and a Zionist. Later the following year his enemies organized a mock "trial" of Madjid, also at the Jakarta Cultural Center. In the course of the event condemnation of Madjid became so heated that officials feared violence, and the proceedings had to be brought to a close. The struggle for civil Islam was greeted here with cries for the trial and imprisonment of one of its most influential proponents.

Conclusion

It would be a mistake to exaggerate the strength of conservative Islamism in Indonesia. In fact, the country remains the strongest center of a liberal-minded, civil Islam in the entire Muslim world. If Indonesia can continue its extraordinary economic expansion, its impressive achievements in the field of education, and—less certainly—its slow steps toward democratization, it may well become a beacon of civil hope for the whole Muslim world.

This much said, it would also be a mistake to gloss over the dimensions of the challenge facing Indonesia and Indonesian Muslims. Having been marginalized from power in the early New Order, the Muslim community in the 1970s adopted a strategy toward national politics quite different from what it had utilized in the 1950s. It concentrated its energies on education, religious outreach, and the strengthening of social institutions, in an effort to deepen Muslim influence on popular society. This effort occurred in the second decade of the New Order economic expansion and thus coincided with the growth of a new, educated Muslim middle class. The period saw growing numbers of pious Muslims entering the ranks of industry and government. Many among their leadership drew on the pluralist ideas of civil Islam to reassure anxious military and government officials that Islam could be a constructive and pacific partner in the project of nation building. Their efforts bore fruit, as the highest echelons of the government—familiar with the Algerian lesson on the drawbacks of driving a revitalized Islam into opposition—changed their policies and channeled ever greater resources into Islamic social and educational initiatives.

Yet the very success of this cultural politics has helped to embolden segments of the Muslim community skeptical about the long-term value of pluralism and tolerance. The strength of the Islamic revival has convinced some that the basic balance of power has changed, or is about to change, in a fashion that will now accommodate demands for a more formal linkage between Islam and government. Animated by the conviction that Islam is an integral and exhaustive system, they are convinced that anything less than this realization represents an irreligious denial of Islam's truth.

For the moment, it seems clear that this latter view is a minority one, and that the great majority of Muslims are committed to a pluralist and civil vision of their religion. Unfortunately, the primary unknown in this unfolding historical experiment is not the various protagonists in the Muslim community but certain factions in government. As the *Republika* incident illustrated, some in government feel they have more to gain from working with conservative Islamists than with democratic pluralists. Muslim conservatives are uncomfortable with the civil pluralists' arguments and feel that such liberal notions as freedom of the press, the dignity of the individual, and the legal equality of religions have little to do with Islam. These attitudes accord well with the views of at least some in the ruling elite. Concerned as they are about challenges to their authority and wealth, these officials prefer a containable "Islam" to a broader commitment to democracy, the rule of law, and civil pluralism.

By way of comparison, one should note that this attitude on the part of power holders resembles that found among ruling elites in a few Middle Eastern countries. There, in the 1970s and 1980s, as elites faced growing challenges from an Islamist opposition, many rushed to clothe themselves in the garb of Muslim piety in an effort to split the opposition by winning some in the Muslim community to their side.[50] Obviously such a divide-and-conquer tactic has more to do with the logic of power politics than it does with Islam per se. The irony in this comparison, however, is that in many of those countries the Islamic opposition is less committed to the ideals of civil pluralism and democracy than it is in Indonesia. In Indonesia, government policies of this sort could very well reverse the impressive steps already taken toward a civil Islam.

There is a larger lesson in this example. The struggle unfolding in Indonesia is part of a long and as yet unfinished regime transition. The early years of the New Order regime caused great soul-searching in the

Muslim community, deepening an extant process of reflective self-criticism on the part of Muslim pluralists. The impasse between government and Islam created the opportunity for these activist intellectuals to distance themselves from power politics and mine their Islamic tradition for new insights and values. As Muslims, they felt a deep obligation to provide religious sanctions for civil values. As defenders of pluralism and the rights of religious minorities, however, they also felt compelled to reformulate these values in a manner responsive to the demands of the modern era.

One of the lessons of this example is relevant far beyond Indonesia. It is that there is a wealth of material in the Islamic tradition with which to construct a normative discourse compatible with the pluralist demands of the modern era. Contrary to certain currently fashionable postmodernist claims or predictions of an irremediable "clash of civilizations," the terms of this discourse are not irreducibly "other" but, with a little work, accessible from a Western perspective. As in the Western tradition of civic republicanism, for example, civil Islam emphasizes that virtue is a vital public as well as private resource. However, again like some variants of modern Western republicanism, civil Islam asserts that one way to promote virtue is to strengthen the role of religion in society while rejecting, however, the establishment of a formally confessional state. None of this is identical to any single version of Western republicanism,[51] nor, least of all, to those hyperindividualistic variants of Western liberalism that have come to the curious conclusion that civility and tolerance are impossible without the withdrawal of religion from public life. However, as a number of social theorists have recently shown, there is nothing intellectually or sociologically *necessary* to such a privatized view of religion. To the degree that it has occurred at all, the privatization of religion in the modern West reflects a historical event peculiar to the region (and only parts of the region at that), not one that is necessary for modern pluralism.[52]

If Indonesia shows that there is a rich vein of Muslim materials to be mined for modern civility, and if it shows that there are systematizers hard at work on their recovery, it also illustrates the more troubling fact that these efforts alone are not sufficient to guarantee the achievement of political civility. Once the recovery and systematization are done, there remains the task of institutionalizing those values in a state effectively committed to their implementation.[53]

It is on this last point that the Indonesian situation is most uncertain. It is not just that some Muslims have different understandings than their civil rivals as to what is essential and what is marginal to their ethical tradition. It is that there are certain actors in state and society who see it as in their own interest to block efforts at the broader institutionalization of civil values within a system of open and constitutional government.

Most of this opposition has nothing whatsoever to do with Islam. But it *does* have the awful potential to upset the climate of opinion in the Muslim community and reverse its extraordinary progress. This would be particularly unfortunate were it to occur, for it would take place at precisely that moment when civil Islam stands prepared to make its most enduring contribution to the nation, and perhaps even to international Islam.

In their preference for backstage deals with a limited pool of players, these state actors reinforce a patron-mediated authoritarianism inimical to efforts to develop a new normative framework for civility and democracy. Their political actions limit the options of other actors, forcing everyone to play, if they want to play at all, by the terms of a secret game that undercuts efforts at public accountability and the rule of law. It is understandable that for a Muslim leadership marginalized from power for more than thirty years, the temptation might be great to give up and merely play with the cards offered. What is remarkable is that, up to now, so many Muslim leaders have politely refused the offer and worked for broader adjustments in the playing field.

Finally, a larger lesson from Indonesia for our understanding of how to mediate normative conflict is that in the modern struggle for civil decency, there can be no detour around the state. However much we enthusiasts of human dignity and civil freedom might wish otherwise, there is no getting around the fact that liberal values alone do not a civil society make. Civil society requires a civil-*ized* state, and vice versa. The good news is that such a state, with its commitment to law and constitutional safeguards, is easily *conceivable* within a variety of traditions, including Islam. Its objective *practicality*, however, depends on the institutionalization of those values in effective political structures, supported by a broader balance of power in society that helps to safeguard their continuing operation. It is this kind of social order for which Indonesia's civil Muslims are currently struggling. For their sake and our own, we should pay homage to their efforts, and hope for their success.

Notes

1. See Lyon 1977 and Hefner 1993a and 1985, pp. 239–265.
2. In earlier times a significant proportion of Chinese migrants to the Indonesian archipelago were in fact Muslim; indeed, there is evidence to suggest that Chinese were among the earliest bearers of Islam to the region. However, in the nineteenth and twentieth centuries, when the great majority of Chinese Indonesians emigrated to the region, few professed Islam. Under the post-1945 Indonesian republic, some in the Chinese community have sought to have Confucianism recognized as an official religion. While officials in the Department of Education and Culture have sometimes supported these efforts, the powerful Department of Religion, domi-

nated by Muslims, has opposed it. Thus, officially at least, all Chinese Indonesians must choose from among one of the five recognized religions.

3. On the role of the Chinese in business during the New Order era, see Robison 1986, especially pp. 271–322; Schwarz, 1994, pp. 98–132; and Mackie, 1992.

4. This idea of a civilizational clash between the Western and Muslim worlds has been enunciated most famously, of course, by Huntington (1993).

5. See Kahin 1952, pp. 65–77; and Benda 1983, pp. 42–47.

6. Anderson 1983, p. 105.

7. Soekarno presented this view in his essay, "Apa Sebab Turki Memisah Agama dari Negara" [Why has Turkey separated religion from state?]. See Soekarno 1964, pp. 404–407.

8. The speed with which reformist ideas spread in the Indies also raises questions about Benedict Anderson's claim that "in complete contrast" to the government schools in which "creole functionaries" were socialized to a nationalist conviction, Muslim religious schools "were always local and personal enterprises"; see Anderson 1983, p. 111. The speed with which reformist ideas spread, and the uniformity of their vision—a vision that typically included a forceful rejection of European colonialism—suggests that the contrast was by no means "complete." On the spread of reformist ideas throughout Muslim Indonesia in the late nineteenth century, see Bowen 1993, pp. 39–73, and Woodward 1989, pp. 134–148. Bowen's work also illustrates the staunchly nationalist elements in much Islamic reform.

9. On the varied connotations of 'asabiyah in traditional and modern Islamic political discourse, see Baali 1995.

10. For an illustration of Muslim arguments against nationalism in the late colonial era, see Noer 1973, pp. 259–266.

11. On the appeal among Islamist radicals of this idea of Islam as a *nizam* ("order," "system"), see Moussalli 1992, pp. 69–70, 87, and Mitchell 1969, pp. 234–245.

12. Perhaps the best example of such a figure was the co-declarer of Indonesian independence and the country's first vice president, Mohammad Hatta. A devout Muslim from the Minangkabau region of Sumatra, Hatta was an early supporter of the nationalist party and a proponent of the idea that Muslims need to renew their political and economic ideas. See Rose 1987.

13. The classic, if now somewhat dated, study of these normative divisions within Javanese Islam is Geertz 1960. For a critique, see Woodward 1989 and Hefner 1987.

14. On the circumstances surrounding formulation of the charter, see Boland 1982, pp. 25–33.

15. On the challenge this requirement has posed for Indonesian Hindus, see Hefner 1985 and Bakker 1993.

16. The single best source on this period remains Feith 1962.

17. See Nasution 1992. For a discussion of the disputes as related to the Jakarta Charter, see Boland 1982, pp. 85–99.

18. For an overview of the campaign, see Mortimer 1974.

19. For an illustration of government interference in party affairs, see Ward 1974.

20. See Feillard 1993, pp. 89–110.

21. On the educational origins of this "systemic" view of religion in the Muslim Middle East, see Eickelman 1992, pp. 643–655. On its role in the thought of

Sayyid Qutb (one of the founding figures of modern Islamist radicalism), see Shepard 1992. For a somewhat less generalizable model of the role of this experience on the rise of Islamist radicalism, see Roy 1994, pp. 89–106.

22. Eickelman 1992, p. 652.

23. See Roy 1994 for an especially forceful statement of this thesis; it should be noted, however, that Roy does not extend his model to Indonesia.

24. Portions of this section are based on my interviews with HMI figures during the summers of 1993 and 1995. For an English-language overview of the early New Order period, see Schwarz 1994, pp. 24–28; for an unusually insightful insider's commentary on the HMI's role during this time, see Sulastomo 1989.

25. For analysis of the violence, see Young 1990 and Hefner 1990, pp. 193–227.

26. Interviews with HMI and other Muslim activists during the summers of 1993 and 1995.

27. Interview, July 4, 1993. By late 1968 Nasution had become a regular critic of the government on matters of human rights and the rule of law; eventually he was imprisoned for his defense of civil liberties.

28. On the relationship between predominantly Islamic student action groups in the anti-Soekarno campaign, see Crouch 1978, especially pp. 158–220, and May 1978, pp. 129–159.

29. Published eight years after his death, Wahib's diaries were a bestseller and remain broadly popular to this day. As discussed later, however, the diaries have also incited broad condemnation in more conservative circles, who see Wahib's questioning of Islamic authorities as an assault on Islam itself. For English-language discussions of Wahib's legacy, see Johns 1987 and Barton 1995.

30. Interview with Dawam Rahardjo, July 1993; see also Barton 1995, pp. 27–28.

31. For a discussion of the political context of Madjid's reflections, see Hefner 1993.

32. The original text of Madjid's article, entitled "Keharusan Pembaruan Pemikiran Islam dan Masalah Integrasi Umat" [The necessity of renewal in Islamic thought and the problem of the religious community's integration], was reprinted in Madjid 1987. An English-language translation of the article is available as Appendix A in Hassan 1982.

33. Hassan 1982, pp. 121–123, discusses the attacks of several of these senior figures from a largely partisan perspective. Ali and Effendy (1986, 134–143) provide a more balanced account.

34. Interview, June 19, 1993.

35. It is interesting to observe that there is a striking similarity between Madjid's argument here on religious renewal in the modern era and that of some religiously disposed Western social thinkers. See, for example, Berger 1992.

36. For an early formulation of the idea of civil religion in the United States, see Bellah 1975; for a more recent and critical reading of the concept, see Casanova 1994, pp. 135–166.

37. For an English-language discussion of the Medina experience, and the charter through which the Prophet and his followers organized this pluralist politics, see Serjeant 1981.

38. From a sociological perspective, the renewal or *pembaruan* group is not so much an organized "movement" as it is a loose network of people with pluralistic

ideas on the nature of Islam and society. Not all of the people conventionally identified with this group identify themselves as *pembaruan*, in part because the term has come to be so closely associated with the "neomodernist" thought of Nurcholish Madjid, Ahmad Wahib, and Djohan Effendi. Thus, for example, Abdurrahman Wahid, the influential leader of the Nahdlatul Ulama, resists explicit identification with *pembaruan;* Dawam Rahardjo does as well. But both are unstinting in their commitment to a strong civil society and a proactively pluralist Islam. For a short but revealing English-language article expressive of Wahid's views, see Wahid 1990.

39. For a discussion of the way in which moral arguments may be derived in traditional Islamic jurisprudence, see Coulson 1964, especially pp. 182–225. For an illustration of some of the debates that have surrounded jurisprudential reasoning in Indonesia, see Jamil 1995, pp. 53–68.

40. Roy 1984, pp. 89–106.

41. Hefner 1993b.

42. For an insightful study of the role of mysticism in Javanese society, see Stange 1980.

43. There were of course proponents of such a mediating rule elsewhere in the government, including in some of the upper echelons of the military, which has also often been misportrayed by some Western observers as uniformly anti-Islamic. One of the earliest and most outspoken proponents of such accommodation was Lieutenant General Sayidiman Suryohadiprojo. In recent years (especially since 1990), as the military has sought to improve its ties with Muslim organizations, Sayidiman has played an important role.

44. On the role of Munawir Sjadzali in the revival, see Effendy 1995.

45. See Pranowo 1990. He observes, "The Islamic groups enthusiastically welcomed these decisions, for they were directed especially toward the Christian missionaries actively carrying out religious propagation among the Muslim community" (p. 493).

46. See Hefner 1993b and Labrousse and Soemargono 1985.

47. See Hefner 1993b.

48. One need only consult the contents of the first issue of the impressive Muslim news biweekly *Ummat*, with its cover photo of President Soeharto behind the headline, "The New Order Has Changed!" ["Orde Baru Berubah"], for a dense sample of Muslim opinion on the depths of this change. See *Ummat* 1:1 (July 10, 1995).

49. For the Indonesian-language text of Madjid's paper, see Madjid 1993.

50. See, for example, Roy 1994, p. 125.

51. For an example of the kind of ethically proactive (as opposed to "procedural") liberalism I have in mind here, see Taylor 1989.

52. On the critique of privatized views of religion in modern civil society, see Casanova 1994. On efforts to recover resources in Muslim tradition compatible with the demands of modern civility, see Eickelman 1993 and Norton 1995.

53. For a related point in terms of general theories of civil society, see Hall 1995.

References

Ali, Fachry, and Bahtiar Effendy. 1986. *Merambah Jalan Baru Islam: Rekonstruksi Pemikiran Islam Indonesia Masa Orde Baru* [To open a new Islamic road: The reconstruction of Indonesian Islamic thought in the New Order era]. Bandung: Mizan.

Anderson, Benedict R. O'G. 1983. *Imagined Communities: Reflections on the Origin and Spread of Nationalism.* London: Verso.

Baali, Fuad. 1995. "'Asabiyah." In John L. Esposito, ed., *The Oxford Encyclopedia of the Modern Islamic World* (New York: Oxford University Press), vol. 1, p. 140.

Bakker, F. L. 1993. *The Struggle of the Hindu Balinese Intellectuals.* Amsterdam: VU University Press.

Barton, Greg. 1995. "Neo-modernism: A Vital Synthesis of Traditionalist and Modernist Islamic Thought in Indonesia." *Studia Islamika: Indonesian Journal for Islamic Studies* 2:3:1–75.

Bellah, Robert N. 1975. *The Broken Covenant: American Civil Religion in Time of Trial.* Chicago: University of Chicago Press.

Benda, Harry J. 1983. *The Crescent and the Rising Sun: Indonesian Islam Under the Japanese Occupation, 1942–1945.* Dordrecht: Foris Publications.

Berger, Peter L. 1992. *A Far Glory: The Quest for Faith in an Age of Credulity.* New York: Free Press.

Boland, B. J. 1982. *The Struggle of Islam in Modern Indonesia.* The Hague: Martinus Nijhoff.

Bowen, John R. 1993. *Muslims Through Discourse: Religion and Ritual in Gayo Society.* Princeton: Princeton University Press.

Casanova, Jose. 1994. *Public Religions in the Modern World.* Chicago: University of Chicago Press.

Coulson, N. J. 1964. *A History of Islamic Law.* Edinburgh: Edinburgh University Press.

Crouch, Harold. 1978. *The Army and Politics in Indonesia.* Ithaca: Cornell University Press.

Effendy, Bahtiar. 1995. "Islam and the State in Indonesia: Munawir Sjadzali and the Development of a New Theological Underpinning of Political Islam." *Studia Islamika: Indonesian Journal for Islamic Studies* 2:2:97–121.

Eickelman, Dale F. 1992. "Mass Higher Education and the Religious Imagination in Contemporary Arab Societies." *American Ethnologist* 19:4 (November):643–655.

_____. 1993. "Islamic Liberalism Strikes Back." *Middle East Studies Association Bulletin* 27:2 (December):163–168.

Feillard, Andrée. 1993. "Les oulémas indonésiens aujourd'hui: De l'opposition à une nouvelle légitimité." *Archipel* (Paris), 46:89–110.

Feith, Herbert. 1962. *The Decline of Constitutional Democracy in Indonesia.* Ithaca: Cornell University Press.

Geertz, Clifford. 1960. *The Religion of Java.* New York: Free Press, 1960.

Hall, John A. 1995. "In Search of Civil Society." In Hall, ed., *Civil Society: Theory, History, Comparison* (Cambridge: Polity Press), pp. 1–31.

Hassan, Muhammad Kamal. 1982. *Muslim Intellectual Responses to "New Order" Modernization in Indonesia.* Kuala Lumpur: Dewan Bahasa dan Pustaka.

Hefner, Robert W. 1985. *Hindu Javanese: Tengger Tradition and Islam.* Princeton: Princeton University Press.

_____. 1987. "Islamizing Java: Religion and Politics in Rural East Java." *Journal of Asian Studies* 46:3 (August 1987):533–554.

_____. 1990. *The Political Economy of Mountain Java: An Interpretive History*. Berkeley: University of California Press.

_____. 1993a. "Of Faith and Commitment: Christian Conversion in Muslim Java." In Hefner, ed., *Conversion to Christianity: Historical and Anthropological Perspectives on a Great Transformation* (Berkeley: University of California Press), pp. 99–125.

_____. 1993b. "Islam, State, and Civil Society: ICMI and the Struggle for the Indonesian Middle Class." *Indonesia* 56 (October):1–36.

Huntington, Samuel P. 1993. "The Clash of Civilizations?" *Foreign Affairs* 72:3 (Summer):22–49.

Jamil, Fathurrahman. 1995. "The Muhammadiyah and the Theory of *Maqasid al-Shariah*." *Studia Islamika: Indonesian Journal for Islamic Studies* 2:1:53–68.

Johns, Anthony H. 1987. "An Islamic System or Islamic Values? Nucleus of a Debate in Contemporary Indonesia." In William R. Roff, ed., *Islam and the Political Economy of Meaning* (London: Croom Helm), pp. 254–280.

Kahin, George Mc. T. 1952. *Nationalism and Revolution in Indonesia*. Ithaca: Cornell University Press.

Labrousse, Pierre, and Farida Soemargono. 1985. "De l'islam comme morale du développement: L'Action des Bureaux de Propagation de la Foia (Lembaga Dakwah) vue de Surabaya." *Archipel* (Paris) 30:219–228.

Lyon, Margaret L. 1977. "Politics and Religious Identity: Genesis of a Javanese-Hindu Movement in Rural Central Java." Ph.D. diss., University of California, Berkeley.

Mackie, Jamie. 1992. "Changing Patterns of Chinese Big Business in Southeast Asia." In Ruth McVey, *Southeast Asian Capitalists* (Ithaca: Southeast Asian Program, Cornell University), pp. 161–190.

Madjid, Nurcholish. 1987. *Islam, Kemodernan, dan KeIndonesiaan* [Islam, Modernity, and Indonesianness]. Bandung: Mizan.

_____. 1993. "Beberapa Renungan tentang Kehidupan Keagamaan untuk Generasi Mendatang" [Several reflections on religious life for future generations]. *Ulumul Qur'an* 4:1:4–25.

May, Brian. 1978. *The Indonesian Tragedy*. Singapore: Graham Brash.

Mitchell, Richard P. 1969. *The Society of the Muslim Brothers*. New York: Oxford University Press.

Mortimer, Rex. 1974. *Indonesian Communism Under Sukarno: Ideology and Politics, 1959–1965*. Ithaca: Cornell University Press.

Moussalli, Ahdmad S. 1992. *Radical Islamic Fundamentalism: The Ideological and Political Discourse of Sayyid Qutb*. Beirut: American University of Beirut.

Nasution, Adnan Buyung. 1992. *The Aspiration for Constitutional Government in Indonesia: A Socio-legal Study of the Indonesian Konstituante, 1956–1959*. Jakarta: Pustaka Sinar Harapan.

Noer, Deliar. 1973. *The Modernist Muslim Movement in Indonesia, 1900–1942*. Kuala Lumpur: Oxford University Press, 1973.

Norton, Augustus Richard. 1995. *Civil Society in the Middle East*. Leiden: E. J. Brill.

Pranowo, M. Bambang. 1990. "Which Islam and Which Pancasila? Islam and the State in Indonesia: A Comment." In Arief Budiman, ed., *State and Civil Society in Indonesia* (Clayton: Centre of Southeast Asian Studies, Monash University), pp. 479–502.

Rose, Mavis. 1987. *Indonesia Free: A Political Biography of Mohammad Hatta.* Ithaca: Southeast Asia Program, Cornell Modern Indonesia Project, Publication No. 67.

Robison, Richard. 1986. *Indonesia: The Rise of Capital.* Sydney: Allen & Unwin.

Roy, Olivier. 1994. *The Failure of Political Islam.* Cambridge, Mass.: Harvard University Press.

Schwarz, Adam. 1994. *A Nation in Waiting: Indonesia in the 1990s.* Boulder: Westview Press.

Serjeant, R. B. 1981. "The Constitution of Medina." In Serjeant, *Studies in Arabian History and Civilization.* London: Variorum Reprints, pp. 3–16.

Shepard, William E. 1992. "Islam as a 'System' in the Later Writings of Sayyid Qutb." *Middle Eastern Studies* 25:31–50.

Soekarno. 1964. "Apa Sebab Turki Memisah Agama dari Negara?" [Why has Turkey separated religion from state?]. In *Dibawah Bendera Revolusi* [Under the flag of revolution] (Jakarta: Panitia Penerbitan), pp. 404–407.

Stange, Paul Denison. 1980. "The Sumarah Movement in Javanese Mysticism." Ph.D. diss., University of Wisconsin, Madison.

Sulastomo. 1989. *Hari-Hari Panjang, 1963–1966* [The long days, 1963–1966]. Jakarta: CV Haji Magasung.

Taylor, Charles. 1989. "Cross-Purposes: The Liberal-Communitarian Debate." In N. Rosenblum, ed., *Liberalism and the Moral Life* (Cambridge: Harvard University Press).

Wahib, Ahmad. 1981. *Pergolakan Pemikiran Islam: Catatan Harian Ahmad Wahib* [Upheaval in Islamic thought: The diaries of Ahmad Wahib], edited by Djohan Effendi and Ismed Natsir. Jakarta: LP3ES Press.

Wahid, Abdurrahman. 1990. "Indonesia's Muslim Middle Class: An Imperative or a Choice?" In Richard Tanter and Kenneth Young, eds., *The Politics of Middle Class Indonesia* (Clayton: Centre of Southeast Asian Studies, Monash University), pp. 22–24.

Ward, Kenneth E. 1974. *The 1971 Election in Indonesia: An East Java Case Study.* Clayton: Monash Papers on Southeast Asia, Centre of Southeast Asian Studies, Monash University.

Woodward, Mark R. 1989. *Islam in Java: Normative Piety and Mysticism in the Sultanate of Yogyakarta.* Tucson: University of Arizona Press.

Young, Kenneth R. 1990. "Local and National Influences in the Violence of 1965." In Robert Cribb, ed., *The Indonesian Killings, 1965–1966: Studies from Java and Bali* (Clayton, Victoria [Australia]: Centre of Southeast Asian Studies, Monash University, 1990), pp. 63–99.

9

The Conflict of Norms and Values in Contemporary Indian Society

André Béteille

Norms, Values, and Interests

Conflict and change are universal features of contemporary societies and may be considered normal and, within limits, even conducive to their well-being. But the limits are easily transgressed, and hence their members are perennially beset by anxieties about total stagnation on the one hand and endemic disorder on the other. Fifty years ago, at the time of independence in India, the anxiety was about the stagnation engendered by an atrophied traditional order. Today, as all the tensions associated with a major social transition become manifest, it is disorder that appears to be the larger threat, although the two kinds of anxiety might be experienced simultaneously.

The turbulence that is endemic in contemporary India is often attributed to the decline of moral values or their displacement by the pursuit of narrow personal or sectional interests. There is a constant refrain that values have gone out of politics, civic life, the professions, and education. These are represented as being driven increasingly by the desire for individual gain as against social well-being.

When people who are placed differently in society strive for the same scarce objects, conflicts of interest are bound to occur, and they tend to overshadow all other conflicts. The focus of this chapter will not be on the conflict of interests but on the conflict over values and norms: over what people consider to be right, proper, and desirable, and what they regard as legally and morally binding. The issue of contending norms and values is not the same thing as that of conflicting interests, but it is difficult to convey a sense of the dynamics of the former without taking some account of the latter.

Though I shall be concerned with the normative order in the broad sense, it will be useful to keep in mind the distinction within that order between values and norms. Here I will follow the convention of terminology established by Parsons and his associates (Parsons and Shils 1951). As Parsons has put it, "On the normative side, we can distinguish between *norms* and *values*. Values—in the pattern sense—we regard as the primary connecting element between the social and cultural systems. Norms, however, are primarily social." For us, as for Parsons, "the structural focus of norms is the legal system," although this too has to be conceived in a broad sense (Parsons 1966: 18).

Following Parsons, Smelser (1962: 24) has described values as the "generalized ends" characteristic of a culture, and norms as the "regulatory rules" prevalent in the corresponding society. As we shall see, one of the reasons for the persistent failure of regulatory rules in contemporary public institutions in India is that they are often at odds with certain generalized ends that are deeply embedded in India's traditional culture.

The diversity of norms and values is related both to the conflict of interests and to the social morphology. Society is not a simple aggregate of individuals but a differentiated structure of groups, classes, and categories. The ideas and values of the individual are shaped in part by his location within this differentiated structure. Even where uniform rules are established, these are refracted by the social morphology so that they are perceived and applied differently by the different sections of society.

Societies differ greatly in their scale and complexity. India has a population of around 950 million, divided by language, region, religion, sect, caste, tribe, wealth, occupation, education, and income. It is also a nation-state with a formal legal and administrative structure designed to maintain some measure of unity without doing violence to the distinctive lifestyles cherished by its major religious and cultural groups. Indians believe, rightly or wrongly, that the tolerance of diversity was a core value within the Indian tradition, which has for that reason a great deal to contribute to the growth of a pluralist democracy.

The tolerance of diversity can accommodate the conflict over norms and values only up to a point. Those responsible for managing the affairs of state in India view such conflicts as clear signals of disorder and impending disintegration. That is not the point of view from which this chapter is written. Firstly, there is no way in which change can come about without the displacement of some norms and values by others. Nor do all conflicts over norms and values end by tearing apart the fabric of society; indeed, the suppression of such conflict may as easily lead to that outcome. It is important to acknowledge their presence and even their necessity, and to create and sustain institutions to negotiate them.

This cannot be done by wishing present conflicts out of existence, or hoping for a future in which no conflicts will arise.

Indian Civilization: Design and Morphology

India is a society with a long past, and many different elements have contributed to its moral and intellectual tradition. It would be fair to say, though, that the organizing principles of its social life came mainly from Hinduism; and the majority of its population, from ancient to modern times, has been, in one sense or another, Hindu.

Hinduism is a religion of many gods and goddesses, each having many different forms. Further, as the noted anthropologist and writer Irawati Karve (1968) observed, the Hindu moral and intellectual climate absorbed new elements of belief and practice while allowing old ones to remain, without too much anxiety about consistency. The accommodation of apparently inconsistent beliefs has been a notable feature of Hindu civilization through the ages.

Society and culture in India have been substantially influenced by Islam, which has had a long presence in the country, large parts of which were under Muslim rule for centuries. Despite the partition of the country in 1947, there are still more Muslims in India than in any other country in the world, Indonesia excepted. The influence of Islam has been manifold—in art, architecture, music, literature, and language. Islam also influenced religious belief and practice, particularly through the formation of syncretistic movements and sects during the long Middle Ages, although sect formation in India goes back to pre-Islamic times.

Though the Muslims dominated large parts of India politically for centuries, they did not destroy the basic design of Hindu society; rather, they adapted themselves to it (Bose 1975). Islam is a religion of equality, Hinduism of hierarchy. Islam softened to some extent the hierarchical basis of Indian social structure by weakening at least a little the legitimacy of the Hindu order of *varnas*. But Muslims came to accept ascribed and invidious social distinctions more or less as the Hindus did; the same holds true by and large for Christians.

Diversity in ideas, beliefs, and practices was encouraged by the system of values, and the tolerance of diversity had an ethical basis in Hinduism. The classical legal texts, or *smritis*, formulate various ideal rules of conduct but also add that where the rules are at variance with *deshachar* (local customs) or *lokachar* (folk customs), those customs should prevail: There is a maxim of Yajnyavalka, one of the principal *smriti* writers, that "one should not practice that which, though ordained by the Smriti, is condemned by the people" (Kuppuswami 1991: 44). *Dharma*, commonly translated as "religion" but better regarded as "right conduct," is classified into *varnashramadharma,* or rules appropriate to particular stations and stages in life, and *sadharanadharma,* or rules common to all; far more stress is given to the former than to the latter (Kane 1974: 3). The classical texts provide little authority for one single and uniform normative standard for all sections of society.

Modern Indians sometimes say that the acceptance of diversity as a core value in Indian civilization gives Indians a special advantage in building a democratic society. However, tolerance of diversity should not be mistaken for individual freedom. Although society as a whole tolerated the widest range of practices among its multifarious groups, the individual had very little freedom to choose his own life plan for himself in work, worship, or even leisure. Classical law stressed duties more than rights (Kane 1974; Karve 1968), and one's most important duty was to uphold the way of life of the group into which one was born. The only legitimate way in which the individual could turn his back on his allotted way of life was by adopting the path of the renouncer (Dumont 1970: 33–60).

What was important in the social ethic was not individual choice but the immemorial tradition by which the life of each particular group was in principle governed. Not that ideas, beliefs, and practices never changed—they changed slowly and imperceptibly, and not generally through the consciously designed action of the individual. Either the group as a whole or, more commonly, a section of it would adopt a new way of life, always claiming that it was its traditional way of life from which its members had deviated in recent times through some accident or misfortune.

Just as the tolerance of diversity did not go with individual autonomy, it also did not go with equality. The diverse ways of life were all considered legitimate in their respective spheres; but they were not all equally esteemed. The various groups that were their bearers had their assigned places in society, but some were at or near its sacred center, and others on the periphery or even beyond it.

The ideological justification of hierarchy was expressed symbolically through the opposition of purity and pollution. These ideas were a central part of the Hindu tradition, but other religious groups, such as Muslims and Christians, did not escape their influence. The two poles of the social hierarchy were represented by the Brahmins, who were the bearers of the highest purity, and the Untouchables, among whom all forms of pollution were concentrated. But even in the traditional order, there was more to social disparity than its expression in the ritual idiom of purity and pollution. It was maintained and perpetuated through extreme inequalities in the distribution of economic and political power, that is, in the control over things and persons. That distribution does not change automatically with a change in religious beliefs and practices, and Indian society today continues to be marked by large inequalities in the material conditions of existence.

An account of the conflicts in contemporary Indian society has to begin with the transformations in it during the past hundred and fifty years, and particularly since independence. What is most striking from the present point of view is the change from a hierarchical normative order to one based on the principle of equality: equality before the law, the equal protection of the laws, and equality of status and of opportunity.

Traditional Hindu society was governed for 2,000 years by the law of the Dharmashastras, whose influence was pervasive and far-reaching. The Dharmashastras in general and the Manusmriti in particular provide the most complete and elaborate design for a hierarchical social order known to human history. In 1950 India adopted a new constitution in which provisions for equality are given a prominent place. No two charters for a social order could be more strikingly different than these. It is no accident that Dr. B. R. Ambedkar, widely regarded as the father of the Indian constitution, publicly burned the Manusmriti, which he viewed as the embodiment of injustice and oppression.

The whole life of a society does not change with the adoption of a radically new constitution. New laws may be enacted, but many old customs and conventions remain. In India these are often at variance, and it cannot be assumed that the law is always more binding than custom and convention. Relations based on kinship, caste, and community have not remained exactly as they were, but they have not changed beyond recognition. Old identities and invidious distinctions based on them continue to be prominent features of the social landscape.

Two features of the traditional social morphology require special attention in view of their continuing presence in contemporary India. The first is the predominance of collective over individual identity; and the second is the unequal placement of individuals and groups in society. Jawaharlal Nehru (1961: 247–248) wrote, "This structure was based on three concepts: the autonomous village community, caste, and the joint family system. In all these three, it is the group that counts; the individual has a secondary place."

The design of traditional Indian society was most fully embodied in the structure of Hindu society, but it has left its mark on Indian society as a whole. Its distinctive morphological feature is the caste system. Caste may be understood either as *varna*, representing the conceptual design of Hindu society, or as *jati*, representing the actual social divisions operating in everyday life. *Varna* and *jati* never fitted together exactly (Srinivas 1962: 63–69), and today *varna* has become anachronistic (Béteille 1996), whereas *jati* continues to be important. Only Hindus had *varnas* in the proper sense of the term, whereas *jatis* existed and continue to exist among Muslims, Christians, and others (Ansari 1959, Ahmad 1973, Caplan 1980, Godwin 1972).

The conceptual scheme of *varnas* divided Hindu society into the four ranked orders of Brahmin, Kshatriya, Vaishya, and Shudra. These divisions were exclusive and in principle exhaustive. The classical texts declared: "Brahmin, Kshatriya, Vaishya, Shudra, these are the four *varnas*, and there is no fifth." In fact there were many groups whose status was interstitial, marginal, or beyond the pale: "sectarian" communities, "aboriginal" tribes, "exterior" castes, and others. All of these were in some sense regarded as *jatis*, similar in their constitution to those that constituted the basic building blocks of traditional Hindu society.

The system of *jatis* lacked the neatness and symmetry of the order of *varnas*. The *varnas* were only four in number, but the *jatis* were innumerable. Moreover, while all Hindus acknowledged the same immutable order of *varnas*, in the same hierarchy of rank, each region had its distinctive complement of *jatis*, although the pattern of differentiation and ranking was broadly the same everywhere. It is clear from the historical record that old *jatis* disappeared and new ones emerged, either by fission or by the absorption of immigrant or aboriginal groups. While the *jatis* were ranked everywhere, the order of ranking was nowhere strictly linear; there were competing claims to superior status, particularly at the middle levels, and *jatis* regularly rose and fell in rank in the course of time.

Over the centuries many tribal groups were absorbed into Hindu society (Bose 1975). In the course of absorption, the tribe discarded many of its practices, including religious and linguistic practices, but still retained the sense of its immutable identity. Thus when a tribe became a caste it was in some sense still the same group, although in a different dress, and it found a niche for itself within the local system of *jatis*. In like manner, conversion to Islam—or to Sikhism or Christianity—might lead to a change of religion, but not necessarily a change of caste. Sometimes the same caste, such as Ahir, Jat, or Rajput, might be found among Hindus, Muslims, and Sikhs, occupying roughly the same rank in each of the three religious divisions (Smith 1996: 465).

Although the framework of *varnas* has today lost much of its coherence and legitimacy, the *jatis*, which were the real building blocks of society, continue to be active among Hindus, Muslims, Sikhs, Christians, and others. The divisions of caste are intersected by other divisions based on language and religion. The hierarchical principle, or even the principle of social gradation in a broader sense, does not apply to all of them. In some contexts, people might refer to Bengali and Tamil speakers as *jatis*, but that does not mean that they regard them as being mutually ranked; the same is to some extent true of the major religious divisions. But there are conditions under which all of these groups might compete for the same scarce resources. They then act in the manner of the ethnic groups familiar in sociological literature (Béteille 1996; Schermerhorn 1978).

Finally, all these divisions, based on language, religion, sect, caste, and tribe, are intersected by other divisions based on the distribution of wealth, income, occupation, and education, or divisions corresponding to class in the broad sense. Making the confusion worse, it is quite common in contemporary India to represent the divisions of caste and community in the language of class, in both law and politics.

Positive Discrimination

Attitudes to hierarchy began to change among the Indian intelligentsia from the middle of the nineteenth century onward (Ganguli 1975). This was a slow and gradual process that encountered many unsuspected obstacles, and it has not by any means reached its terminus. British rule acted as an important catalyst, but Indians began on their own to look into their cultural traditions for support for the ideal of equality. With the approach of independence, the tide turned, and caste came to be widely regarded as the main source of inequity and divisiveness in Hindu society.

Nehru (1961: 521) wrote on the eve of independence: "The spirit of the age is in favour of equality, though practice denies it almost everywhere," adding that "The spirit of the age will triumph." This contradiction between what Nehru saw as the spirit of the age and social practices based on other presuppositions continues to be one of the major sources of conflict in contemporary Indian society. The spirit of the age has not triumphed, at least not in the sense or to the extent that Nehru wished and hoped; nor is it possible to exorcise that spirit today.

The Constitution of India is one of the longest documents of its kind— and it has incorporated some eighty amendments in its brief existence. The length and the number of amendments are good indicators of the ambiguity, uncertainty, and conflict over norms in contemporary Indian society. There are strong provisions for equality in the constitution, although some of them have required amendment. An Indian jurist has said of the guarantee of equality that "it must be appreciated that the scope of the guarantee in the Constitution of India extends far beyond either, or both, the English and the United States guarantees taken together" (Tripathi 1972: 47). What has to be added about these guarantees is that their number and variety have themselves become sources of debate and dissensus, for the idea of equality is seen to have diverse components not always easy to harmonize with one another.

The principal provisions for equality in the constitution are contained in Part III on Fundamental Rights and Part IV on Directive Principles of State Policy. It must be noted first that the provisions in Part III are enforceable by courts of law, whereas those in Part IV are not, even though the latter have acquired increasing strength in recent years, contributing something to the amendments made in the former (Sivaramayya 1984). The provisions in Part III are related to equality before the law (Art. 14), prohibition of discrimination on grounds of religion, race, caste, sex, or place of birth (Art. 15), and equality of opportunity in public employment (Art. 16). Here equality is viewed as a right whose bearers are individual citizens. The provisions in Part IV are related to the distribution of material resources (Art. 39) and the promotion of the interests of the Scheduled Castes, the Scheduled Tribes, and other weaker sections of society (Art. 46). Here equality is viewed as a policy and is addressed to the disparities between classes and castes. It will be seen that these provisions contain a number of tensions, firstly, between different conceptions of equality, and secondly, between the rights of individuals and the claims of communities (Béteille 1987a).

The leaders of independent India saw of course that a new constitution could not by itself secure substantive equality. Many of the old disparities between groups remained, and new inequalities between individuals were emerging. Efforts were set in motion to remove or reduce these inequalities through legislation, through democratic politics at the national, regional, and local levels, and through economic planning. I will now focus on the program of positive discrimination in order to bring to light some of the tensions inherent in the pursuit of equality in contemporary India.

India has one of the oldest and most comprehensive programs of positive discrimination. It has been a source of great social dissension and political strife, leading to the fall of the national government in 1990. The courts have spoken on it in more than one voice, giving judgments that are or appear contradictory (Galanter 1984). The point to note here is that the program has been both supported and opposed in the name of equality.

The broad basis of positive discrimination is the principle of redress: It seeks to redress the bias of past generations in the direction of greater equality. I have given some account of that bias in the past and also indicated its effects on the present distribution of life chances between the different sections of Indian society. The disadvantaged among these are broadly described as the Backward Classes, and positive discrimination has sought to make various special provisions in their favor with a view to securing greater equality overall.

To understand the conflicts brought to the fore by positive discrimination, we need to have some idea of the benefits offered by it, and also of its intended beneficiaries. The intended beneficiaries are designated as the Backward Classes; they are not in fact classes in the accepted sociological sense but rather groups of tribes, castes, and other communities

(Béteille 1991). The intended benefits cover a very wide range, but the most important and also the most contentious are reserved positions in political bodies, public employment, and education; hence positive discrimination has come to be widely known in India as the policy of reservations or quotas.

The Backward Classes are a very large and heterogeneous category, which may be divided into three broad sections: the Scheduled Tribes, the Scheduled Castes, and the Other Backward Classes. The former two share certain features in common, and the constitutional provisions for their betterment are more clear and specific than for the third. The Scheduled Tribes comprise 7.75 percent and the Scheduled Castes 15.75 percent of the population of the country; together, they number over 200 million persons. The traditional hierarchical order imposed numerous hardships on them, from many of which they continue to suffer, the former on account of isolation and the latter because of segregation. If equality of opportunity depends not merely on the absence of disabilities but also on the presence of abilities, positive discrimination may be said to aim at creating some of those abilities.

The constitution requires seats in the lower houses of Parliament and the state legislatures to be reserved for the Scheduled Castes and Scheduled Tribes (Arts. 330, 332) roughly in proportion to their strength in the population; this is political reservation. In addition, Article 335 states, "The claims of the members of the Scheduled Castes and the Scheduled Tribes shall be taken into consideration, consistently with the maintenance of efficiency in administration, in the making of appointments to services and posts in connection with the affairs of the Union or of a State"; this is the job reservation. The provisions for political reservation and for job reservation are somewhat differently phrased, although the various branches of the government have increasingly treated them alike. Finally, there is reservation in education: Seats are reserved in educational institutions, including medical and engineering colleges, for students belonging to the Scheduled Castes and the Scheduled Tribes.

The makers of the constitution were well aware that enlarging the special provisions, whether relating to benefits or to beneficiaries, beyond a certain point might subvert the principle of equal opportunity for which there was general endorsement in the Constituent Assembly. The principle of special opportunities for some, even when designed for reducing social disparities, does not rest easily with that of equal opportunities for all and can be accommodated by it to only a certain extent. The chairman of the Drafting Committee, B. R. Ambedkar, had observed that "we have to safeguard two things, namely, the principle of equality of opportunity and, at the same time, satisfy the demand of communities which have not had so far representation in the State" (Constituent Assembly 1948:

vii, 702). While arguing for some special provisions, he wanted to ensure that they did not "eat up" the general provision of equality of opportunity for all. Hence the provisions for reservation in the constitution apply specifically only to the Scheduled Castes and Scheduled Tribes, leaving aside the token representation granted to the very small Anglo-Indian community.

At the same time it was felt in the Constituent Assembly that some measures for social and economic betterment should be adopted also for other disadvantaged groups in addition to the Scheduled Castes and the Scheduled Tribes. Article 340 provided for the appointment of a commission to "investigate the conditions of socially and educationally backward classes" and to make recommendations relating to them. In fact, reservations in employment and education for these Other Backward Classes had already been introduced by the colonial administration and were in operation in some states when the new constitution was adopted. Those provisions, which were not uniform in their application, appeared somewhat ambiguous in light of the constitution (Béteille 1991). The president appointed a commission (the Kalelkar Commission) in 1953, but its recommendations, submitted two years later, could not be implemented because of sharp disagreements among its members. A new commission (the Mandal Commission) was appointed in 1978, and it submitted its report in 1980 recommending extensive reservations in education and employment for the Other Backward Classes over and above those in force for the Scheduled Tribes and the Scheduled Castes. When the union government sought to implement them in part in 1990 there were massive protests, and the government fell.

The Other Backward Classes are socially, economically, and politically even more diverse than either of the two other divisions. Again, they are not classes, but an assortment of 3,743 castes and communities. Their exact strength in the population is difficult to determine, but they are believed to comprise no less than 50 percent of the population. Some of them occupy lowly positions, not much above the Scheduled Castes in the social scale; others occupy positions of political dominance, despite their low status in the traditional ritual hierarchy. Their individual members vary enormously in income, occupation, and education, much more than do the members of the Scheduled Castes and Tribes. As the law stands now, there is reservation of up to 27 percent of jobs in the government for them, although that limit has been exceeded in a couple of states. There is also reservation in education for them in some, though not all, states, but no reservation of seats in either Parliament or the state legislatures.

The nationwide political turmoil over job reservations for the Other Backward Classes revealed dramatically the conflict between equality as a right and as a policy, between formal and substantive equality. Well before independence, the colonial administration had introduced quotas in education and employment in some parts of the country, which the Congress Party had then viewed as politically divisive rather than as steps toward greater social equality. Moreover, the colonial administration was not hampered in the pursuit of its policies by a constitution guaranteeing equality of opportunity in public employment as a fundamental right. The constitution has had to incorporate, through amendments, enabling provisions to permit some reservation in education and employment, despite the antidiscrimination and the equal opportunities clauses. How these provisions are balanced depends to some extent on day-to-day political pressures. The Supreme Court initially urged restraint in the use of quotas; a landmark judgment in 1962 struck down the rather generous provisions for quotas in favor of the Other Backward Classes in the then state of Mysore in South India as "a fraud on the Constitution." Later judgments have been more accommodating on the ground that Fundamental Rights cannot be interpreted in isolation from the Directive Principles of State Policy (Sivaramayya 1984).

The report of the second Backward Classes Commission, which became the charter of the proponents of job quotas for the Other Backward Classes, maintained that the "real acid test" of equality was equality of result rather than the purely formal principle of equality of opportunity (Government of India 1981: 22). The progress of equality, in the commission's view, had to show in the extent to which all castes were equally represented in positions of respect and responsibility in public institutions; it was forcefully pointed out that they were in fact less than adequately represented. Opponents of job quotas argue, in their turn, that it is a gross violation of the principle of equality when more qualified candidates from the upper castes have to make room for less qualified ones from the lower castes, particularly when the benefits of quotas go, as they frequently do, to the most advantaged and not the least advantaged members of the lower castes. Moreover, it can be questioned whether bureaucracies should be required to meet the test of representativeness in the same way as legislatures.

A second and closely related conflict of norms has to do with the claims of collectivities as against the rights of individuals. The framers of the Constitution of India sought to base the constitution on equality and individual rights, but both inequality and collective identities have survived as obdurate facts in independent India. In the Constituent Assembly, there were some, mainly Gandhians, who wanted the village to be the basic unit in the new social scheme in view of what they claimed had been its central place in the traditional order. Dr. Ambedkar, who was a tireless advocate of the special claims of the Scheduled Castes, opposed their argument, and said, "I am glad that the draft Constitution has discarded the village and adopted the individual as its unit" (Constituent Assembly 1948: vii, 39). Caste was thrown out by the front door, but it has, in the name of equality and social justice, reentered through the back door (Béteille 1987b, 1991).

At the time of independence it was hoped that democracy would undermine the structure of caste in the course of creating a more liberal and equal society through the operation of the political process. But caste has been given a new lease on life by the democratic process to which it has provided an easy basis for the mobilization of support (Srinivas 1962). In India caste politics operates somewhat in the manner of ethnic-group politics in the United States, but on an enormously expanded scale and in a much more pervasive way (Kothari 1969). The traditional ritual basis of caste is certainly being eroded, but nobody can ignore its active role in contemporary Indian politics. It is true that politics is altering caste, but caste too is changing the face of democracy in the country.

What was expected from democracy was also expected from economic development. The general belief among Indian intellectuals was that caste was the social basis of a stagnant, backward, feudal or semifeudal economic system and that it would wither away with the advance of a vibrant economy. There has been some economic development in India, but not a very great deal of it. The question that troubles many today is how the fruits of this development are or ought to be distributed. It appears that increasing numbers of people would like to assess this distribution by taking not just individuals or households but also castes and communities as the units in their reckoning. This leads not to a weakening but a strengthening of the consciousness of caste, at least in the short run.

Writing about affirmative action in the United States, the American jurist Owen M. Fiss (1977: 474) distinguished between the "antidiscrimination" principle and the "group-disadvantaging" principle in the pursuit of equality. Fiss pointed to the strong bias in the United States in favor of the antidiscrimination principle, but in India we see a marked tendency, in politics as well as in law, to invoke the group-disadvantaging principle. In the report of the important Backward Classes Commission for the state of Karnataka, the chairman, L. G. Havanur, argued that in India, equality between castes had to be achieved first before much could be done about equality between individuals. He offered an interpretation of the constitution that is perhaps more surprising than convincing: "Hence the Constitution suggests *recognition of castes for their equalisation*" (Karnataka Backward Classes Commission 1975: 36, italics in original).

Havanur appears to have taken it for granted that wherever the constitution pointed to "socially and educationally backward classes" or even to the "weaker sections of society," it had castes and communities in mind. That view might be accepted by some Indians, including some Indian judges, but by no means by all. Kaka Kalelkar, the chairman of the first all-India Backward Classes Commission, found himself unable to recommend the adoption of caste as the unit in determining the composition of the Other Backward Classes. In forwarding his report to the president, he expressed his misgivings about the continuing use of caste for such purposes: "In a democracy, it is always the individual (not even the family) which is the unit. Democracy thrives best when, on the one hand we recognise and respect the personality of the individual and on the other we consider the well-being of the totality comprising the nation" (Government of India 1955: xiv). Kalelkar was expressing a sentiment that is perhaps shared as widely as that of Havanur. Indeed, the modern educated Indian is deeply divided within himself about what is due to the individual and what is due to caste.

Secularism

It is not uncommon to find both supporters and opponents of caste-based quotas who say that they would like to see an end to caste. The supporters say that caste can never be eradicated so long as such massive disparities remain in society; they maintain that the reduction of these disparities through positive discrimination is bound to lead to the weakening of caste in the long run. The opponents say that the policy of reservation as it is practiced in India can lead only to the reinforcement of the consciousness of caste and is therefore an obstacle to its natural decline.

In considering the persistence of collective identities in India, we have to consider not only caste but also religion. A person may be reluctant to admit to loyalty to his caste, but it is far less common for him to deny loyalty to his religion. Today religion, like caste, not only unites but also divides people. Like caste, religion is a matter of social identity; but, to a large extent unlike caste, it is also a matter of faith and doctrine. People justify their loyalty to their religious community not only in terms of their birth or by invoking "immemorial tradition," but also on grounds of doctrine and faith.

The specter of "communalism" hung over the subcontinent when India became independent in 1947. The country was partitioned in order to achieve some sort of solution to the communal problem, but the specter has not been laid to rest. The Indian case at the time of the partition was that Pakistan might become a country for the Muslims, but India would remain a home for Hindus, Muslims, Christians, and others. Pakistan has become an Islamic state, but India has, at least so far, rejected the idea of being a Hindu state. As indicated earlier, there are in fact more Muslims in India than in Pakistan. Hindus and Muslims have lived together on the subcontinent, in amity and strife, for centuries, but their coexistence within a modern nation-state has brought new normative issues to the fore, related to secularism and the rights of religious minorities.

The Indian state is based on a constitution whose secular character has been reaffirmed by an amendment to its Preamble. It is at the same time mindful of the claims of religion. Hence it grants "the right to profess, practice and propagate religion" (Art. 25) as a fundamental right. How does one simultaneously promote "secularism" and also protect the right to propagate religion?

Many observers from both within and outside the country have commented on the strong and pervasive hold of religion on the people of India. Europeans in the nineteenth and early twentieth centuries generally took this to be an index of their enslavement to superstition, although a few also regarded it as a sign of their superior spiritual quality. In all long-established agrarian civilizations, religion permeates every area of life: family, kinship, work, and leisure, and this was perhaps more true of Hinduism than of the other world religions. While religion maintained a strong hold over everyday life, a slow, diffuse current of secularization had set in among Indians by the end of the nineteenth century. More than thirty years ago, M. N. Srinivas drew attention to the inroads being made by secularization, noting at the same time the presence of countercurrents and the uneven spread of the process among the different sections of Indian society. "Hindus were more affected by the secularization process than any other religious group"; and, further, "Different sections among the Hindus are affected in different degrees by it . . ." (Srinivas 1966: 119).

We have to distinguish between secularization as an outcome of diffuse technological, economic, and other forces operating in society and secularism as a conscious ideology or design for living. It is the ideology of secularism rather than the broad process of secularization that has to be the issue in a discussion of the conflict of norms. The members of the Constituent Assembly by and large took for granted the desirability of having a secular constitution for India; in a sense they had little choice, having committed themselves to the principle that there should be no discrimination among citizens on grounds of religion. In the first two or three decades following independence, there was a general consensus among the intelligentsia that the growth of secular ideas and institutions was both necessary and desirable for the modernization of Indian society. That consensus appears less secure than before, and questions are increasingly raised about the content of secularism as an ideology (Béteille 1994). One of India's more popular intellectuals has even published an "Anti-Secularist Manifesto" (Nandy 1985).

A major source of disagreement, and hence of potential conflict, has to do with the role of the state in the promotion of secularism. It will be useful here to make a distinction, however crudely, between a secular society and a secular state. I will illustrate the distinction by contrasting the United Kingdom with India. In Britain, secularization as a general social process has gone far, and society has acquired a more secular character than in India, where religious beliefs and practices have a much stronger hold over the people. Yet Britain is not a secular state, since it has an established church whose bishops are, by virtue of their office, members of the House of Lords. India is, by contrast, a secular state, without any established church and without any religious representation in the organs of government.

How far can a secular state go in promoting the secularization of life in a society that is deeply permeated by religious beliefs and practices? Is it legitimate for a ruling elite, no matter how well intentioned, to impose its values on a population whose members mostly subscribe to values that are so widely different from its own? Can the state seriously promote secularism without interfering with the religious life of the people? Indeed, can it do so without violating the freedom of religion guaranteed by the constitution itself? (Madan 1987). The British had learned to be cautious about tampering with the religious customs of their Indian subjects after making some false moves. Should not a sovereign independent state act toward its citizens with greater responsibility, if not greater courage? Srinivas (1966) drew attention to precisely this enhanced sense of moral responsibility when he suggested that the abolition of untouchability, in whose practice traditional ritual beliefs and attitudes were deeply implicated, could become a state act only after independence and not before it.

The ship of state has to steer a perilous course in India between the norm of secularism and the norm of religious pluralism. It is becoming increasingly clear that there are two distinct, if not mutually conflicting, ways of viewing secularism. In the first view, secularism means disengagement from religion—not this or that particular religion, but religion as such; this appears to be the generally accepted idea of secularism in the West, and it is not without some adherents among Indians. But there is a second view, believed to be more in conformity with the Indian tradition, which regards secularism as the equal tolerance, if not the equal encouragement, of all religions; here the emphasis is on equality and fairness.

These two views of secularism have coexisted among Indians for some time. Not many appear to have been greatly troubled by their discordance; or, if they were troubled, they perhaps felt that, being Indians, they would somehow manage to square the circle. At any rate, these issues were not widely debated and they did not appear to be seriously divisive. For a variety of reasons, having much to do with developments in Indian politics, the divisions have now come to the fore, without any clear resolution in sight.

In order to understand India's peculiar predicament over secularism, we have to keep in mind not only its composite cultural tradition but also its present demography. The presence of large and populous religious minorities makes it difficult to conceive of a stable social arrangement without some degree of religious tolerance as well as some disengagement of religion from public affairs. Secularism, in one form or another, has become India's destiny, however hard it may be for its present leaders to cope with that destiny.

State-sponsored secularism is exposed to attack from various sides. Where it seeks to neutralize religious excesses, it will be attacked by believers for undermining morality. Where it seeks to promote or even protect a religious community under stress, it will be accused by one set of believers of bias in favor of another. In recent years it is the second kind of allegation that has been the most frequently made, since governments have been far too insecure to wish to alienate any section of voters by appearing to undermine their faith.

Successive governments have in fact been involved in the internal affairs of religious communities and in the administration and maintenance of places of worship and other kinds of religious establishments. Their involvement has originated from a mixture of motives, among which the real or expected gains of politics and patronage have always been present. The publicly expressed view of all the major political parties is that religion and politics should be kept apart in the interest of both, and such would appear to be the spirit behind the Constitution of India. But that is more easily said than done in a society in which the temptations of mobilizing political support by appealing to religious sentiment can be resisted only by saints.

Religious establishments in India vary greatly in their wealth. Some are enormously wealthy while others are too poor to be able to manage on their own. It is not altogether unreasonable for a government to wish to keep an eye on the financial affairs of the former and to provide some financial cushion to the latter. This brings forth allegations of interference on the one hand and favoritism on the other. Religious institutions themselves have not been innocent of complicity in these developments. They would like to be free from government interference, but they would not like to miss too many opportunities for securing government funding. In this they seem to have taken their cue from many public institutions, including universities, which are forever approaching the government for more money and forever reproaching it for violating their autonomy. Where a religious institution is large and wealthy, internal disputes are endemic, and one or another branch of the government has to play the part of arbitrator.

The interface between religion and the state brings in not only the administration but also the law. When the British sought to reform the legal system in the nineteenth century, they were confronted by a bewildering variety of laws. They introduced some uniformity in the law of criminal procedure but proceeded cautiously with civil law. Thomas Macaulay, who came to India as the Law Member on the Supreme Council, wrote: "Our principle is simply this; uniformity where you can have it; diversity where you must have it; but in all cases certainty" (Stokes 1959: 219–220). Between Macaulay and the independence of India, much legal reform took place, but the personal law of Indians, governed largely by religious tradition, still retained an enormous diversity when the constitution was being written.

Article 44 of the constitution says, "The state shall endeavour to secure for all citizens a uniform civil code throughout the territory of India." It is true that this is only a directive principle of state policy and not a law enforceable by the courts, but it has recently acquired great political significance in an unexpected way. Today it is not so much the parties of secularism as the proponents of Hindutva (or the cultural hegemony of Hinduism) that have begun to press for a uniform civil code. This has caught the secularists, both within and outside the government, off guard.

The principal focus of contention today is found in the marriage laws, including the laws relating to the maintenance of divorced women. As is well known, polygamy was allowed by both Hindu and Islamic law, with no restriction as to numbers among Hindus in contrast with Muslims. The Hindu laws relating to marriage, succession, adoption, and guardianship were substantially reformed, with some opposition from orthodox Hindus, in 1955 and 1956. Today polygamy is no longer permitted to Hindus, but it still prevails among Muslims, whose personal laws in India, as elsewhere, have been more resistant to change than those of the Hindus. The party of Hindutva has now begun to accuse the government and the "self-styled secularists" of double standards: acting imperiously in regard to Hindu polygamy, but being coy about Muslim polygamy.

Secularists both within and outside the government now find themselves on the horns of a dilemma, between two conflicting norms: the norm of religious tolerance and the norm of equality between men and women. There is an active and articulate women's movement in India, though confined largely to urban, Westernized, middle- and upper-middle-class women. They are genuinely liberal and secular, perhaps more so than their menfolk, and their anguish is not difficult to comprehend. Their devotion to the cause of equality is sincere, even passionate; at the same time, they have a generous attitude toward the minorities and would not like to see changes imposed on their personal laws by militant Hindus determined to humiliate the Muslims.

The divisions over secularism bring to the fore the complex interplay of ideas and interests in society. People do have basic and fundamental differences over the meaning of tolerance and the meaning of equality, and how far religious tolerance can go in accommodating gender inequality. But adherence to a particular position is an expression not merely of inner faith in a particular doctrine but also of loyalty to the community of one's birth. Such loyalty can gather strength even when the faith is growing weaker. Among both Hindus and Muslims, the most intransigent positions are often adopted by persons who have very little to do with the religious life.

Civil Society and Its Institutions

India has a democratic constitution that stresses equality, liberty, and the rule of law within a secular framework. But does it have a civil society appropriate to the proper and effective functioning of such a constitution? In this penultimate section, I shall discuss the problem of creating and sustaining a civil society in the light of the conflicts over norms, values, and interests on which I have dwelt in the preceding sections.

The concept of civil society is both ambiguous and appealing. I do not wish to propose a definition here, but there are three components that are essential to our understanding of it: state, citizenship, and mediating institutions. It is true that state and civil society are often opposed, but it is difficult to give an adequate account of civil society without keeping the state in mind. Of course what one keeps in mind is not the state as such but the modern constitutional state of the kind that Indians have sought to design for themselves, as I described earlier.

"Citizenship" is a deceptively simple concept. In the contemporary world it is often assumed to be a universal idea, but it is in fact the end product of a long historical evolution. Part I of the Constitution of India is entitled "Citizenship," but one does not create citizens as autonomous moral and political agents simply by recording their existence in a constitution. Theodore Zeldin (1977: 3), the historian of modern France, has described how, as late as 1864, the peasants in a remote rural district in that country still did not think of themselves as Frenchmen; indeed, if the evidence is to be trusted, they did not even know clearly whether they were Frenchmen, Englishmen, or Russians. They thought of themselves as peasants or artisans, as members of a family, a kin group, or a parish rather than as citizens of the republic of France.

The plain fact is that in no country in the world is the peasant converted into a citizen overnight. In the remoter rural districts of France, the conversion had not gone very far nearly a hundred years after the French Revolution. The Indian constitution is not even fifty years old, and it would hardly be realistic to expect that all Indians—rural and urban, peasant and professional, illiterate and educated—will think of themselves as citizens of India.

For centuries the typical Indian had thought of himself as a member of a particular kin group, village, caste, sect, and religious community rather than as a member of a larger society or civilization. For the most part, he had little awareness of what lay beyond his immediate geographical and social horizons. To be sure, there were fairs and pilgrimages, and the depredations of conquering armies that exposed him to the external world. But these were too fitful and intermittent to enable him to incorporate his links with that world as a significant component of his social identity. Being a citizen means adding a new component to one's identity, but that cannot be done without some rearrangement, even displacement, of the old components.

The trajectory from the first formation of the idea of universal citizenship to the attainment of full citizenship is a long, unfinished one. The subject has been examined in great detail by sociologists in Britain, beginning with the work of T. H. Marshall (1977). There it is shown how the content of citizenship became progressively enriched with the creation of first civil, then political, and finally social rights. Marshall's successors have shown how full citizenship still remains a vague and distant goal; and we know today that the entitlements of citizenship may be not only expanded but also abridged.

As I have suggested, the realization of citizenship calls for some degree of social rearrangement. There are many structures that stand between the individual and the wider society of which he is a part. These mediating structures vary enormously from one type of society to another, and they also change in the course of the evolution of each type. Some of them are actual or potential obstacles to the development of civil society; others are necessary and desirable for its sustenance and well-being.

An extreme position, adopted by some secular nationalists, is that if India is to prosper, nothing should be allowed to stand between the individual as citizen and the nation or the state. Such a position is clearly untenable. What makes the inhabitant of this country an Indian today is the fact that he is a citizen of India; but that would amount to little in the absence of the innumerable bonds by which he is tied to particular persons and particular places. Imagine a world of only 950 million Indians and then India, with nothing in between. There would be nothing in it to protect the individual from the arbitrary powers of the state. Also, it would have very little to offer to its members by way of variety, richness, meaning, and purpose in life.

The conception of civil society presented here is one that accommodates a variety of institutions operating at different levels between the individual and the nation. They help to connect individuals to each other and to the wider society. Two features of these institutions deserve special comment: They should be of different kinds, and each, within its own sphere, should enjoy a measure of autonomy in relation to the others and to the state. Civil society, in this conception, is pluralistic in principle; it resists absorption by the state as well as by religion.

By an institution I mean something more than the kinds of informal networks of interpersonal relations that emerge and dissolve continuously in every society. I also mean something more by it than the kind of voluntary association that is merely a registered body without any active or continuous social existence. An institution has a differentiated internal structure; it has a definite and recognizable identity for its members as well as for others; and it has a continuity over time that is longer than the life span of any individual member. I view an institution as some kind of a corporation in the sense given to the term by Henry Maine, who said "Corporations *never die*" (Maine 1931: 104, italics in original). A temple or a monastery is an institution; municipal corporations and universities are institutions. The Bombay Stock Exchange is an institution; an established newspaper with its own traditions, such as *The Times of India*, is an institution. Not all voluntary associations are institutions; but a voluntary association might develop into one after it acquires a definite organizational form and a distinct tradition.

The institutions I have enumerated, more or less at random, cover a very wide range. They include traditional religious institutions because I believe that those should not be placed outside the pale of civil society. However, in countries like India, the real test of the success of civil society will be in the performance of open and secular institutions rather than the rigid and hierarchical ones characteristic of the past. Does Indian society have the resources for creating and sustaining such new institutions?

A variety of new institutions—colleges, hospitals, banks, and so on— began to emerge in India from the middle of the nineteenth century onward under the stimulus of colonial rule. Recruitment to these was on a different basis from recruitment to their traditional counterparts; they were open, at least in principle, to all castes and creeds. Their internal structure and functioning were also different, being governed by secular rather than religious principles. These new institutions did not all at once efface the basic design of traditional Indian society, but they opened up new spaces within it.

In retrospect, it seems remarkable how quickly these new institutions made room for themselves in a society whose basic design and social morphology were so greatly at variance with them. Perhaps there was something congenial in the polymorphous character of Hindu civilization that allowed the accretion of new social and cultural components without fully assimilating them. Moreover, these new institutions were backed by a new type of education and a new occupational system that provided avenues of economic advancement to aspiring individuals from the upper castes. A key role was played in these developments by an emerging middle class imbued with a new outlook on life.

Modern institutions, as I have noted, are open institutions, meaning that membership in them is open to all, irrespective of caste, creed, and gender. This is in principle true of all public institutions in India. But while they are open in principle, the facts clearly show that recruitment to positions of respect and responsibility in them is generally from a rather restricted social base. The consequences of past inequalities between families manifest themselves in the present distribution of persons in even the most open institutions, to a greater or lesser extent, in all societies. It is this that the policy of positive discrimination seeks to correct in India, and in doing so it has reintroduced caste and community as criteria of recruitment to public institutions.

The idea is to make all public institutions—the civil service, universities, medical schools, engineering institutes—representative of the different castes and communities in society, to make each one of them look a little like India. Even where people agree that this should be ideally so, there are disagreements about acceptable ways of bringing it about. Massive political pressure to achieve social justice through equal representation is changing more than the social composition of public institutions; it is changing their internal relations and the focus of their activity. The divisions of caste and community have been carried over into them, and those divisions affect not only the efficiency of work but also the trust and goodwill that are essential to the smooth functioning of every institution.

I have indicated one kind of pressure that modern institutions have to withstand in India. There are other kinds of pressure, actual as well as potential, that cannot be discounted, but here only a passing remark will be made about secularism. I have said that the institutions distinctive of civil society, those on which its well-being largely depends, are both open and secular in nature. The modern institutions to which I have been referring are secular in principle; they are also by and large secular in practice to the extent that their activities are not regulated by religious rules or religious authorities. The peculiar character of Hinduism probably accounts for this relative immunity. It has neither the kind of unified doctrine nor the kind of centralized authority through which religious regulation can be easily imposed on secular institutions. But by the same token, they are open to penetration by diffuse religious values whose long-term effects it is difficult to determine.

The movement away from hierarchy in India is irreversible, even though no clear destination appears in sight. There is no reason to believe that the decline of hierarchy will necessarily be accompanied by a reduction of inequality in the distribution of income. The experience of Western countries in the nineteenth century seems to have been that the decline of a hierarchical social order was accompanied, at least for some time, by an increase rather than a decrease in income inequality (Kuznets 1955: 489). Though there is nothing inevitable about this, it needs to be pointed out that government policies for reducing the inequalities of income have so far met with little success.

Politically, the decline of hierarchy does not result necessarily in the consolidation of constitutional democracy; it can lead as well to the ascendancy of populism. It is only the former and not the latter that requires the institutions of civil society for its sustenance. Populism demands an unmediated relationship between a charismatic leader and the people. It does not need mediating institutions; indeed, they are an encumbrance for both leader and people in a populist regime. The real acid test of nation building in India will lie in the capacity of its new mediating institutions to maintain their open and secular character and to extend their influence.

Conclusion: Considerations for Policy

The normative structure of a society is designed to regulate conflicts of interest between the groups, classes, and categories that are its constituent parts. But what is to regulate the conflicts that inhere in the normative structure itself? I have noted that the values prevalent in contemporary Indian society, or the ends that are considered socially desirable, are often at variance with each other. There is the commitment to equality that is a part of the modern scheme of things; but the commitment to hierarchy that marked the traditional order is still widely manifest beneath the surface. Recognition of the autonomy of the individual and the respect due to him is now an important value; but it is at odds with the strong sense of obligation to the group of which one is a member by birth.

The tolerance of diversity on the plane of values or generalized ends is one thing; quite another is the coexistence of norms or regulatory rules that are unclear, ambiguous, or mutually inconsistent. Whereas the diversity of generalized ends is diffused through society as a whole, the conflict of regulatory rules manifests itself most clearly in particular institutional domains. There is widespread anxiety today over the many problems with which public institutions are beset: misuse of funds, lack of discipline, absenteeism, work stoppages, strikes, and so on. All of these are related in one way or another to the failure of regulatory rules. Allegations about the violation of rules are endemic, calling for the creation of new rules that are in their turn violated.

The courts of law are preeminent among the institutions responsible for interpreting and harmonizing the various regulatory rules by which the other institutions of society are governed. Judicial institutions in India, and in particular the Supreme Court and the high courts, have on the whole maintained a high reputation for rectitude and fair-mindedness throughout the period since independence. It will be safe to say that today the judiciary enjoys a greater measure of public confidence than either the legislative or the executive branches of the state. So the first condition for ensuring that the conflict of norms does not go beyond reasonable limits is the maintenance of the integrity and the autonomy of the courts.

The judiciary has in recent years taken an increasingly active role in an effort to set right the endemic violation of rules, particularly by those holding high public office. This has led to discussions in the press and elsewhere on the possibilities and the limits of judicial activism in a constitutional democracy (Béteille 1996; Baxi 1996). In a thoughtful public lecture, the Chief Justice of India has drawn attention to the unusual nature of legislative and executive failures that has led the courts to take a more active role. But he has also sounded a wise note of caution: "However, by virtue of the fact that the present situation is a corrective measure, the phenomenon of judicial activism in its aggressive role will have to be a temporary one" (Ahmadi 1996).

A new development that has led the courts to take a more active role, as the Chief Justice pointed out in his lecture, is public-interest litigation, which is quite extensive in India. It is now a factor that the state must take into account in ensuring against gross violations of its own norms by its official agents. But such litigation can also put unbearable strains on the courts, which are already overburdened with an enormous backlog of pending cases. Those active in public interest litigation represent diverse interests and act from a variety of intentions. They have had some success in restraining the arbitrary exercise of power by corrupt officials, but the real test of their success will lie in their ability to create the kind of public opinion through which citizens at large become aware of their own rights.

The formation of responsible public opinion is a laborious and demanding task that cannot be left solely to public interest litigation or even to a judiciary with a sympathetic concern for it. Public opinion in India is fragmented, uncertain, and volatile, with a tendency to swing from one extreme to another. The courts address themselves directly to regulatory rules, and only indirectly, and that too not invariably, to the generalized ends that those rules seek to express. Many of the regulatory rules are relatively new and some are against the grain of tradition. New rules cannot be binding unless they are made meaningful through a process of active and continuing education in the widest sense of the term.

Education for meaningful and effective participation in a democratic society and polity is by its nature a many-sided and diffuse process. A variety
of agencies, organizations, and institutions contribute to it. Their contributions are not all of the same kind, and they are not all consciously directed
to the same end. After all, it is in the nature of democracy that such institutions as newspapers, publishing houses, and even schools should express
and articulate different, if not contradictory, points of view. At the same
time, their continuing activity is essential to the widest diffusion of the values on which an open and secular society is sustained.

India has one of the oldest intellectual traditions in the world, with
many remarkable achievements to its credit, but it was among the most
elitist known to human history, in its social base and in the type of
knowledge it favored. Major changes were initiated in the content and
organization of intellectual activity in India in the early part of the nineteenth century (Shils 1961). A new educational system, with new types of
schools, colleges, and universities, was introduced by the British and on
the whole well received by the traditional intellectual elite. What is remarkable in retrospect is the *social* continuity maintained throughout the
nineteenth century, particularly among the Hindus, between the traditional literati and the new educated class, despite important changes in
the content and institutional setting of education. The new middle class
became the bearer of new social values, and it placed the greatest emphasis on the education it received in the new institutions of learning. This
class is growing in number, but it still comprises a small proportion of the
total population.

Following a process of slow but steady growth in education for a hundred years, there was a spurt after independence. The growth of education has been highly uneven in independent India, and this has been a
source of increasing anxiety among planners and policymakers (Karlekar
1983; Tilak 1987). With some simplification, it may be said that secondary
education has grown at the expense of primary education, and higher education at the expense of secondary education. There are several reasons
behind this. Firstly, it takes far greater material and manpower resources
to develop a good system of universal elementary education than to establish a small number of universities and centers of advanced study and
research. Secondly, the effects of a good system of elementary education
show only indirectly and in the long run, whereas universities and research institutes can show some spectacular results in the form of Ph.D.'s
and research publications in a much shorter time. But perhaps the really
decisive factor has been the conservative bias in Indian planning and in
Indian society and culture in favor of established castes and classes.

The neglect of elementary education has been perhaps the single most
important factor behind the poor record of development planning in In-

dia. It has affected economic and political life in general, and it is now beginning to affect higher education itself. The quantitative expansion of colleges and universities continues apace, but they are already under severe strain on account of the woefully inadequate early education of the students and even the teachers they are now compelled under pressure to admit and promote.

When the first census was taken in independent India in 1951 shortly after the new constitution was adopted, the literacy rate was very low, below 20 percent for the general population and much lower in some states where female literacy was abysmally low. The constitution had, under Article 45, already declared as a directive principle of state policy that "The State shall endeavour to provide, within a period of ten years from the commencement of this Constitution for free and compulsory education for all children until they complete the age of fourteen years." The magnitude of the economic as well as political consequences of the state's failure to redeem this pledge has now become plainly manifest.

The literacy rate began to climb very slowly in the first three decades of independence, and then began to pick up. By 1991, the state of Kerala in south India had effectively achieved full literacy. The case of Kerala came to be viewed as exemplary because the same state had, among other things, shown impressive results in population control, and the connection between low fertility and literacy, particularly female literacy, has now come to be generally accepted (Sen 1994). The government has begun to show greater determination to eradicate illiteracy by committing substantial resources to its Total Literacy Mission.

Total literacy is only the first step in the creation of responsible citizenship. Sustaining a credible system of elementary education demands far greater resources in time and money than eradicating illiteracy once and for all. Primary and secondary schools have no doubt increased in number since independence, but they have also become much more differentiated in terms of the quality of education they provide. The good schools have superior facilities, but they are very expensive and outside the reach of the majority; the majority of primary and even secondary schools are inexpensive, but in many of them there are hardly any facilities at all. The expensive schools are privately funded and managed by and serve the metropolitan middle and upper middle classes. The rest depend on government funding, which comes in dribs and drabs and is frequently mismanaged and misappropriated.

Fitful and inadequate schooling does not lead to responsible citizenship. It relaxes the grip of traditional values but does not put anything coherent in their place. Some of the willful disregard for norms witnessed among the urban youth is a result of the failure of schooling in India. A deeper and wider awareness of this certainly helps to clear the atmosphere but does not by itself generate the vast resources required to make available even good quality primary education to all. Private funding will be provided only selectively, and the gap between a few expensive private schools and those accessible to all will remain, but there is no reason why it cannot be narrowed instead of being widened.

Since I attach so much importance to good quality education in the making of civil society, I must in conclusion point to the limits within which it can be expected to work. The effects of good schooling are diffuse, and not specific. Moreover, in a pluralist society, there is no way in which the values imparted by schools can be propelled in a given direction. A technically efficient system of schools, which India seems to need most at present, does not guarantee schooling in liberal and secular ideas. It will be a miracle if the multiplicity of schools through the length and breadth of the country all inculcate a uniform set of values. The same is to some extent true for the press, which is also made up of many diverse strands. Not all newspapers in India propagate the liberal and secular ideology of the constitution; there are some that propagate ideas that are openly violative of its spirit if not its letter.

It is difficult to determine what can be done to regulate the propagation of values contrary to the norms of the constitution in the school, by the press, or elsewhere. Here again the courts have a crucial, though delicate, role. They must act when norms are clearly violated; but they cannot snuff out every form of dissent or anticipate the violation of norms in every dissenting idea.

References

Ahmad, Imtiaz (ed.). 1973. *Caste and Social Stratification Among the Muslims.* New Delhi: Manohar.

Ahmadi, A. M. 1996. "Judicial Activism—I." *The Times of India*, Delhi, 27 February 1996.

Ansari, Ghaus. 1959. *Muslim Caste in Uttar Pradesh.* Lucknow: Ethnographic and Folk Culture Society.

Baxi, Upendra. 1996. *On Judicial Activism, Legal Education, and Research in Globalizing India.* New Delhi: Capital Foundation Society.

Béteille, André. 1986. "The Concept of Tribe with Special Reference to India." *European Journal of Sociology*, vol. 27, pp. 297–318.

———. 1987a. "Equality as a Right and as a Policy." *LSE Quarterly*, vol. 1, no. 1, pp. 75–98.

———. 1987b. *The Idea of Natural Inequality and Other Essays*, 2d ed. Delhi: Oxford University Press.

———. 1991. *Society and Politics in India: Essays in a Comparative Perspective.* London: Athlone Press.

———. 1994. "Secularism and the Intellectuals." *Economic and Political Weekly*, vol. 24, no. 10, pp. 559–566.

_____. 1995. "Judicial Activism." *The Times of India*, Delhi, 11 December 1995.

_____. 1996. "Caste in Contemporary India." In C. J. Fuller, ed., *Caste Today* (Delhi: Oxford University Press).

Bose, N. K. 1975 [1949]. *The Structure of Hindu Society* (translated from the Bengali, with an introduction and notes by André Béteille). Delhi: Orient Longman.

Caplan, L. 1980. "Caste and Castelessness Among South Indian Christians." *Contributions to Indian Sociology*, vol. 14, no. 2, pp. 213–238.

Constituent Assembly. 1948. *Constituent Assembly Debates: Official Report*, vol. 7. New Delhi: Government of India.

Dumont, Louis. 1966. *Homo hierarchicus: Essai sur le système des castes.* Paris: Gallimard.

_____. 1970. *Religion, Politics, and History in India.* Paris: Mouton.

Fiss, O. M. 1977. "Groups and the Equal Protection Clause." In M. Cohen, T. Nagel, and T. Scanlon, eds., *Equality and Preferential Treatment*, pp. 84–154. Princeton: Princeton University Press.

Galanter, Mark. 1984. *Competing Equalities.* Delhi: Oxford University Press.

Ganguli, B. N. 1975. *Concept of Equality: The Nineteenth Century Indian Debate.* Simla: Indian Institute of Advanced Study.

Godwin, C. J. 1972. *Change and Continuity: A Study of Two Christian Village Communities in Suburban Bombay.* Bombay: Tata McGraw-Hill.

Government of India. 1955. *Report of the Backward Classes Commission*, vol. 1. New Delhi: Controller of Publications.

_____. 1981. *Report of the Backward Classes Commission*, Part 1. Delhi: Controller of Publications.

Kane, P. V. 1974. *History of Dharmashastra*, 2d ed., vol. 2, part 1. Poona: Bhandarkar Oriental Research Institute.

Karlekar, Malavika. 1983. "Education and Inequality." In André Béteille, ed., *Equality and Inequality* (Delhi: Oxford University Press), pp. 182–242.

Karnataka Backward Classes Commission. 1975. *Report.* Bangalore: Government of Karnataka.

Karve, Irawati. 1968. *Hindu Society: An Interpretation*, 2d ed. Poona: Deshmukh Prakashan.

Kothari, Rajni (ed.). 1969. *Caste in Indian Politics.* Delhi: Orient Longman.

Kuppuswami, Alladi (ed.). 1991. *Mayne's Treatise on Hindu Law and Usage*, 13th ed. New Delhi: Bharat Law House.

Kuznets, S. 1955. "Economic Growth and Income Inequality." *American Economic Review*, vol. 45, no. 1, pp. 257–287.

Madan, T. N. 1987. "Secularism in Its Place." *Journal of Asian Studies*, vol. 46, no. 4, pp. 747–759.

Maine, Henry Sumner. 1931 [1861]. *Ancient Law.* London: Oxford University Press.

Marshall, T. H. 1977. *Class, Citizenship, and Social Development.* Chicago: University of Chicago Press.

Nandy, Ashis. 1985. "An Anti-Secularist Manifesto." *Seminar*, no. 314, pp. 14–24.

Nehru, Jawaharlal. 1961 [1946]. *The Discovery of India.* Bombay: Asia Publishing House.

Parsons, Talcott. 1966. *Societies: Evolutionary and Comparative Perspectives.* Englewood Cliffs, N.J.: Prentice-Hall.

Parsons, Talcott, and Edward A. Shils (eds.). 1951. *Towards a General Theory of Action*. Cambridge, Mass.: Harvard University Press.

Schermerhorn, R. A. 1978. *Ethnic Plurality in India*. Tucson: University of Arizona Press.

Sen, Amartya. 1994. "Population: Delusion and Reality." *New York Review of Books*, 22 September 1994, pp. 62–71.

Shils, Edward A. 1961. *The Intellectual Between Tradition and Modernity: The Indian Situation*. The Hague: Mouton.

Sivaramayya, B. 1984. *Inequalities and the Law*. Lucknow: Eastern Book Company.

Smelser, Neil J. 1962. *Theory of Collective Behavior*. New York: The Free Press.

Smith, R. S. 1996. *Rule by Records*. Delhi.

Srinivas, M. N. 1962. *Caste in Modern India and Other Essays*. Bombay: Asia Publishing House.

_____. 1966. *Social Change in Modern India*. Berkeley: University of California Press.

Stokes, Eric. 1959. *The English Utilitarians and India*. Oxford: Clarendon Press.

Tilak, J.B.G. 1987. *Economics of Inequality in Education*. London: Sage.

Tripathi, P. K. 1972. *Some Insights into Fundamental Rights*. Bombay: University of Bombay.

Zeldin, Theodore. 1977. *France: 1848–1945*, vol. 2. Oxford: Clarendon Press.

10

Normative Conflicts in Japan

Seizaburo Sato

In this chapter, I will seek to illuminate Japan's principal normative conflicts, to analyze how they are or are not mediated, and to examine how they might develop in the future. Preliminary to this analysis, however, I will conduct a general survey of the principal normative conflicts, observed in a shifting perspective, since the mid–nineteenth century when a conscious modernization effort commenced in Japan. Such a review is pertinent because the normative conflicts in today's Japan remain inseparably intertwined with Japanese society's process of modernization and economic development. This chapter will shed analytical light on this interrelationship.

Principal Normative Conflicts and Their
Mediation in Modernizing Japan Until 1945

Modernization, as defined here, is a total process of social change centering on industrialization, but it also includes the political, economic, cultural, and psychological shifts that facilitate industrialization. Industrialization, which began in England during the second half of the eighteenth century, dramatically heightened the capacity of mankind to control the environment by systematically and cumulatively applying scientific technologies to production processes. As a result, it brought about revolutionary change to human life and society. Between those countries that succeeded in industrialization and those that failed to do so, a profound gap arose in national power and popular living standard. Thus, the latter had to remain under the domination of the former, until a wave of nationalism arose on a global scale and the principles of national self-determination became widely recognized across the world.

In non-Western societies, achieving industrialization was not only a difficult task in itself, but also its process generated a variety of frictions, as modernization accompanied a succession of monumental social changes. Modernization first began in Western Europe, and, at least until quite recently, those societies that succeeded in modernization were always under the predominant influence of Western civilization. Therefore, for non-Western societies, modernization meant Westernization, that is, a process of a large-scale absorption of the technologies and institutions conceived and elaborated in societies with an alien cultural tradition.

Japan's modernization was no exception to this rule. It is well known that by the middle of the eighteenth century national political integration in Japan had progressed to a considerable extent. A bureaucratic system of government had become fairly well organized and the process of nation building was already under way in substance, and popular literacy had reached a level fairly comparable to those of the contemporary Western nations.[1] Commercial activities were spreading across the country, and a uniform currency system was permeating the nation's economic life. In this sense, it can be said that Japan was exceptionally well equipped among the non-Western countries to launch its own industrialization effort, in terms of the necessary preconditions. Nonetheless, it would be far from fact to claim that Japan's modernization was a smooth and easy process without attendant confusion. Indeed, the task was urgent, and the nation's independence hung in the balance; it was a painful process that demanded fundamental changes in traditional institutions and practices. In addition, modernization required a trial-and-error series of experiments in emulating and adopting aspects of a foreign culture that was totally alien to Japan—there existed practically no advance knowledge. In 1877, nine years after the Meiji Restoration of 1868, Erwin von Baelz, a German medical doctor who came to Japan as consultant to the Japanese government to direct the educational and research activities in medicine at Tokyo University, was shocked by the tumults and chaos in the early Meiji Japan and commented that Japan was attempting a "death jump (salto mortale)" in what amounted to a stupendous cultural revolution.[2]

The normative conflicts that confronted modernizing Japan arose above all around the issue of how Japan should proceed with its modernization (or Westernization) program. Attitudes toward modernization can be divided into four major functional positions, as shown in Figure 10.1, as a combination of two factors: one expressed on the axis of whether one is in favor of, or opposed to, the introduction of Western technologies, institutions, and culture (conversely, whether one is in favor of, or opposed to, the preservation of the traditional culture), and the other on the axis of how far and at what speed Japan should proceed with Westernization.

To totally refuse to Westernize was out of the question, as long as modernization was an unavoidable prerequisite to maintaining national inde-

Westernization	Rejective	Receptive
Eclectic	(2) Conservatives	(1) Liberals
Total	(3) Reactionaries	(4) Radicals

FIGURE 10.1   Normative conflict in the Meiji Restoration era: Modernization

pendence and could not be achieved without embracing Western technologies, institutions, and culture. And in Japan, with its long history—since ancient times—of emulating the Chinese and the Indian cultures, there was relatively little resistance to the idea of accepting and adapting to a foreign culture, as long as it was perceived as "more advanced." Consequently, the reactionaries (category 3 in the figure) who were entirely opposed to Westernization were only a small minority. Also, while some radical Westernizers (category 4) went so far as to advocate, for instance, the abolition of the native language in favor of English, this group also remained merely a handful of intellectuals, for the obvious reason that totally replacing one's culture with an alien import was in practice utterly impossible and at best would be destined to cause inordinate social chaos and create a serious hindrance to industrialization as a result. Therefore, most Japanese in those days belonged to the two remaining groups, liberals (category 1) or conservatives (category 2).

One aspect that these two groups shared in common was that they felt that Japan should neither totally embrace nor reject Western civilization, and they accepted the practical necessity of striking a workable compromise between Western civilization and their traditional culture. The difference between the two groups was merely a matter of degree in that the conservatives preferred to keep Westernization to the necessary minimum while the liberals remained fundamentally in favor of Westernization and stood for pushing it to the possible maximum. Thus, Japan's effort to limit the extent of Westernization to the adoption of scientific technologies and administrative and legal institutions under the famous slogan of "Western technology and Eastern morality" typically reflected the former group's position. But neither technologies nor institutions could be conveniently severed from the culture that gave birth to them. As long as emulating Western technologies and institutions accompanied the unavoidable necessity of coming into direct contact with and learning from Westerners, it was practically impossible to prevent the penetration of the underlying Western values into Japanese society.

In addition, progress in industrialization, together with the impact of Westernization, predictably gave rise to labor disputes and a popular demand for greater democratization. The conservatives in modern Japan, therefore, had to live—just as the leaders in Beijing and Pyongyang do to-day—under the constant fear of the collapse of the traditional order. On the other hand, while recognizing that a total, rapid Westernization was impossible, the liberals could not avoid deep frustration at the fact that modernizing Japan was saddled with tenacious remains of its own traditional culture, quite alien to that of the West. In particular, they perceived the still relatively immature stage of economic and technological development and the fragile existence of the newly adopted liberal democracy to be signs of Japan's "backwardness" and the "warps" in its modernization process. Thus, normative conflicts surrounding the issue of Westernization existed not only between the conservatives and the liberals; some irreconcilable, internal normative conflicts plagued each group.

In those days, even the conservatives and the reactionaries had to accept the reality that the Western powers were by far more advanced than the latecomer Japan, both economically and technologically, and in possession of a formidable military capability. This meant in effect that a feeling of inferiority vis-à-vis the West pervaded the society, broadly shared by the Japanese people regardless of their personal attitude toward Westernization. Such perceived inferiority rendered these normative conflicts much more serious, adding fuel to Japan's national effort to "catch up and overtake" the Western powers. In the end, it was destined to provide the hotbed for an "anti-Western" nationalism that became a prominent force in Japan during and after the 1930s.

In the 1930s, not only did a new tide of "anti-Western" nationalism arise, which more often manifested itself in an express form of Asianism, but also the Western model to be emulated by Japan began to split in three directions—into the Anglo-Saxon type of liberal democracy, Nazi Germany's type of totalitarianism, and the Soviet Union's type of communism. Since the onset of the Great Depression in the fall of 1929, while Western capitalism remained confronted by a serious crisis, Hitler's Germany and Stalin's Soviet Union seemed to be making a robust progress, the stark contrast of which was really responsible for the split of the Western model. Thus, the normative conflicts in those days were being transformed into the positions shown in Figure 10.2. Here, the difference between the moderate conservatives of category 1 and the conservatives of category 2 was that the former were fundamentally committed, if not as strongly as the confirmed liberals, to the idea of liberal democracy, while the latter took the position that Japan would have better security by allying itself with Britain and/or the United States from the standpoint of realpolitik even though they were basically anti-West to begin with. Also, for the radicals falling into category 4, the exemplary West was to be found in the Nazi and Marxist-Leninist systems, marking the

	Anti-West	Pro-West
Pro–Liberal Democratic/Pro–Anglo-America	(2) Conservatives	(1) Liberals and Moderate Conservatives
Pro-Totalitarianism	(3) Reactionaries	(4) Radicals

FIGURE 10.2   Normative split in the 1930s

starkest difference from the liberals and moderate conservatives of category 1, who saw their exemplars in Western Europe and the United States. In contrast, the reactionaries of category 3 were Japanists, or Asianists, who meant to reject Western values outright. Indeed, throughout the 1930s the reactionaries kept amassing power, ultimately to plunge Japan into a total war against the West.

In what way, then, were these normative conflicts mediated in those days? Such a mediating role was played most effectively by three major institutional factors: first, a strong rising nationalism; second, the tenacious existence of the traditional communities; and third, but not the least, the fact that the Japanese enterprises that proliferated in the process of industrialization had developed a unique management system incorporating communal values and organizational characteristics. This was later to become widely known as the "Japanese way of corporate governance," or more simply as "Japanese management."

Like most other large ethnic groups, the people of Japan also represent a product of the intermixing of divergent ethnic subgroupings over a long historical timeline. But no large-scale incursion by foreign people has taken place since most of Japan was brought under the rule of a unified government some 1,500 years ago. The Westernization of Japan, as was the case with the introduction of Chinese civilization, did not occur as a result of military conquest or colonization; it was instead undertaken at the initiative of the Japanese people, through a process of learning from the West. And in this sense, Japan has remained, along with Korea, one of the most homogeneous societies in both ethnic and cultural terms among the societies with larger populations.

Moreover, having never been incorporated into the Chinese Empire, Japan was destined to develop an awareness of its national identity as a unique political and cultural entity at an early stage of its history, because it had long been made aware of the overarching existence of China as an advanced major power. The threats that came from the Western countries—far different from China both culturally and ethnically—further intensified Japan's awareness of its own national identity and gave rise to a new tide of nationalism. That Japan alone succeeded in industrialization as a non-Western society, while numerous others became colonized one after another by the Western powers, reinforced Japanese national pride. The Western colonization drive provided Japan a convenient pretext for its own external expansion, which was called an act of "liberating Asia (and non-Western societies as well)," while also strengthening Japan's nationalism. Even the liberal intellectuals, victims of an ambivalent mixture of admiration and sense of inferiority toward Western civilization, had a clear sense of belonging to Japan as members of this "unique" political and cultural entity. It is a recognized fact that the rise of nationalism played a very significant role in Japan to prevent the normative conflicts surrounding the issue of Westernization from producing serious social cleavages.

Second, in pre–World War II Japan, strongly viable traditional communities remained, such as rural village communities and family institutions, all of which played a role in maintaining the existing social order. The majority of the Japanese population then lived in rural villages, and while there was a confrontational relationship between large landlords and their tenants, who lived at mere subsistence levels in some regions, the Japanese rural communities as a whole continued to perform the function of providing traditional mutual assistance. In addition, the Japanese family system also continued to play an important role as the fundamental social building block in rural communities as well as in urban centers. Especially among the families above the middle class, there was an awareness that the primary responsibility of the head of an *ie* household (it really ought to be called *ie* in Japanese, rather than the English translation of "family") was to maintain the continuity of and further build a more prosperous *ie*. It should be especially noted in this context that the Japanese *ie* system was considerably different from the kinship clans in China and Korea.

The basic community in pre-modern China and Korea comprised kinship clans (with membership often reaching several hundreds of thousands), whereas in the Japanese situation such clans dissolved, at least after the thirteenth century, rendering blood relationship less than decisively important. Both in China and Korea, exogamy is still rigorously practiced, and when adoption is contemplated the accepted rule is to find a candidate from among one's kinship relations (and furthermore, of the immediately following generation). But in Japan endogamy was a common practice, and adoption of someone completely unrelated was frequently acceptable. Especially in the case of merchants and artisans, when their own sons were judged less than qualified to assume family businesses, it was not an infrequent practice for the families to adopt able employee managers for the sake of business continuity. In Japan the sustained growth of family business was considered more important than the continuity of blood relationships. To borrow from the famous dichotomy of Ferdinand Tönnies, the Japanese *ie* thus has actually been closer to what might be called *gesellschaftliche Gemeinschaft*. After World War II, under the direction of the U.S. Occupation authorities, the civil code was revised in Japan, eliminating the legal prop for the traditional *ie* system. But as recently as 1953, a public opinion poll indicated that as many as 74 percent of respondents replied in the affirmative to the question "Would you want to adopt someone unrelated to you in blood to assure the continuity of your *ie* when without a child of your own?" and only 16 percent replied in the negative.[3]

With this uniquely Japanese family system in the background, the progress of industrialization in Japan has given rise to a uniquely Japanese enterprise institution, characterized by a strong sense of belonging and loyalty of the employees to their employer organizations. Not infrequently, Western scholars have called this a "familized corporation." The birth of this so-called Japanese management system can be traced to the early years of the twentieth century, and it gradually developed over the following decades. During World War II this form came to be widely adopted by various types of enterprises through strong wartime government guidance that encouraged them to implement this management system to meet the requirements of the general mobilization program.

By the commonly held Western yardstick, Gesellschaft, or association, is organized on the free choice of an individual, or individuals, for specific purposes. As such, it is fundamentally different from Gemeinschaft, or community, which precludes freedom of choice and exists for diffuse purposes. But the Japanese *ie* and business firms possess the characteristics of both association and community. In Japanese society, formed as it is with such groupings as its building blocks, it has been argued that individuality and collectivity function in a mutually reinforcing relationship, rather than in a relationship of opposition and tension, as in the West. In China, in contrast, it is generally the case for business enterprises to be formed on the basis of blood relationship owing to especially strong familial ties.[4]

I believe that such organizational characteristics were intimately related to the historical fact that Japan became an exceptional success case in industrialization among the non-Western societies from the end of the nineteenth century through the early twentieth century, when the transition was taking place from early family capitalism to organized capitalism. Also, the fact that social order was maintained relatively well despite rapid progress in industrialization was due in no insignificant degree to the function and the role played by the Japanese management system.

The Impact of the Defeat and the Influences
of the Postwar Reforms

Japan's defeat in World War II meant a far more serious loss to the Japanese than mere battlefield losses (miserable as they were), devastation of homeland, and the loss of colonial possessions and national wealth. The causes and characteristics of World War II are never so simple, and historians still dispute one another's interpretations. On the part of the victorious Allied nations, the war has been defined as a struggle against totalitarian aggressions (though the fact that the Soviet Union, a member of the Allied powers, was a totalitarian state is often neglected); moreover, the Allied nations' interpretation of the war was accepted at face value by most Japanese. The situation was basically no different in Germany. In other words, the Axis countries not only were roundly defeated in the war but also suffered a moral defeat.[5]

In the case of Japan, the defeat in a foreign war with its homeland in ruins and the occupation of the country by foreign powers were the first such experiences ever in its history. Its impact was therefore especially far-reaching, shaking to their very foundations the traditional order and the legitimacy of the state based upon it. Besides, the affluent and free "American way of life" and "American democracy," as they became known through contact with the U.S. Occupation forces, turned out to be a breathtaking temptation to the Japanese people, who had been exposed to poverty and suppression during the decades before and during the war.

For example, a female writer who was in her teens during the first part of the 1960s remarked as follows on her admiration of the American way of life she intimately learned about through television: "I have come to know about the American lifestyle watching television programs. . . . I said to myself it must be a lot of fun to live in America. And ever since, I have done all I could to Americanize myself . . . a spacious lawn garden, white fence, and a garage. My textbook was that glistening middle-class American family life."[6] For the Japanese in the years immediately after the war, when life was far more difficult than in the early years of the 1960s, American life, as made known through the Occupation forces, newspapers, and magazines, represented a fantastic affluence and an irresistibly attractive allure to most people in Japan. Also, when compared with the wartime repressions, to be occupied by the Allied forces under U.S. leadership was for most Japanese to experience freedom for the first time in their lives. This was the very reason why most Japanese felt they were "liberated" in spite of the fact that their country was occupied by the Allied powers. Such admirations, then, no doubt tended to strengthen the tendency of the Japanese people to criticize the traditional values of their own culture.

Simultaneously, a large number of Japanese who were exposed to the miseries of a modern war for the first time came to harbor a strong pacifist sentiment that such a war should never be repeated. This pacifist sentiment acquired a strong tinge of antistatism when coupled with the negative reaction toward the state by most Japanese who had earlier worked so hard in patriotic fervor, driven by the wartime slogan of "Sacrifice yourself for the interest of your state." The interpretation of the war rendered by the Allied countries and the Occupation authorities that "the real culprits of World War II were a handful of military leaders and the Japanese government, or state, which these men represented, and the ordinary people of Japan were the victims of their propaganda,"[7] was widely accepted in Japan because it provided a convenient excuse for many Japanese to extricate themselves from their war responsibilities, again contributing to the nurturing of antistatist attitudes. That the political system in prewar and wartime Japan was not democratic also made the act of self-exemption an easier psychological process. A scenario writer born in 1936 writes that the image of democracy in post–World War II Japan was a "pattern of thinking and action arising from the idea that 'individuals should be most respected and placed above political system, society, or organization.'"[8] The preamble of the Japanese Constitution, drafted by the Occupation authorities, begins with the paragraph, "We, the Japanese people, resolved that never again shall we be visited with the horrors of war through the action of government," is another salient manifestation of such antistatism lined with a pacifist sentiment.

The Occupation policy for Japan in its early phase was primarily directed at the democratization and demilitarization of Japan, and various reforms aimed at achieving these goals were forcefully implemented by the Occupation authorities. There was a rapid-fire enforcement of reforms, such as the arrest and purge from public offices of Japan's wartime leaders, the promulgation of a new constitution extolling popular sovereignty and respect for human rights and renunciation of war, the dissolution of undemocratic institutions such as the Imperial military establishment and the peerage, agricultural reform aimed at breaking up landlordism, and economic democratization reform involving the dissolution of the giant *zaibatsu* (conglomerates) and other large business combines and the strengthening of labor unions. But as the Cold War began, and especially with the birth of a communist China and the outbreak of the Korean War, the Occupation policy underwent a major redirection, from pursuit of democratization and demilitarization to achieving the social stability and economic recovery of Japan. For the United States (as for the Western camp as a whole), the perceived image of Japan changed from that of a dangerous belligerent state to the most important ally in Asia in waging the Cold War.

	Revision of Postwar Reforms	Promotion of Prewar Reforms
Pro-Statist/Realist	(2) Conservatives and Moderate Reactionaries	(1) Radicals
Anti-Statist/Pacifist	(3) Reactionaries	(4) Moderate Radicals and Liberals

FIGURE 10.3   Normative conflict in the postwar decade

The defeat in the war and the postwar reforms, and then the reversal of Occupation policy after the onset of the Cold War made the normative conflicts in postwar Japan substantially different from those of the prewar decades. There was no longer a situation in which normative orientations differed significantly according to one's attitude toward modernization (Westernization), as had been the case in the prewar era. Instead, the issuing point centered on one's attitude toward the postwar reforms and the state, both of which became the primary factors defining the postwar normative conflicts. Figure 10.3 is a simplified expression of the new kinds of normative conflicts in postwar Japan.

First, attention should be directed to the fact that there have been very few, if any, individuals who demanded the return to the prewar regime with a total negation of the postwar reforms. That postwar Japan was freer and more democratic and more peaceful than prewar Japan was obvious to most Japanese. With the exception of some of the privileged class like the peerage in prewar Japan, the postwar reforms were generally embraced by most Japanese. The affirmative popular attitude became further strengthened as the postwar chaos finally came under control, economic growth took off, and it became obvious that the popular living standard was steadily improving. Accordingly, very few people still fell into category 3 of the figure, and as time passed their number steadily declined. Of those who belonged to category 2, the moderate reactionaries remained more critical of the postwar reforms while the conservatives were usually more readily willing to accept the consequences of the postwar reforms, the difference between the two being merely a matter of degree.

Also, it was inevitable that the reform policies instituted in the early stages of Occupation would be corrected sooner or later, because they had been hurriedly carried out immediately after the war, without a sound understanding of what made the Japanese society tick on the part of those who were determined to introduce American-style democracy into the defeated Japan. Then as the Cold War intensified, the unrealistic nature of the policy of demilitarization of Japan became patently obvious. Thus, as long as one remained a realist, one had to accept some degree of modifications to the postwar reforms, and therefore the position in category 1 in the figure, if valid in the early years of occupation, was bound to lose its validity sooner or later.

Second, the Cold War's outbreak and the reversal of the Occupation policy toward Japan reinforced the bridge between antistatism and pacifism, making it possible for those who held the moderate-radical and liberal positions (category 4) to maintain a significant political influence over an extended period of time. In the meantime the Occupation authorities shifted their policy from purging and suppressing the Japanese wartime leadership to supporting the postwar leaders who fell into category 2 (which included not a few who had been in leading positions in prewar and wartime Japan). Further, they opted for shifting the policy of demilitarizing Japan to that of directing the Japanese government to start building its own Self-Defense Forces. This abrupt policy volte-face caused those who had held to the positions of category 4 to interpret it as an act of emasculating and bastardizing the new postwar constitutional order built on the twin pillars of pacifism and democracy, and consequently to regard the Japanese government supported by the Occupation authorities as the successor of the prewar and wartime state power. Additionally, the sense of continuity linking postwar Japan with prewar Japan was further reinforced—unlike Germany's postwar experience—by the fact that Emperor Showa continued to hold the throne, despite the constitutional revision that reduced the emperor's position from the sovereign and the highest ruler of the land, if only by name, to that of a mere integrative symbol of the state without any real power. In addition, the new constitution—based on a set of principles fundamentally different from those of the old constitution—was introduced in postwar Japan using the amendment procedures set forth by the old Imperial Constitution. These were also the reason why the policy of the Japanese government of modifying segments of the postwar Occupation reforms that had been implemented soon after the war and were later found incompatible with conditions in Japan was criticized by those who were in category 4 as an act of reverting to the days of the prewar regime (the "reverse course" as it was called at the time).

The United States, as the leader of one camp in the era of East-West confrontation, promoted the rearming of Japan dictated by the realistic needs of the Cold War era, which fueled a rising tide of anti-Americanism among those who found themselves in category 4. As a result, their fundamental policy position came to center on an opposition to the Japan–United States alliance and an out-and-out insistence on idealistic pacifism, that is, a policy of "unarmed neutrality." It was indeed an irony of history that those who had subscribed almost blindly to the postwar reforms instituted by the Occupation authorities turned anti-American in the end. Unlike Germany, which as a state remained divided into the East and the West segments and was situated at the forefront of the East-West confrontation, Japan was never divided. Moreover, it was separated by seas from both the Soviet Union and China, and the United States maintained overwhelmingly powerful naval and air forces in this area until the 1970s. Therefore, as long as a trustworthy U.S. commitment to Japan's security existed, Japan's national security remained fully assured, even without having substantial armed forces of its own. This relatively favorable international environment also helped to ensure a continued pacifist position in Japan. It can also be said that, in this sense, the moderate-radical and liberal position of category 4 was practically underwritten by the U.S. commitment to safeguard Japanese security. However, to be anti-American in the context of the East-West confrontation was inevitably to be drawn into a friendly relationship with the Eastern camp. In fact, those who fell into category 4 eventually grew into a grand coalition comprising those who believed in idealistic pacifism and those who subscribed to various hues of political ideology ranging from socialism to communism.

In postwar Japan, Marxism-Leninism continued to have a strong influence among the socialists until quite recently. They should have belonged in categories 1 or 2 rather than category 4 since their platform was to take over state power and build a socialist state in Japan, overriding the postwar reforms aimed at democratizing the country. But in the meantime there was practically no one among them who advocated a socialist constitution or pointed to the unrealistic character of the principle of unarmed neutrality. It was also a tactically comfortable position for those who chose to stand on the Eastern side in the political context of the Cold War to side with those who fell into category 4, well-known for their strong anti-Americanism. Thus, most of those who subscribed to Marxism-Leninism adopted the position of category 4 regardless of their true inner preferences. One can see from this fact just how potent the influence of the thought and attitudes of category 4 remained in those days.

Thus, the normative conflicts in postwar Japan have become more polarized in comparison to the decades preceding World War II. The so-called 1955 Regime, which became firmly established in 1955, was a political consequence of such polarized normative conflicts. This regime functioned on the basis of the confrontational framework between the Liberal Democratic Party (LDP) representing category 2 and the Japan Socialist Party (JSP) and the Japan Communist Party, which championed the positions of category 4. Noteworthy was the fact that the JSP, while under the strong influence of Marxism-Leninism, remained guided by a relatively relaxed and open organizational principle without subscribing to the communist-type control by powerful central leadership. As a result, the Communist Party remained an insignificant minority. The JSP continued to insist on its position of unarmed neutrality and favored the Eastern camp within the power dynamics of the East-West confrontation. Thus it was totally incapable of wresting the seat of power from the LDP, allowing the latter to remain perpetually in power because most Japanese remained in favor of being in the Western camp. This factor notwithstanding, for the reasons already pointed out, the JSP could still maintain the support of about one-third of the people in Japan because the Socialists, while under the influence of Marxism-Leninism, were able best to represent category 4 by remaining an open organization, unlike that of the Communists.

The 1955 Regime was in a way a reflection of Japanese domestic politics in the international East-West confrontation. It must have been due to a set of similar circumstances that in Italy (vanquished in World War II and, like Japan, occupying an important strategic position, but not in the forefront of the Cold War confrontation), the Communist Party, while subscribing to Marxism-Leninism in the postwar world, maintained a position more flexible than its counterparts in most other countries and became the largest opposition party in Italy. This situation gave life to a sustained series of middle-of-the-road coalition governments between the Christian Democratic Party (DC) as the anchor and various other splinter groups, sometimes leaning toward the right-wing and sometimes toward the left-wing groups. The principal difference between Italy and Japan, however, was that in Italy anticommunist political groupings continued to suffer from a much more pronounced tendency to fragment into splinter parties than in Japan. This made it impossible for them to form a unified party like Japan's LDP and left them on rather precarious organizational footings.

The mediating institutions of normative conflicts also underwent major changes as a result of World War II. Of the three major institutions that played an especially important role in mediating normative conflicts in prewar days, in the postwar era both nationalism (aligned with patriotism to the state) and traditional communities lost their power of influence. The popular sense of belonging to the uniquely different cultural and political entity called Japan, however, has been kept intact and remained stubbornly viable throughout the postwar decades, and in fact to this day, as a result of Japan's long history and social homogeneity. But the populace's sense of loyalty to the state was largely destroyed because of excessive wartime emphasis on the "self-sacrificing devotion to the state interest." The Japan Teachers' Union, which provides a strong power base for the JSP, remained strongly opposed until quite recently to the singing of the national anthem and the hoisting of the national flag even in such institutions as the nation's elementary and middle schools. Since neither the anthem nor the flag was changed after Japan's defeat, these symbols of the state became the objects for those who take positions of category 4, which evoked the memories of Japan's wartime aggressions abroad and suppressions at home. In this sense, in the postwar period the concept of Japan as a nation was effectively severed from the concept of Japan as a state. Moreover, these two concepts came to be interpreted often as mutually confrontational.

The following example illustrates the conflict that exists between these two concepts. Upon receiving the Nobel Prize in literature, Kenzaburo Oe, one of the intellectuals who represent category 4, was quoted as saying, "This honor means that the high level of modern Japanese literature has finally been given worldwide recognition." This statement reflects Oe's strong personal sense of belonging to Japan. But at the same time, the same author refused to be decorated when offered an order of cultural achievement by the Japanese government on the ground that "as a believer in Japan's postwar democracy, [I] cannot possibly accept such honor conferred upon me by the Japanese government." Oe's statements are an eloquent example in postwar Japan of a viewpoint in which the nation is severed from and confronted by the state, subscribed to by those in category 4. Thus, nationalism and patriotism became weakened to a serious extent in the postwar period, becoming almost synonymous with the reactionaries in category 2 and clearly no longer capable of mediating the new normative conflicts.

Postwar reforms and the subsequent economic development continued to work as forceful agents for the dissolution of traditional communities. The Occupation authorities' agrarian reform abolished the landlord system, and as a result of redistribution of the appropriated land among the tenant farmers who actually worked the farms, major structural change occurred in the rural community. In addition, rapid sustained growth of the Japanese economy, which began in the 1950s, caused the rural population (especially its younger segment) to migrate in large numbers to urban centers. Whereas the rural population at the end of the war accounted for nearly 50 percent of the total population, it dropped to a meager 10 percent toward the end of the 1960s. Moreover, the rapid progress of motorization enabled a considerable number of the remaining rural residents to give up farming and commute to new workplaces in nearby cities. As a result of these factors, the rural communities have lost much of their traditional function of mutual assistance.

The family system also underwent a major change because of revisions of the civil code and the resulting change in the popular perception of family life it caused as well as because of a rapid population shift spurred by the sustained high economic growth. The preceding illustrates this change. As mentioned earlier, the 1953 opinion poll question, "If you could not have a child, would you want to adopt someone unrelated to you by blood to assure the continuity of *ie*?" resulted in three-quarters of respondents saying "Yes" and a scant 16 percent saying "No." By the end of the 1960s, however, in response to the same question, answers were split 43 percent in the affirmative and 41 percent in the negative. By the early 1980s, 27 percent of those polled answered in the affirmative and more than 50 percent responded negatively.[9] In short, more and more Japanese are inclined to think that one who is childless should not feel obliged to adopt a child to assure continuity of *ie*. This response is in effect a denial of the family system under which the continuity of *ie* was considered most essential.

Of all the institutions that played some significant role in mediating normative conflicts in the prewar period, the only one that not only survived the postwar decades but actually expanded its mediative function is the "Japanese way of corporate governance," or as it is more simply called, "Japanese management." The war's defeat and the postwar reforms inflicted serious injuries upon traditional authority. The Occupation authorities gave positive support to the organization and development of labor unions in postwar Japan.

The rising influence of Marxism-Leninism tended to radicalize the labor movement in the years immediately following the war, forcing labor-management relations to hang in a tense and delicate balance. But as the postwar chaos subsided and Occupation policies were revised by the successive governments representing the positions of category 2 in Figure 10.3, and Japan's economy entered the period of sustained high growth, the Japanese management system as we know it today became a widely established practice. This system was built on three pillars: lifelong employment, wage raise and promotion by seniority, and labor unions that had a strong sense of belonging and loyalty to the enterprise.

It is a phenomenon of profound significance that the labor unions, fostered by the American model by the Occupation authorities, finally yielded a new form of organization called "enterprise unionism," under which the strengthening of the rights of workers have, rather unexpectedly, resulted in the fortification and intensification of their sense of belonging to the companies for which they work. High economic growth, which brought about a labor shortage in Japan, resulted in the improvement of management's attitude toward workers rather than a heightening of the fluidity of the labor market. The improvement in the attitude of management reinforced the institutionalization of the lifelong employment practice. As a result, the Japanese style of corporate governance has expanded its role as a mediating institution of normative conflicts to a still greater extent in postwar Japan.

It should be noted that such employment practices are also compatible with the temperament and values of most Japanese. In this context, there is a very interesting opinion survey that implicitly reaffirms this fact, as follows:

> QUESTION: There are two section managers described below. If you are to choose between them as your superior, which one of the two do you prefer?
> 1. Manager A seldom forces you to do things outside your normally expected job responsibilities, but does not pay much attention to your personal problems, which are unrelated to the workplace.
> 2. Manager B orders you from time to time to do things outside your normally expected job responsibilities, but he (or she) also pays a lot of attention to your personal problems even if they may be unrelated to the workplace.

The distribution of responses to this survey question have never changed, ever since it was instituted in 1953 (including the latest poll, taken in 1993): The proportion of respondents who chose Manager B has always amounted to some 80 percent. This percentage has remained steady irrespective of personal factors such as age, sex, educational attainments, job, or position.[10] These results illustrate that the Japanese management system is fully compatible with Japanese workers, who clearly prefer such a relationship with their superiors in the workplace.

There still are other important mediating institutions in postwar Japan. Among them are the income redistribution mechanism based on the sustained high economic growth, the formation of a de facto cooperative working relationship between the ruling party and the opposition under the 1955 Regime, and the proliferation of new religious organizations that placed the guarantee of the temporal world's benefits at the center of their religious teachings.

As one would expect, economic growth does not take place at the same speed in all sectors of the economy. Therefore, if economic growth is left entirely to the dictates of market forces, it is bound to produce an increasingly unequal pattern of income distribution, threatening the stability of the society if unchecked. Both government's income redistribution policy and the wage negotiations between management and labor are aimed at preventing such an eventuality.

In the case of Japan, after the beginning of the high economic growth of the 1950s and 1960s, income redistribution policy and wage negotiations between management and labor were deployed with close mutual coordination. In addition to the establishment of the 1955 Regime, a new wage negotiating regime was developed and implemented, the scope of which went beyond individual industrial sectors. (This came to be known as the "spring offensive" as the negotiations were held annually in or around April, at the start of Japan's fiscal year.) As a result of this uniform wage negotiation, the ratio of wage raise was allowed to maintain a uniform level across most industrial sectors, despite the varying levels of profitability of individual sectors and enterprises. In addition, the wages paid to government employees as well as the public utilities rates under governmental jurisdiction were also allowed to rise in accordance with the results of the annual spring offensive, contributing to the betterment of the income of those who worked in these sectors as well. In particular, subsidies and preferential tax treatments were liberally awarded to farmers and small businesses, often motivated by election strategy. Largely because of the combined income redistribution mechanism, Japan managed to keep the inequities of real income distribution to a minimum, despite the widespread practice of the Japanese management system and the accompanying lack of fluidity of the labor market. This income redistribution mechanism, however, depended on the sustained rapid growth of the Japanese economy and the viability of the progressive taxation system. Therefore, if these assumptions abruptly changed, the continuation of the mechanism was destined to run into serious difficulties.

As already pointed out, the 1955 Regime was the political consequence of the normative conflicts in postwar Japan. Under this system power could not possibly change to another party, and if the governing party and the opposition had continued to confront each other over political principles, such a party system could only have aggravated the normative conflicts rather than mediating them. But just as the Christian Democratic Union/Christian Social Union and the Social Democratic Party formed the Great Coalition in West Germany, and the Christian Democrats and the Communist Party launched the Historical Compromise in Italy, with the exception of the Japan Communist Party, the LDP and the opposition parties (especially the JSP, the largest opposition party), gradually formed a framework of compromise and cooperation despite their surface confrontation. This de facto working relationship was possible because the LDP, which monopolized power, was willing to maintain a flexible position to accommodate the demands of the opposition as much as possible. For their part, the opposition opted for gaining concessions for their constituents through negotiations with the LDP. Such a relationship was functionally similar to that of the labor unions' wage negotiations at the time of their spring offensive.

Thus, through such functional transformation, the 1955 Regime turned itself into an institution for mediating normative conflicts. It was possible to construct a framework for de facto cooperation between the government party and the opposition because despite their ideological and policy differences, tacit but broad agreement existed between them to give domestic economic growth utmost priority and to keep Japan's military responsibilities to the minimum level by maintaining a low posture toward the outside world. The existence of such an agreement, along with the high level of homogeneity of Japanese society, played a significant role in preventing the further aggravation of normative conflicts. On the basis of his analysis of various opinion surveys, Chikio Hayashi, a well-respected statistician, pointed out: "In Japanese society, decisionmaking by a majority vote is always felt to be overtly confrontational, and as such, is not considered viable as a means for productive decisionmaking. The Japanese people tend to think that attaching a considerable importance to *wa* (harmony) and *chuyo* (middle-of-the-road position) and selecting workable compromises are the style [of decisionmaking] most likely to contribute to meaningful development. Nothing will make life more unsettling for the Japanese than living in a world in which the majority vote will determine everything they do or do not do."[11] Japan's polity is nonmajoritarian, and it is extremely important for the stable management of political affairs to pay serious attention to minority opinions.[12] The 1955 Regime, which was dominated by a stable LDP majority but was also ready to incorporate the demands of the opposition parties such as the JSP as much as possible, was a fitting arrangement compatible with these values peculiar to Japanese society, and for this very reason, the LDP government lasted over an extended period of time despite the severe surface confrontations with the opposition, and this method of decisionmaking functioned well as a mediating instrument for normative conflicts.

However, there was a significant change in the structure of political confrontation under the 1955 Regime after the latter half of the 1960s. First, in the several years following the restoration of Japan's independence in 1952, that part of the postwar reforms that did not at all fit the actual conditions in Japan was largely corrected, and as a result, the fundamental direction of the postwar reforms striving to achieve democracy and pacifism came to be accepted by an overwhelming majority of the Japanese people, rendering the confrontational issues surrounding the postwar reforms practically meaningless by the early 1960s. Secondly, as a result of Japan's economic development, sustained at a high growth rate and with the resultant distribution of income on an increasingly equitable basis, the Japanese living standard as a whole showed a marked improvement during the same period, while the issue of environmental destruction posed a new threat to the Japanese quality of life by the mid-1960s. It was also true that by then the level of popular expectations had risen to a new high, and a strong demand arose for the improvement of

	Alliance with the U.S.	Unarmed Neutrality
Economic Growth Oriented	(2) Conservatives	(1) Liberals
Environment and Welfare Oriented	(3) Conservatives	(4) Liberals and Radicals

FIGURE 10.4   Normative conflict under the 1955 Regime

the social welfare systems such as medical care and retirement pensions. But as long as the Cold War confrontations continued, the old scheme of things had to persist, centering on the confrontation between the realist group in support of the U.S.-Japan alliance with respect to national security policy and the idealist group insisting on unarmed neutrality. Thus, under the 1955 Regime the relationship among these divergent groups shifted to a new pattern, shown in Figure 10.4.

Here, hardly anyone took up the category 1 position. Liberals by definition would be more seriously concerned with the strengthening of environmental protection and social welfare rather than economic growth. Also, the LDP, nonmajoritarian by nature with enough flexibility to incorporate the opposition's demands into its own policy platforms, was quick to respond to the tasks whenever there was a rising popular demand for specific environmental and welfare measures. While the opposition placed a one-sided emphasis on environmental protection and improvement of social welfare, the LDP attempted to strike up a balance between these and economic growth. As a result, the Environment Agency was established in 1972, a variety of environmental protection measures were adopted, and in 1973 an extensive improvement program of the existing welfare system was launched. It was thus no surprise that the flexible LDP government continued to boast its extraordinary staying power. Further, as a result of its alliance with the United States, Japan was able to enjoy an assured security at a relatively low cost, thus making it possible for the LDP government to enjoy a far greater popular support for its security policy than the opposition's.

The Japanese management system came to be widely practiced in postwar Japan, but not all of the Japanese workers were recipients of its benefits and protection. In the process of the high economic growth, among the people who kept moving to urban centers, some could not come under the umbrella of such corporate protection, especially among the employees of smaller firms. In particular, female workers were often kept outside the corporate protective shield. In addition, in the rural village communities, the relatively older generations were left behind as wave after wave of youngsters left their rural homes to seek jobs in urban areas.

The new religions, different from the traditional religious institutions such as temples, shrines, and sect organizations, played a remarkable role in providing these "lonely souls" with a sense of personal satisfaction and solidarity among themselves. In fact, a large number of new religions have sprouted in Japan, in the immediate postwar period, through the ensuing period of chaos, and on into the early stages of the sustained high economic growth. The number of incorporated religious organizations in 1947 was 3,000, but by 1960 it jumped to a whopping 180,000.[13] That so many of these newly organized religious sects placed at the center of their teachings the idea of salvation by faith from such worldly sufferings as poverty and disease reveals the social role these new religions were to perform in postwar Japan.[14]

Conclusions: Japan's Transformation into an Economic Giant and Its Future Perspective

By the end of the 1970s, a quarter of a century after Japan's defeat in World War II, Japanese society had undergone a major transformation. Along with this change, normative conflicts too had undergone a fundamental shift from those of the immediate postwar period. First, as already pointed out, the problems attendant to the postwar reforms were corrected by piecemeal governmental actions through the 1950s, and a Japanized version of liberal democracy gradually became established—and thus the old confrontation surrounding the issue of the postwar reforms lost its original meaning. The fact that the hotly contested issues of the 1950s such as the constitutional amendment had ceased to be political issues by the end of the 1960s is a clear indication of the transformation that had taken place in the interim. Similarly, as a consequence of this transition, the 1955 Regime became firmly established, and the government party and the opposition entered into a period of de facto compromise and cooperation, despite their outward look of confrontation. Also pointing to the shift to a new confrontational issue was the emergence in the 1960s of the so-called middle-of-the-road parties that claimed their positions to be between the Socialists and the Communists, who fell into category 4 of Figure 10.4, and the Liberal Democrats, whose conservative stance is represented in categories 2 and 3.

Second, as a result of sustained economic growth, Japan became one of the world's major economic powers by the 1970s. In particular, after adroitly overcoming the impact of the oil crises, Japan ascended to the position of the world's largest creditor nation with the largest trade surplus. This shift in Japan's status in the international community has given rise to a new sense of self-confidence and an awareness among the people of Japan of the need to play a greater international role. A reputable public opinion poll posed the question: "Do you think Japanese are superior to Westerners?" In 1953 only 20 percent thought so, with some 30 percent responding "inferior," and 14 percent saying "similar." But thirty years later in the 1983 poll, some 52 percent said "superior," 8 percent said "inferior," and 12 percent said "similar." This very high level of self-confidence, almost bordering on arrogance, came to be somewhat moderated in the 1980s as Japan's "bubble" economy collapsed. In the 1993 survey, the proportion of those who chose "superior" dropped to 41 percent, and those who chose "similar" increased to 27 percent. The number of those who replied "inferior," however, again decreased, to an all-time low of 6 percent.[15] This result indicates that while the excessive self-confidence might well be trimmed further, the sense of inferiority commonly held by Japanese since the nineteenth century no longer has any chance for revival. On the other hand, it cannot be denied that such self-confidence, whatever the source from which it springs, has nurtured an awareness among the Japanese people that they should play an international role commensurate with the country's economic capability.

The termination of the Cold War and the experience during the Gulf War in particular have had a significant impact on the Japanese people, creating a higher level of interest in playing a new and more positive international role. But whether Japan's role should be limited to nonmilitary areas or expanded to include a military role still remains sharply contentious. In this sense, the old confrontation of pacifism (unarmed neutrality) versus political realism (alliance with the United States) of the postwar period still lingers, though in the changed context of today. While calls are publicly being issued today to amend Article 9 of the constitution (such a topic was long a virtual taboo) there remains stubborn opposition to such an amendment. This opposition clearly indicates that there is still a lack of national consensus on this issue in Japan.

The end of the Cold War and the collapse of the Soviet Union have, quite ironically, helped to resolve this old issue of confrontation as a result of the spread of popular support in Japan for the U.S.-Japan alliance, with the exception only of the Communist Party. The passive reason that wider support arose for the U.S.-Japan alliance when the clear and ever-present common threat of the Soviet Union disappeared, of course, is that there was no longer any fear of Japan's getting dragged into a war with the Soviets as a result of alliance with the United States, and thus no justification remained for demanding a policy of unarmed neutrality. But the more positive reason is that there remained the flash points with high tensions in East Asia, such as the Korean Peninsula and the Taiwan Straits, and moreover, there still were countries like China and North Korea, which possess nuclear weapons, or the will to develop them, and are not entirely friendly toward Japan. The fact that the JSP has made a 180-degree policy shift on the matter of national security and took up a position not fundamentally different from that of the LDP and on that basis went so far as to form a coalition government with the LDP—toward which it had maintained a sharp confrontational posture in the past, if only on the surface—meant that the useful life of the 1955 Regime had obviously expired. At the time of the 1993 general election, the LDP lost the Diet majority, and therefore the power, not because it was defeated at the polls but because it had suffered from a major party split just before the election. The reason that such action was actually launched was that the LDP splinter group knew that the JSP's security policy shift was already quite predictable and it could regain power by allying with the still powerful JSP and other minor parties. In fact, after the 1993 general election, a non-LDP coalition government was formed centering on the splinter LDP group joined by other minority parties.

Thus, the political confrontation over the issue of Japan's alliance with the United States had been finally resolved, but the security policy itself remains a divisive issue because there still are divergent views and positions on the specifics, such as what Japan ought to be doing in order to maintain the U.S.-Japan alliance given the greatly altered international environment.

Japan's economic success has also nurtured an attitude critical of placing foremost priority on economic growth. As already noted, this attitude has manifested itself in the form of popular concern over environmental destruction that occurred as a result of economic growth. Popular interest in environmental protection has continued to rise since the end of the 1960s. This new trend has been clearly observed in a number of public opinion polls that have consistently confirmed an accelerating decline of acceptance for the idea that "we must conquer nature to build a happier future"—a phrase that had enjoyed growing popular support in the preceding decades.[16] Also during the 1970s and 1980s, such qualities of life as *yutori* (room for relaxation) and *uruoi* (gracefulness) came to be accepted as desirable aspects of the new lifestyle. Furthermore, while the new religions that arose during the 1950s and 1960s placed their main emphasis on helping their followers overcome temporal sufferings such as poverty and disease, the religious activities of their counterparts of the 1970s and 1980s shifted their focus to the overcoming of the individual's sense of helplessness and boredom by giving a new "meaning" to life.

The collapse of the 1955 Regime mirrored the nation's political system at a time in which the principal postwar normative conflicts had become increasingly ambiguous. And the breakdown of the 1955 Regime also signaled the fact that the two basic consensuses that supported the regime,

	Positive Attitude Toward Playing International Role	Negative Attitude Toward Playing International Role
Overcoming Pacifism	(2) Neo-Conservatives	(1) Old Conservatives
Adhering to Pacifism	(3) Neo-Liberals	(4) Old Radicals

FIGURE 10.5   Normative conflict since the 1980s: Pacifism

	Positive Attitude Toward Playing International Role	Negative Attitude Toward Playing International Role
Positive About Economic Growth	(2) Neo-Conservatives	(1) Old Conservatives
Negative About Economic Growth	(3) Neo-Liberals	(4) Neo-Radicals

FIGURE 10.6   Normative conflict since the 1980s: Economic growth

that is, the minimum possible commitment to playing international roles and the predominant emphasis on economic growth, were irreparably lost. As a result, by the 1980s the dominant normative conflicts had shifted to the patterns shown in Figures 10.5 and 10.6. The primary substance at play in both figures is the confrontation related to Japan's international role. Figure 10.5 focuses on the confrontation surrounding the issue of pacifism, and Figure 10.6 centers on the attitudinal differences toward economic growth.

In both Figures 10.5 and 10.6 the influence of categories 1 and 4 is expected to lose its historical usefulness in the near future: At present, as we are moving inexorably toward a multipolar world in the post–Cold War era, it has become all too obvious that Japan's long-term national interest will be poorly served if the country, as an economic giant, continues to take a passive attitude in the international community as it did in the immediate postwar years. Also, with respect to Figure 10.6, a negative attitude toward economic growth will be quite unlikely to strengthen itself in the foreseeable future. Such an attitude (which became quite noticeable during the 1980s) was predicated upon the assumption that continued economic growth was a self-evident fact, or upon the assumption that without further growth, the Japanese people could still enjoy a comfortable life. In the 1990s, however, as Japan sank into the depth of its most serious and prolonged postwar recession and has been challenged by revitalized U.S. as well as other rapidly developing Asian economies, such a negativist assertion has begun to run out of steam. It is true that popular concern over environmental problems will not disappear from the scene. Adequate environmental conservation, however, requires the development of new technologies. Technological development in turn demands adequate R&D funding from the fruits of economic growth. In this context, even the staunchest environmentalists cannot mount a frontal attack on economic development. Also, the shift of personal attention from economic growth to the quality of life can become possible only when there is a material guarantee of daily life, without the fear of unemployment. However, as the bubble economy busted, Japan's unemployment rate began climbing in the early years of the 1990s. True to the tradition of Japanese management, companies in Japan remain unwilling to resort to personnel cuts in restructuring their businesses, and as a result, the unemployment rate still remains rather low in comparison with those in Western Europe. But it is also true that more and more people in Japan are becoming aware that their job security is being exposed to a growing threat.

Thus, it is quite understandable that most Japanese have been tending toward the neoconservatism of category 2 in Figures 10.5 and 10.6 since the beginning of the 1990s. Such a trend, however, does not presuppose the disappearance of normative conflicts in tomorrow's Japan. On the contrary, as a result of the collapse of the broad social consensus that existed until the 1960s, the chaotic situation with respect to personal values is certainly worsening. People will continue to live in different ways in pursuit of new meanings of life, but such a quest is unlikely in the near future to produce any set of clearly defined and mutually distinct normative orientations emerging from a state of confrontational coexistence.

Intimately related to this situation is that of mediating institutions that played important roles during the postwar period: The 1955 Regime has already collapsed, and the income redistribution mechanism has become incapable of performing the same function it used to play, because of the prolonged recession and the ensuing fiscal crisis. The Japanese management system remains viable, however, and is contributing to the lowering of Japan's unemployment. Nevertheless, the system will obviously face a crisis when its existence is threatened by both the continual rise in Japan's overseas direct investment (which is prompting the loss of job opportunities in Japan) as well as by the increasingly rampant downsizing and restructuring of Japanese businesses that is becoming commonplace as international competition intensifies and the recession continues.

In fact, even among Japanese business leaders, there is growing doubt about the viability of the Japanese management system. If and when the postwar normative conflicts become ambiguous, the institutions that formerly mediated them are destined to fall apart and disappear.

There are some noteworthy phenomena emerging in Japan during the latter half of the 1990s with respect to normative conflict. Generally speaking, there is a growing trend of exploring one's identity, both in collective and individual terms. The quest for a collective identity manifests itself most clearly in the attempt to identify the meaning of Japanese nationality in the collective sense. As a result of the defeat in World War II, Japan suffered a serious injury to its pride as a nation, resulting in an injured sense of nationalism. For a long time Japan had the problem—of profound latent importance—of how to define its new national identity, but until quite recently it had remained largely submerged under the more concrete and pressing normative conflicts. By the end of the 1980s, as the hitherto important normative conflicts ceased to have real meaning, this more fundamental issue had came to the surface.

The Democratic Party of Japan (DPJ), formed just before the 1996 general election by a group of dissidents with a considerable number of former JSP members at the center who fought rather well in the election, has become the third largest party. This party, quite interestingly, consciously refuses to use the word *kokumin,* or the people of the country, and uses instead the expression *shimin,* or the citizens. According to the party leaders, this is because *shimin,* as used in such expressions as "world citizens," is more expansive in usage, going beyond national boundary, whereas the expression *kokumin* is narrowly bound up within territorial limits and nationality. In this case, the party is looking for a collective identity in a cosmopolitanism that will take its members beyond their national boundary and nationality. As economic globalization progresses, it is obviously whittling down the roles once considered the prerogatives of the sovereign nation-state, but it is nevertheless true that sovereign states will continue to play the principal role in international relations for the foreseeable future. Therefore, it can be said that there is no possibility in the near future for the stance of seeking the nation's collective identity in cosmopolitanism to become a dominant trend in Japan. But at the same time, the fact that a political party with such a platform should come to acquire a significant number of seats in the Diet is proof enough to show that Japan has entered a new stage in its quest for a new collective identity. The fact that how properly to interpret Japan's own history from the nineteenth century to World War II, especially how to describe it in the history textbooks, has become a hotly debated issue in Japan is yet another indication of the advent of a new normative conflict over the issue of where to discover a new national identity.

The effort to seek individual identity has been most prominently manifested in the rise of new religious movements. As noted earlier, the first phase of new religions, arising in the postwar era prior to the 1960s, concentrated on preaching gospels of freedom from poverty and sickness targeted at those who had lost their secure stations in life as a result of the postwar turmoil and the social upheavals of economic growth. But the "neo–new religions" that have grown during and after the 1980s must be separated from these new religions by their obvious difference—their emphasis on teaching the meaning of life to those who are suffering from personal loneliness and spiritual void.[17] Among these neo–new religions are some radical sects, such as is the case with the Aum Shinrikyo (Supreme Truth), which wishes to destroy the existing political system by force in order to build the "Ideal Society" on the basis of its own faith.[18] Nevertheless, there are a few instances in which the neo–new religions function as agents for mediating normative conflicts arising from the quest for individual identity. At this point, however, it remains an unresolved problem whether or not the normative conflicts surrounding the issues of collective identity or individual identity will ever be mediated, and if so, in what way and by what means and in what forms.

Notes

1. R. P. Dore, *Education in Tokugawa* (London, 1965), chapter 10.

2. This is an expression in Baelz's diary, which was partially published in German under the title *Das Leben eines deutschen Arztes im erwachende Japan* (Stuttgart, 1931), but due to obvious abridgments, the quotation here is derived from the Japanese translation of the entire text. Toku Baelz, ed., *Baelz no Nikki* [Dr. Baelz's diary], vol. 1 (Tokyo, 1979), pp. 45–46.

3. Tokei Suri Kenkyujo (Institute of Statistical Research), ed., *Nihonjin no Kokuminsei* [Japanese national character], vol. 5 (Tokyo, 1992), p. 104.

4. Francis Fukuyama, *Trust: The Social Virtues and the Creation of Prosperity* (New York, 1995), chapter 8.

5. Of the Axis members, Italy had joined the Allied nations before Germany and Japan had surrendered, and in this sense it finds itself in a somewhat different position, able to call itself a member of the Allied nations.

6. Seizaburo Sato, "Amerikanizumu to ajiashugi [Americanism vs. Asianism in today's Japan]," *Hatsugensha* [Monthly Speak-Out Magazine], no. 9, p. 24.

7. Cf. The Potsdam Declaration (July 26, 1945).

8. Mamoru Sasaki, *Sakaki Mamoru Shinario Shu* [Selected scenarios] (Tokyo, 1984), p. 5.

9. Tokei Suri Kenkyujo, ed., op. cit., p. 104.

10. Ibid., pp. 113–115. Also see Chikio Hayashi, *Suji karamita Nihonjin no Kokoro* [Statistical analysis of Japanese attitudes] (Tokyo, 1995).

11. Chikio Hayashi, op. cit., pp. 216–218.

12. Peter J. Katzenstein, *Cultural Norms and National Security: Police and Military in Postwar Japan* (Ithaca and London, 1996), p. 16.

13. Monbusho (Ministry of Education, Science, Culture, and Sport), ed., *Shukyo Nenkan* [Annals of religious organizations], 1948 and 1961.

14. Cf. Kenya Numata, *Gendai Nihon no Shinshukyo* [New religions in modern Japan] (Tokyo, 1988).

15. Tokei Suri Kenkyujo, ed., op. cit., pp. 183–184; Chikio Hayashi, op. cit., pp. 91–94.

16. Tokei Suri Kenkyujo, op. cit., pp. 75–76; Chikio Hayashi, op. cit., pp. 163–164.

17. On the transition from new religion to neo–new religion, refer to Susumu Shimazono's *Shin Shin Shukyo to Shukyo Buum* [Neo–new religions and a new tide of religious activities] (Tokyo, 1992).

18. With respect to the teachings and movement of the Aum Shinrikyo, refer to Masachi Osawa's *Kyoko no Jidai no Hate* [At the end of the Fictitious Age] (Tokyo, 1996).

11

Normative Conflicts in Contemporary Taiwan

Hsin-Huang Michael Hsiao

Introduction

This chapter addresses the two most salient normative conflicts and the prospect of mediation in contemporary Taiwanese society, namely, the controversy over national identity and the conflict between growth and environmental quality. It is not suggested that it is only in these two arenas that Taiwanese society has been experiencing collective value contradictions. As in many other modern societies undergoing political transformations, Taiwan has witnessed an array of emerging views, public debates, and discourses concerning the "redefinition" of the normative character of Taiwanese society's present and future.

In contrast to other sorts of conflicts—those caused by divergent class interests, political aspirations, or ethnic animosities—normative conflicts entail controversies and differences concerning the normative character of the society as a whole. Though frequently associated with the aforementioned social cleavages, conflicts derived from "normative" cleavages have distinctive features. In this chapter, normative conflicts in Taiwan are identified by the following criteria: (1) they should concern the normative definition of Taiwanese society as a whole; (2) they should entail the reorientation of the collective perception and meaning of the past and vision of the future for Taiwan; (3) there should be identifiable competing groups or institutions that aggravate or mobilize the conflicting public discourse or political agenda; and (4) there should be room for mediation, negotiation, and even possible resolution that can be found in the civil society or political institutions. In other words, I will attempt in this chapter, in the course of a sociological exposition of normative conflicts in Taiwan, to shed light on the sociological understanding of mediation in conflicts (cf. Collins 1975; Bornschier and Lengyel 1994; Hunter 1991, 1994).

The contexts within which the conflicts over national identity and the environment along with other less salient normative conflicts have emerged and intensified have their origins in the three great sociopolitical transformations: the class transformation and the rise of the middle classes; the emergence of social movements and the resurrection of civil society; and political democratization. In other words, Taiwanese society's normative conflicts were virtually induced by and resulted from the changing state-society relations since the 1980s. Under these unprecedented changes, the state can no longer monopolize the power to define the normative character of Taiwanese society. In the early 1980s the authoritarian Kuomintang (KMT) state faced challenges from organized political oppositions and middle-class-led social movements for liberalization. The middle-class-led social movements for consumers' rights, gender equality, and the environment in Taiwan's initial phase of liberalization played an instrumental role in undermining authoritarian rule and opened a political space and opportunity for other social groups in civil society to mobilize themselves further. The social-psychological impact was tremendous at the time, as the voice of civil society was finally heard and their demands were taken seriously without political repression. For the first time, social forces had exerted pressure on the state in defining and setting new priorities for Taiwan after two decades of capitalist development.

The formation of a quasi–party organization and then the creation in 1986 of Taiwan's first opposition party, the Democratic Progressive Party (DPP), accelerated the pressure on the authoritarian state to respond along a liberalization path in order to regain its political legitimacy. The option to liberalize chosen by the state ruling elites in resolving the social and political contestation had been made feasible largely by the persuading and mediating capability of the new middle-class professionals and liberal intellectuals. The strategy of the middle-class-initiated social reform movements was formulated in a more-or-less depoliticized fashion in order to avoid drawing immediate repressive action from the state, and the reformers made clear to the state that they sought social reforms and not political power. Such collective sentiment for change was interpreted by the state as a challenge from the rising middle class to its legitimacy, and concessions seemed to be inevitable if the state were to regain middle-class support.

On the other hand, the liberal intellectuals played a critical mediating role in convincing the KMT state to agree to open political dialogues with the new opposition party. This reconciliation move on the part of the state was welcomed by many in the middle classes, since a potential political crisis was thus avoided, and it also prepared the necessary ground for the official lifting of martial law in July 1987. The lifting of martial law represented a watershed in Taiwan's political liberalization and set the stage for the subsequent democratic transition.

In short, via various reform-oriented organized movements, the new middle-class intellectuals and professionals exercised a persuasive influence on the state, leading it to opt for political relaxation and policy changes in what turned out to be the opening stages of political liberalization and democratization. They also successfully mediated between the authoritarian state and the rising political opposition so as to avoid a political crackdown that would otherwise have postponed Taiwan's democratization process.

As it entered the democratic transition phase, civil society was further mobilized by numerous other social movement organizations and pro-democracy actions led by alliances of students, university professors, liberal journalists, and legal professionals. By the early 1990s Taiwanese civil society had already witnessed the following social movements in continuing its momentum for transforming the nature and conduct of the KMT state: consumers' movement (1980–), antipollution movement (1980–), nature conservation movement (1982–), women's movement (1982–), aborigines' rights movement (1983–), students' movement (1986–), the New Testament church protest (1986–1990), labor movement (1987–), farmers' movement (1987–), teachers' movement (1987–), the handicapped and disadvantaged group welfare movement (1987–), the veterans' welfare movement (1987–1990), the political prisoners' human rights movement (1987–1992), the Mainlanders' home visiting movement (1987–1989), the Taiwanese home-returning movement (1988–1992), the anti–nuclear power movement (1988–), the Hakka culture movement (1988–), the non-homeowners' housing movement (1989–), the judiciary reform movement (1990–), and the independent mass media movement (1993–). Excepting those five social movements that have already ceased to operate either because their immediate objectives were accomplished or because their causes were absorbed by the state's responding policies, fifteen social movements are still in existence, comprising numerous civil-society organizations working toward their unfinished goals (Hsiao 1994a).

The mobilized Taiwanese civil society expressed in the twenty social movements since the 1980s has continuously competed with the democratizing state in defining and redefining the norms, values, and goals for both state and society to pursue in Taiwan's current and future development. It is clear that almost all of these social movements have taken the state as the primary target to press their respective demands for "desirable" social and political changes. Though specific adversaries in addition to the state are also identified by different social movements, the state is nevertheless considered to be the most powerful actor, and it is only through necessary change in the state's social and political agenda that new social priorities and goals can be legitimated and achieved. Emerging from the organized social movements' painstaking efforts of engaging in demonstration, protests, public dialogues, and debates, new notions such as human rights, gender equity, cultural survival, welfare, environmental quality, and sustainable development have steadily gained social support from different sectors in civil society. Accompanied by the achievements in shifting and redirecting societal thinking on alternative values and goals, some controversies have also been intensified over the years. Conflicts over the construction of national identity, the applicability and scope of the notion of human rights, the controversy of expanded versus restrained social welfare, feminism and gender equality, cleavages between the construction of national culture and the preservation of minority identity, and finally, continued growth versus the natural environment, are all emerging areas of serious concerns.

What underlies these conflicts is the normative nature of the discourse of adversaries. They do not originate simply in tangible interest conflicts. Among the emerging normative conflicts just listed, the controversy of environment versus growth is the most organized. On the social movement side, three distinct movements have been organized since the 1980s for environment-related causes—the antipollution movement, the nature conservation movement, and the anti–nuclear power movement—and they can be considered the three streams of contemporary Taiwan's environmental movement. Each has its own normative and practical agenda, and they have different social bases and separate leadership circles. What they share is the common normative concern for the environment in terms of the quality of life and future development in Taiwan. Given its magnitude and intensity, the normative conflict of environment versus growth will be subjected to further analysis later on in this chapter.

It was also in the broader context of political liberalization and democratization that the definition of Taiwan's national identity faced open debate for the first time. Conflicting views concerning Taiwan's identity have long existed in Taiwanese civil society—along ethnic lines between the minority Mainlander-controlled state and the Taiwanese ethnic majority ruled by it as well as between the state and the political opposition and dissidents. During the authoritarian phase of Taiwanese rule, however, such a sensitive issue was not allowed in open question and debate. The issue of the normative character of Taiwan as a national society as well as an autonomous and independent state was never brought into the arena of public discourse. The claim long made by the KMT state that Taiwan is a part of China and that China is legitimately represented by the Republic of China (ROC) in Taiwan was finally severely challenged by both external and internal forces.

The People's Republic of China (PRC) on the mainland began to push the drive toward "national unification" in the early 1980s, after having successfully gained international recognition in the early 1970s and aggressively launching its "open-door development policy" in the late 1970s. Under the PRC's national unification scheme, Taiwan is also a part of China—but the Chinese nation is represented only by the PRC state on the mainland and not by the ROC state in Taiwan. Taiwan's identity was thus once again presupposed by another outside state. Naturally the KMT state's previous claim of "one China" was further exploited, this time by the PRC in declaring its sovereignty over Taiwan. Taiwan's identity thus became the focus of conflict between the two rival "Chinese" states. To the ROC state, Taiwan is the only reason for its very existence. Therefore, the KMT was forced to redefine Taiwan's identity vis-à-vis the PRC in order to cope with the latter's aggressive unification pressure. Taiwan was then redefined as a sovereign nation-state rather than a sheer local society, and certainly not a local state of the PRC.

The redefinition within Taiwan of Taiwan's national identity undoubtedly has its roots in the intensified interstate conflict between the two Chinas over Taiwan's sovereignty. How to redefine Taiwan as a sovereign state separate from the PRC and yet without worsening the cross-Strait relations has thus become a primary concern for the KMT state and the opposition parties in Taiwan's political society since the late 1980s. The external pressure from the PRC's unification drive was thus eventually internalized as a source of political conflict over the definition of Taiwan's national identity. The democratization in Taiwan accelerated the competition of power in redefining Taiwan's identity within civil society. Civil society's conflicting discourses on Taiwan's national identity have even gone beyond pragmatic political concerns in resolving the increasing cross-Strait tension and protecting Taiwan's existence and interests; even the history and culture of the past four hundred years in Taiwan was open for reinterpretation along adversary ideological lines. The state, political parties, civil society groups, intellectuals, and the general public all have been, in one way or another, mobilized into the normative conflict of self-definition. Without the democratization and the emergence of civil society, this national identity conflict would not have been developed to such a level of intensity.

The conflict over national identity has been occurring at the national level, whereas the conflict of growth versus environment has by and large taken place in the social arena, often locally. The emergence of both of these normative conflicts was brought about by the changing state-society relations since the 1980s, and their current dynamics and possible resolutions will certainly have even greater implications for the course of the development of the state and of civil society in Taiwan.

The Making of the Normative Conflict over National Identity

Historical Roots and Evolution

The controversy over Taiwan's national identity was an evolving social construction greatly shaped by both internal and external factors. The long-established normative definition of Taiwan made by the occupying KMT regime from the mainland after 1948 was to treat Taiwan as a local society rather than a national society. The purpose of defining Taiwan as a province of the nation of the Republic of China (represented by the KMT state) was to legitimate the KMT's takeover of Taiwan after the war. The notion that China was "one nation," as KMT indoctrination of the Taiwanese people held, did not have real meaning, for two reasons: First, Taiwan was colonized by imperial Japan for fifty years from 1895 to 1945, during which time the Republic was established (in 1911), and therefore the Republic had never ruled Taiwan; second, the Chinese mainland on which the KMT state claimed its legitimacy of rule was occupied by the rival regime of the Chinese Communist Party (CCP) after the war, and the Taiwanese people were of course prohibited from identifying with it. Therefore, between the late 1940s and the early 1980s, Taiwan was left only with "local identity" in real terms, and the "national identity" was either distorted or simply absent.

The majority of the ethnic Taiwanese have long suppressed identifying Taiwan as their "imagined" national community because to do so could carry the political risk of being charged with separatism. Yet the imposed national identity of China also has a catch, for identifying with "China" on the mainland could also lead to the charge of treason. Hence the ethnic Taiwanese have been largely deprived of developing their own national identity, even though Taiwan is the only territory of the ROC over which the KMT state can claim sovereignty. The identity of Taiwan was downgraded to the local and provincial level. On the other hand, the minority of the ethnic Mainlanders who moved to Taiwan with the exiled KMT regime had no difficulties in continuing to identify with the "lost China" as their nation. To them Taiwan was not a complete national community, and no genuine national identity of Taiwan ever developed in the minds of these Mainlander groups until the 1980s.

As a result, prior to political liberalization and democratization in the late 1980s, the issue of Taiwan's national identity was completely denied by the KMT state, and it was not felt by the Mainlander population on the island. But to the ethnic Taiwanese, the imposed image of a Chinese nation versus Taiwanese locality was never easy. They were forced to identify with the Chinese nation that was lost by the KMT before it took over Taiwan. An abstract and symbolic China rather than a real China was constructed and imposed upon Taiwanese minds, but this national identity had no real-world meaning to them. The notion that there is a Chinese nation having only Taiwan as its real national territory but yet the prohibition of identifying Taiwan as a national community has been the very source of conflicts between the Mainlander-KMT state and the Taiwanese political descendants. Obviously the nature of the political conflicts between Taiwanese independent activists and the Mainlander KMT regime was essentially an internal one. Beneath this political struggle were the internal social cleavages along ethnic lines, in which provincial (ethnic) origins were often used by the Mainlander KMT regime as a criterion for political inclusion or exclusion (Chang 1994). A wide range of deliberate policies concerning language, culture, and historical interpretation were also adopted to further institutionalize and jeopardize differences between Mainlanders and Taiwanese (Wachman 1994; Cheng 1994). Prior to political democratization in the late 1980s there were internal ethnic tensions, political conflicts, and the suppressed Taiwanese identity.

The transformation of the KMT state from a predominantly Mainlander-controlled regime from outside through a Mainlander-Taiwanese power-sharing process and then into an indigenous Taiwanese state has had a great impact on the changing nature of the social conflicts in Taiwan's civil society. The original form of ethnic conflicts between the ruling Mainlanders and the ruled Taiwanese was gradually replaced by the emerging democratic struggles between the indigenized state and Taiwanese civil society at large. The suppressed Taiwanese consciousness was liberalized, and the localized Taiwanese identity was upgraded to the national level. The mythified image of Taiwan as an inseparable part of "China" was therefore repudiated and challenged by many Taiwanese and even some among the younger generations of Taiwan-born Mainlanders. The democratization process further helped to foster the normative nature of the competing perceptions and definitions of Taiwanese national identity. In essence, the normative conflicts of national identity after political democratization can be vividly characterized as the conflicts deriving from the process of consensus building concerning Taiwan's new national identity.

Since the early 1970s Taiwan under the imposed image of the ROC began to experience challenges to its "national identity" from the international community. The legitimate status of the KMT state in Taiwan as representing the Chinese nation was questioned by many nations under increasing pressures from the communist state in mainland China. The ROC's severe diplomatic setbacks began in 1971 when its seat at the United Nations was removed in favor of a seat for the PRC, and since then the ROC's legitimate status has diminished in the international political world, while "Taiwan" increased its participation and visibility in the world market. The diplomatic setbacks since 1972 inspired many intellectuals to begin a journey of self-discovery for themselves and for Taiwan as a nation.

The evolution of the development of a prototype of the new national identity for Taiwan can be traced back to the mid-1970s, when several cultural movements were initiated to provoke literature, music, dance, and film with attempts to reflect the realities of postwar Taiwan. The social science community also became more reflective in its research questions and more anxious to make social sciences relevant to Taiwan's social reality. And since the mid-to-late 1970s social realism has established its legitimate status in Taiwan's literature. Taiwanese popular culture received new appreciation and respect, and steps were taken to restore and revitalize them. Popular songs were written to be more reflective of how Taiwanese people live and think. The local Minanese language songs were once again widely received with enthusiasm. New Minanese singers emerged, and their songs were more socially realistic than Mandarin-language songs. Taiwanese reality began to concern many intellectuals, though the national identity issue was not directly and openly posed at the time (Hsiao 1996).

Liberal intellectuals and scholars began to demand political reform, though still on a very limited scale, as a growing sense of "national crisis" brought about an unprecedented collective consciousness, motivated to deal with the problem of survival then facing Taiwan as a nation. Because of external frustration on the diplomatic front and the questioning of national identity posed by international community, serious attention was directed to internal reforms. Though the call for political reform from the intellectuals turned out to be a failure, the cultural movements mentioned earlier served to shape and even to legitimate the growing Taiwanese consciousness. The recognition and construction of Taiwanese reality in the form of Taiwanese consciousness in the 1970s was, in fact, the fertile ground for the development of Taiwanese national identity in the 1980s.

The evolving national identity of Taiwan since the 1980s was no longer targeted to the indigenized KMT state, and it was developed in order to defend Taiwan's very existence from being annexed by the PRC. The indigenized KMT state and Taiwanese civil society were all involved in the reconstruction of Taiwan's own identity, separating it from PRC-ruled China. In this conjuncture, the normative conflicts over Taiwan's national identity can be further characterized as an ongoing construction of the sociopolitical distinction between Taiwan and China.

The Social Base

From this brief historical sketch of the evolution of the conflict over the definition of Taiwan's national identity, it is clear that the normative character of the conflict is indeed a historical construction. The changing nature of the conflict is also evident; it involves the transformation from an internal, ethnicity-based social conflict into a conflict-generating national identity building process induced by external pressures. However, the current status of national identity conflicts is not yet completely free from the legacy of the previous ethnic conflicts that prevailed in the postwar decades. Therefore, ethnic or provincial origins, that is, the Taiwanese and Mainlanders divide, remains a factor in distinguishing the different social bases of the national identity conflict. However, ethnicity can no longer serve as an important social base of internal social conflicts; it has become instead the social foundation of the crystallized conflict over the definition of the normative character of Taiwan as a nation in relation to China across the Taiwan Strait.

Some illustrations of the changing sociological function of ethnic divisions in Taiwan's experience in the succession of normative conflicts are in order. According to a survey in 1990 on the personal experiences of ethnic conflicts and troubles in various aspects of socioeconomic and political life, it was found that after more than forty years of socioeconomic transformations, the ethnic difference had very little effect on everyday social and working life in Taiwan, whereas local and national politics are still shadowed by the ethnic division. For example, measured by the felt troubles in friendship, neighborhood, marriage, job seeking, and career promotion as the five aspects of everyday social and working life, respondents revealed an average of 1.6% (friendship) to 5.4% (promotion) of perceived problems. It is evident that the real-world experience of ethnicity and resulting ethnic conflicts has been marginalized to an insignificant level. But ethnic conflicts are still considered to have a greater effect on Taiwan's national politics than local politics, with reported responses of 24.2% and 17.8%, respectively (Hsiao, 1991).

In a similar survey conducted two years later in 1992, the same pattern of differential perceived seriousness of ethnic tensions was found. The conflict in national politics that were affected by the ethnic factor was again perceived to be higher than in local politics (28.8% and 22.9%, respectively). The responses showed that the public felt that ethnic tension in the political arena had increased between 1990 and 1992. On the other hand, difficulties caused by ethnic differences in both everyday social and working life were significantly fewer than in political life. Reported ethnic tensions and troubles in ordinary life came to 8.3%, and those in work-related experience, 13.4%. In other words, the public also experienced an increase in ethnic tension in their social and working lives in that two-year period.

Does ethnic background make a difference in the experience of ethnic tensions? After further analysis, the ethnicity variables (Minanese,

Hakka, and Mainlanders), like other social and demographic variables, had no significant effect on the experienced conflict levels in everyday social and working life. But the Mainlanders have felt more strongly about the existence of ethnic conflicts in today's Taiwanese national and local politics. Respondents of Minan and Hakka origins have tended to be less sensitive to politicized ethnic tensions (Chang 1992).

From these illustrations, some important observations can be made. First, regardless of the different ethnic backgrounds, the ethnic conflicts in interpersonal experiences and work situations have by and large not concerned the Taiwanese public. What concerns them is the increasing ethnic tensions in Taiwan's political arena, and this is particularly so for the Mainlanders. Second, between 1990 and 1992, a greater degree of ethnic conflict has been felt by the Taiwanese public—and more so in the political realm. Third, the sociological definition of ethnic relations and conflicts manifested in interpersonal, work, and other aspects of socioeconomic life can no longer apply to Taiwan's experience. What is significant is the increase in politicized ethnic conflicts reflected in the broader political and symbolic struggles. Fourth, the emerging conflict over Taiwan's national identity since the late 1980s has intensified the ethnic conflicts in Taiwan's symbolic and political life as observed in the early 1990s (Wu 1993).

Moreover, the construction of national identity starts with the residents' subjective identification with the imagined national community to which they develop a sense of belonging. A new sense of belonging—a sense of Taiwan as a national community—has been growing among the people of Taiwan in the 1990s as a result of both the self-questioning and self-discovery of the 1970s and the democratization and indigenization of the previously Mainlander-controlled regime in the late 1980s. The survey data from 1991, 1992, and 1994 demonstrate, further, that when asked if they identify themselves as Taiwanese or Chinese, the "Taiwanese identity" in comparison to the "Chinese identity" has been growing more rapidly over the years. The proportion of those responding that they are Taiwanese came to 13.6%, 23.7%, and 33.8%, respectively, in the three surveys, whereas those identifying themselves as Chinese came to 13.0%, 23.4%, and 27.3%. The "Taiwanese identity" for each year is higher than the "Chinese identity," with the difference notably greater in 1994. In between the two polarized identities stands the sizable "dual identity"—both Taiwanese and Chinese at the same time. But if we take into account the order in which these are given in the cases of the dual identity—whether Taiwanese or Chinese is given first—we find that more people think of themselves first as Taiwanese, then as Chinese. In either measure, then, the "Taiwanese identity" is greater than that of "Chinese identity" (Social Attitudes Survey Team 1991, 1992, 1994).

Those holding a Taiwanese identity or a Chinese identity also would interpret Taiwan's past and envision Taiwan's future differently. Analysis of the 1994 Social Attitudes Survey data reveals that those who hold the Taiwanese national identity tend to value the historical events that directly concern Taiwan's past much more and to endow them with greater significance. They have a deeper collective memory of Taiwan's past. In comparison with those who hold the Chinese national identity or the dual identity, they tend to identify less with other ethnic Chinese in mainland China, Hong Kong, and Singapore.

More significantly, with different subjective national identities, they also envision different political futures of the Taiwan-China relationship. The option of an independent Taiwan separate from China, provided that no immediate war would break out between the two states, is much more supported by those with Taiwanese national identity. In contrast, the option of the eventual unification of Taiwan with China given that the conditions of two societies would be equal is more supported by the Chinese identity group. On the whole, the majority of Taiwan's public hold very pragmatic attitudes toward future relations between Taiwan and the mainland, preferring to maintain the status quo. Nevertheless, under the pragmatic and security-conscious mentality, there is a growing expectation for Taiwan to become a new nation if both independence and peace can be achieved. The Social Change Survey of 1992 revealed that 25.6% of respondents approved this "conditional Taiwanese independence" option, and the proportion rose to 32.0% two years later. On the other hand, the same surveys also suggested a decline of approval for the unification option even if unification is brought about only after all conditions are comparable between Taiwan and mainland China. In 1992, 56.9% welcomed the "conditional unified China" option, but the figure dropped to 33.7% in 1994. In other words, though a declared independence is not necessarily perceived as a viable immediate future for Taiwan, more and more residents of Taiwan have challenged the mythical view that Taiwan is an inseparable part of China and that the two should be unified on the PRC's terms.

As already analyzed, it is in the political and symbolic world where ethnic conflicts exist at present, and the emergence of the new identity of Taiwan as a national society is a reflection of just such political and symbolic struggles. Therefore, to say that the traditional ethnic division still has a place in the emergence of this new national identity does not mean that the current conflict over national identity formation is purely the manifestation of the ethnic conflicts. The conflict over national identity cannot be reduced to the ethnic conflicts. Moreover, the emerging Taiwanese identity has transformed not only the axis of social cleavages but also the pattern of ethnic division in Taiwan. This is because a new eth-

nic/national notion, namely, the Mainlanders from the PRC regime—
called Mainland-Mainlanders—has been added to the Taiwanese perception. To all the residents of Taiwan (including both Taiwan-Mainlanders
and Taiwan-Taiwanese), the Mainland-Mainlanders are the real "outside" Mainlander Chinese and are considered as a great threat to Taiwanese society. In the 1993 Social Attitudes Survey, 48.5% of respondents
named the PRC as the most likely "outside enemy." Another survey in
October 1994 commissioned by the Council of the Mainland Affairs revealed that 78.7% of respondents expressed that the mainland Chinese
regime was unfriendly to the government of Taiwan, and 56.9% also felt
that the communist regime was unfriendly to the people of Taiwan (*Independence Evening Post*, October 1994). A year later the proportions rose to
88% and 69%, respectively (*United Daily News*, September 18, 1995). So
instead of the internal division along the "old ethnic lines" between Taiwan-Mainlanders and Taiwan-Taiwanese, the divide has now shifted externally to the "new national line": Taiwanese (Taiwan) versus Chinese
(PRC) (Hsiao and So 1994).

Moreover, according to the China Credit Corporation's survey conducted between August and September 1995, more than 80% of respondents disputed the PRC's assertions concerning the status of Taiwan in
relation to China and its accusations of Taiwan's "flexible diplomacy" toward independence. For example, 84.7% disagreed with the PRC's line
that there is only one China and it is represented by the PRC; 89.7% disputed the PRC's assertion that the ROC ceased to exist as a sovereign
state as of 1948; 86.9% were against the charge that direct election of the
president of Taiwan is to push for Taiwan's independence; 80.2% were
against the accusation that to accept the reality of divided rule across the
Strait is to claim independence; and 83.3% did not agree with the PRC's
charge that the purpose of Taiwan's launch of "flexible diplomacy" is to
move toward independence. The survey also found that 67% felt that the
PRC did not understand Taiwan's public will, and 78% even argued that
it was impossible for the PRC to respect the Taiwanese people (*United
Daily News*, September 18, 1995). Strong public distrust of the PRC state
seems prevalent in the minds of Taiwanese.

But beneath the disputes against the PRC's downgrading of Taiwan's
national identity, there are still unsettled, confused, and conflicting conceptions of such an identity. A survey of public views of Taiwan's national identity carried out by the DPP at the same time demonstrated that
nearly one-third of Taiwanese still considered the 1.2 billion Chinese on
the mainland as the citizens of the ROC; about one-third acknowledged
that the territory of the ROC should include mainland China, and 40.9%
opposed giving up the "one China policy" (*Independence Morning Post*,
August 18, 1995). Clearly, although there has been a general consensus

rejecting the PRC's conception of Taiwan's national status, there are still conflicts and even confusion in the minds of Taiwanese as to how to clearly define Taiwan's national identity. A clear and crystallized consensus of Taiwan's national identity is still in the making.

Competing Organizations and Political Agendas

The conflicting definitions of Taiwan as a nation and the competing discourses on Taiwan's political future are highly related, and there is a tendency for the two conflict domains to merge into one larger picture where conflicts in the political agenda are being crystallized. Both areas of normative conflict emerged in a rapidly changing society, with pluralization and democratization internally, and the PRC's pressures externally. They did not arise in a reality vacuum; they were largely mobilized by adversary organizations. It is therefore important to identify these competing institutions and groups and to delineate their respective political agendas. The spectrum of conflicting definitions of Taiwan's national identity ranges from "Taiwanese identity," to "dual identity," to "Chinese identity." On the other hand, the perspectives of Taiwan's political future are the corresponding "Taiwanese independence," "status quo," and "unification with China." The polarized political agenda that reflects the extremes of the two conflicting discourses are "Taiwanese identity (present), Taiwan independence (future)," on the one hand, and "Chinese identity (present), unification with China (future)," on the other. However, there is an intermediate discourse, a pragmatic one, that advocates the "Taiwanese identity (present), status quo (present), unification with China (future)" political agenda. Since the third political agenda is upheld by the indigenized KMT state as its major policy framework, it has become the target of criticism from both extremes of the polarized discourses. For that reason, the following discussion will start with the KMT state and its political agenda.

KMT and Its Political Agenda.   Since the early 1990s under the rule of the "mainstream faction" of Lee Teng-Hui as president, the KMT has pursued a strategy of deferral in dealing with the PRC's unification pressure. The deferral agenda includes recognizing Taiwan's autonomous identity vis-à-vis China, maintaining the status quo as long as it can, and seeking a future peaceful unification with China on an equal basis. It has realized that its long-held "one China policy" has to be changed in order to respond to the growing Taiwanese identity in civil society and to protect Taiwan's interests. The result was the decision not to engage in any immediate unification talk with the PRC. The KMT opened up the cross-Strait trade and economic activities as well as civilian contacts and sought more international recognitions of Taiwan's national identity by employing "flexible diplomacy." In mid-1991 the KMT formulated a "stage model" in its "National Unification Guideline" to counteract the PRC's "one country, two systems" model. The KMT state pointed out that the timing and process of national unification should give priority to the well-being, rights, security, and welfare of Taiwanese residents, and it should be based on rational, peaceful, equal, and mutually beneficial principles. Three stages of long-run unification were proposed.

First, in the short term, there should be mutually beneficial exchange aiming to lessen the hostility on each side, and each side should recognize the other as a legitimate political entity. Second, in the middle term, there should be mutual trust and cooperation, through the development of direct mail, transportation, and trade. In particular, both sides should jointly develop the mainland's coastal region to bridge the existing gap in living standards between the two sides. Moreover, each side should assist the other in participating in international organizations. Third, in the long term, unification talks would be initiated, governed by the principles of political democracy, economic freedom, social justice, and compliance with the wishes of the people in both Taiwan and mainland China. As the KMT state has defined the present period at the first stage, the main concern is to facilitate nonpolitical exchange and to persuade the PRC to recognize Taiwan's status as a legitimate political entity (Hsiao and So 1993).

Clearly, in the KMT's agenda, Taiwan is a sovereign state, with the official name of ROC. Since the KMT has been greatly Taiwanized in its political power structure, the controversy over naming Taiwan internationally is no longer a great concern. It is also quite evident that the KMT has become very sensitive to the possibility of being misinterpreted by the Taiwanese people as too pro-unification, as selling out the interests of Taiwan to the PRC. The deferral political agenda is designed in part to make clear that although the KMT state is for unification in the long run, there is no timetable, and the most important task is to maintain the status quo and sustain Taiwan's de facto independence.

This deferral strategy is used and advocated by the KMT state to gain more room to maneuver. While the PRC wished to incorporate Taiwan by means of economic integration, the KMT wished to use economic cooperation to defer and halt the threat of political unification with China. But this political agenda and its proposals have not received friendly responses from the PRC as Taiwan continues to seek more participation in international organizations and expand its flexible diplomacy. The visit by President Lee Teng-Hui to Cornell University in June 1995 was further interpreted by the PRC as a political move intended by Taiwan to press for independence. The PRC's launch of a series of military exercises and missile testing in the fall of 1995 and the spring of 1996 on the eve of the

direct election of Taiwan's president was a clear sign of China's intoler-
ance to the KMT's deferral strategy. The increasing military threats and
political coercions from the PRC on Taiwan have further intensified the
internal conflicts over Taiwan's national identity and its political future.
The KMT's "Taiwanese identity–status quo–future unification" moderate
agenda has faced attacks from other political camps for very different
reasons.

DPP and Its Political Agenda.   From one end of the spectrum of the
conflicts over national identity and national future has been the opposition DPP's "Taiwanese identity–Taiwan independence" agenda. Since
the late 1980s the DPP has articulated a new political platform in order to
continue to pose challenges to the already transformed ruling KMT state.
It thus redefined the political content of its political struggles and movement: Instead of being simply anti-KMT, the original reason for the establishment of the DPP, it also quickly expressed its opposition to the PRC's
unification plan. The DPP's new political mission has become to protect
Taiwan from the domination of another outside Chinese state. In other
words, the DPP redirected its independence platform from the immediate independence from the then Mainlanders-dominated KMT to the ultimate independence from the PRC.

In April 1988 the DPP first tested the political climate by announcing a
timid proposal of "conditional" independence for Taiwan with "four ifs":
"If the KMT engages in unification talks with the communist China, if the
KMT sells out the interests of the Taiwanese people, if communist China
invades Taiwan, and if the KMT does not carry out democratic reforms,
the DPP will promote Taiwan independence." In October 1990 the DPP
further declared the de facto sovereignty of a Taiwan that excluded mainland China and Outer Mongolia. In August 1991 it even openly proclaimed the title of "Republic of Taiwan" in defiance of the "Republic of
China." Finally, in October 1991, the DPP wrote in its party charter that
the issue of Taiwan's independence should be democratically decided by
a plebiscite of all the residents of Taiwan. The DPP also criticized the
KMT's "stage model" for not giving priority to the Taiwanese people, not
including them as a major player, and not granting them veto power for
any policy concerning possible future unification with China. In the 1996
presidential election, the DPP's underlying campaign platform was set to
be "antiunification."

Such a strong stand on Taiwanese national identity and independence
as the DPP's ideological basis has certainly attracted a substantial number of supporters, as more than 30% of the general votes have gone to the
DPP's candidates in most of the elections since the late 1980s. Yet it also
cost the DPP in preventing it from gaining more public confidence. The
pragmatic and security-conscious general public may feel at home with

the DPP's stand for Taiwanese national identity, but they are not ready to pay for the costs that the move for Taiwan independence might incur. Sensing this social mood, the DPP recently redirected its political agenda by downplaying the Taiwan independence platform. It continues to advocate protecting Taiwan's interests as an independent nation separate from China, charging that the PRC's unification drive is Chinese imperialism, yet it acknowledges that the de facto independent status of Taiwan is acceptable and that declaring de jure independence is unnecessary, and will be so even after the DPP is in power. The pragmatic shift in the DPP's political agenda on the independence issue is thus reconcilable with the KMT's current strategy of deferral by acknowledging that the status quo is not so undesirable after all. Therefore, the focus of the conflicts between the DPP and the KMT lies not in the definition of Taiwan as a nation but in the different visions of Taiwan's future.

The shift toward a bit more pragmatism on the part of the DPP on the national identity–independence issue has been severely criticized by the "fundamentalist" independence groups, such as the Taiwanese Professors' Association (TPA), for softening the most fundamental political ideology. The TPA even criticized the assertions made by one DPP official that the KMT has already been indigenized and that the DPP therefore now has to compete with an indigenized KMT state. The TPA, established in 1990, has a strong and deep conviction in the Taiwanese identity–Taiwan independence agenda, and since its formation it has become one of the most active organizations in promoting Taiwanese independence in civil society. Other pro–Taiwan independence civil society organizations and groups include the Taiwan Independence Union, the Mainlanders' Association for Taiwan Independence, the Taiwan Medical Union, and the Taiwan Environmental Protection Union. During the months of intensified military coercion carried out by the PRC in the fall of 1995 and the spring of 1996, these pro-independence groups, joined by some twenty social-movement organizations, issued public statements denouncing the PRC's aggression and encouraging the Taiwanese people not to be afraid of China's threats and to fight against China in order to protect Taiwan. The civil-society organizations' announcements also demanded that the ruling KMT declare the position of "China is China, Taiwan is Taiwan" and the policy of "one China, one Taiwan." Ironically, the latest aggressive actions from the PRC in the spring of 1996 have further agitated the pro–Taiwanese identity and Taiwan independence civil-society organizations, though they somehow softened the DPP's official agenda on independence.

The Anti-Taiwan Independence Coalition. As a consequence of the Taiwanization of the ruling KMT and the rise of the pro–Taiwanese identity and Taiwan independence movement supported by both the opposition DPP and other civil-society organizations, the opposing side advocating the political agenda of "Chinese identity–Chinese unification" has been rapidly marginalized in today's Taiwan. What is emerging is the discourse of "Chinese identity–anti-Taiwanese independence" represented by the "nonmainstream" faction within the KMT and other prounification civil society organizations. The nonmainstream faction of the KMT was created by the power struggles between the Taiwanese and Mainlander blocs after the death of the KMT's last strongman, Chiang Ching-Kuo, and it consists of members of the old guard under the authoritarian regime and the mid-career Mainlander politicians who were defeated by the Taiwanese-led mainstream faction. The nonmainstream KMT faction was loosely united by their members' resentments toward Lee Teng-Hui, the Taiwanese successor to Chiang Ching-Kuo, and their collective sentiments of Chinese identity and Taiwan's reunification with China. As the years went by, their pro-reunification political agenda was greatly suspected by the Taiwanese people, and even their Chinese national identity was criticized for not identifying with Taiwan's land and people. As a result, their pro-reunification stand was forced to change, and they began to criticize the counterdiscourse of Taiwanese identity and Taiwanese independence from both the ethnocultural and the practical perspectives.

They argued that since both Taiwanese and Mainlanders are Chinese, the overemphasis on the Taiwanese identity will inevitably jeopardize internal ethnic relations and even lead to social conflicts. They also strongly warned of the danger that Taiwanese independence might cause, as the PRC would not tolerate it. On the surface, both arguments in this newly formulated anti-independence agenda were pretty much in line with the mainstream KMT's anti-independence and pro-unification lines. Both sides are against Taiwanese independence, but the mainstream KMT expects the unification process to unfold over the long term, whereas the nonmainstream faction wishes to accelerate the pace of reunification for fear that the Taiwanese-mainstream may not seriously pursue this goal (Wachman, 1994). The nonmainstream faction, for both political and ideological reasons, has even broken its historical ties with the KMT by pushing a competing ticket of presidential and vice presidential candidates. The candidates from the ex-KMT's nonmainstream faction had run their campaign against both the KMT's and the DPP's candidates. These two nonmainstream candidates, both the party vice chairmen, were the heavyweight party leaders of the KMT. The split of the nonmainstream faction with the mainstream KMT power bloc in the recent presidential election demonstrated the peak of noncompromising power struggles within the KMT under the indigenization and democratization processes. What is beneath the obvious power struggles is, again, the underlying conflict over Taiwan's national identity and Taiwan's destinies vis-à-vis China.

The ex-KMT nonmainstream faction's political agenda has been endorsed by the Chinese New Party (CNP), a party founded in 1993 mainly by KMT's former mid-career Mainlander politicians, whose major political inspirations have been anti–Lee Teng-Hui and anti-independence. The expelled KMT nonmainstream force and the CNP have claimed that they are the only legitimate orthodox KMT, accusing the indigenized KMT of having betrayed the party spirit and ideology of the KMT since Sun Yat-Sen and the Chiang families. Another pro-reunification and anti-independence force also came from the KMT's conservatives who resisted the KMT's transformation and democratization. Among them are the New Tung-Men Hui, the Coalition for Anti–Taiwan Independence and Nation Rescue, the Greater Federation of Saving the Nation and the Constitution, and the Patriotic Anti–Independent Action. The alliance of the nonmainstream faction and the CNP was already mobilized under the recent presidential election campaign, but the rest of these anti-independence and pro-reunification civil-society organizations have a limited social base.

The social constituency of the anti-independence civil-society organizations is made up essentially of the Mainlander KMT members who have felt threatened by the ongoing KMT Taiwanization and democratization. As they identify themselves as Chinese, they have deeply feared that the Taiwanese national identity would ultimately lead to the independence of Taiwan, and they would be mistreated by the powerful Taiwanese, as the Mainlanders had done to the Taiwanese in the past. At present the anti-independence coalition, joined by forces in the political and civil societies, has perceived the status quo as a fragile and dangerous situation under the mainstream KMT's deferral political agenda. To them, the deferral strategy has been used by the Taiwanese KMT elites to disguise their ambition to pursue Taiwanese independence. In other words, the social-psychological basis of the anti-independence coalition has been the combination of ethnic anxiety on the part of the minority Mainlanders, the resistance to political democratization, and the fear of the PRC's immediate retaliation upon Taiwan's independence.

If the definition of the status quo is the de facto autonomy and independence of Taiwan, then it can be a possible basis of mediation of the conflicts between the KMT's "Taiwanese identity first, reunification later" and the DPP's "Taiwanese identity first, independence later" political agenda. For precisely the same reason, the current discourse of the status quo has further intensified the normative and political conflicts between the CNP-led anti-independence coalition on the one hand, and the KMT and the DPP's mutually conflicting yet potentially reconcilable political agenda on the other.

The Making of the Normative Conflict over the Environment

The Emergence and the Social Base

Unlike the normative conflicts over national identity, which were rooted in the historical and political processes under which Taiwan has been transformed from a "Chinese" local society into a "Taiwanese" national entity, the conflicts over the environment were created and constructed primarily by the social movements in civil society. As noted at the outset of this chapter, since the early 1980s three distinctive social movements for the environment have been mobilized and organized: The antipollution protest movement, the nature conservation movement, and the anti–nuclear power movement can be considered the three streams of the environmental movement from 1980 to the present. They were staged, first, to raise the Taiwanese people's awareness and consciousness of the worsening environmental/ecological problems caused by rapid industrialization and economic growth as well as to mobilize the public into organized social movements to protect the quality of life and the environment, and second, to engage in the discursive conflicts against the pro-growth state and the profit-seeking industrialists on the values of the environment.

A search of Taiwan's economic planning documents from the early 1950s to the present uncovers no mention of the need for environmental protection or nature conservation until the late 1970s, when the planning bureaucrats began consciously to articulate nature as a resource to be exploited or used for recreation. Some local scientists and intellectuals had done their best in the 1970s to warn the public and the government about environmental dangers, but their voices went largely unheeded (Hsiao 1987). As serious problems have developed at an alarming rate, accumulations of solid and hazardous wastes, air and water pollution, and destabilized natural resource systems have brought discomfort, pain, and loss to ordinary people on a large scale beginning in the 1980s, and people began to experience the cost incurred by the hypergrowth of the postwar era under the authoritarian developmental state of the KMT.

Thirty years of commitment to capitalist growth at any cost has left the environment, almost unprotected, to absorb the by-products of production and consumption. According to one estimate in the late 1980s, if production and consumption were not reorganized to reduce environmental stress, annual growth rates of the gross national product at 6.5% and of the population at 1.1%—the targets set by planners of the Council for Economic Planning and Development (CEPD)—will more than double the current pressure on Taiwan's environment by the year 2000 (Taiwan 2000 Study Steering Committee, 1989). The public has been increasingly aware of, and impatient with, the worsening environmental problems and their effects on quality of life, and public discontent over Taiwan's environmental degradation has become an increasingly important source of discord and even of disorder since the 1980s. Many surveys over the years have found that environmental problems rank high among the social concerns of the Taiwanese people, that environmental consciousness has increased rapidly beginning in the mid-1980s, and that the public is extremely pessimistic about Taiwan's environmental future.

The survey findings in 1983, 1986, 1990, 1991, and 1992 reveal that a steadily growing concern among the public about the worsening environmental problems has been emerging in the ten-year period under study. For example, in 1983, 70% of respondents (surveyed throughout the island) rated environmental problems as serious or very serious; by 1986 the figure jumped to 88%; though it dropped to 77% in 1990, it was still higher than in 1983. In the 1990s the social perception of the seriousness of Taiwan's environmental problems rose again; in 1991 it was 81.1%, and in 1992 just slightly higher at 82.3%. In other words, at present more than 80% of Taiwanese residents consider environmental problems to be serious or very serious. Also, more than 50% expect the problem to become worse over the coming years (Hsiao et al. 1993, 94).

The Social Base of the Local Antipollution Protests

Since the early 1980s the antipollution stream of collective action first became a social movement in many contaminated local communities. They all started as localized pollution victims' protests, organized solely by the victim residents of the communities. With the help of media exposure to the wider public, in the mid-1980s the scattered antipollution protests turned into a noticeable nationwide grassroots social movement. The "success" of the victims' self-mobilization in one locality has an immediate demonstration effect, inspiring other communities to organize to stage similar protests. The primary actors involved in this type of environmental movement have been the local victim residents in villages, townships, or cities. The concerned new middle-class intellectuals and university professors, college students, and the younger generations of newspaper reporters rendered their sympathy and support to the victims' collective action against the polluting industries. The social base of the local antipollution movement consisted of the community residents and their existing social networks and fabrics of kin, neighborhoods, temples, and local voluntary organizations. Though the leadership was in the hands of existing local elites or a new breed of grassroots elites, the supporters consisted of different classes. The new middle-class segment's support from outside served to legitimate the cause of protests from within. Some nationwide environmental organizations, of which the Taiwan Environmental Protection Union (TEPU) and its local chapters are the most notable, have also provided necessary professional know-how and mobilized popular support behind them.

On the basis of the 462 local antipollution protests that took place between 1980 and 1991, Taiwan's environmentalism could be characterized as a victims' activism (Hsiao 1994b; Hsiao, Milbrath, and Weller 1995). The frequency of the victims' protests reflects one critical factor: the retreat of authoritarian control over civil society. Three-quarters of these 462 protests took place in the four years (1988–1991) after martial law was lifted, demonstrating how victims took advantage of the opening of more civil space to voice their grievances. Most of the actions were organized to mitigate or to seek compensation for existing injuries or losses to residents. Existing injuries arouse people much more than potential injuries; 84% of the total protest objectives were reactive rather than preventive or preemptive, with the latter accounting for only 16%. However, the large increase in the number of preventive protests in the post–martial law era indicates the residents' lack of confidence in the state's policies and business pollution control practices. All the local protests were mobilized by the collective "victim consciousness" derived from the immediate or perceived victimization caused by pollution.

The frequency of antipollution populist protests also corresponds with the density of industries in different parts of the island. More than 75% of the protests took place in northern and southern Taiwan, where the polluting industries are concentrated. More than 70% of the local populist movements were organized against existing industrial facilities and corporations. The second largest target has been local government. Though not directly or explicitly, the central state's industrial and pro-growth policies were implicated as the prime cause of many local communities' environmental problems. Sometimes the protests generated the formation of permanent local antipollution or environmental protection organizations. This was not the norm, however, as only 62 cases have established more or less formalized civil-society organizations as the centers for staging long-term struggles against the polluters. In most cases, energetic and persistent organizations that sustained the protests quickly atrophied after the immediate threat had been withdrawn.

Such antipollution populist movements have generated both direct-interest conflicts and normative conflicts between the local residents and ordinary citizens on the one hand, and the business and the state on the other. The victim consciousness has taken a form in which residents suddenly realized that the air they breathed, the water they drank, and the natural commons on which they depended for their livelihoods (as farmers, fishers, and other growers) was being commodified to serve the political and economic needs of the state and industry (Hsu 1995). The rapid industrialization of Taiwan's many localities has also undermined long-existing local institutions, relations, norms, and values, and the new sense of community was constructed in opposition to the state's ideology of economic and industrial growth at the sacrifice of the environment and people's life quality.

The Social Base of the Nature Conservation Movement

The second stream in Taiwan's environmental movement is concerned more with the destruction of Taiwan's natural resources. It became a "movement" also in the early 1980s, shortly after the antipollution protests had begun. Numerous rescue campaigns were organized by nature conservationists, consisting mainly of writers, scholars, and scientists. As of the late 1980s they were joined by many other local concerned middle-class groups. These campaigns have been conducted to rescue the endangered migratory birds, mangroves, rivers, forests, coastal wetlands, and the ecologically significant gorge from excessive industrial development projects and careless human actions. The key actors of this nature conservation movement, in contrast with the antipollution protests, have been nongovernmental organizations, including the Birds Society, the Homemakers' Union and Foundation, the Green Consumer's Foundation, the Society of Wildlife and Nature, and the Nature Conservation Union.

The Birds Society was originally organized by bird-watchers. By the 1990s the Society had developed into one of the largest environmental organizations in Taiwan, with more than a dozen local chapters island-wide. This formerly apolitical organization was gradually drawn into political activism because of the increased destruction of Taiwan's natural environment, which sharply contradicts the society's fundamental values. It is important to note that women make up the membership of several national conservationist groups, and not only the women writers who started the conservation concerns in Taiwanese civil society. Women are not usually the public leaders of local antipollution protests, yet they are often very active in stressing nurturing nature during the protests. But in the conservation movement, they have been playing more important roles. Among the women conservation-environmental groups, the Homemaker's Union and Foundation is the most notable example. With a popular base of middle-class housewives, they are not inclined to take on the controversial political issues and are not interested in the more strictly academic lectures and roundtables of the other groups; they try to root their environmentalism in issues of household and motherhood. More predominantly for them, environmental protection and nature conservation are a means to protect the health and future of their children, not just their own.

A few Buddhist organizations also pursue the appeal to nurturance (Weller and Hsiao 1994). Usually Buddhist organizations for the environment take on no radical issues, addressing instead less controversial issues more within the control of the individual and the household. But they often speak of the need to preserve nature and not to destroy it. A Buddhist monk and his civil-society organization was very active in pushing the formation of the Nature Conservation Union. To the Union, one of the most pressing issues concerning Taiwan's ecological system and natural resource balance is to protect the ecology of Taiwan's west coast and coastal wetlands from the environmentally damaging large-scale industrial projects that have been planned by the state in recent years. The natural ecology along Taiwan's west coast has been severely polluted and eroded by ill-planned industrial development and fisheries. The state's new plan is to build a chain of coastal industrial zones on those ecologically sensitive areas, with a hidden agenda of launching the big redevelopments after the coastal destruction. Hence the nature conservation movement is increasingly taking on the state's pro-growth policies and developing discourse against the state and big industry.

The Social Base of the Anti–Nuclear Power Movement

The third stream of Taiwan's civil-society movement for the environment concentrates on one specific goal: preventing the construction of the fourth nuclear power plant planned by the powerful state-owned Taiwan Power Company. The proposed plant had been approved by the state before it was made public. The debate peaked during a public forum in the summer of 1985 organized by the Consumers' Foundation, the first social movement organization ever established (in 1980). In that heated debate, Taiwan Power Company officials present were critically questioned by the participating concerned scholars and environmentalists about the feasibility of the new plant, in terms of both safety and economic considerations. Later, in late 1985, an accidental fire in the third nuclear power plant on the southern tip of Taiwan once again drew public attention to the nuclear power issue. Local residents even organized meetings and rallies to demand that the authorities promise a safer emergency plan and provide compensation to communities surrounding the plant.

As a result of these developments in 1985 and of the ever-intensive media coverage of nuclear-related issues, people in Taiwan were provided with ample opportunity to learn more about the pros and cons of nuclear power generation. Ironically, this needed public education did not come from the voluntary provision of accurate information from the nuclear power regulatory authority. The Taiwanese people were forced to be educated about nuclear power issues by potential nuclear disasters in Taiwan and abroad. The Chernobyl nuclear power plant accident in the Soviet Union was another lesson by default. Still in the state's pro-growth strategy, nuclear power generation was considered a necessary national industrial project. Before the controversy of the fourth nuclear power plant became public in 1985, the Taiwan Power Company even had planned a total of twenty reactors on this small island by the year 2000. By the early 1980s Taiwan had already constructed three nuclear power plants, with a total of six reactors in operation, that together generated 43% of Taiwan's electricity. This made Taiwan, after France, the world's second highest nuclear power dependent country (Cohen 1988).

The conflicts over the nuclear power issue between the new middle-class liberal intellectuals and concerned environmental groups on the one hand, and the Taiwan Power Company on the other, were intensified after 1986. However, the anti–nuclear power voices came mainly from the academic and social movement circles. From 1988 onward, they were joined by the active participation of the residents around the proposed site of the fourth plant on the northern coast of Taiwan. Since then Taiwan's movement against nuclear power has become a social movement with forces from the new middle-class-led intellectuals and civil-society organizations and local residents. The main force behind the anti–nuclear power movement has been the TEPU, which devoted almost all its organizational resources to combating the proposed nuclear power plant since the mid-1980s. The TEPU was established by volunteers from among university professors and students. It also established a local chapter at the proposed site in order to sustain the mobilization of local residents for this specific cause. As the years have passed, the anti–nuclear power movement has turned into a nationwide "No-Nukes" movement to take on the state's energy development policy and the pro-growth myth behind it.

In 1995 the Taipei County Government, controlled by the opposition DPP, organized a countywide referendum on the fourth nuclear power plant. But the result of the referendum was not validated, because of insufficient turnout. The following year, the capital Taipei City Government, also controlled by the DPP, held another referendum on the nuclear power issue at the same time as the presidential election, on March 23, 1996. The result was that 52% of the Taipei voters cast "no" votes on the issue. Obviously, the anti–nuclear power movement has developed a clear coalition with the opposition political party. The opposition DPP has even written the anti–nuclear power position into its charter in opposing any further construction of nuclear power facilities on the island. The CNP is also inclined against nuclear power generation for Taiwan's future energy needs. In other words, the conflicts of nuclear power generation have even emerged into a political conflict between the pro-nuclear KMT and the anti-nuclear DPP and CNP. Recently the movement also adopted a more confrontational approach, commonly used by the antipollution protests, in staging protests against the Taiwan Power Company and the state. A coalition between the anti–nuclear power and the nature conservation movements has also been developed, as both are concerned with the protection of Taiwan's nature and ecology, and both have targeted the state and its pro-growth and antienvironment ideology.

The Impact of the Environmental Discourse

The impact of Taiwan's three environmental movement streams can be evaluated in several different aspects. The first is to see how the environmental movement has been understood and supported by the general public. The second is to assess what normative and organizational impact it has had on individuals, communities, and the overall society. The third aspect is to focus on the policy effects the environmental movement has produced on the state.

Compared to other social movements, the environmental movement as a whole has been perceived by the Taiwanese people with the highest level of understanding, and it has also enjoyed the greatest public support. The Social Attitudes Surveys conducted in both 1991 and 1992 clearly revealed the public's positive attitude toward the environmental movement. In both years, the environmental movement topped nine other social movements in the rank-ordering of the publicly understood movements. In 1991, 68.3% of the respondents reported that they were aware of and understood the environmental movement; the figure rose to 79.5% the following year. Again, in both 1991 and 1992, the environmental movement was the most supported social movement among the ten listed, with 82.4% and 87.7%, respectively, of the respondents expressing their support (Hsiao 1994a).

Though the survey data cannot directly distinguish the differential awareness and support each of the three streams has actually gained, it can be hypothesized that among the three, the nature conservation movement is likely the most understood and supported and the anti–nuclear power movement the least. The social consensus on the nature conservation cause is the least questionable. The misunderstanding and mistrust on the part of some individuals and groups toward the two "anti" causes in the environmental movement are often detected. Generally speaking, the middle classes, especially the new middle-class segment, have greater empathetic understanding and positive support of the environmental movement as a whole.

The victims have learned that protesting brings results; the majority of the local antipollution protests achieved their immediate objectives. The polluting factories were either forced to improve conditions or pay compensation to the victims or their communities. Some factories were even forced to shut down or move to another location. A few preemptive protests succeeded in stopping planned construction projects or delaying them for further evaluation. But what is unclear is the long-term impact in terms of transforming the shortsighted "victim consciousness" into a broader and farsighted "environmental consciousness" by which the people of Taiwan can continue their self-mobilization to safeguard the future environmental and living qualities. As noted earlier, more often than not, once the immediate source or cause of pollution has been removed the local antipollution effort soon ceased to exist and no further pro-environment collective action was sustained. Nevertheless, the emerging sense of community that has been induced by collective protest experiences in many local communities should serve in the future as the normative foundation for constructing a sustainable pro-environment consciousness.

The nature conservation and anti–nuclear power movements have successfully raised the overall social consciousness about one of the most pressing problems facing Taiwan. The public has become more aware of the high environmental costs incurred by rapid industrialization and modernization. Public debates have been staged on the environmental impacts of several large-scale industrial projects, including the state-backed nuclear power plants. More and more people in Taiwan are forced to realize that beneath the modern and efficient lifestyle they enjoy are the increasingly intolerable environmental and living conditions. The people of Taiwan are now caught between two equally desirable values for both individuals and society—the good material life, and a clean and safe environment for them and their children and grandchildren. In other words, the nature conservation and anti–nuclear power movements have successfully forced people to face the normative dilemma of which of the two values should take priority for the society. At the least, the Taiwanese people are no longer single-minded about the pro-growth beliefs and values that were so deeply embedded in the society's accepted notions. A slow yet firm emergence of the public's recognition of the dialectics of economic growth and environmental quality has been observed.

The policy impacts of the three streams of Taiwan's environmental movement are again varied. The widespread local antipollution protests have forced the central government to speed up necessary changes of various environmental policies. Tougher measures of pollution controls were adopted, a specific Pollution Disputes Resolution Law was passed, the Environmental Impacts Assessment Act was enacted, and the Environmental Protection Basic Law is being reviewed in the Legislative Yuan. Though the local and central governments are also more responsive and accountable in dealing with local environmental problems, their pro-growth ideology has not been effectively challenged. That the state is willing to take care of immediate environmental problems does not mean the pro-industry and pro-growth strategies it pursues are to be modified as well. It is quite evident, judging from the continued and even more ambitious industrial polices already planned, that the democratizing KMT state has no clear intention of redirecting its national development priorities in the near future.

The nature conservation movement faces the same difficulties in truly influencing the state's pro-growth policy. This movement, with the timely help of global conservation groups' applying pressure as well, was able to push the state to pass the Wildlife Protection Law. But because of the lack of supporting manpower and of political determination on the part of local governments to implement the protection of wildlife and natural resources, the new law has become only an empty promise. As noted earlier, the state and its capitalist allies have even planned to construct numerous additional industrial zones along the already endangered coastal areas of the island. The nature conservation groups have voiced their disagreement, and the conflict over the proposed large-scale coastal industrial facilities was intensified, but the state's determination has not been affected as of yet. If the ambitious and ruthless plan of building up a chain of coastal industrial zones is eventually implemented, Taiwan's natural coastal ecology is doomed to be destroyed completely. The few remaining wetlands will be wiped out as well. The Nature Conservation Union and many other environmental-conservation organizations, with the support of many concerned intellectuals and scientists, are now fighting to rescue Taiwan's coastal areas from being turned into the "Great Wall" built along the west coast. The movement is confronting not only the KMT state but also local governments and industrial interests, all of which see these great projects as necessary for upgrading Taiwan's industrial capability and increasing Taiwan's competitiveness in the world manufacturing market.

Finally, the anti–nuclear power movement, though in alliance with the opposition parties, is still struggling to postpone, if not to stop all together, the construction of the fourth nuclear power plant. The ruling KMT still controls more than half of the seats in the Legislative Yuan (the Legislative Assembly of Taiwan), and it won the votes in the legislative body to approve the first-year budget for the proposed plant in 1995. The DPP and the CNP legislators have declared that they will continue the war against the 1996 nuclear power plant budget. In other words, the battlefield of the conflicts on future nuclear power generation has now moved from civil society to political society. Again, no one can predict the eventual destiny of this increasingly politicized stream of the environmental movement either.

Conclusions: Prospects of Mediation

The latest developments of the conflicts over Taiwan's national identity and Taiwan's political future have been redefining the Taiwanese national identity and acknowledging Taiwan's de facto independence. The ruling KMT and the opposition DPP currently seem to share a common national-identity view concerning Taiwan's present status but are still split over the vision of Taiwan's political future vis-à-vis China. The sustaining internal disputes over Taiwan's eventual unification with China or independence between the civil society's pro-independence organizations and the political society's KMT and DPP are further intensified by the PRC's incomprehensible external aggression. The changing political agenda of the KMT's stand on Taiwan's national identity and the more pragmatic standpoint on Taiwanese independence on the part of the DPP have prepared the grounds for possible mediation and reconciliation between the two rival political parties. To acknowledge the de facto independence of Taiwan with its own rights and to take the status quo as a dynamic situation rather than a static end state can be a normative basis for further political dialogues to reach the consensus necessary for formulating feasible strategies to deal with the external pressure from the PRC. The prospect of such consensus building within Taiwan's political society and civil society is further supported by the fact that Taiwan has largely succeeded in its democratic transition process. The direct presidential election despite the PRC's military threat in March 1996 further marked Taiwan's progress into democratic consolidation. The consolidated democracy of Taiwan will greatly enhance the possibilities of the conflicts over Taiwan's national identity.

Furthermore, the diminishing social conflicts based on ethnic divisions also bode well for establishing effective mediation. The everyday life experiences shared by the residents of Taiwan of different ethnic and provincial origins have, to a great extent, fostered a new sense of national community. The opposition DPP's call for the construction of a new communalism based on shared interests, norms, and values that have developed over the postwar era in Taiwan has been adopted by the ruling KMT as well to legitimize its rule. It is quite clear that the postwar Taiwanese experience of economic growth, affluence, lifestyles, social mobility, political stability, and democratic institutionalization all will serve as the bonding ties in the further construction of a new Taiwanese national identity distinct from China. A new sensitivity to the politicized ethnic conflicts— derived not from interpersonal or social life experiences but from the normative conflicts over national identity and national future, aggravated by the external pressure from the PRC, has induced the Taiwanese people further to reassess the very nature of such internal social and political cleavages. With the development of this sensitivity and realization, the use of the ethnic factor for political mobilization and political struggles is now considered unfounded and distasteful. Therefore, with the increasing assimilation and the avoidance of manipulating ethnic divisions as the base of internal political conflicts, ethnicity will soon cease to be an obstacle to the building up of a new Taiwanese *conscience collective.*

In sum, the normative bases for the possible mediation of national identity conflicts were not deliberately created by the existing civil-society institutions or organizations founded to legitimate such mediation. The life experiences of Taiwan's postwar development, shared by the people of Taiwan, actually comprise the most important institutionalized norms that could eventually legitimate the construction of a national communalism. More important, in Taiwan's case, some common ground for mediation could be reached by the intensive competition of the adversary political agendas mobilized by the rival political parties. Of course the civil-society organizations such as the nonpartisan liberal intellectual groups, journalists, and religious establishments (especially the Buddhist groups) have also contributed to mobilizing shared life experiences into the basis for consensus-building discourse. In this sense, the civil-society institutions have succeeded in inducing the rival political parties to realize that the shared life experiences and norms of the people of Taiwan are the ultimate base from which to construct Taiwan's national identity and even for envisioning the nation's future.

Taiwan's environmental movement has since the 1980s successfully generated the value conflicts of environment versus growth in the minds of the Taiwanese people, which is necessary for the possible and sensible mediation between the civil society's demands for a better environment and the state's and industry's insistence on continued growth. It is clear too, though, that without more extensive and sophisticated public discourse and debates on the choices and stakes, the state's pro-industry and pro-growth ideology and policies will not easily be challenged. The state and the strong industrial interest groups have a long-established power bloc that sustains the pro-growth ideology embedded in postwar Taiwanese society. However, the results already achieved by the civil-society environmental movement in pressing the state to be more responsive to existing environmental problems can be seen as one area where mediation has been practiced. As for any eventual changes in the state's pro-growth ideology, the environmental movement has achieved its only serious challenge thus far by imposing into discourse the reality of environmental and human costs incurred by unchecked growth. However, it has also presented potential political threats to the local and central governments.

One prospect for mediation of the normative conflict over the environment is by means of much more organized and stronger civil-society pressure to demand that the state opt for "sustainable development" to replace "hypergrowth" as a desirable national development goal. Following that line of thinking, the challenge for the environmental movement organizations would be first to convince the self-proclaimed pro-environment DPP-ruled local governments to adopt the "sustainable development" notion and to put it into practice in balancing the local needs of industrial development with the need for a clean environment. The potential is already there, as some DPP-ruled county governments have begun to formulate the "environmental constitution" as guiding principles to precede "sustainable development" policies for their own local societies. Therefore, the prospect of successful mediation to bring about a healthy and balanced course of development for the people and society of Taiwan remains a task for the environmental movement to undertake in the immediate future.

In the final analysis, it is the conflicting discourse brought about by the great transformations experienced in Taiwan since the 1980s that have created and accelerated the normative conflicts over national identity and environmental values. The changing social reality has generated conflicting definitions of the meaning of the past and visions of the future for Taiwanese society. And it is this social reality that has also fostered the possibilities and feasible directions for mediation in resolving the two most salient normative conflicts in contemporary Taiwan.

References

Bornschier, Volker, and Peter Lengyel (1994). *Conflicts and New Departures in World Society* (New Brunswick, N.J.: Transaction Publishers).

Chang, Mau-Kuei (1994). "Toward an Understanding of the Sheng-chi Wen-ti in Taiwan: Focusing on Changes after Political Liberalization." In *Ethnicity in Taiwan: Social, Historical, and Cultural Perspectives*, edited by Chen Chung-Min, Chuang Ying-Chang, and Huang Shu-Min (Taipei: Institute of Ethnology, Academia Sinica), pp. 93–150.

Chang, Ying-Hwa (1992). "Ethnic Problems" (in Chinese). In *Social Attitudes Survey Report, 1992* (Taipei: Institute of Social Science and Philosophy, Academia Sinica), pp. 31–38.

Cheng, Robert L. (1994). "Language Unification in Taiwan: Present and Future." In *The Other Taiwan: 1945 to the Present*, edited by Murray A. Rubinstein (Armonk, N.Y.: M. E. Sharpe), pp. 357–391.

Cohen, Marc J. (1988). *Taiwan at the Crossroads: Human Rights, Political Development, and Social Change in the Beautiful Island* (Washington, D.C.: Asia Resource Center).

Collins, Randall (1975). *Conflict Sociology: Toward an Explanatory Science* (New York: Academic Press).

Hsiao, H. H. Michael (1987). "Who Cares About Taiwan's Natural Environment? The Formation and Evolution of Nature Conservation" (in Chinese). In *We Have Only One Taiwan*, by H. H. Michael Hsiao (Taipei: Yuan Shen Pub. Co.), pp. 81–104.

_____ (1989). "The Rise of Environmental Consciousness in Taiwan." *Impact Assessment Bulletin*, vol. 8, no. 1/2, pp. 217–231.

_____ (1991). "Ethnic Identification and Ethnic Issues" (in Chinese). In *Social Attitudes Survey Report, 1991* (Taipei: Institute of Social Science and Philosophy, Academia Sinica), pp. 41–50.

_____ (1994a). "Social Movements and Civil Society in Taiwan: A Typological Analysis of Social Movements and Public Acceptance." Paper presented at the Twenty-third World Congress of Sociology, Bielefeld, Germany, July 18–23.

_____ (1994b). "The Character and Changes of Taiwan's Local Environmental Protection Movement: 1980–1991" (in Chinese). In *Environmental Protection and Industrial Policies*, edited by Taiwan Research Fund (Taipei: Vanguard Pub. Co.), pp. 550–573.

_____ (1996). "Changing Literary Images of Taiwan's Working Class." In *Putting Class in Its Place: Bases of Worker Identity in East Asia*, edited by Elizabeth Perry (Berkeley: Institute of East Asian Studies, University of California).

Hsiao, H. H. Michael, P. C. Chiang, L. Severinghaus, and Y. P. Chu (1993). *Taiwan 2000* (in Chinese) (Taipei: Commonwealth Pub. Co.).

Hsiao, H. H. Michael, and Alvin So (1993). "Ascent Through National Integration: The Chinese Triangle of Mainland–Taiwan–Hong Kong." In *Asia-Pacific and the Future of the World-Economy*, edited by Ravi Palat (Westport, Conn.: Greenwood Press), pp. 133–147.

_____ (1994). *Taiwan-Mainland Economic Nexus: Socio-political Origins, State-Society Impacts, and Future Prospects*. Occasional Paper No. 37, Hong Kong Institute of Asia-Pacific Studies, The Chinese University of Hong Kong.

Hsiao, H. H. Michael, and Hagen Koo (1995). "The Middle Classes and Democratization in East Asia: Taiwan and South Korea Compared." Paper presented at an International Conference on Consolidating the Third Wave Democracies, Institute for National Policy Research, Taipei, August 27–30.

Hsiao, H. H. Michael, L. Milbrath, and R. Weller (1995). "Antecedents of an Environmental Movement in Taiwan." *Capitalism, Nature, Socialism*, vol. 6, no. 3, pp. 91–104.

Hsu, Shih-Jung (1995). *Environmental Protest, the Authoritarian State, and Civil Society: The Case of Taiwan*. Ph.D. diss., University of Delaware.

Hunter, James Davison (1991). *Culture Wars: The Struggle to Define America* (New York: Basic Books).

_____ (1994). *Before the Shooting Begins: Searching for Democracy in America's Culture War* (New York: The Free Press).

Lee, Hsiao-Fung (1995). *Fourteen Debates on Unification and Independence* (in Chinese) (Taipei: Yi Shan Pub. Co.).

Social Attitudes Survey Team (1991, 1992, 1994). *Social Attitudes Survey Report* (Taipei: Institute of Social Science and Philosophy, Academia Sinica).

Taiwan 2000 Study Steering Committee (1989). *Taiwan 2000: Balancing Economic Growth and Environmental Protection* (Taipei: Taiwan 2000 Study Steering Committee).

Wachman, Alan (1994). *Taiwan: National Identity and Democratization* (Armonk, N.Y.: M. E. Sharpe).

Weller, Robert, and H. H. Michael Hsiao (1994). "Culture, Gender, and Community in Taiwan's Environmental Movement." Paper presented at the Workshop on Environmental Movements in Asia, IIAS, Leiden, October 27–29.

Wu, Nai-Teh (1993). "Ethnic Relations, Political Support, and National Identity" (in Chinese). In *Ethnic Relations and National Identity*, by Chang Mau-Kuei, et al. (Taipei: Institute for National Policy Research), pp. 27–51.

Conclusion:
General Observations on
Normative Conflicts and Mediation

Peter L. Berger

This book contains analyses of normative conflicts in eleven national societies, with a rich supply of what anthropologists call "thick description." The purpose of these observations is not to attempt a summary (which would be a futile exercise), nor to present a general theory (which would require a book of at least equal length). Rather, it is simply to step back and ask what wider lessons can be learned from these cases, both in terms of intellectual understanding and of policy implications.

Normative conflicts are nothing new in history. Human beings have fought over the norms governing both public and personal life throughout history. In the case of Western civilization, one need only recall the wars of religion that followed the Protestant Reformation, which submerged Europe in an ocean of bloodshed and which took several centuries to mediate (not to mention the fact that there are places where the conflicts are as virulent as ever, such as the Balkans and Northern Ireland). Analogous conflicts can be found in every other civilization. Modernization, however, has brought about a certain globalization of such conflicts (which is precisely why the cross-national comparisons in this book are instructive). Modernization carries with it certain normative freight that leads to conflicts virtually everywhere—such as the undermining of traditional values, the ethos of rationality, a strong tendency toward individuation, and what Danièle Hervieu-Léger has called the "ecumenism of human rights." Modern education and the modern communications media ensure that normative disputes in one part of the world are rapidly diffused to other parts, reappearing there in forms that are often indistinguishable from those in their places of origin, at other times modified in terms of indigenous traditions and local problems. As far as the normative order of society is concerned, the single most important consequence of modernization is the pluralization of beliefs and values. Despite various challenges, including the bloody ones, premodern societies frequently had a reasonable chance of maintaining a unified system of norms that could command allegiance (be it by force or more or less freely) from the great majority of the population. Modernization makes such a project more and more difficult. Thus pluralism becomes not just a fact but a virtue—to wit, the ideal of people with different beliefs and values living together in a state of civic peace. Accordingly, normative conflicts in modern or modernizing societies commonly revolve around the question of the outer limits of pluralism. There will always be beliefs and values that are beyond the pluralistic thresholds of tolerance: Which are they, and how is society to deal with the people who adhere to them?

In this connection it is interesting to look at the manner in which the European wars of religion were mediated. Where neither violent suppression nor conversion worked, the mediation was in the form of territorial separation—the formula *"cuius regio eius religio"* of the Peace of Westphalia. Either Catholicism or Protestantism was declared to be dominant in a particular territory, and those who did not accept this had the option of emigrating. This formula of, as it were, normative partition rarely works in a modern society. In its place must be found some formula of institutional separation or diversification—if you will, *"cuius institutio eius religio."* That too is nothing altogether new. The system of confessional "pillarization" *(verzuiling)* in the Netherlands was an earlier version of this—the different religious groups, and the additional group adhering to "humanism," each having its own set of officially recognized institutions that overlapped geographically. The Turkish *millet* system (the institutional base of the "Ottoman civility" discussed by Serif Mardin), which granted wide jurisdiction to the officially accepted religious groups, is a non-Western example of a similar formula. Again, the question here is the threshold of tolerance: Which groups are to be accepted into the system of institutional pluralism? Conversely: Which beliefs and values are beyond the pale of tolerance?

One disputed point of sociological interpretation must be briefly touched upon here, namely, the issue of the degree of normative consensus that is necessary for social order. A central school of thought in sociology, most cogently represented by Emile Durkheim and his disciples, has always maintained that any society will fall apart that does not have a "collective conscience"—that is, a common body of norms adhered to by most of its people. This view has been challenged by some who have argued that a modern society cannot aspire to such normative unity and can function adequately without it, as long as there is agreement on a set of procedures by which conflicting interests and ideologies can be adjudicated. In a democracy, of course, these procedures are institutionalized in the political and legal systems. It is in everyone's interest to adhere to these procedures, and as long as they are followed, the resultant outcome will be deemed legitimate by all or nearly all concerned. In a somewhat extreme form this can be described as a traffic-system model of social order: In modern urban traffic, most people stop at red, go at green; they do so not because of shared normative convictions, and usually not from fear of the traffic police, but because it is in everyone's interest to follow the rules.

Franz-Xaver Kaufmann's interpretation of the German case comes close to such a view. One may have some doubts about his interpretation (for example, the events commonly subsumed under the heading of "1968" would seem to contradict it), but it is clearly the case that, at least until the incorporation of the former German Democratic Republic, West Germany had developed very effective processes to mute and to "civilize" normative conflicts. The constitution *(Grundgesetz)* had become a sort of civil religion, and normative conflicts could be mediated through legally recognized procedures. The transformation of the Greens from a disruptive movement to a political party among others is a prime example of this. However, it is instructive that Kaufmann also mentions "normality" as an important element in this case. "Normality," as he interprets it, is an aspiration. But it is also a factual situation: A society that is economically prosperous and free from immediate external or internal threats to its political stability (there was, of course, the Soviet threat, but the presence of North Atlantic Treaty Organization [NATO] forces was evidently enough of a reassurance for most Germans to feel reasonably secure). So far, so good. In such a situation the traffic-system model of society has a certain plausibility. "Normality," alas, is rarely a permanent state of affairs. When it becomes threatened, for whatever reasons, the question of shared norms quickly attains a new urgency. A central Durkheimian insight is relevant here: Whenever members of a society are called upon to make sacrifices for the common good, the presence of a "collective conscience" is essential. But even in a more-or-less "normal" situation, there is the ongoing imperative to reconcile the beliefs and values of individuals with the legitimacy of the public order. When the gap between these two spheres of social life becomes too large, legitimacy is slowly but surely undermined. The public order becomes progressively meaningless. For a while, under "normal" conditions, this may not matter much. When the society comes under threat, the lack of legitimacy can very quickly become very serious indeed.

"Normative order," "normative conflicts," "normative mediation"— these are concepts that at first glance may seem to be far removed from the social realities with which ordinary people live every day. Social scientists can discuss these matters in various esoteric languages, the use of which may well be doubted. Yet in the end these concepts refer to realities that are very close indeed to the concerns of ordinary people. Essentially the notion of "normative order" means the way in which any human group tries to answer two fundamental questions: *Who are we?* And, *How are we to live together?* One or both of these questions can be found in every one of the cases analyzed in this book. The answers, of course, are very different, and the normative conflicts are rooted in the differences.

Normative Fault Lines: Who Are We?

The American case, as analyzed here by James Hunter, is in many ways paradigmatic. It contains all the essential elements of a societywide normative conflict: Two diametrically opposed sets of normative convictions; a debate over the fundamental nature of the society (in Hunter's words, a struggle over how to define America); opposed delineations of who "we Americans" are and how "we" are supposed to live; different social locations of the two normative systems (by class, education, region) and corresponding sets of associated vested interests; and, last but not least, a complicated set of institutions, most of them in the so-called voluntary sector, mobilized to support one or the other side in the conflict. Finally, attitudes toward religion and the place of religion in the society are a key determinant of who stands where in the conflict. The opposing norms span the most private and the most public concerns, personal morality (sexual behavior, abortion), and the legitimacy of the state (religious symbols in public places, prayer in the public schools). It is indeed, as Hunter named it, a "culture war." This does not mean, of course, that everyone in the country is manning the opposing barricades; this is not the case at all (and is one of the grounds for optimism as to the final outcome). But the battle lines are clearly drawn. Both the democratic political process and the courts are favored battlefields, as each side tries to enlist the vast powers of the state on its behalf. There is a good deal of irony in this development—a relatively recent one, being only some three decades old. America long prided itself as the shining exemplar of successful pluralism; the very word "pluralism" was coined in the United States (in the 1920s, by the American philosopher Horace Kallen), to describe both a fact and an ideal. This very pluralism has now generated a deeply divisive conflict of beliefs and values.

It is instructive to reflect that the phrase "culture war" is actually an Americanization of the German *"Kulturkampf,"* the term applied to the struggle between Bismarck's government and the Catholic Church in the late nineteenth century. Here too (though the word was unknown then) the conflict was over the permissible boundaries of pluralism. In its overwhelmingly Protestant home territories, the Prussian government had been tolerant of religious diversity (allowing, in the words of Frederick the Great, everyone to be saved in his own fashion—*"nach eigener Façon selig werden"*) while at the same time being keenly alert to the dangers of religious conflict. The latter attitude led to the Prussian Church Union earlier in the century, the enforced unification of the Lutheran and Calvinist churches in the Prussian lands. But as Prussia expanded west, incorporating large Catholic populations into its state, this mixture of tolerance and control ran into serious difficulties. The Catholic Church, with its tightly organized international structure centered in Rome, could not so easily be absorbed into what could be called the "Prussian agenda" (the title of the liturgy of the united Protestant church). Bismarck's attempt to do so, both in Prussia proper and in the newly founded Second Reich, failed. In consequence, the definition of who "we Germans" are had to be revised.

In one way or another most of the cases discussed in this book involve conflicts over the nature and the boundaries of the national community, over just what "we" are in each case. In the United States, consonant with the highly moralistic heritage of its history (the Puritan heritage, if you will), this question is closely related to issues of personal morality. As in Europe and all societies with high immigration, the question also involves all the issues associated with so-called "multiculturalism": How much cultural diversity can the nation-state accommodate? The French case is particularly poignant. After more than a century of struggle between "the two Frances"—one conservative and Catholic, the other republican and *laïque*—a reasonable compromise had emerged out of the crucible of World War II, only to be challenged anew in recent years. A major factor in this new challenge has been the introduction of a new reality in French society—the massive presence of an increasingly self-conscious Muslim community. It had become fairly clear what it means to be a French Catholic, a French Protestant, a French Jew, or a French atheist. Given a tradition of racial tolerance, it was also reasonably clear what it means to be a French citizen of North African ancestry, as long as this citizen had thoroughly assimilated to French language and culture. But what does it mean, what could it mean, to be a French Muslim who turns to Mecca in prayer five times a day and who wishes to live in accordance with Islamic religious law? As Hervieu-Léger points out, the very definition of the republican state is now on the table.

The German case is interesting in another way. As Kaufmann shows, in the old Federal Republic, prior to reunification, the question of national identity had been shelved quite successfully. German nationalism had been thoroughly discredited by the events of the Nazi period and in any case seemed implausible in a state containing only a part of the national community. The West German state was exceedingly careful to avoid the symbols and memories of German nationalism (this was particularly difficult as a new West German army was created). The dramatic and rapid reintegration of East Germany necessarily reintroduced the question of national identity, especially since (once again verifying a previously mentioned Durkheimian proposition) West Germans were asked to make considerable sacrifices on behalf of their brethren in the former German Democratic Republic. This intra-German problematic came on top of the problems of multiculturalism that most European societies have been forced to deal with.

In Hungary, as in other countries of the former Soviet empire, the collapse of the Communist regime (the "refrigerator," as János Kovács puts it) brought out once more an old quarrel between "populists" and "urbans" with sharply opposed ideas as to the nature of the national community. South Africa presents a particularly dramatic case of the rapid collapse of a state defined in terms of race and ethnicity, followed by the urgent need to redefine just who "we South Africans" are. The Asian cases as well involve, albeit in different forms as dictated by the different historical backgrounds, the need to redefine the national "we." India has been struggling with this question at least since independence, against the tremendous odds posed by a subcontinent containing a multitude of languages, castes, and religions (not to mention immense class inequalities). Japan had to reinterpret its national identity in the wake of defeat and foreign occupation. In Taiwan, of course, there has been the distinctive problem of an emerging Taiwanese identity in a state that officially understood itself as the exiled government of all of China—the "we Taiwanese" hence colliding in dangerous ways with the official identity of "we Chinese" (on which, paradoxically, the Kuomintang regime in Taipei agreed with the Communist regime in Beijing).

Through most of human history the boundary between "us" and "them" has been defined in religious terms: "We" served these particular gods; "they" served others. Despite the inroads of modern secularity, there continue to be strong connections between national identity and religion in many places. In the Western cases studied, the issue of religion in society occupies an important place in the normative conflicts in two countries, the United States and France. They are not the only ones in the West, but they illustrate the issue very sharply. Religion enters into virtually every disagreement between "conservatives" and "progressives" in the United States, the final disagreement being over the question of whether the nation is to consider itself as being "under God" (a traditional formula, but which, curiously, was only added after World War II to the oath of allegiance used at solemn ceremonies such as the inauguration of new citizens). And if America is indeed a nation "under God," just what does this mean in terms of collective symbols and morally permissible behavior? Can one still speak of a "Judeo-Christian tradition" underlying the American political creed? And what is the status within American pluralism of people who repudiate the traditional "Judeo-Christian" morality (such as gay or lesbian couples insisting that their partnerships be legally recognized as marriages)? In France, after many decades of struggle, the notion of the *laïque* state had finally brought about an uneasy settlement between the "two Frances," when all at once this "republican compact" was challenged from an unexpected source.

If Islam poses a problem for the democratic state in France, it does so much more radically, of course, in all the predominantly Muslim countries. Two of the latter cases analyzed in this book, Turkey and Indonesia, have had relatively robust experience with secular government and religious pluralism, but even there, as was shown, there are powerful movements to redefine the state and the national community in explicitly Islamic terms. The Indonesian case, as discussed by Robert Hefner, is particularly interesting in that one finds here an important movement led by intellectuals who are rethinking Islam in its relationship to modernity, pluralism, democracy, and the market economy. Such rethinking is rarer in the Arab Middle East and in Iran, where a resurgent Islam is much more unyielding in its confrontation with modernity. And religious issues, of course, are pervasive in all the normative conflicts in India that André Béteille reports on, most recently in the disputes on the status of Hinduism within the state, the way of dealing with caste, and the recognition by the state of Islamic personal law. It is instructive to observe that there is one feature of these conflicts that reappears cross-nationally—a highly secularized cultural elite in conflict with a general population that continues to be deeply religious. In a democracy there is the inconvenient fact that the non-elite religious types (the "great unwashed," if you will) have the vote—and there are usually many more of them. Embarrassingly, in a number of countries (notably in the Muslim world) more democracy has meant more power for "fundamentalists" (thus, among other things, creating a dilemma for U.S. foreign policy, which has generally been *for* democracy and *against* "fundamentalism").

Normative Fault Lines: How Are We to Live Together?

If the first focus of normative conflict is the definition of a society's identity, the second focus is the delineation of its moral boundaries: Given some sort of notion as to who "we" are, how are we to live together? Once again, of course, modern pluralism makes it much more difficult to answer this question. A number of normative fault lines have been uncovered in the foregoing analyses.

Ever since the French Revolution a principal fault line has been between the "Right" and the "Left"—conservative, traditional, typically religiously defined forces arrayed against forces representing the faith in progress, radical reconstruction of society, and usually a secular orientation. More precisely describable contents of "Right" and "Left" positions have shifted over time. For a long period the "Left" was primarily determined by an allegiance to socialist ideals. The collapse of Soviet-style socialism and (probably just as important in the long run) a capitalist transformation in China under a regime that still calls itself Communist brought about a considerable decline in the plausibility of socialist ideals, at least for the time being. But the old divides are still there, even if the socialist rhetoric has been muted. Traces, more or less clear, of the old "Right"/"Left" dichotomy can be found in every one of the country cases. In the Chilean case, as reported by Arturo Fontaine Talavera, the old divide attained civil-war dimensions in the very recent past, and the mediation efforts he describes were aimed precisely at the overcoming of this divide. In the South African case, as described by Ann Bernstein, the resistance movement that attained power in the recent transition to multiracial democracy has an explicitly Leninist history, which it is only now, with some difficulty, trying to leave behind. But even if Marxism and other overtly socialist ideologies have not been having a good season of late, the old "Right"/"Left" fault line is prone to reemerge whenever there are sharp conflicts over distribution and equity. Partly as a result of economic globalization, such conflicts are presently on the increase everywhere, including all the industrial democracies. The current debate over "shareholder versus stakeholder capitalism" illustrates this phenomenon very clearly. Among Western and Westernized cultural elites the head may no longer think socialism, but *"le coeur est toujours à la gauche."*

In the West the conflict between "traditional" and "progressive" moral values is a continuation of the conflict unleashed more than two centuries ago by the Enlightenment. In other parts of the world (including Eastern Europe, as in the Hungarian case) the same conflict is, as it were, translated into geographical terms: Traditional values, typically legitimated by reference to religion, are defended against a more-or-less mythical West, perceived as an undifferentiated carrier of a perverted modernity. This is clearly the case in India and in all Muslim countries (including Turkey and Indonesia). In northeastern Asia, where a highly successful modernization process has occurred, the situation was the same until very recently: Traditional Chinese and Japanese values were defended against the "cultural imperialism" of the West. This neat dichotomy has become less plausible and the normative conflicts are defined in a manner not very different from their definition in Western Europe and in the United States. The cases of Japan and Taiwan, as analyzed by Seizaburo Sato and Hsin-Huang Michael Hsiao, are instructive in this regard. But the normative conflicts are not just over theoretical formulations of morality; rather, they concern the enforcement of this or that morality in law. The conflict over abortion in the United States (arguably *the* normative conflict in that society) may be taken as paradigmatic in this sense as well.

A related but yet distinct conflict is between particularistic and universalistic values. The French republican ethos, as discussed by Hervieu-Léger, embodies Enlightenment universalism in a pure form—a radical egalitarianism, in which the individual citizen confronts the state having divested himself, as it were, of all religious or ethnic particularities. This universalism has always been in tension with various particularisms—Catholic or Protestant, regional, most recently Islamic.

In many countries today this conflict is concretized in terms of individual rights versus group rights: Are human rights only ascribable to individuals, or do collective entities of one kind or another have rights too? This conflict comes out sharply in at least three of the countries discussed here, in the debates over "affirmative action"—the United States, South Africa, and India. In all these cases previously discriminated-against groups have been accorded rights that, at least on occasion, may supersede the rights of individuals. In the American and South African cases the collective rights are accorded to racial groups, in India to the so-called "scheduled castes, scheduled tribes, and other backward classes." In all three countries there are legal and political problems coming out of the delicate efforts to balance these particularistic strategies against the universalistic rights enshrined in constitutions, in laws, and in the democratic ethos. To date, at any rate, the conflict has been sharpest in India, where there is the additional problem of reconciling modern notions about equality with a deeply hierarchical culture.

One normative conflict, that between growth and the environment, has appeared in only two of the foregoing case studies—Germany and Taiwan. It is a very recent conflict, having little anchorage in older cultural battles. However, it is becoming more and more important in a broad array of countries, often criss-crossing earlier normative fault lines. The contemporary environmental movements have generally been perceived, and have perceived themselves, as being "on the Left." They have certainly been marked by a considerable anticapitalist animus. However, environmentalism also appeals to deeply conservative people, who (quite correctly) see modern economic growth as corroding traditional ways of life. And the "organic" view of life that environmentalists tend toward—man as part of nature rather than standing over and against it—has always had an affinity with traditional, anti-Enlightenment worldviews.

Norms and Interests

It would of course be an egregious error to think that normative conflicts take place in some kind of Platonic heaven segregated from vested interests. History is not an ongoing philosophical seminar, and philosophical disputes are most of the time closely connected with conflicts over power, privilege, and prestige. Often the philosophical positions are put forth cynically to legitimate the hard-nosed interests at issue; at other times, people genuinely believe (and often enough are ready to both kill and die for) the ideals and values they uphold. But, fortunately or unfortunately, the question of whether these ideals and values are held sincerely or cynically is often irrelevant to one's understanding of a particular conflict situation.

In the foregoing analyses it is very clear how vested interests of different sorts have attached themselves to normative conflicts (or, as Max Weber would have said, how there has developed an "affinity" between certain norms and certain interests). In most countries the conflict between traditional and "progressive" moralities has specific class locations. The "carriers" (another Weberian term) of the cultural radicalisms of the late 1960s have had a very specific social character in all Western countries— overwhelmingly belonging to an upper middle class with higher education. In the United States the cultural conflict analyzed by Hunter has been interpreted as raging between the so-called new knowledge class and the rest of society; this new class is roughly coextensive with the cultural elite and those farther down on the status ladder wishing to belong to it (say, Harvard professors of psychiatry and social workers with therapeutic ambitions). Very similar class dynamics can be observed in Germany (and indeed in all Western European societies). In Hungary the class divide has strong ethnic overtones (specifically, through the role of Jews in the culture). In Chile and South Africa there are regional, racial, and ethnic interests in addition to class interests. In Turkey there is the conflict between "center" and "periphery," with regional, class, and cultural interests involved. And in India there is a huge cacophony of vested interests hanging from the normative conflicts.

Polarizing and Mediating Institutions

One of the major objectives of the present book has been to identify two sets of institutions—those that polarize normative conflicts and those that seek to mediate them. And here has occurred a surprising insight: It is the *same* institutions that, depending on the case, can play the one or the other role. Thus it is not plausible to make one list of institutions that polarize and then contrast it with a list of institutions that mediate. The crucial variable determining which of the two roles an institution will play is not the sociological structure of the institution but rather the ideas and values inspiring it—and, needless to repeat, these ideational contents will typically be linked to specific vested interests. There has been an additional, very useful implication to this insight: At the outset of the project there was a

clear prejudice in favor of "civil society institutions," also known as "intermediate" and "mediating" institutions—that is, those institutions that are
neither governmental nor economic, and which stand between the personal life-world of individuals and the macro-institutions of a modern society. These, of course, are the institutions in which much hope has been invested in modern social thought ever since Edmund Burke and Alexis de
Tocqueville. The expectation here was that it is institutions such as these
that may play a mediating role in conflict situations. And so they may—in
some cases. In other cases, though, it is precisely such institutions that feed
normative conflicts and serve to polarize society. Conversely, such puta-
tively alienating forces as the institutions of government and the market
economy may serve to mediate between conflicting parties.

The American case, as described by Hunter, shows a marked absence
of *any* mediating institutions, except perhaps of a widely diffused culture
of civility that so far has led to a largely violence-free conduct of the "culture war." But the driving forces in the conflict have been, precisely, intermediate institutions of civil society, institutions of the "voluntary sector."
Hunter has coined the sadly apt phrase "adversary philanthropy" to refer to some of these institutions. As to the macro-institutions of the law
and the democratic political process, they have in the main been battlefields of the conflict rather than agencies of mediation. A very similar picture emerges for France (though the episode in New Caledonia shows a
formal government-based agency playing a successful mediating role).
But it is the German and Japanese cases, as analyzed by Kaufmann and
Sato, that most clearly illustrate the aforementioned insight.

In both West Germany and Japan a formal corporatist system has
muted all sorts of conflicts and thus served to stabilize the social order.
The system has, precisely, been based on the macro-institutions of government, organized business, and organized labor. By contrast, it is, precisely, intermediate institutions of civil society—movements and groupings committed to strong normative positions—that have generated
conflicts and disrupted the social order. Kaufmann makes this very useful point most sharply, so that one is tempted to subhead his paper "How
to Defend the Social Order Against Civil Society." Now, it would be fool-
hardy to generalize from these two cases. The apparatus of corporatist
mediation has recently come under considerable strain in both countries,
and even before this happened it was clear that very specific historical
circumstances not replicated elsewhere had given birth to these institutional arrangements. It is also very likely that sustained economic growth
coupled with a generous distribution of its benefits is a precondition for
such a system to succeed (current economic difficulties are what now
threatens the system in both countries). All the same, the German and
Japanese cases are important enough to put in question an easy dichotomy between "bad" macro-institutions and "good" civil society.

In the cases analyzed, deliberate mediating efforts have been made by a great variety of institutions—political parties, courts, institutions of corporate capitalism, educational institutions, the media, religious institutions. Intellectuals—the people who produce and disseminate the ideas by which society defines itself—have played both polarizing and mediating roles. The polarizing role can be seen in every case analyzed. Arturo Fontaine Talavera gives the most dramatic account of intellectuals and their institutions playing a strategically important mediating role in Chile. A similar role for intellectuals can be observed in South Africa. But the most startling feature of the South African case, in Ann Bernstein's account, is the crucial mediating role of big business—an institution that is commonly depicted as a major villain in conflict situations.

Put simply: In terms of social order and the peaceful resolution of normative conflicts, there are both "good" and "bad" macro-institutions, both "good" and "bad" civil-society institutions. An analogy suggests itself here: For a time it was believed that all cholesterol was injurious to health; more recently, medical research came to distinguish between "bad" and "good" cholesterol. In the case of institutions, it is not enough to ask whether they are "macro" or "intermediate"; one must also ask what ideas they "carry" and what interests they represent. Put differently: Civil-society institutions are "good" to the extent that they are animated by civic virtues.

This is not to repudiate the theory (put forward most recently by Thomas Luckmann and the present author) that intermediate institutions are essential for the well-being of modern societies. There must be the "mediating structures" that protect the individual from alienation and the macro-institutions (especially the state) from loss of legitimacy. But the same intermediate institutions can also "go bad," polarizing instead of mediating and thus destabilizing the social order. A further distinction may be useful here: The social function envisaged in the earlier theory is that of "vertical mediation"—that is, mediation between personal life-worlds and the macro-institutions. The concern of the present project has been with what could be called "horizontal mediation"—that is, mediation between conflicting segments in the overall society. What is "good" for one function may be very "bad" indeed for the other function. Thus, for example, a movement propagating racial or ethnic hatred may indeed bridge personal meanings and public concerns, and may do a lot to protect individuals belonging to it against feelings of loneliness and impotence. At the same time, of course, it could have devastating effects in creating conflicts and subverting social order.

A further useful distinction may be made between deliberate efforts of mediation and processes of de facto mediation that no one has planned or organized. The aim of the project, very legitimately, has been to investigate the former kind, but the importance of the latter should not be overlooked. There is, for one, mediation imposed coercively by political or legal fiat. People then come to accept this and become habitualized to acting accordingly. With the passage of time, they may also accept the norms underlying the imposition; this is what Hans Kelsen called the "normative power of facticity." The role of the federal government in imposing desegregation in the American South may serve as an example. There is also spontaneous, undirected cultural change, with large numbers of people changing their attitudes so as to be "with it" culturally. The decline of religious and ethnic prejudices (notably anti-Semitism and anti-Catholicism) in the United States is a case in point (though, of course, there were also deliberate "antidefamation" processes involved in this). The causes of such cultural change are hard to assess. There may be the "invisible" influence of certain institutions, which modify the attitudes and behavior of individuals without making visible efforts in the public arena. Religious and educational institutions often play this role. Thus it is an interesting question (hard to research) to what extent the strength of Christian churches in South Africa has contributed to the relatively peaceful demise of apartheid. There is also the presence of a long-established culture of tolerance, significant in the case of the United States, France (Hervieu-Léger's "ecumenism of the rights of man"), Turkey (Mardin's "Ottoman civility"), Indonesia (the relaxed Islam of traditional Javanese culture), and India (a centuries-old history of religious pluralism). Then there is "normality" and the idealization of this condition, as Kaufmann stressed in his analysis of the German case. Economic prosperity or the reasonable prospect of such prosperity is very probably helpful in generating a climate of tolerance, though, on the other hand, people whose material needs have been met may find the leisure to indulge in the pursuit of potentially conflict-producing "postmaterialist" needs. Finally, in many of the cases analyzed, there is the memory of catastrophe or the specter of threatening catastrophe that may motivate people to look for compromises. This applies to every one of the cases studied, with the possible exception of the United States.

Practical Implications

The present project had from the beginning a practical as well as a theoretical interest—not only to obtain a better understanding of normative conflicts but also to explore possibilities of mediation that could be embodied in policies. What, then, are the practical implications of the foregoing analyses?

If one wishes to mediate any conflict, it is obviously important first of all to acquire a clear understanding of its ideational and social features. This does not necessarily assume research of the social-science variety; often a good journalist does better than a team of sociologists or political scientists (who all too often get bogged down in methodological esoterica). Whoever does the analysis, there is no great mystery as to what must be understood—the contents of the norms on both sides of the conflict, and the way in which these are embedded in a wider worldview (say, a religious one); the way in which the parties in the conflict perceive the situation in which they find themselves (their "cognitive maps," as it were); the vested interests that are attached to the normative positions; the institutions through which people are mobilized to engage in the conflict; and finally, the actual or potential mediating institutions and processes, if any. It is not possible to generalize about the depth of research needed or its duration; this will obviously depend on the given situation, not least on the available literature or other sources of information.

Equally obviously, the next step would have to be an assessment of the institutional options for successful mediation. Choices will have to be made. One may hope that the preceding research will be helpful in making these choices. If no existing institutions seem plausible, there is always the possibility of inventing new institutions—a difficult option, but by no means an impossible one.

Perhaps the most important choice to be made concerns the *type* of mediation one intends to pursue. To clarify this choice, three types can be suggested. The following typology represents a simplification of the very useful one developed by Hervieu-Léger in her chapter.

There is, first, *imperative mediation*. This is a mediating process, normally through political and legal agencies, that eventuates in a clear-cut decision that is then imposed on everyone. In labor relations this is the process known as arbitration—all sides are heard, compromises are weighed, but in the end the arbitrator decides what is to be done and this decision is binding. In the end, this type of mediation is based on coercion—however understanding and open-minded the process leading up to the decision may be, when the decision is made everyone's compliance is enforced under the threat of sanctions (normally by force of law).

Occasionally special agencies may be set up to pursue the mediation/arbitration process (for example, parliamentary commissions or special courts), but most of the time the ordinary institutions of the political system and of law undertake this task. In a democracy the public debates leading up to legislation constitute the forum of mediation. In countries such as the United States where the courts play a strategic constitutional role, litigation provides another method by which a decision is sought. The rules of the game here are well-known to all the parties and they make use of them as their resources allow. As with every policy option, there are benefits and costs to this type of mediation. The major benefit is that, once a decision is made, the matter is ended at least for a while, and all parties are obliged to comply—a law is passed, a court has handed down its decision, and resistance can be legitimately quelled. The cost is that the decision may leave a significant number of people feeling themselves to be oppressed; in the extreme case this may lead them to question the legitimacy of the political and legal institutions through which the decision was made. This, of course, will be especially so if the losing party has a deep commitment to the normative position that has been rejected. An example of this is the sense of disenfranchisement felt by large numbers of Americans as a result of Supreme Court decisions on public prayer and on abortion. Another example is the feeling of oppression of Muslims when a secular state denies or relativizes their conception of what the public morality should be (as in Turkey under Kemalist government).

A second type is *pragmatic mediation*. This, quite simply, is a process of uncoerced negotiation by which the parties themselves seek compromise solutions. This may take place under both democratic and nondemocratic regimes, and it usually means a bargaining behind closed doors between elite groups. Depending on circumstances, this could occur in informal settings (the proverbial smoke-filled rooms—at least in places not yet dominated by the antismoking movement!), or it could make use of any number of specially created mediation agencies. The transitions to democracy in Eastern Europe, in Chile, and in South Africa provide excellent examples of the latter possibility. In all these cases there sprang up a multiplicity of roundtables, think tanks, forums, and the like, where possible compromises were hatched by key participants from the contending parties. As F. van Zyl Slabbert, a leading South African political figure who himself played an important role in the negotiations, recently put it: "We have talked our way through a revolution." In the United States a number of institutions have been created with the express purpose of offering such mediating services on an international scale, such as the Carter Center or Search for Common Ground.

There is a rich and generally useful literature on how such mediation is to be handled—the literature on so-called "conflict resolution." However complicated the particular issues, the strategy here is to set normative disagreements aside, to determine everyone's bottom-line positions, and then to work out a pragmatic compromise. Broadly speaking, this involves converting norms to interests. Once this is done, a sort of "proceduralism" is established: People stop pushing their normative agendas in the public arena, and if the agreed-upon procedures are followed, everyone can be reasonably happy. An example of this, discussed in Kaufmann's paper, is the conversion of the Greens in Germany from a quasi-messianic movement to a political party among others: Environmentalism, while still a faith to many of its adherents, is now one of many competing interests.

The principal advantage of this type of mediation is that the conflict is resolved by the participants themselves, without recourse to coercion. One disadvantage is the potential split between the negotiating elites and their followers who are left out of the mediating process. The latter may feel that their leaders have betrayed them and that, consequently, they need not feel bound by the agreements made. But the principal disadvantage of pragmatic mediation is that it is least likely to work when very deeply held norms are at stake. In ordinary management/labor negotiations it is often possible to arrive at a compromise by "splitting the difference." But how is one to do this when diametrically opposed moral convictions are at stake? Examples would be the debate over abortion in the United States and elsewhere, over genital mutilation of girls in France and other European countries with significant African immigration, or over the status of Islamic religious law in a long list of countries with large Muslim populations. How does one "split the difference" between those who believe that abortion is murder and those who understand it as a woman's right to control her own body? Or between people who believe that God's law supersedes any democratic decisionmaking and those willing to submit their beliefs to the democratic process? Converting norms to interests is likely to be very difficult in such cases. One will either have to have recourse to coercion— which is to imperative mediation—or take a chance with the third, and most difficult type of mediation.

This is what may be called *dialogic mediation*—that is, an effort to engage the normative differences head-on and to seek not just a pragmatic but an ideational compromise.

Needless to say, such cases are rather rare. What is involved here is no less than a redefinition of the "collective memory" (as Hervieu-Léger would put it). The resolution of the conflict in New Caledonia probably comes closest to this type of mediation among the cases discussed in this book. However, the "dialogue" need not always take the form of actual face-to-face negotiation between the contending parties. The creation of new symbols, representing a new postconflict identity, could also be called a kind of dialogic mediation. South Africa again comes to mind here, with the quest for new national symbols in the new democracy, beginning with the flag and the national anthem (actually two anthems at that point). This need not be the result of negotiations but could be effected by imaginative political leadership that shows respect to all the relevant parties. South Africa has been very fortunate in having Nelson Mandela presiding over the transition process, who, as Bernstein points out, has been a mediating institution all by himself. The ingenious adoption of a non-Javanese Malay dialect as the national language of Indonesia, by the otherwise singularly inept Sukarno regime, is another example of the invention of a new national symbol. One may compare this with the unsuccessful attempts to make Hindi the official language of India or Tagalog of the Philippines, resented in both cases as the languages of politically dominant regions.

Once again, this third type of mediation could in principle be carried on in any number of institutions. By definition, it could only be participated in by people prepared to submit their beliefs and values to reasoned discussion; it is not possible to have a dialogue with militant fanatics. Most often this type of mediation occurs spontaneously within processes that have much more mundane purposes, such as those going on under the first two mediation types proposed, rather than in enterprises explicitly defined in terms of this sort of philosophical exchange. There is no body of literature that would instruct us on approaches and methods. It is possible that some methodological lessons could be drawn from the experiences of interreligious dialogue, which has multiplied in recent decades.

It should be pointed out that there has been at least one institution, created in Germany in the wake of World War II, that explicitly intended what has here been called dialogic mediation. This is the Evangelical Academy, a Protestant institution with centers throughout Germany, which has as its avowed aim the bringing together in an uncoerced and searching dialogue of parties that normally only meet each other in confrontational situations. Eberhard Mueller, the founder of the Academy movement, tried to formulate some very tentative ideas on method, but he was far too much engaged with political and social problems of the day to carry these ideas very far. The Academy continues as an institution in Germany today, though it is arguable whether it still fulfills the functions it did in its beginnings. In the 1950s, at any rate, the Protestant Academy (especially in its three major centers of Bad Boll, Loccum, and Tutzing) performed a strategically important role in the new Federal Republic. Two important decisions of that period, the establishment of workers' participation in management (initially in the mining industry) and the establishment of the new West German army, were greatly influenced by discussions at Academy centers.

Of the three types of mediation just discussed, it is clearly the third that would appeal most to intellectuals. It is here, if anywhere, that mediation becomes a vehicle for new insights into the human condition. For just this reason it is likely to appeal *least* to those concerned with achieving practical results. Imperative or pragmatic mediation would appear to be more plausible in most situations. A certain amount of overlap between the three types is also, of course, possible. Genuine dialogue may thus make an appearance in unexpected places, as in bargaining sessions between hard-nosed politicians. In those cases the seeds of a redefined normative order will have been planted. Whatever one's practical priorities may be, it is certainly worthwhile to reflect about the prospects and the possible institutional avenues for the dialogic mediation of normative conflicts.

International Dimensions

As already indicated in the introduction to this volume, pluralism today is not only a phenomenon within but also between societies, and normative conflicts are a visible component of international relations. Samuel Huntington's recent book *The Clash of Civilizations and the Remaking of World Order* has made this fact the centerpiece of his analysis of the contemporary international scene. He concludes his book with a call for dialogue between civilizations. This is but another term for what in this book we called normative mediation.

Some of the normative conflicts raised to our attention in this report as well as the strategies of mediating them have deep implications for the scope of international and intercultural conflict as well. They refer to notions of national identity, common history, visions of the future, and perceptions of progress or traditionalism, which are equally at stake in international relations between nations and cultures. It is the same processes of mobility (geographical and social) that undermine normative homogeneity in a society and at the same time delineate cultural cleavages in international terms. It is not only the processes of economic globalization, media communication, and intellectual cross-fertilization that confront traditional normative patterns within a society with alternatives or challenges; these processes are also the causes for intercourse between members of different cultures in various societies to an extent unprecedented in earlier history.

Many chapters of this volume refer to national identity. In relation to religion, progress, modernization, globalization, and cross-cultural communication, societies are facing the challenge of coming to terms with their self-perception and of reassuring their identity. This process does not always proceed without friction and is not always successful. Radical nationalism and outbursts of violence—both with internal and external effects—are the consequences. This study did not investigate clearly nationalistic conflicts. Nevertheless, the intrasocietal conflicts examined clearly shed some light on arguments referring to national identity. On the one hand, societal dynamics call into question traditional notions of identity, and on the other hand, nationalistic conflicts conducted in an aggressive manner lead to new movements of migration. This in turn challenges social integration and peaceful coexistence across cultural and national borders.

Processes of migration and immigration not only affect social cohesion within societies but also have an impact on relations between societies.

They are interrelated with conflicts of interest, and whenever "clashes" between civilizations are called into question, it is of particular importance to distinguish conflicts of interest and underlying normative divides. What already holds for attempts at solving these conflicts within society is all the more true as regards the international domain. Nevertheless, some inferences can be drawn from the cases in this report if one makes an attempt to find solutions to such intercivilizational conflicts; here the cases are to some extent telling as to the chances of mediation.

It is absolutely crucial to seek ways of establishing communication between the contending parties or between actors that may legitimately represent them. It is equally important to build up some shared experience, to allow some time to pass so that trust and understanding may develop. It is necessary to decide whether there is a chance of disentangling issues of interest from those of norms and cultural patterns. It must be decided which kind of mediation may have a chance to succeed. And answering this question may in turn require the definition of responsible and trustworthy actors. Therefore, in the international domain imperative mediation will be very difficult to pursue because of a lack of plausible candidates for such a function. In a few cases of international intervention, they had to be aggregated on an ad hoc basis in a very difficult process. A system of world governance is beyond perception, and multinational organizations, such as the UN or NATO, or ASEAN or MERCOSUR, are bound to express interests but are in trouble when they have to deal with normative questions.

Pragmatic mediation may be the most promising course allowing for a process of building trust to involve those who are willing to join. In the course of time an already established framework of communication may offer the advantage of having been in existence for some time so that some *conscience collective* may have developed. Whatever the issues to be considered will be, it is important to allow sufficient time to let the process continue. It is quite obvious that a major achievement of any such communication would have to be a considerable degree of exchange of information on each other to provide a more sound basis of mutual normative judgment. As in the case within societies, the first aim will not be the tackling of normative divides itself but rather the dealing with agreed-upon questions that may be consequences of normative clashes and that can nevertheless be tolerated as part of an agenda.

As in the intrasocietal case, dialogic mediation will be the most difficult case to be achieved because it will require dealing with everyone's otherness without simply seeking the least common denominator. The great discovery will not be the one that finds some shared normative elements in the civilizations in question but rather one that finds a legitimate way in each of them to accept that there are others who have their own legitimate claims to identity and existence. The definition of one's own identity and the drawing of lines of distinction from others are necessarily interdependent processes. It would be futile to define one's identity (or that of a civilization, a nation, any collectivity) without any recourse to difference—without the background of other options against which a distinction can be drawn.

The cases of the Muslim countries in our report as well as the countries in transformation processes to democracy and market economies provide clear evidence that the self-definition of a society's identity and answering the question "Who are we?" cannot be effected without recourse to international relations. Normative clashes in all these cases make reference to modernity as represented in models abroad, to "the West" as a model or as a case distinct from the desired path into the future, to democracy as opposed to more culturally "apt" forms of governance, to populist notions of a tradition-rooted development to be distinguished from an alienated, imported model of development. South Africa could not have taken the option it did had it not been for the position that both the Western world and the potential economic partners of the country took with regard to apartheid and that South Africa's neighbors took with regard to the chances of the black population in that country. The business community could not have played its part as it did had it not had the chance to expect backing from its partners abroad. And it is again for this very web of interrelatedness with international relations that South Africa is not a model case for transformation processes in the rest of the continent.

The same holds for the attitudes that allowed the Chilean intellectual elites to play their part in the transition to democracy—again based on notions of the responsibility that they shared with members of the academic elite in many countries of the world. And this in turn raises the more general question of the responsibility or the quality of leadership that has to be provided by trustworthy individuals who may bridge the gap until institutions have sufficiently gained in legitimacy or even efficiency to perform a mediating role. In other words: The Indonesian as well as the Indian case, the South African as well as the Turkish case have shown the great importance of charismatic figures to represent normative positions and to provide a focus for the *conscience collective* on the one hand, but of this very capacity's being able to mediate on the other hand. The successful cases illustrate the relationship between leadership and institutions—reminding us of the fact that neither of them could hope for success without the other.

Even the very telling cases of Japan and Germany as postwar societies cannot be read without keeping in mind that their normative self-perceptions were formulated with reference to external sources—regarding democracy, American occupation played a crucial role; regarding economic development as an integrating force of these societies, their integration into the world economy was vital; and regarding the prevailing notions of "Left" and "Right," nothing could be stated without reference to the Cold War situation. For this very reason their admirable quality of being able to transform normative clashes into conflicts of interest that the political system could legitimately deal with started to crumble at the very moment when the framework of external reference changed totally. These cases tell the story that the case of normality is defined with reference to other cultural and normative patterns, and the case of emergency by the very lack of that. Contrary to currently fashionable assumptions, the difference between civilizations is not a threat in itself but rather a precondition to formulating identities that are characterized by a certain degree of stability.

The pivotal question that arises from an attempt at setting up strategies of mediation in international normative clashes is related to the experience that within societies the macro-institutions of the state play a crucial role: Which could be the international equivalent of national governance? Which institution could be appropriate to provide such services? What sort of design would have to characterize them and from what sources could they derive their legitimation? Under what conditions would they have a chance to develop without being burdened with the necessity of being fully effective from the beginning while having to build up their credibility first? Which could be the forms of leadership that this system could have to rely on or could bear without being thrown out of balance? These are questions yet to be answered but far beyond the scope of this report. The first insights into the conditions for a dialogue between the cultures could be gained from this report, but the great task still lies ahead of us.

Yet there is one conclusion that can be drawn from these considerations with considerable confidence: No matter whether one is primarily concerned with the social cohesion within nations or with the stability of the international order, one will not be able to ignore the normative conflicts that threaten to undermine both. Consequently, the search for possible mediating processes and institutions is of eminently practical significance. It is hoped that the present volume will make a contribution to this concern.

Executive Summaries

1. United States of America

James Davison Hunter

The American Culture War

At the end of the twentieth century, the United States finds itself in the midst of an extensive "culture war" dividing progressives and conservatives on nearly every domestic issue under discussion. Rooted as it is in fundamentally different philosophical assumptions and competing moral visions, the contemporary American culture war challenges democratic institutions in profound ways. This chapter explores the role of civic institutions in mediating these conflicts. In particular, the chapter explores the institution of private philanthropy in providing a bridge between contending forces. Rather than mediating disputes, however, the extensive network of private foundations in the United States engage in this conflict as partisans, on one side or the other. In effect these foundations become de facto special interest groups themselves. Instead of mediating conflict, the involvement of private philanthropy in the United States tends to aggravate it, rendering democratic solutions to normative tensions that much more difficult.

2. France

Danièle Hervieu-Léger

The Past in the Present: Redefining Laïcité *in Multicultural France*

The normative conflicts characteristic of a given society emerge at the precise point where the ideological process of definition and redefinition of collective orientations (which are at once induced by change and generators of change) meets the concrete processes involved in the readjustment of relations between social agents. Accordingly, these conflicts must be seized not as dysfunctions or miscarriages of the social system but as the very dynamic through which society creates itself. In a given society, the truly significant normative conflicts are those that call into question the definition that the society gives of itself—in other words, conflicts that strongly influence the construction of collective identity, the management of memory, and the definition of the foundations on which social cohesion is, or should be, based. Taking into account one of the most decisive changes that have occurred in France since the beginning of the 1980s, this chapter examines the process of redef-

inition of the republican referents in a society in which the most radically foreign element to the national culture is now emerging: that is the claim for communitarian
difference. The question of Islam, which has become the second religion in France
after Catholicism—ahead of Protestantism and Judaism—constitutes the highly
sensitive point of crystallization of a problem that is much more vast: the relation
between particularity and universality in the very definition of French identity. The
main dimension of this problem is the reevaluation of both the ideological and
practical meanings of *laïcité*. The very notion of *laïcité* seems often mysterious (and
untranslatable) outside of France. It has been, for more than a century, a highly specific constituent of the French identity, and it retains today—even though its stakes
have changed considerably—a remarkable capacity to crystallize public debate. Via
the apparently abstract question of the redefinition of *laïcité* comes to light the
whole range of problems related to the construction and preservation of social ties,
in a society whose historical ideal of integration (political, administrative, linguistic, administrative, ideological, and cultural) is now confronted with a new configuration of social and cultural relations characterized by pluralization and fragmentation. The redefinition of *laïcité* today constitutes neither a new point of conflict
between the Catholic Church and the State nor a new episode of the old historical
"War of the Two Frances": hierarchical, conservative, and Catholic on the one hand,
and modern, progressive, and republican on the other. It concerns rather the relation of national common values (shaped at the crossroads of a Catholic civilization
and a revolutionary-republican tradition) to community values held by minority
groups that claim their right to be different in the very name of democracy. In relation to these phenomena of the self-assertion of communities, the state, the Catholic
Church, and Protestant and Jewish institutions representing minorities assimilated
into a republican culture that they have helped to create are striving to re-create,
from the standpoint of their own traditions, a body of common values. Among
themselves, they are entering into unprecedented levels of cooperation, through
which has come into play a redefinition of relations between the Republic and the
different spiritual families that constitute the French identity. In these redistributions, the question of the memory of the different traditions that make up French
identity is particularly important: These traditions are once again elaborated and
re-created with regard to present problems. Taking into account several crucial conflicts marking out this process (the school debates, the conflict in New Caledonia,
etc.), this chapter emphasizes the different mediating processes through which the
normative conflicts giving rise to the redefinition of *laïcité* are capable—under certain conditions—of contributing to the formation of a common identity in today's
multicultural France.

3. Germany

Franz-Xaver Kaufmann

Normative Conflicts in Germany: Basic Consensus,
Changing Values, and Social Movements

If the degree of normative conflict in Germany since World War II is measured by
the virulence of traditional areas of conflict—religion, ethnic origin, class—then

the level of conflict proves to be surprisingly low. Overt normative conflicts have emerged primarily in connection with the formation of new social movements, which have left a characteristic mark on the "old" Federal Republic and its politics. However, more recent developments in the period since the unification of the two postwar Germanies raise the question of whether normative conflicts of the older type are not reemerging. Controversy has flared up in particular over the too-high ancillary wage costs in Germany; the restricted scope for the distribution of income has resulted partly from the growth in competitiveness of other countries with considerably lower wage levels and partly from the rise in ancillary wage costs caused by the unification.

Conflicts that have been made into longer-term political issues by the new social movements have developed above all in the area of environmental risks and the relation between armament and peace. With the exception of the controversy surrounding nuclear power, which connects these two areas and is still virulent today, these conflicts have largely lost their urgency or adopted more conventional forms.

An overview is presented of the most important factors contributing to the hitherto relatively low level of normative conflict in Germany—a fundamental consensus within the major political parties comprising support for the Basic Law (the German constitution); the market economy; the principles of a welfare state; and a corporatistic system of wage negotiation. Essential features include the right to self-organization for groups that represent different normative concerns and their integration into the political decisionmaking process, provided that they form political parties. Beyond this a complex system of negotiating and decisionmaking bodies has developed, particularly in the area of the relationship between capital and labor, in which both parties to the wage agreements are represented. In this the role of state legislation is restricted to procedural regulation. Similarly, the concerns of the new social movements have been defused by the establishment of numerous procedures to ensure the consideration of these concerns. The dominant strategy could then be defined as the linking of the self-organization of normative-oriented groups to the proceduralization of their conflicts.

4. Hungary

János Mátyás Kovács

Uncertain Ghosts: Populists and Urbans in Postcommunist Hungary

In 1989 optimistic observers believed that the century-long cleavage between the so-called "Populists" (nationalists) and "Westernizers" (liberals) would fade from the intellectual and political life of Eastern Europe. Today we know that the rapprochement of the national(ist) and liberal strains of anticommunism was due to the common enemy rather than to normative cohesion. The optimistic prognosis of a sweeping victory of "liberalism with national face" in Eastern Europe had to be revised. Today, instead of a kind of *Verfassungspatriotismus*, nationalism, authoritarianism and neosocialism are ascendant in many of the new democracies. The major normative conflicts are still ritually attached to comprehensive visions of nativist-traditionalist or West-oriented development.

Is it appropriate to use the old designations and call the current confrontation a struggle between "Populists" and "Westernizers"? A widely used hypothesis describes this old dichotomy in terms of the "refrigerator metaphor," according to which communism only froze the old normative conflicts in Eastern Europe, which reappeared in full strength after the refrigerator door had been opened in 1989. However, I prefer the metaphor of the ghosts who were periodically allowed by the Communist rulers to rise from their graves, to scare each other and see the world develop. To put it simply, the Populists were reactivated when the Communist elite needed patriotic legitimation, and the Westernizers were sought when the nomenklatura wanted to initiate limited market reforms and open up a little to the West.

Following the 1989 Revolution, the Populists had to realize not only the costs of ethnic conflict but also those of advocating isolationist policies, an agrarian orientation, and anticonsumerism. At the same time, the Westernizers found themselves confronted with a West imbued with postmodern relativism and scared by the challenge of globalization and its own indecision concerning the future of the welfare state. Interestingly enough, democracy in Hungary first contributed to the sharpening of the conflict, and then—paradoxically—helped to bridge the normative cleavages.

The chapter demonstrates this cyclical process with the example of Hungary, a country in which the normative conflict between the Populists and the Westernizers can be observed both in a transparent dichotomic breakdown and in a surprising historical continuity. In Hungary one finds two large camps of intellectuals and politicians concentrated in the capital who still call themselves "Populists" or "National-Populists" and "Urbans" or "Westernizers." Today they use terms that were coined back in the nineteenth and the early twentieth century. The chapter also examines why reconciliation has proved unsuccessful so far, and how truce can be converted into peace.

Modern democratic politics has instrumentalized—revitalized, exploited, and partly moderated—a traditional normative conflict in Hungary. While the Populists and Urbans were quarreling, the Neo-Socialists emerged as a successful political force that marketed itself as a pragmatic "third party" that ignores ideological strife. By cooperating with the liberals, they cross-cut the boundaries of the old conflict. Nonetheless, the recent cease-fire is only partly intentional: It stems to a large extent from the common frustration experienced in parliamentary realpolitik.

In addition to a growing trust in the benefits of civil society, established democratic procedures had a lasting impact on the mediation of the conflict. Since 1989, democracy taught the participants of the conflict to negotiate with each other and honor second-best solutions in the political process. Conflicting norms were translated into conflicting interests; business groups entered the scene; new buffer zones emerged; and it turned out that there *are* common solutions. Parliamentarism urged many Populists to accept bargaining as such, to obey constitutional procedures, and to exchange romantic language for professional discourse. Similarly, it convinced the Urbans that the Populists are inferior partners in a rational discussion only until they learn to accept the rules of the game.

In 1994 the Hungarian citizens voted for a desacralization in party politics and thus started to "civilize" the conflict, that is, to keep the hostilities under control (or outside the Parliament). The former enemies feel a bit uneasy in the new atmosphere of partial tolerance. With the passage of time, however, the repeated political compromises between them may result in some cultural synthesis of national-conservativism and social liberalism.

5. Chile

Arturo Fontaine Talavera

Revolution from the Top and Horizontal Mediation: The Case of Chile's Transition to Democracy

Chile was governed by General Pinochet for seventeen years. Profound cleavages in society allowed the assumption that peaceful transition would not be possible. The open wounds, the violations of human rights, and in particular, incompatible visions of the past and the future suggested that agreement and negotiation would prove to be either fruitless or ephemeral formalities. Nevertheless, the nation has advanced toward democracy in a covenanted and bloodless way. Manifold factors play a part in the mediation process of a controversy so intense and so radical. This case study attempts to show that Chile's transition to democracy was not simply the consequence of economic growth. It will focus first on the impact of economic and institutional transformations that originated in the government—"the revolution from the top"—and then on the work of private academic institutes devoted to the social sciences who played a mediating role.

The chapter shows that the institutional changes initiated by the Pinochet regime to stabilize its power and to destroy the perspective of a socialist transformation of society had consequences that reached far beyond their original intentions. These changes did not simply support the process of economic modernization, which also led to new constitutional fundamentals, but they also caused a reorganization of basic interests and values in the society as a whole. The result of the dictatorship, therefore, was not a homogenized vision of the future but—in a rather dialectical process—the development of new social and political cleavages. These cleavages contained a variety of impulses for democratization that, by transcending the Pinochet regime, established important prerequisites for the successful transition to democracy.

Private academic institutes devoted to social research played an important role in mediating these new social and political cleavages by serving as an institutional platform where new visions of the future could be negotiated. Although it would be wrong to give the impression that the intellectual elite in Chile had overthrown the dictatorship by means of discussion and producing papers, the academic institutes did offer a peculiar opportunity to propose new ideas that in the long run helped to overcome the social cleavages. In addition, many of the intellectual architects of a "New Chile" who worked within these institutes advanced to political office after the democratization, where they could contribute to the rearrangement of Chilean society. As a result of this process, new visions of the future gained influence, which helped to overcome the heritage of the dictatorial regime as well as the socialist utopia.

6. South Africa

Ann Bernstein

South Africa: Normative Conflict, Social Cohesion, and Mediating Institutions

South Africa in the 1990s is a society undergoing a fundamental transformation. This transformation is taking place in every aspect of South African society and is radical in its implications. This chapter thus explores a society undergoing a profound, albeit negotiated, revolution. The chapter begins with a discussion of the historic and central South African conflict of apartheid and the way in which it affected South African life. This fundamental conflict generated a series of important strategic, political, and ultimately normative divides among apartheid's opponents about how to oppose the system. Next the chapter considers the remarkable political transition that took place in the country. In assessing the transition, many commentators have concentrated on the dramatic and highly visible political developments since F. W. de Klerk announced the lifting of the ban on the African National Congress, the South African Communist Party, and others, and the release of Nelson Mandela. By contrast, this chapter emphasizes two related but different processes that are important in this transformation, namely, the "silent revolution" of de facto desegregation and growing black empowerment, and the "small miracle" of political negotiation and the relatively peaceful introduction of democracy to South Africa for the first time in its history.

The role of business as a mediating institution is highlighted, under apartheid and during the transition toward a new democratic order. The business sector played an unusual and remarkable role in the fight against apartheid and the transition to a new political and social order. Three different aspects are explored: business and its growing opposition to apartheid laws; business and the political negotiations; and business and the peace process.

To conclude, the chapter focuses on new normative conflicts and major issues that confront South Africa now. One particular challenge, the reestablishment of the rule by law inside the country, is spotlighted. The important mediating role of the legal system and the punishments that flow from its abrogation are looked at in this context. The concluding section of the chapter focuses on mediating institutions more generally.

7. Turkey

Serif Mardin

Some Notes on Normative Conflicts in Turkey

Some years ago, Seymour Martin Lipset and Stein Rokkan analyzed[1] both the continuing cleavages in European politics and their partial integration into "centers"[2] by highlighting some of the historical thresholds Europe had had to cross. Among these they counted the confrontations and subsequent negotiations between state and church, between nation builders and locals, and between owners and nonowners of the means of production. The outcome of these contrapositions and mediations was the partial alleviation of the conflict component of the original difference. Lipset and Rokkan's venue has the immense advantage of enabling one to study the influence of fundamental sociopolitical and concomitant cultural cleavages across time in specific national settings, in a manner that differentiates it from the diffuse and panoramic sweeps of Samuel P. Huntington.

In the case of Turkey, what sets the terms of one's analysis in the present is the continuing centricity of center-periphery cleavages in modern times. I have described elsewhere[3] the historical background of this focalization and its modern transformation. What I have attempted to show more recently, as in my contribution to this volume, is the manner in which, in the past four decades, this opposition has been partially turned into a confrontation between the bureaucratic center (i.e., the elite in historical perspective) and Islam (i.e., the folk). Turkish Jacobin officials have perceived this confrontation as one between "backwardness" and "progress" and have acted in consequence. The bureaucrat's originally sincere, if naive, conviction that the introduction of democracy in Turkey would automatically sanitize Islam and expand support for the secular foundations of the state they had built was not borne out. The general astonishment that the revitalization of Islam caused among *bien-pensant* intellectuals of the Turkish Republic since the 1970s can—paradoxically—be attributed to the superficiality of their knowledge of Western social science, a science which they believed they were using as an analytical tool for their projects of modernization but out of which they had left Weber and dismissed the later work of Durkheim.

In this exercise I have attempted to disclose some of the current manifestations of the encounter between the Turkish officials' clouded view of the place of religion in society and Islamist revival, and the way in which this official denial has created basic value conflicts in Turkish society. Elsewhere,[4] I have attempted to show that this very denial has enabled a parallel religious sociopolitical and economic universe to develop in contemporary Turkey, often showing the marks of what in the West one would describe as "civil society."

What we must keep in mind if we are to go on the policy recommendations in the situation I have described is that we nevertheless observe a set of uncoordinated but forceful emergents in Turkey, such as a multifaceted public opinion, which may well work in the direction of synthesis rather than that of continued conflict between secular and religious values.

Notes

1. Seymour M. Lipset and Stein Rokkan, "Cleavage Structures, Party Systems, and Voter Alignment: An Introduction," in *Party Systems and Voter Alignment: Cross-National Perspectives*, ed. S. M. Lipset and S. Rokkan, New York, 1967, pp. 1–64.

2. Edward Shils, "Center and Periphery," in *The Logic of Personal Knowledge: Essays Presented to Michael Polanyi on his Seventieth Birthday*, Glencoe, Ill., 1961, pp. 117–130.

3. *Daedalus*, Winter 1973, pp. 169–190.

4. "Civil Society and Islam," in *Civil Society: Theory, History, Comparison*, ed. John A. Hall, Cambridge, Polity Press, 1995, pp. 278–299.

8. Indonesia

Robert W. Hefner

Islamic Tolerance: The Struggle for a
Pluralist Ethics in Contemporary Indonesia

The largest majority-Muslim nation in the world, the Southeast Asian country of Indonesia has for most of its modern history been racked by political disagreements between supporters of a nonconfessional state and those committed to establishing an Islamic state. Today, however, Indonesia is home to the world's largest and most influential movement for a democratic and pluralist Islam. This movement has been preoccupied with developing normative sanctions for democracy and religious tolerance; it has also rejected the idea that Islam requires the establishment of an Islamic state. In its place, these "civil Muslims" advocate the substantive realization of the values they regard as most intrinsic to Islam— equality, freedom, and social justice—through the strengthening of civil society and constitutional government. This development is of potential importance not only for Islam in Indonesia but also as a model for Muslim pluralism in the rest of the world.

This chapter examines the social and historical background to this effort to develop a modern Islamic tradition of pluralism and tolerance. It also assesses the challenges the movement now faces, which have more to do with structural tensions within the Indonesian political system than with anything peculiar to Islam. At a time when some Western observers speak of a potential "clash of civilizations" between Islam and the West, the Indonesian example provides a local illustration of efforts widespread in the Muslim world to devise an Islamic framework for democratic pluralism and tolerance.

9. India

André Béteille

The Conflict of Norms and Values in
Contemporary Indian Society

Indian society is undergoing a major transformation in which a new order seeking to establish itself on the basis of a liberal and secular constitution has to confront the residues of a traditional hierarchical order. There is in the present context not only a variety of ends considered socially desirable but also much ambiguity, diffuseness, and inconsistency in the regulatory rules for the governance of society and its many institutions. Hence the conflict of norms and values manifests itself in many domains, though not over the same issues in every domain.

The two issues considered in detail in this chapter are related to the pursuit of equality in a hierarchical society, and the viability of secular arrangements in a society permeated by religion. The Constitution of India emphasizes equality within a secular framework, but the programs adopted for securing its objectives encounter various obstacles. India's massive experiment with positive discrimination has brought to light the tensions lodged within the ideal of equality, and the promotion of secularism has not proved easy to combine with the freedom of religion. These conflicts are examined in relation to the prospects of civil society in India, and the concluding section points to the crucial role of judicial and educational institutions in maintaining the conditions for the resolution of conflict.

10. Japan

Seizaburo Sato

Normative Conflicts in Japan

Japan was a late modernizer with a distinctively different cultural tradition from the West's, where modernization first started. As modernization meant Westernization until recently, the normative conflicts that confronted Japan as it modernized arose, above all, around the issue of how Japan's traditional culture, on which its national identity was firmly based, would fare in the process, and hence on what the nature of Japan's modernization program would be. It was by no means an easy task. In order to catch up with the more advanced West, it was impossible for Japan to reject totally the West's industrial civilization. At the same time, the threats from the Western powers fostered a strong anti-West sentiment in Japan. Japan's anti-West nationalism became all the more agitated in the early 1930s as economic confrontation among the major economic powers intensified, only to plunge Japan into a total war against the West.

In pre–World War II Japan, there were three major institutional factors that played a useful role in mediating these national normative conflicts: a strong rising nationalism; the tenacious existence of the traditional communities; and the fact that Japanese enterprises developed a unique management system incorporating communal values and organizational characteristics.

The defeat in World War II and the democratic reforms carried out by the U.S.-led Occupation authorities of the Allied powers shook to their very foundations the traditional order and legitimacy of the state based upon it. The miseries caused by wartime destruction also fostered a strong pacifist sentiment with a strong tinge of antistatism. At the same time, the reality of the Cold War forced the Occupation authorities to modify their policy in order to make Japan a reliable ally against the communist camp. Japan had no alternative but to ally with the United States if it did not want to become a satellite of the Soviet Union. Thus, the major normative conflicts in postwar Japan came to center on one's attitude toward the postwar reforms and the state on the one hand, and the alliance with the United States on the other. By the early 1960s the postwar reforms, through some modifications initiated first by the Occupation authorities and followed up by consecutive Liberal Democratic Party governments, became firmly established in Japanese society. As a result, the confrontational issues surrounding the postwar reforms became meaningless. On the other hand, the runaway economic growth made environmental destruction and welfare the new focus of normative conflicts.

The mediating institutions of normative conflicts also underwent major changes as a result of World War II. Of the three major mediating institutions in the prewar days, both nationalism and traditional communities lost their power of influence in postwar Japan. Only the Japanese way of corporate governance survived through the postwar decades to expand its influence throughout the 1950s and 1960s, aided by the rapid economic growth throughout this period. In postwar Japan, in addition to the Japanese management system, there emerged three new mediating institutions: a new income redistribution mechanism based on sustained high economic growth; the formation of a de facto cooperative working relationship between the ruling LDP and the opposition parties under the 1955 Regime of the LDP's stable one-party dominance; and the proliferation of new religious organizations that placed the guarantee of the temporal world's benefits at the center of their religious teachings.

By the 1980s Japan had become the world's largest creditor nation, enjoying the largest trade surplus. The termination of the Cold War has also produced a higher level of interest among the Japanese in playing a larger international role. But whether Japan's role should be limited to nonmilitary areas or expanded to include a military role remains sharply contentious. Since the early 1990s Japan has sunk into a prolonged recession that has proven to be the most serious since the end of World War II. This economic difficulty has aroused a new strong interest in economic recovery and made the confrontation between economic growth and environmental protection almost meaningless. How these new normative conflicts can be mediated and by what kind of institutions, however, remains to be seen.

11. Taiwan

Hsin-Huang Michael Hsiao

Normative Conflicts in Contemporary Taiwan

This chapter addresses the two most salient normative conflicts in contemporary Taiwanese society, namely, the controversy over Taiwan's national identity and the conflict between growth and environmental quality. The historical origins, the social bases of competing groups and actors, the different public discourses and political agendas, and the prospects for mediation for these normative conflicts are explored.

It is found that the common ground for possible mediation in the normative conflicts over Taiwan's national identity has actually evolved during the course of the intensive competition between adversary political agendas mobilized by the conflicting political parties and civil-society groups. It is also found that the life experiences of the postwar development shared by the people of Taiwan are the most important institutionalized norms that may legitimate the further construction of a new Taiwanese national identity distinct from China.

On the other hand, the conflict between growth and environmental values was primarily generated by the rise of the environmental movement, and this civil-society-led new social movement has succeeded in calling into question the state's pro-growth ideology and policies. Though the state and its industrialist allies have been forced to be more responsive to environmental problems, without more vigorous public discourse and more organized challenge from the civil society the long-lasting pro-growth state strategy will not easily be changed.

In the final analysis, it is the conflicting discourses brought about by the great transformations experienced in Taiwan since the 1980s that have created and accelerated the normative conflicts over national identity and environmental values. The changing social reality has generated conflicting definitions of the meaning of the past and visions of the future for Taiwanese society. And it is this social reality that has also fostered the possibilities and feasible directions for mediation in resolving the two most salient normative conflicts in contemporary Taiwan.

Bibliography

Ahmad, I., ed., 1973, *Caste and Social Stratification Among the Muslims*, New Delhi.

Ali, F., and Bahtiar, E., 1986, *Merambah Jalan Baru Islam: Rekonstruksi Pemikiran Islam Indonesia Masa Orde Baru* (To Open a New Islamic Road: The Reconstruction of Indonesian Islamic Thought in the New Order Era), Bandung.

Anderson, B. R., 1983, *Imagined Communities: Reflections on the Origin and Spread of Nationalism*, London.

Ansari, G., 1959, *Muslim Caste in Uttar Pradesh*, Lucknow.

Bakker, F. L., 1993, *The Struggle of the Hindu Balinese Intellectuals*, Amsterdam.

Ballion, R., 1982, *Les consommateurs d'école*, Paris.

Banac, I., ed., 1991, *Eastern Europe in Revolution*, Ithaca.

Barton, G., 1995, "Neo-modernism: A Vital Synthesis of Traditionalist and Modernist Islamic Thought in Indonesia," *Studia Islamika: Indonesian Journal for Islamic Studies* 2(3), pp. 1–75.

Baubérot, J., 1990a, *Vers un nouveau pacte laïque?* Paris.

———, 1990b, *La laïcité, quel héritage? De 1789 à nos jours*, Geneva.

———, 1988, *Le protestantisme doit-il mourir?* Paris.

Baxi, U., 1996, *On Judicial Activism: Legal Education and Research in Globalizing India*, New Delhi.

Bellah, R. N., 1985, *Habits of the Heart: Individualism and Commitment in American Life*, Berkeley.

———, 1975, *The Broken Covenant: American Civil Religion in Time of Trial*, Chicago.

Berger, P. L., and Luckman, T., 1995, *Modernität, Pluralismus und Sinnkrise, Die Orientierung des modernen Menschen*, Gütersloh (English: *Modernity, Pluralism, and the Crisis of Meaning*, 1995).

———, 1992, *A Far Glory: The Quest for Faith in an Age of Credulity*, New York.

Bernstein, A., ed., 1995, "Post-Apartheid Population and Income Trends," *CDE Research*, No. 1, Centre for Development and Enterprise, Johannesburg.

Bernstein, A., et al., 1996, "Business and Democracy: Cohabitation or Contradiction?" Development and Democracy, No. 10, Centre for Development and Enterprise, Johannesburg.

Béteille, A., 1996, "Caste in Contemporary India," in C. J. Fuller, ed., *Caste Today*, Delhi.

———, 1994, "Secularism and the Intellectuals," *Economic and Political Weekly*, vol. 24, no. 10, pp. 559–566.

———, 1991, *Society and Politics in India: Essays in a Comparative Perspective*, London.

———, 1987a, "Equality as a Right and as a Policy," *LSE Quarterly*, vol. 1, no. 1, pp. 75–98.

———, 1987b, *The Idea of Natural Inequality and Other Essays*, 2d ed., Delhi.

———, 1986, "The Concept of Tribe, with Special Reference to India," *European Journal of Sociology*, vol. 27, pp. 297–318.

Bibó, I., 1992, *Die Misere der osteuropäischen Kleinstaaterei*, Frankfurt.

———, 1990, *Zur Judenfrage: Am Beispiel Ungarns nach 1944*, Frankfurt.

Birnbaum, P., 1995, *Destins juifs: De la Révolution française à Carpentras*, Paris.

———, 1992, *Les fous de la République: Histoire politique des juifs d'État, de Gambetta à Vichy*, Paris.

———, 1988, *Un mythe politique: La "république juive,"* Paris.

Boland, B. J., 1982, *The Struggle of Islam in Modern Indonesia*, The Hague.

Borbándi, G., 1976, *Der ungarische Populismus*, Munich.

Bornschier, V., and Lengyel, P., 1994, *Conflicts and New Departures in World Society*, New Brunswick, N.J.

Bös, M., 1993, "Ethnisierung des Rechts? Staatsbürgerschaft in Deutschland, Frankreich, Großbritannien und den USA," *Kölner Zeitschrift für Soziologie und Sozialpsychologie* 45, pp. 619–643.

Bose, N. K., 1975, *The Structure of Hindu Society*, Delhi (translated from the Bengali edition of 1949).

Boussinesq, J., 1994, *La laïcité française: Memento juridique*, Paris.

Bowen, J. R., 1993, *Muslims Through Discourse: Religion and Ritual in Gayo Society*, Princeton.

Bozóki, A., 1993, "Hungary's Road to Systemic Change: The Opposition Round-table," *East European Politics and Societies*, Spring.

Brand, K.-W., et al., 1983, *Aufbruch in eine andere Gesellschaft: Neue soziale Bewegungen in der Bundesrepublik*, Frankfurt am Main and New York.

Brisebarre, A. M., 1989, "La célébration de l'Ayd-el-Kabir en France: Les enjeux du sacrifice," *Archives de Sciences Sociales des Religions* 68(1), July-December.

Bruner, J., 1990, *Acts of Meaning*, Cambridge, Mass., and London.

Budiman, A., ed., 1990, *State and Civil Society in Indonesia*, Clayton, Australia.

Casanova, J., 1994, *Public Religions in the Modern World*, Chicago.

Castoriadis, C., 1987, *The Imaginary Institution of Society*, Cambridge.

Chang, Mau-Kuei, et al., 1993, *Ethnic Relations and National Identity*, Taipei.

Chang, Ying-Hwa, 1992, "Ethnic Problems" (in Chinese), in Institute of Social Science and Philosophy, *Social Attitudes Survey Report 1992*, pp. 31–38.

Charney, C., 1994, *Political Violence, Local Elites, and Democratic Transition: Business and the Peace Process in South Africa*, unpublished paper commissioned by the Development Strategy and Policy Unit, Urban Foundation.

Chen, Chung-Min, et al., eds., 1994, *Ethnicity in Taiwan: Social, Historical, and Cultural Perspectives*, Taipei.

Cheng, R. L., 1994, "Language Unification in Taiwan: Present and Future," in M. A. Rubinstein, ed., *The Other Taiwan: 1945 to the Present*, Armonk, N.Y., pp. 357–391.

Chikio Hayashi, 1995, *Suji karamita Nihonjin no Kokoro* (Statistical Analysis of Japanese Attitudes), Tokyo.

Cohen, M., 1993, "Les juifs de France: Affirmations identitaires et évolution du modèle d'intégration," *Le Débat*, no. 75, May-August.

Cohen, M. J., 1988, *Taiwan at the Crossroads: Human Rights, Political Development, and Social Change in the Beautiful Island*, Washington, D.C.

Collins, R., 1975, *Conflict Sociology: Toward an Explanatory Science*, New York.

Constable, P., and Valenzuela, A., 1991, *A Nation of Enemies: Chile Under Pinochet*, New York.

Cooper, C., et al., 1992, *Race Relations Survey*, South African Institute of Race Relations, Johannesburg.

Coq, G., 1995, *Laïcité et République: Le lien nécessaire*, Paris.

Coulson, N. J., 1964, *A History of Islamic Law*, Edinburgh.

Csizmadia, E., 1995, *A magyar demokratikus ellenzék (1968–1988)* (The Democratic Opposition in Hungary), Budapest.

Davie, G., and Hervieu-Léger, D., eds., 1996, *Les identités religieuses des européens*, Paris.

Dettling, W., 1995, *Politik und Lebenswelt, Vom Wohlfahrtsstaat zur Wohlfahrtsgesellschaft*, Gütersloh.

Diamond, L., and Plattner, M. F., eds., 1993, *Capitalism, Socialism, and Democracy Revisited*, Baltimore and London.

Dore, R. P., 1965, *Education in Tokugawa*, London.

Doumergue, J. P., 1994, "L'enracinement des mouvements politiques en Nouvelle-Calédonie," *Acta Geographica*, no. 98, pp. 20–42.

Dumont, L., 1970, *Religion, Politics, and History in India*, Paris.

_____, 1966, *Homo Hierarchicus*, Paris.

Edwards, S., and Cox, A., 1991, *Monetarism and Liberalization*, Chicago.

Efe, M., 1993, *Mizraksiz Ilmihal*, Istanbul.

Effendy, B., 1995, "Islam and the State in Indonesia: Munawir Sjadzali and the Development of a New Theological Underpinning of Political Islam," *Studia Islamika: Indonesian Journal for Islamic Studies* 2(2), pp. 97–121.

Everatt, D., and Orkin, M., eds., 1993, *Growing Up Tough: A National Survey of South African Youth*, Community Agency for Social Enquiry, Johannesburg.

Falcoff, M., et al., 1988, *Chile: Prospects for Democracy*, New York.

Feith, H., 1962, *The Decline of Constitutional Democracy in Indonesia*, Ithaca.

Fukuyama, F., 1995, *Trust: The Social Virtues and the Creation of Prosperity*, New York.

_____, 1992, *Das Ende der Geschichte: Wo stehen wir?* Munich.

Furet, F., 1995, *Le passé d'une illusion*, Paris.

Gabriel, C., and Kermel, V., 1988, *Nouvelle-Calédonie: Les sentiers de l'espoir*, Paris.

Gabriel, O. W., 1986, *Politische Kultur, Postmaterialismus und Materialismus in der Bundesrepublik Deutschland*, Opladen.

Galanter, M., 1984, *Competing Equalities*, Delhi.

Ganguli, B. N., 1975, *Concept of Equality: The Nineteenth Century Indian Debate*, Simla.

Gaspard, E., and Khosrowkhavar, F., 1995, *Le voile et la République*, Paris.

Gauchet, M., 1985, *Le désenchantement du monde: Une Histoire politique de la religion*, Paris.

Gauthier, G., 1994, *Un village, deux écoles*, Paris.

Geertz, C., 1960, *The Religion of Java*, New York.

Gellner, E., 1994, *Encounters with Nationalism*, Oxford.

_____, 1992, *Nationalismus in Osteuropa*, Vienna.

Giddens, A., 1991, *Modernity and Self-Identity*, Stanford.

Godwin, C. J., 1972, *Change and Continuity: A Study of Two Christian Village Communities in Suburban Bombay*, Bombay.

Gole, N., 1992, *Modern Mahrem*, Istanbul.

Greenfeld, L., 1992, *Nationalism: Five Roads to Modernity*, Cambridge, Mass.

Greiffenhagen, M., et al., 1993, *Ein schwieriges Vaterland: Zur politischen Kultur im vereinigten Deutschland*, Munich and Leipzig.

Greskovits, B., 1995, "Demagogic Populism in Eastern Europe?" *Telos*, Winter.

Hale, W., 1994, *Turkish Politics and the Military*, London and New York.

Hall, J. A., ed., 1993, *Civil Society: Theory, History, Comparison*, Cambridge.

Hanf, T., et al., 1981, *South Africa: The Prospects of Peaceful Change—An Empirical Enquiry into the Possibility of Democratic Conflict Regulation*, London.

Hanioglu, M. S., 1995, *The Young Turks in Opposition*, New York and Oxford.

Haraszti, M., 1987, *The Velvet Prison: Artists Under State Socialism*, New York.

Hassan, M. K., 1982, *Muslim Intellectual Responses to "New Order" Modernization in Indonesia*, Kuala Lumpur.

Hefner, R. W., 1993a, "Of Faith and Commitment: Christian Conversion in Muslim Java," in R. W. Hefner, ed., *Conversion to Christianity: Historical and Anthropological Perspectives on a Great Transformation*, Berkeley.

_____, 1993b, "Islam, State, and Civil Society: ICMI and the Struggle for the Indonesian Middle Class," *Indonesia* 56 (October), pp. 1–36.

_____, 1990, *The Political Economy of Mountain Java: An Interpretive History*, Berkeley.

_____, 1985, *Hindu Javanese: Tengger Tradition and Islam*, Princeton.

Hellmann, K.-U., 1996, *Systemtheorie und neue soziale Bewegungen*, Opladen.

Hervieu-Léger, D., ed., 1990, *La religion au lycée: Conférences au lycée Buffon*, Paris.

Hof, B., 1991: *Für mehr Verantwortung—Langzeitarbeitslosigkeit und soziale Marktwirtschaft*, Cologne.

Hsiao, H.H.M., 1996, "Changing Literary Images of Taiwan's Working Class," in E. Perry, ed., *Putting Class in Its Place: Bases of Worker Identity in East Asia*, Berkeley.

_____, 1994a, "Social Movements and Civil Society in Taiwan: A Typological Analysis of Social Movements and Public Acceptance," paper presented at the Twenty-eighth World Congress of Sociology, Bielefeld, Germany, July 18–23.

_____, 1994b, "The Character and the Changes of Taiwan's Local Environment Protect Movement, 1980–1991" (in Chinese), in Taiwan Research Fund, ed., 1994, *Environmental Protection and Industrial Policies*, Taipei, pp. 550–573.

_____, 1991, "Ethnic Identification and Ethnic Issues" (in Chinese), Institute of Social Science and Philosophy, Academia Sinica, *Social Attitudes Survey Report 1991*, pp. 41–50.

_____, 1987, "Who Cares About Taiwan's Natural Environment? The Formation and Evolution of Nature Conservation" (in Chinese), in H.H.M. Hsiao, *We Have Only One Taiwan*, Taipei, pp. 81–104.

Hsiao, H.H.M., and Koo, H., 1995, "The Middle Classes and Democratization in East Asia: Taiwan and South Korea Compared," paper presented at an International Conference on Consolidating the Third Wave Democracies, Institute for National Policy Research, Taipei, August 27–30.

Hsiao, H.H.M., and So, A., 1993, "Ascent Through National Integration: The Chinese Triangle of Mainland–Taiwan–Hong Kong," in R. Palat, ed., *Asia-Pacific and the Future of the World Economy*, Westport, Conn., pp. 133–147.

Hsiao, H.H.M., et al., 1995, "Antecedents of an Environmental Movement in Taiwan," *Capitalism, Nature, Socialism*, vol. 6, no. 3, pp. 91–104.

Hsu, Shih-Jung, 1995, *Environmental Protest, the Authoritarian State, and Civil Society: The Case of Taiwan*, Ph.D. diss., University of Delaware.

Hunter, J. D., 1994, *Before the Shooting Begins: Searching for Democracy in America's Culture War*, New York.

_____, 1991, *Culture Wars: The Struggle to Define America*, New York.

Huntington, S. P., 1996, *The Clash of Civilizations and the Remaking of World Order*, New York.

_____, 1993, "The Clash of Civilizations?" *Foreign Affairs* 72(3) (Summer), pp. 22–49.

Hunyadi, M., 1995, *La vertu du conflit: Pour une morale de la médiation*, Paris.

Inalcik, H., 1973, *The Ottoman Empire: The Classical Age, 1300–1600*, London.

Ionescu, G., and Gellner, E., eds., 1969, *Populism, Its Meanings and National Characteristics*, London.

John, L., ed., *The Oxford Encyclopedia of the Modern Islamic World*, New York.

Johns, A. H., 1987, "An Islamic System or Islamic Values? Nucleus of a Debate in Contemporary Indonesia," in W. R. Roff, ed., *Islam and the Political Economy of Meaning*, London, pp. 254–280.

Kahin, G., 1952, *Nationalism and Revolution in Indonesia*, Ithaca.

Kalberg, S., 1994, *Max Weber's Comparative-Historical Sociology*, Chicago.

Kane, P. V., 1974, *History of Dharmashastra*, Poona.

Kane-Berman, J., 1990, *South Africa's Silent Revolution*, Johannesburg.

Karlekar, M., 1983, "Education and Inequality," in A. Béteille, ed., *Equality and Inequality*, Delhi, pp. 182–242.

Karve, I., 1968, *Hindu Society: An Interpretation*, 2d ed., Poona.

Katzenstein, P. J., 1996, *Cultural Norms and National Security: Police and Military in Postwar Japan*, Ithaca and London.

Kaufmann, F.-X., 1989, "Die soziale Sicherheit in der Bundesrepublik Deutschland," in W. Weidenfeld and H. Zimmermann, eds., *Deutschland-Handbuch: Eine doppelte Bilanz 1949 bis 1989*, Munich, pp. 308–325.

Kenya Numata, 1988, *Gendai Nihon no Shinshukyo* (New Religions in Modern Japan), Tokyo.

Kepel, G., 1987, *Les banlieues de l'islam: Naissance d'une religion en France*, Paris.

Kitschelt, H., 1980, *Kernenergiepolitik—Arena eines gesellschaftlichen Konflikts*, Frankfurt am Main and New York.

Knoke, D., 1986, "Associations and Interest Groups," *American Review of Sociology* 12, pp. 1–21.

Konrád, G., and Szelényi, I., 1979, *The Intellectuals on the Road to Class Power*, New York.

Kothari, R., ed., 1969, *Caste in Indian Politics*, Delhi.

Kovács, J. M., 1993, "Which Institutionalism? Searching for Paradigms of Transformation in Eastern European Economic Thought," in H.-J. Wagener, ed., *The Political Economy of Transformation*, Heidelberg.

_____, 1992, "Compassionate Doubts About Reform Economics (Science, Ideology, Politics)," in J. M. Kovács and M. Tardos, eds., *Reform and Transformation: Eastern European Economics on the Threshold of Change*, London.

Kovács, J. M., ed., 1994, *Transition to Capitalism? The Communist Legacy in Eastern Europe*, New Brunswick, N.J.

_____, 1991, "Rediscovery of Liberalism in Eastern Europe," *East European Politics and Societies*, special issue, Winter.,

Kuppuswami, A., ed., 1991, *Mayne's Treatise on Hindu Law and Usage*, 13th ed., New Delhi.

Lampert, H., 1995, *Die Wirtschafts- und Sozialordnung der Bundesrepublik Deutschland*, 12th edition, Munich.

Langlois, C., 1988, "L'héritage de la Révolution française: Les trois cercles de laïcisation," *Projet*, September-October.

Le Bras, G., 1955–1956, *Etudes de sociologie religieuse*, 2 volumes, Paris.

Lebrun, F., ed., 1980, *Histoire des catholiques en France*, Paris.

Lepsius, M. R., 1966, "Parteiensystem und Sozialstruktur: Zum Problem der Demokratisierung der deutschen Gesellschaft," in W. Abel, ed., *Wirtschaft, Geschichte und Wirtschaftsgeschichte*, Stuttgart, pp. 371–393.

Leveau, R., and Kepel, G., eds., 1988, *Les musulmans dans la société française*, Paris.

Lewis, B., 1968, *The Emergence of Modern Turkey*, 2d ed., London.

Lipset, S. M., 1959, *Political Man: The Social Bases of Politics*.

Lodge, T., and Nasson, B., 1991, *All Here and Now: Black Politics in the 1980s*, Cape Town.

Luhmann, N., 1991, *Soziologie des Risikos*, Berlin and New York.

Lyon, M. L., 1977, "Politics and Religious Identity: Genesis of a Javanese-Hindu Movement in Rural Central Java," Ph.D. diss., University of California, Berkeley.

Mackie, J., 1992, "Changing Patterns of Chinese Big Business in Southeast Asia," in R. McVey, ed., *Southeast Asian Capitalists*, Ithaca, pp. 161–190.

Madan, T. N., 1987, "Secularism in Its Place," *Journal of Asian Studies* 46(4), pp. 747–759.

Maître, J., et al., 1991, *Les Français sont-ils encore catholiques?* Paris.

Mamoru Sasaki, 1984, *Sakaki Mamoru Shinario Shu* (Selected Scenarios), Tokyo.

Mardin, S., 1988, "Freedom in an Ottoman Perspective," in M. Heper and A. Evin, eds., *State, Democracy, and Military: Turkey in the 1980s*, Berlin and New York, pp. 23–35.

_____, 1964, *Jon Turklerin Siyasi Fikirleri*, Ankara.

Mardin, S., ed., 1994, *Cultural Transitions in the Middle East*, Leiden.

Marshall, T. H., 1977, *Class, Citizenship, and Social Development*, Chicago.

Martin, D., 1979, *A General Theory of Secularization*, London.

Masachi Osawa, 1996, *Kyoko no Jidai no Hate* (At the End of the Fictitious Age), Tokyo.

May, B., 1978, *The Indonesian Tragedy*, Singapore.

Messner, F., ed., 1995, *La culture religieuse à l'école*, Paris.

Mitchell, R. P., 1969, *The Society of the Muslim Brothers*, New York.

Monbusho (Ministry of Education, Science, Culture and Sport), ed., 1948 and 1961, *Shukyo Nenkan* (Annals of Religious Organizations), Tokyo.

Mortimer, R., 1974, *Indonesian Communism Under Sukarno: Ideology and Politics, 1959–1965*, Ithaca.

Moussalli, A. S., 1992, *Radical Islamic Fundamentalism: The Ideological and Political Discourse of Sayyid Qutb*, Beirut.

Müller, H. P., 1992, *Sozialstruktur und Lebensstile*, Frankfurt am Main.

Nehru, J., 1961, *The Discovery of India*, Bombay (first published 1946).

Noer, D., 1973, *The Modernist Muslim Movement in Indonesia, 1900–1942*, Kuala Lumpur.

Norton, A. R., 1995, *Civil Society in the Middle East*, Leiden.

Ozouf, J., 1973, *Nous les maîtres d'école: Autobiographies d'instituteurs de la Belle Époque*, Paris.

Ozouf, M., 1989, *L'homme régénéré: Essais sur la Révolution française*, Paris.

Parsons, T., 1966, *Societies: Evolutionary and Comparative Perspectives*, Englewood Cliffs, N.J.

Parsons, T., and Shils, E. A., eds., 1951, *Towards a General Theory of Action*, Cambridge, Mass.

Poulat, E., 1987, *Liberté, laïcité: La guerre des deux France et le principe de la modernité*, Paris.

———, 1977, *Eglise contre bourgeoisie*, Paris.

Price, R., 1991, *Apartheid State in Crisis: Political Transformation in South Africa, 1975–1990*, New York.

Puryear, J., 1994, *Thinking Politics*, London.

Rémond, R., 1984a, "La laïcité n'est plus ce qu'elle était," *Etudes*, April, pp. 439–448.

Robison, R. 1986, *Indonesia: The Rise of Capital*, Sydney.

Roller, E., 1992, *Einstellungen der Bürger zum Wohlfahrtsstaat der Bundesrepublik Deutschland*, Opladen.

Roy, O., 1994, *The Failure of Political Islam*, Cambridge.

Rubinstein, M. A., ed., 1994, *The Other Taiwan: 1945 to the Present*, Armonk, N.Y.

Saktanber, A., 1994, "Becoming the 'Other' as a Muslim in Turkey: Turkish Women vs. Islamist Women," *New Perspectives in Turkey*, no. 11 (Autumn), p. 99.

Savary, A., 1985, *En toute liberté*, Paris.

Schermerhorn, R. A., 1978, *Ethnic Plurality in India*, Tucson.

Schlozman, K. L., and Tierney, J. T., 1985, *Organized Interests and American Democracy*, New York.

Schmidtchen, G., 1996, *Lebenssinn und Arbeitswelt, Orientierung im Unternehmen*, Gütersloh.

Schnapper, D., 1994, *La communauté des citoyens: Sur l'idée moderne de nation*, Paris.

Schulze, G., 1992, *Die Erlebnisgesellschaft: Kultursoziologie der Gegenwart*, Frankfurt am Main.

Schwarz, A., 1994, *A Nation in Waiting: Indonesia in the 1990s*, Boulder.

Seligman, A., 1992, *The Idea of Civil Society*, New York.

Serjeant, R. B., 1981, *Studies in Arabian History and Civilization*, London.

Shils, E. A., 1961, *The Intellectual Between Tradition and Modernity: The Indian Situation*, The Hague.

Sivaramayya, B., 1984, *Inequalities and the Law*, Lucknow.

Six, J. F., 1995, *Dynamique de la médiation*, Paris.

Smelser, N. J., 1962, *Theory of Collective Behavior*, New York.

Srinivas, M. N., 1966, *Social Change in Modern India*, Berkeley.

_____, 1962, *Caste in Modern India and Other Essays*, Bombay.

Szacki, J., 1995, *Liberalism After Communism*, Budapest.

Sullivan, J., et al., 1982, *Political Tolerance and American Democracy*, Chicago.

Susumu Shimazono, 1992, *Shin Shin Shukyo to Shukyo Buum* (Neo–new Religions and a New Tide of Religious Activities), Tokyo.

Tanter, R., and Young, K., eds., 1990, *The Politics of Middle Class Indonesia*, Clayton, Australia.

Taylor, C., 1989, "Cross-Purposes: The Liberal-Communitarian Debate," in N. Rosenblum, ed., *Liberalism and the Moral Life*, Cambridge.

Tekeli, S., ed., 1995, *Women in Modern Turkish Society*, London and New Jersey.

Tokei Suri Kenkyujo (Institute of Statistical Research), ed., 1992, *Nihonjin no Kokuminsei* (Japanese National Character), vol. 5, Tokyo.

Touraine, A., 1973, *Production de la société*, Paris.

Tripathi, P. K., 1972, *Some Insights into Fundamental Rights*, Bombay.

Turner, V., 1969, *The Ritual Process: Structure and Anti-Structure*, Chicago.

Valenzuela, A., 1978, *The Breakdown of Chilean Democracy*, Baltimore and London.

Venturi, F., 1972, *Les intellectuels, le Peuple et la Révolution: Histoire du populisme russe*, Paris.

Wachman, Alan, 1994, *Taiwan: National Identity and Democratization*, Armonk, N.Y.

Walicki, A., 1975, *The Slavophile Controversy*, Oxford.

_____, 1969, *The Controversy over Capitalism*, Oxford.

_____, 1967, *Legal Philosophies of Russian Liberalism*, Oxford.

Willaime, J. P., 1992, "La laïcité française au miroir du foulard," *Le Supplément*, no. 181, July.

Winock, M., 1989, "Les combats de la laïcité," *L'Histoire*, no. 128, December.

Woodward, M. R., 1989, *Islam in Java: Normative Piety and Mysticism in the Sultanate of Yogyakarta*, Tucson.

Wu, Nai-Teh, 1993, "Ethnic Relations, Political Support, and National Identity" (in Chinese), in Chang Mau-Kuei et al., *Ethnic Relations and National Identity*, Taipei, 27–51.

Wuthnow, R., ed., 1991, *Between States and Markets: The Voluntary Sector in Comparative Perspective*, Princeton.

Yalcin-Heckmann, L., 1991, *Tribe and Kinship Among the Kurds*, Frankfurt.

Zurcher, E. J., 1993, *Turkey: A Modern History*, London and New York.

About the Contributors

Peter L. Berger

Born 1929 in Vienna; since 1985 Director of the Institute for the Study of Economic Culture, Boston University.

1955–56 Research Director, Academy of the Protestant Church, Bad Boll, Germany; 1956–58 Professor at the Women's College, University of North Carolina; 1958–63 Director at the Institute of Church and Community, Hartford Theological Institute of Church and Community, Hartford Theological Seminary; 1963–70 Professor at the Graduate Faculty, New School for Social Research, New York; 1970–79 Professor at Rutgers University; 1979–81 Professor at Boston College; since 1981 Professor at Boston University.

Publications:

Invitation to Sociology: A Humanistic Perspective, 1963; *The Social Construction of Reality* (with Thomas Luckmann), 1966; *The Sacred Canopy: Elements of a Sociological Theory of Religion,* 1967; *A Rumor of Angels: Modern Society and the Rediscovery of the Supernatural,* 1969; *The Homeless Mind: Modernization and Consciousness* (with Brigitte Berger and Hansfried Kellner), 1973; *Pyramids of Sacrifice: Political Ethics and Social Change,* 1975; *The Heretical Imperative,* 1979; *Sociology Reinterpreted* (with Hansfried Kellner); *The War over the Family* (with Brigitte Berger), 1983; *The Capitalist Revolution,* 1986; *A Far Glory,* 1992; *Modernity, Pluralism, and the Crisis of Meaning* (with Thomas Luckmann), 1995.

Ann Bernstein

Since 1995 Executive Director of the Centre for Development and Enterprise, Johannesburg.

Head of the Urbanisation Unit and of the Development Strategy and Policy Unit of the Urban Foundation; 1989–95 Executive Director of the Urban Foundation; 1991 visiting scholar at the Institute for the Study of Economic Culture, Boston University; 1994 member of the Development Bank Transformation Team and in 1995 member of the Transitional Board of the Development Bank of Southern Africa.

Publications:

Policies for a New Urban Future: Urban Debate 2010 (in conjunction with the Private Sector Council on Urbanisation); Urban Foundation Research, a series of executive summaries on national policy issues; *Development and Democracy,* a journal of opinion and debate.

André Béteille
Born 1934; since 1959 Professor of Sociology at the University of Delhi.

Fellow at the British Academy; 1965–66 Simon Fellow at the University of Manchester; 1978–79 Commonwealth Visiting Professor at the University of Cambridge; 1984 held the Tinbergen Chair at Erasmus University, Rotterdam; 1986 Visiting Professor at the London School of Economics; 1988 Visiting Scholar in Residence at the University of California, Santa Barbara; 1989 Fulbright Distinguished Lecturer; 1989–90 Fellow at the Institute of Advanced Study, Berlin; 1991 Visiting Fellow at the Institute for Advanced Study in the Humanities, Edinburgh; 1992 Distinguished Visiting Lecturer at the University of California.

Publications:

Class and Power, 1965; *Castes: Old and New*, 1969; *Studies in Agrarian Social Structure*, 1974; *Inequality Among Men*, 1977; *Ideologies and Intellectuals*, 1980; *The Idea of Natural Inequality and Other Essays*, 1983; *Essays in Comparative Sociology*, 1987; *Society and Politics in India*, 1991; *The Backward Classes in Contemporary India*, 1992; *Social Inequality*, 1969; *Equality and Inequality*, 1983.

Arturo Fontaine Talavera
Born 1952; Director, Centro de Estudios Públicos, Santiago.

Writer and essayist; studied at the University of Chile and at Columbia University, New York; Professor of Political Philosophy at Catholic University, Santiago.

Publications:

Oír su voz, 1992; *Tu nombre en vano*, a collection of poems, 1995; author of various articles: "Nadie ha de Obligarme a Ser Feliz a Su Manera: Un Punto de Vista Liberal," 1986; "Sobre el Pecado Original de la Transformación Capitalista Chilena," 1991; "The Future of an Illusion," 1992; "Significado del Eje Derecha-Izquierda," 1995.

Robert W. Hefner
Born 1952; since 1989 Associate Director, Institute for the study of Economic Culture, Boston University.

1979–80 Visiting Lecturer, Department of Anthropology, Gadjah Mada University, Yogyakarta, Indonesia; 1980 Teaching Assistant, University of Michigan; since 1982 Associate Professor, Department of Anthropology, Boston University; 1990–96 Fellowship Reader, Woodrow Wilson Center, Washington D.C.

Publications:

Hindu Javanese, Tengger Tradition, and Islam, 1985; *The Political Economy of Mountain Java: An Interpretive History*, 1990; *Conversion to Christianity: Historical and Anthropological Perspectives on a Great Transformation* (editor), 1993; *ICMI dan Perjuangan menuju Kelas Menengah Indonesia* (ICMI and the Struggle for the Indonesian Middle Class), 1995; *Islam in an Era of Nation-Building: Politics and Religious Renewal in Muslim Southeast Asia* (coeditor, with Patricia Horvatich), 1997; *Market Cultures: Society and Morality in the New Asian Capitalisms* (editor), 1997.

Danièle Hervieu-Léger
Born 1947; Director, Centre Interdisciplinaire d'Etudes des Faits Religieux, Ecole des Hautes Etudes en Sciences Sociales, Paris.

Academic degrees in Political Science, Law, and Sociology; Professor at the Ecole des Hautes Etudes en Sciences Sociales, Paris; editor-in-chief of the journal *Archives de Sciences Sociales des Religions.*

Publications:

De la mission à la protestation: L'évolution des étudiants chrétiens en France (1965–1970), 1973; *Le retour à la nature: Au fond de la forêt, l'Etat* (with Bertrand Hervieu), 1979; *Le féminisme en France*, 1982; *Des communautés pour les temps difficiles* (with Bertrand Hervieu), 1983; *Vers un Nouveau Christianisme? Introduction à la sociologie du christianisme occidental*, 1986; *De l'émotion en religion* (editor, with F. Champion), 1990; *Christianisme et modernité* (editor, with R. Ducret et P. Ladrière), 1990; *La religion au lycée* (editor), 1991; *Religion et écologie* (editor), 1993; *La religion pour mémoire*, 1993; *Identités religieuses en Europe* (editor), 1996.

Hsin-Huang Michael Hsiao

Born 1948 in Taipei; since 1984 Professor, Department of Sociology, National Taiwan University.

Since 1983 Research Fellow, Institute of Ethnology, Academia Sinica; 1983–84 Fulbright Senior Visiting Scholar, Center for Asian Development Studies, Boston University, and Fairbank Center for East Asian Research, Harvard University; 1988 Visiting Professor, Department of Sociology and Center for International Studies, Duke University; 1989–94 Deputy Director, Institute of Ethnology, Academia Sinica; since 1994 Executive Director, Foundation for the Advancement of Outstanding Scholarship; 1992–93 President, Chinese Sociological Association of Taiwan; 1994 Visiting Chair Professor, Leiden University; since 1995 Research Fellow, Institute of Sociology, Academia Sinica; since 1996 Director, Program for Southeast Asian Area Studies, Academia Sinica.

Publications:

Government Agricultural Strategies in Taiwan and South Korea, 1981; *The Development of Agricultural Policies in Post-war Taiwan*, 1986; *In Search of an East Asian Development Model* (coeditor), 1987; *Taiwan: A Newly Industrialized State* (coeditor), 1989; *Taiwan 2000*, 1989; *The Middle Classes in the Changing Taiwan Society* (editor), 1989; *Discovery of the Middle Classes in East Asia* (editor), 1993; *Southeast Asia Collection in Academia Sinica* (coeditor), 1995; *State and Society in Taiwan* (coeditor), 1996; *East Asian Middle Classes in Comparative Perspective* (editor), 1997.

James D. Hunter

Born 1955; since 1994 William R. Kenan Professor of Sociology and Religious Studies, University of Virginia.

1982–83 Assistant Professor of Sociology, Westmont College; 1983–89 Assistant Professor of Sociology, University of Virginia; 1989–94 Professor of Sociology and Religious Studies, University of Virginia; 1994–2000 Director "The Post-Modernity Project"; 1986–94 principal investigator on "The Religion and Power Project"; 1990–92 principal investigator on "Moral Education in America"; since 1995 President, In Medias Res Educational Foundation.

Publications:

American Evangelicalism: Conservative Religion and the Quandary of Modernity, 1983; *Evangelicalism: The Coming Generation*, 1987; *Culture Wars: The Struggle to De-*

fine America, 1991; *Before the Shooting Begins: Searching for Democracy in America's Culture War*, 1994; *Lessons in Self-destruction: On the Moral Education of Children*, 1997; *Fighting Words: An Essay on Extremism in Public Discourse*, in progress; Coauthored books: *Cultural Analysis: The Work of Peter Berger, Mary Douglas, Michel Foucault, and Jürgen Habermas*, 1984; *Making Sense of Modern Times: Peter L. Berger and the Vision of Interpretive Sociology*, 1986; *Articles of Faith—Articles of Peace: The First Amendment Religion Clauses and the American Public Philosophy*, 1990.

Franz-Xaver Kaufmann

Born 1932 in Zurich; since 1969 Professor of Sociology at the University of Bielefeld.

1956 Licentiate; 1960 Doctorate in Economic Sciences at the University of St. Gallen; 1960–63 Ciba AG, Basle; 1963–68 Social Research Institute at the University of Münster; habilitation in sociology and social politics at the University of Münster; 1979–83 Director, Centre for Interdisciplinary Research, University of Bielefeld; 1980–92 Director, Institute for Demographic Research and Social Politics, University of Bielefeld; 1993 Dr. theol.h.c.; member of the Academia Europea; foreign member of the Royal Academy of Sciences of Belgium.

Publications:

Sicherheit als soziologisches und sozialpolitisches Problem, 1970; *Religion und Modernität: Sozialwissenschaftliche Analysen*, 1989; *The Public Sector* (editor), 1991; *Der Ruf nach Verantwortung*, 1992; *Zukunft der Familie im vereinten Deutschland: Gesellschaftliche und politische Bedingungen*, 1995.

János Mátyás Kovács

Born 1950 in Budapest; since 1991 permanent fellow at the Institute for Human Sciences, Vienna.

Since 1973 member of the Institute of Economics, Budapest; since 1984 Professor of Economics at the Eötvös Lóránd University, Budapest; since 1987 Professor at the Diplomatic Academy, Vienna. Fellowships: 1981 Ecole des Hautes Etudes en Sciences Sociales; 1983 British Academy; 1984 Friedrich Ebert Stiftung; 1986–87 Harvard University; 1987–90 Institute for Human Sciences.

Publications:

The Reform of the Self-Management System and Economic Policy Changes in Yugoslavia, 1975; *Rediscovery of Liberalism in Eastern Europe* (editor), Winter 1991 issue of *Eastern European Politics and Societies*; *Reform and Transformation: Eastern European Economics on the Threshold of Change* (editor with M. Tardos), 1992; *Transition to Capitalism? The Communist Legacy in Eastern Europe* (editor), 1994; coeditor *Transit 2000*; various essays on transformation in postcommunist countries.

Serif Mardin

Since 1988 Ibu Khaldun Chair of Islamic Studies, School of International Service, American University, Washington, D.C.

1958 Ph.D. Political Science, Stanford University; 1954–72 Professor of Political Science, Ankara University; 1958–60 Research Associate, Princeton University; 1960–61 Harvard University; 1965–66 Visiting Professor, Columbia University; 1970–71 Princeton University; 1976 University of California, Berkeley; 1972–88

Professor of Sociology and Political Science, Boğaziçi University; 1979–82 Fellow, St. Antony's College, Oxford University.

Publications:

The Genesis of Young Ottoman Thought, 1962; *Religion and Social Change in Modern Turkey*, 1989; author of various articles in *Daedalus, Comparative Studies in Society and History, International Journal of Middle Eastern Studies.*

Seizaburo Sato

Born 1932; since 1988 Research Director, Institute for International Policy Studies, Tokyo.

1960–63 Research Fellow, Faculty of Law, University of Tokyo; 1963–67 Lecturer and Associate Professor, Rikkyo University, Tokyo; 1967–76 Associate Professor, School of Liberal Arts and Graduate School of Law and Political Science, University of Tokyo; 1970–72 Research Fellow, East Asian Research Center, Harvard University; 1971 Visiting Professor, El Colegio de Mexico; 1977–92 Professor, University of Tokyo; 1979–80 Member of the Prime Minister's Study Groups on Pacific Corporation and on Comprehensive Security; 1983–84 Member of the Japan-U.S. Advisory Commission; 1981–86 Member of the Prime Minister's Commission for the Promotion of Administrative Reform; 1992–95 Professor at Keio University; since 1993 Professor Emeritus, University of Tokyo; since 1995 Professor, Graduate School of Policy Science, Saitama University.

Publications:

United States–Japanese Security Cooperation, 1991; *Japanese Perceptions of the New Security Situation*, 1992; *Korean Peninsula Development and U.S.–Japan–South Korean Relations* (coeditor), 1993; *Prospects for Global Order* (coeditor), 1993; *Korean Peninsula Issues and U.S.–Japan–South Korean Relations* (coeditor), 1993; *Security in the Asia-Pacific Region: Threats, Risks, and Opportunities*, 1994; *Future Sources of Global Conflict* (coeditor), 1995; *The Birth of the Murayama Government*, 1995; *Japan's Democracy in Crisis*, 1995; *Three Major Twentieth Century Trends and Japan's Future Role*, 1996; *Clarifying the Right of Collective Self-defense*, 1996.

Volker Then

Born 1961; since 1995 Director of Cultural Orientation at the Bertelsmann Foundation, Gütersloh.

Studies in History, Economics, and Sociology at the Universities of Tübingen, Bielefeld, Oxford, and Berlin (Free University); since 1994 at the Bertelsmann Foundation.